INTRODUCTION TO MARKETING MANAGEMENT

Text and Cases

THE IRWIN SERIES IN MARKETING

Consulting Editor
Gilbert A. Churchill, Jr.   University of Wisconsin, Madison

INTRODUCTION TO MARKETING MANAGEMENT

Text and Cases

James D. Scott
Professor Emeritus of Marketing

Martin R. Warshaw
Professor of Marketing

James R. Taylor
Sebastian S. Kresge
Professor of Marketing

All of the Graduate School of Business Administration
The University of Michigan

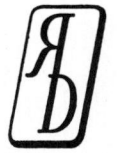

Fifth Edition 1985

RICHARD D. IRWIN, INC.   Homewood, Illinois 60430

ISBN 0-256-03236-X
Library of Congress Catalog Card No. 84–62315

Printed in the United States of America

2 3 4 5 6 7 8 9 0 MP 2 1 0 9 8 7 6 5

To the memory of Stewart H. Rewoldt

PREFACE

The fifth edition of this text, like its predecessors, is designed for a first course in marketing management. It introduces students to the approaches and problems of marketing decision making under conditions of uncertainty. The viewpoint is that of a marketing manager responsible for the planning and execution of a complete marketing program. It recognizes that marketing planning must be accomplished in a changing economic, social, and legal environment that poses many constraints and requirements for the marketing manager. The text draws upon economics, the behavioral sciences, and quantitative analysis wherever these are helpful in the solution of marketing problems. No one of these orientations to the teaching of marketing management predominates. Rather, all are utilized to provide the student with all the tools available to a present-day marketing manager.

In general, an analytical rather than a descriptive approach is taken; only essential descriptive material necessary to marketing decision making is provided. The text material focuses on basic concepts and methods of analysis. By applying these to the analysis of cases, the student will come to appreciate their relevance and value. The student learns marketing decision making by making marketing decisions. There is no other way to train marketing managers that works as well.

The 29 cases included present fundamental issues in marketing man-

agement. Of these 29 cases, 12 are completely new, while 17 others (many of them revised) have been carried over from the previous edition. The cases provide students with valuable experience in exercising their analytical powers and their judgment; they develop the student's capacity to make decisions. The cases follow each major section of text material and are designed to deepen and extend the student's understanding of the challenges that the marketing manager faces in carrying out his or her responsibilities. Additional factual background about marketing and its environment is also gained from case study.

The fifth edition is divided into seven parts, as were the previous editions. Part 1—which has been extensively rewritten for this edition— introduces the student to marketing management by emphasizing the role of marketing planning as a prelude to developing marketing strategy. Marketing research, including demand forecasting—areas which are basic to marketing planning—is also covered in Part 1. Buyer behavior as a key determinant of marketing strategy is stressed in part 2. This part has also been extensively revised, not only in its coverage of behavioral concepts, but also in its explanation of how these concepts can provide a better understanding of buyer behavior in both consumer and industrial markets. Parts 3 through 6 deal with the major decision areas of marketing management—product strategy, distribution strategy, promotional strategy, and pricing strategy. Part 7 is a series of longer cases that can be used to integrate these strategies into an overall marketing program for the firm.

The fifth edition of *Introduction to Marketing Management* is intended for a one-semester course; hence coverage has been limited to essentials. It is assumed that greater depth of coverage will be accomplished by personal input from the teacher, the use of additional readings, and the assignment of cases from other readily available sources. Our aim has been to design the book to be flexible and usable in a variety of situations.

This edition is the by-product of the teaching experience of the authors at both the graduate and undergraduate levels. Having taught introductory marketing management at the University of Michigan, we all have tested both text material and cases in the classroom and revised these materials in the light of our experience. Our thinking about the content of this revision has been much influenced by discussions with our faculty colleagues about ways in which previous editions could be improved. We are especially grateful for the comments of Professors C. Merle Crawford and Thomas C. Kinnear, who have been the respective coordinators of the undergraduate and graduate core marketing courses at Michigan. We have also received valuable input from our students, from the many teachers who have adopted previous editions, and from the intensive reviews commissioned by our publisher. We wish to express our sincere appreciation for all of these contributions.

We are indebted to the Graduate School of Business Administration of the University of Michigan, and particularly to the Division of Research, for financial support for the collection of case materials included in this volume. The Leo Burnett Foundation through its Burnett Scholars Program at Michigan also provided support to students who wrote case histories used in this edition. The cases were collected by the authors or by individuals working under the supervision of the authors or by certain of our colleagues.

We are especially indebted to Paul Arney, Danny Bellenger, Ken Bernhardt, Thomas Ingram, Steven Hartley, Tom Kinnear, William Rudelius, and the Graduate Schools of Business at Minnesota and Stanford for allowing us to use their cases.

The index of cases at the end of the text lists each of the authors and faculty supervisors. To each we extend our hearty thanks. We also are indebted to the many business executives who cooperated with us in our case research activities and shared their experiences in order to provide a realistic learning experience for students. Although these individuals must go unnamed in order to protect confidential information, we nevertheless deeply appreciate their unselfish contributions.

The original authors are pleased to welcome aboard as a coauthor our dear friend and colleague, Jim Taylor. His ideas were increasingly reflected in this book over the years and it seemed only logical for him to replace Stewart Rewoldt, who died shortly before the fourth edition was published.

James D. Scott
Martin R. Warshaw
James R. Taylor

Contents

PART TWO   BUYER BEHAVIOR   121

4. Consumer Buyer Behavior   123

Example of Consumer Behavior. Model of Consumer Behavior: *Stages in Purchase Decision Process. Types of Decision Processes.* Influences on Consumer Behavior: *Psychological Factors. Personal Factors. Social Factors. Cultural Factors. Social Class.* Models of Consumer Buyer Behavior: *The Howard-Sheth Model.*

5. Industrial Buyer Behavior   157

Nature of the Industrial Market. Classification of Industrial Goods. Marketing Patterns. Nature of Demand for Industrial Goods. Extent of Demand for Industrial Goods and Services. Buyer Behavior in the Industrial Market: *Individual and Organizational Goals. Stages in the Buying Process. Multiple-Influence Groups. Types of Buying Situations. The Search Process.*

PART THREE   PRODUCT STRATEGY   213

6. Product Choice Decisions   215

Basic Concepts: *Product Line and Product Mix. Product Life Cycle.* Decision to Offer a New Product. What New Products to Offer: *Objective of Profit Maximization. Profitability Formula. Estimate of Demand. Price Estimates. Cost Estimates. Life-Cycle Estimates. Net Revenue. Compound Profitability Formula. Resource Utilization: Its Relationship to Product Planning. Ultilization of Production Resources. Decision Matrix: Utilization of Production Resources. Utilization of Marketing Resources.*

Decision Matrix: Utilization of Marketing Resources. Summary: Resource Utilization. Dropping Products.

Distribution: *Rising Costs. Cost-Saving Potential. Promotional Potential. Implications. A Physical Distribution System.* Managing the Physical Distribution Function.

Cases for part four

PART FIVE　PROMOTIONAL STRATEGY

10.　Promotional Strategy Decisions

Determination of Basic Promotional Strategy: *Promotion Involves Communication. How Communication Works. Determining the Promotional Mix. Choice of Promotional Methods.* Advertising: *Appraising the Opportunity to Make Profitable Use of Consumer Advertising. When Should Advertising Receive the Main Emphasis in the Promotional Mix? Other Problems of Advertising Management.* Personal Selling: *Factors Influencing the Use of Personal Selling. When Should Personal Selling Receive Main Emphasis? Other Problems of Sales Force Management.* Dealer Promotion: *Increasing Importance of Point-of-Purchase Promotion. When Should Dealer Carry the Main Burden? When Advertising Is Emphasized, How Necessary Is Dealer Promotion? When Retail Personal Selling Is Emphasized, How Necessary Is Dealer Promotion? Methods of Encouraging Dealer Promotion.* Consumer Promotions. Publicity. New Ways to Reach Your Customers. Determining the Promotional Mix.

11.　Determining the Promotional Appropriation

Theoretical Analysis of the Problem. Common Approaches to Determining the Appropriation: *Percentage of Sales. All Available Funds. Competitive Parity. Research Objective. Advertising as an Investment. Research to Determine Expenditure Levels. Relation of Advertising Outlays to Market Share Objectives. Relation of Communication Objectives to Sales Results. Decision Models for Setting Promotional Appropriations. Empirical Analyses of Why Promotional Costs Vary.*

PART SEVEN   INTEGRATED MARKETING PROGRAMS   743

Cases for part seven

MARKET PLANNING AND STRATEGY

The marketing function identifies the desires of customer segments and decides on appropriate products, services, and supporting programs to meet the needs of these markets. Marketing is a critical link between the desires of society and the ability of organizations to respond. Consequently, marketing is an important area of study for several reasons: (1) it represents a large component of the economic system—the careers of most people will directly or indirectly deal with the marketing function; (2) in today's dynamic and hostile environment, the success or failure of an organization can be determined by the effectiveness of its marketing programs; and (3) marketing is an essential aspect of our personal activities as consumers and citizens.

Part One of this text introduces the student to marketing management, marketing planning, marketing strategy, and marketing research. Part Two focuses on buyer behavior. It takes an intensive look at buyer behavior and various approaches to understanding buyer behavior. Parts Three through Six deal with the major decision areas of marketing —product strategy, distribution strategy, promotion strategy, and price strategy. Part Seven integrates strategies discussed in each of these decision areas into an overall marketing program for the firm.

MARKETING AND MARKETING PLANNING

1

This chapter presents a discussion of marketing and the marketing planning process. Upon completion of this chapter you will be able to: (1) define marketing and the role of marketing management, (2) understand the nature of the marketing planning process, and (3) describe the internal and external factors that comprise the situational analysis.

DEFINING MARKETING

Marketing has been defined in similar ways by contemporary marketing scholars.[1] The following definition captures this perspective.

Marketing is the process by which individuals and organizations undertake activities to facilitate the identification, development, and exchange of products and services to satisfy the desires of the parties involved.

The central concept of this definition is that of *exchange*. Exchange involves acquiring a product or service from a person or organization

---

[1]Thomas C. Kinnear and Kenneth L. Bernhardt, *Principles of Marketing* (Glenview, Ill.: Scott, Foresman, 1983), p. 8; and Philip Kotler, *Marketing Management,* 5th ed. (Englewood Cliffs, N.J.: Prentice-Hall, 1984), p. 4. This section follows the discussion of these authors.

by offering something of value in return. Figure 1–1 presents examples of this exchange process. These examples show that exchange can involve money, physical products, services, and psychological feelings of pride, accomplishment, and guilt reduction. The important concept is that *something of value* is involved in the exchange process. The objective of the exchange could be to stimulate or change attitudes, beliefs, or behavior. This could take the form of increased consumption behavior or decreased consumption behavior (demarketing).

There has been a trend among organizations to adopt what is known as the *marketing concept*. Organizations which have adopted this concept are referred to as marketing-oriented. The marketing concept implies that the fundamental purpose of all organizational activity (manufacturing, finance, R&D, and marketing) is the satisfaction of the consumer. A marketing-oriented organization believes that focusing on customer needs and integrating all organizational activities to satisfy these needs will result in long-term profits and growth.

FIGURE 1–1   Examples of marketing exchange transactions

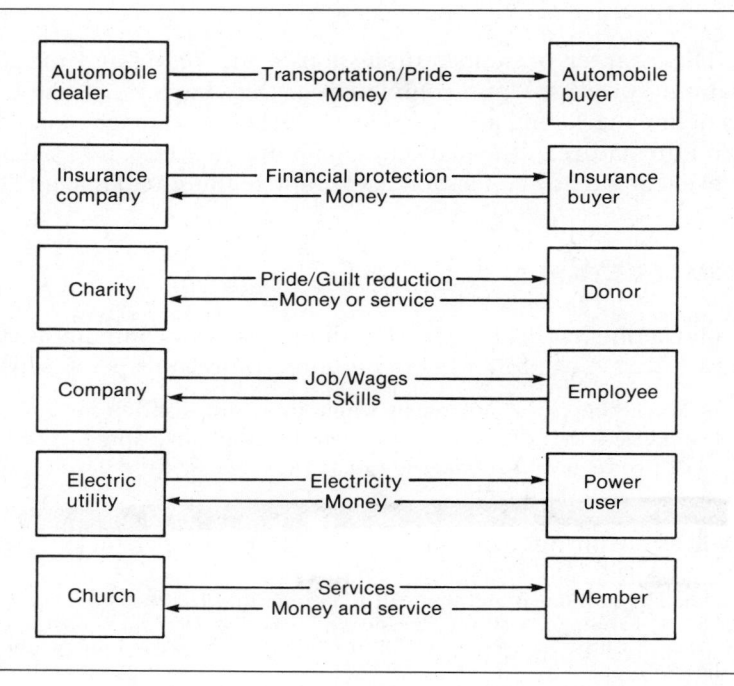

MARKETING MANAGEMENT

Marketing management is that part of an organization which is responsible for the formulation and implementation of a marketing progam to satisfy the needs of a market segment and to attain organizational objectives. Decisions must be made as to the product offered, the distribution system, the promotional campaign, and the pricing structure.

These four decision areas are referred to as the *marketing mix*—the main tools of marketing management. These four areas are often referred to as the 4Ps: product, place (distribution), promotion, and price.[2] The nature of the activities to be considered in these areas include:

1. Product decisions—product planning (quality, features, style, name, packaging); product development (marketing research, product testing); and pre- and post-sales service (product specifications, installation, warranties).
2. Distribution (place) decisions—types of distribution channels; channel coverage and location; warehousing and inventory control; and physical distribution.
3. Promotion decisions—advertising; personal selling; sales marketing; sales promotion; and publicity.
4. Pricing decisions—price level; channel discounts; allowances; payment period; and legal issues.

The majority of the chapters of this book are devoted to explaining the types of marketing mix issues involved in formulating a marketing strategy and plan. In planning a marketing strategy, the marketing manager faces certain inherent environmental constraints. These constraints are situational variables or factors which are uncontrollable by marketing management. They operate both inside and outside the organizations.

In essence, marketing strategy consists of changing those variables that the marketing manager can control and adapting optimally to those variables that cannot be controlled, to most effectively attain objectives. Those variables that can be controlled are, for the marketing manager's purposes, the relevant marketing strategy variables. The uncontrollable variables are environmental. They, in a sense, limit the strategy choices available in trying to achieve a favorable purchase decision by the consumer. Figure 1–2 attempts to portray this approach to achieving an integrated marketing effort. It is debatable whether the skills and resources of the firm are truly uncontrollable. It was decided to include them here because, in the short run, control may be very difficult, if not impossible.

---

[2]E. Jerome McCarthy and William D. Perrault, Jr., *Basic Marketing: A Managerial Approach,* 8th ed. (Homewood, Ill.: Richard D. Irwin, 1984).

FIGURE 1–2   Controllable and uncontrollable variables in marketing

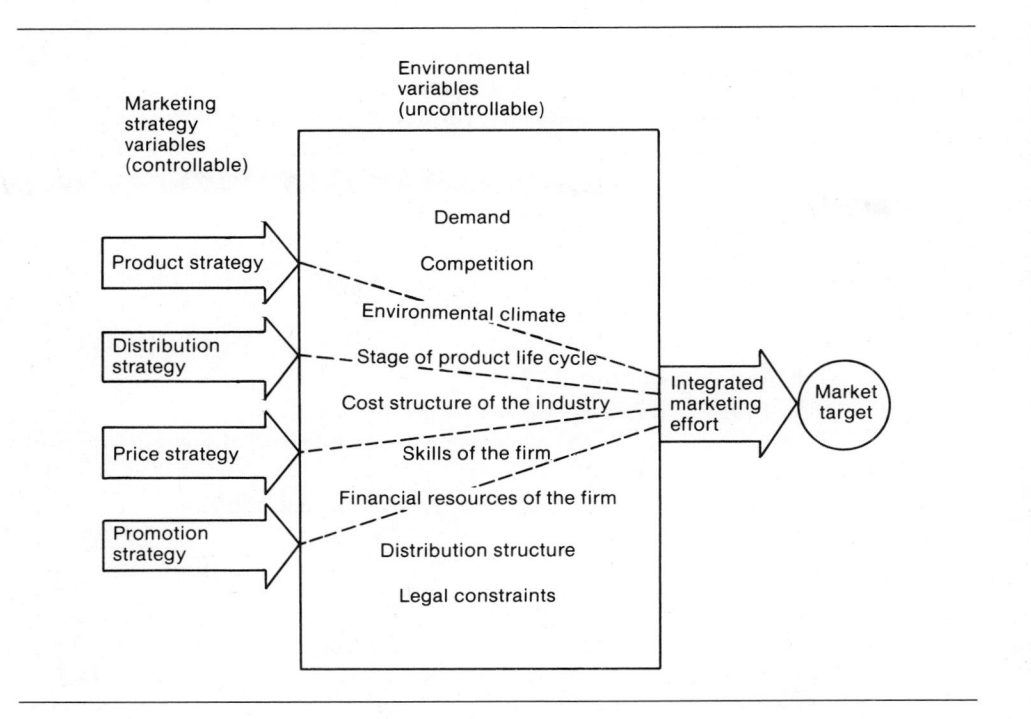

SYNERGISM AND MARKETING

Synergism is a popular word in business management literature. It is defined by *Webster's* as: "Cooperative action of discrete agencies such that the total effect is greater than the sum of the effects taken independently."[3] Nowhere in business management is synergism more important than in management of the marketing function. The effectiveness of action taken with regard to one controllable variable depends greatly on what is done with regard to others. For example, the effectiveness of advertising depends on the adequacy of distribution of a product. Even favorable responses to advertising appeals cannot lead to customer purchase if the product is not available in the marketplace. Personal selling can have its effectiveness blunted if advertising has not been used to lay the groundwork for the approach of the salesperson. A price cut may

---

[3]*Webster's Eighth New Collegiate Dictionary.* Copyright © 1974, by G. & C. Merriam Co., Springfield, Mass.

fail to have the hoped-for effect if it is not promoted effectively. In short, the total effect of marketing effort is very much a function of the integration a firm manages to achieve in developing and carrying out its marketing program.

The concept of synergism applies not only to the marketing function but to the total operation of a business. The marketing concept involves the orientation of the entire business to the needs of the consumer. This means that production must be integrated with marketing requirements and that finance must provide the capital resources required to serve these consumer needs. It is the special role of marketing not only to assure that the marketing function is so oriented but also to guide the other business functions in serving the same goal.

Approaches used to achieve synergism in business vary widely. In the small enterprise, important decisions are usually made by one person. This, in itself, provides some measure of an integrative approach. As a firm grows in size, effective integration usually requires more and more committees and staff meetings. At some level of size, these somewhat casual approaches to integration are no longer adequate, and achievement of this goal becomes difficult and perplexing. In the large firm, achievement of the synergistic effect is accomplished by formal planning. Although planning is important to the small firm, it is indispensable to the large one. In the smaller firm, close interpersonal contact overcomes some defects in organization; ability to change course quickly overcomes some inadequacies in planning.

MARKETING PLANNING

Marketing planning is a subfunction of business planning.[4] An inevitable result of the complex business environment in which change is the order of the day is the need for both short-range and long-range planning. A business firm, in order to survive and prosper, must know where it is going and how it is going to get there. It needs clearly defined goals and well-thought-out courses of action to achieve these goals. Without them, efficient employment of resources is not possible.

A business firm may have many goals, either implicit or clearly stated. It may choose to maximize long- or short-range profits, to achieve steady but not necessarily maximum growth, to provide maximum security for management personnel, to maximize dividend payments to stockholders, and so on. The merit of these or other goals is not at issue here. What is at issue is the fact that these goals must be known before mar-

---

[4]For a description of the process of setting up a strategic planning system for the entire firm, see Peter Lorange and Richard F. Vancil, "How to Design a Strategic Planning System," *Harvard Business Review*, September–October 1976, pp. 75–81. (See the Appendix for an outline of approaches to planning system design issues.)

keting planning can proceed. Planning for marketing activities must be consistent with the overall goals of the company.

The role of marketing planning is a special one in overall business planning. Marketing is the major link between the business firm and its environment. In order to achieve the orientation of the business firm to its market, marketing must study and interpret consumer needs and then guide the firm in serving those needs. A marketing plan can be thought of as a company's battle plan. It surveys the environment, isolates marketing opportunities, and states the courses of action to be followed in taking advantage of those opportunities. Other parts of the overall business plan (for example, those relating to production and finance) are more in the nature of support plans—things that must be done to carry out the marketing plan which has been agreed upon. Obviously, however, no part of the overall plan for a business is independent of the other parts.

THE MARKETING PLANNING PROCESS

Figure 1–3 presents the components of the marketing planning process. The process begins with an assessment of the situation facing the organization. This *situational analysis* includes an assessment of environmental factors *external* and *internal* to the organization. These environmental factors represent circumstances that marketing management must consider in developing a marketing strategy and marketing plan.

External factors include nature and extent of demand, competition, environmental climate, stage of product life cycle, cost structure of industry, distribution structure, and legal constraints. These factors represent problems and opportunities which directly influence the development of a marketing strategy.

Internal factors represent organizational skills and resources which characterize the organization's ability to compete effectively. These factors include marketing, production, research and development, finance, and management. These areas represent elements of the organization where objectives and programs are being implemented. An assessment of the organization's skills and resources can identify strengths and weaknesses which determine its future competitive capability.

The second component of the marketing planning process involves identifying *key* problems and opportunities from the external environment and key strengths and weaknesses from the internal environment. While many factors can be identified in the situational analysis, this stage requires the marketing manager to prioritize and delimit these factors to those most important to the development of an effective marketing strategy and plan. This is a critical stage in the planning process since

FIGURE 1—3 Marketing planning process

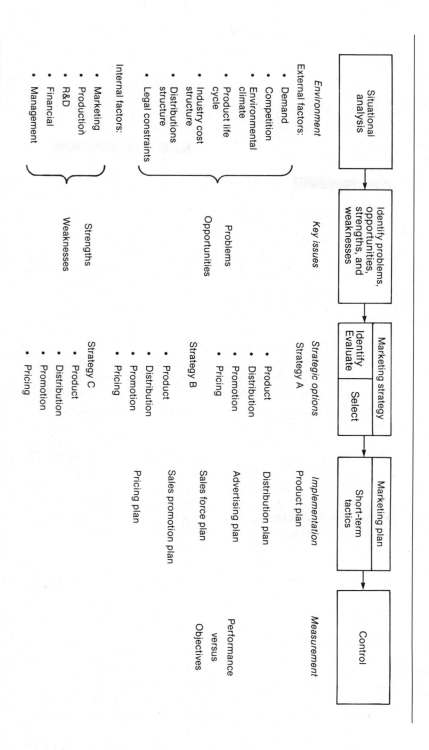

the depth and quality of this analysis directly influence the logic of the marketing strategy and plan.

The remaining components of the marketing planning process—marketing strategy, marketing plan, and control—will be discussed in the following chapter.

Before turning to these topics, let's review the anatomy of the marketing planning process.

ANATOMY OF A MARKETING PLAN

There is an important distinction to be made between marketing planning and a marketing plan. Marketing planning is a continuous function and is never completed. A marketing plan is an expression of the output of the planning process as of a particular moment for a particular period of time. Our discussion to this point has emphasized the planning process, with particular emphasis on the steps involved in this process. We shall now shift our attention to the structure of a marketing plan.

There is a trend in business toward formal, written marketing plans. Usually both long-range and short-range plans are prepared. The appropriate time span for marketing plans will vary with each industry, but the long-range plan should cover the longest predictable period ahead for which objectives can be identified. Short-range plans must be in harmony with the long-range plan. They are steps on the way to achieving the long-range objectives.

Although no one plan is necessarily the best, there are certain things that must be encompassed in any marketing plan. The structure discussed below incorporates these things. It is built around the controllable and uncontrollable marketing variables. These are integrated with other factors to form a plan structure that has wide applicability.

GENERAL STRUCTURE OF A MARKETING PLAN

An appropriate skeletal structure for a marketing plan might appear as follows:

   I.   Situation analysis.
       A.   External factors.
           1.   Demand.
               a.   Nature of demand.
               b.   Extent of demand.
           2.   Competition.
           3.   Environmental climate.

4. Stage of product life cycle.
5. Cost structure of the industry.
6. Distribution structure.
7. Legal constraints.
B. Internal factors.
1. Skills of the firm.
2. Financial resources of the firm.
II. Problems, opportunities, strengths, and weaknesses.
III. Marketing strategy.
A. Objectives.
1. Target market segments.
2. Volume to be sold.
3. Profit goals.
B. Marketing mix/program decisions.
1. Product strategy.
2. Distribution strategy.
3. Price strategy.
4. Promotion strategy.
a. Advertising.
b. Personal selling.
c. Sales promotion.

The Situation Analysis

Basic to marketing planning is an understanding of the environment in which marketing effort is to be expended. The environment determines not only what must be done but what it is possible to do. Situational variables are multitudinous. One useful way of classifying them is suggested in the outline.

The purpose of the situational analysis is, in a sense, to take a picture of the external and internal environment for marketing planning. It cannot, however, be a still picture that merely depicts what exists at the time it was snapped. It must be a moving picture that reveals trends and helps us to forecast what the environmental situation will be throughout the planning period. It is really the future situation in which we are most interested.

Demand.   Demand is the most significant situational variable because it is least known and least predictable, yet it has the greatest impact on what can or cannot be done in marketing. Some analysis areas and questions that might be asked about the nature of demand are the following:

1. How do buyers (consumer and industrial) *currently* go about buying existing products or services? What are the main types of behavior patterns and attitudes?

a. Number of stores shopped or industrial sources considered.
b. Degree of overt information-seeking.
c. Degree of brand awareness and loyalty.
d. Location of product category decision—home or point of sale.
e. Location of brand decision—home or point of sale.
f. Sources of product information and current awareness and knowledge levels.
g. Who makes the purchase decision—male, female, adult, child, purchasing agent, buying committee, and so on?
h. Who influences the decision maker?
i. Individual or group decision (computers versus candy bar).
j. Duration of the decision process (repeat, infrequent, or new-purchase situation).
k. Buyer's interest, personal involvement, or excitement regarding the purchase (hairpins versus trip to Caribbean).
l. Risk of uncertainty of negative purchase outcome—high, medium, or low (specialized machinery versus hacksaw blades, pencil versus hair coloring).
m. Functional versus psychosocial considerations (electric drill versus new dress).
n. Time of consumption (gum versus dining room furniture).

The key to such an analysis of the nature of demand is to uncover the implications for marketing programs. For example, if the purchase (brand) decision is made in the store and the brand is not important to the buyer, what implication does this have for national TV advertising versus in-store display? What does it suggest as to the number of stores in which distribution should be sought?

2. Can the market be meaningfully segmented or broken into several homogeneous groups with respect to "what they want" and "how they buy"? A few of the criteria for segmenting the market might be:
a. Age.
b. Family life cycle.
c. Geographic location.
d. Heavy versus light users.
e. Nature of the buying process.
f. Product usage.

Consideration should be given to whether a different marketing program should be developed for each segment or whether one program should be designed to reach all segments. Tailoring a program for each segment may give a competitive advantage. On the other hand, there may be negatives to this strategy in terms of volume and cost consideration.

The extent of demand must be either measured or assumed. The sales potential for a product or service determines product and marketing resources that must be committed. It also determines profit opportunity. It is essential that such questions as the following be answered:

1. What is the size of the market (units and dollars) now, and what will the future hold?
2. What are the current market shares, and what are the selective demand trends (units and dollars)?
3. Is it best to analyze the market on an aggregate or on a segmented basis?

Competition.   Failure to evaluate competition correctly is one common reason for unprofitable marketing programs. If competition is intense, a diffferent marketing program might be required than if it is moderate. The bases of competition in an industry (for example, price versus nonprice) help determine the appropriate marketing strategy. The following are illustrative questions about competition that might be asked:

1. What is the present and future structure of competition?
   a.   Number of competitors (e.g., 5 versus 2,000).
   b.   Market shares.
   c.   Financial resources.
   d.   Marketing resources and skills.
   e.   Production resources and skills.
2. What are the current marketing programs of established competitors? Why are they successful or unsuccessful?
3. Is there any opportunity for another competitor? Why?
4. What are the anticipated retaliatory moves of competitors? Can they neutralize different marketing programs that we might develop?

Environmental climate.   It is not hard to identify marketing programs that have been highly disrupted by a changing environmental climate. The energy crisis together with pollution, safety, and consumerism concerns can bring many such examples to mind. Oil companies and utilities changed their marketing programs drastically in the mid-1970s. Some firms have benefited from the energy crisis, others have been hurt. The basic point is that the environment is constantly changing and that the firms which can adapt to change are the ones which enjoy long-run success. In developing a marketing program, such questions as the following might be asked:

1. What are the relevant social, political, economic, and technological trends?
2. How do you evaluate these trends? Do they represent opportunities or problems?

Stage of product life cycle.   The stage of the product life cycle influences the effectiveness of marketing programs. If the product category is in the early stages of its life cycle, effective promotion may be more important than price and restricted distribution may be more desirable. Such questions as the following should be asked:

1.   What stage of the life cycle is the product category in?
     a.   What is the chronological age of the product category? (Younger more favorable than older?)
     b.   What is the state of the consumers' knowledge of the product category? (More complete the knowledge—more unfavorable?)
2.   What market characteristics support your evaluation of the life-cycle stage?

Cost structure of the industry.   The amount and composition of marginal or additional cost of supplying increased output help determine the marketing program that should be followed. It can be argued that the lower these costs, the easier it may be to cover costs of developing a marketing program designed to increase volume. The garment industry and many service industries have high variable costs. This limits the ability to decrease price in an attempt to boost sales. The hotel and telephone industries have high fixed costs and low variable costs. Hence hotels offer special weekend and off-season rates, and telephone companies offer special evening and weekend rates to attract business. This is profitable to them because their high fixed costs are incurred anyhow, and any rate that more than covers their low variable costs contributes to profits.

Distribution structure.   No marketing program can be successful unless a firm can effectively move its product forward to consumers. A choice of the wrong channel can spell disaster because it can affect both costs and revenues. Therefore, asking the following questions is appropriate:

1.   What channels exist, and can we gain access to the channels?
2.   Cost versus revenue from different channels?
3.   Feasibility of using multiple channels?
4.   Nature and degree of within- and between-channel competition?
5.   Trends in channel structure?
6.   Requirements of different channels for promotion and margin?
7.   Will it be profitable for particular channels to handle my product?

Legal constraints.   Often a marketing program deemed desirable because of its predicted effectiveness cannot be fully implemented because of restraints imposed by antitrust laws, antipollution laws, truth-in-lending laws, truth-in-advertising laws, and many more. Legal constraints have been imposed to protect the public interest, and a company must design a marketing program within this framework. Many com-

panies end up in court each year because they overstep the line of legality.

Skills of the firm. Failures by companies that venture into unfamiliar fields are numerous, as many of the cases in this book will illustrate. Just as an unskilled person finds it difficult to compete with a skilled person in work or sports, so a company that lacks certain important skills finds it difficult to compete with companies that possess these skills. Therefore, such questions as the following should be asked:

1. Do we have the skills and experience to perform the functions necessary to be in this business?
   a. Marketing skills.
   b. Production skills.
   c. Management skills.
   d. Financial skills.
   e. R&D skills.
2. How do our skills compare to those of competitors?
   a. Production fit (see Chapter 6).
   b. Marketing fit (see Chapter 6).

Financial resources of the firm. Many a firm is hampered in its marketing by inadequate financial resources. When resources are slim, a marketing program must of necessity reflect this fact. An expensive promotional campaign, for example, may seem called for, but it must also be paid for. Therefore, such questions as these must be asked:

1. Do we have the funds to support an effective marketing program?
2. Where are the funds coming from, and when will they be available?

PROBLEMS, OPPORTUNITIES, STRENGTHS, AND WEAKNESSES

The next phase is listing problems, opportunities, strengths, and weaknesses. It is extremely helpful to combine and summarize the most important things that have been discovered in doing the situational analysis and to assign some kind of weight to each item.

Problems represent those external factors that cause the organization's performance to be below objective. Opportunities represent the presence of external factors where performance can be improved by undertaking new activity. Organizational weaknesses represent internal factors which limit competitive capabilities, while strengths represent distinctive advantages of the organization relative to competitors.

Marketing Strategy

Marketing strategy, covered only briefly at this point, will be explored more fully in Chapter 2. Actually, the remainder of this book is con-

cerned with the marketing strategy variables, with one or more chapters devoted to each. The following outline of this section of the marketing plan, which will later be expanded upon, gives a preview of what is to follow. This list is not meant to be complete but, rather, is illustrative.

Objectives defined

1. Target market segments identified.
2. Volume to be sold (dollars or units).
3. Profit analysis (contribution analysis, break-even analysis, ROI, etc.).

Marketing mix/program decisions

1. Product decisions.
   a. Develop new product(s).
   b. Change current product(s).
   c. Add or drop product from line.
   d. Product positioning.
   e. Branding (national, private, secondary).
2. Distribution decisions.
   a. Intensity of distribution (intensive to exclusive).
   b. Multiple channels.
   c. Types of wholesalers and retailers (discounters, and so on).
   d. Degree of channel directness.
3. Promotion decisions.
   a. Mix of personal selling, advertising, dealer incentives, and sales promotion.
   b. Branding—family versus individual.
   c. Budget.
   d. Message.
   e. Media.
4. Price decisions.
   a. Price level (above, same, or below).
   b. Price variation (discount structure, geographic).
   c. Margins.
   d. Administration of price level.
   e. Price leadership.

The planning of marketing strategy consists of making decisions about the use of controllable marketing variables to achieve predetermined goals. If goals have not been clearly established, there is little point to planning. If you don't know where you are going, any road will take you there, and there is no meaningful basis for choice between one route and another. Therefore, the first step in planning marketing strategy is to establish goals.

To be useful, goals should be reasonably specific, and performance in

achieving them should be measurable. A goal of maximizing profits does not fit these criteria when the achievable maximum is not known. Growth is not a meaningful objective unless it is expressed as a specific growth rate, which is either achieved or is not. The most common ways of stating marketing strategy objectives are: (1) sales volume, expressed in either dollars or units; (2) market share, expressed as a percentage of the total market for a product or service; and (3) profit, expressed as a return on investment. These objectives are concrete, and the degree to which they are achieved can be calculated.

The heart of the marketing plan is the section on methods of strategy. Here decisions are made about the manner and extent of use of each controllable marketing strategy variable and how these variables should be meshed together into a total strategy. How this is done will be discussed in Chapter 2. Again, decisions should be reasonably specific and should be consistent with the kind and amount of resources available. Plans must be consonant with budget considerations and often must be modified to fit budget constraints.

CONCLUSION

Marketing is an important determinate of the success or failure of organizations, and it is a predominant aspect of the economy and society. The key aspect of marketing is the exchange process; marketing is concerned with the activities involved in facilitating exchange. The marketing concept focuses the organization on customer needs by requiring the integration of all organizational activities to this end.

The marketing manager uses the marketing mix variables (4Ps) to create products and services of value to meet the desires of customer segments. In making marketing mix decisions, the marketing manager analyzes the internal and external factors (situational analysis) that influence the effectiveness of alternative marketing strategies and then develops a marketing strategy/plan to meet a set of predetermined objectives. This procedure is called the marketing planning process.

QUESTIONS

1. In what ways is marketing different from selling?
2. The marketing concept implies orientation of the business firm's total operation to the needs, wants, and desires of the consumer. What are the implications of this concept for consumer welfare?
3. The planning and execution of marketing strategy have been described as a "synergistic" process. What does this mean?

4. What is the relationship between marketing planning and corporate planning?

5. Why must a situation analysis precede the planning of marketing strategy?

6. Given the uncontrollable environmental variables identified in Figure 1–2, what steps could the marketing manager take to reduce their adverse impact on marketing programs?

7. Failure to analyze any external factor in a situational analysis can be costly, but which two or three factors are the most important? Give reasons for your choices.

DEVELOPMENT OF MARKETING STRATEGY

$$2$$

In Chapter 1 the marketing planning process was discussed, focusing on the situational analysis and identification of key problems, opportunities, strengths, and weaknesses. We now focus on the remaining components of the planning process—marketing strategy, marketing planning, and control.

Our understanding of strategy and control can be developed more completely by an understanding of the concept of strategic market planning.

STRATEGIC MARKET PLANNING

Strategic market planning is a broader concept than the marketing planning process described in Chapter 1. (See Figure 1–3.) Figure 2–1 presents this expanded planning process. Strategic market planning is broader in that the mission of the business or business definition precedes the development of a marketing strategy. The formulation of a business definition is based upon a comprehensive situational analysis which includes the internal and external factors discussed in Chapter 1.

FIGURE 2–1   Strategic market planning process

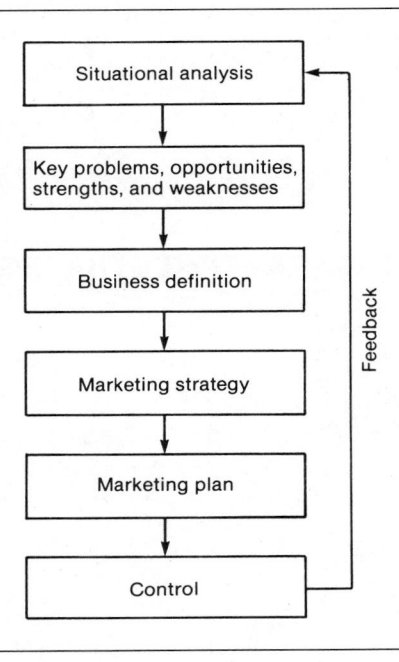

Business Definition

Business definition is a rather difficult concept to grasp. It has been described as a vision of what the organization is all about.[1] The concept must be operationalized when addressing the question, "What business are we in?" For example, is it better to think of IBM as being in the computer or communications business? Is General Motors in the automotive or the transportation business? Is MGM in the film or entertainment business?

Levitt, in "Marketing Myopia," emphasized the risk of defining the business narrowly with a product focus.[2] In describing the decline of the railroads, he argued that automobiles took customers away from trains because management narrowly viewed their business as the railroad business rather than the transportation business. The lesson to be

[1]Robert T. Davis, *Marketing Strategy: A Note* (Stanford: Graduate School of Business, Stanford University, 1975), pp. 2–4.

[2]Theodore Levitt, "Marketing Myopia," *Harvard Business Review*, September–October 1975.

learned is that a business definition should focus on the needs of customer groups rather that focusing on the product or manufacturing technology.

A useful business definition must strike a balance between being so narrow that market and competitive dynamics are missed and so broad as to outstrip the organization's skill and resource base. Consequently, a good business definition should be (1) specific enough to have impact upon the behavior of the organization, (2) focused more upon the satisfaction of customer needs than characteristics of the product being produced, (3) able to reflect the essential skills of the organization, (4) attainable, and (5) flexible.[3]

Business definition is important to marketing strategy in that it guides the strategic thrust of the organization. Consequently, business definition precedes the formulation of a marketing strategy.

Marketing Strategy

Marketing strategy involves a statement of long-term competitive thrust which specifies objectives, target markets, and marketing mix guidelines. This statement does not specify the detailed plans or tactics on how the organization will compete in the short term. The *short-term marketing plan* specifies the details and may be subject to modification as day-to-day market realities evolve. This component of the planning process will be discussed in more detail later in the chapter.

It is important to recognize that the marketing strategy selected can be no better than the best strategic option under consideration. Consequently, a critical step in the marketing planning process is the identification of alternative marketing strategies. It is fairly easy to identify a good strategy, but it is difficult to identify an innovative strategy which has a decisive competitive advantage. A comprehensive *situational analysis* is the key to identifying innovative strategic options. In addition, the situational analysis provides insights to the evaluation of the alternatives. Typically, a listing of pros and cons of each strategic option is a useful format for evaluation. As a rule, at least three strategic options should be evaluated.

A marketing strategy is subject to change when fundamental internal and/or external factors change. Sometimes these environmental factors change rapidly. Examples include technological advances, government deregulation, oil prices, and changes in inflation. Effective marketing planning must be prepared to respond to such fundamental changes through the use of *contingency planning*. Here alternative strategies are formulated which best anticipate changes in internal and external factors. When changes occur, the contingency/strategy plan can be implemented.

---

[3]Davis, *Marketing Stategy,* p. 3.

Objectives.   The strategy statement provides guidelines as to objectives. *Objectives* involve the specification of future performance in terms of one or more measures. The measures can be marketing-related, such as sales, share of market, distribution coverage, and advertising effectiveness. They can be financially related, such as net profit, return on sales, or earnings per share.

Objectives provide the expectations against which actual performance can be measured. The expectations of future performance need to be attainable if they are to be used effectively in a control system. Unrealistic objectives result in loss of control over marketing performance.

Effective objective statements must (1) be quantifiable, (2) specify a target market, and (3) define a time horizon. For example, the statement "To be more aggressive in our marketing activities" does not meet these three criteria. However, the statement "To increase Diet Coke share of market by one share point in the Boston market in the next six months" does meet the three criteria.

If the organization has a mix of performance measures, it is important that the objective statement maintain consistency among them. For example, the statement "Increase share of market and increase cash flow" is not consistent.

Target market.   The strategy statement provides guidelines as to the market target. It is important to recognize that an effective marketing strategy is directed toward a specific group of customers. If the marketing strategy is not directed to a clearly defined target segment, it does not provide the focus essential for directing marketing mix guidelines and tactical decisions (product, distribution, promotion, and price).

The guidelines for market targets should address the following questions:

1.   How can the market be segmented in a meaningful manner?
2.   What are the requirements or needs of the segments?
3.   Where is the best fit between what the organization can offer and the needs of the segments?
4.   Can these needs be satisfied better by competitors?

The topic of market segmentation will be discussed in more detail later in the chapter.

Marketing mix.   The third component of a marketing strategy statement involves marketing mix guidelines. Here the marketing manager has a wide range of options regarding the four elements of the marketing mix—product, distribution, promotion, price. One set of options deals with the relative importance or leverage of the four elements in the marketing strategy. While the leverage of the four elements can vary due to market and competitive factors, it is generally recognized that product decisions and distribution decisions are high-leverage areas for an innovative marketing strategy.

Within each of the four marketing mix elements several options exist. While these options are specific to each of the four elements, it is very important to recognize the interdependence of these options and the need for synergy in formulating an effective marketing strategy. The options for each of the marketing mix elements will be discussed next.

Product decisions.   There are two basic issues in product decisions: (1) the degree of product/market fit and (2) the breadth of product/market relationships.

Degree of product/market fit refers to the extent to which a strategy will recognize the market segments and differentiate products across segments. One option is to not recognize market segments and offer a single product to all segments. This is called *mass market strategy.* A second option is to recognize market segments and target a single product to a segment. This is called *focused strategy.* The third option is to recognize market segments and target two or more segments with two or more product offerings. This is called a *differentiated strategy* in that the products are changed or differentiated to fit the varying needs of the segments.

Breadth of product/market relationships refers to the scope of business activity and the commonality among activities. The issues discussed here relate closely to the previous discussion on *business definition.*

Figure 2–2 presents a classification scheme for product/market relationships. The growth options are:

1. *Market penetration*—Increase sales for present products in present markets through more efficient and effective marketing efforts. This can be accomplished by increasing usage rates, attracting competitor customers, and attracting nonusers.

FIGURE 2–2   Growth options

Market \ Product	Present	New
Present	Market penetration	Product development
New	Market development	Diversification

Source: H. I. Ansoff, *Corporate Strategy* (New York: McGraw-Hill, 1965), p. 109.

2. *Product development*—Increase sales by developing improved products for present markets. This can be accomplished by new-product features, quality variation, new models and sizes, and new concepts.
3. *Market development*—Increase sales by taking present products into new markets. This can be accomplished by new geographic markets and new channels.
4. *Diversification*—Increase sales by developing or acquiring new products for new markets.

There are several types of diversification, depending on: (1) the degree to which the new-product technology is related to the technology base of the organization and (2) the degree of similarity of the new market entered. Figure 2–3 presents these types of diversification. The specific types of diversification are:

1. *Vertical integration.* This option is intended to increase profitability, efficiency, and/or control by moving backward in the system to produce within the company those components which were previously purchased or forwarded into channels of distribution. Here the organization becomes its own customer.

FIGURE 2–3   Diversification options

		New products	
Products Markets		Related technology	Unrelated technology
Firm its own customer		Vertical integration	
Same type of market		Horizontal diversification	
Similar type of market		Marketing-and technology-related concentric diversification	Marketing-related concentric diversification
New type of market		Technology-related concentric diversification	Conglomerate diversification

(left axis label: New markets)

Source: H. I. Ansoff, *Corporate Strategy* (New York: McGraw-Hill, 1965), p. 132.

2. *Horizontal diversification.* This option broadens the line of products offered to present customers through technology unrelated to the company's present products.
3. *Concentric diversification.* This option attracts new classes of customers by adding new products that have technological and/or marketing synergies with the existing product line.
4. *Conglomeraete diversification.* This option attracts new classes of customers by diversifying into products that have no relationship to the company's current technology, products, or markets.

The growth options presented under breadth of product/market relationships differ in their probability of success. The high-success option should be market penetration. Here the organization is expanding its growth in areas it knows best—present products and markets. The low-success option should be diversification. Here the organization is moving away from its skill and resource base to grow in areas it knows less well—new products and markets. Consequently, as the organization moves further from its current markets/customers and products/technology, the decreased probability of success must be counterbalanced by increased rewards.

Existing products in existing markets (market penetration) can be classified using product portfolio analysis developed by the Boston Consulting Group (BCG). Figure 2–4 presents a two-dimensional array called a *product portfolio matrix.* The horizontal dimension is defined by relative share of market (i.e., a product's share of market relative to the largest competitor). The vertical dimension is the market growth rate.[4]

An organization's products (and competitive products) can be classified in the product portfolio matrix on the two dimensions of relative share of market and market growth rate. Each product is represented in this matrix by a circle. The size of the circle corresponds to the product's relative sales volume compared to the organization's total sales volume.

BCG argued that a product's location in this matrix is related to its cash flow position because high relative share of market is associated with cost advantages over a low-share product. Consequently, the product with market share dominance should have lower total unit cost than a product with a low-share position. Lower unit cost implies higher margins and higher profit and cash flow capabilities.

The relationship of market growth rate and cash flow comes from our understanding of accounting and finance. Products in rapidly growing markets are heavy users of cash to fund investments in working capital, manufacturing, R&D, and marketing. Products in mature or declining markets should be net cash generators.

---

[4]This section follows Derek F. Abell and John S. Hammond, *Strategic Market Planning* (Englewood Cliffs, N.J.: Prentice-Hall, 1979), pp. 173–80.

FIGURE 2–4   Product portfolio matrix

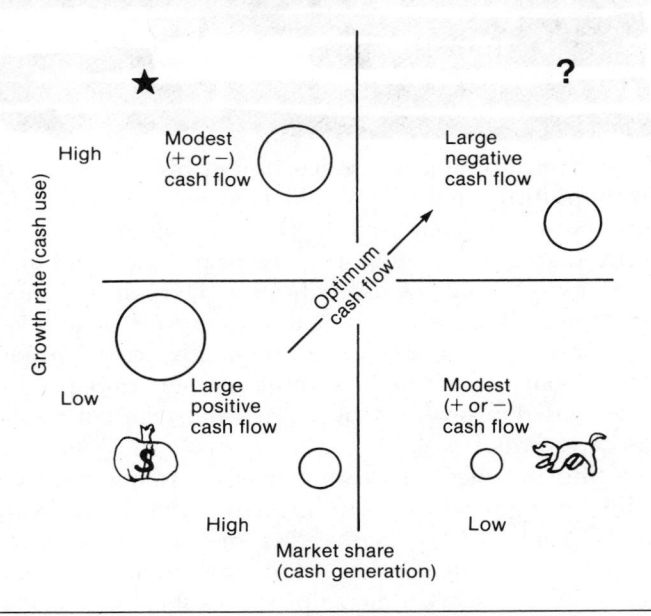

Source: Derek F. Abell and John S. Hammond. *Strategic Marketing Planning* (Englewood Cliffs, N.J.: Prentice-Hall, 1979), p. 178, as adapted from "The Product Portfolio" (Boston Consulting Group, 1970), Perspectives No. 66.

Using this logic, BCG gave colorful names to the quadrants in the product portfolio matrix: cash cows, dogs, question marks, and stars.

Cash cows are higher-share, low-growth products. These two factors contribute to the product's positive cash flow position. Cash cows tend to generate cash beyond their needs.

Question marks, sometimes called *wild cats* or *problem children,* are products with low share of market in a rapidly growing business. These two factors suggest that the product cannot generate enough cash flow to support the investment required to maintain or increase its share of market. Possibly the excess cash flow from a cash cow could be used to fund the investment opportunities of a question mark.

Stars are high market share products in high-growth businesses. These two factors suggest that the cash flow generation and needs are in near balance. Over time, as the market matures and growth rates slow, the product will become a cash cow—assuming that relative share of market is maintained.

Dogs have a low share of market in a low-growth business. These two

factors suggest that cash flow generation and needs are in near balance, but the low-share position can cause poor profitability.

The product portfolio approach to managing existing products in existing markets suggests cash cows should not be allowed to retain all of their cash flow due to the lack of opportunities for profitable growth. Rather, excess cash flow from cash cows should be used to fund growth opportunities present in question marks. The objective for a question mark is to gain share of market, move to the start position, and then to attain a cash cow position as market growth matures. This is called a *success sequence*. A *disaster sequence* involves having a star lose share of market and move to a question mark position. As the market growth matures, the question mark becomes a dog. The loss of share market for a cash cow would result in a disaster sequence to a dog position.

Marketing management generally cannot influence market growth rate but can influence relative share of market. Four share of market options are available to marketing management.

1. Building market share—This option is appropriate for question marks or stars which need to strengthen their share position.
2. Holding market share—This option is appropriate for stars and cash cows. The objective is to maintain their relative position and build barriers around their positions.
3. Harvesting or milking market share—This is appropriate for dogs and selected question marks where limited growth opportunities exist. A cash cow in a declining business may be harvested under certain circumstances.
4. Withdrawal or divesting market share—This is appropriate for dogs when their assets can be deployed more profitably in other areas. The same is the case for question marks.

Distribution decision.   There are two basic issues in distribution decisions: (1) the number of channel levels and (2) the degree of market exposure.

Number of channel levels.   The marketing manager has the option of selling directly to the final consumer (direct marketing) or selling through intermediaries (indirect marketing). One advantage of direct marketing is control over the selling effort; while the advantage of indirect marketing is that it provides lower costs of distribution.

Degree of market exposure.   The second channel issue involves deciding the number of channel outlets or intermediaries needed for the desired market exposure. This requires determining the intensity of distribution to be used.

Intensive distribution is where the maximum market coverage in an area is desired. For example, a manufacturer may attempt to persuade as many retailers in an area as possible to carry the product. *Exclusive distribution* involves the use of a single intermediary (wholesaler, retailer,

or manufacturer's agent) in a market area. *Selective distribution* falls between the extremes of intensive and exclusive distribution. It involves the use of a selective number of intermediaries in a market area. An advantage of intensive distribution is high availability of the product to the consumer; while the advantage of exclusive distribution is increased intermediary cooperation in selling and servicing the product.

Promotion decisions.   There are two fundamental issues in promotion decisions—*push* versus *pull* strategy.

A *pull strategy* directly communicates (usually by advertising and sales promotion) to the end consumer with the expectation of stimulating demand. The promotional objective is to have consumers demand that intermediaries carry the product. This process is called *pulling* the product through the channel of distribution.

The alternative is *push strategy.* Here the promotional objective is to develop programs (usually personal selling, higher margin, and sales promotion) for intermediaries which gain their cooperation in exposing and selling the product to consumers.

Pricing decisions.   When setting the price for a new product, there are two issues: skimming and penetration.

Skimming involves setting a high entry price for a new product targeted to a price-sensitive segment. The objective is to "skim the cream" off the top of the market. Over time, the price is lowered to penetrate successively price-sensitive segments. This is called "sliding down the demand curve."

Penetration involves pricing low to penetrate all segments rapidly. The objective is to gain a large share of the mass market.

Figure 2–5 summarizes the marketing strategy options discussed above. These strategy options must be considered in formulating marketing strategy guidelines.

Evaluating Marketing Strategies

After alternative marketing strategies have been formulated in terms of (1) objectives, (2) target markets, and (3) marketing mix guidelines, the next step is evaluating the strategy options. While the nature of the pros and cons associated with evaluating alternative strategy options is conditional upon the details of the situational analysis, the following guidelines are suggested for evaluating an effective marketing strategy: (1) must be consistent with the business definition/mission; (2) must be consistent with the organization's skills and resources; (3) must exploit and be consistent with external trends and influences; (4) must be flexible enough to respond to rapid changes in external factors; (5) must incorporate carefully developed objectives and market targets; and (6) must possess meaningful benefits which differentiate the marketing mix from competition.

FIGURE 2–5   Marketing strategy options

    I. Product
        A. Degree of product/market fit
        B. Breadth of product/market relationships

   II. Distribution
        A. Number of channel levels
        B. Degree of market exposure

  III. Promotion
        A. Pull
        B. Push

  IV. Price
        A. Skim
        B. Penetration

Marketing Plan

The short-term marketing plan specifies the details of how the marketing strategy will be implemented. There are many possible ways to implement a strategy. Consequently, alternative tactical approaches must be identified and evaluated. These tactical approaches represent specific decisions regarding the marketing mix elements of product, distribution, promotion, and pricing.

The marketing plan can be seen as a composite of several tactical decisions or tactical plans. These tactical plans include the following:

- Product plan—Specific items in the product line, warranty, service, quality, and packaging.
- Distribution plan—Selection of intermediaries and specific programs to support and stimulate them.
- Advertising plan—Selection of creative approach, specific media (TV versus magazine), specific media vehicle (TV or radio programs), type of coverage (national, regional, local), monies, and time schedule.
- Sales force plan—Selection, training, compensation, and assignments of who will do what, where, when, and how.
- Sales promotion plan—Selection of type, timing, and allocation of promotions by products and channel of distribution.
- Pricing plan—Specific price on product line items, quantity discounts, and special price deals.

It is important to remember that an effective marketing plan can only

be developed after the marketing strategy is set and communicated. The tactics should reflect the realities of the situational analysis and be sensitive to changes in assumptions. Finally, the tactical marketing mix decisions must be tied to a carefully developed system for implementation and control.

Marketing Control

Marketing control provides feedback on the implementation of the marketing plan. This feedback allows marketing management to compare expected performance with actual performance. When gaps occur, the manager must decide whether or not adjustments are needed in the short-term marketing program. It is essential that the causes of this gap be identified. If the underlying causes represent changes in the situational analysis, a change in the marketing strategy could be required.

Control of the long-term marketing strategy is achieved by a periodic appraisal called the *marketing audit*. This is an objective and comprehensive evaluation of the marketing strategy in the context of internal and external factors which influence the effectiveness of the strategy. The dynamic nature of the internal and external situational factors triggers the need to reappraise the marketing strategy periodically to determine whether the current strategy and objectives are still appropriate. It is best to have this appraisal done by individuals independent of those directly responsible for implementing the strategy/plan. This assures that critical questions can be asked in a more systematic and unbiased manner.

Control of the short-term marketing plan is achieved by developing specific performance measures for critical aspects of the marketing plan (product, distribution, promotion, and price). Typical measures include: (1) sales (units and dollars), (2) share of market, (3) marketing costs, (4) advertising effectiveness, (5) sales call reports, (6) distribution measures (out-of-stock, shelf space), (7) price levels (manufacturer, wholesaler, and retailer), and (8) profit margins.

These performance measures are typically specific to (1) product lines, (2) target segments (customer size, type, or location), (3) distribution level (wholesale versus retail), and (4) sales territory. Measurements of this nature are available quarterly, monthly, and weekly, in some cases.

Imagine you are the marketing manager for IBM's personal computer. You could measure sales performance by sales territory and compare this performance to a sales objective for the territory. Sales could be higher or lower than this objective. If the deviation is significant, you would want to discover its cause. Sales higher than objectives could result from opportunities not recognized in the marketing plan. Conversely, lower sales might be caused by constraints not anticipated in the plan.

Both situations could result in tactical adjustments in the plan or raise questions about the soundness of the long-term marketing strategy.

The control process just described is an example of *exception management*. Here the control system focuses on the comparison of expected performance versus actual performance. Deviations from expected performance (objectives) are ranked by direction and magnitude for management consideration and potential analysis and action.

MARKET SEGMENTATION

Successful marketing strategies are characterized by marketing programs which have a differential advantage over competition. A differential advantage involves offering a benefit(s) to a significant segment of customers which cannot be obtained elsewhere. The key to developing a differential advantage is to segment the market and identify the unfulfilled desires of the segment. Consequently, market segmentation is a central component in developing a marketing strategy. It can be defined as identifying a group of potential customers who respond similarly to the differential advantage offered by the marketing program.

Requirements for Segmentation

Market segmentation requires that the market be divided into identifiable segments. Thus there is a measurability requirement attached to the segmentation. The variables to be measured may be concerned with geography, demography, or some aspect of consumer behavior. Regardless of the market characteristic or characteristics upon which segmentation is to be based, without the ability to identify segments and to measure their various dimensions, little progress can be made.

Even if a subset of the market is readily identifiable and measurable, it must be reachable by the manufacturer. This "reachability" includes both the promotional and the physical aspects of the marketing strategy mix. It does little good to identify and measure a segment of the market if no channels of distribution are available to reach its occupants or if no economic way exists to communicate with them.

Third, the subset of the market must be of sufficient size, in terms of purchasing power, to offer a profit potential consonant with the extra effort required to design and implement a unique marketing strategy.

Cost–benefit trade-off.   Following a strategy of market segmentation is neither easy nor inexpensive. A great deal of expertise is required in the area of market research as well as in marketing strategy design. Economies of scale are lost as the firm tailors its marketing mix to the needs of a smaller audience group in each of several different market subsets.

On the other hand, the benefits to be derived from a segmentation strategy may be considerable. The manufacturer is closer to each of the submarkets and can react more rapidly to changing tastes or consumption trends. He or she can compare the effectiveness of different strategy variable mixes and can experiment in a submarket with less risk than in a mass market. The manufacturer can design offerings to meet the customers' needs more closely and, in so doing, may capture a larger share of each of the submarkets which he or she is attempting to serve.

As more and more firms find that the payoff from segmentation strategy is highly favorable, the move toward seeking competitive advantage through adapting to the needs of submarkets is accelerating. At present it appears that the question facing most marketing managers is not whether or not to engage in segmentation strategy, but rather on what basis or bases the market should be divided.

If the preliminary situation analysis indicates that a segmentation strategy is desirable, then two questions must be answered. These are: (1) Which bases for segmentation are most likely to provide identifiable, reachable, and substantial submarkets? and (2) What marketing strategy is most likely to gain maximum results from each target segment?

Bases for Market Segmentation

The number of variables that might be used for market segmentation is almost limitless. To help the marketing manager with the selection process, these variables have been classified into categories such as geographic, demographic, psychographic, and behavioristic. These categories and typical breakdowns associated with each are illustrated in Figure 2–6.

As seen in the figure, the demographic variables include such dimensions as age, sex, family size, income, occupation, education, family life

---

FIGURE 2–6   Major segmentation variables and their typical breakdown

Variables	Typical breakdowns
Geographic	
Region	Pacific, Mountain, West North Central, West South Central, East North Central, East South Central, South Atlantic, Middle Atlantic, New England
County size	A, B, C, D
City or SMSA size	Under 5,000; 5,000–19,999; 20,000–49,999; 50,000–99,999; 100,000–249,999; 250,000–499,999; 500,000–999,999; 1,000,000–3,999,999; 4,000,000 or over.
Density	Urban, suburban, rural
Climate	Northern, southern

FIGURE 2–6 (concluded)

Variables	Typical breakdowns
Demographic	
Age	Under 6; 6–11; 12–19; 20–34; 35–49; 50–64; 65 +
Sex	Male, female
Family size	1–2; 3–4; 5 +
Family life cycle	Young, single; young, married, no children; young, married, youngest child under six; young, married, youngest child six or over; older, married, with children; older, married, no children under 18; older, single; other.
Income	Under $3,000; $3,000–$5,000; $5,000–$7,000; $7,000–$10,000; $10,000–$15,000; $15,000–$25,000; $25,000 and over.
Occupation	Professional and technical: managers, officials, and proprietors; clerical, sales; craftsmen, foremen; operatives; farmers; retired; students; housewives; unemployed
Education	Grade school or less; some high school; graduated high school; some college; graduated college
Religion	Catholic, Protestant, Jewish, other
Race	White, black, Oriental
Nationality	American, British, French, German, Scandinavian, Italian, Latin American, Middle Eastern, Japanese
Social class	Lower-lower, upper-lower, lower-middle, upper-middle, lower-upper, upper-upper
Psychographic	
Lifestyle	Straights, swingers, longhairs
Personality	Compulsive, gregarious, authoritarian, ambitious
Behavioristic	
Purchase occasion	Regular occasion, special occasion
Benefits sought	Economy, convenience, prestige
User status	Nonuser, exuser, potential user, first-time user, regular user
Usage rate	Light user, medium user, heavy user
Loyalty status	None, medium, strong, absolute
Readiness stage	Unaware, aware, informed, interested, desirous, intending to buy
Marketing-factor sensitivity	Quality, price, service, advertising, sales promotion

Source: Philip Kotler, *Marketing Management: Analysis, Planning, and Control*, 5th ed., © 1984, p. 256. Reprinted by permission of Prentice-Hall, Inc.,Englewood Cliffs, New Jersey.

cycle, religion, race, nationality, and social class. The geographic variables are those which pertain to region, climate, size of city and county, and whether the location of the potential customer is in an urban, suburban, or rural area.

Demographic or geographic segmentation bases are easy to understand, and data collection and analysis are usually straightforward. For example, suppose that a beer manufacturer were interested in applying a segmentation strategy. Market research indicated that the sales of beer were strongly correlated with such demographic variables as age of head

of household and level of income. In addition, beer sales appeared to be related to the geographic variable that described the population density. Given this information, the market for this manufacturer's beer might be segmented into 36 submarkets, as illustrated in Figure 2–7. Each submarket might then be evaluated in terms of market potential, and strategy could be devised to reach those segments most likely to produce the most profitable sales volume.

FIGURE 2–7   Segmentation of beer market by two demographic and one geographic variable

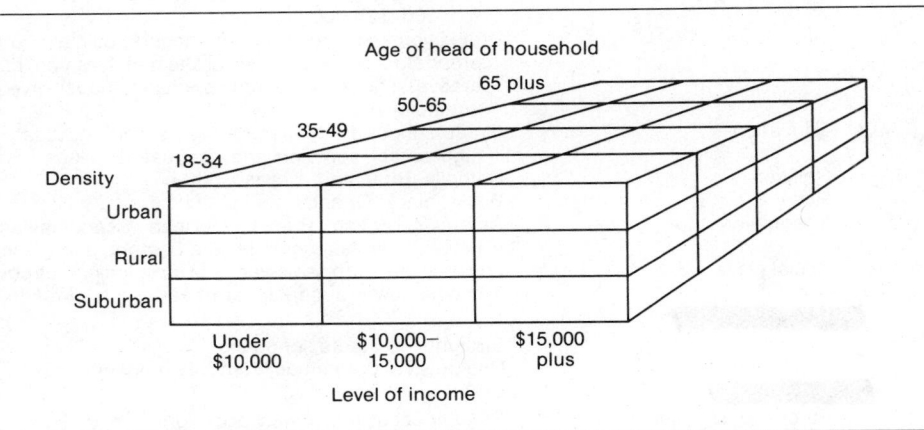

Geographic and demographic variables have been defined as those that describe the consumer's "state of being."[5] In contrast, those variables that describe the consumer's "state of mind" may be termed psychographic. Some typical breakdowns of this latter category, such as degree of compulsiveness, gregariousness, and autonomy, are illustrated in Figure 2–6. The use of such personality variables to isolate segments of the market has not proved feasible—even after almost two decades of research following a highly controversial study reported by Evans in 1959 in which he concluded that personality variables were of little value in

[5]Ben M. Enis, *Marketing Principles: The Management Process* (Santa Monica, Calif.: Goodyear Publishing, 1974), p. 281.

differentiating owners of Ford automobiles from persons owning Chevrolets.[6]

Perhaps more useful psychological variables are those that describe the "lifestyle" of potential buyers. Lifestyle measurement for the purpose of providing bases for market segmentation is usually accompanied by means of AIO (Activities, Interests, and Opinions) rating statements.[7] Specifically, lifestyle research is aimed at measuring people's activities "in terms of (1) how they spend their time; (2) their interests, what they place importance on in their immediate surroundings; (3) their opinions in terms of their view of themselves and the world around them; and (4) some basic characteristics such as their stage in life cycle, income, education, and where they live."[8] Proponents of lifestyle segmentation claim that it provides a more fully detailed view of the target markets and allows for more effective product positioning, communication, and media selection.

In contrast to psychographics, the use of buyer behavior variables for segmentation purposes has a longer history of success. The usage rate, readiness stage, benefits sought, end use, and brand loyalty dimensions have proved to be effective means of identifying submarkets in each of which consumers behave in a unique manner. For example, the behavior of consumers who are heavy users of a product type and have strong loyalties is different from the behavior of infrequent users who show little or no loyalty to a given brand.

Closely allied to both psychographic and buyer behavior bases for market segmentation is the use of data on consumer perceptions of various products and their preferences for certain brands. The ability of marketing researchers to utilize computers to apply what are known as "multidimensional scaling" techniques enables them to determine how products or brands are perceived with respect to similarities or dissimilarities on several dimensions, to find out whether or not existing brands or products are meeting consumer needs, and to locate opportunities for the introduction of new products or brands or for the modification and/or repositioning of existing ones.

An example of the application of these techniques to an analysis of the Chicago beer market is illustrated in Figure 2–8. The two-dimensional product space was obtained by asking consumers to rate various

[6]Franklin B. Evans, "Psychological and Objective Factors in the Prediction of Brand Choice: Ford versus Chevrolet," *Journal of Business,* October 1959, pp. 340–69. In this study, Evans tested the hypothesis that Ford owners were "independent, impulsive, masculine, alert to change, and self-confident," while Chevrolet owners were "conservative, thrifty, prestige-conscious, less masculine, and seeking to avoid extremes."

[7]William Wells and Doug Tigert. "Activities, Interests, and Opinions," *Journal of Advertising Research,* August 1971, pp. 27–35.

[8]Joseph T. Plummer, "The Concept and Application of Lifestyle Segmentation," *Journal of Marketing,* January 1974, pp. 33–37.

beers on appropriate scales of mildness and lightness. The computer program averaged these ratings to produce a rectangular space with products positioned as illustrated by the solid black dots. Reading this "perceptual map" indicates that Schlitz and Budweiser are viewed as being quite similar products. Both are prestige beers and are somewhat on the heavy side. Miller and Hamm's are perceived as being somewhat lighter than Schlitz and Budweiser.

FIGURE 2–8   A two-dimensional product space for the Chicago beer market

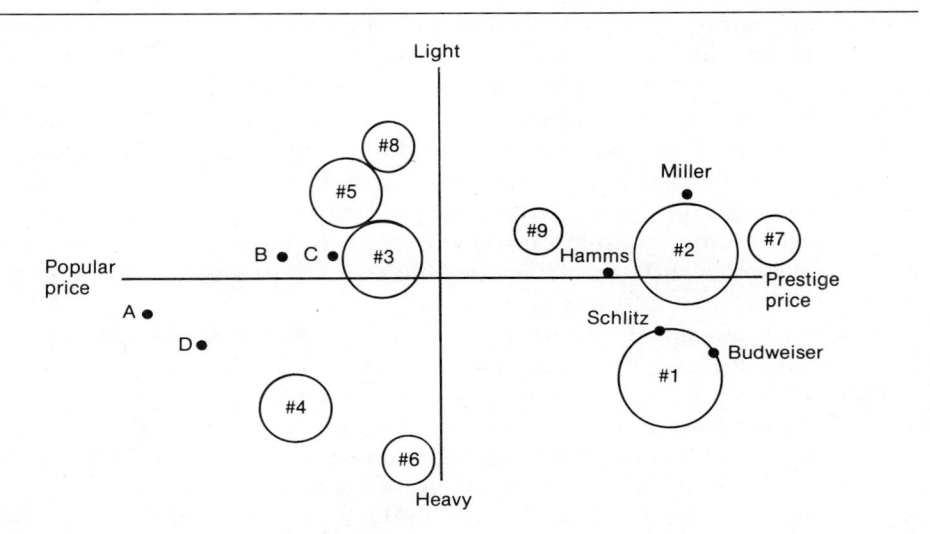

Source: Adapted from Richard M. Johnson, "Market Segmentation: A Strategic Management Tool," *Journal of Marketing Research,* February 1971, pp. 13–18, with permission of the publisher, the American Marketing Association.

The second purpose of the study was to determine consumer preferences for beer. To accomplish this goal, consumers were asked to rate their "ideal" brand of beer on similar scales. These ratings were then processed by the computer to identify the location of "ideal" points on the preference map. The points clustered in several locations in the space, and these clusters have been identified by the numbered circles. Clusters 1 and 2 are the largest and are positioned near the largest-selling brands. Several clusters are not near any brand, and thus the map suggests that there might be an opportunity for the entry of a new brand which meets the needs of a specific group of consumers. In addition, the analysis indicates that brands A, B, and D might be reformu-

lated and repositioned to be closer to the clusters of "ideal" points on the popular-price half of the preference map.[9]

Moving from consumer reaction to a specific product or brand, we must also consider consumer reaction or sensitivity to the various elements in the marketing strategy mix. Marketing factor sensitivity is the name given to the variable that can be used to segment a market on the basis of how consumers react to product quality, service, advertising, and other aspects of the sales promotion program. Using this basis, the manufacturer might identify a market segment composed of consumers very sensitive to price, and another segment in which potential buyers were concerned with quality and service.

Two versions of the product might be designed, and an economy-priced model would be marketed by means of a strategy mix that emphasized price. Retail outlets would be discount stores or basement departments of leading department stores. In contrast, a more costly version of the product would be directed to the market segment in which consumers emphasized quality and service. The marketing strategy mix would be varied accordingly, with greater emphasis placed on gaining distribution through full-service, quality retail outlets.

CONCLUSION

Marketing strategy establishes the competitive thrust but not the specific marketing mix details or tactics of how the organization will compete. It identifies objectives, target markets, and marketing mix guidelines. Once the marketing strategy has been determined, the marketing plan specifies the tactical details for each element of the marketing mix. This is the organization's one-year marketing plan. The implementation of the plan is controlled by establishing detailed marketing mix measures where performance can be compared to objectives.

Strategic market planning is a broader concept than the marketing planning process. It contains a statement of business definition or mission before the marketing strategy is formulated. Business definition defines the organization in terms of customer groups and needs while recognizing the need for consistency with the internal skills and resources of the organization.

QUESTIONS

1. Why does the business definition logically precede the formulation of a marketing strategy?

---

[9]In addition to the Johnson study noted previously, see Edgar A, Pessemier and H. Paul Root, "The Dimensions of New-Product Planning," *Journal of Marketing*, January 1973, pp. 10–18.

2. Why should a firm have more than one strategic option to evaluate?

3. Comment on the following statement of marketing objectives: "We are committed to broader sales and increased profit through aggressively capturing market share from competition."

4. Given the growth options in Figure 2–2, which option is the most risky and which is the least risky? Why?

5. List some advantages and disadvantages of the BCG portfolio analysis concept.

6. Using Figure 2–5 as a guide, identify the strategic options used by Procter & Gamble in marketing Ivory bar soap.

7. Differentiate between long- and short-term marketing control.

8. Why do different companies in the same industry, selling comparable products, often use different marketing strategies ?

9. Compare and contrast demographic segmentation bases with bases of a psychographic or behavioral nature.

MARKETING RESEARCH

3

A primary task of a marketing manager is to make decisions. In the marketing planning process, decisions must be made as to the markets to be served as well as what combination of marketing strategy variables will be most effective in these markets. The dynamic nature of marketing requires continual appraisal of the situation and frequent decisions about whether changes should be made in the market targets previously selected or in the strategy mixes developed to reach them.

Marketing decisions are not made in a vacuum. Executives responsible for making such decisions require a wide variety of informational inputs that, when combined with their collective experience, allow them to make decisions that effectively advance the firm toward attainment of its marketing objectives.

Informational inputs have been classified as (1) facts, (2) estimates, (3) predictions, (4) generalized relationships, and (5) rumors.[1] Facts are events or conditions that are directly observed; estimates are pieces of information based on inference and/or statistical procedures rather than on direct observation and enumeration. Predictions deal with the future, in contrast to facts and estimates, which deal with the past and the

---

[1]Robert D. Buzzell, Donald F. Cox, and Rex V. Brown, *Marketing Research and Information Systems: Text and Cases* (New York: McGraw-Hill, 1969), p. 11.

present. Generalized relationships are linkages among variables that may be used as the bases for estimation and prediction. An example of a generalized relationship may be the connection between the birthrate and the demand for baby food. Finally, there are rumors, or information from sources of unknown reliability.

Based on the classification scheme utilized above, the following broad definition of information in a management context has been suggested:

> *Information* consists of all objective facts *and* all beliefs that affect a decision maker's perceptions of the nature and extent of the uncertainties associated with a given management problem or opportunity.[2]

Note that a key word in the above definition is *uncertainties*. The successful manager is one who has learned what types of information will reduce the uncertainty associated with a decision and is able to obtain the information at a cost consistent with the value of reduced uncertainty. More about the cost-benefit aspect of information will be said later in this chapter.

GETTING INFORMATION INTO MARKETING DECISIONS

Granted that information of many types is important for effective marketing decision making, the problem is how to insure the actual use of such information in planning marketing strategy. This problem is critical because of the substantial progress that has been made in recent years in developing new and more powerful concepts and tools for use in gathering information. This "new technology" of marketing relates not only to information about buyer behavior, but also to other data that are potentially helpful in planning, executing, and monitoring marketing programs.

While better research tools are now available to supply information to aid in the solution of marketing problems, not enough is known about how to put them to work effectively in the decision-making process. Among the impediments to progress, Newman lists (1) the limited backgrounds of certain marketing executives; (2) the fact that some business executives see research as a threat to their personal status and therefore resist its use; (3) the absence of systematic planning in some organizations; (4) the inability of some executives to make productive use of specialists from such disciplines as psychology, anthropology, sociology, semantics, economics, mathematics, and statistics; and (5) the isolation of some marketing departments from management.[3]

---

[2]Ibid., p. 13.

[3]Joseph W. Newman, "Put Research into Marketing Decisions," *Harvard Business Review,* March–April 1962, pp. 105-12.

If we are going to correct this situation, according to Newman, we must first do two basic things:

1. Think more specifically in terms of an ongoing process of decision making that requires a flow of inputs.
2. See research as the systematic application of a variety of concepts and methods that can be useful in generating these inputs.

Stated differently, "The main point is that research is not simply a matter of having a survey done from time to time, as has been so typical in the past. Instead, it should be a continuous program designed to help management set its objective, plan for its accomplishment, implement the plans successfully, and evaluate the outcome so that still better programs may be undertaken in the future." In short, one way to get relevant information into the marketing decision-making process is through the development and use of a marketing information system, which would provide the data needed by marketing managers to plan, execute, and control more effectively.

CONCEPT OF A MARKETING INFORMATION SYSTEM

A firm's *marketing information system* consists of "a structured, interacting complex of persons, machines, and procedures designed to generate an orderly flow of pertinent information, collected from both intra- and extrafirm sources, for use as the basis for decision making in specified responsibility areas of marketing management."[4]

The components of a marketing information system are visualized in Figure 3–1.[5] This diagram shows the marketing information system as the connecting link between the environment and the marketing executive. The system generates a *marketing data flow* concerning the noncontrollable variables in the environment. The marketing information system converts this flow of data into a *marketing information flow,* which is made available to marketing executives for use in planning, execution, and control. Using this information, the executives then develop marketing plans and strategies that result in a flow of information back to certain elements in the environment.

As Figure 3–1 indicates, a marketing information system includes four subsystems: (1) the internal accounting system, which provides measures of current activity and performance; (2) the marketing intelligence system, which gathers and makes available information on devel-

---

[4]Samuel V. Smith, Richard H. Brien, and Jerome E. Stafford, eds., *Readings in Marketing Information Systems* (Boston: Houghton Mifflin, 1968), p. 7.

[5]Adapted from Philip Kotler, *Marketing Management: Analysis, Planning, and Control,* 4th ed. (1980), p. 603. Reprinted by permission of Prentice-Hall, Inc., Englewood Cliffs, New Jersey.

FIGURE 3–1   Components of the marketing information system

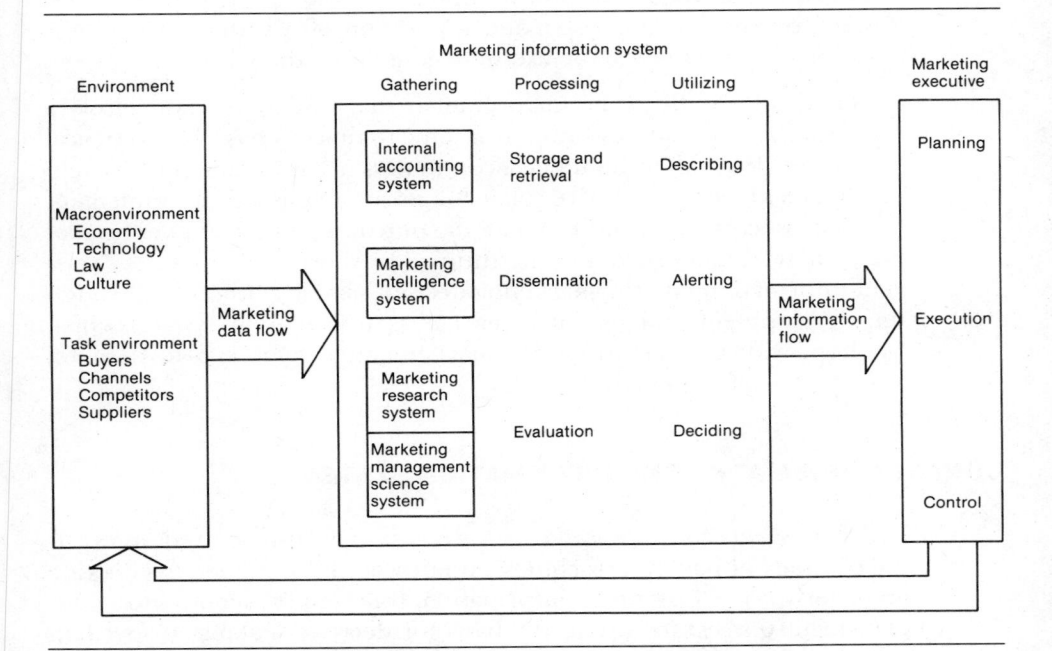

Source: Adapted from Philip Kotler, *Marketing Management: Analysis, Planning, and Control,* 4th ed. (1980), p. 603.
Reprinted by permission of Prentice-Hall, Inc., Englewood Cliffs, New Jersey.

opments in the environment; (3) the marketing research system, which gathers, evaluates, and reports information required by executives for problem solving, planning, and the development of marketing strategy; and (4) the marketing management science system, which assists executives in analyzing complex marketing problems and operations, often through the use of analytical models.

MARKETING RESEARCH

In this chapter we shall concentrate on the marketing research subsystem of the marketing information system. While the number of firms having well-developed marketing information systems is limited at present, many firms engage in marketing research. A recent study of 798 companies of diverse sizes and representing many industries was made under the auspices of the American Marketing Association. In a report

published in 1978, the findings indicated that 76 percent of the respond-ing firms had formal marketing research departments.[6] The wide vari-ety of research activities undertaken by these firms is illustrated in Figure 3–2.

FIGURE 3–2   Research activities of 798 companies

Type of research	Percent doing
Advertising research	
Motivation research	48
Copy research	49
Media research	61
Studies of ad effectiveness	67
Business economics and corporate research	
Short-range forecasting (up to one year)	85
Long-range forecasting (over one year)	82
Studies of business trends	86
Pricing studies	81
Plant and warehouse location studies	71
Product mix studies	51
Acquisition studies	69
Export and international studies	51
MIS (management information system)	72
Operations research	60
Internal company employees	65
Corporate responsibility research	
Consumers "right-to-know" studies	26
Ecological impact studies	33
Studies of legal constraints on advertising and promotion	51
Social values and policies studies	40
Product research	
New-product acceptance and potential	84
Competitive-product studies	85
Testing of existing products	75
Packaging research—design or physical characteristics	60
Sales and market research	
Measurement of market potentials	93
Market share analysis	92
Determination of market characteristics	93
Sales analysis	89
Establishment of sales quotas, territories	75
Distribution channels studies	69
Test markets, store audits	54
Consumer-panel operations	50
Sales compensation studies	60
Promotional studies of premiums, coupons, sampling, deals, etc.	52

Source: Dik Warren Twedt, ed., *1978 Survey of Marketing Research* (Chicago: American Marketing Association, 1978), p. 41.

---

[6]Dik Warren Twedt, ed., *1978 Survey of Market Research* (Chicago: American Market-ing Association, 1978), p. 41.

The simplest definition of marketing research is "the systematic collection of information for the purpose of decision making."[7] It is the way in which a firm gets and tests ideas. Marketing research is not a part of the marketing mix but rather an aid to management in making decisions about the marketing mix and the market targets at which it is aimed.

TYPES OF MARKETING RESEARCH

Not all marketing research activities are the same. They differ in purpose, extensiveness, research design, mode of data analysis, and format of presentation. In the following discussion we shall attempt to cover some of these aspects of the marketing research process in more detail. We shall classify research activity in terms of whether it is *exploratory* in nature, aimed at a *specific* problem, or used to provide *routine feedback*. Our goal is to familiarize future marketing managers with the importance and complexity of marketing research. Although few marketing managers actually conduct research, the most effective ones, in our opinion, are those who understand the research process and stay involved through the various stages from problem definition to final reporting.

To illustrate better the different types of research, we must move from the generality that marketing research is aimed at getting and testing ideas to something more specific. Take, for example, a situation in which a sales promotion that appears to offer a good value to the consumer does not live up to expectations. Marketing management thus has a problem but does not know its exact nature or causes. Without such information it is difficult to prescribe an effective solution. What is needed is some type of research of an "exploratory" nature aimed at more precise problem definition and perhaps the uncovering of hypotheses that might lead to an effective solution.

Exploratory research. An example of exploratory research may be illustrated by relating the experiences of a large manufacturer of food products who was promoting a newly developed dehydrated chicken noodle soup by offering a premium to each purchaser of the product. In each plastic package of soup the manufacturer placed printed material offering a pair of women's hosiery at a discounted price to those women who would return the coupon. The printed material included a picture of a pair of legs wearing the hosiery being offered; it was clearly visible through the packaging. The promotion was a failure in that nei-

[7]Milton P. Brown, Richard N. Cardozo, Scott M. Cunningham, Walter J. Salmon, and Ralph G. M. Sultan, *Problems in Marketing*, 4th ed. (New York: McGraw-Hill, 1968), p. 409.

ther sales of the soup nor requests for the premium came anywhere near expectations.

It was decided to undertake exploratory research in the form of depth interviews with small groups of potential customers for the product. These interviews suggested the hypothesis that the hosiery promotion elicited images of "feet in the soup," a highly unattractive picture for many potential buyers.[8] When the premium was changed, the sales response was as expected and the problem was solved.

Specific research. Another type of research is termed "specific research." When a problem has been defined, a different type of information input is needed to enable management to make decisions concerning alternative ways of solving the problem. Specific questions that might be posed include: What changes should be made in the marketing mix? Is the product positioned properly? What are the likely responses of the leading competitors, and what effect will these responses have on the market share? Questions such as these lead to specific research. Returning to the chicken soup situation, specific research by management might be used to determine the most effective premium to use instead of the hosiery. Such research might be conducted by test marketing in several representative but geographically separated areas. Specific research generally involves the use of larger samples and is more costly than exploratory research. That is because while exploratory research is aimed at suggesting hypotheses, specific research is used to enable management to accept or reject hypotheses with predetermined levels of confidence.

Routine feedback. A third type of research is routine feedback. It is an attempt to monitor on a continuous basis certain dependent variables such as sales, market share, or consumer sentiment. Firms with well-operating marketing information systems would be receiving such information through the marketing intelligence subsystem. Firms without such sophisticated means of conducting routine feedback research have two options. The first is to utilize the marketing research department to engage in gathering and assessing routine feedback. Such a course of action is utilized by certain members of the Bell System in a continuous appraisal of customer attitudes with respect to the various aspects of telephone service offered.[9] Companies without the necessary internal resources may avail themselves of commercial services such as those offered by the Nielsen Retail Audit, which monitors movement of goods off of the shelves of retail stores, or by the Market Research Corporation

---

[8]See Edward H. Weiss, "How Motivation Studies May Be Used for Creative People to Improve Advertising," in *Advertising Conference: Contributed Papers* James D. Scott, ed. (Ann Arbor: Bureau of Business Research, The University of Michigan, 1954), pp. 47–49.

[9]See TELSAM (telephone service attitude measurement), a series of studies undertaken by the Michigan Bell Telephone Company, 1974.

of America, which is one of several private research firms that maintain a continuous consumer panel to monitor consumer preferences for specific brands and consumer reactions to existing marketing programs.

The relationships among the three types of research and the decision process sequence followed by marketing managers are illustrated in Figure 3–3. The research terminology of hypothesis formulation and testing has been replaced by the management concepts of problem recognition, the identification and evaluation of alternative courses of action, and the selection and implementation of the course of action deemed most likely to resolve the problem under consideration.

ROLE OF THE MARKETING MANAGER IN THE RESEARCH PROCESS

In support of the thesis that the more effective marketing managers are those who are intimately involved with the marketing research

---

FIGURE 3–3   Types of research

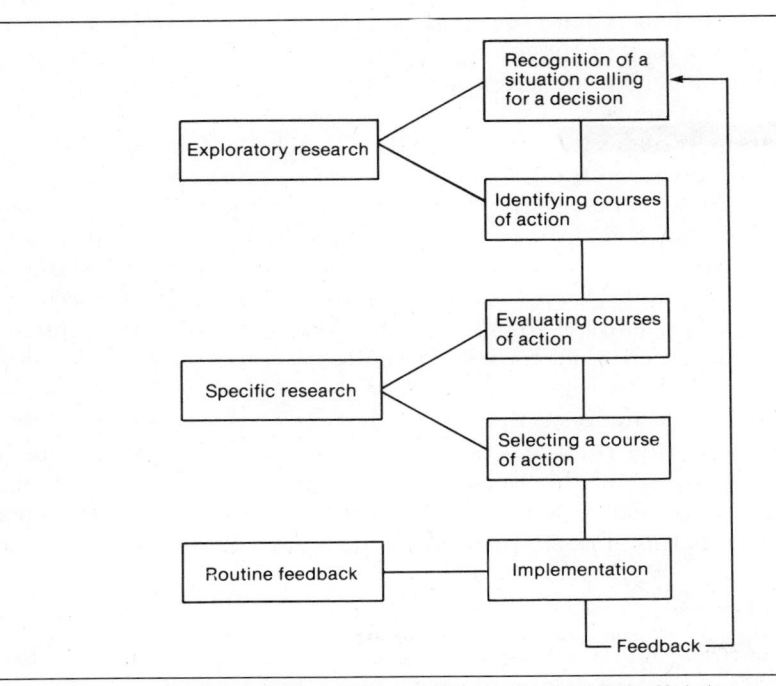

Source: Adapted from Thomas C. Kinnear and James R. Taylor, *Marketing Research: An Applied Approach* (New York: McGraw-Hill, 1983), p. 84. Reprinted by permission.

process, although they may not actually do the research, this section will consider the nature of managerial responsibility, given the various activities that make up marketing research. Perhaps the following questions will best illustrate the role of the marketing manager in instigating and utilizing research.

What is the nature of the problem?   This is the first and perhaps the most important of the questions that must receive consideration from management. Indications that a problem (or problems) may exist may come from a situation analysis made prior to a decision on a specific marketing strategy or may emanate from an appraisal of the results of an existing strategy. Regardless of its source, a problem must be defined in such a way that not only is it researchable but that the information evoked by research will be useful in its solution. For example, asking a researcher to measure brand acceptance in market X is a feasible request. If the problem is that the market share of the product in market X has been falling for the past year, then it is doubtful that the information as to brand acceptance will be sufficient to indicate a course of action that will remedy the problem of declining market share. It is therefore crucial at this stage of the marketing research process that the marketing manager and the researcher work together. The manager can then explain the type of problem perceived and indicate the type of information needed to make a decision, which, hopefully, will provide a solution to the problem. The researcher, in turn, can indicate various ways in which the problem can be specified to aid in the gathering of data and its analysis. In many cases a slight reformulation of the problem will allow the use of specific techniques that will provide a better payoff for the research dollar spent.

Failure of collaboration at the problem definiton stage of the process is so costly in terms of wrong questions asked and irrelevant answers provided that some firms have insisted that their product managers be fully responsible for the marketing research activities needed for their decision making.

Is the problem researchable?   Although problem definition is most crucial to the success of the marketing research project, often a well-defined problem is not researchable. There are several reasons why a seemingly legitimate problem is not a candidate for research activity. First, considerations other than research findings may be the determinantes of a specific course of action. Budgetary limitations, for example, may preclude a specific marketing strategy, although research would probably indicate that it would be the most effective way of generating sales. Second, when variations in the results of research, even if sizable, would not influence the choice of alternatives, it would be a waste of resources to engage in the project. Third, when the cost of information is out of proportion to the benefits to be attained by solving the given problem, the problem may be deemed to be nonresearchable. Fourth,

when the value of achieving the marketing objective is limited, even a small expenditure on research may not be justified. Fifth, and last, research takes time. In a dynamic business activity such as marketing, time is usually of extreme value, and thus delaying a decision to gain more information may be risky. Competitors may be alerted to a proposed strategy by noting the type of research being undertaken and may make changes in their own strategies to counter the effects of the proposed strategic moves. On the other hand, the risk of failure of a proposed strategy may be so great that the time delay for research must be accepted so that the quality of the decision will be improved.

The central purpose of the above discussion is to lay to rest the myth that research is always a desirable course of action. Both students and practitioners, when faced with difficult marketing problems, will seek haven in a call for more research. Such a call is only valid when the results of research will influence the course of action, when the value of the information obtained from research is greater than its cost, and when the time delay occasioned by research can be justified on a risk-benefit basis.

What type of research should be used?   This question can only be answered after problem definition has been attempted and the question of researchability resolved. Then the choices are among the three types of research discussed previously: exploratory, specific, and routine feedback.

Exploratory research should be considered when management cannot define the problem in specific terms. It is a way of uncovering hypotheses that can then be tested by specific research. When the situation analysis provides a reasonably clear idea of the nature of the problem, specific research can be undertaken without the need for any additional exploratory efforts.

In contrast, routine feedback research is aimed at finding out how well current strategy is working in the marketplace. In addition to letting management know how well current goals are being met, it can alert management to incipient problems arising out of changes in demand or competitive conditions.

How much to spend on research?   This question is easier to answer in theory than in practice. Let us consider a conceptual approach to the problem, and then we will attempt to illustrate a practical way of handling the problem. Figure 3–4 illustrates a graph on which the payoff of research is plotted against the cost of research.

In this graph, the payoff of research is plotted against its cost. The vertical axis indicates the dollar amounts of costs and payoffs, while the horizontal axis indicates the number of units of information purchased. The assumption is made that as the number of units of information available increases, the degree of uncertainty decreases.

FIGURE 3–4   Relationship between cost and payoff of research

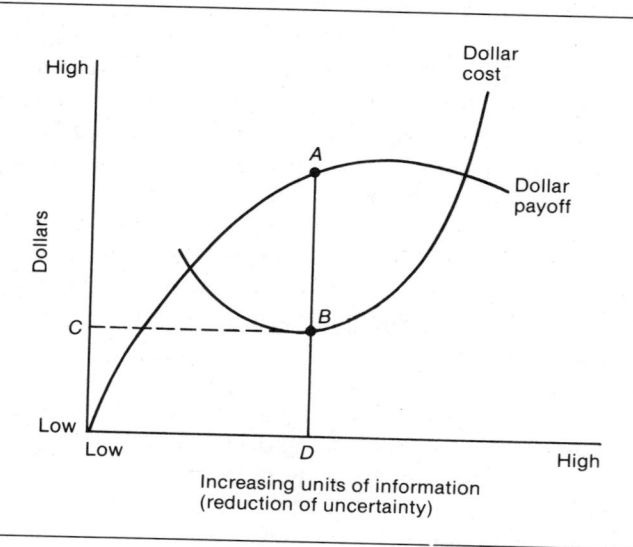

Source: Adapted from Milton P. Brown et al., *Problems in Marketing*, 4th ed. (New York: McGraw-Hill, 1968), p. 416.

When the cost curve is above the payoff curve, the initiation of research is not indicated. When the payoff curve is above the cost curve, research is economically feasible. The optimal expenditure for research *C,* is found by locating where the vertical distance between the curves is greatest (*A* minus *B*). In like manner, by reading from the horizontal axis, the number of units of information that would be purchased by this expenditure is found to be *D*.

Although the approach described above is of value conceptually, it is extremely difficult in practice to assign payoff values to increments of information. The model does indicate, however, the need for management to evaluate the probable payoff of a research project against the cost of engaging in it. There are sophisticated methods of doing this by using subjective probabilities. Although we will not go into detail as to these methods in this book, the essence of this approach is to estimate the value of a decision, assuming it to be a correct one. Then an estimate is made of the loss that would be incurred if the decision were incorrect. Given these estimates of probable gains and losses and the likelihoods of the decision being either correct or incorrect, a judgment can be made about whether a proposed investment in research is reasonable in light

of the expected value of a correct decision or the expected loss resulting from a wrong one.[10]

DESIGNING THE RESEARCH PROJECT

Most marketing managers delegate the detailed design and implementation of research projects to specialists either within or outside their organizations. The principal reason for such delegation is that most marketing managers do not have the time or the expertise to engage in market research activities. They must, to a greater or lesser extent, depend on the efforts of others. It is therefore most important that managers know enough about research design and methods of implementing research to be effective in commissioning research and to be capable of appraising the quality and cost effectiveness of its results.

Problem definition. As has been noted earlier in this chapter, problem definition is the most important step in the research process. Without a clear definition of the problem to be studied, the rest of the process will not produce much of use to the decision maker. If it is apparent that the problem area has not been defined with sufficient clarity, then the only recourse is to continue exploratory research until problem definition allows a statement of hypotheses which can be tested by specific research.

Information gathering. For purposes of exposition, let us assume that the research project is still in the exploratory stage. What is needed is additional information which will aid to define the problem more clearly. The most widely used practice to gain this needed information is to search for data which have already been collected, but for other purposes. These data are termed "secondary," and they may be found in company records, government publications, university publications, trade association studies, scholarly journals, and so forth. Most university business school libraries have lists of sources of secondary data which are useful to marketing researchers. Annotated lists of sources may be found in some texts in marketing research.[11]

If data which shed some light on the problem cannot be found in secondary sources, then steps must be taken to collect data which are specifically relevant to the investigation. Such data are termed "primary" because they have never been used before for the purpose at hand.

Data collection from primary sources. If the research is in the exploratory stage, three methods of data collection which can be used

---

[10]For further information on this approach, see Paul E. Green and Donald S. Tull, *Research for Marketing Decisions*, 3d ed. (Englewood Cliffs, N.J.: Prentice-Hall, 1975), pp. 16–37.

[11]See Thomas C. Kinnear and James R. Taylor, *Marketing Research: An Applied Approach* (New York: McGraw-Hill, 1983), pp. 145–56, 169–84.

include observation, casual interviews, and focus group interviews. If the research has progressed to the specific stage, then experimental or survey research methods are more suitable. A hypothetical case history will be used to illustrate the data collection process.

A manufacturer of frozen gourmet soups sold his product through selected specialty food stores. In order to increase his sales volume he was considering marketing the product to a broader array of consumers who purchased food in supermarkets. To determine whether the strategy proposal was feasible, the manufacturer could have engaged in exploratory research to uncover potential problems (and opportunities) which might be faced if the proposed change in strategy were implemented. A small team of observers could have been sent to study the behavior of soup purchasers in supermarkets. Of special interest might have been the extent and nature of the search process by which consumers located soup in the store and the length of the deliberations, if any, at the point of purchase.

These and other observations could then have been supplemented by casual interviews with selected shoppers as well as with store personnel concerned with the stocking and display of soup products. Questions that might have been asked would include: Can you understand and accept the product concept? What are your attitudes about the placement of soup in the freezer section? What benefits would you expect to receive from this product?

A third research option would be to assemble a small group of a dozen or so persons representative of the target market audience into what is termed a "focus group." In-depth interviews could then be held with this group to develop and further clarify insights gained through observation and casual interviews. In a well-directed focus group interview new ideas and insights should surface, thus throwing more light on the situation under study.

The purpose of these methods is to gather sufficient information from primary sources to move the research to the specific stage. Given researchable hypotheses, experimental or survey research methods can be used to accept or reject them.

Experimental methods.   The experimental approach is used to determine whether or not a cause-and-effect relationship exists between an independent variable and a dependent variable. In the context of the frozen gourmet soup example, let us assume that one result of the exploratory research was the development of the hypothesis that location of the product within the supermarket had an important effect on the sales activity of the product. With the experimental method the researcher creates a situation in which the manipulation of an independent variable such as the in-store location of the product allows cause-and-effect statements to be made about a dependent variable such as the sales volume of the product. Imagine an experimental design in which

frozen gourmet soup would be placed in the soup sections of three supermarkets and in the frozen food departments of three other but similar supermarkets. Price, promotion, and packaging would all be identical, so that the only variable being manipulated would be in-store location.

The dependent variable would be sales of the product over a predetermined time period, say three months. If at the end of this time it could be shown that sales were greater in those stores in which the product was located in the soup section than in the stores in which it was placed with frozen foods, a statement could be made that the experimental results supported the hypothesis. The results could also serve as a more general test of the market acceptance of the product and could indicate whether or not the product with its associated marketing program appeared likely to meet its volume and profit goals.

Survey method.   An approach in which a research instrument such as a questionnaire is used to obtain information from a large number of respondents is known as survey research. As is the case with the experimental method, survey research is most effective as a form of specific research in which information is gathered for the acceptance or rejection of hypotheses.

Returning once again to the frozen gourmet soup example, let us assume that several hypotheses are available for testing. Some of these might be: H_1—most consumers perceive that the costs and inconveniences of the new product outweigh its benefits; H_2—supermarket managers will require margins equal to those obtained on frozen foods before they will stock the product.

The next step is the development of the research instrument or questionnaire that will be used to collect information from the sample and that will enable the hypotheses to be accepted or rejected. Devising such a questionnaire requires considerable skill. It is highly advisable to pretest the questionnaire on a small sample of respondents to make sure that it is working as desired. If not, changes can be made to increase its effectiveness; and, after another pretest, it is ready to be used on the larger sample.

The next part of the survey research procedure deals with the sampling plan. How large should the sample be? How will the sample be chosen? Will the survey be made by field interviewers, by telephone, or by mail? The answers to these questions are very important, but the detailed discussion of these technical aspects of survey research is beyond the scope of this text. Fortunately, several excellent sources cover these areas in considerable detail.[12]

Continuing with the frozen gourmet soup example, let us assume that the researchers in the company have decided to mail a questionnaire to

---

[12]See Kinnear and Taylor, *Marketing Research.*

selected customers and supermarket buying personnel. The decision has been made to cover 100 percent of the supermarket buyers in the area. Given the size of the sample and the number of persons responding, statistical statements about the significance of the findings of the survey can be made after the data have been analyzed.

The final step in the survey process is the tabulation and analysis of the data. If the questionnaire has been prepared properly, the responses can be transferred to a coding sheet and thence to computer punch cards. Once the data are in this form, many techniques for data analysis are available, including simple cross-tabulation, simple or multiple regression, and more sophisticated multivariate analytic methods such as factor and discriminant analyses. Again, the details of the methods are beyond the scope of this text, but the objective in using these methods is to be able to support or reject the research hypotheses.

Presentation format. The format of the presentation of the research results also flows from the nature of the research project and the reason it was undertaken. For example, specific research on consumer attitudes about a proposed new type of product that will be used continuously for a considerable period of time will require a much more detailed and lengthy presentation than will the results of exploratory or routine feedback research. With respect to the latter, management will usually accept short reports on sales, share of market, and/or profit figures unless a marked deviation from projected levels is seen. Indeed, given the increasing dependence on computers, this type of information may be made available to interested executives on a continuous basis by means of teletype terminals or cathode-ray tube readout devices. When and if an "exception" is noted, management may then request a more detailed report or even some specific research to uncover the cause and the possible remedy for, say, a drop in sales or market share.

DEMAND FORECASTING

— DONT SPEND MUCH TIME ON THIS JUST KNOW THE BASIC STEPS OF THE TOP DOWN & BUILD UP METHOD

Our discussion of marketing research up to this point has emphasized obtaining information of a qualitative rather than a quantitative nature, although these two types of information cannot be clearly separated. It has focused on answering such questions as: (1) Why do people buy? (2) What criteria do they use to discriminate among products? and (3) How do they seek information? Now our emphasis will be tilted toward answering such questions as: (1) How much of a product will the market purchase? (2) Where will consumers purchase? and (3) When will they purchase? The research done to answer these and similar questions is usually referred to as *demand forecasting*. It provides the information needed to set goals for the planning of marketing strategy discussed in Chapter 1.

A marketing manager has no choice but to forecast demand, however clouded the future and difficult the task. Every move that he or she makes in planning and executing marketing strategy involves an implicit assumption about the quantitative aspects of demand. For example, a decision to launch a new product assumes that future demand will be adequate to support profitable operations; a decision to enlarge a sales force implicitly assumes a demand adequate to support the increased level of expenditure. If demand is assumed to be lower than it really is, insufficient resources will be utilized to cultivate it, and profit opportunities will be lost. Thus, demand forecasting is an essential prerequisite to effective planning of marketing operations.

Before demand forecasting can begin, the target market must be clearly defined. If we are following a product-differentiation strategy, the total market is our target and we will try to forecast the total demand for a type of product. If we are following a strategy of market segmentation, our forecast should relate to the market segments we wish to reach.

BASIC APPROACHES TO DEMAND FORECASTING

Many different techniques are used in demand forecasting; they cannot all be discussed here. For pedagogic reasons it is better to oversimplify and discuss two fundamental approaches to demand forecasting. In practice, these two methods can be combined or modified in many ways. Some of the cases in this book will make this abundantly clear.

The two basic approaches to demand forecasting are the "top-down" method and the "buildup" method.[13] The top-down method is a deductive approach to forecasting, proceeding from general demand estimates to demand estimates for small market segments. It begins with a forecast of business conditions, derives therefrom a forecast of industry demand, and then breaks this forecast down to arrive at an estimate of demand for the individual company and for each segment of its total market.

In contrast, the buildup method is an inductive approach to forecasting, beginning with demand estimates for small segments of the market and ending with demand estimates for the total market served by a company or an industry. Individual market segments are studied separately, demand estimates are made for each, and then total demand is arrived at by the process of addition. An overall comparison of the two approaches is shown in Figure 3–5. The terminology used in the listing

---

[13]Demand forecasting terminology is very loose. The top-down method is also known as the "overall-forecast approach," the "index method," and the "breakdown method." The buildup method is also known as the "individual-unit approach," the "direct-evaluation method," and the "bottom-up" method.

FIGURE 3–5   Steps in demand forecasting

Top-down method	*Buildup method*
1. Forecast of business conditions. 2. Determination of market potential. 3. Determination of sales potential. 4. Determination of preliminary sales forecast. 5. Measurement of geographic distribution of demand. 6. Determination of sales quotas. 7. Determination of final sales forecast.	1. Division of total market into market segments. 2. Measurement of demand in individual market segments. 3. Summing of demand by market segments to arrive at total demand.

of steps for the top-down approach will be foreign to most students at this point but will be explained as this method is described.

Top-Down Method of Demand Forecasting

Variations in the specific steps involved in the top-down approach are common. There is no set of steps that is right, with all others being wrong. Nevertheless, the top-down approach will generally proceed somewhat along the lines of Figure 3–5. These steps will now be discussed in order.

Forecast of business conditions.   What can be expected in terms of sales for most products is a function of the general state of the economy. When general levels of employment and income rise, people buy and consume more goods and services. The purchase of luxury products may fluctuate widely with swings in business conditions; the fluctuations for basic staples may be very little. The assumption implicit in beginning the top-down method with an economic forecast is that a known relationship exists between changes in business conditions and changes in demand for a given type of product. Regression analysis can be used to determine the degree of correlation that existed in the past between, say, fluctuations in levels of income and the demand for automobiles. If this relationship between levels of income and automobile purchases is expected to continue, then a forecast of future income level has a high relevance to the expected demand for automobiles.

The character of the economic forecast that is made will depend on the product under consideration. Levels of employment and income may be most significant for automotive demand, but expected new-home construction and number of family formations may be more relevant to expected demand for appliances. Expected demand for agricul-

tural equipment will depend more on the outlook for agriculture than on the outlook for business conditions generally. A general economic forecast will include these and other components of total economic activity. However, a forecast of the peculiarly relevant components is most useful in demand forecasting.

Market potential.   Market potential is "the capacity of a market to absorb a product or a group of products of an industry in a specified period of time."[14] It is, for example, the capacity of the market to absorb the output of the automotive industry during a given model year. It is an industry–market concept in contrast to the term *sales potential,* which relates to the capacity of a market to absorb the output of a given firm. Sales potential will be discussed separately.

If a forecast of business conditions that includes those factors causally related to past sales of a given industry has been made, derivation of the market potential figure is, in theory, a simple task. For example, if observation of past relationships reveals that each 10 percent increase in disposable income has consistently produced a 10 percent increase in demand for automobiles, then it is reasonable to conclude that a forecasted 5 percent change in disposable income would have a 5 percent effect on the demand for automobiles. Unfortunately, in the real world things are not this simple. Usually, many economic factors influence demand for a given industry, and multiple-correlation analysis must be used to discover and weight them. Past relationships often do not extend into the future. Subjective factors, such as the appeal or lack thereof of new-car styles, muddy the waters. Hence, deriving market potential from a forecast of economic conditions is not a simple mechanical process, but one involving much expert judgment.

Sales potential.   Sales potential is the capacity of a market to absorb the output of a given firm. It is the firm's share of the market potential. A good starting point in determining sales potential is a firm's past share of total industry sales. If over an extended period of years it has consistently sold 25 percent of total industry sales, it would be reasonable to conclude, in the absence of additional information, that its most probable sales potential for the year ahead is 25 percent of market potential. If there is an increasing or decreasing trend in its market share, this should be taken into account. Having started with the benchmark of past market share, we should analyze all available information that might cause that share to change. If a firm's competitors are expected to introduce new models of their products but they themselves have no such plans, this may suggest that a decline in market share be anticipated. Conversely, if a company plans to increase advertising in relation to the rest of the industry, an increase in market share may be expected.

Preliminary sales forecast.   It is not uncommon for demand fore-

---

[14]K. R. Davis and F. E. Webster, Jr., *Sales Force Management* (New York: Ronald Press, 1968), p. 258.

casters to speak of sales potential and the sales forecast as if they were synonymous. In practice they are sometimes equal quantitatively, but conceptually they are very different things. Sales potential refers to the capacity of a market to purchase a product, while the sales forecast is the sales goal decided upon. If we set as our sales target all potential sales available to us, the two values will be equal. However, in many cases there are reasons why the sales forecast may be set below potential demand. It may be considered too costly to strive for all potential sales. Profits may actually be enhanced if the sales target is set at a lower level if some potential sales can only be achieved at a marginal cost in excess of marginal revenue. An anticipated labor strike may cause an expectation of a limitation on production, which makes it prudent to set a sales forecast figure below the sales potential. Limitations of other resources, such as sales force and promotional funds, may have the same effect.

A sales forecast is a function of more things than sales potential. It is a result of the opportunity for sales, the amounts and kinds of resources committed to exploit this sales opportunity, and the effectiveness with which these resources are employed. If no significant forces constrain the last two of these factors, then the sales forecast can be equal to the sales potential. If such constraints do exist, it might well be less than the sales potential.

Geographic distribution of demand. Demand for a company's product is largely uniform throughout the total market. Generally, it is distributed very unevenly, depending on how the demand-causing forces for the product are distributed over the market. If demand is in part a function of disposable income, the distribution of demand over the market will be at least partially correlated with the distribution of disposable income. If demand varies with age, the distribution of demand will vary with the age makeup of the population by geographic areas.

A company must know how demand is spatially distributed in order to allocate its salesmen, to direct its advertising and sales promotions, and to locate its inventories. It must select wholesalers and retailers in accordance with the amount of demand in the areas they serve. In order to gain this needed information, the demand forecaster must employ some means to break down the total sales forecast by geographic areas.

In the top-down approach the sales forecast (or possibly the sales potential or the market potential) is broken down geographically by application of an index. There is an infinite number of indexes that might be used for this purpose, ranging from very simple single-factor indexes to highly involved multiple-factor indexes. The index chosen should reflect the demand-causing factors for the product under consideration. Regression analysis should be used to determine what these factors are. No attempt will be made here to describe all the indexes available, but attention will be focused on several major types of indexes.

These will be classified into two categories: (1) market-factors indexes and (2) past-sales indexes.

Market-factor indexes are indexes in which the variables are factors in the market that produce demand for goods and services. A very simple market-factor index, for example, might be composed of population data. The total population in the United States would be broken down into the population of each county as a percentage of the total population. If a given county had a population of 2 million and the total U.S. population were 200 million, the index factor for that county would be 1 percent. Such an index would be useful in determining the distribution of demand for a product like table salt. If salt consumption per capita is relatively constant, then the demand for table salt could be expected to be distributed over the market in accordance with the distribution of the population. Other single-factor indexes of this sort might be such things as age, income, urban population, and rural population.

The most widely used market-factor indexes are those published by *Sales Management* magazine. The *Sales Management Survey of Buying Power*, published annually, includes a population index, an income index, a retail-sales index, and a "buying-power" index. The last index is a composite of the first three, with income weighted 5, retail sales 3, and population 2. The buying-power index is included as a convenience because of its applicability to a broad range of popularly priced goods. An illustration of this index is provided in Figure 3–6. The demand forecaster can use any one of these indexes that regression analysis reveals is appropriate. They can be combined, using suitable weights, to form new indexes. If none of these indexes fits the forecaster's needs, there are many others to choose from.

The distribution of the past sales of a firm or an industry over the market are sometimes used as indicators of the distribution of demand that can be expected in the future. In theory, this approach is unsound. Past sales indicate what has been achieved but not necessarily the opportunities of the future. Used without judgment, past sales can be the basis for ludicrous conclusions. For example, zero sales of television sets in an area because no television station served that area in the past are not indicative of sales opportunities once a station has been established. Also, the sales of a single firm may be very poorly correlated with its true sales opportunities. They reflect how the company distributed its marketing efforts in the past, and if they were poorly distributed in relation to potential, past sales may not have reflected the actual distribution of potential demand.

Past industry sales also may not have been distributed in direct proportion to the distribution of potential demand, but maldistribution is less likely for an entire industry than for a single firm. In the case of basic staples, such as bread and toothpaste, it is likely that past sales opportunities have been reasonably fully exploited over the many years

FIGURE 3–6   *Sales Management Survey of Buying Power*

Michigan estimates		Effective buying income, 1978						
Metro area County City		Total EBI ($000)	House-hold EBI	A*	B*	C*	D*	Buying power index
Ann Arbor		2,066,319	21,077	4.2	12.4	29.8	38.7	0.1367
Washtenaw		2,066,319	21,077	4.2	12.4	29.8	38.7	0.1367
Ann Arbor		945,467	20,056	4.7	13.7	27.2	37.8	0.0625
Suburban total		1,120,852	21,772	3.7	11.3	32.0	39.6	0.0742
Battle Creek		1,166,788	16,918	5.4	16.0	25.7	21.7	0.0789
Barry		232,179	15,449	5.7	18.7	37.0	15.1	0.0143
Calhoun		934,609	17,424	5.3	15.2	35.3	23.6	0.0646
Battle Creek		229,460	13,935	6.6	16.7	30.4	16.0	0.0216
Suburban total		937,328	17,663	5.0	15.7	37.4	23.4	0.0573
Bay City		762,553	18,195	4.3	13.5	37.6	25.5	0.0554
Bay		762,553	18,195	4.3	13.5	37.6	25.5	0.0554
Bay City		308,232	16,491	5.4	14.8	34.0	21.9	0.0237
Suburban total		454,321	19,407	3.4	12.4	40.5	28.3	0.0317
Benton Harbor–St. Joseph		1,166,947	14,285	6.4	21.1	34.2	12.6	0.0872
Berrion		932,961	14,391	6.2	20.7	34.2	13.0	0.0718
Benton Harbor		67,855	11,179	6.9	20.7	26.9	7.0	0.0105
St. Joseph		83,240	15,401	6.2	18.0	31.3	20.2	0.0063
Cass		233,986	13,890	7.3	22.4	34.0	10.8	0.0154
Suburban total		1,015,852	14,447	6.4	21.4	35.0	12.4	0.0704
Detroit		34,907,796	21,600	3.8	10.7	31.0	39.2	2.2585
Lopeer		332,895	15,607	5.4	19.4	38.1	14.9	0.0231
Livingston		480,600	15,721	6.1	20.2	37.5	16.0	0.0326
Macomb		5,462,418	24,413	2.6	7.9	32.9	47.7	0.3422
East Detroit		348,268	24,209	2.6	8.1	31.6	47.1	0.0218
Roseville		422,983	22,949	3.0	9.0	37.1	41.2	0.0325
St. Clair Shores		697,105	25,209	2.5	7.5	31.1	50.8	0.0403

*Percent of households by EBI group:
  A: $ 8,000–$ 9,999
  B: $10,000–$14,999
  C: $15,000–$24,999
  D: $25,000 and over.
Source: © 1978 *Sales & Marketing Management Survey of Buying Power.*

that such products have been on the market. Hence, past industry sales for such products are widely used as an index of potential demand.

Past sales of a given type of product (for example, appliances) do indicate the opportunity for replacement demand. As a product matures and sales are more and more for replacement, past sales become an increasingly valuable index. If brand loyalty is strong, past sales of a single company are useful in estimating the market share it can expect. Past sales of another product may be indicative of the sales opportunities for a given firm's product. A most obvious case is that past sales of

automobiles indicate sales opportunities for automotive parts. Past sales of cameras create opportunities for the sale of film.

Sales quotas. A sales quota is a sales goal for a segment of the total market. It is not necessarily identical with the sales potential for that market segment as revealed by application of an index of relative potential demand. The sales quota may be set below 100 percent of potential for a variety of reasons. Perhaps wholesale and retail dealers have gone over to a competitor. Both of these events might cause a quota to be set below full potential. Each territorial potential figure must be carefully evaluated; and realistic goals, reflecting not only potential demand but the commitment of a firm's resources, must be established. Quotas are the basis for all allocation decisions in the marketing planning process, and they can be used as standards of performance for many marketing activities.

Final sales forecast. The whole must equal the sum of its parts; the sales forecast must equal the sum of territorial quotas. If quotas deviate from territorial potential figures derived by application of an index, the company's total sales forecast must be revised to reflect this fact. In a very real sense, this is a way of saying that an accurate forecast of sales depends on an objective and painstaking evaluation of each segment of a firm's total market.

Buildup Method of Demand Forecasting

The top-down method of demand forecasting is the most widely used method of setting marketing goals. However, it has several basic limitations that restrict its application. In order for it to be an effective forecasting tool, three conditions must be met:

1. There must be an observed correlation between forecastable economic variables and the quantity demanded of a given product.
2. This observed past relationship must be expected to continue into the future.
3. There must be a means available to break down total expected sales to expected sales for segments of the total market.

The first of these conditions is not present when demand for new products is being forecast. Because the product has not been on the market before, no correlation can be observed between its sales and economic conditions. Intuition may suggest that certain relationships will hold, but there is no empirical evidence in support of such a view.

There is always the chance that observed past relationships between economic variables and product demand will not hold into the future. Consumers continually change their patterns of behavior and come under the influence of different forces. When products change greatly in

styling or other features, the assumption that past relationships will continue is particularly risky.

If a forecast of total sales cannot be broken down to reveal relative potential demand by market segments, there is no good basis for allocating marketing effort. As we have seen, this is usually done by application of some sort of an index. The distribution of demand for some products, specialized capital equipment, for example, is not reflected on any existing index. Furthermore, there is no source of readily available information from which such an index can be built. For this reason, industrial marketers often resort to the buildup method.

New consumer products.   The buildup method, outlined in Figure 3–5 requires as a first step the selection of some segment of the total market to study. The market segment chosen will, in the case of new consumer products, usually be some very small portion of the total market. It may be a scientifically chosen sample of consumers who are interviewed about their reaction to a new product. On the basis of their response an attempt is made to determine their probability of purchase. The sample, because of convenience and cost considerations, is often opportunistically selected. It may be composed of all people attending an event such as a builders' show or an auto show who can be induced to fill out a questionnaire. It may consist of women's clubs, church groups, and the like, whose members can be interviewed at one time and in one place. It may, however, also be a representative sample of all consumers in a market segment, who are scientifically selected and interviewed in their homes.

Demand estimates based on test marketing are a use of the buildup method. Sales in the test market are audited. If the test market is representative of the total market, sales in the test market will provide the basis for at least a rough estimate of total demand. The audit procedure in the test market should consist of more than just measuring unit or dollar sales. Studies should be made to relate sales results to basic market factors. For example, information may be gathered about purchasers (age, income, etc.) and compared with like data about nonpurchasers. If a profile of probable purchasers can be constructed in terms of basic demand-causing characteristics, then the distribution of demand over the total market can be estimated. This is done by use of a basic market-factors index, such as the *Sales Management Survey of Buying Power,* which reveals the relative presence of these causal demand factors by geographic area.

Demand forecasts based on consumer surveys and test-marketing data are not models of precision. General Motors' sales forecast for the "X" car indicated that there would be greater consumer preference for the six-cylinder engine than for the four-cylinder engine. The increasing cost of gasoline, however, increased demand for the smaller engine.

Unfortunately, production capacity was planned in accordance with the forecasts and there was a shortage of four-cylinder models during most of the introductory year.

New industrial products. The top-down approach is no more applicable to new industrial products than it is to new consumer products. Fortunately, the buildup method can be employed with more precision for industrial products. There are several reasons for this. First, potential industrial buyers can be more readily identified than potential consumer buyers. Many industrial goods are specialized products with specific applications. This means that there is usually a much smaller universe for which demand must be estimated, thus simplifying the forecasting task. Second, demand for industrial goods depends on more easily identified and measured factors. Consumer purchase often depends on unknown subjective considerations, whereas industrial buying depends on more tangible cost and profit considerations. Third, there is a greater geographic concentration of demand for industrial goods than for consumer goods. This, too, simplifies the use of the buildup method and keeps cost at a reasonable level.

Established industrial goods. For industrial goods that have been on the market for some time, the top-down approach is often applicable. Observable correlations between forecastable economic factors and product demand may well be present. Demand for office equipment, for example, is very likely to be correlated with business activity. Indexes for determining the geographic distribution of demand can be composed from available sources. For office equipment, Social Security data on office employment by geographic regions and type of industry are readily available.

Unfortunately, demand forecasts cannot be made for all established industrial goods with the top-down approach. This is particularly true of specialized capital equipment. Total demand, as well as the geographic distribution of demand, depends on specific investment decisions of individual potential buyers. General business conditions do not indicate that a certain company will build a new plant this year to produce a new product. No available index will indicate that the potential buyer in company X is likely to go ahead with his expansion plans but that the potential buyer in company Y is not. Under these circumstances the "sales-force composite method" of demand forecasting, which is a special form of the buildup method, is widely used.

Conceptually, the sales-force composite method is very simple. Each company salesman is asked to evaluate each present and potential customer and to estimate his or her purchases for a specified time period, usually one year. These estimates are then totaled, reviewed, and adjusted, and become the sales forecast. This approach is possible because buyers are likely to be few, because they plan their own future activities and are likely to know their needs, and because their buying decisions

are made on objective grounds. The method makes use of the special knowledge of the salesperson, the one closest to the market and, indeed, often the only person who has the knowledge necessary to predict the actions of particular buyers. Sampling error is avoided because the entire market is surveyed. Salespeople who will probably be judged by performance against quota, will have more confidence in sales goals that they have participated in formulating. The method lends itself to easy development of product, territory, customer, and sales personnel breakdowns.

The sales-force composite method is often criticized on the ground that salespeople are often poor estimators, being either too optimistic or too pessimistic, depending on how their sales are going at the moment. Of course, they have an incentive to keep quotas low if their performance is to be judged against them. This method requires a lot of time on the part of the sales force, and it may detract from their sales efforts. However, often no other method will provide the information needed for demand forecasting.

CONCLUSION

Marketing research is essential to the planning and execution of marketing strategy because it provides the information base for marketing decision making. Without adequate marketing research, a firm is "flying blind" in making marketing decisions. Marketing research is not a luxury, but a necessity.

QUESTIONS

1. What are the various types of information that management might need in order to make decisions under conditions of uncertainty?

2. What is a marketing information system, and how does it differ from a marketing research system?

3. How might one classify marketing research activities? Give an example of each type of activity that you have identified.

4. What are the principal responsibilities that should be assumed by a marketing manager with regard to the marketing research process?

5. What are the key considerations in attempting to establish a marketing research budget for a specific project?

6. What is the difference between data collected from secondary sources as contrasted with data collected from primary sources?

7. When would you use observation as opposed to experimental methods to collect primary data?

8. What are the components of a sampling plan?

9. What are the advantages of using probability sampling?

10. Because demand forecasting is an imperfect art and many forecasts prove to be not fully accurate, some companies fail to make demand forecasts. Is their position sound?

11. Is it possible that a demand forecast that is inaccurate because it understates actual market demand may serve as a factor that holds down a company's sales? Explain.

12. Define and contrast (*a*) market potential, (*b*) sales potential, and (*c*) sales forecast.

13. Contrast market-factors indexes and past-sales indexes. Under what circumstances is it reasonable to use a past-sales index to determine the geographic distribution of demand?

14. Why is it necessary, considering the difficulties involved, to break down a company sales forecast of the total market into demand by geographic segments?

Cases for part one

AMES

Mr. George Orr, Jr., president of Ames Company, Inc., a wholly owned subsidiary of Miles Laboratories, sat at his desk studying the information at his disposal regarding a young, innovative firm, Berkeley Medical Instruments (BMI). BMI had produced its first major product called the BMI Blood Analyzer. The Blood Analyzer offered the physician a reliable, automated, convenient piece of equipment which could perform up to 14 standard blood chemistry tests[1] with great speed and ease, right in his office. The Blood Analyzer gave both qualitative and quantitative results for each test, results that were highly accurate, reproducible, and arrived at usually in less than 15 minutes. The Blood Analyzer equipment was smaller than a portable typewriter, yet it contained an integrated system of colorimeter and incubator with capillary pipettes, cuvettes, and reagents. However, the system was so easy to operate that its proper use required only a few hours of training. The operator needed only to insert a prepared sample into the test well and read the results. Tests averaged two minutes of operator time and cost

---

This case was prepared by Constance M. Kinnear under the supervision of Professor James R. Taylor. Copyright © 1984 by James R. Taylor.

[1]Tests performed by the BMI Blood Analyzer were for Albumin, Alkaline Phosphatase, Bilirubin, Blood Urea Nitrogen, S.G.P.T., S.G.O.T., Cholesterol, Creatinine, Globulin, Hemoglobin, Total Protein, Phenolsulfonthalein, True Glucose, and Uric Acid.

about $1 per test based on reagent costs only. The BMI Blood Analyzer equipment itself was priced at $700 per unit. The use of BMI's Blood Analyzer would provide a physician with on-the-spot meaningful information which could be used in combination wih clinical judgment to aid in a patient's diagnosis and treatment.

Ames' internal research and development personnel had confirmed for Mr. Orr the claims BMI made about its Blood Analyzer. The product was fast, convenient, accurate, reliable, and economical. Yet, Mr. Orr's financial consultants pointed out that BMI lacked the marketing and sales structures necessary to bring this product to its market. Marketing analysis showed Mr. Orr that the Blood Analyzer had a potential market of approximately 108,000 units, or nearly half the total physicians' offices in the country at the time.

It was estimated that a physician interested in buying the Blood Analyzer would use the instrument to aid in disease diagnosis for approximately one quarter of his daily patient load and use an average of five tests per patient. The technology which produced the Blood Analyzer was new. However, five other firms had already entered the market or planned to do so in the near future. Ames' marketing staff believed that only one of these firms had the marketing abilities that Ames had and that the company could reasonably set a goal of reaching a 50 percent market share for the product within five years.

Mr. Orr's information pointed to the conclusion that BMI was a prime candidate for acquisition by a firm that could offer it the marketing and sales skills it lacked. The concerns for Mr. Orr were many. Would the sales potential of the Blood Analyzer be enough to allow Ames' sales growth to continue to double in the next five years as it had in the past five? Did the BMI product fit the abilities and sales patterns of Ames' current sales force? Did the BMI product fit into Ames' current product line? Was acquisition the right road for growth for Ames? Should R&D personnel be given more resources to develop new spin-off products from Ames' current line? Mr. Orr was faced with a decision of whether or not to take Ames into a new business line, that of blood chemistry, through acquisition, or seek growth through other means.

COMPANY HISTORY

Ames Company began in the early 1940s as Effervescent Products Company. The technology which developed Miles Laboratories' Alka-Seltzer was used to produce Effervescent Products' first two products, Clinitest and Bumintest. Clinitest tablets were a simple test for sugar in urine. In each test, a tablet was dropped into a test tube containing urine. The resulting reaction produced a color change which was almost instantaneous.

By 1944, the company had added a line of therapeutic products, products used to relieve or treat illness, to its original line of diagnostic, or illness detection, products. These products did not work through an effervescent reaction, and the name of the company was changed to Ames Company, Inc., as a result.

When Mr. Orr came to Ames in 1951, the company's annual sales had reached $1.5 million, of which $1 million was produced by sales of Clinitest. The remaining sales were produced by the therapeutic product called Decholin. Decholin was used to treat certain biliary tract conditions.

Later Product Additions

In 1956, Ames introduced CLINISTIX, a new test based on enzyme chemistry which greatly simplified urine-sugar testing. CLINISTIX were elongated filter paper sticks, shaped like paper matches but larger. One end of the CLINISTIC was impregnated with chemicals that produced a color change in 10 seconds when dipped in urine containing sugar. However, CLINISTIX did not provide a reliable estimation of the amount of sugar present, as CLINITEST did, so Ames marketed it only as a qualitative test.

Ames researchers built on the CLINISTIX technology, producing "banded" sticks which tested simultaneously for two, three, and more substances when dipped in urine. By the late 1960s, Ames had expanded its stick testing product line to include five product families. BILI-LABSTIX Reagent Strips provided a qualitative measure of urine pH, glucose, protein, ketones, blood, and bilirubin, all in only 30 seconds. Results gave a physician information about urinary tract and kidney status, carbohydrate metabolism, and liver and biliary tract status. URO-BILISTIX Reagent Strips tested for urine urobilinogen, aiding physicians in diagnosing types of hepatic, biliary, and hemolytic disease. AZOSTIX Reagent Strips tested for blood urea nitrogen, important for diagnosing kidney function. DEXTROSTIX Reagent Strips provided rapid determination of blood glucose levels. DIASTIX, KETO-DIASTIX, CLINITEST, and KETOSTIX were used in home testing programs by diabetic patients to test for urine-sugar levels.

In 1963, Ames purchased Atomium Corporation which manufactured and marketed two instruments, the Volemetron and Gammacord, which were used in certain medical and other diagnoses.

The Volemetron was a computerized radiation detector for estimating the volume of blood circulating in a human being, using principles developed from nuclear physics and electronics. The main use of the machine was for estimating blood volumes before, during, and after surgery, so that the amount of blood lost during surgery could be measured and a proper amount replaced. In using the Volemetron, a small

quantity of radioactive iodine (a "dose") was injected into the patient's circulatory system, where it would mix with the blood and diffuse evenly throughout the circulatory system. The Volemetron would give a reading of blood volume within five minutes by calculating the degree to which the radioactive tracer had been diluted in the blood stream. The machine was described as "a portable, completely self-contained system combining radioactivity detectors, transistor electronics, and digital computer precision. . . . It could easily be operated after a few minutes of instruction.

The other product purchased with Atomium, the Gammacord, could be used medically to measure thyroid functioning and the "uptake" of certain drugs by several body organs by introducing a radioactive tracer into the drug prior to its consumption. The Gammacord was used only in hospitals.

From the technology used in these products, Ames researchers developed the Thyrimeter. This was a semiautomatic, self-calculating, gamma-counting instrument which made routine thyroid testing feasible and convenient for the clinical lab and in the physician's office. A Thyrimeter sold for $1,800 and used radioactive tracer "doses" which cost $1.50 per test.

AMES' SALES

Before the purchase of Atomium in 1963, Ames' total sales had reached the $8 million range. The diagnostic line contributed $7 million to this total with the therapeutic products contributing the remaining $1 million. Ames' market share of the diagnostic business was 47 percent.

Atomium, before its purchase by Ames, had sold an estimated 200 Volemetrons at a purchase price of $4,600 each. In addition, each time a Volemetron was used, a disposable "dose" of radioactive iodine, selling for about $5, was consumed. Atomium had also sold approximately 12 Gammacords for $2,600 each.

Mr. Orr estimated that every hospital in the United States of 100-bed size or larger was a potential customer of a Volemetron. He believed that there were more than 2,000 such hospitals when Ames purchased Atomium and that that number had grown to nearly 3,000 by the end of the 1960s. The selling process for this product was complicated. He said,

> This is a rather specialized thing to sell. . . . It requires a good deal of technical training. . . . You've got to sell the surgeon (on the necessity of measuring blood loss rather than simply guessing at it), and the final decision to purchase will probably rest with the hospital's chief of surgery. . . . But the anesthesiologist may often be the person who will most promote its use, since he's the one who really has the worry about keep-

ing the patient alive during an operation. . . . Maybe you can start with the anesthesiologist, and then bring the surgeon in. . . . Then, the instrument might actually be under the jurisdiction of either the radiologist or the pathologist . . . In any event, you have to demonstrate the instrument, perhaps several times, before you can sell it. . . . And after you demonstrate, and get a hospital interested, you are highly vulnerable to competition (for the "dose" used).

The problems don't stop when you sell the instrument . . . You have to keep them using it. Sometimes it is just too much trouble, and sometimes it is the cost. . . . Blue Cross won't always pay for a blood volume determination . . . I've found that several of the instruments which have been sold are being used infrequently—and primarily for research . . . with lab animals . . . By and large, the attitude toward routine blood volume determination is one of apathy, lethargy . . . and indifference. . . . Physicians are not really convinced of the need. . . . This takes a fantastic amount of promotion . . . truly educational selling.

The nature of the line is such that it must be sold direct. Even the disposable Volemetron doses must be sold direct. Several other pharmaceutical companies—among them two of the largest—make doses also and sell them direct. There is also another blood volume instrument available, made by the nation's largest manufacturer of x-ray equipment, which lists for about $700 more than the Volemetron. But that company always cuts prices.

When the Thyrimeter was first introduced, there was only one competitor for the product. Market analysis available to Ames showed that this type of product would fill a very clear diagnostic need for physicians. Estimates showed that the average physician could be expected to perform 30 tests a month if the Thyrimeter was in his office. Estimates of hospital and commercial clinical usage were for 10 to 12 times that of the average physician. Mr. Orr believed that Ames' strength in the market would come from sales to physicians' offices but that some sales would also come from hospitals and labs. He set a 50 percent market share as a goal for this product line by the mid-1970s.

By the late 1960s, Ames' sales force had sold an estimated 300 Volemetrons at $5,000 each, while giving an additional 300 units to hospitals where it was believed potential use was high enough to warrant such action. Radioactive iodine "dose" sales reached $1 million per year as a result. Ames had also sold approximately 850 Gammacords at $2,500 each. By the same time, nearly 3,000 Thyrimeter units were sold. Thyrimeter "dose" sales rose to $4 million a year.

At the end of the 1960s, Ames' sales of diagnostic products had grown to approximately $17 million per year, representing nearly 60 percent of the market for such products. Total sales for the company reached the $23.5 million per year level, with sales of therapeutic products contributing the difference.

Under Mr. Orr's direction, Ames' sales had more than doubled their

1963 level by the end of the decade. He believed that the goal of doubling sales every five years was attainable. He planned to increase sales to over $90 million annually by the end of the 1970s.

MARKETING AT AMES

Mr. Charles Owens, Ames marketing vice president, described Ames's marketing department, saying,

> We have all of the usual functions. However, we do not have product managers, and there is no corporate marketing function (at Miles). All of our division and regional managers' jobs, and most of our marketing jobs, are staffed with former Ames detail men. We have tried since 1951 to staff our sales force with potentially promotable people. We have been successful at this . . . About 40% of our salesmen are definitely promotable. We have been on a merry-go-round of being told growth could come either internally or externally but that, when it came, we should be in a position people-wise to take advantage of it. Because of this, the competition between these good people has been keen . . . however, we have lost almost none of them and have been able to supply some first-class people to other operating divisions. . . . As the company has grown, it has changed repeatedly—patterns, policies, ideas . . . we are most anxious here about adapting to new environmental factors, but some of the changes have met with the usual resistance.

Ames products were advertised only to the medical profession and allied fields. They were not advertised directly to consumers. Ames salesmen (or "detail men," as pharmaceutical salesmen are commonly referred to) called on physicians, hospitals, commercial clinical laboratories, drug stores, physicians and hospital supply dealers, and surgical supply dealers to encourage them to stock and recommend (or prescribe, as the case might be) Ames products. The company did not sell its products direct to retail drug stores; these stores were supplied by drug wholesalers who, in turn, bought from Ames.

SALES FORCE ACTIVITIES

In the late 1960s, Ames' 144 detail men faced a complicated sales task. All sold the company's therapeutic and diagnostic products and Volemetron. Gammacord, and Thyrimeter clinical laboratory equipment and supplies. All were to cover all sales markets in their assigned teritories. These markets included sales to physicians, hospitals, clinical laboratories, drug wholesalers, surgical supply wholesalers, and physicians and hospital supply dealers, as well as calls on drugstores in the area. As

EXHIBIT 1   Partial organization chart

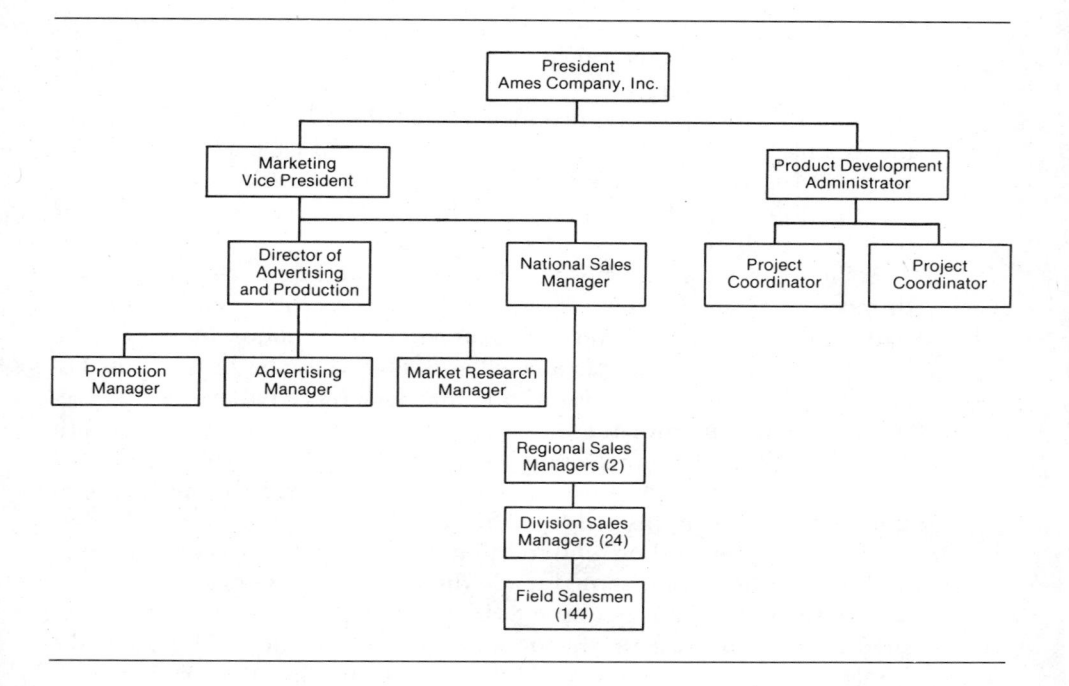

Mr. Owens summarized it, "There is no other detail man quite like the Ames man."

On average, each Ames salesman had 1,500 physicians in his territory in 1970. This number had grown from approximately 1,300 per salesperson in 1963. In selling diagnostics to a physician, the number of physicians a salesman called on was more important than the frequency of calls on any one office. Once a physician began using a product, the sales task became one of maintenance. Required frequency of calls became less, but the sales task became one of getting the physician to do the test routinely. Salesmen found that the physician would buy any test you asked him to buy; he looked a bit old-fashioned if he didn't.

Ames found that changes in how a physician's medical practice ran were affecting how products were sold to the physician. They found that the use of diagnostic tools in the office was related to sophistication in the practice of medicine. As sophistication increased, the use of diagnostics increased. However, physicians were becoming busier. They had less

time to talk to detail men; often an appointment was necessary. Product advertising became more important for reaching the physician, informing him of product capabilities, and developing a need for the product. Furthermore, more and more physicians were becoming specialists. With this, their practices were becoming more oriented to the hospital. And with increased medical coverage, more patients could be admitted to hospitals for testing.

The sale of therapeutic products to the physician required very frequent calls at each office. Each therapeutic product had many substitutes, and a competitor could be expected to be knocking on the door right behind you. If the salesman didn't keep at the physician, he was likely to switch brands.

Selling products to a hospital was very complex. Each hospital was different; each had its own rules, regulations, and personalities. Before making his first sales call, the salesman had to determine what diagnostic tests the hospital already performed as well as what new testing possibilities existed. Often the division sales manager played a key role in preparing a detail man for these calls. He put the salesman in contact with staff marketing personnel, company research staff, and special hospital men who spent all their time calling on hospitals. With all this information, the detail man was prepared for the initial call, knowing the "rules" of the hospital including who to call on, in what order to contact them, and which hospital personnel made the final purchase decision. Hospitals were often change-resistant. If hospital personnel believed their present methods were satisfactory, they stayed with them. Thus, to make a sale, the salesman probably had to talk to the head pharmacist, the pathologist, the chief lab technician, the chief resident physician, the chief of service, and the head floor nurse. Many hospitals were decentralizing. Therefore, many tests were conducted by the nurse or resident on the hospital floor without ever getting to the laboratory. In this case, multiple sales were possible, but the sales task involved even more personnel contacts.

Selling to commercial clinical laboratories had some of the characteristics of selling to physicians and selling to hospitals. There were fewer people involved in the sales decision than in a hospital sale, but the owners of clinical labs were more cost-conscious than their hospital counterparts and often just as resistant to change. Still, clinical labs needed to be able to offer the physician a full range of his desired tests. Therefore, labs wanted to be able to offer the newest tests on the market. In the early 1960s, an Ames detail man could expect to find five clinical labs in his territory.

Ames detail men also called on the drug stores, drug and surgical supply wholesalers, and physicians and hospital supply dealers in their territories. When calling on a drug store, it was the detail man's job to make sure that the store has an adequate stock of Ames diagnostic and

therapeutic products. While Ames did not sell direct to drug stores, the detail men could write "turnover orders"—orders for Ames products to be shipped and billed to the store by a drug wholesaler.

Drug wholesalers, surgical supply wholesalers, and physicians and hospital supply dealers were sold direct. The drug wholesalers' primary function was to supply retail drug stores, although some drug wholesalers also sold to certain hospitals.

The prime suppliers of Ames products to physicians and hospitals, however, were the surgical supply wholesalers and physicians and hospital supply dealers. Many of these firms maintained their own sales forces who called on physicians and hospitals and offered a full line of diagnostic products, office and operating room supplies, and medical equipment.

"One of the jobs we have undertaken in the last few years," commented Mr. Owens, "is that of training the surgical supply and physicians and hospital supply salesmen to sell our diagnostic products. These dealers now account for over 30 percent of our diagnostic products volume, but we must keep learning how to work better with these people. . . . We will sell direct to any drug, surgical supply wholesaler, or physicians and hospital supply dealer who meets two criteria: he must have an obvious franchise in his own right—in his own market—and he must be able to pay his bills."

An average salesman would make calls in the ratio of six physician visits and three drug store calls to one hospital call.

MARKET PLANNING

Planning was accomplished in a series of meetings attended by the marketing vice president, the advertising manager, the promotion manager, and the field sales manager. The function of these meetings was to set targets for the company's sales volume and to translate the targets into specific plans for each product in the Ames line. These plans included allocation of detailing effort, journal advertising, direct mail advertising, and articles in Ames' direct mail publications. Long-range planning was primarily the responsibility of Mr. Orr. Ultimate responsibility for the development of new products belonged to Mr. Orr.

A new Ames product usually began as an idea in the head of a research worker in one of Ames' laboratories. It was the option of the research department's management to reject the suggestion or go ahead. If they decided to study the idea's possibilities, a "working model" would be developed for presentation to Ames' Product Development Committee. The idea would then be tested for such factors as stability and resistance to environmental changes in performance and statistical evaluations. If the "working model" was approved, a project proposal would

be made up. This represented a commitment to the idea and objectives for its further development from the research, marketing, medical, and administrative departments of the company. New products at Ames were not just a function of the research department. They were company business.

Mr. Orr had spent considerable company resources to construct an extensive research department. Researchers included specialists in chemistry, biochemistry, enzymology, immunology, physiology, pharmacology, pharmacy, microbiology, pathology, toxicology, molecular biology, physics, and electrical engineering.

THE DECISION FACING MR. ORR

Mr. Orr knew that the decision as to whether or not to purchase Berkeley Medical Instruments was his alone to make. He realized that the decision had to be made in the light of his long-range plans for the company. He commented:

> BMI's product represents a good direction for us. It is in blood chemistry, where we have little experience, but it's testing—measurement . . . diagnosis. In this sense, it is the business we are really in.
>
> But are we in medicine or in a broader mensuration business. Our future is in testing and measuring devices. Our research department has already presented us with many new product possibilities, all extensions of our present reagent strip technology. They are developing tests to determine whether and at what levels certain pollutants are present in air and water; if contaminants are present in food; and to allow such industries as dairy, wine, and petroleum to screen and process product samples to determine if quality standards are being achieved. Why we even have under consideration a test strip to allow pool owners to easily and instantaneously check the pH level and chlorine content of their pools! Maybe we should move in this direction, altering our present formulas and color scales to specific uses. It is easier to take a technology you already have and shove it in new directions . . . than it is to develop new technology.
>
> I don't know, though . . . Do we look at this acquisition from the point of view that we are already in this business or not? We have been thinking more in terms of a machine to automatically perform the tests we are already selling.
>
> Maybe our research focus could be changed to concentrate on medical applications for new products. We could move our energies into developing products aimed at disease or disorder detection, before symptoms present themselves. It may be important to us to move into preventive medicine tests.
>
> The consensus of business thinking seems to be that diversification can produce greatest benefits if there is some relation in the technology. . . . But is the BMI technology the same?

What it all boils down to is that the kinds of biochemical tests we are selling are fine, but that is not all we should be doing.

Then, what about our therapeutics? Our growth in the past few years has come about largely through diagnostics. Our volume in therapeutics has remained pretty flat. If we are going to develop the therapeutics business, we need to compete with some specialties with characteristics of usefulness and distinctiveness comparable to those of our diagnostics. We have some research in progress which may develop products of this nature . . . But, we can't be sure. . . ."

QUESTION

Identify and evaluate the strategic options which confront Ames.

TODD COUNTY PACKING COMPANY*

Evaluation of marketing strategy

The Todd County Packing Company was a medium-sized, well-established canner of a wide variety of food products with an annual sales volume of about $50 million. The company was founded in central Indiana in the 1880s by John A. Wagner. It was then, and continues to be, family-owned and -operated. Tomatoes were a major crop in the area in which the company was originally established. It is not surprising, therefore, that the company concentrated in its early years on the packing of tomato-based products. Through the years, as the company grew, it gradually broadened its list to include a wide variety of other vegetable and meat products. Tomato products, plus baked beans, however, continued to be its major products.

The vegetable- and meat-canning industry were dominated by a small number of very large, integrated, and well-known firms. Among these were Heinz, Green Giant, and Del Monte. In addition, however, there were a large number—variously estimated at 1,000 to 2,000—of small and medium-sized canners. Most of these served local and regional markets under brands which did not possess national recognition. The Todd County Packing Company was one of the largest of the canners without a well-known brand name. By 1977, it was operating six plants, all in the Midwest.

---

*Written by Stewart H. Rewoldt, late Professor of Marketing, Graduate School of Business Administration, The University of Michigan.

BRAND POLICY

Todd County Packing Company sold its products both under its own brands and under the private labels of wholesalers and retail grocery chains. Over the years, its products were sold under as many as 250 different brands. Its brand policy, if it can be said to have had one at all, was to sell to any distributor who wanted to buy its products under any brand that the distributor wanted to use. This was a common policy among small canners. Private brand sales tended to be primarily to smaller chains, but some sales were to the larger chains, usually for only a portion of their requirements. Large chains usually bought from different canners in each area in which they operated in order to minimize transportation costs.

The company had over 50 company-owned brands, none of which was well-known among consumers. Most of these brands were marketed in only a small portion of the company's total market, where a particular brand had built up a local following.

Some of the items marketed under Todd County brands were of high quality, some medium quality, and some of low quality. The company's brands were applied rather indiscriminately to products of different quality, so that there was no uniformity of quality under any particular brand. As a result, there was no brand/quality association in the consumer's mind. Todd County catsup, when graded by government standards, was one of the highest quality catsups on the market. It compared favorably in quality with such well-known brands as Heinz and Hunt's. Some other products under the Todd County label barely met the minimum government standards. As a result of the use of the Todd County brand and other company-owned brands on products that differed vastly in quality, consumers were willing to accept all of the company's products only at relatively low prices. For example, Heinz and Hunt's catsup usually sold at retail for 45 cents to 50 cents per 14-ounce bottle; the chains' private brands sold in the 40-cent to 45-cent range; and Todd County catsup sold in the 30-cent to 40-cent range.

COMPANY ORGANIZATION

The Todd County Packing Company's organization was relatively simple. The only member of the founding family still active in the firm served as its chief executive officer, holding the title of both chairman of the board and president. Reporting to him were vice presidents of production, finance, research and development, and sales. The vice president for sales had two assistant sales managers reporting to him. The sales vice president and his assistants worked with food brokers, through whom almost all sales were made. There were no marketing staff func-

tions within the organizational structure. Corporate planning was considered a function of the chairman of the board. Primary emphasis was placed on producing and selling the maximum volume at the minimum cost each year. The inactive members of the founding family, who dominated the board of directors, were becoming increasingly unhappy with the company's return on investment.

STIMULUS FOR CHANGE

Harold West, son of the vice president for sales, John West, had just completed the first year of an MBA program at a leading midwestern university. During the summer between the first and second year of his program, he worked for his father. John West had for some time been concerned that sales had reached a level at which continuation of the marketing practices common to small, local canners was no longer appropriate to the Todd County Packing Company. For this reason, and also because he wanted his son to receive as broad an exposure to real-life marketing as possible, he gave Harold the assignment of making an in-depth study of Todd's marketing practices and recommending a marketing plan for the future.

Harold was elated with this assignment. He had just completed a case course in marketing management and had done well, receiving a grade of B +. During the course he had been required to analyze several cases which focused on the marketing of packaged food products. He believed that this background would be very helpful to him in studying the situation of the Todd County Packing Company.

ASSESSMENT OF COMPANY PROBLEMS

Harold West spent his first week on the job thinking about how he would approach his assignment. He decided to set two goals for himself:

1. To develop a list of the problems facing Todd County Packing Company.
2. To come up with suggestions for overcoming the problems he uncovered.

Harold devoted about one month to searching out Todd's problems. He had ready access to all the top executives as well as employees at lower levels. He followed no specific format in his interviews. He felt that he would get maximum insight into the company's problems by just getting people to talk about the company, the industry, their specific job roles, and the difficulties they had in fulfilling those roles. He was somewhat surprised to discover that the people he interviewed did not seem

to be aware that the company was at a critical juncture in its growth pattern, that some of its past practices did not lend themselves to today's market realities, that little planning for the future was going on, or, in general, that anything was wrong and needed changing. The general feeling seemed to be that the company had been growing steadily and was earning a profit. True, profits could be better, but they would probably improve as population and consumer incomes rose.

Harold began to feel he was getting nowhere with the approach he was taking. He remembered his marketing professor saying that management was often so close to its problems that it "couldn't see the forest for the trees." He then decided on a different approach. He would first review what he had learned in his marketing class and then produce his own list of problems. He had gained substantial knowledge of Todd's operations by this time, and he could now set down on paper a more objective list of the company's problems than management itself seemed able to provide.

In short order, Harold came up with the following list of problems facing Todd County Packing Company:

1.   Todd's management had no understanding of "the marketing concept." Its practice was to pack the raw materials available in whatever quantities that were available, and then to sell the output on the most favorable terms it could get.

2.   Little attention was given to planning for the future. Management personnel focused their attention primarily on day-to-day affairs. In general, things were done today as they had been done for many years.

3.   Todd had no real consumer franchise for its products. Its brands and the company were relatively unknown.

4.   The large number of company-owned brands made it difficult to devote much marketing support to any particular brand. Todd's management had to some extent recognized this as a problem. For about 10 years it had been slowly shifting emphasis to the Todd County brand and had given that brand some advertising support. Whenever possible, it had attempted to shift wholesale and retail customers to the Todd County brand from the other brands that they had been buying. As a result of these efforts, 20 percent of Todd's sales were now made under the Todd County label. Some of Todd's other brands had been dropped entirely. Distribution of the Todd County brand was primarily in the Southeast, but within this region it continued to have spotty distribution. It held a stronger position in smaller towns than in larger urban areas.

5.   The quality of the products packed under each brand, including the Todd County brand, varied widely. These brands, therefore, did not accomplish one of the basic purposes of brands: that is, to serve as a guide to quality.

6.   Todd County Packing Company was heavily dependent on pri-

vate brand accounts, which represented 50 percent of the company's sales. Because these accounts could obtain identical merchandise from many sources, the bidding for this business was fierce. A difference of less than one cent per case could result in the loss of an order. Profits on this part of Todd's business, therefore, were extremely low.

7. The company engaged in no marketing research. It had no information on who bought its products or why the products were bought.

Harold West pondered these problems and wondered what he should do next. He could write a formal report, detailing his findings and offering a set of recommendations. Would this, however, really accomplish anything? He was conscious of the apathy and resistance to change that existed within the management. Any report, he felt, would at best be skimmed, then filed away and forgotten. He believed that he must demonstrate how the problems he had outlined could be overcome. What action could he take that would serve this purpose?

THE CATSUP EXPERIMENT

Harold West was convinced that a basic need of the company was to make Todd County products distinctive in the consumer's mind. At present they were just me-too products that consumers would accept if the price were right, but there was no basis for establishing a preference for them.

Harold decided to concentrate on catsup. It was Todd County's major product and of high quality. How could a preference, or at least equal acceptance, be gained for Todd County catsup? Heavy promotional expenditures were out of the question because of the narrow profit margins now being realized on the company's products.

Todd County catsup was sold in both the consumer market and the institutional market. In the consumer market, catsup was traditionally sold in long-necked, 14-ounce bottles. In the institutional market, it was usually sold in large-sized cans because of the lower cost involved. The institutional market offered little opportunity for product differentiation. Competition was fierce, and it centered on price. The consumer market, however, offered some product-differentiation opportunities.

The more Harold thought about the typical long-necked catsup bottle, the less satisfactory a package it seemed to be. The contents were often difficult to remove. The all-or-nothing results of consumer attempts to put catsup on hamburgers, hot dogs, french fries, or other items were a standard comedy routine in cartoons, situational comedies, and the like. Such attempts were also all-too-frequent experiences for all consumers, day in and day out. The problem of removing catsup from its container was compounded by the fact that consumers seemed

to prefer a thick catsup. Catsup was also a common ingredient in cooking. Measuring out a precise quantity, say, one tablespoonful, was not an easy task. A partially used catsup bottle was not a particularly attractive item to place on the table. The more Harold thought about the catsup bottle, the more he wondered how such an impractical container had come into such universal use.

If canned catsup could be sold successfully in the institutional market, why would this not work in the consumer market? Such a transition had been pioneered in the packaging of beer and soft drinks. Tomato juice, orange juice, and other fruit juices were commonly sold in cans. The big difference between these products and catsup was that the contents of the container were usually consumed all at once, so that resealing was not a problem. Canned coffee, however, was a product consumed over time. Coffee producers had solved this problems by providing a plastic lid for resealing the can after a portion of its contents had been used. Why wouldn't this work for catsup?

Further investigation by Harold revealed that using cans instead of bottles for catsup would offer a number of advantages. Attractive lithographed cans, similar to those long used for beer and soft drinks, were somewhat cheaper than bottles. Cans permitted easier handling than bottles, and breakage, which was a major cost item for bottled catsup, would be virtually eliminated. It was also felt that the retailer would prefer to have catsup in cans. This would simplify his handling of the product and reduce his breakage. Also, cans could be stacked and displayed more effectively than bottles. The consumer, too, would benefit. Since a can is more stable than a narrow bottle, using a can instead of a bottle would reduce the danger of spilling. The large opening of the can would permit access to the contents by spoon, eliminating the awkward problem of getting catsup out of narrow-necked bottles. Of course, breakage by consumers would also be reduced. Most important, placing catsup in cans would make Todd County catsup a unique product, thus establishing a basis for consumer preference. Table use of the product would present few problems. An attractive can could itself be placed on the table. However, consumers could, if they wished, transfer the contents of the can to a plastic squeeze bottle for table use. Such containers were available in most supermarkets at relatively low prices, ranging from 39 cents to 59 cents.

REACTION TO HAROLD WEST'S IDEA

Harold talked over his plan for selling catsup in cans with his father and other top management officials. He had expected an enthusiastic reception and was surprised by the skepticism with which his idea was received.

They raised several objections to his scheme. The most commonly mentioned objections were:

1.   The long-necked bottle catsup package had a long tradition. Consumers were so accustomed to it that they would resist changing to a new catsup package.
2.   Consumers judged catsup in part by its color. The see-through bottle permitted such an assessment; the can did not.
3.   Consumers might resist both serving catsup from a can at the table and transferring the can's contents to a plastic container.
4.   Todd was too small to be a pioneer. If the big fellows tried it and it worked, then Todd could follow their example. Hunt's had lost millions of dollars in its effort to market flavored catsups. Todd was too small to afford such risks.

Harold's summer break was near an end, and he had to get ready to return to school. He was discouraged with the outcome of his efforts during the summer. He felt that he had accomplished little, if anything, in changing the course of the Todd County Packing Company. He was not ready, however, to drop the matter. He planned to discuss his experience with his marketing professor and to get his professor's reactions. He hoped that his professor would allow him to sign up for an individualized research course so that he would be able, under the professor's supervision, to pursue the project further.

QUESTIONS

1.   Evaluate Harold West's approach to his summer assignment.
2.   If you were offered such an opportunity, how would you handle it?
3.   Is Harold West's idea for marketing catsup in cans worth pursuing? If so, what steps would you take to further evaluate his proposal? If not, why not?

VERNORS INC. (A)*

Marketing strategy for Vernors' soft drinks

VERNORS' CURRENT POSITION

"Mention Vernors ginger ale to almost anyone who has lived in the Detroit area, and you will usually get a warm smile and a one- to five-minute reminiscence of good things that have happened around a cold (or hot) Vernors." (So began the 1954 article in the *Mid-Continent Bottler Magazine,* which went on to describe the company's tradition-filled 80-year history and its newly opened Detroit bottling plant and company headquarters—the pride of the industry.)

In the 20 years that followed the appearance of this article, many people continued to enjoy drinking Vernors; however, their numbers had diminished significantly. New soft drink competitors achieved distribution in Detroit and promoted their brands heavily. The increased competition caused Vernors' market share to fall from 30 percent in the 1950s to less than one third of that in 1974. The company also went through several management changes in the years since 1954. Vernors, which had been family-owned and -operated since its beginning in 1865, went public in the 1950s. In 1966, the business and its assests were

---

*Written by Peter E. Robinson, research assistant, under the direction of James D. Scott, Sebastian S. Kresge Professor of Marketing, Graduate School of Business Administration, The University of Michigan, Ann Arbor.

acquired by a group of institutional investors which in turn sold out to the company's current owner, American Consumer Products, Inc.

Although the company had experienced modest but sustained profits for its first 80 years under the Vernors family, it had to cope with rocky financial times under each of its new management teams. After significant losses in fiscal 1970 (July–June) and 1971, Vernors rebounded to show successive profits in fiscal 1972 and 1973. Based on these profits, and with much greater profits in mind, Vernors' management geared up for new additions to the product line (ice-cream parlors and new soft drink flavors, primarily) and backed its effort with substantial increased advertising expenditures. The expenditures, however, failed to produce needed sales, and Vernors found itself losing in the six figures per month for the first half of fiscal 1974.

In December 1974, the parent company, American Consumer Products, Inc., sent Leonard Heilman to investigate the profit situation. As a result of his efforts, Heilman was asked to take and accepted the presidency of Vernors in January 1975. He immediately enacted widespread cost-cutting procedures to bring the company's profits and cash flow back into the black. All advertising was immediately suspended; the new-product additions were shelved; and a number of managerial and staff positions were eliminated until only a selected management team remained. The company succeeded in its climb back to profitability and positive cash flows during the last quarter of fiscal 1974, but for the year as a whole it was heavily in the red.

Setting its sights on a turnaround, the new management group established as its primary objective the recapture of Vernors' market share for fiscal 1975 and thereafter. In its attempt to increase sales, there were several questions that it believed should be answered:

Where should the product be positioned?

Which consumer segment should be targeted?

How can the product be effectively promoted?

Can more sales be produced through the existing distribution channels?

COMPANY HISTORY

As company history has it, the Vernors story started with the firing of a cannon at Fort Sumter in 1861. James Vernor put on his blue uniform and went off to war. But before he left, he mixed some secret ingredients and put them in an old wooden keg for safekeeping until he returned.

Four years later the war came to an end, and James Vernor returned to Detroit to open a pharmacy on Woodward Avenue. It was then traditional for pharmacists to create their own special fountain drinks which

customers drank both for pleasure and for relief of upset stomachs. And so James Vernor opened his four-year-old keg of secret ingredients (gingers and oils), and customers took to the new soft drink "like a sponge to water." The product became so successful that within a few months Vernor found himself in the business of providing his drink to soda fountains throughout the area. Customers were enthusiastic, and the gingery soft drink was unique.

By 1896, the soft drink had a name, Vernors, and it had been on sale at the family drugstore in Detroit for over 30 years. That same year saw the entry into the business of the second James Vernor and marked the start of a second generation of progress. The popularity of the drink necessitated the closing of the family pharmacy and the opening of a larger store dedicated exclusively to the manufacture and sale of Vernors. Consumer demand continued to grow, and summertime Boston Cooler (Vernors plus vanilla ice cream) became a family tradition in downtown Detroit. By 1915, James Vernor II was operating a full-scale bottling plant and the product and its president were becoming well-known, respected names throughout the industry.

The founder died in 1927, but realization of his dream was perpetuated by his son. In 1941, the firm purchased a large building on the waterfront and set up a plant which became a landmark in downtown Detroit. Visitors by the thousands came to watch the men and equipment at work, mixing the soft drink, and the soda fountain was said to have had over 5,000 visitors on a single weekend. The company stated with pride that there had been no parallel in the soft drink industry.

In 1954, eight years after its 80th birthday, the company again expanded its operations and moved into the former Detroit Convention Hall on Woodward Avenue. An entire city block of buildings was converted into a vast and innovative bottling plant with over 250,000 square feet of working space plus 2½ acres of parking lots. Each of the four completely automatic bottling lines had a capacity of 750 cases per hour. The Vernors extract was also manufactured at the plant and stored for four years. Vernors' second story housed management's offices, which were all lined with expensive foreign woods and air-conditioned. Outside, the largest neon sign of its kind in the world was erected. The dream plant of the Vernor family had become a reality.

In 1974, the physical facilities remained much the same as they were when the plant was first opened. One of the bottling lines had been replaced by a canning line with a capacity of 1,500 cases of 12-ounce cans per hour. During 1974, the bottling lines produced about 750–1,000 bottled cases per hour. Not only was Vernors bottled in Detroit, but the company had become the franchised bottler for RC and Diet Rite Cola, Weight Watchers beverages, a line of "100 percent naturals" (lemon lime, orange, grape, cherry cola, berry cola, raspberry red pop, and black cherry). It also produced a line of private label soft drinks for

area supermarkets. However, despite the diversity of the company's product lines, Vernors and 1-Cal Vernors continued to account for approximately 75 percent of its sales.

THE PRODUCT

The formula for Vernors, named the best ginger ale in America by *Esquire* magazine in 1974, has existed unchanged since 1865. During that time the Vernors formula has been a tightly guarded secret which has been made available only to the company's president.

Vernors and 1-Cal are a combination of 3 types of gingers and 17 other ingredients. The ingredients go through a variety of processing steps before they are combined to resemble a syrup. The entire formulation is placed in 47-gallon oak barrels, where it is stored for at least four years. During this long storage period, chemical reactions cause the ingredients to combine and produce a syrup extract. The extract is bottled in one-gallon units and either sent to franchised Vernors bottlers around the country or combined with water and sugar and bottled at Vernors' own Woodward Avenue bottling plant.

The aging process is considered the key to Vernors' "deliciously different"® flavor, as it has been described in advertising campaigns. The four-year process has also discouraged any successful imitation of the product. Although other golden ginger ales have been produced in the past, the taste of Vernors is still unique unto itself. The other ginger ales used a different production process which eliminated the need for aging and subsequently resulted in a taste much different from that of Vernors. Even if Vernors' competitors had been willing to take the time and spend the money to age their product for four years, it would have been exceptionally difficult for them to analyze and duplicate the ingredients in Vernors' final bottled product. During the aging process subtle changes occur due to chemical reactions which make the original blend almost indistinguishable.

Outside Detroit, the word *ginger ale* conjures up a vision of Canada Dry, which is a pale, dry ginger ale. In comparison to the golden ginger ales, the dry has less caramel coloring, less natural sweetness, and more acidity. Many people consider the golden better for refreshment and the dry better for mixing with alcoholic beverages.

Vernors has also enjoyed considerable popularity as an ingredient in food recipes. Vernors' sales have been exceptionally strong during Christmas and Easter seasons, when the product is used to glaze turkeys and hams. During the winter it also has considerable appeal served hot.

"V and V's" (Vernors and vodka) is sometimes served in Detroit bars and Vernors and whiskey is known to be popular at weddings. Some people combine a small amount of Vernors with their beer, and they allege that this allows them to drink more beer.

Drinkers of Vernors have traditionally ascribed certain medicinal benefits to the product. Served hot, Vernors is said to relieve sore throats. Hot or cold, it has been used to relieve fevers and calm upset stomachs. (See Appendix C for market research reports: (1) a 1971 study covering Boston and Minneapolis; and (2) a 1973 project dealing with the Detroit market.)

DISTRIBUTION

From its Detroit bottling plant, Vernors ships Vernors extract syrup to franchised bottlers nationwide and bottled product to its 11 independent distributors in eastern Michigan and northern Ohio.

At one time, the eastern Michigan and northern Ohio distributor territories were owned and operated by Vernors itself, but in 1972 these areas were turned over to independent distributors. Vernors wholesales bottled product to each distributor, who is responsible for the functions and costs necessary to sell the product to the retailer. These costs include hiring and paying a sales force, buying or leasing the delivery trucks, and maintaining a warehouse and office. The territories serviced by independent distributors are (Exhibit 1):

1. Saginaw.   5. Jackson.
2. Marysville.   6. Ann Arbor.
3. Lansing.   7. Pontiac.
4. Flint.

The Detroit and Toledo distribution areas are owned and operated by Vernors. The Toledo warehouse services the following independent distributor areas:

1. Defiance.   3. Findlay.
2. Lima.   4. Sandusky.

The sales force for the distributor (and the Vernors') areas typically includes a team consisting of a preseller, a route driver-salesman, and a driver's helper. Usually the distributor subdivides his territory and assigns a team to each subarea. The preseller is responsible for contacting and selling to the retailer. A good preseller uses suggestive selling to convince the retailer to carry more of his product and also attempts to get the best shelf position available (on the lower shelf between Coke and Pepsi) and the greatest possible amount of shelf space. The preseller is also responsible for the placement of point-of-purchase promotional and merchandising materials. The driver-salesman and his helper are responsible for delivering the presalesman's orders and collecting the returnable bottles. The salaries and commissions for each position differ from one distributor area to the next.

Vernors employs three district managers to maintain liaison between

EXHIBIT 1   Detroit major market area basic statistics

Counties included:

Michigan	Michigan (continued)
Genesee	St. Clair
Lapeer	Sanilac
Lenawee	Washtenaw
Livingston	Wayne
Macomb	Ohio
Monroe	Lucas
Oakland	Ottawa
Saginaw	Wood

Total population (000): 6,093.5
Percent of U.S. population: 3.0%
Percent of U.S. households: 2.9%
Per capita income: $3,367
Total grocery sales: $2,074,600,000
Total drug sales: $445,493,000

Total number of grocery stores: 4,826 (1967 count) by store type:

	Number	Percent of total	1967 Sales ($000)		Percent of total
Chains	784	16.2%	$1,361,806		65.6%
Independents	4,042	83.8	712,791		34.4
Extra large		284		$331,153	
Large		1,208		249,980	
Medium		1,327		93,497	
Small		1,223		38,164	

Commercial TV stations (1969):

CKLW	WKBD	WTOL
WDHO	WKNX	WWJ
WJBK	WSPD	WXON
WJRT		WXYZ

Percent of TV households (1969): 98%

Newspapers (1969—circulation 75,000 or over):
Detroit Free Press
Detroit News
Flint Journal
Toledo Blade

Total number of drugstores: 1,741 (1967 count) by store type:

	Number	Percent of total	1967 Sales ($000)		Percent of total
Chains	258	14.8%	$116,276		26.1%
Independents	1,483	85.2	329,217		73.9
Large		637		$240,725	
Medium		448		67,047	
Small		398		21,445	

Source: *Sales Management Survey of Buying Power,* 1969 data.

the Detroit office and the distributors. The district managers work with the distributors to develop area sales potential, analyze local problems, and train the distributors' personnel. They oversee all promotional and merchandising activity in the area and report its results to Detroit on a monthly basis.

Chain store sales are considered a key to profitability, and for this reason Vernors employs a key account executive based in Detroit. The key account man arranges all of Vernors' chain store promotions and calls on all chains which have a central buying office in Detroit. If a Vernors' promotion is accepted by the chain's central office, all stores within its jurisdiction are required to carry the promotion. Chains that have stores in a distributor's area but do not have a central buying office in Detroit are usually called on by the distributor and the district manager together.

Vernors also monitors the price structure in the distributor territories, and the district managers keep a close watch over the competition's prices to the retailer. The Detroit office establishes suggested prices to the retailer, seeking to keep them competitive with Coke, Pepsi, and 7up.

All dealer promotions originate from the Detroit office, and the cost of the allowances offered to retailers is divided between the Detroit office and the distributor. The distributor usually pays for 25 percent of the allowance, which is added to his invoice price. The Detroit office pays for all advertising costs and attempts to utilize media whose coverage includes the Detroit area and all areas covered by the Vernors distributors.

The Vernors distribution system in the cities of Detroit and Toledo is company-owned and -operated. Because distribution coverage in Detroit to the chains and independents is close to 100 percent, the primary objective is to get more product onto the shelf and better shelf position.

The city of Detroit is divided into 20 areas or routes, each with its presalesman, driver-salesman, and driver's helper. The sales force has a pay scale which makes the driver-salesman's job the most desirable, with the driver's helper and the presalesman following, in that order. All three receive a base pay that depends primarily on seniority. In addition, the driver-salesman receives 8 cents a case commission and his helper receives 6 cents a case for every case delivered, and the presalesman receives 4 cents a case for each case sold to his customers. Vernors believes that an effective sales pitch to the retailer can boost his purchases 15–40 percent, and for this reason Vernors has embarked on a sales training program for its driver-salesman in order to supplement the presalesman's efforts.

SALES (Exhibit 2)

By Season

As with all soft drink producers, Vernors' sales are highly seasonal. The warm summer months usually produce the highest per capita consumption for the soft drink industry. Industry analysts have established direct correlations between annual soft drink consumption and the

EXHIBIT 2   Case sales of Vernors and Vernors 1-Cal

	July	August	September	October	November
Vernors total product line:					
73–74	229,187	199,624	194,279	186,462	251,722
72–73	172,811	240,363	185,655	184,434	214,291
71–72	189,277	208,659	172,934	185,781	167,090
70–71	212,516	240,168	180,141	169,096	169,181
69–70	252,220	248,003	170,485	205,226	216,126
68–69	235,955	269,996	180,346	229,542	172,159
8-oz. R					
73–74	7,446	8,413	7,081	6,006	5,510
72–73	11,994	11,265	9,819	8,700	8,673
71–72	20,924	18,687	17,059	15,350	14,614
70–71	24,664	25,529	22,876	21,290	16,126
69–70	62,356	52,794	41,356	44,235	33,023
68–69	87,937	86,080	64,797	71,018	54,535
10-oz. NR					
73–74	80,206	22,420	23,236	16,963	23,275
72–73	47,230	54,171	46,617	40,341	84,168
71–72	56,804	76,527	48,614	50,227	54,469
70–71	71,848	63,507	51,794	50,251	54,599
69–70	59,028	50,258	48,308	54,837	59,900
68–69	40,661	43,209	33,732	40,105	31,447
12-oz. R					
73–74	8,194	8,697	6,435	6,345	6,234
72–73	9,678	9,856	6,963	7,616	7,730
71–72	11,170	12,171	11,098	8,396	7,598
70–71	17,482	16,042	12,626	11,873	9,223
69–70	12,114	11,726	9,300	9,397	12,966
68–69	5,910	5,919	4,324	4,724	3,952
24-oz. R					
73–74	5,434	4,940	5,576	4,971	5,940
72–73	9,509	7,919	7,603	10,746	10,844
71–72	11,515	13,356	13,602	12,807	16,322
70–71	16,260	23,850	16,618	13,476	12,962
69–70	36,741	41,352	15,544	23,860	28,385
68–69	46,752	69,645	26,485	51,808	35,701
12-oz. cans					
73–74	55,387	61,717	54,799	41,228	42,913
72–73	37,969	88,849	44,035	56,875	28,681
71–72	50,033	47,290	41,621	59,818	25,162
70–71	47,134	50,156	39,724	35,224	33,539
69–70	51,964	49,159	40,153	40,786	37,930
68–69	46,480	47,910	36,115	41,053	29,604
28-oz. NR					
73–74	43,278	34,690	42,257	40,121	103,396
72–73	42,342	51,608	54,262	44,110	61,472
71–72	38,831	40,628	40,960	39,183	48,925
70–71	35,128	61,084	36,503	36,982	42,732
69–70	30,017	42,714	4,334	3,562	2,089
68–69	8,815	17,418	3,885	5,054	4,050

December	January	February	March	April	May	June	Total
263,411	148,937	174,515	191,394	255,086	205,817	200,526	2,496,256
288,650	160,497	164,816	193,162	241,302	181,786	211,937	2,439,704
305,777	114,387	139,488	293,068	136,954	240,054	222,450	2,375,939
322,013	161,419	191,859	231,263	277,837	207,881	217,577	2,580,951
385,793	189,537	201,643	277,957	196,063	207,648	256,127	2,806,828
342,659	193,808	177,950	246,029	220,294	212,612	211,054	2,692,404
4,612	4,015	5,443	4,718	5,342	5,014	4,800	131,943
9,208	7,802	6,868	7,657	6,942	7,269	8,254	104,451
17,919	3,669	5,111	13,479	10,790	13,389	12,828	163,819
21,867	15,581	15,093	21,882	22,305	18,372	22,251	247,836
40,893	29,840	28,043	28,959	30,364	29,856	39,071	460,790
77,618	65,466	55,337	60,941	64,987	61,342	55,224	805,282
33,925	23,661	4,453	4,996	4,443	5,553	10,411	248,948
46,535	53,911	41,509	41,351	42,039	41,728	51,299	590,899
72,007	35,066	45,446	60,537	43,730	52,533	52,537	650,497
76,515	61,794	59,049	61,357	77,350	104,108	63,010	795,182
92,189	60,996	59,782	63,896	66,072	58,520	73,546	743,332
57,430	41,526	37,418	44,543	45,269	47,023	49,098	510,681
4,762	5,498	7,010	6,267	6,460	5,935	8,637	80,019
7,083	8,611	7,360	7,393	6,658	6,821	7,508	93,277
10,629	9,680	8,948	10,215	7,567	8,544	9,693	115,709
11,673	9,002	8,749	11,012	12,242	9,712	13,921	143,627
18,592	15,264	14,329	14,532	10,518	13,918	15,998	164,654
6,238	5,036	4,133	4,729	5,516	6,050	7,496	64,027
8,534	3,810	5,870	4,596	7,038	2,856	2,507	56,729
22,720	5,862	6,188	6,565	19,014	3,598	7,175	117,743
37,756	4,336	4,943	22,232	6,543	8,407	8,846	160,565
36,854	9,680	11,953	32,215	43,634	9,322	21,369	248,193
74,943	15,367	25,680	54,619	15,051	17,069	23,520	372,131
100,267	30,313	30,572	60,683	42,270	30,880	31,989	557,360
48,606	33,235	35,417	42,115	43,280	78,364	57,881	595,012
34,150	38,533	34,017	37,541	39,337	81,187	51,328	572,494
36,056	22,642	33,602	36,016	36,333	102,121	80,633	571,327
41,952	32,277	32,926	48,017	59,829	36,531	52,774	505,083
52,062	37,517	36,296	43,303	39,558	41,040	57,577	527,343
42,813	35,348	31,474	36,138	37,337	50,494	43,553	478,389
102,350	28,473	58,888	53,079	106,451	35,296	39,212	681,491
154,112	28,812	45,256	42,530	111,974	23,177	65,388	725,043
129,520	18,491	36,650	147,430	18,605	43,650	41,946	644,819
133,152	33,055	64,089	61,710	64,477	29,836	44,252	643,000
107,114	30,553	37,513	72,648	28,500	37,791	46,425	443,260
58,223	16,119	19,016	37,995	24,965	26,277	23,694	246,461

EXHIBIT 2 *(concluded)*

	July	August	September	October	November
16-oz. NR					
73–74	27,909	22,402	20,627	30,963	50,261
72–73	14,089	16,695	16,356	16,046	12,723
71–72					
1-Cal total product line					
73–74	121,338	111,018	93,155	100,547	105,670
72–73	79,620	112,862	80,510	88,342	91,576
71–72	88,136	95,888	81,591	92,487	66,615
70–71	110,573	101,967	86,312	77,649	74,939
69–70	100,949	91,619	77,434	48,602	22,890
68–69	93,287	93,778	75,552	88,785	67,966
10-oz. NR					
73–74	50,451	18,845	13,305	14,243	14,138
72–73	33,280	37,019	31,778	30,362	47,361
71–72	36,339	45,282	33,606	35,171	31,434
70–71	51,503	42,573	36,487	32,970	34,495
69–70	31,352	27,356	25,147	16,237	3,980
68–69	21,682	23,875	19,939	23,019	17,767
12-oz. R					
73–74	6,638	6,217	5,467	5,328	5,118
72–73	7,215	6,941	6,323	6,102	5,962
71–72	10,645	10,430	10,397	8,649	8,045
70–71	16,304	15,354	13,807	11,968	8,897
69–70	24,520	20,746	16,991	10,569	4,935
68–69	29,551	28,893	21,939	25,287	19,266
Cans					
73–74	38,206	47,488	36,007	33,908	32,807
72–73	27,361	54,857	26,859	39,085	23,085
71–72	34,034	32,988	30,249	41,518	18,550
70–71	36,066	35,464	30,590	27,066	25,304
69–70	39,272	36,486	30,962	18,234	11,836
68–69	37,881	37,723	29,962	35,425	26,883
28-oz. NR					
73–74	113,891	7,528	8,494	8,974	18,113
72–73	8,866	10,251	11,973	9,497	11,364
71–72	7,118	7,188	7,339	7,149	8,586
70–71	6,703	8,576	5,428	5,645	6,183
69–70	5,804	7,031	4,334	3,562	2,089
68–69	4,173	3,287	3,885	5,054	4,050
16-oz. NR					
73–74	11,615	9,060	8,092	13,558	15,980
72–73	2,894	3,794	3,577	3,306	3,804
71–72					

Note: 24 cans/bottles per case for sizes less than 24 ounces. Sizes greater than or equal to 24 ounces contain 12 bottles per case.
Source: Company records.

December	January	February	March	April	May	June	Total
42,704	21,278	20,575	24,417	31,626	22,730	34,460	350,082
14,842	16,966	23,564	50,125	15,338	18,006	20,993	235,743
1,890	48,503	14,788	3,159	13,316	11,410	16,067	69,203
101,320	82,779	92,627	106,486	98,791			
82,613	89,239	96,408	113,402	118,772	119,555	105,878	1,178,477
87,108	52,262	77,420	99,808	75,058	116,055	105,034	1,037,462
90,820	77,915	84,544	100,470	108,668	110,174	103,549	1,127,583
22,890	85,003	108,624	122,553	120,909	118,818	130,354	1,051,838
90,183	77,235	75,532	88,459	89,216	93,494	90,660	1,024,147
21,273	16,254	3,064	3,545				
30,208	38,659	36,219	39,169	41,313	36,956	39,632	441,960
38,396	25,530	33,39	41,644	29,961	40,859	36,829	428,792
40,892	38,025	39,204	43,290	47,850	61,496	43,501	512,286
2,986	43,012	51,837	55,983	58,031	49,742	57,001	422,664
27,520	22,033	21,550	25,914	26,717	28,398	27,940	286,354
4,264	4,505	5,829	5,630	6,131			
5,895	7,510	7,015	6,899	7,581	6,632	7,019	81,094
7,849	6,604	6,604	7,122	9,168	7,709	8,627	103,888
10,791	9,028	9,028	9,554	11,753	12,229	12,647	143,227
3,643	14,462	14,462	15,138	17,190	17,964	19,294	183,227
23,173	21,545	21,545	20,205	22,635	23,966	21,645	281,973
34,942	25,617	31,631	36,537				
23,260	30,615	31,500	35,503	37,618	59,877	37,136	426,756
26,327	16,649	24,813	26,246	28,490	56,834	48,413	385,111
28,380	24,678	26,854	35,485	40,284	30,692	38,875	379,788
16,227	24,727	35,359	40,193	38,730	44,457	46,696	383,181
3,304	28,759	28,735	33,114	33,206	35,237	35,149	365,378
15,360	6,064	13,184	10,413				
19,561	7,713	10,529	10,281	24,131	7,624	12,324	144,104
14,536	3,479	12,094	20,609	6,006	6,385	7,747	108,236
10,757	6,184	8,832	9,942	8,315	7,024	8,526	92,215
1,277	2,802	6,290	9,187	6,184	6,844	7,363	62,767
6,186	4,898	5,042	6,886	5,327	5,991	5,926	60,615
14,298	10,092	10,005	10,866	14,308			
3,689	4,742	11,145	21,550	7,829	8,466	9,767	84,563
			2,141	2,892	3,334	3,418	11,785

average temperature—the higher the average temperature, the higher the sales.

Holidays are also prime periods for soft drink sales. Christmas, New Year's Day, Easter, Memorial Day, the Fourth of July, Labor Day, and Thanksgiving are all big-volume periods. Vernors is considered by most in the industry to be the champion of the holidays. Indeed, it is November, December, and the Easter month, not the summer months, that are Vernors' biggest sales periods. Officials attribute this to Vernors' diverse cooking uses, which include a basting sauce for turkeys and hams, and its inclusion in Jell-O and dessert recipes.

By Package Size

Vernors comes in 12-ounce cans; 8-, 12-, and 24-ounce returnables; and 10-, 16-, and 28-ounce nonreturnables. The returnable business was once forecast to be the bulk of Vernors' future sales due to the widespread appeal of the ecological movement. However, the shift to returnable sales did not materialize.

The bulk of Vernors' business is in nonreturnables (NRs) and cans. The 12-ounce cans have accounted for 25 percent of Vernors' unit sales in the past few years, and management anticipates a strong demand in the future, although it worries about the rising cost of the aluminum container. The 16-ounce and 28-ounce NRs have become big-volume items, as recent consumer trends have been toward the larger bottles. The industry recently witnessed the introduction of 48-ounce and 64-ounce containers, and Vernors was considering the inclusion of such items in its product line.

Vernors versus Vernors 1-Cal

Throughout the last five years, Vernors' case sales have been twice as high as those of 1-Cal. However, the sales of 1-Cal have increased somewhat faster than those of regular Vernors.

By Geographic Area (Exhibit 3)

The city of Detroit consumes over half of Vernors' sales. However, its percentage of Vernors' sales has been decreasing in recent years. The Toledo distributorship, also owned by Vernors, is a distant second in volume, with 8 percent of company sales. The other seven distributorships are all locally owned and account for about 35 percent of company sales.

By Distribution Channel (Exhibit 4)

Food stores.   Vernors has achieved nearly 100 percent distribution in food stores in the Detroit area. The product has been well accepted

EXHIBIT 3   Sales in cases by geographic area: Distributor breakdown

	1973–74 Sales	Percent	1972–73 Sales	Percent
Vernors				
Total	2,496,256	100%	2,440,672	100%
Detroit	1,428,242	57%	1,488,525	61%
Toledo	184,438	8	174,190	7
Pontiac	205,005	8	179,424	7
Flint	159,052	7	149,723	6
Saginaw	134,511	5	124,194	5
Jackson	67,898	3	55,515	2
Ann Arbor	147,893	6	125,761	5
Lansing	75,576	3	67,757	3
Marysville	83,249	3	76,551	3
1-Cal				
Total	1,255,267	100%	1,178,745	100%
Detroit	625,913	50%	637,281	54%
Toledo	110,064	9	93,542	8
Pontiac	120,122	10	102,037	7
Flint	89,290	7	74,576	6
Saginaw	89,667	7	80,868	7
Jackson	41,731	3	33,585	3
Ann Arbor	89,268	7	79,420	7
Lansing	49,980	4	44,347	5
Marysville	39,232	3	33,092	3

Source: Company records.

by chains and independents alike, a crucial variable if a soft drink operation is to become profitable, since food stores produce the bulk of soft drink sales. Approximately 84 percent of Vernors' unit volume is sold via the food stores, and Nielsen surveys give Vernors and 1-Cal together 8.9 percent of all soft drink sales in food stores.

Restaurants. Vernors' distribution in restaurants is considered spotty. This facet of the business is handled by independent business which was given the restaurant distribution rights through a long-term agreement that was made several years ago. The independent organization buys Vernors in syrup form and is solely responsible for selling it to and through various restaurants and institutions in the area. At one time Vernors was available in almost every restaurant in town. However, company officials believe that its distribution coverage is now less than 50 percent. Restaurant sales account for 13.5 percent of Vernors' volume in comparison to 21 percent for the industry.

Vending. The vending operation is controlled by Vernors and accounts for 0.9 percent of company volume versus 19 percent for the

EXHIBIT 4   Sales by distribution channel: Detroit—1972–1973 sales breakdown and share of market*

	Vernors		1-Cal		Combined	
	Units	Percent	Units	Percent	Units	Percent
Sales distribution						
Sales to food stores	3,657,995	84.2	1,694,231	96.6	5,352,226	87.7
Sales to restaurants	587,197	13.5	19,054	1.1	606,251	9.9
Sales by vending machines	40,661	0.9	11,302	0.6	51,963	0.9
Other sales (estimated)	60,000	1.4	30,000	1.7	90,000	1.5
Total	4,345,853	100.0	1,754,587	100.0	6,100,440	100.0

	Units	Percent
Share of market in food stores		
Detroit major market	60,250,000	100.0
Vernors	3,657,995	6.1
1-Cal	1,694,231	2.8
Combined Vernors/1-Cal	5,352,226	8.9

*All sales figures in eight-ounce-equivalent units.
Source: Company records.

industry. The company estimates that it has 707 vending machines in the city of Detroit (458 can machines, 249 bottle), although not all of the locations are known. A five-slot machine holds 11 cases of cans, and the machine costs approximately $750.

COST STRUCTURE

The maintenance of margins in fiscal 1973–74 was an ever-increasing struggle. Sugar, a major ingredient in regular Vernors, rose in price from $15 to $31 per 100 pounds in a six-month period. Soft drink producers had to pass on the increases to their customers to a point where they feared that the price of soft drinks might be approaching the consumer resistance level.

Vernors' contribution margins were:

	Regular	1-Cal
10 NR	50.7%	64.6%
16 NR	41.6	56.4
28 NR	51.5	64.3
12-oz. cans	46.3	57.9

Vernors' prices to the retail outlets were identical for both brands.

10 NR	$4.20 per case of 24
16 NR	5.00 per case of 24
28 NR	5.10 per case of 12
Cans	4.85 per case of 24

Retail prices charged by the various Detroit area food stores varied from store to store, but each store generally charged the same for both varieties.

10 NR	$1.69 per eight-pack
16 NR	1.55 per six-pack
28 NR	0.53 per bottle
Cans	1.45 per six-pack

COMPETITION (see Appendixes)

Traditionally, Vernors has been priced as a national brand soft drink, making it competitive with Coke, Pepsi, and 7up. Second and third tiers of soft drink competition come from regional soft drinks such as Faygo, which are priced below the national brands, and the private labels, which are the lowest-priced soft drinks on the market.

Pepsi has developed a strong position in the Detroit market, with a commanding market share in the food stores of 27.3 percent for regular Pepsi and 2.6 percent for Diet-Pepsi. Pepsi has been positioned as the soft drink that perks you up, and it attempts to appeal to the 18–24-year-old segment of the population, the group that has the largest per capita consumption. Its position is executed through radio and television commercials and printed ads which emphasize sociability and vitality.

Coke, the leading brand nationally, is a distant second in the Detroit food store market, with 15.7 percent of the market. Its recent advertising efforts have centered on "The Real Thing," and it too tries to appeal to the 18–24 age group. Coke's image is one of refreshment and good times.

Seven-Up has achieved notable success by positioning itself against colas in general. The primary target for the "Uncola" campaign is all persons 13 and up, with the major emphasis on the young. An absence of jingles has made the execution of the Uncola positioning markedly different from that of the colas.

VERNORS' PROMOTION

Vernors has never established a strong position for itself. For its first 100 years it was promoted in the soft drink market simply as a ginger ale. The same has been true of 1-Cal since its introduction in 1961.

EXHIBIT 5   Advertising expenditures, 1971–1974, by types of media ($)

			Detroit 40	Toledo 41	Pontiac 47	Flint 48	Saginaw 49
1973–74:	Outdoor	43–130					
		43–730					
	TV	43–131	21,112.98	6,310.00		6,805.00	
		43–731	27,528.13	3,070.00		3,520.00	
	Print	43–132	4,254.44	1,097.17		500.00	500.00
		43–732		22.11			
	Radio	43–133	28,211.37	930.00		1,380.00	
		43–733					
	Promotion: Trade 43–150 and 151		216,746.94	19,326.79	24,993.98	20,340.51	12,818.13
	43–750 and 751		50,759.11	1,445.70	11,058.64	5,095.79	3,386.34
	Promotion: Consumer 43–152 and 153		9,980.63	363.82			
	43–752 and 753		311.79	14.38			
1972–73:	Outdoor	43–130	25.67				
		43–730					
	TV	43–131	14,745.00	6,365.00		2,478.55	
		43–731	23,393.75	5,130.00		4,461.20	
	Print	43–432	1,253.94	310.00			
		43–732	1,115.75				
	Radio	43–133	24,690.25	3,868.50		2,920.29	
		43–733					
	Promotion: Trade 43–150 and 151		239,034.64	370.63)	21,251.79	20,686.95	17,204.05
	43–750 and 751		70,144.35	335.80	8,487.16	4,483.09	7,581.40
	Promotion: Consumer 43–152 and 153		17,228.06	277.67	49.28	18.21	3.32
	43–752 and 753		4,771.82	77.99			1.55
1971–72:	Outdoor	43–130					
		43–730					
	TV	43–131	38,265.00				
		43–731					
	Print	43–132	133.25	27.85	383.50		
		43–732	6,857.10			820.80	
	Radio	43–133	23,177.50	1,890.00		1,482.30	
		43–733					
	Promotion: Trade 43–150 and 151		152,254.73	14,968.62	14,796.10	21,461.87	16,697.30
	43–750 and 751		17,787.30		3,420.80	2,252.95	2,431.10
	Promotion: Consumer 43–152 and 153		3,041.55	217.76	49.26	171.37	
	43–752 and 753						

Source: Company records.

In June 1973, Vernors broke from its ginger ale tradition and positioned itself simply as "Vernors." The containers bore a label with the Vernors name; above the name was printed "original," and below the name, "it's different."

In the past months there has been considerable discussion as to where the soft drink would be correctly positioned. Some have argued that Vernors is simply a ginger ale; others regard it as unique and think that it should be considered a soft drink all its own; a third group believes that Vernors should be considered a golden ginger ale to distinguish

	Jackson 52	Ann Arbor 54	Lansing 59	Marys-ville 60	Central office 99	Total year
1973–74:						
TV			5,190.00		39,417.98 Vernors	Vernors 77,983.41
			2,420.00		38,958.13 1-Cal	1-Cal 38,980.24
Print	250.00	250.00	460.00		153.68 7,465.29 Vernors	
					22.11 1-Cal	
Radio			566.25		12.52 31,100.14 Vernors	
Prom: Trade	5,881.35	18,482.97	9,433.47	8,049.89	336,074.03 Vernors	Vernors 346,422.04
	2,042.37		470.76	3,210.19 1,657.89	83,363.64 1-Cal	1-Cal 83,689.81
Prom: Consumer					3.56 10,348.01 Vernors	
					326.17 1-Cal	
1972–73:						
					25.67 Vernors	Vernors 82,108.63
TV			1,919.00		14,294.87 39,202.42 Vernors	1-Cal 38,685.91
			3,529.25		837.83 37,352.03 1-Cal	
Print					3,388.50 4,952.44 Vernors	
					165.00 1,280.75 1-Cal	
Radio	173.13		1,107.60		5,168.33 37,928.10 Vernors	
	53.13				53.13 1-Cal	
Prom: Trade	3,655.65	19,177.68	4,752.09	5,011.36	3.39 330,406.59 Vernors	Vernors 350,486.40
	1,414.53	6,042.13	1,773.16	1,669.84	101,931.46 1-Cal	1-Cal 106,784.59
Prom: Consumer	3.00		43.15	11.68	2,445.44 20,079.81 Vernors	
					1.77 4,853.13 1-Cal	
1971–72:						
TV					38,265.00 Vernors	Vernors 67,433.20
						1-Cal 925.10
Print					544.60 Vernors	
	410.40	410.40	752.40		9,251.10 1-Cal	
Radio	25.00		2,648.80		28,623.60 Vernors	
Prom: Trade	2,765.23	10,947.25	3,698.60	4,423.39	242,013.09 Vernors	Vernors 246,185.27
	380.80	2,277.15	471.65	482.50	29,504.25 1-Cal	1-Cal 29,692.65
Prom: Consumer	345.98	36.17	304.56	4.80	4,172.18 Vernors	
			181.40		181.40 1-Cal	

itself from the better-known Canada Dry; and the last group thinks that it should be placed in the mold of "deliciously different."

In the last decade, over 10 different media campaigns were attempted, and all of the positioning alternatives were tried to some extent. Radio, television, and billboards were the basic advertising tools (Exhibit 5). Consequently, Vernors achieved significant awareness of its brand. However, individual ad campaigns produced little recall. For the last few years Vernors has spent roughly $80,000 for Vernors advertising and $40,000 for 1-Cal. About $15,000 was spent in the Detroit area

for promotions in conjunction with local groups and activities. Due to its long history in the city of Detroit, the company was often approached to participate in local promotional activity before any of its competition was approached.

The greatest portion of the advertising budget was the $430,000 spent on trade promotions. On each of the major holidays, as well as at other times, Vernors would encourage the local chains to give Vernors a special point-of-purchase display which would feature Vernors at a reduced price. The store would also advertise the special in the local newspaper along with its other special items for the week. Vernors, in turn, would sell its product to the wholesalers at a specially reduced price, or it would give them one case free for every five or six cases purchased. Chain store promotions are actively solicited by all soft drink producers due to their ability to generate a high volume of sales during the promotional period.

APPENDIX A

Soft Drink Industry Statistics

Section 3 (Midwest)

Minnesota	Illinois
Michigan	Indiana
Wisconsin	Ohio
Iowa	Missouri

84 plants reporting

Sales	Number of plants	Average percent
Increased	57	+8.6
Decreased	15	−4.5
Profits		
Increased	39	+17
Decreased	18	−15.1

Costs	Percent of increase
63 plants report increase* (average 8.6%)	
Ingredients	7.3
Distribution	5.5
Packaging	6.9
Labor	8.6
Taxes	8.6

Low-calorie sales
1973 volume: 8.7%
60 plants report volume up (average 13.5%)

Section 4 (Southwest)

Utah	New Mexico
Colorado	Arizona
Kansas	Texas

36 plants reporting

Sales	Number of plants	Average percent
Increased	21	+13.6
Decreased	9	−4.0
Profits		
Increased	12	+10.0
Decreased	6	−6.0

Costs	Percent of increase
27 plants report increase (average 6.9%)	
Ingredients	3.1
Distribution	3.1
Packaging	3.4
Labor	5.8
Taxes	3.6

Low-calorie sales
1973 volume: 9.07%
6 plants report volume up (average 9%)

Section 3 (Midwest)
Low-calorie sales
5 plants report volume
   down (average 2.8%)
Average number of
   flavors: 2.8

Sizes	Percent of volume
6–8 oz.	8.8
10 oz.	16.7
12-oz. cans/bottles	31.3
16. oz	16.1
Over 26 oz.	36.9

Size trends	Average change
6–8 oz.	40% decrease
10 oz.	No change
12-oz. cans/bottles	8.7% decrease
16 oz.	5.8% decrease
Over 26 oz.	59.2% increase

Market share by package type	Percent of volume
Returnables	66.0
Nonreturnables	9.9
Cans	14.1
Bulk	9.9

Flavor shares of market	Percent of volume
Cola	46.7
Lemon-lime	17.3
Orange	6.5
Ginger ale	1.7
Root beer	5.2
Grape	3.4
Grapefruit	2.3
Chocolate	—
Strawberry	5.1
Club soda	—
Bottled water	—
Others*	10.5

Vending
Average share of volume: 22.2%

Most important outlets	Percent of volume
Food stores (chains, 34.9%; independent, 22.2%)	57.1
Bars, taverns, and restaurants	13.7
Service stations	13.8
Recreational outlets	3.7
Beverage distributors	1.7
Discount stores	2.4
Cash and Carry	5.7
Others	1.6

Section 4 (Southwest)
Low-calorie sales
6 plants report volume
   down (average 2.9%)
Average number of
   flavors: 1.8

Sizes	Percent of volume
6–8 oz.	3.9
10 oz.	25.5
12-oz. cans/bottles	39.0
16 oz.	17.3
Over 26 oz.	13.8

Size trends	Average change
6–8 oz.	7.1% decrease
10 oz.	8.2% decrease
12-oz. cans/bottles	15.7% increase
16 oz.	16.1% increase
Over 26 oz.	89% increase

Market share by package type	Percent of volume
Returnables	43.5
Nonreturnables	19.8
Cans	30.3
Bulk	6.3

Flavor shares of market	Percent of volume
Cola	39.8
Lemon-lime	3.2
Orange	4.8
Ginger ale	1.0
Root beer	11.3
Grape .	5.1
Grapefruit	.6
Chocolate	.5
Strawberry	3.4
Club soda	.5
Bottled water	—
Others*	29.3

Vending
Average share of volume: 22.8%

Most important outlets	Percent of volume
Food stores (chains, 42.1%; independent, 25.3%)	67.4
Bars, taverns, restaurants	2.2
Service stations	9.4
Recreational outlets	12.7
Beverage distributors	1.1
Discount stores	2.3
Cash and carry	2.7
Others	.3

*Note: the "others" category includes all other flavors plus Dr. Pepper and similar soft drinks.

Source: "Softdrinks 17th Annual Sales Survey," *Softdrinks*, December 1973. Copyright by Softdrinks, Keller Publishing Corp., 10 Cutter Mill Rd., Great Neck, N.Y. Section 3 (Midwest); section 4 (Southwest).

APPENDIX B

Sales by Types of Distribution Channels

Flavor mix. Regular (nondiet) soft drinks represented 91 percent of packaged sales in the United States in 1973, a share unchanged from the 1972 level. Cola was the predominant flavor, with 65 percent share of this market. Lemon-lime was reported at 11 percent. Orange and root beer both attained market shares of 3 percent. Ginger ale and grape both accounted for 2 percent of the regular drink sales. All other flavors constituted 14 percent of packaged regular soft drinks. The survey indicated that diet soft drinks represented 9 percent of packaged drinks, maintaining their share from the previous year. Cola was the dominant low-calorie flavor, accounting for 65 percent of the total diet market.

Distribution. The survey indicated that food stores were the predominant outlets, accounting for 52 percent of packaged sales on a unit basis, slightly below the ratio recorded a year earlier. Vending machines dispensed 19 percent of the soft drinks sold. Retail stores other than food stores represented 21 percent of packaged sales, and other outlets constituted 8 percent of unit sales. These national distribution patterns differ markedly by region.

Employment and investment spending. According to the survey, employment in the industry rose 2.5 percent in 1973 and approximated 125,000 persons. Plant and equipment spending by the bottlers is projected to rise at least 2 percent in 1974 over 1973 and approach $215 million.

Outlook. The 1973 sales survey indicated that the bottlers anticipate a growth of 9.6 percent in soft drink dollar sales in 1974. One-way containers are expected to outpace returnables in unit sales, with cans increasing an estimated 8 percent. Bottlers anticipate one-trip bottle unit sales to increase 4 percent. Soft drinks in returnable containers are projected to rise 4 percent.

APPENDIX C

Market Research Reports

PART 1.   MARKET RESEARCH: 1971 BOSTON/MINNEAPOLIS SUMMARY FINDINGS

Product Perception

Initial reaction to Vernors' taste was very favorable, with almost two-thirds of the people giving positive responses.

The youngest age group responded most favorably to Vernors' taste, while the oldest group was most critical. Blacks responded more favorably than whites.

National sales distribution

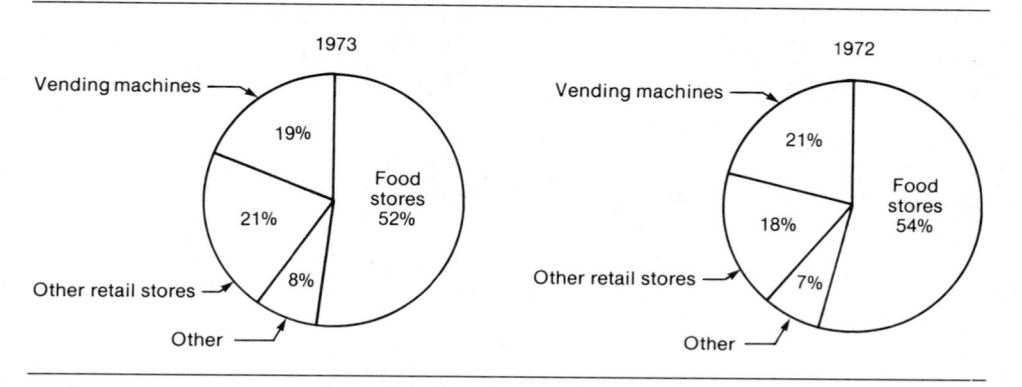

1973

Vending machines — 19%

Food stores 52%

21%

8%

Other retail stores —

Other —

1972

Vending machines — 21%

Food stores 54%

18%

7%

Other retail stores —

Other —

Source: National Soft Drinks Association, "1973 National Summary," *Survey of 1973 Sales*, p. 5.

Product attributes were perceived as "just right" by 79 percent to 91 percent of the respondents. The attributes receiving the most criticism (too much) were sweetness and carbonation; sweetness primarily from the older group and carbonation from both younger groups.

Buying Intentions

An extremely high majority of respondents probably or definitely will buy Vernors, ranging from 69 percent of the older group to 88 percent for the younger group.

Exposure to four promotional concepts about Vernors raised the likelihood of purchase to 75 percent for the older group and 98 percent for the younger group.

After home use, the likelihood of purchase dropped considerably, but still came out to two-thirds of the respondents who would probably or definitely buy Vernors (compared with 82 percent and 86 percent on previous measures).

Blacks show a slightly higher probability of purchase than whites, especially after exposure to promotional statements.

Promotional Statements

Natural wholesome ingredients is the preferred promotional statement, with unchanged formula a distant second.

This same relationship holds for both blacks and whites, all age groups except the 8–12-year-olds, and also regardless of favorite soft drink.

Uniqueness

Vernors is perceived as a unique ginger ale by a small but consistent majority of respondents.

All age groups, both blacks and whites, and all groups of "favorite" soft drink users, except ginger ale, perceived Vernors as a unique ginger ale. Ginger ale drinkers perceived Vernors as a unique soft drink by a small margin.

PART 2.   1973 MARKET RESEARCH, DETROIT

VERNORS INC.
INTEROFFICE CORRESPONDENCE

To: Mr. J. C. Becker   *Date:* October 4, 1973
From: R. H. Evans   *Subject:* Vernors Copy Development

Per your request, this is to summarize the copy planning phase prior to our meeting and evaluating copy for testing. The information which you requested is contained in this document and includes:

A summary of the attitude research conducted in Detroit after reviewing it carefully to determine the greatest potential for Vernors advertising.

Copy plans for Vernors and 1-Cal in both Detroit and the franchise areas.

A point of view as to whether or not Vernors and 1-Cal should be consolidated or treated separately in Detroit and the franchise areas.

A remommended media approach for the two brands in and out of Detroit.

ATTITUDE RESEARCH SUMMARY

A total of 599 people in Detroit were surveyed to determine their reaction and point of view toward soft drinks and Vernors in particular. The composition of the sample size was as follows:

Age	Composition	Number
10–14	Half male/half female	198
15–21	Half male/half female	203
25–40	All housewives	198
		599

In addition to the above, all respondents must have consumed at least one glass of soft drink during the week previous to the study. A copy of

---

Mr. J. C. Becker   October 4, 1973

the questionnaire utilized is attached to this report and shows the actual questions in the order they were asked.

OVERVIEW AND MAJOR RECOMMENDATIONS

Vernors' awareness and trial are both at near-maximum levels, and the challenge to the brand is one of achieving greater frequency of use. About half of the respondents in all three age groups drink Vernors once every three months or less, and this is clearly where the problem and opportunity exist.

While a substantial number of people see Vernors as a ginger ale, this is less true among younger respondents. People who drink Vernors often (once a week) like Vernors most for its robust, hardy flavor and the fact that Vernors is so different. Equally important, those who drink Vernors about once a month (about 33 percent of teens) have no particular dislike, and only about one in six of this group thinks the flavor is too strong or a reason for not drinking Vernors more often. This group represents potential for conversion to greater frequency as evidenced by the fact that about half of them have "nothing" as a dislike about Vernors.

While there are data in this survey which indicate that Vernors is more popular among older people (25–40) in terms of their favorite brand (21 percent versus 11 percent and 9 percent for the younger groups), there is nothing to indicate that teenagers dislike Vernors. On the contrary, 53 percent and 51 percent of those aged 10–14 and 15–21, respectively, drink Vernors once a month or more compared to 38 percent for those 25–40. Additionally, both age segments of teenagers respond in nearly the same manner as adults when questioned why they do not drink Vernors more often or what they dislike about it.

Over half of all age segments who drink Vernors once a week use it as an additive to ice cream, and nearly half of adults who purchase at this frequency use the product as a mixer. Both of these avenues should be pursued to gain increased usage. In addition, about 60 percent of those surveyed believed Vernors to possess medicinal benefits, perhaps explaining why everyone had drunk Vernors but a substantial proportion drink it less than once in three months.

My recommendations are:

1. Advertise and merchandise Vernors to the 15–21-year-old market since 63 percent of this group consume more than five glasses of pop per week compared to 47 percent and 48 percent of the 10–14-year-olds and 25–40-year-olds, respectively. Additionally, the 15–21-year-olds rate Vernors slightly higher than the 10–14-year-olds in terms of favorite flavor and brand being Vernors, and this group cites flavor as a reason for dislike of Vernors to a lesser extent than do the other two age groups.

Mr. J. C. Becker   October 4, 1973

2. Provide via advertising a reason for drinking Vernors more often centered on its difference (or strong flavor if this positioning is testing successfully).

3. Vernors is in dire need of reintroduction. Radio is recommended as the medium to do this because of the age target. However, from a judgmental point of view it is recommended that radio be used after an initial television approach is aired. Reasons for this recommendation are discussed below.

MAJOR FINDINGS

A. Awareness and trial of regular Vernors are at near-maximum levels, and the advertising assignments should not be addressed to this area:

	10–14	15–21	25–40
Aware of Vernors	100%	100%	100%
Vernors trial	96.4	94.6	96.9

B. Awareness and trial of 1-Cal are at much lower levels than regular Vernors. Additionally, users of 1-Cal consume it on an infrequent basis:

	10–14	15–21	25–40
Aware of 1-Cal	55.4%	76.7%	87.0%
1-Cal trial	65.6	62.8	67.4

	Frequency of use		
	10–14	15–21	25–40
Within last week	6.5% } 14.6%	6.8% } 17.3%	15.5% } 24.1%
Within last month	8.1	10.5	8.6
Over one month	11.8 } 15.6	19.4 } 25.7	19.3 } 32.7
Over one year	3.8	6.3	13.4
Never	34.3	37.2	32.6

C. *Pop* is the term Detroiters use to describe carbonated beverages:

	Term used to describe carbonated beverages		
	10–14	15–21	25–40
Pop	90.4%	88.7%	86.9%

D. The challenge to Vernors is one of increasing the brand's saliency and at the same time increasing frequency of use, as the following tables demonstrate:

	First and second favorite flavor of pop		
	10–14	15–21	25–40
Cola	37.4/24.2 = 61.6	39.9/26.6 = 66.5	53.0/22.2 = 75.2
Grape	10.1/17.2 = 27.3	13.3/15.8 = 29.1	15.7/16.7 = 32.4
Root beer	9.6/ 9.1 = 18.7	8.9/12.3 = 21.2	5.1/ 8.6 = 13.7
Red pop	7.1/ 7.6 = 14.7	4.4/ 4.4 = 8.8	2.5/ 4.5 = 7.0
Vernors	1.5/ 3.5 = 5.0	2.0/ 3.4 = 5.4	5.1/ 6.1 = 11.2

Mr. J. C. Becker   October 4, 1973

First and second favorite brand of pop

	10–14	15–21	25–40
Coca-Cola	25.3/13.6 = 38.9	20.2/17.7 = 37.9	21.2/16.2 = 37.4
Pepsi-Cola	18.2/16.7 = 34.9	24.6/13.8 = 38.4	26.8/11.1 = 37.9
Faygo	36.9/16.7 = 53.6	25.6/15.8 = 41.4	19.7/20.2 = 39.9
7up	2.0/ 9.6 = 11.6	8.9/10.8 = 19.7	5.1/10.1 = 15.2
Vernors	2.0/ 5.1 = 7.1	3.0/ 7.9 = 10.9	8.1/13.1 = 21.2

Flavor drunk within past two weeks

	10–14	15–21	25–40
Cola	69.2%	72.9%	71.2%
Root beer	15.7	21.2	16.7
Red pop	17.2	12.8	13.1
Vernors	8.6	14.3	15.7

When did you have Vernors last?

	10–14		15–21		25–40	
Last week	25.3%		28.3%		34.2%	
Last month	33.3	58.6%	30.9	59.2%	18.7	52.9%
Over one month	32.3		26.7		29.4	
Over one year	8.6	40.9	14.1	40.8	17.6	47.0

How often do you drink regular Vernors?

	10–14	15–21	25–40
At least one/week	19.4%	16.2%	18.2%
At least one/month	33.3	34.6	19.8
Once/three months	17.7	15.2	11.2
Less than once/three months	27.4	31.4	47.6

E.   The target age group for regular Vernors advertising should be those between 15 and 21 years old because of greater consumption of soft drinks and the fact that they rate Vernors slightly higher than do 10–14-year-olds.

How much pop have you drunk in the past week?

	10–14	15–21	25–40
5–7 glasses	22.2%	27.1%	19.7%
8–13 glasses	15.2 47.0%	11.3 63.0%	11.1 48.0%
Over 14 glasses	9.6	24.6	17.2
Favorite flavor of pop (Vernors)	1.5/3.5 = 5.0	2.0/3.4 = 5.4	5.1/6.1 = 11.2
Favorite brand (Vernors)	2.0/5.1 = 7.1	3.0/7.9 = 10.9	8.1/13.1 = 21.2

Dislike about Vernors*

	10–14	15–21	25–40
Flavor	16.7%	12.9%	16.0%
Nothing	44.2	51.5	47.9

*Among those who do not drink Vernors at least once a week.

Mr. J. C. Becker   October 4, 1973

	For those who have not had Vernors for at least a month		
	10–14	15–21	25–40
Don't like flavor	35.9%	31.3%	32.6%
No good reason	14.6	14.8	13.6
Not bought by person who shops	13.6	5.2	0.8

F.   Awareness of Vernors advertising lags all other major brands:

	Aware of advertising within past week		
	10–14	15–21	25–40
Coca-Cola	43.3%	27.9%	25.8%
Pepsi	44.4	37.9	30.8
Faygo	34.8	19.2	22.2
7up	20.2	26.1	17.7
Vernors	10.1	9.9	6.1

Of those who did recall Vernors advertising within the past three months (approximately 50 percent of each age segment), over 60 percent (by far the highest number) remembered seeing it on television.

G.   Older people see Vernors as a ginger ale to a greater extent than do younger people:

	What is Vernors?		
	10–14	15–21	25–40
Popular soft drink	51.8%	32.7%	28.5%
Ginger ale	37.3	59.9	63.7
Aged in wood	1.0	1.5	2.1

	Description of Vernors		
	10–14	15–21	25–40
Ginger ale	33.3%	41.9%	46.0%
Different	5.9	10.5	9.6
Other (see verbatims)	53.8	46.1	48.1

H.   Vernors is used as an additive to a large extent by frequent users (those who drink Vernors once a week):

	Use Vernors in:				
	Food recipes	With ice cream			Alcoholic drinks
	25–40	10–14	15–21	25–40	25–40
Often	22.0%	30.8%	39.5%	30.0%	40.0%
Seldom	30.0	28.2	27.9	20.0	8.0
Never	26.0	28.2	18.6	28.0	32.0

I.   Frequent Vernors users like the fact that Vernors is robust in flavor and different:

	What do you like most about Vernors?		
	10–14	15–21	25–40
Robust, hearty	20.5%	20.9%	20.0%
Different	25.6	34.9	34.0

Mr. J. C. Becker　　　　　　　　　　　　　　October 4, 1973

J. Among all age segments and among both frequent and infrequent
users in each segment, an astonishingly high percentage of respondents believe that Vernors is medicinally beneficial or aids in relief
of a nervous or upset stomach.

	Percent saying that Vernors is medicinally beneficial		
	10–14	*15–21*	*25–40*
Total	57.5%	63.9%	74.1%
Frequent	58.3	80.6	91.2
Infrequent	60.3	66.5	74.3

In summary, the research indicates expanded usage as a goal among
all segments, with particular volume leverage existing in the 15–21
group. Given no real expressed barrier to increased usage among those
who do not drink Vernors at least once a week and the lack of any
advertising awareness, opportunity exists to build volume with the right
message and sufficient advertising exposure. Extra flavor and/or difference in taste are seen as viable copy messages. It is also recommended
that via consumer promotion, recipe and ice-cream usage ideas be used
to gain extra volume.

QUESTIONS

1. Analyze the situation faced by the new management group which has
taken charge of the marketing of Vernors soft drinks. What problems and
opportunities can you identify?

2. What marketing strategy (objectives; marketing mix) would you recommend for the coming year? Keep in mind that specific questions of promotional strategy will be considered later, when Part B of the Vernors
case (Case 5–1) is analyzed.

MODERN PLASTICS (A)*

Institutional sales manager Jim Clayton had spent most of Monday morning planning for the rest of the month. It was early July, and Jim knew that an extremely busy time was coming with the preparation of the following year's sales plan.

Since starting his current job less than a month ago, Jim had been involved in learning the requirements of the job and making his initial territory visits. Now that he was getting settled, Jim was trying to plan his activities according to priorities. The need for planning had been instilled in him during his college days. As a result of his three years' field sales experience and development of time management skills, he felt prepared for the challenge of the sales manager's job.

While sitting at his desk, Jim recalled a conversation that he had a week ago with Bill Hanson, the former manager, who had been promoted to another division. Bill told him that the sales forecast (annual and monthly) for plastic trash bags in the Southeast region would be

---

*Written by Professor Tom Ingram, University of Kentucky, and Professor Danny N. Bellenger, Texas Tech University.

due soon as an initial step toward developing the sales plan for the next year. Bill had laughed as he told Jim, "Boy, you ought to have a ball doing the forecast being a rookie sales manager!"

When Jim had asked what Bill meant, he explained by saying that the forecast was often "winged" because the headquarters in New York already knew what they wanted and would change the forecast to meet their figures, particularly if the forecast was for an increase of less than 10 percent. The experienced sales manager could throw numbers together in a short time that would pass as a serious forecast and ultimately be adjusted to fit the plans of headquarters. However, an inexperienced manager would have a difficult time "winging" a credible forecast.

Bill had also told Jim that the other alternative meant gathering mountains of data and putting together a forecast that could be sold to the various levels of Modern Plastics management. This alternative would prove to be time-consuming and could still be changed anywhere along the chain of command before final approval.

Clayton started reviewing pricing and sales volume history (see Exhibit 1). He also looked at the key account performance for the past two and a half years (see Exhibit 2). During the past month Clayton had visited many of the key accounts, and on the average they had indicated that their purchases from Modern would probably increase about 15–20 percent in the coming year.

EXHIBIT 1   Plastic trashbags—sales and pricing history, 1975–1977

	Pricing dollars per case			Sales volume in cases			Sales volume in dollars		
	1975	1976	1977	1975	1976	1977	1975	1976	1977
January	$6.88	$7.70	$15.40	33,000	46,500	36,500	$ 227,000	$ 358,000	$ 562,000
February	6.82	7.70	14.30	32,500	52,500	23,000	221,500	404,000	329,000
March	6.90	8.39	13.48	32,000	42,000	22,000	221,000	353,000	296,500
April	6.88	10.18	12.24	45,500	42,500	46,500	313,000	432,500	569,000
May	6.85	12.38	11.58	49,000	41,500	45,500	335,500	514,000	527,000
June	6.85	12.65	10.31	47,500	47,000	42,000	325,500	594,500	433,000
July	7.42	13.48	9.90*	40,000	43,500	47,500*	297,000	586,500	470,000*
August	6.90	13.48	10.18	48,500	63,500	43,500	334,500	856,000	443,000
September	7.70	14.30	10.31	43,000	49,000	47,500	331,000	700,500	489,500
October	7.56	15.12	10.31	52,500	50,000	51,000	397,000	756,000	526,000
November	7.15	15.68	10.72	62,000	61,500	47,500	443,500	964,500	509,000
December	7.42	15.43	10.59	49,000	29,000	51,000	363,500	447,500	540,000
Total	$7.13	$12.25	$11.30	534,500	568,500	503,500	$3,810,000	$6,967,000	$5,694,000

*July–December 1977 figures are forecast of sales manager J. A. Clayton and other data comes from historical sales information.

EXHIBIT 2   1977 key account sales history (in cases)

Customer	1975	1976	First six months 1977	1975 monthly average	1976 monthly average	First half 1977 monthly average	First quarter 1977 monthly average
Transco Paper Company	125,774	134,217	44,970	10,481	11,185	7,495	5,823
Callaway Paper	44,509	46,049	12,114	3,709	3,837	2,019	472
Florida Janitorial Supply	34,746	36,609	20,076	2,896	3,051	3,346	2,359
Jefferson	30,698	34,692	25,044	2,558	2,891	4,174	1,919
Cobb Paper	13,259	23,343	6,414	1,105	1,945	1,069	611
Miami Paper	10,779	22,287	10,938	900	1,857	1,823	745
Milne Surgical Company	23,399	21,930	—	1,950	1,828	—	—
Graham	8,792	15,331	1,691	733	1,278	281	267
Crawford Paper	7,776	14,132	6,102	648	1,178	1,017	1,322
John Steele	8,634	13,277	6,663	720	1,106	1,110	1,517
Henderson Paper	9,185	8,850	2,574	765	738	429	275
Durant Surgical	—	7,766	4,356	—	647	726	953
Master Paper	4,221	5,634	600	352	470	100	—
D.T.A.	—	—	2,895	—	—	482	—
Crane Paper	4,520	5,524	3,400	377	460	566	565
Janitorial Service	3,292	5,361	2,722	274	447	453	117
Georgia Paper	5,466	5,053	2,917	456	421	486	297
Paper Supplies, Inc.	5,117	5,119	1,509	426	427	251	97
Southern Supply	1,649	3,932	531	137	328	88	78
Horizon Hospital Supply	4,181	4,101	618	348	342	103	206
Total cases	346,007	413,217	156,134	28,835	34,436	26,018	17,623

SCHEDULE FOR PREPARING THE FORECAST

Jim had received a memo recently from Robert Baxter, the regional marketing manager, detailing the plans for completing the 1978 forecast. The key dates in the memo began in only three weeks:

August 1	Presentation of forecast to regional marketing manager.
August 10	Joint presentation with marketing manager to regional general manager.
September 1	Regional general manager presents forecast to division vice president.
September 1–September 30	Review of forecast by staff of division vice president.
October 1	Review forecast with corporate staff.
October 1–October 15–	Revision as necessary.
October 15	Final forecast forwarded to division vice president from regional general manager.

COMPANY BACKGROUND

The plastics division of Modern Chemical Company was founded in 1965 when Modern Chemical purchased Cordco, a small plastics manufacturer with national sales of $15 million. At that time the key products of the plastics division were sandwich bags, plastic tablecloths, trash cans, and plastic-coated clothesline.

Since 1965 the plastics division has grown to a sales level exceeding $200 million with five regional profit centers covering the United States. Each regional center has manufacturing facilities and a regional sales force. There are four product groups in each region:

1. Food packaging: Styrofoam meat and produce trays; plastic bags for various food products.
2. Egg cartons: Styrofoam egg cartons sold to egg packers and supermarket chains.
3. Institutional: Plastic trash bags and disposable tableware (plates, bowls, and so on).
4. Industrial: Plastic packaging for the laundry and dry cleaning market; plastic film for use in pallet over-wrap systems.

Each product group is supervised jointly by a product manager and a district sales manager, both of whom report to the regional marketing manager. The sales representatives report directly to the district sales manager but also work closely with the product manager on matters concerning pricing and product specifications.

The five regional general managers report to J. R. Hughes, vice president of the plastics division. Hughes is located in New York. Although Modern Chemical is owned by a multinational oil company, the plastics division has been able to operate in a virtually independent manner since its establishment in 1965. The reasons for this include:

1. Limited knowledge of the plastic industry on the part of the oil company management.
2. Excellent growth by the plastics division has been possible without management supervision from the oil company.
3. Profitability of the plastics division has consistently been higher than that of other divisions of the chemical company.

THE INSTITUTIONAL TRASH BAG

The institutional trash bag is a polyethylene bag used to collect and transfer refuse to its final disposition point. There are different sizes and colors available to fit the various uses of the bag. For example, a

small bag for desk wastebaskets is available as well as a heavier bag for large containers such as a 55-gallon drum. There are 25 sizes in the Modern line with 13 of those sizes being available in 3 colors—white, buff, and clear. Customers typically buy several different items on an order to cover all their needs.

The institutional trash bag is a separate product from the consumer grade trash bag which is typically sold to homeowners through retail outlets. The institutional trash bag is sold primarily through paper wholesalers, hospital supply companies, and janitorial supply companies to a variety of end users. Since trash bags are used on such a wide scale, the list of end users could include almost any business or institution. The segments include hospitals, hotels, schools, office buildings, transportation facilities, and restaurants.

Based on historical data and a current survey of key wholesalers and end users in the Southeast, the annual market of institutional trash bags in the region was estimated to be 55 million pounds. Translated into cases, the market potential was close to 2 million cases. During the past five years, the market for trash bags has grown at an average rate of 89 percent per year. Now a mature product, future market growth is expected to parallel overall growth in the economy. The 1978 real growth in GNP is forecast to be 4.5 percent.

GENERAL MARKET CONDITIONS

The current market is characterized by a distressing trend. The market is in a position of oversupply with approximately 20 manufacturers competing for the business in the Southeast. Prices have been on the decline for several months but are expected to level out during the last 6 months of the year.

This problem arose after a record year in 1976 for Modern Plastics. During 1976, supply was very tight due to raw material shortages. Unlike many of its competitors, Modern had only minor problems securing adequate raw material supplies. As a result the competitors were few in 1976, and all who remained in business were prosperous. By early 1977 raw materials were plentiful, and prices began to drop as new competitors tried to buy their way into the market. During the first quarter of 1977 Modern Plastics learned the hard way that a competitive price was a necessity in the current market. Volume fell off drastically in February and March as customers shifted orders to new suppliers when Modern chose to maintain a slightly higher than market price on trash bags.

With the market becoming extremely price competitive and profits declining, the overall quality has dropped to a point of minimum standard. Most suppliers now make a bag "barely good enough to get the

EXHIBIT 3   Competitive factors ratings (by competitor)*

Weight	Factor	Modern	National Film	Bonanza	South-eastern	PBI	BAGCO	South-west Bag	Sun Plastics	East Coast Bag Co.
.50	Price	2	3	2	2	2	2	2	2	3
.15	Quality	3	2	3	4	3	2	3	3	4
.10	Breadth	1	2	2	3	3	3	3	3	3
.10	Sales coverage	1	3	3	3	4	3	3	4	3
.05	Packaging	3	3	2	3	3	1	3	3	3
.10	Service	4	3	3	2	2	2	3	4	3

Overall weighted ranking†

1.	BAGCO	2.15	6.	Southeastern	2.55
2.	Modern	2.20	7.	Florida Plastics	2.60
3.	Bonanza	2.25	8.	National Film	2.65
4.	Southwest Bag (Tie)	2.50	9.	East Coast Bag Co.	3.15
5.	PBI (Tie)	2.50			

*Ratings on a 1-to-5 scale, with 1 being the best rating and 5 the worst.
†The weighted ranking is the sum of each rank times its weight. The lower the number, the better the overall rating.

job done." This quality level is acceptable to most buyers who do not demand high quality for this type of product.

MODERN PLASTICS VERSUS COMPETITION

A recent study of Modern versus competition had been conducted by an outside consultant to see how well Modern measured up in several key areas. Each area was weighted according to its importance in the purchase decision, and Modern compared to its key competitors in each area and on an overall basis. The key factors and their weights are shown below:

		Weight
1.	Pricing	.50
2.	Quality	.15
3.	Breadth of line	.10
4.	Sales coverage	.10
5.	Packaging	.05
6.	Service	.10
	Total	1.00

As shown in Exhibit 3, Modern compared favorably with its key competitors on an overall basis. None of the other suppliers were as strong

---

EXHIBIT 4   Market share by supplier, 1975 and 1977

Supplier	*Percent of market 1975*	*Percent of market 1977*
National Film	11	12
Bertram	16	0*
Bonanza	11	12
Southeastern	5	6
Bay	9	0*
Johnson Graham	8	0*
PBI	2	5
Lewis	2	0*
BAGCO	—	6
Southwest Bag	—	2
Florida Plastics	—	4
East Coast Bag Co.	—	4
Miscellaneous and unknown	8	22
Modern	28	27
	100	100

*Out of business in 1977.
Source: This information was developed from a field survey conducted by Modern Plastics.

as Modern in breadth of line nor did any competitor offer as good sales coverage as that provided by Modern. Clayton knew that sales coverage would be even better next year since the Florida and North Carolina territories had grown enough to add two salespeople to the institutional group by January 1, 1978.

Pricing, quality, and packaging seemed to be neither an advantage nor a disadvantage. However, service was a problem area. The main cause for this, Clayton was told, was temporary out-of-stock situations which occurred occasionally primarily due to the wide variety of trash bags offered by Modern.

During the past two years, Modern Plastics had maintained its market share at approximately 27 percent of the market. Some new competitors had entered the market since 1975 while others had left the market (see Exhibit 4).

The previous district sales manager, Bill Hanson, had left Clayton some comments regarding the major competitors. These are reproduced in Exhibit 5.

EXHIBIT 5   Characteristics of competitors

National Film	Broadest product line in the industry. Quality a definite advantage. Good service. Sales coverage adequate but not an advantage. Not as aggressive as most suppliers on price. Strong competitor.
Bonanza	Well-established tough competitor. Very aggressive on pricing. Good packaging, quality okay.
Southeastern	Extremely price competitive in southern Florida. Dominates Miami market. Limited product line. Not a threat outside of Florida.
PBI	Extremely aggressive on price. Have made inroads into Transco Paper Company during 1977. Good service but poor sales coverage.
BAGCO	New competitor in 1977. Very impressive with a high-quality product, excellent service, and strong sales coverage. A real threat, particularly in Florida.
Southwest Bag	A factor in Louisiana and Mississippi. Their strategy is simple—an acceptable product at a rock-bottom price.
Sun Plastics	Active when market is at a profitable level with price cutting. When market declines to a low profit range, Sun manufactures other types of plastic packaging and stays out of the trash bag market. Poor reputation as a reliable supplier, but can still "spot-sell" at low prices.
East Coast Bag Co.	Most of their business is from a state bid which began in January 1976 for a two-year period. Not much of a threat to Modern's business in the Southeast as most of their volume is north of Washington, D.C.

DEVELOPING THE SALES FORECAST

After a careful study of trade journals, government statistics, and surveys conducted by Modern marketing research personnel, projections for growth potential were formulated by segment and are shown in Exhibit 6. This data was compiled by Bill Hanson before he had been promoted.

EXHIBIT 6   1978 real growth projections by segment

Total industry	+5.0%
Commercial	+5.4
Restaurant	+6.8
Hotel/motel	+2.0
Transportation	+1.9
Office users	+5.0
Other	+4.2
Noncommercial	+4.1
Hospitals	+3.9
Nursing homes	+4.8
Colleges/universities	+2.4
Schools	+7.8
Employee feeding	+4.3
Other	+3.9

Source: Developed from several trade journals.

Jim looked back at Baxter's memo giving the time schedule for the forecast and knew he had to get started. As he left the office at 7:15, he wrote himself a large note and pinned it on his wall—"Get started on the Sales Forecast!"

QUESTIONS

1. What techniques might Mr. Clayton employ to prepare the 1978 forecast for trash bags?

2. What is your forecast for 1978 sales of trash bags? How did you arrive at this forecast, and what assumptions are made about competition, pricing, the economy, etc.?

███████████████

BUYER BEHAVIOR

The chapters in Part One emphasized that building an effective marketing strategy requires information concerning buyers' desires and behavior. Marketing research can provide marketing management with this type of information.

The chapters in Part Two examine consumer and industrial buyer behavior. Buyer behavior is the study of human behavior in the context of the marketplace. Certain fundamental concepts which come from the behavioral principles of psychology, social psychology, and sociology are essential for an understanding of human behavior. The following chapters will present these concepts in the context of our knowledge of buyer behavior.

It will be helpful to discuss the factors that influence the purchase of consumer goods separately from those resulting in the purchase of industrial goods.

Consumer goods are those destined for use by ultimate consumers or households, and these goods are in such form that they can be used without commercial processing. *Industrial goods* are products destined to be sold primarily for use in producing other goods or rendering services, as contrasted with goods destined to be sold primarily to the ulti-

mate consumer.[1] Since executives responsible for purchasing industrial goods are professionals who make their decisions in the context of a complex organization, the factors that influence their buying tend to differ from those that influence the buying of the ultimate consumer. Accordingly, we shall deal with consumer buyer behavior first and then turn to a consideration of the behavior of the industrial buyer.

---

[1]Reprinted by permission from *Marketing Definitions*, compiled by the Committee on Definitions, American Marketing Association, Ralph S. Alexander, Chairman (Chicago: American Marketing Association, 1960), pp. 11, 14.

CONSUMER BUYER BEHAVIOR

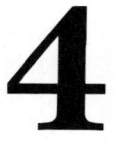

Marketing management must have an accurate and insightful understanding of consumer desires and behavior in order to develop and implement a successful marketing strategy. This chapter will examine the many factors that influence the dynamics of consumer behavior. Our objective is to identify these influences and understand how they affect the consumer's decision-making process.

EXAMPLE OF CONSUMER BEHAVIOR

The study of buyer behavior is the study of the decision process leading to the purchase and consumption of products and services. Consumer and industrial behavior are included in this definition. To understand consumer behavior, let us consider the following situation:

The time is 8:00 on Friday evening. The location is Giant supermarket in Washington, D.C. The following episodes take place:

Episode A.   A couple and their younger son enter the cereal section. The mother goes directly to Kellogg's Corn Flakes and puts a box in the cart. The son asks the father, "Can't I have some cereal?" The father

advises, "Ask your mother." The mother frowns and says, "OK, but none of the sugar-coated stuff." The boy smiles and picks out a box of Cheerios.

Episode B.   A woman pulls a half-full cart by the front along with her down the aisle to the cereal section. She picks up a box of Kellogg's Fruitful Bran and inspects the box thoroughly while turning it around. She puts the box back and picks up a box of Post Raisin Bran for inspection. Replacing the Post cereal, she returns to the box of Kellogg's Fruitful Bran, inspects it again, and puts it in her cart.

The two episodes illustrate several aspects of consumer behavior. While products were purchased in both episodes, the process and influences are different. Many questions are left unanswered in both episodes regarding the nature of the purchase decision process and the underlying influences.

In episode A, the mother automatically purchased Kellogg's Corn Flakes. Why did she do this? Was this a repeat purchase or did she have a promotional coupon for trial purchase? Why did the mother, rather than the father, determine whether the son could purchase cereal? Why did she not allow the purchase of a presweetened cereal? Were the Kellogg's Corn Flakes for the family or just the mother? What influences, if any, did the father have in the purchase of cereals?

In episode B, what was the woman looking for on the two cereal packages? Was price important? Was she looking for information on nutrition, fiber content, or calories? Was she a previous user of Post Raisin Bran who has decided to switch to another bran cereal? If so, what caused this switch? Was it the influence of a friend or promotion?

The questions raised in these two episodes illustrate the types of issues important in the study of consumer behavior. These include topics from the fields of psychology, social psychology, and sociology such as motivation, perception, learning, attitudes, family, and reference groups. Before turning to a discussion of these topics, let us examine the consumer purchase decision process in more detail.

MODEL OF CONSUMER BEHAVIOR

There are two ways marketing managers can understand the nature of consumer behavior. First, they can directly observe and interrogate consumers as part of the implementation of the marketing strategy and program. In earlier times, marketing managers acquired this understanding through their daily contact with customers. Today, growth in the size of markets and organizations prevents most marketing managers from having direct contact with their customers. Marketers have increasingly turned to indirect means to understand their customers. This involves marketing research. Here, the marketing manager relies

on professional researchers to portray consumer behavior using qualitative and quantitative research procedures. The basic questions addressed are: Who buys? How do they buy? When do they buy? Where do they buy? Why do they buy?

Answers to these questions are essential to evaluate the effectiveness of a marketing strategy and supporting programs. The organization that understands how consumers respond to variations in marketing mix (product, distribution, promotion, and price) can often gain a competitive advantage in the marketplace.

Figure 4–1 presents a model of consumer behavior. This model shows the relationship between the marketing strategy/program and the con-

FIGURE 4–1   Model of consumer behavior

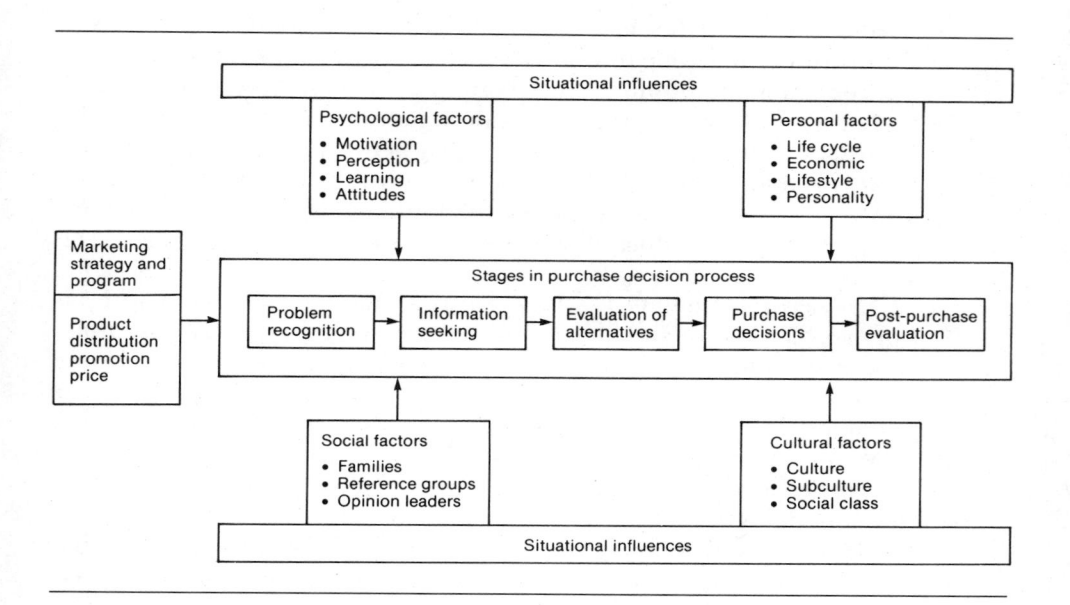

sumer decision-making process. The decision-making process is influenced by a series of psychological, personal, social, and cultural factors. It is essential to understand these influences—which will be discussed in detail later in this chapter—if we are to learn the who, how, when, where, and why of the buying process. Let us turn now to a better understanding of the stages in the consumer purchase decision process.

Stages in Purchase Decision Process

The purchase decision process is a series of stages consumers go through in the process of buying a product. Figure 4–1 shows the consumer passing through five stages: problem recognition, information seeking, evaluation of alternatives, purchase decision, and post-purchase behavior. The model emphasizes that the buying process begins long before the purchase decision and has consequences long after the purchase. Consequently, the marketing manager must understand the complete buying process and not just focus on the purchase decision in isolation.

The five-stage model is most relevant to complex decision making such as that required for the purchase of an expensive product, which demands emotional and intellectual involvement. The purchase of a personal computer, stereo equipment, or ski equipment might involve these five stages. We will use this model in our discussion because it illustrates the complete range of considerations for an important new purchase. Later in the chapter we will consider alternative models where the consumer may skip or even reverse the sequence of stages.

Problem recognition.   The buying process begins with the recognition of a problem. Two situations can trigger this recognition. First, the consumer can be confronted with a gap between what is desired and what is actual. Here the consumer recognizes that something is wrong and needs attention. He or she may be running low on gasoline, or have product failure, product obsolescence, or a new job which triggers the need for new housing.

The second situation is where the consumer is confronted with an opportunity to raise or change consumption expectations. For example, he or she could receive a salary increase, triggering the need for a better automobile, or could read a book on French cooking and then develop an interest in taking French cooking classes or even a vacation in France.

Many situations can trigger problem recognition. The marketing manager needs this information to estimate future market demand and develop marketing strategies to stimulate demand.

Information seeking.   After the consumer recognizes a problem, the next stage is to seek information. The amount of information gathered will vary depending on (1) the importance of the desire, (2) the amount of information already known, (3) the availability of information, and (4) the satisfaction the consumer has in processing information.

For a highly involved purchase such as a personal computer, a great deal of information could be gathered. The search process may be quite limited for the less important purchase of a new paper stapler, or nonexistent in the case of a repeat purchase of toothpaste.

The consumer can use several sources to obtain information, the

logical first source being his or her own memory. Next, the consumer may proceed to the next stage of the purchase decision process or turn to additional sources of information to supplement that available in memory. These major sources of information are:

1. *Personal sources*—family, friends, neighbors, and acquaintances.
2. *Marketing-dominated sources*—advertising, salespersons, dealers, packaging, and displays.
3. *Public sources*—mass media and consumer rating organizations such as *Consumer Reports.*
4. *Experience sources*—handling the product, examining features, and trial use of the product.

These four information sources vary in their relative influence by product type (personal computer versus toothpaste) and by consumer characteristics. Marketing-dominated sources provide the consumer with the most information exposure. However, the most effective exposures come from personal sources. Marketing-dominated sources tend to create awareness and provide information, while personal sources tend to validate information and facilitate the evaluation of products or services.

Evaluation of alternatives. The evaluation process begins with identifying alternative purchase options. From seeking information, the consumer becomes acquainted with some of the market's purchase options and their characteristics. This is called an *evoked set* or a group of brands that a consumer will consider when deciding to purchase.[1] It is unlikely that the evoked set will include all of the purchase options available in the product category; consumers usually limit the number of purchase options to a relatively small number for evaluation.

The marketing implication of the evoked set concept is that an organization must develop a strategy to get its product or service in the customer's evoked set. If the strategy fails, the organization has lost its opportunity to sell to the customer. If the strategy is successful, information is needed on the competitive products or services in the set.

Once the consumer has determined an acceptable set of purchase options, the next issue is how to choose among the alternatives. There are many potential choice models the consumer can use.[2] We will discuss the basic characteristics of a choice model but will not discuss specific models.

A basic concept is that the consumer perceives a choice option as a set

---

[1]John A. Howard and Jagdish N. Sheth, *The Theory of Buyer Behavior* (New York: John Wiley & Sons, 1969).

[2]For a discussion of these models, see Paul E. Green and Yoram Wind, *Multiattribute Decisions in Marketing: A Measurement Approach* (Hinsdale, Ill.: Dryden Press, 1972), chap. 2.

of product or service attributes. The attributes perceived by consumers in various product categories might be:

Automobile: Style, price, economy, dependability, service, accessories, color, safety, prestige.

Mouthwash: Taste/flavor, color, germ-killing capacity, package, price.

Insurance: Protection, price, whole life versus term, company reputation.

Hotel: Cost, location, food, atmosphere, image, cleanliness.

It is important to recognize that consumers will vary in how they perceive the importance of these attributes. The importance of an attribute is related to how it satisfies consumer needs. A married couple with two children might consider a four-door car more important than a two-door car. The opposite could be true for a single person. Consequently, the market for a product or service can often be segmented according to the importance different segments place on attributes.

Once the consumer has identified various attributes and determined the relative importance of each one, each product or service must be characterized as to where it stands on each attribute. The consumer's perception of the product or service in terms of attribute levels is referred to as *brand image*. In Chapter 2, Figure 2–8 presented the brand images of Budweiser, Schlitz, Hamm's, and Miller. Budweiser was positioned higher in "prestige price" than Hamm's, while Miller was positioned as "lighter" than Budweiser.

It is important to recognize that the consumer's brand image or beliefs about a product or service may be at variance with the correct or desired positioning. Information on brand images can be very important in formulating or evaluating the effectiveness of a marketing strategy.

Purchase decision.   Figure 4–2 presents an example of an evaluation procedure leading to the decision to purchase an automobile. The consumer has identified four decision options: automobiles A, B, C, and D (evoked set). The automobiles are positioned on the attributes of mileage, price, safety, and accessories. Each attribute has five levels: high, somewhat high, medium, somewhat low, and low. For example, in Figure 4–2A, the consumer has positioned automobile A as high (H) on mileage, somewhat low (SL) on price, low (L) on safety, and somewhat low (SL) on accessories.

Figure 4–2B presents the evaluation procedure used by the consumer to select an automobile. The consumer has identified a utility function for each attribute. This function describes how the consumer's satisfaction varies by attribute level. The attribute levels range from 1 (low satisfaction) to 5 (high satisfaction). Level 5 is associated with high mileage, low price, high safety, and high accessories.

The consumer finds some of the attributes more important than oth-

FIGURE 4–2   Automobile purchase decision

A. *Product positioning*

Attributes	Automobiles			
	A	B	C	D
Mileage	H	M	L	SL
Price	M	SL	M	SH
Safety	L	SH	SL	SH
Accessories	SL	L	H	L

B. *Evaluation procedures*

Weight*	Attributes	Automobiles			
		A	B	C	D
10	Mileage	5(50)	3(30)	1(10)	2(20)
8	Price	3(24)	4(32)	3(24)	2(16)
4	Safety	1(4)	4(16)	2(8)	4(16)
5	Accessories	2(10)	1(5)	5(25)	1(5)
		(88)	(83)	(67)	(57)

Key: H = High; SH = Somewhat high; M = Medium; SL = Somewhat low; L = Low.
*10 is most important.

ers. The attribute importance weights are 10 for mileage, 8 for price, 4 for safety, and 5 for accessories (see Figure 4–2B).

The evaluation procedure involves multiplying each attribute weight by the utility of the attribute level and adding the combined score for each automobile. The automobile with the highest summated score is the most preferred and the one chosen. For example, in Figure 4–2, automobile A is chosen.

Post-purchase evaluation.   Post-purchase evaluation refers to the consumer's level of satisfaction or dissatisfaction with the product or service after the purchase and the resulting actions of consumers. These actions can be important to marketers and can directly influence the success of the marketing strategy.

If the consumer is satisfied that product performance is consistent with expectations, this favorable experience will be remembered and will directly influence the search for information for subsequent purchases in that product category. In addition, the consumer will tend to say favorable things about the product or service to other consumers who are also searching for information. There is a marketing saying that, "The best advertising is a satisfied customer."

If the consumer is dissatisfied, a different set of actions can result. High dissatisfaction could result in the consumer's returning the prod-

uct or even abandoning it. A dissatisfied customer may eliminate the product from the evoked set in subsequent purchase decisions and may expand the number of purchase options considered by looking more extensively for information. In addition, a dissatisfied consumer would probably say unfavorable things about the product or service to other consumers who are searching for information.

Types of Decision Processes

The nature of the consumer decision-making process varies with the type of buying situation. The behavior of a consumer purchasing a personal computer can be significantly different from one purchasing a soap powder. The more expensive, complex, and new the product category, the more involved the consumer will be with the purchase process. Two types of buying processes have been identified: low and high involvement.[3]

High-involvement buying involves a decision process characterized by the sequence of awareness, knowledge, liking, preference, conviction, and purchase. An example would be the purchase of a personal computer. Consumer involvement would be high due to high expense, product differentiation, low information in memory, and infrequency of purchase.

Low-involvement buying involves a decision process characterized by the sequence of awareness, knowledge, purchase, liking, preference, and conviction. An example would be the purchase of a soap powder. Consumer involvement would be low due to low expense, product similarity, high information in memory, and high frequency of purchase.

Marketing strategies for low-involvement products or services may be different from those for high-involvement products or services. Low-involvement products may find effective use of promotion and price as an incentive to switch buyers to a new brand. High-involvement products require a strategy consistent with high information-seeking and evaluation behaviors. The strategy must assist the consumer in learning about product attributes and the relative importance of attributes in the purchase decision. The product positioning of the product or service and the key points of differentiation over competition must be communicated to the consumer.

INFLUENCES ON CONSUMER BEHAVIOR

The consumer's purchase decision process is influenced by many factors, primarily psychological, personal, social, and cultural. We will explore in detail each of these influences.

---

[3]Adapted from Walter B. Wentz, *Marketing* (West, 1979), p. 240.

Psychological Factors

Motivation. The starting point in the purchase decision-making process is the recognition of a need (or a buying motive). *Motives* are "all those inner striving conditions variously described as wishes, desires, needs, drives, and the like. Formally, then, a motive is an inner state that energizes, activates, or moves (hence 'motivation'), and that directs or channels behavior toward goals. Hunger, the quest for power or status, the desire to land on the moon or to own a new car—all these are motives according to this definition." A *goal,* in turn, may be thought of as "the object, condition, or activity toward which the motive is directed; in short, that which will satisfy or reduce the striving.[4]

Motivational theory received its greatest impetus from Freud. Nearly all theorists who have worked with clinical data have accepted part of the Freudian scheme but have rejected other portions.[5] One of the more recent theories is that developed by Maslow, who has integrated most of the leading approaches to motivation into an overall scheme designed to conform to the known facts—clinical and observational, as well as experimental. He refers to his synthesis as a "holistic-dynamic theory." It is especially interesting to marketing people, since it is based primarily upon a study of normal people rather than upon the abnormal subjects who have been the concern of most other theorists.

Maslow classifies motivational life in terms of fundamental needs or goals, rather than in terms of any listing of drives in the ordinary sense of instigation (the "pulls" rather than the "pushes"). He lists the following five levels of needs, arranged in order of their basic importance to the individual:[6]

1. The physiological needs—for example, to satisfy hunger and thirst.
2. The safety needs—for example, security, order, and stability.
3. The belongingness and love needs—such as affection and identification.
4. The esteem needs—such as prestige, success, and self-respect.
5. The need for self-actualization—for example, to do what one is best fitted for.

Also identified are two classes of cognitive needs, which are not definitely located in the need hierarchy but which are believed to exist,

---

[4]Reprinted by permission from Bernard Berelson and Gary A. Steiner, *Human Behavior* (New York: Harcourt, Brace & World, Inc., 1964), pp. 239–40.

[5]See D. C. McClelland, *Personality* (Hinsdale, Ill: Dryden Press, 1951), pp. 388–410, for a brief summary of Freud's motivational system, an evaluation of his conceptual scheme, as well as contributions of other scholars to motivational theory.

[6]Adaptation of "The Basic Needs," pp. 80–101 in *Motivation and Personality* by A. H. Maslow. Copyright 1954 by Harper & Row, Publishers, Inc. Reprinted by permission of the publishers.

perhaps as a function of intelligence and of gratification, fairly high up the scale of lower-order needs:

6. The desire to know and understand (an essential precondition to the satisfaction of basic needs).
7. The aesthetic needs—for example, the craving for beauty.

Maslow believes that the five basic needs develop in such a way that the most important—that is, physical needs—must be satisfied before the safety needs, which are next in importance, can fully emerge in a person's development; and so on up the ladder from the lower needs (most important) to the higher needs (least important) in the hierarchy.

For example, he explains that the physiological needs are the most prepotent of all needs:

> What this means specifically is that in the human being who is missing everything in life in an extreme fashion, it is most likely that the major motivation would be the physiological needs rather than any others. A person who is lacking food, safety, love, and esteem would most probably hunger for food more strongly than for anything else.
>
> It is quite true that man lives by bread alone—when there is no bread. But what happens to man's desires when there is plenty of bread and when his belly is chronically filled? *At once other and (higher) needs emerge* and these, rather than physiological hungers, dominate the organism. And when these in turn are satisfied, again new (and still higher) needs emerge, and so on. This is what we mean by saying that the basic human needs are organized into a hierarchy of relative prepotency.[7]

Maslow explains that the need hierarchy is not as rigid as may be implied by the above explanation. While most people feel the needs in about the order indicated, there may be exceptions in individual cases. Also, it would be a mistake to conclude that each need must be satisfied 100 percent before the next need emerges. Instead, all the basic needs of most normal members of our society are partially satisfied and partially unsatisfied at the same time. A more realistic description of the hierarchy would be in terms of decreasing percentages of satisfaction as we go up the hierarchy of prepotency. To illustrate it is as if the average citizen were satisfied perhaps 85 percent in physiological needs, 70 percent in safety needs, 50 percent in love needs, 40 percent in self-esteem needs, and 10 percent in self-actualization needs.

Maslow's hierarchy of needs is useful in identifying the motives underlying consumer behavior. The hierarchy concept suggests that lower-order needs must be satisfied before higher-order needs can emerge. For the vast majority of U.S. consumers, lower-order physiological needs have been satisfied by our high standard of living. Higher-order needs are thus the driving force in consumer behavior.

---

[7]Ibid., pp. 82, 83.

Perception. The actions taken by a motivated consumer will be influenced by his or her perception of the situation. If two consumers perceive the same product differently, they are likely to behave differently with respect to the product.

Consumers have different perceptions of the same situation for several reasons. Perception begins with the apprehension of a stimulus object (product or advertisement) through our five senses: sight, hearing, touch, smell, and taste. Differences in perception result from the alternative way consumers attend, organize, and interpret the object. Perception can be defined as "the process by which an individual selects, organizes, and interprets information inputs to create a meaningful picture of the world."[8] Consumers can emerge with different perceptions of the same product or service because of three perceptual mechanisms: selective exposure, selective distortion, and selective retention.

Selective exposure is a process by which consumers screen out most of the stimuli to which they are exposed. For example, consumers can be exposed to several hundred advertisements (television, magazines, newspapers, billboards, and radio) a day, yet perceive only a small number of them. Most of the advertisements are screened out.

There are important marketing implications of selective exposure. The marketing program must attract the consumer's attention. Here the promotional message must relate to a real consumer need, and the promotional format must be designed to stand out from the competing advertisements.

Selective distortion describes a process where consumers change or fit information into their personal meaning. Information which challenges consumers' existing attitudes may be distorted so that it is supportive of preconceptions.

Selective retention suggests that consumers remember information that is consistent with preconceptions and forget information which is inconsistent. Consumers are likely to remember the positive information about products they have a preference toward and forget negative information.

Perception is a concept useful in understanding the risk associated with a purchase. "Consumer behavior involves risk in the sense that any action of the consumer will produce consequences which he or she cannot anticipate with anything approximating certainty, and some of which at least are likely to be unpleasant."[9]

There are two types of perceived risk. *Functional risk* is concerned with whether the product will perform as expected. *Psychosocial risk* is

---

[8]Bernard Berelson and Gary A. Steiner, *Human Behavior: An Inventory of Scientific Findings* (New York: Harcourt Brace Jovanovich, 1964), p. 88.

[9]Raymond A. Bauer, "Consumer Behavior as Risk Taking," in *Dynamic Marketing for a Changing World,* ed. R. S. Hancock (Chicago: American Marketing Association, 1960), pp. 389–98.

concerned with whether the product will be supportive of the consumer's self-image and whether it will be accepted positively by others whose opinion the consumer values.

Consumers strive to reduce perceived risk by reducing the negative consequences of the purchase or by reducing the probability that negative consequences will occur. If the purchase process involves high perceived functional risk, the consumer will seek information on performance attributes from impersonal sources (magazines, advertisements). If the purchase process involves high perceived psychosocial risks, the consumer will seek information from personal sources (friends, salespeople).

Learning. After a need has been recognized, alternative products and brands have been evaluated, and a purchase has been made, the consumer arrives at one of the most significant aspects of the entire sequence. With the use of the brand, some degree of satisfaction of the initial need will be experienced. If the consumption of the brand leads to gratification of the initiating needs, then "reinforcement" will occur. If the same need is aroused at some later date, the consumer will tend to repeat the purchase of the same product and brand. We have described here the process of *learning*, which is defined as any change in behavior which results from experience or practice in similar situations.

Almost every aspect of the consumer purchase decision process is affected by learning. Experience in purchasing a product will enable the consumer to rely on memory for the information search rather than on an external source of information. The evaluation process can be simplified and the consumer may exhibit habitual or routine purchase behavior when buying the product category.

Learning can be conceptualized as a stimulus–response model. The major components are drive, cue, response, and reinforcement. *Drive* is defined as a state of tension caused by an unfulfilled need (problem recognition stage). Drive will stimulate action to reduce tension. A *cue* is a stimulus that triggers the response to a drive. Examples would include a soft drink advertisement, promotional coupon, or store display. *Response* is the consumer's action resulting from a cue. The purchase of a product or service is a response in this model. *Reinforcement* is the reduction in a drive resulting from a satisfying response. The probability that the same response will occur again is increased with reinforcement. Repeated reinforcement leads to *habit formation*. If the response is not reinforced, *extinction* occurs and the learned habit decreases.

Routine or habitual purchasing behavior is typical of low-involvement products which are reinforcing. Here there is a linkage between the learning model and the concept of brand loyalty. *Brand loyalty* exists when there is a favorable attitude toward and consistent purchase of a single brand over time.[10]

---

[10]Henry Assael, *Consumer Behavior and Marketing Actions* (Boston: Kent Publishing, 1981), p. 65.

It is clear from the above discussion that learning theory helps us understand consumer buying behavior. Indeed, theories of stimulus–response learning are important elements in the Howard model of consumer behavior, which is discussed later in this chapter.

Attitudes. *Attitudes* are learned tendencies to perceive and act consistently toward a given object or idea, such as a product, service, brand, company, store, or spokesperson.[11] This is a broad concept and impacts on our previous discussion of factors that influence the consumer purchase decision process. This definition implies that attitudes are learned, in that they are derived from experiences and information. Attitudes are perceptions, and they influence the formation of brand images and product positioning.

Attitudes have three components—a *cognitive* component (perceptions and beliefs), an *affective* component (liking or feeling and evaluation), and a *behavioral* component (intentions, preference, or purchase).[12] These three components have been seen as a sequence of steps—from not knowing about a product or service to its final selection. The steps in this *hierarchy of effects* are: awareness, knowledge, preference, conviction, and purchase.

How are attitudes formed? To a very considerable extent they are learned in the process of interaction with other people. Factors that tend to develop and change attitudes may include the following: (1) In the satisfaction of basic desires, the individual will develop favorable attitudes toward people and objects that satisfy his or her needs and unfavorable attitudes toward those that block the attainment of those needs. (2) Attitudes are based in part upon the kind and amount of information that the individual receives and upon the nature of the sources of this information. (3) Many attitudes held by individuals come either directly or indirectly from the groups of which they are members—for example, family, work, and social. (4) Personality factors (such as intelligence, appearance, activity levels, withdrawal tendencies, and dominance) have some effect upon attitudes. (5) Actual experience with the object—favorable or unfavorable—will have a profound effect upon attitudes toward it.[13]

Evidence on the relationship between consumer attitudes and their buying decisions comes from the work of the Survey Research Center of the University of Michigan. The center has been making surveys of consumer finances since 1946. The information is secured through annual personal interviews with the head of each spending unit in a na-

---

[11]Martin Fishbein and Icek Ajzen, *Belief Attitude, Intention, and Behavior: An Introduction to Theory and Research* (Reading, Mass.: Addison-Wesley Publishing, 1975), p. 6.

[12]Milton J. Rosenberg et al., *Attitude Organization and Change* (New Haven: Yale University Press, 1960).

[13]Adapted from D. Krech, R. S. Crutchfield, and E. L. Ballachey, *Individual and Society* (Copyright 1962 by McGraw-Hill Book Co.), chap. 6. Used with permission of McGraw-Hill Book Company.

tional sample of dwelling units selected by area probability sampling to represent the population of the United States. Through these surveys, data are gathered on consumer attitudes; income; ownership, purchases, and purchase plans of automobiles, durable goods, and houses; assets; debts; and personal characteristics. Our special interest is the center's studies dealing with the measurement of consumer attitudes and their relationship to spending.

Two measures of attitudes toward spending are used by the center. The primary measure is an index of consumer attitudes based upon answers to six attitudinal questions: (1) whether the family is better or worse off than a year earlier; (2) its personal financial expectations for the coming year; (3) its one-year expectations regarding business conditions; (4) its longer-range economic outlook; (5) its appraisal of buying conditions for household goods and clothing; and (6) price expectations. The six components of the index have equal weight.

A second measure of attitudes toward spending is an index of buying intentions. Data have been collected on expressed intentions to buy houses, cars, and durable household goods; to make home improvements or repairs; and to make major nondurable goods expenditures. Only plans that respondents rated as having at least a fair chance of fulfillment were considered.

To what extent do consumer attitudes influence spending? According to Katona:

> Changes in consumer attitudes are advance indications of changes in consumer spending on durable goods and make a net contribution to the prediction of such spending after the influence of income has been taken into account.[14]

The work of the Survey Research Center deals with the relation of consumer attitudes to primary demand—that is, to the purchase of *alternative* types of products such as automobiles, durable goods, and houses. Let us now consider the relationship between attitudes and the purchases of individual brands.

Significant evidence is reported by Alvin A. Achenbaum in discussing an attitude measurement system developed by the marketing research department of Grey Advertising, Inc., in which 24 studies were conducted over a period of eight years. This system was designed to measure attitude as a predispositional response—one that is indicative of future behavior. According to Achenbaum:[15]

---

[14]From George Katona, *The Powerful Consumer* (Copyright by McGraw-Hill Book Co.), pp 52–53. Used with permission of McGraw-Hill Book Company.

[15]Reprinted by permission from Alvin A. Achenbaum, "Knowledge Is a Thing Called Measurement," in *Attitude Research at Sea,* Lee Adler and Irving Crespi, eds., published by American Marketing Association, 1966, pp. 112–14.

We start with the point of view that attitudes reflect needs or motivation and are predictive of behavior. There is a growing abundance of marketing data which suggest that this is a tenable point of view.

In our own work, we have found in every study we have done—and there has not been a single exception—that there is a very direct relationship between attitudes and usage behavior. The more favorable the attitude, the higher the incidence of usage; the less favorable the attitude, the lower the incidence of usage [see Figure 4–3, Current users column].

In an effort to inject dynamism into the analysis, we also looked at the relationship in regard to former triers and never triers of the product. As we would expect, the more unfavorable people are toward a product, the more likely they are to stop using it. The interesting thing is that if you look at people who have never tried the product, their attitudes tend to fall in a normally shaped curve [see Figure 4–3, Never users column].

FIGURE 4–3   Relationship between attitudes and usage for a dental product

Attitudes toward dental product	Current users	Former users	Never users	Line total
Excellent	78	8	14	100
Very good	56	15	29	100
Good	29	26	45	100
Fair	14	35	51	100
Not so good	8	53	39	100
Poor	8	76	16	100

Source: Reprinted by permission from Alvin A. Achenbaum, "Knowledge Is a Thing Called Measurement," in *Attitude Research at Sea*, Lee Adler and Irving Crespi, eds., published by American Marketing Association, 1966, pp. 113–14.

While the above evidence shows that there is a direct relationship between attitudes and usage behavior, Figure 4–3 indicates that a portion of the respondents with favorable attitudes toward the dental product (brand) were "never users": excellent, 14 percent; very good, 29 percent; good, 45 percent. Why haven't these people purchased the brand? There are a number of possibilities: (1) Considerable time may elapse between the formation of a favorable attitude toward a brand and the date when an actual purchase decision is made. Thus, advertising and word-of-mouth comment may lead a consumer to form a favorable attitude toward the Toyota compact automobile in September, but the consumer may then own a year-old Volkswagen and not wish to trade it

in until it is three years old. (2) Lack of money may lead the consumer to purchase a less expensive brand, which is the second choice, rather than the more expensive brand, which is really preferred. (For example, consumers may buy a Panasonic color television set at a lower price than they would have to pay for the RCA model that they really prefer.) (3) The preferred brand (e.g., Maxim freeze-dried coffee) may be out of stock when the housewife goes to make a purchase, and she may therefore accept a substitute that does not rate as high on her preference scale, rather than seek the desired brand in another store. (4) Attitudes may be more favorable to a competing brand than to the one "never-tried." For example, a portion of the 45 percent who rated the brand "good" may rate a competing brand "excellent," and some of these may buy the competing brand when a purchase decision is finally made. (5) Other inhibiting forces such as social influences and time pressure may also prevent the purchase of the preferred brand. In recognition of the fact that a number of forces other than consumer attitudes influence the purchase decision, Howard has suggested the measurement of intention (to buy) as an intervening construct in explaining buyer behavior.[16]

The previous discussion has indicated that consumer attitudes have an important influence on the purchase decision. If this is the case, the question then arises as to how the firm can lead prospective buyers to adopt more favorable attitudes toward the type of product it manufactures (for example, air conditioners) as well as to its own brand, as opposed to competing brands (for example, Frigidaire versus General Electric).[17]

There are two basic approaches to this problem. One is to undertake research to determine current desires and attitudes of prospective buyers with regard to the product and the brand. Once this information is known, the firm may redesign its product so that it more adequately conforms to these buyers' desires and preferences. The firm may also modify its promotional approach in the light of this information.

A second method is to attempt to change the consumer's desires and attitudes with regard to the product and the brand. This is a more difficult task than the first, but it is necessary where the product represents an innovation, as was true with television when it was first introduced commercially after World War II. Such would also be the case where a product used primarily by women, such as hair coloring, is first marketed for use by men.

A marketer wishing to change attitudes toward his or her brand should choose an approach only after consideration of the factors that

---

[16]The relationship between the constructs of attitude, intention, and purchase is discussed later in this chapter. See also Howard and Sheth, *Theory of Buyer Behavior*, pp. 132–33.

[17]Based upon Myers and Reynolds, *Consumer Behavior*, pp. 165–66.

influence the formation of attitudes: biological needs, information, group affiliations, personality, and experience. Analysis indicates that certain of these attitude-forming factors cannot be changed by the marketer. Certainly this is true of basic needs, personality characteristics, and group affiliations. Under certain circumstances, the experience of consumers with the brand may be changed. For example, people who have never used it may be given free samples for trial—provided that the item is a consumable product of low unit price subject to repeat purchase (for example, toothpaste). If the product is superior, and its want-satisfying qualities may be evaluated through usage, experience with a free sample may indeed modify consumer attitudes toward the brand. Distribution of free samples, however, is not suitable for all types of products.

Of the various attitude-forming factors, therefore, the possibility of changing the information that the consumer has about the brand is often the most effective approach. The effective use of communication through personal selling, promotion, and publicity is therefore worthy of careful study.[18] While space does not permit a discussion of this topic here, we shall deal with the subject of building an effective promotional mix by which to influence consumer desires and attitudes in Chapter 10. Crane summarizes a discussion of this topic, however, as follows:[19]

> Attitudes are not easy to change. First, because there seems to be a tendency to restore balance when it is upset and, second, because there is a tendency to avoid an upset by avoiding exposures to messages inconsistent with the existing attitude structure. Accidental exposure does occur, however. A communicator who knows existing attitude structures and the ways in which people react to their upset, can choose the method and point of attack most likely to produce, in the end, the new attitude structure most favorable to his objectives.

Personal Factors

Consumer decisions are also influenced by personal factors, notably stage of life cycle, economic circumstances, lifestyle, and personality.

Life cycle.   Individuals purchase different goods and services over their lifetimes. Babies, teenagers, adults, and the elderly differ in their consumption of food, clothing, furniture, and recreation.

The nine stages of the *family life cycle* are presented in Figure 4–4, along with the financial circumstances and product interests of each

---

[18]For an interesting discussion of five broad strategy alternatives that advertisers may use to change attitudinal structures, see Harper W. Boyd, Jr., Michael L. Ray, and Edward C. Strong, "An Attitudinal Framework for Advertising Strategy," *Journal of Marketing*, April 1972, pp. 27–33.

[19]Reprinted by permission from E. Crane, *Marketing Communications* (New York: John Wiley & Sons, Inc., 1965), p. 66. See this source for a discussion of ways to change attitudes through communication.

FIGURE 4–4   An overview of the family life cycle and buying behavior

Stage in family life cycle	Buying or behavioral pattern
1. Bachelor stage: Young, single people not living at home.	Few financial burdens. Fashion opinion leaders. Recreation oriented. Buy: basic kitchen equipment, basic furniture, cars, equipment for the mating game, vacations.
2. Newly married couples: Young, no children.	Better off financially than they will be in near future. Highest purchase rate and highest average purchase of durables. Buy: cars, refrigerators, stoves, sensible and durable furniture, vacations.
3. Full nest I: Youngest child under six.	Home purchasing at peak. Liquid assets low. Dissatisfied with financial position and amount of money saved. Interested in new products. Like advertised products. Buy: washers, dryers, TV, baby food, chest rubs and cough medicines, vitamins, dolls, wagons, sleds, skates.
4. Full nest II: Youngest child six or over.	Financial position better. Some wives work. Less influenced by advertising. Buy larger-sized packages, multiple-unit deals. Buy: many foods, cleaning materials, bicycles, music lessons, pianos.
5. Full nest III: Older married couples with dependent children.	Financial position still better. More wives work. Some children get jobs. Hard to influence with advertising. High average purchase of durables. Buy: new, more tasteful furniture, auto travel, unnecessary appliances, boats, dental services, magazines.
6. Empty Nest I: Older married couples, no children living with them, head in labor force.	Home ownership at peak. Most satisfied with financial position and money saved. Interested in travel, recreation, self-education. Make gifts and contributions. Not interested in new products. Buy: vacations, luxuries, home improvements.
7. Empty nest II: Older married. No children living at home, head retired.	Drastic cut in income. Keep home. Buy: medical appliances, medical-care products that aid health, sleep, and digestion.
8. Solitary survivor, in labor force.	Income still good but likely to sell home.
9. Solitary survivor, retired.	Same medical and product needs as other retired group; drastic cut in income. Special need for attention, affection, and security.

Source: William D. Wells amd George Gubar, "Life Cycle Concepts in Marketing Research," *Journal of Marketing Research,* November 1966, pp. 355-63, here p. 362. Also see Patrick E. Murphy and William A. Staples, "A Modernized Family Life Cycle," *Journal of Consumer Research,* June 1979, pp. 12–22.

stage. Marketing strategies are often targeted to a specific life-cycle group.

Economic circumstances.   Consumers' economic resources directly affect their consumption of goods and services. This includes their spendable income, savings and assets, borrowing power, and attitude toward spending versus saving. Marketers of goods and services which are sensitive to changes in the consumer's economic circumstances must monitor trends in income, savings, and interest rates and adapt their marketing programs accordingly. Examples of products which are income-sensitive include automobiles, housing, and vacation travel.

Lifestyle.   Lifestyles can be defined as the patterns in which people live and spend time and money.[20] A person's lifestyle is measured by activities, interests, opinions, and demographics. These dimensions are used to portray the person's pattern of living and interaction with the environment.

When developing a marketing strategy for a good or service, marketers seek a relationship between a product or brand and lifestyle profiles. Here is an example of a person's lifestyle profile:

> He lives in one of those modern, high-rise apartments and rooms are brightly colored. He has modern, expensive furniture, but not Danish modern. He buys his clothes at Brooks Brothers. He owns a good hi-fi. He skis. He has a sailboat. He eats Limburger and any other prestige cheese with his beer. He likes and cooks a lot of steak and would have a filet mignon for company. His liquor cabinet has Jack Daniels bourbon, Beefeater gin, and a good Scotch.[21]

Boyd and Levy describe the implications of the lifestyle concept:

> Marketing is a process of providing customers with parts of a potential mosaic from which they, as artists of their own lifestyles, can pick and choose to develop the composition that for the time seems the best. The marketer who thinks about his products in this way will seek to understand their potential settings and relationships to other parts of consumer lifestyles, and thereby to increase the number of ways they fit meaningfully into the pattern.[22]

Personality.   The field of psychology has not been able to agree on a definition for personality. The concept characterizes the consumer's own dimensions—extrovert–introvert, aggressive–submissive, impulsive–orderly, or compliant–dominant.

For the last 20 years, marketers have conducted studies to determine

---

[20]James Engel and Roger Blackwell, *Consumer Behavior,* 4th ed. (Hinsdale, Ill.: Dryden Press, 1982), p. 188.

[21]Sidney J. Levy, "Symbolism and Lifestyle," in *Toward Scientific Marketing,* ed. Stephen A. Greyser (Chicago: American Marketing Association, 1964), pp. 140–50.

[22]Harper W. Boyd, Jr. and Sidney J. Levy, *Promotion: A Behavioral View* (Englewood Cliffs, N.J.: Prentice-Hall, 1967), p. 38.

the relationship between personality dimensions and consumer behavior. These studies have focused on purchase behavior, segmentation criteria, media exposure, and many others. An article which reviewed these studies concludes, "A few studies indicate a strong relationship between personality and aspects of consumer behavior, a few indicate no relationship, and a great majority indicate that if correlations do exist they are so weak as to be questionable or perhaps meaningless.[23] Consequently, we must conclude that the influence of personality on the consumer purchase decision process is minimal.

Social Factors

In our discussion of buying behavior up to this point, we have focused attention upon the individual consumer. Drawing upon psychology and social psychology, we have traced the influence of motives, attitudes, and learning upon buying decisions. But the individual consumer lives in an environment that exerts important cultural and social influences upon his or her behavior. Indeed, both motives and attitudes of the consumer are patterned by the culture and the social institutions in which he or she lives. Accordingly, to assist in explaining certain uniformities in motives and attitudes of consumers which influence their buying behavior, we shall now draw on the fields of anthropology and sociology for a number of helpful concepts relating to cultural and social influences. We shall consider first the social factors of families, reference groups, and opinion leaders.

Families.   Early in this chapter a family shopping together in a supermarket for cereal was described. The interaction among the mother, father, and child demonstrate how purchase decisions are influenced by family members. Accordingly, let us examine the framework in which buying decisions are made within the family and some of the factors that influence brand choice in this setting. According to Coulson, there are three sources of influence on brand and product choices: the purchaser, the user, and the authority.[24]

In this context, it is clear that the purchasing agent (generally the housewife) has the strategic role in the brand decision, since she acts as the "gatekeeper" controlling the channel through which products flow from the stores to consumption within the family. Coulson developed

---

[23]Harold J. Rasserjean, "Personality and Consumer Behavior: A Review," *Journal of Marketing Research*, November 1971, pp. 409–19.

[24]Adapted by permission from John S. Coulson, "Buying Decisions within the Family and the Consumer–Brand Relationship," from Joseph W. Newman, ed., *On Knowing the Consumer* (New York: John Wiley & Sons, Inc., 1966), pp. 59–66. For an interesting study of the prevalence of conflict in household decision making and the tactics employed by spouses to resolve their conflict, see Jagdish N. Sheth and Stephen Cosmas, "Tactics of Conflict Resolution in Family Buying Behavior," *Faculty Working Paper* no. 271, College of Commerce and Business Administration, University of Illinois at Urbana-Champaign, September 16, 1975.

some tentative propositions about how the household "purchasing agent" accommodates the user and the authority in making her brand decisions. These propositions were based on the results of previous research and also upon a pilot study among 100 housewives in Chicago. The study covered 10 top product classes that have a high percentage of their sales in food stores. These were: beer, cake mixes, candy bars, canned peas, canned spaghetti, chewing gum, cigarettes, cold cereals, deodorants, and margarine. A selection of Coulson's propositions follows:

1. Other members of the family exert considerable influence on the housewife in making brand decisions.
2. In the role of purchasing agent, the housewife knows the family's brand preferences better for some product classes than for others.
3. In the role of purchasing agent, the housewife takes more account of the family's brand preferences for some product classes than for others.
    a. On products with the brand name clearly visible in use, she is more receptive to her husband's brand preferences than to those of her children. (If she thinks a brand is not good for a child, she may veto the child's request.)
    b. The housewife is most receptive to the brand preferences of her family for products in which the brand is clearly visible, and least receptive for products in which there is a substantial change in the product before use. (If the family cannot identify the brand during consumption, the housewife is free to select the brand she desires.)

This study calls our attention to the different roles played in the buying process, distinguishing among users, influencers, and buyers.

Another study of husband/wife influence in buying decisions found that relative influence depends upon the item being purchased. Figure 4–5 presents the results of this study of married couples in four U.S. cities.

Reference groups.   "Reference groups" are those groups that individuals use as a point of reference in determining their own judgments, beliefs and behavior.[25] Note that the individual may not be a member of a group that serves as a frame of reference for his or her judgments, beliefs, and behavior. It may be a group to which he or she aspires; by adopting its dress, habits, and attitudes, he or she may hope to be invited to membership.

Our interest is in the influence which reference groups may have

---

[25]Reprinted from Tamotsu Shibutani, "Reference Groups as Perspectives," *American Journal of Sociology,* May 1965, pp. 562, 563, and 565, by permission of The University of Chicago Press. Copyright 1955 by The University of Chicago.

FIGURE 4–5   Involvement of husbands and wives in selected household decisions

Decision/activity	Husband would be more involved (percent)	Equally involved (percent)	Wife would be more involved (percent)
1. Determining what make of stereo to buy.	65	33	2
2. Shopping at different automobile dealers.	61	34	5
3. Determining what make of car to buy.	57	41	2
4. Determining whether to get a 4-channel or 2-channel stereo.	50	46	4
5. Suggesting a new car be bought.	46	44	10
6. Selecting the brand of TV to buy.	39	59	2
7. Deciding how much to spend for a new car.	39	57	4
8. Deciding how much to spend for a new stereo.	39	56	5
9. Suggesting a new stereo be bought.	39	49	12
10. Shopping for a stereo.	38	56	6
11. Deciding how much to spend for a new TV.	28	66	6
12. Determining whether or not to get air conditioning in a new car.	28	62	10
13. Suggesting a new TV be bought.	25	60	15
14. Deciding amount to spend on a new refrigerator.	23	64	13
15. Shopping for a new TV.	19	74	7
16. Deciding whether to get a black-and-white or color TV.	18	75	7
17. Deciding what make of refrigerator to get.	18	49	33
18. Choosing the color of a new car.	15	53	32
19. Deciding whether or not to get an automatic ice cube maker in the refrigerator.	12	49	39
20. Shopping for a new refrigerator.	7	55	38
21. Suggesting a new refrigerator be bought.	7	37	56
22. Choosing the color for a new refrigerator.	2	28	70

Source: H. Davis, "Research Explores Further Aspects of Family Purchasing Power," *Marketing Today* 16, no. 1 (1978), p. 2.

upon buying behavior. (1) Reference group influence is particularly potent in an informational vacuum. Where the individual has little or no knowledge about the attributes of a product, reference group influence is at its strongest. (2) The conspicuousness of the product is perhaps the most general attribute bearing on its susceptibility to reference group influence.[26]

---

[26]Adapted by permission from Francis S. Bourne, "Group Influence in Marketing," in Rensis Likert and Samuel P. Hayes, Jr., eds., *Some Applications of Behavior Research* (UNESCO, 1957), chap. 6.

The susceptibility of various products and brands to reference group influence is summarized in Figure 4–6. Note the following examples.

1.   Reference group influence may operate with respect to both product and brand (product +, brand +), as in the upper right cell of Figure 4–6. With respect to cars, both the product and the brand are socially conspicuous. Whether or not a person buys a car, and also what brand he or she buys, is likely to be influenced by what others do.

FIGURE 4–6   Reference group influence (relatively weak [−]; relatively strong [+])

	Weak − [−]	*Product*	Strong + [+]	
Brand or type [+] [−]	Clothing Furniture Magazines Refrigerators (type) Toilet soap		Cars* Cigarettes* Beer (premium versus regular)* Drugs*	*Brand or type* [+] [−]
	Canned peaches Laundry soap Refrigerators (brand) Radios		Air conditioners* Instant coffee* TV (black and white)	
	[−]	*Product*	[+]	

*Products and brands of consumer goods may be classified by the extent to which reference groups influence their purchase. The classification of all products marked with an asterisk (*) is based on actual experimental evidence. Other products in this table are classified speculatively on the basis of generalizations derived from the sum of research in this area and confirmed by the judgment of seminar participants.

Source: Bureau of Applied Social Research, Columbia University. Reprinted by permission.

---

2.   Reference group influence may operate with respect to product but not brand (product +, brand −), as in the case of instant coffee. Whether it is served in a household depends upon whether the housewife, in view of her own reference groups and the image she has of their attitudes toward this product, considers it appropriate to serve it. The brand itself is not conspicuous or socially important and is largely a matter for individual choice.

3.   Where a type of product is owned by virtually all people, reference groups may influence the selection of the brand, but not the product (product −, brand +). In this cell are classified clothing, furniture, magazines, refrigerators (type), and toilet soap.

4.   Purchasing behavior for "product −, brand −" items is governed by product attributes rather than by the nature of the presumed users. Examples are laundry soap, canned peaches, refrigerators (brand), and radios. In this group, neither the product nor the brand tends to be

socially conspicuous. Reference groups, accordingly, exert very little influence over purchasing behavior.

Opinion leaders.   Opinion leaders are able to influence consumers in the purchase of products or services due to their expert knowledge and experience. As consumers, we all have been influenced by individuals who we believe have such special knowledge. The golf or tennis pro may influence our selection of sporting equipment. We may seek the advice of our dentist as to the most effective toothpaste.

Marketers use a *two-step flow of communication* to reach opinion leaders. This is a process of using the mass media to communicate information to opinion leaders who then influence consumers.[27] Opinion leaders are often consumers who first purchase new products and then discuss their reactions and recommendations to followers.

Opinion leaders are difficult to identify. There are few psychological and demographic characteristics that distinguish opinion leaders from followers.[28] The product-related characteristics that differentiate opinion leaders from followers are: (1) more knowledge about the product category, (2) more interest in the product category, (3) more active in receiving communications about the product from personal sources, and (4) more likely to read magazines and print media in their area of product interest.[29] Opinion leadership is specific to a product category. An individual who is an opinion leader in the purchase of golf balls may have no leadership in the purchase of tennis rackets.

Cultural Factors

Culture is a set of customs, values, attitudes, and habits that are learned from one generation to another within a given society. These cultural patterns are transmitted to individuals through such social institutions as the family, school, church, and social class, by means of language, parents' attitudes and behavior, reading, and public school instruction. As a result, the cultural patterns that consumers learn influence their ideas and values, the roles they play, the way in which they carry those roles out, and the manner in which their needs and desires are handled.

Culture provides patterns that guide individuals in the satisfaction of their biological needs. Thus, children learn the diet pattern of their culture, modesty and hygiene of elimination, proper conduct in sexual affairs, patterns of propriety in dress. The requirement for food, for example, is met in every society. But the specific foods that an individual

---

[27]Elihu Katz and Paul F. Lazarsfeld, *Personal Influence* (New York: Free Press, 1955).

[28]James H. Myers and Thomas S. Robertson, "Dimensions of Opinion Leadership," *Journal of Marketing Research,* February 1972, pp. 41–46.

[29]Henry Assael, *Consumer Behavior and Marketing Action* (Boston: Kent Publishing, p. 382).

regards as acceptable are determined by the culture. The Chinese, for instance, dislike milk and milk products, while dairy products make up an important part of the American diet.

Culture not only patterns the way in which people satisfy their needs but also creates desires that exert a strong influence upon their buying behavior. The learned desires of certain consumers for cigarettes or alcohol, for example, may be just as compelling as their requirements for food. So, too, the desires for a late-model automobile or television set, which are learned from the American culture, may occupy a position high in the list of products wanted by a newly married couple—perhaps even ahead of the need they may feel for a home of their own. In the United States, some of the cultural changes include (1) the changing role of males and females, (2) orientation toward experiences rather than possessions, (3) emphasis on individuality instead of conformity, (4) increased importance of leisure time, and (5) desire for a higher quality of life.[30]

The success of marketing strategy can depend on how well the marketer understands the culture of new markets to be entered. International marketing has many examples of unsuccessful strategies resulting from failure to understand cultural differences between domestic and foreign markets. In domestic markets, it is also important to anticipate cultural trends and adapt marketing strategies accordingly. These trends can be identified by understanding subcultures or groups that exist within a culture.

Subcultures. In recent years, marketers have targeted marketing strategies to the unique needs of subcultures. These subcultures may be defined in terms of such factors as geographic location, rural or urban residence, ethnic background, race, and religion. For example, marketing strategies have been targeted to the Hispanic and black segments of the market. In general, subculture is most important for product categories such as food products, clothing, and furniture.

Subcultures typically have differences in media habits. These media differences allow marketers to target specific subculture groups. Examples include Spanish language radio stations and also television programs which appeal to blacks and religious groups. Marketers will continue to target marketing programs to subcultures as the economic importance of these groups grows.

Social Class

In addition to being molded by culture, the attitudes and needs of the consumer are patterned by the social class to which he or she belongs. *Social classes* are relatively permanent and homogeneous divisions

---

[30]Leonard L. Berry and Ian H. Wilson, "Retailing: The Next 10 Years," *Journal of Retailing*, Fall 1977, p. 19.

in a society into which individuals or families sharing similar values, lifestyles, interests, and behavior can be categorized.[31] Even though American political ideology is based upon the concept that "all men are created equal," studies of many communities in all the regions of the United States clearly demonstrate the presence of a well-defined class structure.

Pioneering research dealing with the existence of social class in America and how it may be measured was done by Warner and his associates. Warner conceived of social class as "two or more orders of people who are believed to be, and are accordingly ranked by the members of the community, in socially superior and inferior positions.[32] Associated with this definition are the ideas that the individual must participate in the social interaction of the class and must be accepted as a peer by its members. After considerable investigation, Warner and his associates came to the conclusion that a family's position in the social structure of a community is determined by the following criteria: occupation, amount of income, source of income, house type, neghborhood, and education. Under Warner's approach, individuals are classified as to social class by other people who know them.

Using this research design, Warner identifies six social classes as follows:[33]

> *Upper-upper* (1.4 percent): Members of "old families," the aristocracy of birth and inherited wealth, born into their positions of prestige, with enough wealth to maintain a large house in the best neighborhood.
>
> *Lower-upper* (1.6 percent): Similar to the upper-upper in costly homes in the best neighborhood and in design for living, but lacking in distinguished ancestry. While their incomes average somewhat larger than families in the upper-upper class, their wealth is newer and not inherited.
>
> *Upper-middle* (10.2 percent): Respectable, achieving, solid citizens of high moral principles and personal integrity; moderately successful business and professional men and their families. Their incomes average somewhat less than the lower-upper class, and these incomes are derived predominantly from salary rather than from invested wealth. Some education and polish is necessary, but lineage is unimportant.
>
> *Lower-middle* (28.1 percent): Clerks, white-collar workers, small businessmen, schoolteachers, foremen in industry; people who live in small homes on side streets; frequently homeowners.
>
> *Upper-lower* (32.6 percent): "Poor but honest" workers, usually in

[31]Engel and Blackwell, *Consumer Behavior,* p. 111.

[32]Reprinted by permission from W. Lloyd Warner and Paul S. Lunt, *The Social Life of a Modern Community* (New Haven, Conn.: Yale University Press, 1959), pp. 81–91.

[33]Adapted from W. Lloyd Warner, Marchia Meeker, and Kenneth Eells, *Social Class in America* (Torchbook edition), pp. 11–15, 31, 35, 174, 181. Copyright 1919 by Science Research Associates, Inc., Chicago. Copyright © 1960 by Harper & Row, Publishers, Inc. By permission of Harper & Row.

semiskilled occupations, who participate less in the educational and other advantages of our society, and who spend a large percentage of their income on food and shelter. This class and the lower-middle class are closely related in tastes, problems, and beliefs. Together, these two classes are regarded as "the common man."

Lower-lower (25.2 percent): Semiskilled and unskilled workers; families who live in the worst homes in poor neighborhoods, people who are often on relief, who have low incomes, and who are lacking in ambition or opportunity to improve their lot.

Our interest, of course, is in the value of social class stratification to the marketing executive. Because Warner's research had been done in smaller communities, there was concern that the same social class system might not exist in more complex metropolitan centers. If some such system did exist, would the Warner research approach uncover it? Then, too, many marketers did not see the relevance of social class to consumer buying behavior, since previous research in this area had been concerned with broad differences in patterns of living, moral codes, and mental illness, as well as other behavioral science goals.

With this in mind, the *Chicago Tribune* undertook several extensive studies during the mid-1950s exploring social class in a metropolitan city and the relevance of this factor to the individual family's buying behavior. The studies were carried out under the direction of Pierre Martineau, research director of the *Chicago Tribune,* and W. Lloyd Warner. In this study, interviewing was done in metropolitan Chicago and involved 3,880 households. The data used to calculate the "Index of Status Characteristics" were: (1) occupation (weighted by 5), sources of income (weighted by 4), and housing type (weighted by 3). Martineau reported the following conclusions:[34]

1. There is a social class system operative in metropolitan markets, which can be isolated and described.
2. It is important to realize that there are far-reaching psychological differences between the various classes.
3. Consumption patterns operate as prestige symbols to define class membership, which is a more significant determinant of economic behavior than mere income. Income has always been the marketer's handiest index to family consumption standards. But it is a far-from-accurate index. Social class position and mobility–stability dimensions will reflect in much greater depth each individual's style of life.

Social classes show distinct product and brand preferences in such areas as automobiles, sporting equipment, clothing, home furnishings, and food products. Marketers of ski and golf equipment, air travel,

---

[34]Reprinted by permission from Pierre Martineau, "Social Classes and Spending Behavior," *Journal of Marketing,* October 1958, p. 130, published by the American Marketing Association.

financial investments, and china often define their target markets as "upscale" social classes. Products such as bus travel and bowling appeal to lower social classes. Imported wines are targeted to the upper-middle social class, while the largest market for beer is the upper-lower social class.

Social classes differ in their use of advertising media. Magazines tend to have a higher social class profile than radio and television. However, social class differences exist within each of these media. For example, late-evening television audiences have a middle-class composition, while early evening audiences have a heavier working-class composition. Consequently, marketers can target social classes by selecting appropriate media.

MODELS OF CONSUMER BUYER BEHAVIOR

We now have the conceptual background to enable us to understand the more complex theoretical models of buyer behavior that have developed during the past 18 years. These models tie together in a logical structure a large number of variables known to operate in purchase behavior. Emphasis is on the explanation of the relationships among these variables. Theoretical constructs are defined in such a way as to facilitate measurement through research. A basis is thus provided for formal expression of these models in mathematical terms.

While several comprehensive models of buyer behavior have been developed, we shall limit ourselves to the discussion of the Howard-Sheth model since it has received wide attention in marketing circles and has been subjected to several large-scale validation tests. Those interested in learning about other notable comprehensive models should consult the references cited below.[35]

The Howard-Sheth Model

The Howard-Sheth model is a general theory of buying behavior designed to apply to most people buying most products.[36] The theory may be used to understand industrial buying as well as consumer purchasing. It attempts to explain the brand choice behavior of the buyer over time. It postulates that buying behavior is caused by a stimulus in either the buyer or the buyer's environment. This stimulus is the input to the system. The outputs are a variety of responses that the buyer is

---

[35]See Francesco M. Nicosia, *Consumer Decision Processes* (Englewood Cliffs, N.J.: Prentice-Hall, 1966), chap. 6; James F. Engel, Roger D. Blackwell, and David T. Kollat, *Consumer Behavior*, 3d ed. (Hinsdale, Ill.: Dryden Press, 1978), chap. 3.

[36]From John A. Howard and Jagdish Sheth, "A Theory of Buyer Behavior," in Harold H. Kassarjian and Thomas S. Robertson, eds., *Perspectives in Consumer Behavior*. Copyright © 1968 by Scott, Foresman and Company. Used by permission.

likely to manifest, the most important of which is the purchase of the brand. Accordingly, buying is explained in the context of stimulus-response theory upon which a more elaborate structure has been built. The model integrates ideas from learning theory, cognitive theory, and the theory of exploratory behavior, among others. (See Figure 4–7 for a diagram of this model.)

Stimulus input variables.[37]   Let us examine this model more closely, beginning with the inputs shown at the upper left-hand corner of the diagram. Assume that the buyer becomes aware of a need and expects to satisfy it by the purchase of a brand from a generic product class. Three types of inputs may furnish stimuli designed to influence the choice of an individual brand from among five alternatives that are available. Through their marketing activities, the five competitors attempt to communicate information (stimulus display) to the buyer in the hope that it may influence the choice. Examining an automobile in the dealer's showroom, for example, would communicate "significative" stimuli to the prospective buyer. Likewise, the prospect who reads, views, or hears advertisements for different brands of cars is receiving "symbolic" stimuli.

A third input is social stimuli, that is, the information that the buyer's social environment provides concerning the positive and negative aspects of the alternative brands under consideration. Word-of-mouth communication is the most obvious example.

Internal variables (hypothetical constructs).   We now turn to the central rectangular box which identifies the various internal-state variables and processes that explain how the buyer responds to the three types of stimuli that come from the environment. These constructs are divided into two classes: (1) those having to do with perception and (2) those having to do with learning.

When a need has been aroused, a buyer who is familiar with a product class will call to mind several alternative brands (or goal objects) capable of satisfying that need. These brands constitute the *evoked set,* and they may represent only a few brands out of the many that are available on the market. *Brand comprehension* is a learning construct that refers to knowledge about the existence and characteristics of the brands in the purchaser's evoked set.

Choice criteria are the buyer's mental rules for matching alternative brands with motives and ranking them in terms of their want-satisfying capacity. In the choice process, *attitude* (brand preference) and *confidence* (ability to estimate the reward from buying the brand) lead to *intention* to buy. *Intention,* in turn, may lead to *purchase.* The resulting *satisfaction,* or its absence, will feed back influence to future buying decisions.

---

[37]The description of the Howard-Sheth model that follows is summarized by permission from John A. Howard and Jagdish N. Sheth, *The Theory of Buyer Behavior* (New York: John Wiley & Sons, Inc., 1969), chaps. 2 and 3.

FIGURE 4–7

Simplified description of the theory of buyer behavior

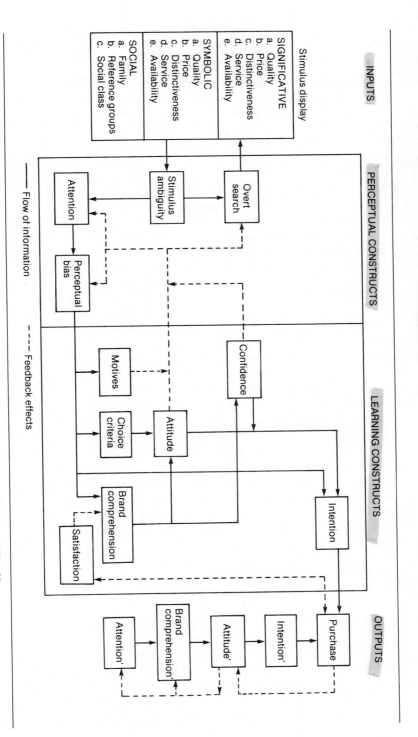

INPUTS

Stimulus display

SIGNIFICATIVE
a. Quality
b. Price
c. Distinctiveness
d. Service
e. Availability

SYMBOLIC
a. Quality
b. Price
c. Distinctiveness
d. Service
e. Availability

SOCIAL
a. Family
b. Reference groups
c. Social class

PERCEPTUAL CONSTRUCTS

Attention

Stimulus ambiguity

Overt search

Perceptual bias

LEARNING CONSTRUCTS

Motives

Choice criteria

Attitude

Confidence

Brand comprehension

Satisfaction

Intention

——— Flow of information

– – – – Feedback effects

OUTPUTS

Attention'

Brand comprehension'

Attitude'

Intention'

Purchase

Source: Reprinted by permission from John A. Howard and Jagdish Sheth, *The Theory of Buyer Behavior* (New York: John Wiley & Sons, Inc., 1969), p. 30.

Output variables. While the act of purchase is the culmination of the processing of the input stimuli explained above, other types of buyer responses are important to executives in evaluating past marketing strategy and in planning future programs. As Figure 4–7 shows, there are five output variables: (1) attention', (2) brand comprehension', (3) attitude', (4) intention', and (5) purchase. These variables are operationally well defined and may be used in research designed to measure the results of marketing effort.[38]

Decision-making process. While the Howard-Sheth model is complex, an important feature of the theory is that the buyer tends to simplify the buying process as a result of the learning that comes from past experience and information processing. Past experience includes generalization from similar buying situations and repeat buying of the same product class. Information comes from the buyer's commercial and social environments. The changes in the decision-making process over time are especially significant.

Howard and Sheth classify the buying decision process as (1) extensive problem solving (EPS), (2) limited problem solving (LPS), and (3) routinized response behavior (RRB), depending upon the amount of information needed to make a decision. In *extensive problem solving*, attitude toward the brands is low, because the buyer is first being confronted with an unfamiliar product class. Brand ambiguity is high, with the result that the buyer actively seeks information. The time interval from the initiation of the decision process until its completion is greater than with LPS or RBB. *Deliberation*, or reasoning, will be high, since the buyer lacks a well-defined product class concept. The buyer is also apt to consider many brands as part of the evoked set; brand comprehension will be extensive, but shallow, on any one particular brand; and stimuli coming from the commercial environment are less likely to trigger any immediate purchase reaction.[39]

When attitude toward brands is moderate, the buyer's decision process can be called *limited problem solving*. Here the buyer is familiar with the product class but unfamiliar with the brand (brand ambiguity still exists). The buyer is likely to seek information, but not to the extent as that in EPS. Fact gathering is to aid in comparing and discriminating among different brands. Deliberation is much less, since choice criteria are tentatively well defined. Brand comprehension will consist of a small number of brands, each having about the same degree of preference.

---

[38]For a stripped-down version of the model and its application, see John A. Howard, *Consumer Behavior: Application of Theory* (New York: McGraw-Hill, 1977), fig. 11–1 and chaps. 2, 3, and 5.

[39]When a family moves to a new city, this triggers a number of purchase decisions, the most important of which may be buying a new residence. For a discussion of information seeking under these circumstances, see Donald J. Hempel and William J. McEwen, "The Impact of Mobility and Social Integration on Information Seeking," paper presented at the 1975 *National Conference of the Association for Consumer Research,* 7 pp.104–9.

In *routinized response behavior,* the buyer will have a high level of attitude toward brands in the evoked set. Furthermore, the buyer has now accumulated sufficient experience and information to have no brand ambiguity and will, in fact, discriminate among brands enough to show a strong preference toward one or two brands in the evoked set. The buyer is unlikely to seek any information actively. Whatever information is passively or accidentally received will be subject to selective perceptual processes, so that only congruent information is allowed. Very often the congruent information will act as "triggering cues" to motivate the buyer to manifest purchase behavior. (Much impulse buying may be explained in this way.) The evoked set will consist of a few brands toward which the buyer is highly predisposed. However, there will be greater preference toward one brand in the evoked set and lesser preference toward others.

Situational variables and buyer behavior.   In recent years it has become evident that recognition of situational variables can substantially increase the ability to explain and understand buyer behavior. A consumer situation may be viewed as comprising "all those factors particular to a time and place of observation which do not follow from a knowledge of personal (intra-individual) and stimulus (choice alternative) attributes and which have a demonstrable and systematic effect on current behavior."

The following five groups of situational characteristics illustrate this concept: (1) physical surroundings (location, sounds, aroma, weather, among others); (2) social surroundings (other persons present); (3) temporal perspective (time of day, season of the year, time since last purchase, last meal, last payday, among others); (4) task definition (an intent or requirement to select, shop for, or obtain information about a purchase); and (5) antecedent states (momentary moods such as anxiety, pleasantness, hostility; momentary conditions such as cash on hand, fatigue, and illness).

A number of empirical tests of situational influence in consumer behavior have been conducted using inventories of situational scenarios and choice alternatives. These inventories ask subjects to rate the likelihood that they would choose each of several alternative products or services under each of several sets of situational conditions. These studies have covered beverages, leisure activities, meat products, motion pictures, snack products, and fast food. The results suggest the importance of including situational variables in undertaking research on buyer behavior.[40]

---

[40]Adapted by permission from Russell W. Belk, "Situational Variables and Consumer Behavior," *Journal of Consumer Research* 2, no. 3 (December 1973), pp. 157–64. See also J. A. Russell and A. Mehrabian, "Environmental Variables in Consumer Research," *Journal of Consumer Research* 3, no. 1 (June 1976), pp. 62–63; and Russell W. Belk, "A Reply to Russell and Mehrabian" 3, no. 3 (December 1976), pp. 175–77.

Concluding comments.   The Howard-Sheth model appears to be a powerful tool for explaining consumer behavior, especially for frequently purchased items, where past experience is likely to influence future attitudes. While it works better when used to guide research on the marketing of established products, rather than new ones, it has been useful in planning, executing, and analyzing test markets for new brands. There is also hope that further developmental work with the model may improve its usefulness in these applications. The results of validation tests of the model have been encouraging, but Howard and his associates indicate that further testing is needed before some of the more advanced applications envisioned for the model become feasible.[41]

CONCLUSION

Information on buyer behavior has been shown as an important input for use in planning marketing strategy. Initially, we have limited our analysis to the purchase of consumer goods, but we will deal with industrial goods in the next chapter. Consumer buying behavior is treated as a decision-making process involving: (1) recognition of a problem (a felt need); (2) the search for alternative solutions to the problem; (3) evaluation of alternatives (brands); (4) the purchase decision; and (5) post-purchase feelings and evaluation.

In seeking to understand those aspects of the individual consumer's psychological makeup that are relevant to the buying decision, we discussed the concepts of motives, attitudes, and learning. It was shown how motives and attitudes are patterned by the culture in which the individual consumer lives, the social class to which he or she belongs, as well as by family and reference groups. The position of the person in the life cycle was shown to have significant influence upon the types of products and services that are purchased at any given time. Knowledge of the interplay of the buyer's motives and attitudes with the cultural and social influences in his or her environment is important in understanding why, how, where, and when people buy.

Finally the Howard-Sheth theoretical model has been presented to tie together, in a unified structure, the many variables that affect the purchase of a brand. Empirical tests indicate that this model appears to have substantial validity, but it still requires additional development and further validation studies before its full potential can be realized. With such a theoretical model of buyer behavior in mind, the executive and the

---

[41]For a report on the comprehensive research project designed to test the validity of the Howard-Sheth theory of buyer behavior and to facilitate its continuing development, see John U. Farley, John A. Howard, and L. Winston Ring, *Consumer Behavior: Theory and Application,* Marketing Science Institute Series (Boston: Allyn & Bacon, 1974).

market researcher can work together in deciding (1) what information to gather in order to provide data needed for planning marketing strategy for the year ahead and (2) what output measurements to secure as a means of evaluating the effectiveness of the program. Weaknesses identified through such audits can then serve as an input in planning improved strategy for the following year. In short, an ongoing program of research, which feeds essential information to those responsible for the planning of marketing strategy, has the potential of making possible significant improvements in the effectiveness of marketing effort. A research program of this kind would constitute part of a modern marketing information system such as that described in Chapter 3.

QUESTIONS

1. Differentiate between the purchase of consumer goods and the purchase of industrial goods.

2. Why should the marketing manager not focus on the purchase decision in isolation from the other stages of the buying process?

3. What determines the amount of information sought by the consumer in the buying process?

4. Discuss the implication of the fact that there can be a difference between the consumer's brand image and the producer's desired image for a brand.

5. Why is the concept of perception so important in understanding consumer behavior?

6. Name some products associated with the two types of perceived risk.

7. Why should marketers incorporate the concept of lifestyle into their strategy for a product or service?

8. How can an understanding of cultures and subcultures help a marketer establish effective target market strategies?

9. Distinguish between extensive, limited, and routinized problem solving as described in the Howard-Sheth model.

10. What are situational variables and what impact do they have on buyer behavior?

INDUSTRIAL BUYER BEHAVIOR

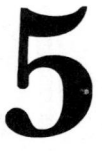

5

The previous chapter dealt with buyer behavior in the consumer market, where the purchasing units are individuals who buy goods and services for the satisfaction of their own needs or those of their families. The consumer market is large, varied, and widely dispersed geographically. Because we all participate in the consumer market to some extent, our knowledge of its working is rather extensive. Any discussion of buyer behavior in the consumer market can be related to concepts that are generally understandable in light of our own experience with the purchase decision process.

There is, however, another market that is even larger than the consumer market but about which the average person knows very little. This other market is the industrial market, and it is composed of the individuals and organizations that purchase goods and services necessary for the production of goods and services—which they, in turn, sell or lease to others. Because this market has not received the attention from the press or from marketing writers that has been given to the consumer market, the average college student is somewhat hazy about the industrial market and how it operates. A brief review of the nature, importance, and organization of this vast "other" market will, therefore, precede the discussion of how buyers behave in an industrial, rather than a consumer, setting.

NATURE OF THE INDUSTRIAL MARKET

The industrial market is composed of almost 12 million producer units that buy (or lease) goods and services that enter into or support their productive process. Although this number is small when compared with over 230 million individuals organized into approximately 70 million family purchasing units in the consumer market, the 12 million producer units account for a considerably larger volume of sales than do their consumer counterparts. For example, over half of all the manufactured goods produced in this country is sold to industrial users. These sales amounted to $600 billion in 1976.[1] In addition, it has been estimated that 80 percent of the total output of domestic farms and mines enters the industrial market. Thus, another $150 billion of sales must be added to the industrial market total.[2]

Of course, one of the reasons that the industrial market has such large sales volume is that so many transactions are required to convert raw materials into finished products and to make these products available at local outlets. Even though some double counting may occur as goods move through the production and distribution processes, the measurement of the value added at each stage in the journey validates the economic contribution of the producer units involved. Suffice it to say that a market employing over 80 million people and generating a trillion dollars in national income is too large and important to be ignored by any marketing manager.

The industrial market, as commonly defined, encompasses a wide range of industries including: agriculture, forestry and fishing, mining, construction, manufacturing, transportation, communications, public utilities, wholesale and retail trade, finance, insurance and real estate, services, and federal, state, and local governments.

Under this broad definition every wholesaler or retailer is an industrial customer, as is any contractor or public utility. In like manner, any governmental entity is considered to be part of the industrial market.

One writer prefers to define the industrial market as a subset of what is termed the "organizational" market. Other key subsets would be the reseller market as well as the government market.[3]

Although there is considerable merit in the three-market approach, based on the fact that industrial, reseller, and governmental customers may differ widely in buying motives, behavior, and mode of operation, for our purposes in this chapter the broader definition of the industrial market will be used. The industrial market will be viewed as containing

---

[1] *Survey of Current Business,* May 1977, p. 5–5.

[2] William J. Stanton, *Fundamentals of Marketing,* 7th ed. (New York: McGraw-Hill, 1984), p. 145.

[3] Philip Kotler, *Marketing Management: Analyses, Planning, and Control,* 5th ed. (Englewood Cliffs, N.J.: Prentice-Hall, 1984), p. 162.

all of those customers who are not in the consumer market. But construing the industrial market to be so all-encompassing does not mean that it is homogeneous. Indeed, the opposite is true, and those differences that are found in the industrial market provide many meaningful bases for market segmentation. This process will be discussed later in the chapter.

Regardless of whether one views the government market as a separate entity or as a segment of the industrial market, it is an area worthy of brief discussion. The government sector is of special interest simply because it uses such vast quantities of goods and services. The federal government consumes over 20 percent of the gross national product, while state and local governmental units use another 10 percent. Thus, almost one third of everything produced in this country each year is sold to some agency of government.

Although government purchases are large, it is not necessarily easy to sell to government. The average marketer finds it difficult to make contact with those persons who influence decisions as to what the government will buy and from whom it will buy. Of course, a great deal of government procurement must, by law, be on a bid basis. Under the bidding system, the government advertises for bids from suppliers, stating the specifications of the goods and services desired. The order goes to the lowest bidder who meets the specifications. In a growing number of situations where a good deal of research and developmental work is required or where there is no feasible competition to support a bid procedure, the government will enter into a negotiated purchase contract either on a cost-plus or incentive basis.

The average marketer does not want to get involved in the red tape and other complications entailed by selling to government. Those firms that have taken the time and trouble to develop specialized marketing skills have found the government market segment to be extremely profitable.

CLASSIFICATION OF INDUSTRIAL GOODS

Goods sold in the consumer market are often classified in terms of how buyers behave when they seek out these goods. Thus, the commonly used classifications such as convenience goods, shopping goods, and specialty goods refer to the amount of time and effort the average potential buyer will expend in order to find, investigate, and finally purchase a specific item. Such a classification approach has only limited application in the industrial market. Producer units do not shop in the usual sense. In most cases, vendors seek them out.

A more useful way of classifying industrial goods is in terms of how these goods enter the production processes and cost structures of the

various producer customers. With this type of information, marketing executives can identify more readily the persons involved in the buying process and can develop a marketing strategy mix to reach these people and to influence them to buy their product. A classification schema that aids in the analysis of the industrial market, in terms of the entry characteristics of specific goods and services, has been suggested by Kotler.[4] In Figure 5–1, wide arrays of goods and services sold in the industrial market have been placed in three major categories shown as Types I, II, and III producer (industrial market) goods.

FIGURE 5–1   Classification of industrial goods

I. *Goods entering the product completely—materials and parts*
  A. Raw materials
      1. Farm products (examples: wheat, cotton, livestock, fruits, vegetables)
      2. Natural products (examples: fish, lumber, crude petroleum, iron ore)
  B. Manufactured materials and parts
      1. Component materials (examples: steel, cement, wire, textiles)
      2. Component parts (examples: small motors, tires, castings)

II. *Goods entering the product partly—capital items*
  A. Installations
      1. Buildings and land rights (examples: factories, offices)
      2. Fixed equipment (examples: generators, drill presses, computers, elevators)
  B. Accessory equipment
      1. Portable or light factory equipment and tools (examples: hand tools, forklifts)
      2. Office equipment (examples: typewriters, desks)

III. *Goods not entering the product—supplies and services*
  A. Supplies
      1. Operating supplies (examples: lubricants, coal, typing paper, pencils)
      2. Maintenance and repair items (examples: paint, nails, brooms)
  B. Business services
      1. Maintenance and repair services (examples: window cleaning, typewriter repair)
      2. Business advisory services (examples: legal, management consulting, advertising)

Source: Philip Kotler, *Marketing Management: Analysis, Planning, and Control*, 4th ed. © 1980, p. 172. By permission of Prentice-Hall, Inc.

The Type I goods enter the product completely. Thus their costs are assigned directly to the manufacturing process. In contrast, Type II goods are generally large and expensive. They are capitalized as assets, and as they are used up or worn out over time, a portion of their original

---

[4]Ibid. p. 172.

cost is assigned to the production process as depreciation expense. Type III goods are those that do not enter the production process at all, but which facilitate operations. The costs of such goods (and services) are treated as expenses in the periods in which they are used.

MARKETING PATTERNS

The physical nature of an industrial good and the way in which it is used by the buyer have an important influence on the manner in which it is marketed. Over time, therefore, certain patterns of marketing have become associated with classes of industrial goods. It is possible, given these patterns, to describe the nature of the marketing strategy mix used by most sellers of a specific class of industrial raw material, product, or service.

Raw materials.   The marketing pattern associated with agricultural raw materials results from the fact that these materials are usually supplied by many small producer units located some distance from the points of consumption. Although the amounts of these materials that can be supplied in total each year are, to a large extent, under the control of man, these quantities cannot be changed quickly. In addition, production is seasonal and the goods produced are perishable. Thus the marketing strategy mix emphasizes distribution in its broadest sense. Long channels of distribution include specialists who perform the functions of accumulating, storing, standardizing and grading, warehousing, and transportation.

Because agricultural raw materials are sold on a contractual basis with product specifications clearly stated, price is extremely important. Because the product itself is a commodity that cannot be physically differentiated from the offerings of other suppliers, the seller does not engage in branding, advertising, or other forms of demand creation for his product. Rather, the seller earns patronage by gaining a reputation for meeting his quality and delivery commitments while charging competitive prices over a period of time.

Natural products have their own marketing patterns, which are somewhat different from agricultural raw materials, especially in the area of distribution. As supplies of these goods are limited by nature and are usually concentrated geographically, producers tend to be large and few in number. The product is standardized, bulky, generally of low unit value, and costly to transport. As a result, channels of distribution tend to be short—often direct from producer to user. Price is important, and it is influenced greatly by transportation costs, thus placing a premium on locational advantage for the seller. Demand creation opportunities are again limited by the commodity nature of the goods, and emphasis

is placed by the seller on consistent quality and service at competitive prices.

Manufactured materials and parts.   These items share many of the marketing characteristics of raw materials. They are usually purchased in large quantities, generally on a contractual basis, and in most industries directly from the manufacturer. Smaller users or hand-to-mouth purchasers may avail themselves of industrial distributors or other marketing middlemen. Price and service are still the basic appeals used by sellers; but the products in this category are often less standardized than are raw materials, and thus some opportunity does exist for product differentiation and demand creation activity. Branding, advertising, and personal selling are all utilized by certain manufacturers to gain patronage for their products. Catalogs and trade publications are important sources of information for potential buyers. In some instances, promotional messages are directed at the consumer market to create brand awareness for materials and parts that enter a consumer product such as an automobile, a refrigerator, or a piece of wearing apparel.

Installations.   These are the large, expensive items of capital equipment that affect the scale of operation of the buyer. The marketing of installations is a difficult and complicated business in which a number of highly qualified salespeople and technicians work with prospective customers over a long period of time. Channels of distribution are generally direct because of the need for close communication between buyers and sellers. Some less costly standardized installations may, however, be sold through middlemen.

The criteria for purchase considered by the buyer include the nature of the installation and how well it can be adjusted to fit the specific needs of the buyer, the nature of the service offered by the seller (not only presale, but also during installation or construction and post-sale follow-up), and the price. It should be noted that the price for an installation is viewed by the buyer as having a close relationship to the cost savings that will be provided by the installation over its life. Thus a higher price will be paid to gain an even higher cost savings.

In terms of the marketing strategy mix, the product ranks first in importance when installations are sold. There is an opportunity, however, for demand creation activity, and in this area personal selling is the main vehicle. Trade advertising, catalogs, and direct mail are used to supplement the efforts of the sales force and to reach those members of the buying team who cannot be reached in person. The highest levels of management are generally involved in the purchase decision for installations.

Accessory equipment.   Items of accessory equipment facilitate the production process without changing a buyer's scale of operation. Accessory items are more standardized, generally cost less, and are purchased by lower levels of management than are installations. Although

some distribution is on a direct basis, a great deal of accessory equipment is sold through industrial distributors. Markets for these items run across industry lines, and therefore broader coverage is required than can be attained economically by the manufacturer alone. In addition to the importance of the distribution variable to provide availability, personal selling has a large role to play in the marketing strategy mix. Greater emphasis is placed upon selling skills than upon technical skills, unlike the situation in the installations market.

Price is also a very important factor, and to gain some freedom from price competition, many sellers of accessory equipment engage in a strategy of promoting product differentiation. Personal selling and advertising are both used to emphasize product advantages and to de-emphasize direct price comparisons with competing products.

Supplies and services.   Operating supplies of one type or another are used by almost all producer units. Thus broad distribution is a necessity if availability requirements in the market are to be met. Because operating supplies are fairly well standardized, if one manufacturer is not represented in the market because of lack of coverage or because of a stockout, the product of another manufacturer can be substituted quite easily. Although distribution is generally through middlemen, some large buyers are served on a direct basis. In addition to availability, price is an important consideration for the potential user. Catalog listings, advertising to resellers as well as final users, and personal selling are all utilized to gain sales for the branded or nonbranded goods of selected suppliers.

Services are marketed in ways that are different from those used to sell operating supplies. Because buyers tend to value quality and the reputation of the provider of services, price is less important in the seller's marketing mix. What is important is personal selling to explain the capabilities of the supplier and to negotiate a purchase contract. Sales efforts are directed at higher levels of management for services than for operating supplies. Thus personal selling efforts are often supplemented by direct mail or business periodical advertising of a professional nature. The appeals used emphasize quality of performance rather than price.

NATURE OF DEMAND FOR INDUSTRIAL GOODS

Demand for industrial goods and services has several characteristics that differentiate it from demand in the consumer market. These characteristics are an outgrowth of the fact that the demand for industrial goods is derived from the demand for the goods and services of which they are a part. For example, the demand for automobile tires is derived both from the demand for new cars and from the replacement needs of

those car owners whose tires have worn out. The simple illustration that follows provides a basis for discussion of the impact that derived demand has upon the industrial market and thus upon marketing strategy formulation.

Derived demand.   Let us assume the existence of a company that manufactures bottles for sale to the soft drink industry. This company has a factory containing 10 bottle-producing machines, each with a capability of turning out 100,000 bottles per year. Each machine has a useful life of 10 years, and the ages of the machines are conveniently staggered for this example, so that one machine must be retired at the end of each year. The history of the demand for bottles faced by this company, as well as its own demand for bottle-producing machinery for the past five years, is illustrated in Figure 5–2.

FIGURE 5–2   Company demand history for bottles and bottle-producing machinery

Year	Bottles demanded	Percent change	Machines demanded	Percent change
−5	1,000,000	0	1 replacement	0
−4	1,000,000	0	1 replacement	0
−3	1,100,000	+10	1 replacement + 1 expansion	+100
−2	1,300,000	+18	1 replacement + 2 expansion	+ 50
−1	1,200,000	− 8	0	−100

Changes in demand for bottles, which do not exceed 18 percent in any one year, are translated into very large changes in demand for bottle-producing machinery. These fluctuations, which reflect year-to-year changes of as much as 100 percent, are typical of demand for capital goods. Sellers of these goods face a feast-or-famine situation, depending on whether forecasts of future demand for end products in a particular industry are favorable or unfavorable.

In contrast, demand for component parts or operating supplies shows a lesser degree of fluctuation than does demand for capital goods. In addition, demand for these goods is linked to the level of general business conditions rather than to the fortunes of any particular industry or group of industries. Finally, as the production process for these goods is shorter than that for capital goods, and because these goods can be stockpiled more economically, estimates of demand for the end product

need not be carried as far into the future as would be the case with capital goods.

Demand for component or supply-type items is also affected by the inventory-holding policies of the users. Generally, these policies specify that sufficient goods will be purchased and on hand to support a specified number of days of production. Increases in demand for the output of the firm will trigger a need to add to inventories. Conversely, a fall-off in demand will cause a moratorium on buying until stocks on hand fall into line with the needs of the production line.

Elasticity of demand.   Derived demand and the psychology of the industrial buyer interact to cause unusual things to happen with respect to the influence of price upon the quantities of goods and services demanded by the industrial users. Let us examine first the impact of price changes on the demand for capital equipment such as expensive, specialized machinery.

Purchasers of such machinery are seeking a way to increase the profitability of their operations. They are, in effect, buying cost-saving capability. When demand for the end product is depressed, there is no need to purchase machinery for expansion purposes. Indeed, even the replacement of old machines may be delayed. If the buyer faces such a situation, a reduction in price by the seller of capital equipment will have little effect in stimulating sales. This is because the cost of any particular piece of capital equipment typically represents a very small part of the price of the ultimate consumer product. A price reduction which can affect the price of the end product in a price-sensitive market may accelerate the replacement of existing machinery. The price cut required may be so large, however, that the seller often prefers to redesign the machine to increase its cost-saving potential instead of reducing its price.

In the face of a forecast upswing in final demand, users of capital equipment will add to capacity at prices which allow them profitable operations. Moderately high prices will not deter them from buying, as the profit potential, not the price, is the important consideration. Thus, whether viewed from the downside or the upside, derived demand for capital goods is relatively inelastic. Price plays a secondary role in the marketing strategy mixes of sellers of such equipment, while product design to afford cost savings to users, personal selling, and service dominate the strategies of marketers of capital equipment.

Demand for raw materials and component parts, although derived, is more sensitive to price changes than is demand for capital goods. In the short run, demand for these types of goods may exhibit reverse elasticity in that when prices decline, buyers may sit on the sidelines until they can determine whether or not the price declines are temporary or are a prelude to a continued succession of price reductions. On the other hand, if prices start to rise, buyers may accelerate their purchases to beat what they believe will be even higher prices in the future. Of course, in

the long run the laws of economics will prevail, and lower prices will result in larger quantities of materials and parts being utilized, while higher prices will have the opposite effect. When an individual seller in an industry lowers his price, one would expect his sales to increase at the expense of his competitors. This does not always happen. Industrial customers do not change sources on the basis of price alone. Quality of product and service and the existence of a long-standing relationship between source and user cause demand to be sticky and a price reduction, even if unmatched by competitors, to be a less effective way of gaining patronage.

As one moves from capital goods to materials and parts and thence to supplies and services, the sensitivity of demand to changes in price increases. As goods become more standardized and service requirements lessen, more emphasis may be placed upon price in the seller's marketing mix. A price reduction is especially effective when the material or part being sold is important in terms of the cost composition of the finished product of which it is a part. In such a situation, a price reduction may enable the seller of the end product to reduce his price and gain a competitive advantage in his market.

Because demand in the industrial market is different from demand in the consumer market (in that it is derived, it fluctuates more, and it is relatively inelastic), special industrial marketing plans must be developed. Industrial marketers who have borrowed planning processes from the consumer market have, to a large extent, achieved disappointing results.

EXTENT OF DEMAND FOR INDUSTRIAL GOODS AND SERVICES

As noted previously, there are approximately 12 million buying units in the industrial market. This is a relatively small number of potential customers when compared with the 200 million individuals in the consumer market. The market seems even smaller to the average industrial seller who is concerned not with the total industrial market but rather with a smaller segment of the total, composed of buyers for his or her specific offerings. For example, sellers of component parts for use in the manufacture of textile machinery may find that the most recent census data indicate that only 639 such establishments exist. Sellers of supplies used by meatpackers will discover that their market is limited to approximately 2,600 firms.[5] A major problem facing the industrial marketer is, therefore, the identification and location of those firms that are likely prospects for the goods and services offered for sale.

To aid in the identification and location process, the federal govern-

---

[5]*U.S. Census of Manufactures: 1977*, vol. 1.

ment has developed the Standard Industrial Classification (SIC) system, under which all business and governmental organizations are classified in terms of 10 groups. Each of these groups is assigned a range of two-digit numbers, as illustrated below.[6]

01–09	Agriculture, forestry, fishing
10–14	Mining
15–18	Contract construction
19–39	Manufacturing
40–49	Transportation and other public utilities
50–59	Wholesale and retail trade
60–67	Finance, insurance, and real estate
70–89	Services
90–93	Government—federal, state, and local
99–	Others

A separate two-digit number is then assigned to each major industry within the group, and three- and four-digit numbers are used to identify specific segments within each industry. For example:

SIC 20	Food and kindred products
SIC 201	Meat products
SIC 2013	Sausages and other prepared meat products

While the industrial market is composed of relatively few firms that are potential users of the offerings of specific suppliers, these few firms represent a great deal of purchasing power. An examination of the size distribution of manufacturing establishments, as illustrated in Figure 5–3, shows that approximately 10 percent of the firms employ 75 percent of the persons involved and account for almost 80 percent of the value added.

In addition to the concentration of demand within an industry in terms of size of firms, demand in the industrial market is concentrated on a geographic basis. As seen in Figure 5–4, almost half of the total value added by manufacturing in the United States in 1977 was accounted for by eight states in the middle Atlantic and East North Central census regions. Of equal interest is the fact that 25 percent of the U.S. total of value added by manufacturing in 1977 was accounted for by only 10 Standard Metropolitan Statistical Areas (SMSAs).

---

[6]*Standard Industrial Classification Manual* (Washington, D.C.: U.S. Government Printing Office, 1972).

FIGURE 5–3   Size distribution of manufacturing establishments in the United States by number of employees, 1977

Number of employees	Number of establishments	Percent of firms	Percent of value added	Percent of employees
1-4	140,612	40.1	1.0	1.2
5-9	48,003	13.7	1.4	1.7
10-99	126,468	36.1	18.1	22.4
100-499	29,907	8.5	30.4	33.6
500-999	3,677	1.0	14.8	13.5
1,000-2,499	1,480	0.4	14.4	11.8
2,500 or more	581	0.2	19.9	15.7
Total	350,756	100.0	100.0	100.0

Source: *Census of Manufacturers, 1977.*

FIGURE 5–4   The United States in proportion to value of manufactured products

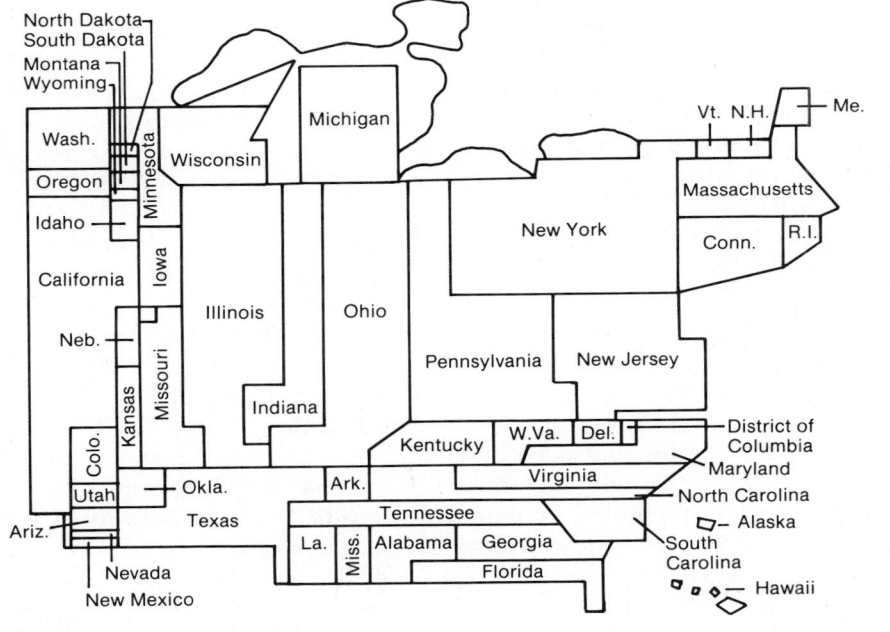

Source: *Census of Manufacturers Area Statistics, 1971.*

Data are available from governmental or private sources which indi-cate the extent of activity for most SIC classifications in each of the nation's counties or Standard Metropolitan Statistical Areas (SMSAs). This latter classification is especially important because the SMSAs, 263 in number, accounted for about 78 percent of value added by manufac-turing in 1972. By utilizing the information on geographic concentra-tion of industrial demand in conjunction with the SIC system, industrial marketing managers can identify and locate the most likely markets for their offerings. In addition, by noting the type, number, and location of individual firms that are likely prospects, an effective distribution and promotional strategy can be developed.

BUYER BEHAVIOR IN THE INDUSTRIAL MARKET

The first part of this chapter dealt with the more descriptive and quantitative aspects of the industrial market. This section will consider the qualitative aspects of demand in the industrial market—those aspects analogous to buyer behavior in the consumer market, yet somewhat different because of the industrial environment in which the behavior takes place.

Buying decisions in industry are made by people who are paid to solve buying problems and who usually function as part of an organized group. To gain insight into the nature of the industrial buying process, accordingly, requires both an understanding of individual buying behav-ior and a knowledge of how that behavior is influenced by the structure and goals of the organization of which the individual is a part.

Individual and Organizational Goals

The idealized picture of those engaged in the industrial purchasing process is that of a group of people dedicated to the advancement of the profit position of their company. They seek to achieve this corporate goal by purchasing goods and services in such a way that the combina-tion of product quality, price, and service received is an optimal one.

A less idealized picture is that which portrays the industrial buyer as a self-seeking individual who is not above accepting gifts or other consid-erations in exchange for favoring certain suppliers with orders for goods that may, or may not, best meet the needs of the firm. In actuality, the average industrial buyer is neither a calculating machine whose ration-ality is above question nor a totally selfish person, always willing to sub-ordinate the needs of the organization to his own. A more honest de-scription is that of a human being who is trying to do a good job for the company but is also interested in advancing his own career. Thus, the industrial buyer has two goals: to further the interests of his company and to further his own position within the organization.

At some times these goals overlap, while at other times they may be in conflict. It has been suggested that the organizational-factors model developed in a political context by Thomas Hobbes offers a useful interpretation of the relationship between organizational goals and individual goals.[7] The Hobbesian view is that although each man is "instinctively" oriented toward preserving and enhancing his own well-being, fear of a "war of every man against every man" leads men to unite in a corporate body.[8]

Perhaps if the various blendings of goals were illustrated by a Venn diagram, the marketing implications of these goal relationships might become clearer. Such an attempt is made in Figure 5–5, which illustrates three situations. Situation A is one in which there is a high degree of overlap between individual goals and organizational goals. In situation B, there is very little overlap. In situation C, there is considerable overlap, but there are still some areas in which the individual and organizational goals do not coincide.

FIGURE 5–5   Individual goals (*I*), group or organizational goals (*O*), and areas of goal mutuality (*M*) in three situations

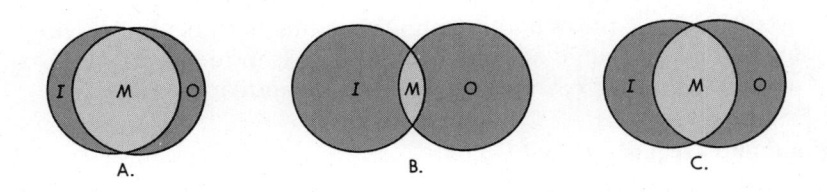

In situation A, there is a great deal of overlap between individual goals and organizational goals. In such a situation, the use of rational appeals illustrating how the product will help in organizational goal achievement should receive a great deal of acceptance from purchasing personnel. Such is the case when individuals responsible for the buying decision perceive that the best way to achieve their personal ends is to seek attainment of organizational goals. Thus, promotional efforts that emphasize the congruence of goals should be most effective here. The seller's slogan in situation A might be, to paraphrase a rather famous

---

[7]Philip Kotler, "Behavioral Models for Analyzing Buyers," *Journal of Marketing,* October 1965, pp. 44–45.

[8]Thomas Hobbes, *Leviathan,* 1651 (London: G. Routledge & Sons, Ltd., 1887).

quotation, "What is good for General Wickets Corporation is also good for its buyers."

In situation B, there is very little overlap. This is not a desirable state of affairs from the standpoint of the buying organization. If the true nature of the goal relationship is perceived by sellers, then their promotional activity will be directed to stimulation of efforts by individuals to achieve their personal goals even at the expense of corporate well-being.

Situation C is a more normal one. There is a better balance between individual and organizational goals. The area of goal mutuality, *M,* is larger than the area of either segment *I* or segment *O.* Given this type of situation, the perceptive seller will depend heavily on rational product arguments but will supplement these appeals with others of a more emotional nature, aimed at the egos of the individuals involved in the buying process.

It must be recognized that goal overlap is a matter of degree. The type of product being purchased, the type of organization being considered, and the relative strength of individual drives to achieve specific goals influence the blend, in a given situation, of individual and organizational goals. Ability on the part of the seller to sense the blend correctly will enable him or her to develop a more effective promotional strategy. An appraisal of the relative importance to the individuals involved in the purchase process of attaining the two goals will indicate whether the promotional appeals should be based on rational product advantages or whether there is some opportunity to utilize appeals to the self-interest of the individuals concerned.

Stages in the Buying Process

The specific buying processes of individual firms or institutions vary widely. For example, no two companies seem to follow the same purchasing procedures. Indeed, within a given firm the purchasing processes appear to vary according to the kind of need being filled or the type of product being sought. In spite of this seeming diversity, investigation of the industrial buying process has indicated that it is, in reality, an orderly one consisting of several clearly defined steps or phases.[9]

A classic study has termed these steps in the industrial buying process "buyphases" and has suggested that for analytic purposes the buying process might be broken down into eight distinct stages which, although generally sequential, may occur concurrently. These buyphases are:

1. The anticipation or recognition of a problem (need) and the awareness that such a problem may be solved by a purchase.

---

[9]John H. Platten, Jr., Scientific American research study, *How Industry Buys.* Copyright © 1950, 1955, by Scientific American, Inc.

2. The determination of the characteristics and the quantity of the needed item.
3. The description of the characteristics and the quantity of the needed item.
4. The search for and qualification of potential sources.
5. The acquisition and analysis of proposals.
6. The evaluation of proposals and the selection of suppliers.
7. The selection of an order routine.
8. Performance feedback and evaluation.[10]

Time element.   The stages or buyphases in the procurement process may take a considerable length of time for their completion. In Figure 5–6 a period of almost four months elapses between recognition of the need and delivery of the order. This rather long time was required, although the purchase was for a standard type of item that had been purchased many times in the past.

The term *straight rebuy* in Figure 5–6 refers to a type of buying situation in which there is a recurring or continuing requirement that is handled on a routine basis. Other types of situations may be termed *modified rebuys* or *new tasks,* and we shall talk about these a little later in this chapter.

Multiple-Influence Groups

Each buyphase of the industrial purchase process is the responsibility of several individuals performing different functions within the organization. Top management has routinely delegated authority to these persons to make the necessary decisions based on their evaluation of the pertinent factors.[11] Three aspects of the process, which have been verified by the research findings of Platten, are: (1) that top management rarely takes a direct hand in the buying process, (2) that few buying decisions are made by individuals, and most buying decisions are group decisions, and (3) that the composition of these groups characteristically changes from phase to phase.[12]

The groups of individuals involved in the purchase process are called "multiple-purchase influence groups." They are, for the most part, composed of middle-management people.[13] The major task of industrial marketers is to find out the composition of the multiple-influence group in a given company and at a specific point in time so that the correct type of promotional effort can be directed to the group members.

---

[10]Patrick J. Robinson, Charles W. Faris, and Yoram Wind, *Industrial Buying and Creative Marketing* (Boston: Allyn & Bacon, 1967), p. 13.

[11]Platten, *How Industry Buys.*

[12] Ibid.

[13]"Who Makes the Purchasing Decision?" *Marketing Insights,* October 31, 1966, p. 16.

FIGURE 5–6   A decision network diagram of the procurement process
(a straight rebuy: drills)

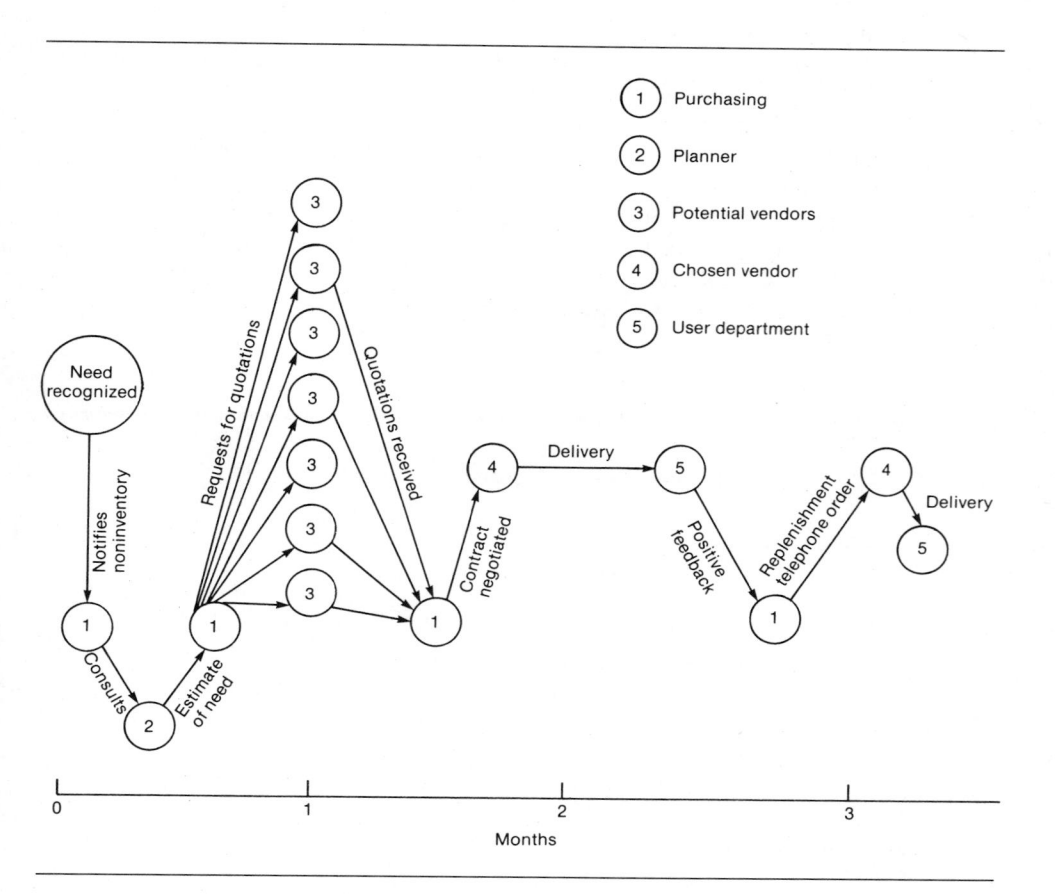

Types of Buying Situations

Members of a multiple-purchase influence group at a given buyphase
may find that their decision-making process is a function of the type of
buying situation with which they are involved. The degree of newness
of the problem, the amount of information required before an acceptable solution can be found, and the extent to which alternative ways of
solving the problem are considered, all go to make up or define a specific
type of buying situation.

The terms *new task, modified rebuy,* and *straight rebuy* have been suggested as describing three distinct types of buying situations or "buy-

classes."[14] The *new task*, for example, describes a buying situation in which the problem encountered is a new one, information requirements are high, and the consideration of alternatives is very important.

Those situations characterized by an essentially recurring problem which has certain new aspects, by moderately high information requirements, and by limited importance of considering alternatives may be called *modified rebuys*.

Finally, if the problem faced is not a new one, if information requirements are minimal, and if there is no consideration of alternatives, then the situation may be termed a *straight rebuy*.

To understand better how buyphases and buyclasses interact, let us examine the matrix in Figure 5–7—which has been termed the "Buygrid" framework. Here we see that in a new-task situation the buying decision passes through all of the buyphases. In the case of a modified

FIGURE 5-7   The Buygrid framework for industrial buying situations

Buyphases	Buy Classes		
	New task	Modified rebuy	Straight rebuy
1. Anticipation or recognition of a problem (need) and a general solution	Yes	Maybe	No
2. Determination of characteristics and quantity of needed item	Yes	Maybe	No
3. Description of characteristics and quantity of needed item	Yes	Yes	Yes
4. Search for and qualification of potential sources	Yes	Maybe	No
5. Acquisition and analysis of proposals	Yes	Maybe	No
6. Evaluation of proposals and selection of supplier(s)	Yes	Maybe	No
7. Selection of an order routine	Yes	Maybe	No
8. Performance of feedback and evaluation	Yes	Yes	Yes

Source: Adapted from Patrick J. Robinson, Charles W. Faris, and Yoram Wind, *Industrial Buying and Creative Marketing* (Boston: Allyn & Bacon, 1967), p. 14.

---

[14]See Robinson et al., *Industrial Buying*, p. 25.

rebuy the decision may or may not incorporate all of the phases, depending on how different the new buy is from the straight rebuy across all eight buyphases. In the straight rebuy situation, in contrast, so much is already known about the circumstances of the buy that only the third and eighth buyphases are operative.

Management generally faces its greatest difficulties during the beginning phases of a new-task buy. That is because in the problem recognition and solution determination stages the influence groups are the largest and the buying influences the most numerous. After these phases have been completed, the buying process becomes more routinized, multiple-influence groups grow smaller, and the number of buying influences decreases. In most cases after the problem has been defined and the solution concept agreed upon, the technical people can develop specifications for the type of product or system to do the job and the purchasing people can select the sources most able to meet the specs.

The Search Process

Having considered the impact of the buyphase, the origin of need, and the type of good being sought upon the composition of the multiple-purchase influence group, and having noted briefly that the decision process may differ with respect to the nature of the buying situation, we now turn our attention to that part of the buying process known as the search procedure. The search, which is conducted by those persons who are involved at a given buyphase, may be for a specific type of good, for selection criteria, or for qualified sources of supply.[15] Figure 5–8 is a schematic representation of one buyer's search for the latter.

An examination of the figure reveals that once a stimulus is received, the buyer may search as many as six different areas in order to gain sufficient information to solve the problem of where to buy. The marketing implications of understanding the nature of the search process are quite evident. Information input by a prospective seller in any of the six areas can direct the searcher to a specific answer. As there is no way of predicting the sequence of the buyer's search, the seller's best strategy is to make certain that information about his or her qualifications as a source is well dispersed among the areas most likely to be searched by the prospective buyer. The fact that not all of these areas can be reached by salespeople means that the promotional mix must include advertising, direct mail, and other methods of nonpersonal sales promotion, including the use of catalogs.

Search with learning.   Given a sequence of searches by the same buyer (or group of buyers) for a source to supply goods to fill a recurring

---

[15]See Frederick E. Webster, Jr., "Modeling the Industrial Buying Process," *Journal of Marketing Research*, November 1965, p. 371.

FIGURE 5–8   The process of a buyer's search for a source of supply

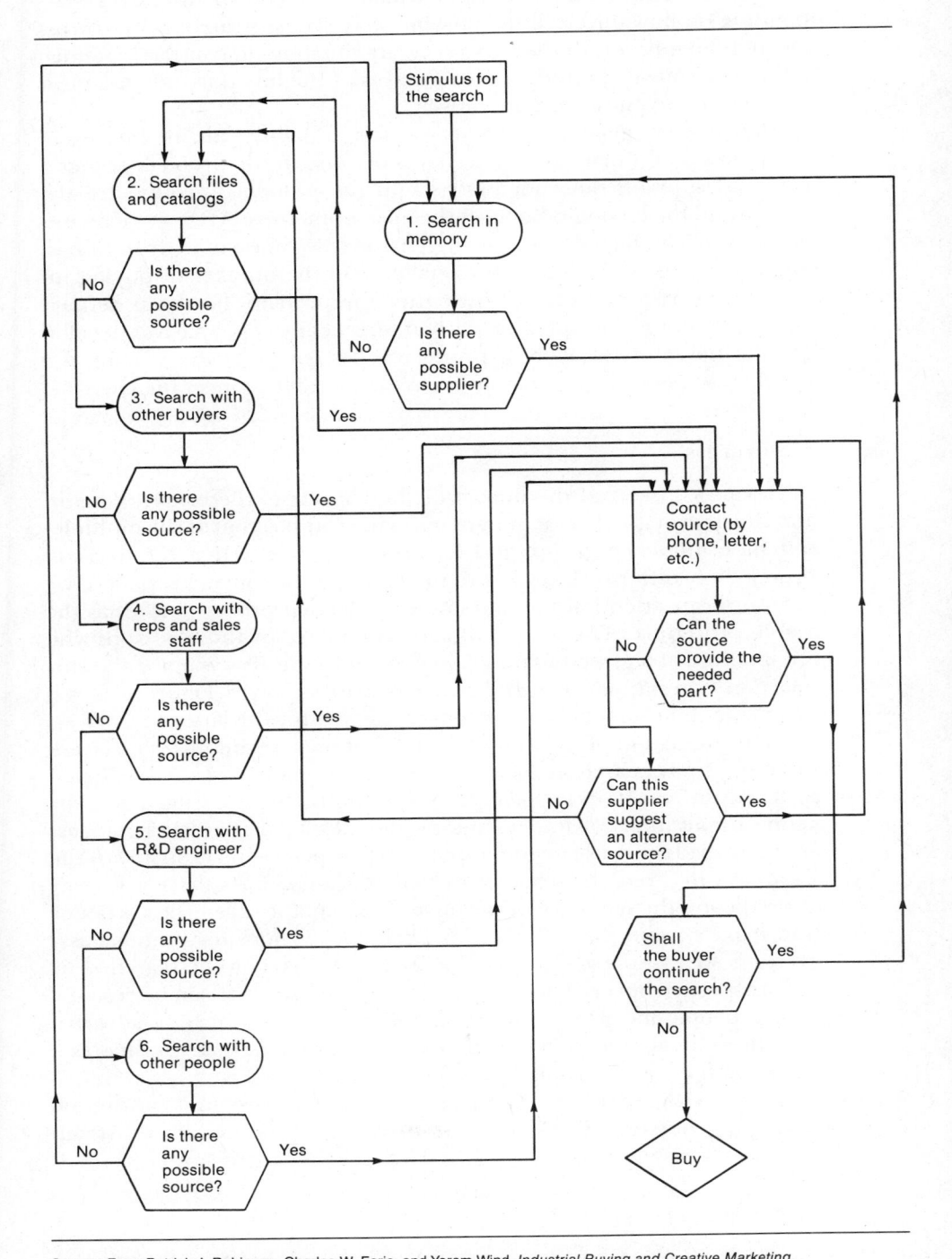

Source: From Patrick J. Robinson, Charles W. Faris, and Yoram Wind, *Industrial Buying and Creative Marketing*, p. 107. Copyright © 1967 by Allyn & Bacon, Inc., Boston. Reprinted by permission of the publisher and the Marketing Science Institute.

need, one would expect that with time the search process would become more efficient. Memory would lead the prospective buyer to a source that had performed well in the past. If prior experience with a source had been less than satisfactory, then memory would enable the buyer to start the search process with the most effective route used last time. Figure 5–9 illustrates such a search when learning from past experience is involved.

The Howard-Sheth model of consumer behavior discussed in Chapter 4 is a stimulus–response model involving learning. By substituting the concept of source for that of product, the Howard-Sheth model becomes readily applicable to an industrial buying situation. One value of looking at the industrial buying process in terms of a learning model is that the implications of the various buyclasses are readily seen.

For example, the straight rebuy, which generally represents the bulk of a firm's buying transactions, is characterized by behavior which is closely akin to what Howard and Sheth have termed *routinized response behavior* (RRB). In this type of buying situation, a great deal of learning has occurred, very little if any searching is required, and the buyer's response to a need stimulus is largely automatic. The purchasing department has a "list" of approved suppliers, and orders are routinely placed with these firms when needs arise. In many cases, straight rebuys are made by computers that track stock levels or reorder points.

The modified rebuy situation is one in which changes have taken place with respect to the buyer's requirements and/or some aspect of the nature of supply. Instead of a recurring problem with a "learned" solution, the buyer is faced with the need to have more information, to consider alternative solutions to the problem, and to conduct a search in order to find the best way of solving the problem at hand. Again we see a parallel with what Howard and Sheth have termed *limited problem-solving* (LPS) *behavior.*

Faced with this type of buying situation, the buyer is hopeful that once the problem has been solved, sufficient learning will have occurred to shift a modified rebuy back to a straight rebuy, which is easier and more economical to handle. Howard and Sheth would describe the same process in terms of movement along the learning curve from limited problem solving to routine response behavior.

The sellers who are not active suppliers to the buyer's firm might wish to delay this shift.[16] In fact, they might even develop a strategy of moving buyers from a straight buy situation to a modified rebuy situation. This is because under a modified rebuy these suppliers may be in the "evoked set" of possible alternatives, while in a straight rebuy they may not be considered at all.

Given a new-buy or new-task situation, information requirements are

---

[16]Ibid., p. 28.

FIGURE 5–9   A buyer's search process when learning is involved

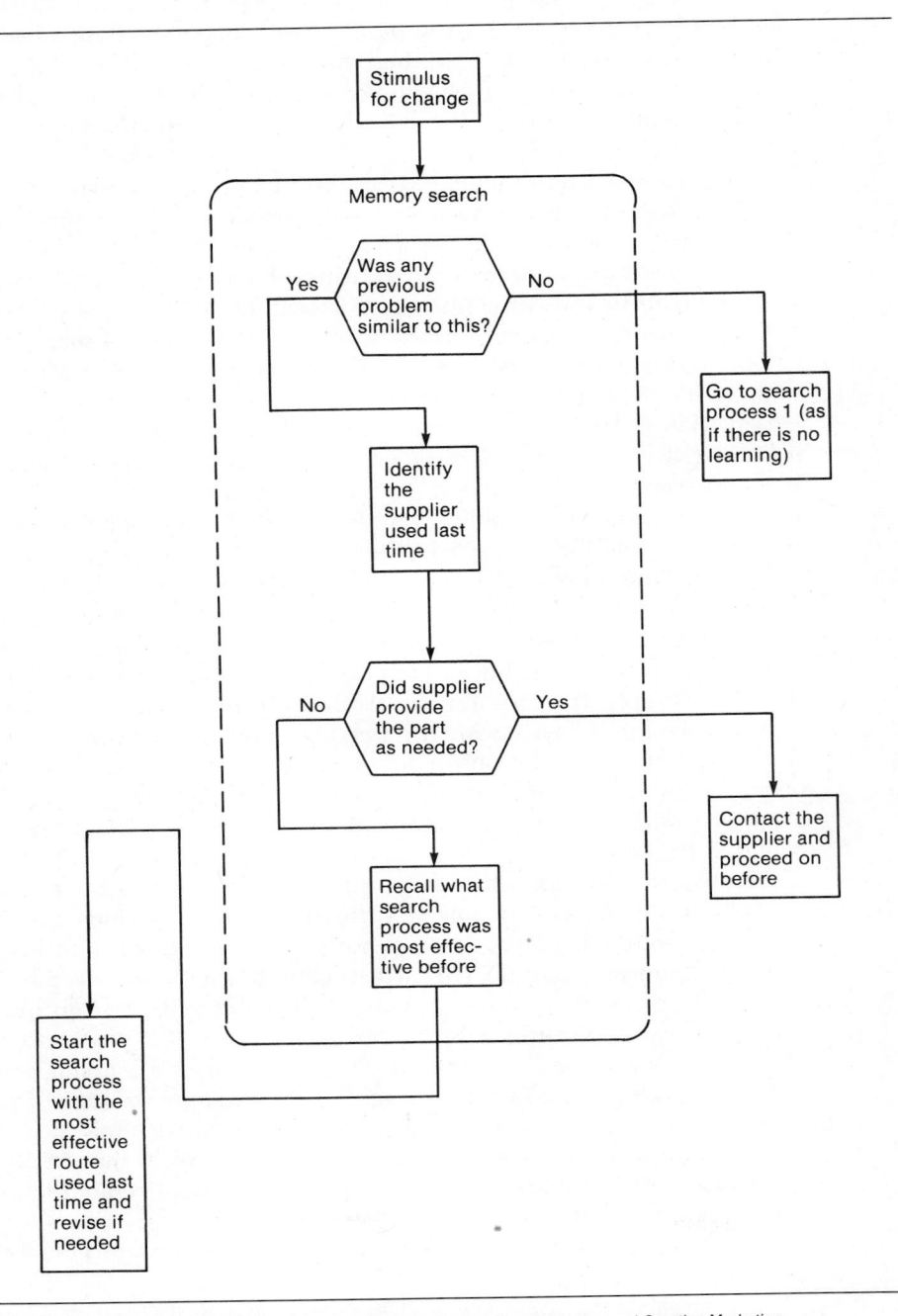

Source: From Patrick J. Robinson, Charles W. Faris, and Yoram Wind, *Industrial Buying and Creative Marketing*, p. 107. Copyright © 1967 by Allyn & Bacon, Inc., Boston. Reprinted by permission of the publisher and the Marketing Science Institute.

very heavy, and the consideration of many alternatives is necessary. The buyer behavior here is very close to what Howard and Sheth have described as *extensive problem-solving* (EPS) *behavior*. Very little learning has occurred, and a great deal of ideation is necessary. The process takes time and is expensive because of the information needs and the extensiveness of the search process.

An understanding of the Howard-Sheth model can help the marketing manager to direct the controllable variables of product, distribution, promotion, and price so that they can influence the industrial buying decision most effectively. For example, personal selling and advertising efforts can have a triggering effect in that they increase the potential buyer's awareness of needs to the point that the buying process starts. Moreover, if the buyer is required to search for clarification of alternatives by seeking additional information from personal or impersonal sources, promotional effort can be directed to these sources so that the information which the sellers want to impart about their offerings is available during the buyer's search.

In those situations where alternatives are known but must be compared, product quality, availability, and price are the important considerations. It is in these areas that the other variables of product design, distribution strategy, and pricing play their roles.

CONCLUSION

Knowledge of the industrial buying process provides insight as to where promotional effort should be directed with respect to different *phases* of the buying process. The recognition that decision making is carried on by groups of changing composition is a prerequisite to the design of an effective promotional strategy.

Buying decisions also differ with respect to the *kind* of buying situation faced. The amount of information needed by a buyer, the number of alternatives to be considered, and the extent of the search process all influence whether the buyer's behavior will be oriented toward a routinized response or toward what has been termed limited or extensive problem-solving behavior.

Finally, an understanding of the nature of the buying process, be it in the industrial or consumer market, is essential to the development of an effective marketing strategy. The controllable variables of product, distribution, promotion, and price, which were mentioned in Chapter 2, must be blended together in such a way that the product attributes, including quality, availability, and price, place the product in competition with other alternatives. In addition, the promotional strategy must be designed to inform potential buyers of the product's existence and to persuade them to buy.

QUESTIONS

1. Why does the industrial market have a larger volume of purchases than the consumer market, even though the number of industrial purchasing units is relatively small?

2. How do the producer, reseller, and governmental markets differ? In what ways are they similar with respect to marketing considerations?

3. Why do many businesses not seek governmental business?

4. Compare and contrast the classification criteria for consumer goods with those suggested for industrial goods.

5. What is derived demand, and how does it affect elasticity of demand in the industrial market?

6. Does the impact of derived demand fall evenly on each category of industrial goods? Explain.

7. What is the Standard Industrial Classification system, and how may it be of use to an industrial marketer?

8. Of what value, if any, is a knowledge of the goals of industrial buyers in the formulation of marketing strategy for a line of industrial goods?

9. What is meant by a multiple-purchase group? Under what circumstances may the composition of such a group change? Why is the ability to identify the membership of the relevant group so important to an industrial marketer?

10. What assumptions might be made about the composition of multiple-purchase influence groups concerned with buying major plant equipment, as contrasted wth groups concerned with the purchase of component parts?

11. How might different types of buying situations be contrasted in terms of the search process required? Explain the implications of search with learning for a seller of a "new" type of industrial product.

12. What is meant by the terms *new task, modified rebuy,* and *straight rebuy?* Relate these concepts to the Howard-Sheth model of buyer behavior.

13. Of what help is a model of buyer behavior in developing a marketing strategy for selling to the industrial market? What is required to adapt a consumer market model to an industrial market model?

Cases for part two

GOOD FOODS, INC.*

Introduction of electrical appliances

Good Foods, Inc., primarily a food manufacturer, was considering a long-range plan to undertake the manufacture and marketing of small electrical appliances.

PRODUCT LINES

Good Foods marketed a wide range of food products. Among the best known were the Ann Anderson line of cake, frosting, and brownie mixes. Good Foods also marketed a number of cereals, flour products, and frozen and refrigerated foods. Recent acquisition had diversified the company into the fast-food business, toys, and women's fashion clothing.

Good Foods also manufactured and distributed underwater mechanical devices plus baking ovens and mixers used by food manufacturers and institutional kitchens. These two product lines represented 2 percent of Good Foods' revenue and 0.1 percent of its before-tax profits.

---

*Written by James R. Taylor, Sebastian S. Kresge Professor of Marketing, Graduate School of Business Administration, The University of Michigan, Ann Arbor.

Good Foods had been in this business since World War II and now considered both product lines to be a poor return on investment.

BRANDING POLICIES

The name Ann Anderson was one of Good Foods' prime assets. It had been carefully cultivated, with over $10 million having been spent to put the name across to the public. So successful had this campaign been that a company survey revealed that 89 percent of the housewives in the United States recognized the name Ann Anderson, and 4 percent correctly identified it with Good Foods, Inc.

ADVERTISING MIX

The total Good Foods advertising expenditures for this year were estimated to be about $50 million. Almost half of the money was for television ($25 million), with newspapers ($10 million) and magazines ($15 million) accounting for the bulk of the remainder.

SMALL APPLIANCE PROJECT

A special project was started in which a group of engineers were asked to develop prototypes of various electrical appliances. Four products—a toaster, an electric frying pan, an iron, and a coffee maker—were developed.

Several consumer tests of these four appliances had been conducted throughout the product development process. All four appliances compared favorably with those of competitors during home-use tests. These tests were conducted with appliance owners throughout the United States.

While the new appliances were not major breakthroughs in design, they did incorporate the most up-to-date features that characterized competitive appliances. All of Good Foods' home-use tests were conducted blind, in the sense that the appliance owner was not told who manufactured the new appliances.

The competition in the appliance business was characterized as intense, with many firms sharing the market. Several large manufacturers, such as General Electric, Sunbeam, and Toast Master, were well established in the traditional appliances distribution channels (appliance outlets, discount houses, hardware outlets, etc.). Several manufacturers followed the policy of franchising the retail outlets for their entire line of appliances. Other manufacturers followed an intensive distribution policy allowing their products to be sold in an array of retail outlets, including discount houses.

The small appliance business showed rapid expansion after World War II. During the 1960s and early part of the 1970s, the rate of growth slowed to an expansion rate of 5 percent a year.

Exhibit 1 indicates the pattern of sales for the last few years by product type. Good Foods' executives considered a 10 percent penetration of this market potential a real possibility. This estimate was based in part on their unique distribution strategy for the new appliance line.

EXHIBIT 1   Kitchen electrics sales patterns (units)

Product type	Last year	This year	Next year (estimated)
1. Irons	9,915,000	9,475,000	9,600,000
2. Coffee makers	8,200,000	8,500,000	8,800,000
3. Toasters	5,800,000	6,200,000	6,600,000
4. Blenders	4,900,000	6,100,000	5,900,000
5. Can openers	5,100,000	5,500,000	5,800,000
6. Mixers	4,560,000	4,900,000	5,100,000
7. Frying pans	2,975,000	3,300,000	3,500,000
8. Broilers	2,770,000	2,640,000	2,500,000
9. Corn poppers	1,850,000	2,200,000	2,600,000
10. Slicing knives	2,500,000	2,100,000	2,000,000

Source: *Merchandising Week.*

The marketing department had debated the question of appropriate channels of distribution for their appliance line. Since Good Foods was well established on the food distribution channel, it was argued that this channel offered the best opportunity for the new line. As far as the marketing executives knew, supermarkets were not carrying appliances, and this offered an excellent opportunity to open a new channel of distribution for the sale of appliances. In recent years, supermarkets had expanded into new areas, including kitchenware items. Homemakers appeared to be willing to buy items like cake pans and regular pots and pans in supermarkets. An additional factor was that the appliance line could carry the Ann Anderson brand, which was well established in the mind of the average supermarket shopper. All in all, the marketing executives were convinced that the regular grocery channel of distribution was the logical place to distribute the new appliance line.

The new line was to be priced competitively with the leading sellers in the field. The average unit selling price at retail was $16, and the unit costs were approximately the same for all four products. This pricing policy allowed approximately a 50 percent margin for the supermarkets.

This markup represented a substantially higher margin than supermarkets received on items such as cereals and canned goods. Management expected this margin to be a major incentive for the supermarkets to handle the new appliance line.

Since Ann Anderson was such a well-established brand name, only moderate advertising was planned for the new line. It was argued that homemakers visit supermarkets at least once a week and that they naturally notice the appliance display. An advertising budget of $2 million a year was proposed for the first few years of new-product introduction.

Good Foods' executives were excited about the new appliance line and were anticipating long-term success in the appliance business. A product manager from the cereal division was chosen to handle the marketing of the new line. (Cost data for the project are given in Exhibit 2.)

EXHIBIT 2   Cost data

	Cost per case*	Total
Variable costs		
Transportation	$ 3.60	
Broken goods	0.30	
Warehousing	1.00	
Parts and materials	28.00	
Packaging	3.10	
Labor and overhead	6.00	
Fixed costs		
Building machinery and equipment†		$4,850,000
Start-up costs‡		650,000
Maintenance		100,000
Other expenses		50,000

*Six items were included in a case. For example, six coffee makers were to be shipped in one case.
†To be depreciated over 10 years.
‡To be amortized over 10 years.

QUESTIONS

1. Evaluate the decision of Good Foods' management to enter the appliance business. What factors weigh in favor of the decision, and what factors weigh against the decision?

2. Has an adequate market/financial analysis been presented? Support your position.

DENNIS D'ANGELO LOOKS FOR AN APARTMENT

When Dennis D'Angelo was about to begin his MBA program at Midwest University in Irwinton, the 1983 winter term was fast approaching. At age 21, Dennis was one of the youngest people entering that term. He had just graduated from a small engineering school in upstate New York, and he wasn't sure he wanted to begin graduate work right away. Time constraints during his final semester as an undergraduate, however, had forced him to decide between attending Midwest U, one of the top 10 MBA schools, and turning down that opportunity in hopes of acquiring a job. His conservative attitude made him choose a sure thing and start school right away. Beginning in January meant that he would have to attend school during the summer in order to catch up with the Class of 1984, which had entered the program in the fall of 1982. With the decision made to start school, Dennis was determined to do well.

FIRST SEARCH FOR AN APARTMENT

It was a 12-hour drive from his parent's home in New Jersey to the town of Irwinton. Dennis made the trip the Monday before orientation. His most important problem at the time was finding housing, both for

the first night and for the 16 months he would be living there. For the first night Dennis decided to stay at a fraternity, as he used to do when hitchhiking. This seemed best for two reasons. First, it was the least expensive way he could think of to spend the first night. Second, it provided the opportunity to talk to other students who knew the area and could give him some helpful advice about finding housing.

The address he received at the Student Union took him to the north side of campus on a small one-way street. Dennis had chosen a graduate fraternity since he felt that its members would be of more help in finding permanent housing. Leaving almost everything he owned in the car, Dennis took only what he would need for the night and settled on the living room sofa of the two-story house.

Later, after Dennis had explained his situation, the brothers of the house came to the conclusion that the best way to find housing, on or off campus, was through the Campus Housing Office. They explained that very little housing would be available since most people were situated for the full school year. Irwinton had a population of 110,000, of whom 30,000 were students attending Midwest University. Most of the nonstudents who worked in town worked for the university. There was no major industry in town, and the closest industrial center was 50 miles away. The next day, with directions from the fraternity brothers, Dennis set out on foot for the Campus Housing Office.

As an undergraduate, Dennis had spent three years in the same dormitory room with a friend he had met during his freshman year. The room was ideally situated—close to classrooms, the Student Union, and a shopping center. Its one disadvantage, as he saw it, was the rule against cooking in the rooms. The hot plate and toaster oven which they had used had to be kept unplugged and often had to be hidden.

After three years of this, Dennis felt that it was time to have an apartment in which he could cook and relax. The only other requirement for his housing was that it be inexpensive. Since his father was funding his education and living expenses, Dennis did not want to burden him any more than absolutely necessary. This would be his first apartment, though, and he didn't know what to look for in features. He could only wait and see the apartment to know whether it was right for him. His intention was to find an apartment which would serve him the entire time that he was at Irwinton. Therefore, he was depending heavily on the information and help he obtained at the Campus Housing Office.

The crowd at the office when Dennis arrived was not conducive to individual attention. Apparently a substantial number of students were entering at the same time, all of whom were seeking housing. Dennis, happy that he had not stayed another day in New Jersey as he had originally intended, was quickly handed the appropriate forms and shown a desk at which he could fill them out. Listening to the students

around him, he soon realized that the openings left were in short supply. Instead of making a decision on the best apartment for him, he found himself choosing among the few university-owned apartments left on campus. The off-campus apartments available through the office had already been taken. Waiting anxiously for his assignment, Dennis watched more and more students file in, looking for housing.

The apartment he finally was offered was listed as a four-man apartment for $433 per person per semester and was located on the outskirts of campus. The woman getting signatures on leases could offer no other assistance or information, which left Dennis with the choice of either signing the lease or seeking housing elsewhere. He decided in favor of the sure thing and signed the lease.

Dennis considered what he had just done all the way back to the fraternity house. He finally came to the conclusion that it was the only decision he could have made under the circumstances. No one at the fraternity house could give him any indication of the merits of his choice since the fraternity members were unfamiliar with the apartment building, but they did give him directions for getting there.

On the way over, Dennis had absolutely no idea what type of apartment to expect. Without knowing the age of the building, he couldn't imagine what it looked like. When he got to the building, however, he saw that it was a modern brick apartment complex. As he entered the lobby, he saw a TV set with several couches and chairs arranged in front of it.

Dennis had been instructed to report to the resident director for his key. She seemed to be a pleasant middle-aged woman, but she wasted no time in laying down the rules and regulations for the building before handing over the key.

After this short encounter, Dennis headed up the stairs to the third floor to inspect his new apartment. He was met there by Ken, one of his new roommates, who had lived there previously. Ken showed Dennis around the apartment but made it clear that he didn't like the idea of having new roommates. His original roommates had found new housing arrangements for reasons unknown to Dennis. Ken was a junior in mechanical engineering with interests in football and racquetball. However, it didn't look as if they would get along well except by avoiding each other.

The apartment was also a disappointment. The kitchen contained a half-size refrigerator, a sink, and a stove, all of which needed cleaning. The dining room/living room/kitchen was approximately 10' × 10'. The bedroom contained two double-bunk beds, the two desks which could fit into the room, and a one-piece dresser and closet for four, which spanned one wall. The only thing he could compare it to was the dormitory at the summer camp that he had stayed at as a child.

More and more, Dennis found himself questioning his decision to

attend Midwest University. He was unsure of continuing his education so soon without work experience. It had snowed since his arrival. And now it looked as if his apartment would not be an escape.

While Dennis considered these things, Ken left, indicating that he would be back in a week. Soon after that, Carl walked in. He was a junior transfer student from one of Midwest University's other campuses. Although Dennis and Carl were both pilots and could talk forever about flying, Dennis found Carl boring. At this point Dennis decided that he was being too critical. He felt that it was time to make the best of things since it seemed as though he was trapped there. Still, he didn't find moving in enjoyable. Nor did he look forward to the approaching school term.

Dennis spent the rest of the week exploring the campus and attending orientation meetings. At the same time, he decided to look into the possibility of finding a new apartment. He didn't have much hope of doing so, considering the lack of openings at the housing office. In addition, he would have to find someone to take over his present lease.

It was at this point that Dennis was introduced to Paul Morton. Paul had arrived at Irwinton too late to find campus housing but was interested in moving into Dennis's building in order to be close to friends.

SECOND SEARCH FOR AN APARTMENT

Without making a definite commitment to sign over the lease until he had found a new apartment, Dennis began a more intensive search for a new place to live. His previous experience had taught him a few things about what to look for in apartments. He decided that he wanted a furnished apartment, in off-campus housing, with a private bedroom and a parking lot, as inexpensive as possible, and close enough to campus to be able to walk to school.

Friends in the apartment building at which Dennis was staying told him to keep away from two of the major realty companies but could offer no further assistance. Talking to other MBA students also turned out to be unhelpful. Many had arrived as early as September. Some lived in unfurnished apartments or too far from campus. Most were of the opinion that there was little or no housing left in town. Those who hadn't found their housing through friends had found it through advertisements in newspapers.

Although he knew that there was little housing available in town, Dennis decided to try looking for advertisements posted on the bulletin board in the Student Union. While at the Union, he found advertisements that either did not satisfy his requirements or didn't mention the features in which he was interested. He decided to answer the latter type. Of the seven people he called, only one seemed to offer something

interesting enough to explore further. The others were either looking for groups or were located in a neighboring town. One two-bedroom apartment, however, was within easy walking distance and offered the option of renting a single bedroom for $90 per month or sharing the other bedroom for $80 per month. The two current tenants had signed the lease with a third person who had never shown up in the fall, leaving them to split the rent which they couldn't afford by themselves. Dennis made an appointment for the following day to look over the apartment and meet the tenants.

George was a junior in mechanical engineering. During the summer he was employed in the design department of a large firm near his home. Harry was also a junior, but in computer engineering. While at school he had a job with a research group in the university. Both seemed extremely friendly and easygoing.

The apartment also impressed Dennis as being more in line with what he wanted. It had a full kitchen with a full-size refrigerator, garbage disposal, stove, oven, and dishwasher. The kitchen was separated from the living room by a bar which served as the dining table. The living room alone was larger than the kitchen/living room in the other apartment. The two bedrooms were approximately the same in size, and each contained a dresser, a desk, a chair, and a bed with box springs and a mattress. There was a parking lot with enough space for all of the tenants. Overall, the apartment seemed ideal for what Dennis wanted. He decided to search no further and arranged to move in that Saturday after orientation and registration were completed. However, no lease was ever signed and no commitment was made as to the length of stay.

Dennis enjoyed moving in this time. With the lease to the other apartment signed by Paul Morton and the Campus Housing Office, Dennis made himself comfortable in his new home. From January through mid-March he was happy with his decision. Living 20 minutes from the main section of town, 10 minutes from school, and 10 minutes from the gym allowed him to walk everywhere except the grocery store. His next-door neighbors, one a junior in political science and the other a graduate student in public administration, soon became close friends. In addition, Dennis found several other MBA students living in the area.

Late in March, however, George began to annoy Dennis. It was little irritating things which caused Dennis to avoid George more and more. In short, a personality clash brought his joy to an end. By the end of March, Dennis's neighbors had decided to move to a new apartment with a lower rent. He tried to join them, but they already had enough people to fill the apartment. At school, friendships which had been formed during the semester tended to become living arrangements. Finally, Dennis found a friend, Jeff Sanderson, also an MBA student, who was looking for a roommate.

Considering all of these things, Dennis felt like moving again. At first,

this was just a thought. However, in April, as the winter term was coming to a close, Jeff's position became urgent. He was living in a dormitory which was closing for the summer. With one week before final exams, there was little time to find an apartment.

THIRD SEARCH FOR AN APARTMENT

On Friday night, before the week of final exams began, Dennis and Jeff got together to find an apartment. Comparing criteria for a desirable apartment, they found themselves in agreement on all points. They were looking for an inexpensive apartment, near the school, with separate bedrooms for each of them. Dennis also needed a place to park his car. And it was desirable, but not necessary, to have a fall option on the lease.

Irwinton is relatively empty in the summer. Most of the 30,000 students leave for home and summer work. Another factor affecting the availability of housing at that time is that most leases are for the period from August through July. Therefore, a lot of apartments are open for sublet at great discounts during the summer months, since students are happy to get any contribution they can toward the rent they are liable for while on vacation.

This time Dennis and Jeff knew exactly where to find information on available apartments. They decided that the library offered the best selection of "for rent" signs. Keeping in mind the requirements that they had agreed upon, they searched the entire bulletin board, collecting 17 phone numbers to call for more information.

The phone conversations were similar to those that Dennis had had before. Some of the apartments were too expensive or too far or were not available for two persons. However, Dennis and Jeff made five appointments to visit apartments the same night.

The field narrowed somewhat after they inspected the apartments. A few were too expensive for what they offered. By the end of the night Dennis and Jeff had decided on one apartment as their primary choice and on two others as second and third choices. The first-choice apartment was unofficially taken. However, the prospective tenants were still looking for a better place. With a little pressure from Jeff, a firm offer of $150 per month was accepted.

The apartment was at least as large as the one Dennis was living in. There were two bedrooms, a bathroom separated into a shower/toilet area and the sink area, a large kitchen, a separate dining area, and a living room. Sliding screen doors opened onto a gravel patio since the apartment was on the ground level.

The second-choice apartment was upstairs in the same building. Its occupants said that they had been offered $180 for it. As it turned out,

they had never been offered more than $160 by other MBA students who soon moved in for the summer.

Without a fall option, Dennis and Jeff had to look for another apartment for the fall. Although they were happy with their present apartment, which was only two minutes' walking distance from campus, it commanded a substantial price. Its tenants during the fall and winter terms paid $375 a month for the apartment.

Now the problem was to find a new apartment. Although Dennis and Jeff had the advantage of experience and knowledge of the area, they expected the search to be difficult because of the scarcity of housing which would again develop with the influx of approximately 30,000 students.

Even though their desired requirements for a new apartment remained the same, they recognized that these would be difficult to meet. It would not be a buyer's market for the fall term. In addition, they wished to rent an apartment which they could dispose of at graduation in April. Therefore, they wanted a lease which ended in April. This would be a difficult combination of criteria to satisfy.

QUESTIONS

1. Evaluate Dennis D'Angelo's search for an apartment. What mistakes did he make? How would you have done it differently?

2. Develop a search plan for Dennis and Jeff to follow in locating a suitable apartment for the fall and winter terms.

HINESBURY MILLS (A)*

In spring 1978, executives at Hinesbury Mills, Inc., a leading foods manufacturer, were concerned over competitive developments which posed a potentially severe threat to their brand's share of the United States cake mix market. Hinesbury was one of three major brands in this market; it also faced competition from several minor brands and private label brands.[1]

Until recently, all brands had been selling essentially the same product line of regular cake mixes in which shortening cake predominated. Each brand offered a basic core of staple flavors such as chocolate, yellow, and white cakes, to which were added a variety of minor flavors which changed periodically. The strategy of the three major brands was essentially one of flavor proliferation; minor and private labels offered less choice, competing primarily on the basis of price. In January 1978, Hinesbury Mills had introduced a new line of premium cake mixes, containing superior quality ingredients which included real butter. How-

---

*Reprinted from *Stanford Business Cases 1978* with permission of the Publishers, Stanford University Graduate School of Business, ©1977 by the Board of Trustees of the Leland Stanford Junior University.

[1]The brand names and some of the data in this case have been disguised.

ever, before the company had time to evaluate the impact of the new line on the market and conduct any meaningful market research, its two major competitors both introduced new cake mixes. While priced at the same level as existing standard mixes, the new entrants appeared as though they might also offer the higher-quality appeal of HM's new premium line, achieved in their case through requiring purchasers to add their own butter.

THE CAKE MIX MARKET

At that time, American consumers had three major sources of cake available: (a) ready-made cakes purchased from bakeries or supermarkets; (b) entirely home-made cakes; (c) cakes prepared at home from manufactured mixes. Total cake consumption per capita had remained fairly constant over the years, with cake mixes accounting for about one third of all cakes consumed. Three main types of cake mix products were available: regular two-layer size, loaf or one-layer size, and angel/chiffon type.

The product category of immediate concern to Hinesbury executives was the two-layer type which, with an annual market of some 30 million 12-pack cases, accounted for the major portion of the total cake mix market. Although experiencing a modest annual growth rate, the long-term outlook for the two-layer cake mix market suggested that the product might be reaching the mature stage in its life cycle. Management knew that the per capita consumption of this type was declining gradually in the face of increasing competition for the consumer's dollar from other prepared desserts.

HINESBURY'S MARKET STRATEGY

Hinesbury Mills had pioneered the development of modern cake mixes in the mid-1950s. Over the years, the company had faced strong competition from Allied Foods Corporation and Concorn Kitchens, Inc. and, to a lesser extent, from a number of regional and private label brands—generally referred to as "price brands" since this formed the basis of their competitive strategy. The other two major brands (Allied and Concorn) focused their marketing efforts on a strategy of heavy and consistent promotion aimed at building up distinctive images of themselves in consumers' minds. Allied Foods emphasized the "moistness" characteristic of cakes made with its mix, while Concorn's advertising concentrated on the flavor quality of its product. Hinesbury's response to these competitive attitudes was to adopt a strategy of proliferating its product line by offering an even wider range of flavors and by building

markets through widespread use of deals.[2] By combining a continuous program of product improvement with new flavor introductions and heavy promotional expenditures, HM had been able to maintain their position as the market leader.

In the late 1970s, however, Hinesbury began to find itself faced with a disturbing loss of market share and weakened distribution. The company fought back with strategic actions which included curtailing the proliferation of flavors, intensively pushing sales, and making heavy promotional expenditures with an emphasis on price deals. Most important of all, in the view of HM executives, was the introduction of a premium line of high-quality cake mixes with superior ingredients including real butter and a guaranteed shelf life of 24 months. This was a technological breakthrough and was designed to appeal to an identified consumer need, capitalizing on that large section of the existing market whom research had shown to want a moister, higher-quality end product. It was also the first product innovation to disturb the existing structure of the market.

Although it retailed at a recommended price of 99 cents, as against a recommended 79 cents for the standard mix, initial acceptance of the premium line appeared very favorable and the decision was soon made to expand distribution nationwide. Like all cake mixes, heavy emphasis was placed on price deals. However, it was anticipated that six months would be needed to build up the product and obtain conclusive data on its impact on both regular cake mix sales and HM's overall market share.

COMPETITIVE ACTION

To the dismay of Hinesbury executives, their premium line had only been in national distribution seven weeks when both major competitors countered with strategic moves which posed a severe threat to Hinesbury's own strategy. Virtually identical product lines were launched within a few days of each other by Concorn (into a midwestern test market) and by Allied Foods (which immediately went national). Their entries were both regularly priced (recommended retail price of 79 cents) cake mixes in two flavors called Butter Chocolate and Butter Yellow. Unlike the standard mix, which contained an inexpensive shortening, or Hinesbury's premium mix with its butter content, these new products contained no shortening at all. Instead, they called for the consumer to *add her own butter* to their "specially prepared formula,"

---

[2]Deals are cut-price offers to consumers, such as "10 cents off," "three for the price of two," etc. Dealing is widely practiced in the packaged foods industry as well as in certain product areas of the drug and cosmetics industries, notably when there are several large brands competing with essentially similar products.

thus allegedly producing the same end product for which Hinesbury was asking consumers to pay an extra 20 cents. In practice, there were certain distinguishable differences between the premium and add-butter end products. Premium mix cakes, while perceived by many as being of higher quality and more moist than the standard mix versions, still retained the latter's light and fluffy consistency. The add-butter cakes, by contrast, tended to have a somewhat denser and closer-grained texture, more akin to brownies or cupcakes. Again, it was believed that many consumers regarded the add-butter end product to be of higher quality than standard mix cake.

It was assumed by HM executives that if the initial move with chocolate and yellow flavors was successful, the two competitors would subsequently introduce add-butter versions in other flavors. Moreover, management noted three significant strengths to the competition's approach. First, ingredient costs to the manufacturer were reduced in that no shortening need be placed in the mix. Since the add-butter product sold at the same price as the standard mix, this meant higher unit profits. Second, the new products possessed a similar appeal to Hinesbury's premium line—that of the higher quality resulting from inclusion of butter as an ingredient—but with the further characteristic of allowing consumers to add their own butter to the prepared mix and thus "individualize" the cake. On the other hand, of course, this method lacked the convenience inherent in a complete mix. Third, it appeared likely that many consumers would not perceive the addition of an ingredient such as butter, which they already had in the home, as an incremental cost. If the cost of butter were added to the price of the competitive mix, this would bring the total cost of the cake up to the same level as Hinesbury's premium offering, but it seemed probable that in many cases the consumer would still see the cost of the cake as 79 cents.

HINESBURY MILLS' REACTION

HM was now offering two lines of cake mix (standard and premium) while its two major competitors were offering standard and add-butter lines. No information existed on how market share might break down among these three lines and among the different brands once the situation stabilized. The principal question for Hinesbury management was how the introduction of the new add-butter line by the competition would affect its own brand standing, but there were other problems too. Would the add-butter line appeal to the same consumers as HM's premium line? Should Hinesbury Mills also have an add-butter offering? To what extent would consumers be willing to pay a higher pack price for a better quality, convenience product? In essence there was a myriad

of possible alternatives HM could follow in terms of the flavor, texture, quality, price, and convenience of the mix itself. Beyond that, there existed a wide variety of marketing strategies which might be undertaken.

It was felt imperative to respond quickly to the competitive threat, but the problem was considered to be the need to quickly obtain sufficient information to permit an early strategic decision. At that point in time, nobody really had any firm information at all on the current state of the market. However, following an all-day conference, three immediate actions were decided upon.

First, the Research and Development department was told to begin developing an add-butter line in case it was subsequently decided to offer such a product on the market under the Hinesbury Mills label. Second, a contract was to be initiated with the A. C. Nielsen Company to monitor the performance of both the Allied Foods and Concorn Kitchens add-butter lines in the market. Last, it was decided to undertake development of a computer model of the cake market. Executives believed that by actually simulating, in a computer-based model, the decision process that various consumer types make in buying a cake, they could develop an understanding of the purchase process and how decisions were arrived at under different circumstances. This might then permit predictions of the market performance of standard, premium, and add-butter lines. The simulation approach had the added advantages of being much faster and cheaper than actual market testing of different product formulations under differing marketing strategies, as well as keeping HM actions secret from the competition.

The Marketing Research department was assigned the task of building the simulation model. After some discussion, it was decided that they should begin by developing an explicit but fairly simple representation of the consumer decision process involved in the purchase of a cake mix. At the same time, it was decided to identify clearly some of the principal needs that a consumer might have concerning cakes. To help them in this task, executives in the department proposed to draw on transcripts of some interviews with housewives on their cake-buying and cake-making habits. These interviews were recently conducted for the company by a well-known research firm. Some extracts from the interviews are shown in Exhibit 1.

QUESTIONS

1. Identify the important product characteristics which affect choice decisions in this product category. What are the differences between regular cake, premium, and add-butter in terms of these characteristics?

2. What are the important segmenting variables in the cake mix market?

3. What is the role of price in consumer choice given that there is a great deal of dealing and given that the consumer is often called upon to add expensive ingredients?

4. Develop a flow chart of consumer choice in the cake mix market. Exhibit 1 should be of help in developing this process model.

5. How could your process model, developed in Question 4 above, be used to evaluate strategic alternatives for Hinesbury?

6. What alternative strategies should Hinesbury consider?

EXHIBIT 1   Research company's report on housewives' cake-buying and cake-making habits

---

Extracts from interviews conducted with housewives

1. "Yes, I use quite a lot of cake mixes. You know how it is with three boys—they like to have something sweet at dinnertime, so I often quickly whip up a cake for them. My husband likes them too, but I won't let him have too much if it's one of those rich, heavy ones: he's really got to watch his weight these days (laughs) . . . I guess I bake about one cake a week, sometimes two. Generally I get Concorn's. I think their flavors are nicer than the other brands, and the quality's good, too. But usually I'll look first to see if any of the main brands have got any special offers. My husband's been on short time at the plant for nearly three months now, so I have to watch the pennies. Can't afford to be too extravagant. Cake's quite a good buy really."

2. "No, I don't buy cake mixes that often—usually it's just for some special occasion, and when I do I like to get the best, and then take a bit of time and trouble over it. You know, even with a good brand like Hinesbury or Concorn you've got to be prepared to put in a few ingredients of your own. I've got a special recipe I use adding sour cream—makes a delicious cake, you know, rich and moist."

3. "I bake a lot of cakes. We often have them with the evening meal. Most times we prefer to have a light spongy cake which I serve with ice cream. For special occasions though, I'll make an extra fancy one and decorate it really nicely. I enjoy doing my own cooking, but just can't give it the time that I'd like to. So I want something that's quick and fairly foolproof."

4. "I've got two kids—and they're always demanding sweet things, so I try to have some sort of cake around most of the time. Mostly, I just put it on the table at dinnertime and let them have as much as they want. Don't care for it much after a meat dish myself, but sometimes I'll make myself a snack during the day and have a sandwich and some cake with a glass of milk when the kids are off at school and I can't be bothered to cook myself lunch . . . No, I really don't worry about the brand, can't say I can tell the difference myself, especially when there's a frosting on top. They're all good enough. I just look to see if any brand has a few cents off, same as I do with detergent."

5. "I'm pretty choosy about the brands I buy—the quality does vary. Allied Foods makes the best lemon I think, but I don't like their chocolate so well—Hinesbury is much the nicest there . . . One thing, though, I like to put in a few extra touches of my own—makes me feel it's my cake and not just some home economist's. That way I feel I can still take some of the credit for the way it turns out. I've still got all of my mother's old cookbooks and sometimes I get ideas out of these, particularly if I want to make a really rich cake for some special occasion."

6. "Yeah, I guess we occasionally have cake with the evening meal. They're pretty quick

EXHIBIT 1 *(concluded)*

and easy to make and my nine-year-old likes putting on the topping. Usually I pick up two or three packages of mix at the market whenever I notice there's a good deal on. Quality? No I don't think there's really much difference between the main brands, though I guess some of the others mightn't be too hot. I tried a private label once because it was cheaper, but it was pretty bad. Came out all heavy and taste-less. So now I stick with brands like Con-corn, Hinesbury, and Allied. Better to be safe than sorry, I guess."

7. "I reckon the only time we have cake is just three or four times a year when it's some-one's birthday or something. I'm not much of a cook, but if you stick with one of the quality brands and get a flavor you know people like, it's pretty hard to go wrong if you just follow the instructions. Mind you, there was the time I forgot to set the timer . . ."(giggles)

8. "My husband says I spend more time on gas driving around the different markets than I save on discounts and special of-fers. But I get a real charge out of looking for bargains. If I see something like Con-corn cake mix with a really good offer on it, I just can't resist it. D'you know, last week I bought *six* packets of some new flavors they were bringing out—they were offering *10 cents off* a pack. I guess we'll all be eating cake now every day for the next three weeks."

9. "I like to make a rich fudge cake as a treat for my grandchildren when they visit me, but personally I prefer something lighter and not so sweet to have with coffee around mid-morning."

10. "There are four of us sharing this apart-ment, see, and we take turns doing the cooking. It's really neat the way it works out—we each do a week at a time. I can never get over how good the two boys are at it. I'm the only one who makes cake though—it's a fun thing to do and I like ex-perimenting with different types of cake and adding little touches of my own . . ."

11. ". . . I like a cake with a nice fluffy consist-ency. Not one of those heavy ones you get in some flavors . . ."

12. "Generally, I make a cake about once a month. My husband has a sweet tooth and likes cake at dinner sometimes or for a quick bite when we get home from after-noon classes. I like a fairly moist consist-ency, not too sickly sweet, with lots of flavor and a pretty appearance. I guess they're all fairly easy to make. Usually, I get Hinesbury, except I watch out for spe-cials—I'd buy any major brand on special. Some of the really cheapo ones haven't much taste. Too dry, too."

13. "We often have cake for dinner. Person-ally, I prefer buying the frozen kind—the ready-made ones. They taste nicer and they're much easier. My daughters'll bake a cake from a mix recipe sometimes. I really don't know why, because they al-ways seem to manage to have them crum-ble all over. So if I'm buying a mix, I just look for something cheap."

14. "The two things I look for in a good cake are taste and consistency. I don't like eat-ing something that looks and tastes like a bathroom sponge, but want a cake I can get my teeth into."

MICROSTAR, INC.*

Developing a marketing plan

Bob Nederlander approached fraternity brother Sean Deson in November 1983 about the possibility of a partnership in a computer consulting firm. Bob, whose first attempt at establishing the business had not been successful, already incorporated the firm under the name of Microstar Services, Inc. He had hoped to operate as a profitable business for the summer of 1983 but was unable to attract any customers. He realized that Microstar's failure was due to a lack of strategic planning with regard to the customers he planned to attract and the services he planned to offer. The second time around, he was determined to run a successful venture, and he was willing to devote much time to planning the business before it actually began to operate in May 1984.

Sean accepted Bob's offer of a partnership in Microstar. The company now comprised Bob Nederlander, Sean Deson, and Paul Dworkin. Bob, an economics and computer science major at The University of Michigan, served as a manager at Pine Knob Music Theater for six years and as an asset treasurer at the Pine Knob box office for two years. As original founder, he is now president of Microstar, responsible for man-

---

*Written by Leo Burnett Fellow Sarah Deson under the direction of Professor Martin R. Warshaw, Graduate School of Business Administration, The University of Michigan.

agement functions and obtaining customers. Sean, a computer technology and management major at The University of Michigan, was employed as the manager of an amusement game room for two years, and for the past year he has been tutoring other computer science students at Michigan. As executive vice president, he is responsible for managerial duties and sales of Microstar's services. Paul is the computer genius of the business, having completed general-purpose programming for Beaumont Hospital in Detroit during the summer of 1983. He is presently a computer and communication sciences major at Carnegie Mellon University. He has had no managerial experience. As vice president, his duties are completely technical. He is in charge of all systems designs, programming, and any other computer-related functions.

As a first step in establishing a successful venture, Sean and Bob wanted a clear definition of their business. After numerous informal discussions with small businessmen, they reached the conclusion that these consumers would prefer "one-stop shopping" when purchasing and implementing a computer system. At present, in order to implement a computer system, a consumer will first go to a computer retail outlet to decide on a system. He then may hire a consultant from a different place, have the system installed, as well as find someone else to teach the employees how to use the system or send the employees to class. Finally, he may purchase the software from either the same or a different retailer. Sean and Bob felt that there was a niche in the market for a company that would offer all the services a business would require to become computerized. Microstar would promote complete computer solutions which would include computer services such as consulting, systems configurations, instruction, installation, repairs, and programming, in addition to retailing hardware and software.

Originally Bob had arrived at the idea of a computer consulting business after observing the improving business economy and the decreasing (thus more affordable) prices of computer hardware and software. In the geographic area of Southfield, West Bloomfield, Farmington Hills, Bloomfield Hills, and other small northwest suburbs of Detroit, many office buildings were being built. Small businesses were leasing most of these offices. Observing that there seeemed to be a growing trend toward office computerization, Bob felt that these small businesses in the northwestern suburbs comprised a prime target for a computer consulting business.

INDUSTRY BACKGROUND

While it is difficult to estimate the growth potential and demand for Microstar's specific market, it is possible to make an estimation using available data on office automation, desktop computer sales, and other

somewhat related markets. According to Standard & Poor's outlook on the office equipment industry, desktop computer growth on the business/professional markets should increase at 50 percent annually through 1986. Unfortunately, annual growth rates for the small business systems market are only forecast at 10 percent through 1986. Sean and Bob feel that although these were logical forecasts when made in 1981, the outlook for future growth in the small business systems market is much brighter now (1984). The advent of the IBM PC and the Apple Macintosh has whetted this market's appetite for business computers. Additionally, there is a desire for increased office productivity due to the increasing expense of employees. Improved software with many more applications is available, and the price of hardware is decreasing. One obvious result of the expanding market for business computers is the large amount of advertising for them directed toward a businessperson. In fact, the March 1984 issue of *Business Week* contained 11 computer-related advertisements. In the same issue it was stated that a recent computer startup company, Compaq Computer Corporation, reached $100 million in its first year of production. Due to these factors and the economy's general upswing, Sean and Bob forecast annual growth of this small business segment at 40 percent through 1988.

Furthermore, Standard & Poor's forecasts that the U.S. office automation market will grow to $40 billion in 1986. Office automation includes data processing, word processing, and communication equipment for the office. According to industry sources, only 10 to 15 percent of this market is being serviced presently. As there is no information available on computer consultants, Sean and Bob feel safe in assuming that this is also an untapped market and that their specific Detroit area target market has much promise. They also feel that the small business segment growth rate is a good indication of Microstar's potential growth rate.

Although the computer industry itself was growing at a fantastic rate and although there were over 250 retail computer outlets in the *Northwest Detroit Telephone Directory* Yellow Pages alone, there were no computer consultants listed as such. After extensive calls, Sean and Bob discovered that very few retail outlets offered any form of consulting and that none offered software customizing. The two partners felt that this phenomenon—a computer retail outlet on every corner combined with the lack of visibility of any consultants—could provide a key opportunity for their business.

A small businessman typically begins his search for an office computer by going directly to a retail outlet such as Computerland. Buying a computer is a high-risk decision. It is an expensive purchase, and one that involves great uncertainty as to whether or not the computer will live up to expectations and actually help the office. Therefore, usually the buyer will try to obtain as much information as possible on a wide

variety of alternatives. He will generally go to more than one store—where conflicting information may increase his uncertainty. The diversity among products and advice can be so overwhelming that Sean and Bob believe the prospective user will want to contact an expert to assist him to purchase and implement the correct system for his business. Examples of how some purchasing decisions were made can be seen in Exhibit 1.

EXHIBIT 1

Interview with travel agent

Mr. K owns a very profitable travel agency with many offices in the Detroit area. Because he mainly wanted a computer for word processing to facilitate correspondence, he simply went to the closest computer store that advertised the best price. He bought a Saber. The agency is rapidly expanding, and he would like to computerize many of its operations such as payroll, for example. Mr. K now regrets that he did not seek the advice of a consultant before purchasing the computer, and he will certainly do so if he decides to expand his computer network.

Interview with small businessman

Mr. Carl hired a consultant to provide advice on what to purchase in order to computerize his small business. He was advised to buy two computers and specific software, subsequently purchased from Computerland. He was willing to pay Computerland higher-than-average prices as he expected to receive excellent follow-up services. Mr. Carl is now the proud owner of two computers and software which he and his employees are unable to use because Computerland is not able to provide adequate training on the system. The consultant was only hired to provide purchase advice and is not capable of providing instruction on system use. Mr. Carl's advice to anyone considering computerizing an office is to go to a consultant who will work with you on a survey of what needs to be computerized and on making the actual purchase decision, and who can provide the instruction necessary to run the system. Mr. Carl is presently negotiating with Microstar for instruction on how to run the system he purchased.

Interview with optometrist

Dr. Roll is an optometrist who owns a very fashionable eyeglass store. He has many customers and decided to look into the purchase of a computer for filing purposes. Dr. Roll went to a few nearby retail outlets and felt that the installation of a computer system would require too much time on his part. He personally handwrites all the files—which are illegible to anyone but himself. He believes that it will take six months to enter all the files into a computer, and he decided it was more economic to hire an employee to spend four days a week maintaining customer files by hand.

COMPETITION

Approximately 250 computer retail outlets are listed in the *Northwest Detroit Telephone Directory*. Sean and Bob believe that these retail outlets are not Microstar's direct competition. Most of these distributors do not

offer consulting services. The dealers listed who do offer consulting services are generally knowledgeable only in regard to the brand of hardware they sell. For example, Computerland considers its salesmen consultants. Very limited assortments of software, usually consisting of spread sheet and general ledger programs, are sold by these retailers. As there were no listings under computer consultants in the telephone directory, a computer search of a special data bank found companies that provide consulting services, programming, and software. Thirteen such establishments were listed.

Sean and Bob contacted the 13 companies and found that only 9 of them provided computer products or related services. Three of these nine companies have gone out of business. One company deals only with credit unions. Two companies only provide keying and dumping on tape for $9 per hour. Two companies provide computer accessory products such as ribbons, paper, and diskettes. Computer Five, Inc., retails Honeywell hardware and software and provides consulting and programming only for Honeywell products at a cost of $36 per hour.

Only 2 of the 13 listed companies seem to provide any competition for Microstar. Both provide programming and consulting for any brand of hardware or software. Technalysis Corporation has rates of $30 an hour for programming and $35 an hour for consulting. Analysis International Corporation is the major competition that Microstar will face. They have 30 consultants and 30 technicians located in 18 offices. They charge $35 an hour for consulting, design specification, and software. They do not retail any hardware or software.

The two partners are not naive enough to think that these businesses are their only competition. Oftentimes a small business will want to computerize its accounting operations. Many reputable accounting firms now provide consulting services for the purpose of computerizing a business' accounting procedures. Sean contacted numerous accounting firms in the area and found that many would only set up time-sharing systems. With one exception, none sells computer hardware or software. One company provides computer instruction at a cost of $30 per hour but offers no other services. Only one man, Robert Karle, provides consulting, original software development, programming, teaching, and retailing of hardware and software. For programming and teaching he charges $25 an hour.

Microstar also considers other forms of computer services to be competitors. Service bureaus, which do a firm's data processing in a batch mode at their location, are very real rivals. There are four types of service offerings: mainframe (only offered by NCR and Control Data), independents, unused time on another firm's system, and time brokers. There seems to be a trend toward the diminishing use of these services as businesses want the availability of a computer at their fingertips. An advantage of having a computer in the office is that information can be

continuously fed into the computer and the results can be seen immediately. Thus, Sean and Bob are optimistic that these centralized services will provide no large threat.

SERVICES OFFERED BY MICROSTAR

Microstar will offer consulting, systems configurations, installation, instruction, repairs, programming, and retail services. As computer consultants providing a complete solution, they will first make sure that the services the customer wants will truly aid his or her business. If the services will help the business, they will then design a computer system to provide these services. This step would include deciding upon the appropriate software needed to provide these services. After deciding upon the software, Microstar can then choose the hardware that will be compatible with the software. Next comes the installation and any instructions necessary for the business to operate the computer. Also, some of the software may have to be customized for the specific business. Microstar will be capable of providing any repair services that may be required by the customer.

In order to provide their complete package of services at a competitive cost, Microstar entered into dealership arrangements with hardware and software retailers. Many consultants appear to be biased toward a specific manufacturer because they can obtain dealership prices. Sean and Bob wanted to choose a system because it would be best for their client, not because it was best for Microstar's profit margin, so they decided to make dealership arrangements with many different manufacturers.

Entering into arrangements with software manufacturers such as Microsoft, Lotus, and Peachtree allowed them to obtain software at 50 percent of retail price. Arrangements made with the hardware manufacturers Columbia, Televideo, Altos, and Eagle to enter into dealership relations enabled them to obtain their hardware at approximately 40–50 percent discounts from retail prices. Through the retailer Rent-A-Byte, Microstar arranged to obtain hardware at almost dealership prices for IBM, Apple, NEC, and Hewlett-Packard. Through the retailer Albon, Microstar can obtain Wang and DEC hardware. Both of these retailers will provide a service contract along with any hardware Microstar purchases. Substantial cost savings are expected from these dealership arrangements. Microstar will have two different price structures for the products and services it offers. In order to discourage potential clients from using Microstar solely as a retailer, consultant, or instructor, they will charge higher prices when the customer is not contracting with them to develop an entire office system. In this case, they will charge retail prices for all hardware and prepackaged software. For any of their other services, Microstar will charge $50 per hour.

When developing a complete office computer system, Microstar will give the client slight discounts on software. The hardware will be sold to the client at 25 percent below retail cost. All services will cost $40 an hour except for consulting, which will remain priced at $50 per hour. The consulting cost is higher because it will be done whether or not the client accepts Microstar's bid to develop a system. If Microstar's bid is accepted, the consulting cost will become part of the bid price. Three repair visits for any problems besides hardware are also included in the bid price. The hardware is covered by 90-day manufacturer warranties.

MARKETING STRATEGY

Sean and Bob realize that they have to make small businessmen aware that Microstar exists and has an array of services to offer. As there were no listings under computer consultants in the Yellow Pages, their first course of action was to have Microstar put under that very general heading, because they have reached a decision not to directly target specific businesses at first.

Approaching the market on an aggregate basis is believed to be Microstar's best initial approach. Microstar is thus able to provide complete office computerization for any small business. However, in order to provide superior work they have to research extensively any business with which they contract. A major complaint about consultants is that they do not know enough about the business they are hired to help and, as a result, cannot really aid the business to the extent promised. Sean and Bob believe that after completing a small number of jobs they will then have the knowledge and experience to specialize in specific business areas. Many benefits will arise from this ability. For instance, there will be a large reduction in research time needed to complete subsequent jobs. Even more important, promotion of computer consultants is primarily through word of mouth. As Microstar successfully completes a job for one business, its executives are likely to inform others in the trade of Microstar's abilities. Microstar can also attend specific trade shows and conventions in order to increase these markets' awareness of their specialized knowledge.

Although Sean and Bob are approaching the market on an aggregate basis, they feel that they already have considerable knowledge with respect to the appraisal profession. Sean's father is a builder and appraiser, and is currently president of Detroit's chapter of the American Society of Appraisers. Sean and Bob have spent quite a bit of time discussing computer uses for the appraisal field. They have also completed a presentation to the chapter on the advantages of computerizing such a business. Microstar hopes that this presentation will stimulate word-of-mouth promotion within the field.

Another possible market is U of M faculty members currently in-

volved in research or outside businesses with whom Sean and Bob have had discussions. They also feel that the legal field could be a good market for them to enter. Bob's father is a lawyer and has shown an interest in future computerization of his office.

FINANCIAL SITUATION

Lack of financial resources is a major problem confronting Microstar. Financing the business venture will come directly from the personal assets of Sean, Bob, and Paul, who believe that they will be able to contribute a total of $9,000 toward the capital of Microstar.

According to Sean and Bob, the $9,000 will be adequate to start up and operate the company. As Sean says,

> Our overhead should be very minimal. Bob, Paul, and I are not taking any salaries out of the company until we feel we are on our feet. We figured that to maintain a professional appearance we should rent an office. We leased one in our area for $300 a month, including utilities and computer system. We'll have to install a phone, but after installation fees we have no reason to believe that our phone bills will ever be higher than $40 to $50 per month. We are using some family connections to obtain our office furniture for free. To be listed in the *Northwest Detroit Telephone Directory* Yellow Pages costs only $27 per month, and to be listed in any of the smaller, suburban Yellow Pages costs only $15 per month. We don't even have to worry about large travel expenses because our target market area is not that large, so we don't have to do a lot of driving around. We estimate that at most we will travel 100 miles per week at a cost of 18 cents per mile. Fortunately for us, two extremely bright computer majors have offered their programming services to us for free. Not only do they want experience, but they also have faith in Microstar and want to get in the company on the ground floor. If not for them, we would have had to hire a programmer at $400 per week. We also would have to hire a consultant at $400 per week because either Bob or I would have had to help with the programming. Annually, our largest expense will be our one full-time employee—at $20,000. We are also hiring a secretary at $3.35 an hour, 15 hours a week, for 12 weeks during the summer. We don't even have to worry about retaining backup labor as Bob, Paul, and I are capable of filling in for any of these people who can't complete a job. We should even have a small amount of money available for some newspaper or radio ads and some printed brochures.

(See Exhibit 2 for a typical project cost. See Exhibit 3 for a pro forma income statement.)

Sean and Bob do realize that one very large problem they will encounter will be in the area of credit—extending credit as well as obtaining credit. They will have to work out a payment policy for their services where the client pays half in advance or something similar so that Mi-

EXHIBIT 2   Typical project cost (small–medium-size business)

Hardware costs		
Printers (1 @ $1,200, 1 @ $1,300)	$ 2,500	
Computers (10 @ $3,200)	32,000	
Hard disk computer (1)	6,500	
Modem (1)	600	
Total hardware costs		$41,600
Programming costs		
Prepackaged software (20 @ $400)	8,000	
Customized software ($40/hour × 100 hours)	4,000	
Blank floppy disks (500 @ $3.50)	1,750	
Total programming costs		13,750
Consulting costs		
Consulting ($50/hour × 40 hours)	2,000	
Computer analysis	200	
Total consulting costs		2,200
Systems configuration costs ($40/hour × 120 hours)	4,800	
Instruction costs ($40/hour × 80 hours)	3,200	
Installation costs ($40/hour × 24 hours)	960	
Repair costs ($40/hour × 24 hours)	960	
		9,920
Average revenue		$67,470

crostar can purchase the necessary software and hardware to complete the job. Microstar will not be able to make these purchases on credit as they have no inventory and no assets to back them up, nor, for the same reason will they be able to obtain funds from any financial lending institutions.

The way the partners look at the financial situation is that they don't have too much to lose if the business fails. The most they will have invested is $3,000 apiece and one summer of time. They believe that all they need is one profitable job to give them adequate capital to start the business really going.

LEGAL CONSTRAINTS

Sean and Bob are aware of the many liabilities they can incur if the system they install does not function as promised. They want to come up with a standard format for a contract which will address many of the liabilities and protect them from lawsuits. At the present time they are hoping to work out a contract and discuss many of the legal implications

EXHIBIT 3   Pro forma income statement

Revenue ($67,470 × 9*)		$607,230
Cost of goods sold		
Hardware costs ($30,000 × 9)	$270,000	
Prepackaged software ($4,000 × 9)	36,000	
Blank floppy disks	9,000	
Total cost of goods sold		(315,000)
Direct labor costs		
Programmer/instructor ($400/week)	20,000	
Consultant/systems configurator ($400/week)	20,000	
General duties	20,000	
Total direct labor costs		(60,000)
Gross profit		232,230
Overhead		
Rent (includes utilities and computer system)	3,600	
Secretary ($3.35/hour × 15 hours × 12 weeks)	603	
Phone	600	
Travel (18 cents/mile × 100 miles/week)	900	
Advertising		
Yellow Pages	$ 348	
Business cards	100	
Mail	200	
Miscellaneous expenses	2,000	2,648
Office supplies		1,000
Miscellaneous expenses		5,000
Total overhead		(14,351)
Net income before taxes		217,879
Taxes (@ 41%)		(89,330)
Net income		$128,549

*A typical job requires 218 total labor hours. Forty hours of initial consulting is required first, then 30 hours of systems configurations, after which the 100 hours of programming can be completed simultaneously with the remaining system configurations. Installation requires 24 hours followed by 24 hours of instruction, totaling 218 hours. Microstar will operate 2,000 hours a year, which will enable them to complete nine average jobs.

of their business with Bob's father, who is a practicing attorney. They also believe that they will need help with their corporate taxes and have requested the advice of a graduating accounting major. Both Bob's father and the accounting major are willing to help Microstar for free.

ISSUE

Sean and Bob are anxious to begin the operation of Microstar and have set their starting date as May 14, 1984. They believe that this will

give them two weeks after school has ended to set up the office and take care of any other pre-operation business. Many decisions as to their marketing strategy must be reached before they begin operation. As the deadline approached they sat down to develop a final version of their marketing plan for this first year of operation.

QUESTION

1. Based on your analysis of the situation, what marketing strategy do you recommend for Microstar's first year of operation? Be specific about market targets, marketing objectives, and the elements of the marketing mix.

PRODUCT STRATEGY

Modern marketing management views the product as a controllable variable in the planning of marketing strategy. Products can be improved to make them more acceptable to the market; new products or services can be added to the company's line; and weak products or services can be dropped. In a sense, product decisions are more basic than decisions about other marketing variables. A product that effectively meets consumer needs reduces problems associated with decisions on distribution, pricing, advertising, and personal selling. A poorly conceived product, on the other hand, creates many problems for other decision areas in marketing.

Demand is increasingly dynamic, and product life cycles are getting shorter. A company that hopes to grow and prosper over the long run must have a capability for product innovation. Marketing management, facing today's market situation, is repeatedly required to answer a very basic question: "What new product or service should we offer?" A company's survival depends on its ability to answer this question correctly. An approach to providing this answer is the key subject of Chapter 6.

Sellers face a dilemma with regard to product policy. New products are essential to survival, yet many new products fail in the marketplace. Thus, another requirement for today's business firm is a product development process that maximizes the probability of success. This is the topic considered in Chapter 7.

PRODUCT CHOICE DECISIONS

6

Product decisions are concerned with changes in a firm's product or product line (or service). For our purposes, the term *product* will be thought of in the inclusive sense as being all that the consumer receives when making a purchase. It is not only a physical entity but also a complex of tangible and intangible attributes, including such things as warranties, packaging, color, design, and even psychic stimulation, as well as services. Product policy involves the adjustment of this complex of product variables to the needs and requirements of the market, on the one hand, and to the capabilities of the firm, on the other, along with the attendant activities of procedure and control.

Product decisions may relate to changes in existing products or their use, or to the offerings of products or services new to the firm. These decisions are not fundamentally different, for in either case a "new" product emerges. The difference is only in the degree of newness involved. However, the greater the degree of newness, the more uncertain is the outcome of the product decision. The focus of this chapter is on decisions concerning essentially new products, but the decision-making process is basically the same, albeit somewhat easier, for modification of existing products.

BASIC CONCEPTS

Product Line and Product Mix

In addition to decisions relating to the individual product, we shall also be concerned with those involving building a product line. A *product line* is a group of products that are closely related, either because they function in a similar manner, are sold to the same customer groups, are marketed through the same types of outlets, or fall within given price ranges. Thus, Kellogg Company produces a line of breakfast foods. Mattel, Inc. produces a line of toys.

The executive responsible for managing a product line has to decide on product line length. The line is too short if profits can be increased by adding items. It is too long if profits can be increased by dropping items.

A firm with several product lines has a product mix. A *product mix* consists of all the individual product lines and items that a particular seller offers to buyers. General Electric is a firm with a very broad product mix. The firm sells light bulbs, small appliances, major appliances, heavy equipment like power plant generators, small electric motors, repair service, and electrical parts. Kellogg Company offers a very narrow product mix, marketing a limited number of product lines. Kellogg's product mix is deep, however, since they market a number of different brands of cereal, each in different sized packages.

As a means of illustrating the concepts of breadth and length of product mix, see Figure 6–1, which is descriptive of Procter and Gamble's product mix.[1]

The *width* of P&G's product mix refers to how many different product lines the company carries. Figure 6–1 shows a product mix width of six lines. (In fact, P&G produces many additional lines, including mouthwashes, toilet tissue, and so on.)

The *length* of P&G's product mix refers to the total number of items in its product mix. In Figure 6–1, it is 31. We can also talk about the average length of a line at P&G. This is obtained by dividing the total length (here 31) by the number of lines (here 6), or 5.2. The average product line at P&G as represented in Figure 6–1 consists of 5.2 brands.

The *depth* of P&G's product mix refers to how many variants are offered of each product in the line. Thus, if Crest comes in three sizes and two formulations (regular and mint), Crest has a depth of six. By counting the number of variants within each brand, the average depth of P&G's product mix can be calculated.

---

[1]This section adapted from Philip Kotler, *Principles of Marketing*, 2d ed. ©1980, pp. 270, 273, 274. Reprinted by permission of Prentice-Hall, Inc., Englewood Cliffs, N.J. General Electric and Kellogg examples from Thomas C. Kinnear and Kenneth L. Bernhardt, *Principles of Marketing* (Glenview, Ill.: Scott, Foresman, 1983), p. 263.

FIGURE 6–1   Product mix width and product line length shown for Procter & Gamble products

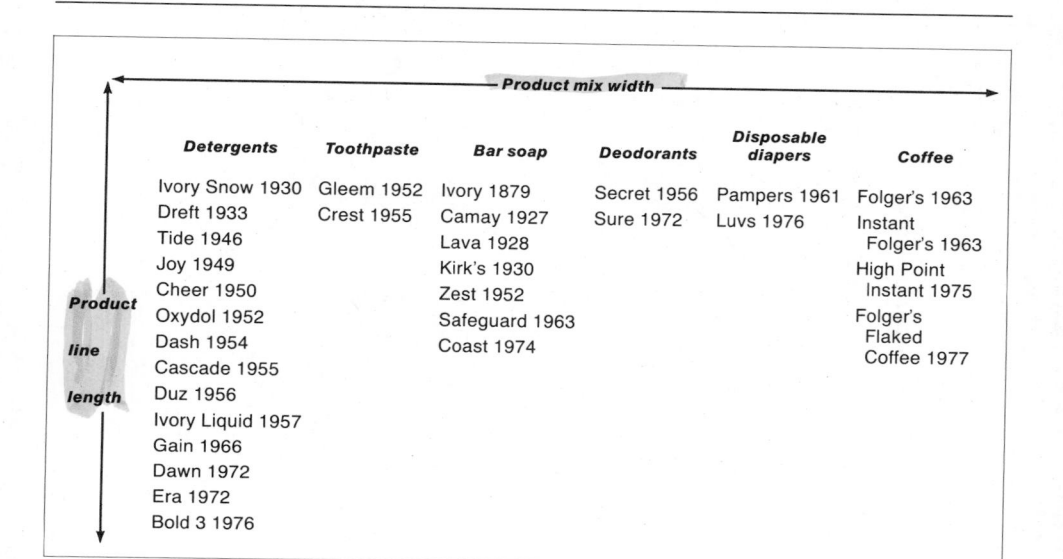

Source: Philip Kotler, *Principles of Marketing*, 2d ed. (Englewood Cliffs, N.J.: Prentice-Hall, 1983), p. 274.

Product Life Cycle

In planning product policy it may be helpful to make discriminating use of the concept of the product life cycle (PLC). This concept sees the life of a product as analogous to the life of an organism in that it progresses through stages of birth, growth, maturity, decline, and death.[2] According to its proponents, the typical life cycle is an S-shaped curve, as illustrated in Figure 6–2. Product life cycles are said to have four identifiable stages: (1) Introduction—sales growth is slow and losses or low profits are reported; (2) Growth—sales volume and profit both rise as market acceptance is achieved; (3) Maturity—sales volume stabilizes, profits start to fall, and increased marketing spending may be needed to sustain the brand; and (4) Decline—obsolescence begins, sales volume declines, profits erode, and the brand quietly dies.

How well does the S-shaped curve fit the sales histories of various

[2]Adapted from Yoram J. Wind, *Product Policy: Concepts, Methods, and Strategy*, © 1982, Addison-Wesley, Reading, Massachusetts. Pp. 45, 46, 50. Reprinted with permission. For details on empirical studies see R. D. Buzzell and V. Cook, *Product Life Cycles* (Cambridge, Mass.: Marketing Science Institute, 1969), pp. 29-35. Also see R. Polli and V. Cook, "Validity of Product Life Cycle," *The Journal of Business* 42 (October, 1969), p. 390.

FIGURE 6–2   The basic life cycle for new products

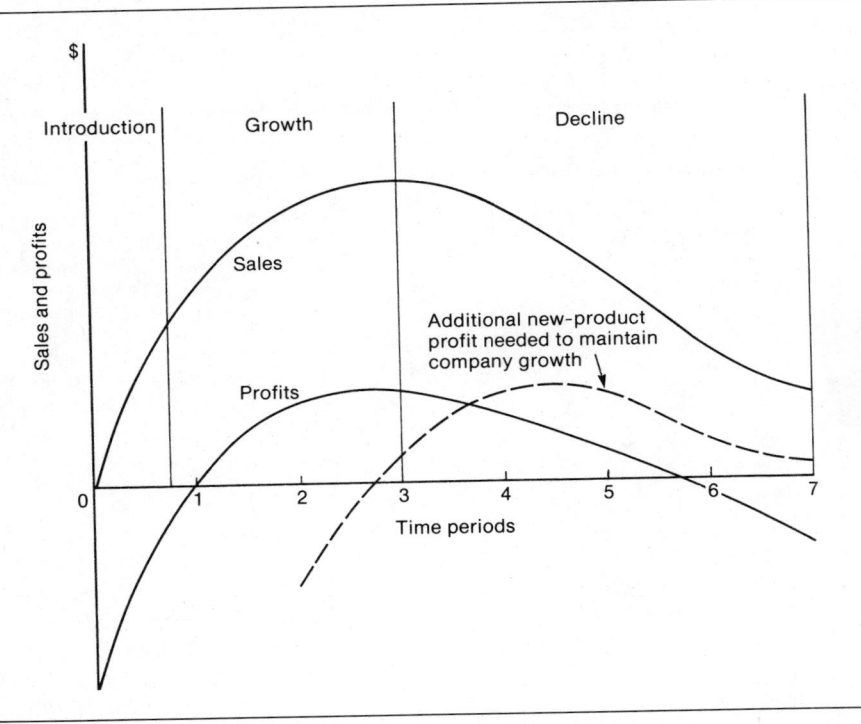

Source: Douglas J. Dalrymple and Leonard J. Parsons, *Marketing Management*, 2d ed. (New York: John Wiley & Sons, 1980), p. 253.

products? Evidence from empirical studies is mixed. In 1969 Buzzell and Cook examined the sales histories of 192 consumer products and found that 52 percent of the products (nonfood grocery products, food products, and durables) followed the general pattern of the PLC model. Note, however, that 48 percent did not. Also in 1969, Polli and Cook tested the sales behavior of 140 consumer nondurable products and found that less than half of the products exhibited sales consistent with the PLC model. In commenting on these results, it was concluded that the fit of the life-cycle model depends heavily on the definition of the product used and the relevance of the product class partitioning.

Thus, the PLC concept may be used to describe a product class (television sets), a product form (black-and-white sets versus color), or a brand (RCA). The PLC concept has a different degree of applicability in each case. In a critical review of the PLC concept, Dhalla and Yuspeh

concluded that with respect to product class, the PLC model does not hold:

> Many product classes have enjoyed and will probably continue to enjoy a long and prosperous maturity stage—far more than the human life expectancy of 3 score years and 10. Good examples are Scotch whisky, Italian vermouth, and French perfumes.
>
> As for product form, it tends to exhibit less stability than does product class. Form is what most PLC advocates have in mind when they speak of a generalized life-cycle pattern for a "product." Even here the model is not subject to precise formulation. Theoretically, it presumes the existence of some rules indicating the movement of the product from one stage to another. However, when one studies actual case histories, it becomes clear that no such rules can be objectively developed. [Evidence is presented showing life cycles of product forms of cigarettes, makeup bases, toilet tissues, and cereals to support the above conclusion.]

* * * * *

> When it comes to brands, the PLC model has even less validity. Many potentially useful offerings die in the introductory stage because of inadequate product development, or unwise market planning, or both.[3]

Clearly it is questionable to generalize which "product" definitions to use in attempting to apply the PLC concept in market planning. The wiser course in planning the marketing strategy for a new brand is to gather data on sales trends over time for both the product class and the product form where the items will compete to determine whether a life cycle can be identified and what stage of the cycle has been reached for either the class or the form.

Even when there is evidence that sales of a product form appear to be moving along the S-shaped curves, Dhalla and Yuspeh remind us that "The PLC is a *dependent* variable which is determined by marketing actions; it is not an *independent* variable to which companies should adapt their marketing programs. Marketing management itself can alter the shape and duration of a brand's life cycle.

"Unfortunately, in numerous cases a brand is discontinued, not because of irreversible changes in consumer values or tastes, but because management—on the basis of the PLC theory—believes the brand has entered a dying stage. In effect a self-fulfilling prophecy results."[4] Such mistakes may be avoided if we recognize that appropriate marketing strategy may not only extend the phase of maturity but avoid the untimely death of the brand.

---

[3]Reprinted by permission of the Harvard Business Review. Excerpt from "Forget the Product Life Cycle" by Nariman K. Dhalla and Sonia Yuspeh (January-February 1976). Copyright ©1976 by the President and Fellows of Harvard College; all rights reserved.

[4]Ibid., p. 105.

If preliminary research suggests that a product class or product form may be expected to follow a life cycle of introduction, growth, maturity, and decline, how may this information be used as helpful background in marketing planning?[5] One approach is to ask, What strategies may lead to extending the life of the brand? Action may be taken to promote more frequent use of the brand among current users. Another strategy is to suggest new uses for the item. Then, too, improving the product may increase its appeal to prospective buyers and provide a basis for a more effective promotional program. Again, consumer research may lead a firm to identify a new market segment for its brand. This approach led the Gerber Company to consider a program of marketing its baby food to adults—women who work; college students who prepare their own lunches; single individuals, 50 to 64 years old, living alone; and others.

A second approach to overcoming some of the limitations of the product life-cycle concept involves incorporating information on the market share and profitability along with data on sales trends in evaluating its performance. This provides a basis for evaluating the brand's current and likely performance for consideration in the design of marketing strategy.[6]

DECISION TO OFFER A NEW PRODUCT

Not all firms engage in product development. In the array of product policy choices available to a firm, one is the null choice: that is, to stick with existing products in their present form and forego product innovation. Company management, having observed the risks involved in the development and introduction of new products, may decide that this is the prudent course to follow. Around 98 percent of new-product concepts die in the development process between an original positive reaction and the point of marketing. Only 2 percent of early projects end up going to market. Then too, when the success or failure of actually marketed new products since World War II is examined, the results are: around 25 percent of all new industrial products significantly fail to meet the expectations of their developers, and 30 to 35 percent of all consumer products fail to do so.[7] When this failure rate is considered along with the often high cost of developing and launching a new

---

[5]Based upon Yoram J. Wind, *Product Policy,* © 1982, Addison-Wesley, Reading, Massachusetts. Pp. 60–63. Reprinted by permission.

[6]For additional background on the product life cycle, see "Special Section, Product Life Cycle," *Journal of Marketing,* Fall 1981, pp. 60–123. Nine articles dealing with the managerial value of the PLC are presented.

[7]C. Merle Crawford, *New-Products Management* (Homewood, Ill.: Richard D. Irwin, 1983), pp. 25–26.

product, the risks associated with product development appear high indeed.

On the other hand, there is risk and potentially high cost associated with not offering new products. Mature brands in the firm's line may lose sales and profits because of changes in consumer demand, product forms may be modified as a result of technological change, competing brands may be improved and gain share of market, and competition may strengthen. To maintain profits, accordingly, aggressive action must be taken to improve mature brands and to increase the effectiveness of the marketing strategy supporting such items.

Does a firm have a real choice insofar as product innovation is concerned? *In the short run,* the answer is yes. Given the substantial costs and high risks associated with product change, plus uncertainty about the present phase and future course of the life cycle of existing products, short-run profits may well be maximized by a decision not to offer new products. On the other hand, *long-run survival of a firm precludes choice* about product innovation. Without improvement the eventual decline in the market acceptability of virtually all mature products is certain.

Even if survival over an extended period were possible without product innovation, most firms are not content with mere survival. They want to grow and to prosper. New products are customarily a major factor in company growth. Therefore, if a firm desires both survival and growth, its fundamental choices concerning product innovation narrow to two: (1) what (not whether) new products should be offered; (2) whether these new products should be gained through internal development or external acquisition.

WHAT NEW PRODUCTS TO OFFER[8]

New products are "new" in varying degrees. They may be minor or major modifications of a firm's existing products. They may be new to the particular firm but not new to the market. If new to the firm, they may be closely related, loosely related, or totally unrelated to the firm's existing products. Or a product may be new to the market, something not previously available in any form. If a product is both new to the market, so that there is nothing by way of guidance to be found in the experience of others, and also unrelated to a firm's existing products, so that there is little carry-over of experience from these, then the risks of product innovation are great. In order to minimize these risks, yet keep alive the opportunity for survival and growth that accompanies product innovation, a well-formulated "add-and-drop" policy is necessary.[9]

---

[8]See Crawford, *New-Products Management,* for a comprehensive discussion of product choice decisions.

[9]Although the emphasis here is on the adding of new products, decisions to drop existing products are governed by the same factors.

Objective of Profit Maximization

The most basic goal of business in a free-enterprise society is the maximization of long-term profit. Therefore, the basic test to be applied in deciding which new product should be added is contribution to the overall profit position of the firm. Unfortunately, such a test is not easily applied. Profit is a function of many things, such as the nature and extent of demand, the activities of competitors, and the costs of production and distribution. Furthermore, when deciding whether to add a new product, it is the future, not the present, condition of such variables that counts. Profit calculations relating to new products must be based on forecasting, an art that mankind has not yet mastered.

In spite of the difficulty of applying a profit test in product choice decisions, a profit calculation cannot be avoided. Any decision to add a new product *implicitly* involves an assumption concerning profitability. Other standards, if used, are at best only substitutes assumed to be correlated with long-term profitability. If initial profit calculations are necessarily very crude, there is opportunity to refine them as the product development process evolves. At this stage, however, we are concerned only with the initial decision of which new product should be selected for development.

Profitability Formula

The total profit directly (but not indirectly)[10] attributable to a new product addition is expressed by the formula:

$$P = D \times (R - C) \times L$$

in which

P = Total long-term net profit in dollars
D = Average total unit sales per year
R = Average sales price per unit (revenue)
C = Average cost per unit
L = Expected life (in years)

Estimate of Demand

The existence of an adequate demand for a potential new product is basic to profit opportunity. An attempt must be made to measure the extent of demand, its strength and location, the segmentation which may be present, and other demand variables. Estimates of future demand for established products are difficult to make because of the many factors, both tangible and intangible, which affect sales opportunities. Demand estimates for a projected new product, at the time a decision must

---

[10]Indirect contributions to a firm's total profits by a new product are discussed later.

be made whether or not to undertake its development, are far more difficult. Just how difficult depends on the nature of the demand determinants (for example, automotive replacement parts versus a new style of clothing). Still, such a decision is implicit in the choice process and cannot be avoided.

Management must estimate future market potential for the type of product it expects to add, as well as the share of the market it expects to serve. Because of the uncertainty associated with sales forecasts at this early stage in the product development process, several forecasts, involving various degrees of optimism and pessimism, might be made. Figure 6–3 shows three sales forecasts for a proposed new product —one highly pessimistic, one optimistic, and one considered most likely to occur. This process might be refined by assigning probabilities to the several estimates, thus making possible the derivation of expected values of unit sales for each product under consideration.

Sales of most new products can be expected to grow for a time, gradually achieve more stability, and eventually decline. If the respective sales of several products are to be compared, it is useful to convert sales data to average sales per year over the expected life cycle of the product. Such a figure can be readily calculated and easily fitted into the profitability formula above. The value of this figure, of course, depends on the expected life of the proposed new product as well as on the trend of sales during its time on the market.

FIGURE 6–3   Estimates of alternative sales volumes, proposed new product

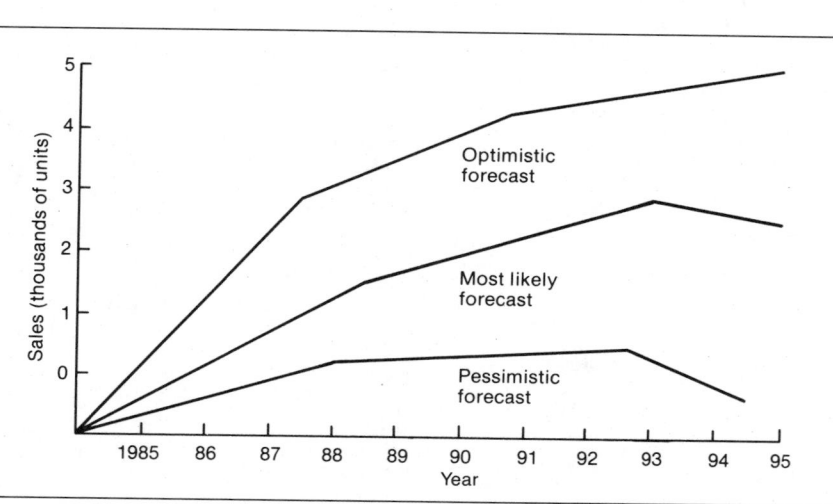

Price Estimates

Management must have some idea of the price to be obtained for a new product throughout its life cycle in order to estimate the product's profit contribution. Valuable price information can usually be gained from demand studies, for price is basically a demand-determined variable. Needless to say, uncertainties of demand cause uncertainties in the price-estimating process. Price is quite likely to vary through time, by size and type of customer, by markets, and so on. As was suggested for estimates of sales volume, it might be useful to make price estimates that range from optimistic to pessimistic and to attempt to derive the "most likely" behavior of price over the life cycle of the projected product. This approach is illustrated in Figure 6–4.

The price received for the new product and its behavior over the product life is a function not only of demand but also of price strategies followed, activities of competitors, changes in the cost structure, and so on. Obviously, the expected price can only be a "best guess." Again, however, it can be pointed out that such a decision is inherent in the product choice process and that it must be made, regardless of its diffi-

FIGURE 6–4   Alternative price expectations, proposed new product

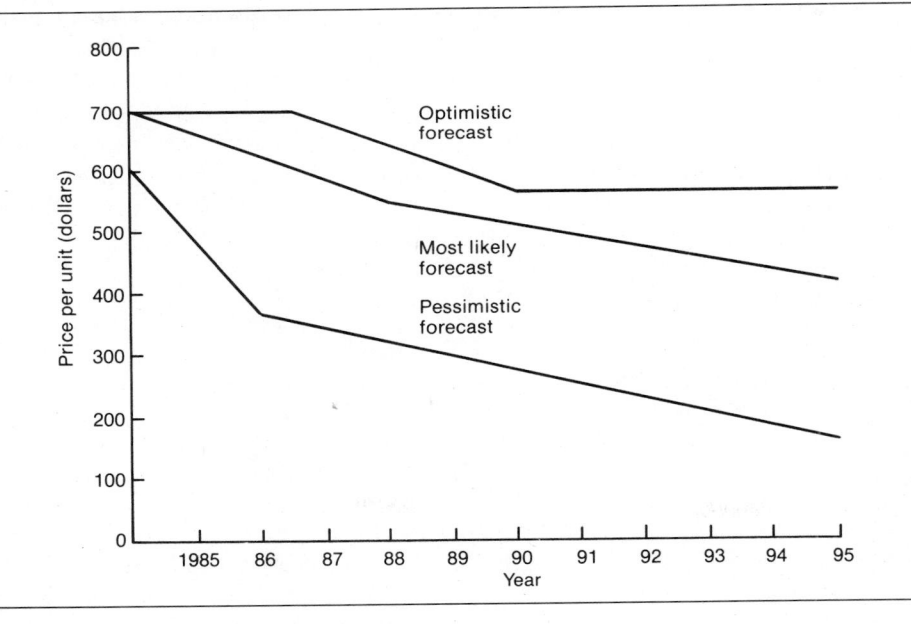

culty. As was suggested for sales volume estimates, it is useful to convert price estimates into an average unit price throughout the life cycle of the product. This value can be inserted directly into the profit formula.

Cost Estimates

Price received per unit, less cost per unit, determines the profit contribution of each unit sold. Cost per unit includes both variable and fixed costs, so the sales forecast must precede any estimate of unit costs. It is in the area of production and marketing costs per unit that a firm adding a new product has a major opportunity to influence the volume of profits that a new product will generate. If it chooses a new product whose production and marketing "fit" with its present products, it can obtain more efficient utilization of resources in two ways. First, fixed costs are spread over a larger volume of operations, thus reducing costs per unit. Second, proper fit may have a favorable effect on demand for both the new product and for existing products, thus increasing the total scale of the operations on which profits depend.

Life-Cycle Estimates

The life cycle of a proposed product may well be the most difficult variable in the profit formula to estimate. The anticipated time period may be long, and the factors that might affect it (change in consumer taste, actions of competitors, changes in technology, for example) may be almost impossible to predict. Nonetheless, such an estimate is highly relevant to the decision at hand. Generally speaking, management would want to avoid products whose life cycles are expected to be short and to favor those whose life cycles are expected to be long, other things being equal.

The difficulty of estimating life cycles varies greatly by type of product. In some fields, fairly uniform cycles may be observable in past sales. These may then be used as a guide to the expected life cycle of the proposed product. In other fields, no such uniformity in life cycles may be observed. Here, perhaps, some arbitrary time period may be chosen for purposes of the profit calculation. For example, 10 years may be established as the maximum time period to be considered. All new products will be judged only on the profits generated in that time span. If the life cycle is expected to be shorter than this, the values of other variables in the formula will have to be higher in order to compensate.

Net Revenue

The total long-term net profit in dollars to be expected over the life cycle of the projected product can now be calculated. Because both the length and shape of life-cycle curves vary greatly among products, the

total profit figure should be converted to "present value" for purposes of comparison. A quick return not only has a higher present value but also a higher probability of being realized because of the greater uncertainty of longer-term forecasts.

Compound Profitability Formula

If a firm is starting from scratch with a new product and has no existing products, the above analysis may be sufficient for the product choice decision. Such, however, is rarely the case. Most new products are introduced to the market by going concerns that are already producing and selling one or more products. In this circumstance, it is axiomatic that what counts is the effect of adding the new product on the overall profitability of the firm. If new-product sales are entirely at the expense of continued sales of existing products of equal profitability, there is no net gain.[11] Conversely, the new product may favorably affect the profitability of existing products because it complements them in some way. A manufacturer of automatic washers who did not also produce dryers might find it difficult to sell the washers because of the demand among consumers for matched pairs of these products. A manufacturer of a car wax who did not offer a car cleaner might find sales difficult because consumers believe such products "go together" better if made by one company.

Because of such considerations, the profitability formula should be expanded as follows:

$$P = [D \times (R - C) \times L] \pm [d \times (r - c) \times l]_1$$
$$\pm [d \times (r - c) \times l]_2 \ldots \pm [d \times (r - c) \times l]_n$$

This formula recognizes that the proposed product may either increase or reduce the profitability of every other product in a firm's product line, ranging from the product designated as 1 up to product n. The effect on profits may be a result of the influence of the new product on any of the variables involved. The new product may either increase or reduce the demand (d) for an existing product. It may make possible the receipt of a higher price (r) or cause a need to lower price. If the new product is wisely chosen, it may well serve to reduce the average cost per unit (c) of producing and marketing present products. The life cycle of existing products (l) may be affected favorably or unfavorably. Any one or more of these effects would cause variation in anticipated overall profits.

---

[11]This assumes that the present product sales would continue if the new product were not added. If a competitor is likely to offer a new product that will cut into sales of the existing product(s), this assumption is not valid.

Resource Utilization: Its Relationship to Product Planning

A business firm employs various resources (inputs) in order to produce revenues (outputs). In the short run, many of these inputs are relatively fixed in amount (for example, plant capacity, size of sales force, and advertising expenditures) and do not vary proportionately with the scale of operations. Profits will be maximized at that point where the marginal cost of the total inputs is equal to the marginal revenue of the total output. For any *given* scale of operations, profit will be maximized when the ratio of the total output to the total input is greatest. Therefore, if profit maximization is assumed to be a firm's objective, new products should be chosen so as to optimize resource utilization. It should be borne in mind that this concept emphasizes the optimum utilization of all resources, employed in combination, rather than the optimum use of each resource.

A great variety of resources are utilized in the average business firm. For purposes of simplicity, these are here divided into production resources and marketing resources. On the production side are such resources as plant, equipment, and technical know-how. On the marketing side are such resources as distribution facilities, the sales force, and established relationships with middlemen. If a proposed product and established products "converge" in production in the sense that they can share the use of production resources, then production costs per unit can be expected to decline. Shared use of marketing resources (for example, sale of a new product through an established sales force) will produce the same result. In addition, a good marketing fit among products may have a favorable influence on demand.

Production and marketing "fit" is one of the more controllable factors in product planning. An individual firm's influence on demand, price, and the product life cycle is likely to be slight. By assuring that new products have good production and marketing fit, input cost can be minimized and output may also be expanded. This not only serves to maximize profits in the short run but also affects the probability of a firm's survival and growth. The efficient firm has all the advantages in a competitive environment.

Utilization of Production Resources

Many production resources are employed in the production of revenues, and these vary greatly by industry classification. Among the more important resources employed in production are the following: (1) physical capacity, (2) labor skills, (3) technical know-how, (4) raw materials, and (5) by-products. Some of these are relatively tangible and fairly easy to measure, while others are less tangible and more difficult to measure.

Physical capacity.   Every manufacturing firm has a certain physical

capacity for production in the form of plant and equipment. If this capacity is not fully utilized and sales of present products cannot be increased because of demand limitations, new products which can be manufactured with the same plant and equipment will spread fixed costs and reduce production cost per unit.

Labor skills.   The skills of a labor force are as real an asset as buildings or machinery and often more difficult to expand or modify. A firm employing highly paid, and perhaps underutilized, fashion designers would not be optimizing the use of its styling resources if it added a new product for which style was not a critical factor. Many technical skills are in short supply and perhaps unavailable to a firm seeking them for the first time. The use of existing skills avoids this problem.

Technical know-how.   If technical knowledge built up over many years is transferable to a newly added product, a firm has an advantage not possessed by others. Past production of military electronic gear may aid a firm in turning out civilian electronic ware. Technical knowledge derived from manufacturing stainless steel cutlery may be an asset to a firm that elects to produce stainless steel razor blades. Although it is difficult to assign a value to technical know-how, this intangible can be a very real asset.

Common raw materials.   If new products can be added that make use of the same raw materials as existing products, several advantages may accrue. First, this may make possible a lower cost for raw materials because acquisition cost tends to be a function of volume purchased. Second, there tends to be a relationship between the use of the same raw materials and common production facilities and distinctive know-how.

By-product factor.   The most obvious case of underutilization of resources occurs when potentially valuable by-products of present production activities are not used. The chemical, petroleum-refining, and meat-packing industries are excellent illustrations of the opportunity to improve the total output–input ratio by finding profitable uses for by-products.

Decision Matrix: Utilization of Production Resources

Isolation of a firm's tangible and intangible resources and the exposure of each new-product idea to the light of these criteria are essential to a sound product policy. However, the decision of which new product to choose is complicated by the almost infinite number of product alternatives that are sometimes available. Management may be in the position of having to select the product that best utilizes company resources out of hundreds or even thousands of possible alternatives. Also, in practice, the number of criteria used in making a judgment may be far greater than the number employed here. For this decision-making process to be

manageable, a practical basis for weighting the several criteria employed, and for assigning an evaluation score to each product considered, is necessary. Then the various alternative choices can be compared. In order to do these things, a reasonably objective evaluation scheme is desirable. This is the purpose of using a decision matrix.

Product choice decisions are made under conditions of uncertainty. Even for such intangible criteria as, for example, the ability of a proposed new product to use existing plant and equipment, there may be a significant degree of uncertainty. Perhaps the product can be physically produced with these facilities, but there is doubt whether costs will be competitive. Perhaps certain desirable features cannot be produced if present equipment is used, and modifications in the product will have to be made that may adversely affect demand. On such intangible factors as the application of technical knowledge gained from producing existing products, there may be even less certainty. Thus, there is need to consider the *probability* that a new product will, or will not, produce the benefits expected. A decision matrix facilitates such consideration.

If a proposed product is rated on conformance to each of the suggested criteria, and a probability estimate is assigned each of these ratings, then the "estimated value" of the proposed product for each criterion can be calculated. If these estimated values are totaled, an estimated value for each new product for total production resource utilization is obtained. The values so obtained for each of the products being considered can then be compared.

Example: Proposed new-product X. Assume that a hypothetical new-product X is under consideration and that a decision matrix is used to evaluate its contribution to optimum use of the firm's production resources (Figure 6–5). In constructing the matrix, weights have been assigned to the several relevant criteria discussed above. These weights are based on management's best judgment of the relative importance of conformance to each standard for the particular company. Arbitrary values have been assigned to the possible ratings, ranging from 10 for "very good" down to 2 for "very poor."[12]

Management must now estimate the probability that the proposed new product will qualify for each of the possible ratings on each of the five criteria used in the evaluation. Note that achievement of any particular rating is not a certainty. For example, the illustrative figures included in the matrix (Figure 6–5) for utilization of physical capacity assume a 20 percent chance of a "very good" fit, a 60 percent chance of a "good" fit, and a 20 percent chance of a fit of only "average" quality. This range of possibilites is possible only because of uncertainty that exists at this early stage of the product development process. For the

---

[12]In addition, precise definitions should be framed for each possible rating on each of the several criteria. As these must differ greatly by industry, they are omitted here.

FIGURE 6–5   Decision matrix: Utilization of production resources (proposed new-product X)

Decision criterion	Criterion weight	Very good (10)		Good (8)		Average (6)		Poor (4)		Very poor (2)		Total	Criterion evaluation (Total EV × Weight)
		P	EV	P	EV	P	EV	P	EV	P	EV		
Physical capacity	0.20	0.2	2.0	0.6	4.8	0.2	1.2	0	0	0	0	8.0	1.60
Labor skills	0.30	0.2	2.0	0.7	5.6	0.1	0.6	0	0	0	0	8.2	2.46
Technical know-how	0.30	0	0	0.2	1.6	0.2	1.2	0.6	2.4	0	0	5.2	1.56
Common raw materials	0.10	0	0	0	0	0.7	4.2	0.3	1.2	0	0	5.4	0.54
By-product	0.10	0	0	0	0	0.1	0.6	0.6	2.4	0.3	0.6	3.6	0.36
Total production resources value													6.52

second criterion (labor skills), the stated probabilities may reflect uncertainty about the adaptability of the labor force to the production requirements of the new product. It is estimated that there is a 20 percent chance that the labor force will adapt with no difficulty. If so, a "very good" rating would be achieved. However, it is more likely (probability 0.7) that the labor force will require some, but not expensive retraining (rating: good). It is possible (probability 0.1) that extensive, and expensive, training will be required (rating: average).

The probabilities decided upon for ratings on each criterion are similarly recorded in the decision matrix. Each probability is multiplied by the respective rating value (ranging from 2 for "very poor" to 10 for "very good") to arrive at the "expected value" (*EV*) for each rating. By adding across, the total expected value of each criterion is obtained. The difference in importance of the several criteria are now taken into account by multiplying the total *EV*s by the criteria weights. The resulting evaluation scores are recorded in the right-hand column. The separate criteria evaluation scores are in turn totaled to obtain the "total production resources" value. The illustration in Figure 6–5 shows a final value of 6.52 out of a possible 10. This is an index number that can now be compared with values similarly derived for other products under consideration. In general, the higher the score for utilization of production resources, the lower the production costs per unit can be expected to be.

Utilization of Marketing Resources

A going concern has marketing resources which, though often less tangible, are no less real than its production resources. These, too, can be underutilized by present products, thus again providing an opportunity for a new product to optimize a firm's input–output ratio. The marketing resources of firms are many and varied. Discussed here are four basic resources that are important in a wide array of product choice decisions. These are: (1) goodwill, (2) marketing know-how, (3) physical facilities, and (4) distribution channels.

Goodwill. In many cases, the most valuable asset a firm possesses is the goodwill that it has built up among consumers through its present products. If this goodwill could be tapped for the support of a new product without undermining the sale of existing products, it is an underutilized resource just as much as is physical plant operated at less than capacity. General Mills, when it undertook the sale of small household appliances some years ago, did so in part because it felt that the goodwill attaching to the General Mills name would help support the sale of appliances. A new Heinz food product probably finds a measure of market acceptance just because of its association in name with products already favored by consumers. A favorable association in the minds of consumers between a new product and existing products can influence the input–output ratio for the entire product line.

This relationship between new and present products can work both ways. The new product may sell better because of its association with present products. On the other hand, and at the same time, existing products may sell better because the new product helps to "round out" the line, sheds prestige on present products (for example, addition of the Continental Mark V to the Ford–Mercury–Lincoln line), or in some other way makes present products more acceptable to consumers. Unfortunately, a negative association between the new and present products in a line will produce opposite, and potentially disastrous, effects. For this reason such product relationships must be carefully considered in product choice decisions.

Marketing know-how.   The knowledge that management has gained through experience in the marketing of certain types and classes of products is often a very important asset. Knowledge of promotional strategies, pricing, dealer buying practices, consumer purchasing patterns, and so forth, can be the critical factor determining the success or failure of a new product. New products similar in marketing requirements to established products trade on this knowledge, thus greatly increasing the chances of success. It is far less risky for Procter & Gamble to introduce a new detergent than, for example, for Monsanto Chemical Company to move into this field. Monsanto did introduce a new detergent, All, which it later sold to Lever Brothers because of the difficulties it experienced in marketing a product with which it was unfamiliar. The rate of failure is high among new products introduced by firms unfamiliar with their marketing requirements.

Physical facilities.   Perhaps the most obvious opportunity for spreading marketing costs over a greater volume occurs when a new product can utilize physical distribution facilities that may contain excess capacity. Such facilities may be warehouses, truck fleets, retail outlets owned by the manufacturer, and so on. When Standard Brands, Inc., decided to distribute camera film to grocery stores along with its yeast, coffee, puddings, and other products, the dominant motivating factor was excess capacity in the direct distribution facilities that it maintained.

Distribution channels.   If the new product can be sold through the same channel of distribution as existing products, it probably can be handled by the same sales force. This will increase average order size and reduce costs as a percentage of sales. If a new channel is required, then an entirely new sales organization may be necessary. Because the cost of this sales force will have to be borne entirely by the new product, distribution costs as a percentage of sales will tend to be high. Also, it is difficult for a firm to break into new channels with a new product. Middlemen are naturally reluctant to add products without an established demand. Normally they are already carrying competitive brands, and they are not eager to assume the risks involved in replacing established products with new and untried brands. Of course, the same fac-

tors may apply even to the channels now used for existing products, but at least the innovating firm has an established relationship with its channels which helps in getting its new product accepted.

Decision Matrix: Utilization of Marketing Resources

A decision matrix of the same type as that used to evaluate the utilization of production resources is now employed to evaluate the use of marketing resources. Weights are assigned to the four decision criteria; the probabilities of various ratings for each are estimated; and the estimated values are calculated, adjusted for criterion weight, and summed to determine the total marketing resources utilization value of the proposed new product (Figure 6–6). There is now an objective basis for comparing it with other proposed new products.

Summary: Resource Utilization

With the aid of a decision matrix, two values relating to the efficiency with which a new product would use the resources of a firm have been arrived at—one for production resources and one for marketing resources. At this point, two pertinent questions arise: (1) What do these values mean? and (2) What does one do with them?

Probably the major value of these figures lies in the analysis that has been necessary in order to derive them. In this process, careful consideration has been given to the potential effects that adding a new product will have on all operations of the firm. Problem areas which might have been overlooked have been thought about by company management. Much of this analysis has been subjective, but often no other approach is possible in the real world.

The value for utilization of production resources and the value arrived at for use of marketing resources are not necessarily equal in significance. Which is more important in influencing the product choice decision depends on the area in which the potential benefits from proper fit between new and old products are greatest. A steel company, for example, has high fixed costs of production and, because of fluctuation in the demand for steel, is often faced with excess production capacity. Its marketing costs, on the other hand, tend to be more variable. Hence, optimizing the use of production resources through the addition of new products offers it the greatest opportunity to reduce average unit costs. A company manufacturing soaps or toiletries would usually have low production costs and high marketing costs. Consequently, a proper marketing fit among its products is of most importance.

A value for the utilization of total company resources can be obtained by combining these two figures. In the process, greater weight can be given to optimizing use of resources in the area with the greatest poten-

FIGURE 6—6   Decision matrix: Utilization of marketing resources (proposed new-product X)

Decision criterion	Criterion weight	Very good (10)		Good (8)		Average (6)		Poor (4)		Very poor (2)		Total	Criterion evaluation (Total EV × Weight)
		P	EV	P	EV	P	EV	P	EV	P	EV		
Goodwill	0.20	0	0	0.2	1.6	0.5	3.0	0.2	0.8	0.1	0.2	5.6	1.12
Marketing knowledge	0.20	0.1	1.0	0.5	4.0	0.3	1.8	0.1	0.4	0	0	7.2	1.44
Distribution facilities	0.30	0.3	3.0	0.5	4.0	0.2	1.2	0	0	0	0	8.2	2.46
Distribution channels	0.30	0	0	0.2	1.6	0.6	3.6	0.2	0.8	0	0	6.0	1.80
Total marketing resource utilization value													6.82

tial benefits. For example, if it is desired to give 50 percent greater weight to use of production resources than to utilization of marketing resources, then a value for efficiency of use of total company resources can be derived as shown in Figure 6–7.

FIGURE 6–7   Utilization of company resources

	Value	Weight	Weighted value
Production resource utilization	6.52	0.60	3.91
Marketing resource utilization	6.82	0.40	2.72
Company resource utilization			6.63

The major impact of efficient utilization of production and marketing resources is on cost. Both manufacturing and marketing costs may be reduced because of the spreading of fixed costs which this fit brings about. This cost advantage may result either in higher profit margins or in an opportunity to charge a lower price and thus increase the number of units sold.

A final word of caution is now in order about the interpretation and use of these numbers. The appearance of objectivity that such numbers give can be misleading. Underlying them is a great deal of subjective analysis, much of it based on inadequate information. Small differences in derived values are therefore of little significance. Even larger differences should be looked at as only rough approximations. On the other hand, the calculated values constitute a useful tool. Alternative product choices can be ranked in order and sorted and classified as desired. However, the main value of these numbers continues to lie in the analysis that is required to derive them.

DROPPING PRODUCTS[13]

The same procedure for adding new products can be used to determine whether products should be dropped. If a change in the demand outlook for a product, the price attainable, and the costs of producing and marketing it become less favorable, then profits might be improved by dropping it. Again, consideration should be given to the effect of

---

[13] For a fuller discussion of this topic, see Wind, *Product Policy,* chap. 18.

discontinuing one product on the profitability of the product line as a whole.

CONCLUSION

Because all products have a life cycle, survival of the business firm depends on the infusion of new products into the market. In a broader sense, the economic welfare of society is based on this same economic function. Long-term growth in labor-hour productivity is due primarily to development of new machines and processes, not to people working harder. The affluent society owes its present comfort more to the new products developed by this and preceding generations than to attempts to lower production costs. One automatic washing machine is worth, in terms of its effect on our way of living, an infinite number of old-fashioned washboards.

QUESTIONS

1. Distinguish between a product line and a product mix.

2. What marketing strategies may lead to extending the life of a mature brand?

3. A manufacturer of central home-heating equipment is considering the possibility of adding a line of electric space heaters selling at $19.95, $24.95, and $49.95. The company's present line is sold through heating contractors and is used both in new-home construction and in the renovation of older homes. The electric space heaters are portable, and it is thought that a large market for them exists among homeowners who require a source of supplemental heating, in cottages and resorts, and as the major heat source in parts of the country which do not require central heating.
   What factors should be considered by the firm before it commits itself to the manufacture and marketing of these electric space heaters?

4. The National Safety Razor Company is a major producer of safety razors, razor blades, shaving creams, and men's toiletries. Management is now considering a proposal to add a line of electric razors. One executive doubts the wisdom of this move. He points out that the Gillette Safety Razor Company failed in its attempt to introduce an electric razor. The reason for this failure, he says, is that electric razors did not fit well with the rest of the Gillette line. Is this executive's reasoning sound? Explain.

5. This chapter emphasized the importance of a good production and marketing fit between a company's present products and a new addition. Yet many companies, particularly the so-called conglomerates, have in recent years entered businesses completely unrelated to their present businesses. Is a decision to do this necessarily unsound?

6. When deciding to add a new product, is it more important that there be a good production fit or a good marketing fit between present products and the proposed addition? Explain.

7. Business firms have a substantial degree of choice in the amount of emphasis they place on product innovations in planning their long-term marketing strategy. What arguments can you offer in favor of relatively heavy stress on this strategy variable?

8. "When a company produces a wide line of products, management should take care to determine that each product covers its full costs and yields a satisfactory rate of profit." Appraise this statement.

9. It has been stressed that "ability to innovate" is vital to the continued success of a business firm. By what criteria do you judge whether or not a firm possesses such capability?

PRODUCT MANAGEMENT DECISIONS

7

In the previous chapter we discussed the considerations involved in choosing the best product to be added to the company's line. When making such a decision it is important to consider the market segment to which the new product is to appeal and to decide how management would like to have prospective customers perceive the position which the product is to occupy in competition with existing brands already available in the market.

In choosing a product to be added to an existing line, previous discussion has emphasized the need to consider the extent to which the new brand may be able to utilize both the production and marketing resources currently available. This, in turn, will influence the investment likely to be required in the development of the new product and its introduction to the market. What management is willing to commit to the new product should be made in the context of the funds currently being allocated to the various items in the current product line. This suggests, accordingly, that a product portfolio analysis may be a useful approach to assist in maintaining the proper balance in the support given both to the new product and to items making up the existing line.

Accordingly, the concepts of product positioning and product portfolio analysis will be discussed before turning to a consideration of the product development process which receives important emphasis in this chapter.

PRODUCT POSITIONING

In the earlier discussion of market segmentation we mentioned the concept of product positioning of new products and the modification and/or repositioning of existing ones. *Product positioning* refers to consumer perceptions of the place a product occupies in a given market relative to competing brands. This can be done by eliciting (*a*) consumers' perceptions using a variety of available procedures for similarity measurement, (*b*) consumer preference—overall and under a variety of usage and purchase conditions—or (*c*) both perceptions and preferences.

In developing a positioning strategy, management can use a number of alternative bases for positioning. These include:

1. Positioning on specific product features (examples: Chevette as an economy car or VW's "Think small").
2. Positioning on benefits, problem solution, or needs (examples: Crest's anticavity positioning or TWA's on-time performance).
3. Positioning for specific usage occasions. Consider, for example, the Schaffer positioning ("The one beer to have when you're having more than one"), Campbell's positioning for soups for cooking.
4. Positioning for user category (example: "The Pepsi Generation").
5. Positioning against another product. Avis never mentions Hertz explicitly, but its positioning—"Avis is Number 2 in rent-a-car, so why not go with us? We try harder!" is an example of implicit positioning against a leader.
6. Product class dissociation. Such positioning is especially effective when introducing a new product which differs from the typical products in an established category. Lead-free gasoline is a new-product class positioned against leaded gasoline. At the brand level probably the most successful antiproduct class positioning is that of 7up with its "UnCola" positioning.
7. Hybrid bases. Still another possibility is a hybrid approach incorporating elements from more than one base for positioning.[1]

Given the variety of bases which can be used to position a firm's products, the question is which one to use. The choice depends upon the distinctive characteristics of the firm, the product, the target market, and the environmental setting.

As a means of deciding upon the initial positioning of a new brand, or the repositioning of an existing brand, it is helpful to make use of a product positioning map. Figure 7–1 is an illustration of a positioning map for 12 brands of automobiles based upon consumers' perceptions

---

[1]Yoram J. Wind, *Product Policy*, © 1982, Addison-Wesley, Reading, Massachusetts. Pp. 74–75, 87–88 (exhibit 4–12), and 108. Reprinted with permission.

FIGURE 7–1   Product positioning map of 12 brands of automobiles

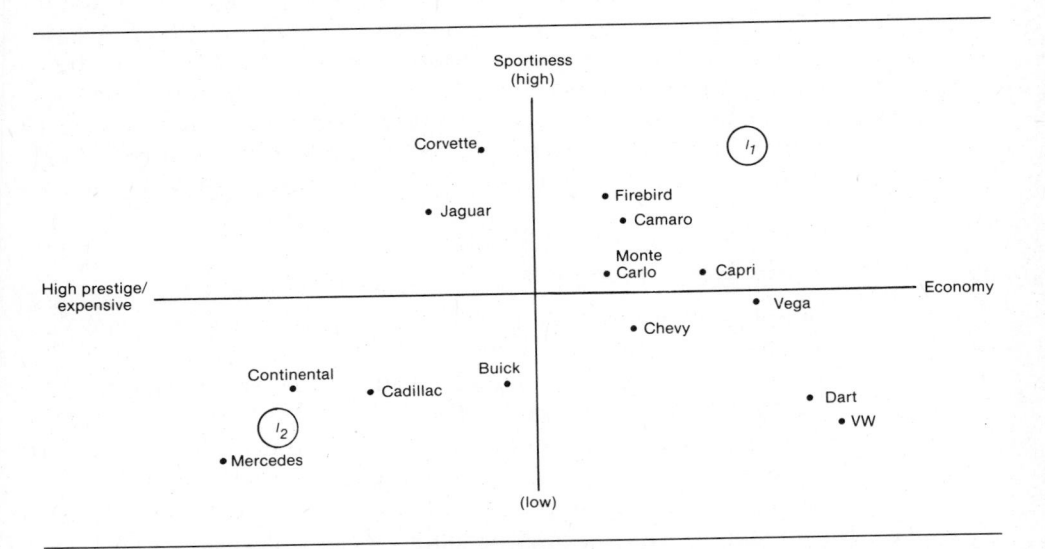

Source: Yoram J. Wind, *Product Policy: Concepts, Methods, and Strategy* (Reading, Mass.: Addison-Wesley Publishing, 1982), p. 87.

of their similarities plus data showing the rank order of the brands according to consumer preferences.[2]

Also shown are "ideal points." The ideal point represents the point in space which satisfies the condition that the distance of all brands from it will correspond to the respondents' rank order of the brands from the most to the least preferred.

In this illustrative map, brands are positioned according to how consumers perceive their degree of sportiness and economy. Note that respondent 1 (whose ideal point is identified as I_1) prefers sporty-type cars such as Camaro, followed by Firebird and Capri. Respondent 2 (ideal point I_2), on the other hand, prefers the luxury-type cars such as Mercedes, followed by Continental and Cadillac.

Understanding consumers' perceptions and evaluations of the firm's products is an essential ingredient in planning marketing strategy. It provides management with a clear understanding of *where its products are* versus the positions of competing products (by segment). It further provides some insights into *why* the products are where they are and can suggest directions for *where they may consider going.*

---

[2]Yoram J. Wind, *Product Policy,* © 1982, Addison-Wesley, Reading, Massachusetts. Pp. 87–88 (exhibit 4–12). Reprinted with permission.

PRODUCT PORTFOLIO CONCEPT[3]

Where a firm has a number of product lines competing in several different markets, a critical part of product policy involves the assessment of the company's portfolio of products and markets and deciding on the best allocation of resources among them. Without explicit attention to the entire product portfolio, the likelihood of suboptimization is high, especially in product-management-organized firms.

Product portfolio analysis evaluates the current products of the firm on a number of key dimensions (such as profitability, growth, and risk) and provides the input to management decisions on addition of products, modification of existing products, or deletion of products, and allocation of resources among the various products and markets.

The product portfolio management approach has its roots and analogies in financial investment portfolio theory. The portfolio problem in financial investment management consists of determining the "optimal" portfolio of stocks and bonds. The typical steps involved in the development of a portfolio of stocks and bonds, which are also required for the development of any product portfolio, are:

1. Determine the objectives of the investor/manager, the trade-off between risk and return in the case of the financial portfolio, and any other management objectives such as market share, or growth, in the case of a product portfolio.
2. Evaluate each item in the portfolio (product in the case of a product portfolio) in terms of the objectives specified above.
3. Decide on the desired portfolio and recommend that certain holdings be reduced or increased in order to give the portfolio balance and conformity with the objectives; i.e., the desired portfolio offers guidelines for the allocation of resources among products (and any other items such as markets included in the portfolio analysis).

NEW-PRODUCT DEVELOPMENT[4]

The process of developing a new product is broad in scope. Directly or indirectly, the process must involve all operations of the business firm—marketing, production, research and development, finance, and even the legal department. Because of its inherent risk feature, top management is usually intimately involved in it. In order for so complex

---

[3]Yoram J. Wind, *Product Policy,* © 1982, Addison-Wesley, Reading, Massachusetts. Pp. 108–109. Reprinted with permission.

[4]For a comprehensive treatment of new-product development, see C. Merle Crawford, *New-Products Management* (Homewood, Ill.: Richard D. Irwin, 1983).

a task to be carried out effectively, it is imperative that a sound program for product development be formulated and then followed.

The most basic and critical decision involved in the product development process is the one discussed in the preceding chapter—selection of the product which provides the best profit opportunity for the particular firm in question. If this decision has been made wisely, with due consideration given to all of the variables involved, the remaining steps in the process are made much easier and the chances of success are greatly enhanced. Still, much remains to be done and many opportunities for error remain after this choice has been made.

Product development is, in essence, the process of fitting the proposed product to the requirements and opportunities of the market. The decision to produce, say, a sports car still leaves unanswered questions about styling and configuration, size, color, convenience options, the image to be projected, and so on. An almost infinite number of specific decisions must be made to provide this market adaptation. If they are made wisely, the profit opportunity visualized will be realized. If not, the profit opportunity will be lost.

Selection of the best product for development is, as previously explained, a procedure fraught with uncertainty—uncertainty concerning demand, price, cost, and the product life cycle. In a very real sense, the product development process is a procedure for gradually reducing this uncertainty by increasing the information available to the decision maker.

THE PRODUCT DEVELOPMENT PROCESS

The product development process is not, and cannot be made, uniform for all companies. Each company is unique, and this uniqueness finds expression in differences in goals, requirements, and procedures. Figure 7–2 shows how the product development process might be carried through in a hypothetical firm. Although not necessarily applicable to situations faced by all companies, it will serve as a useful frame of reference for discussion of the types of decisions involved in product development.

Characteristics of Product Development

An overview of the product development process as depicted in Figure 7–2 reveals certain important characteristics.

Process span.   Product development begins with the conception of an idea for a new product and does not end until an established sales position for the new product has been achieved in the market. In a very real sense, a product has not been "developed," nor has a true innova-

FIGURE 7–2   Steps in conversion of new-product idea into new business

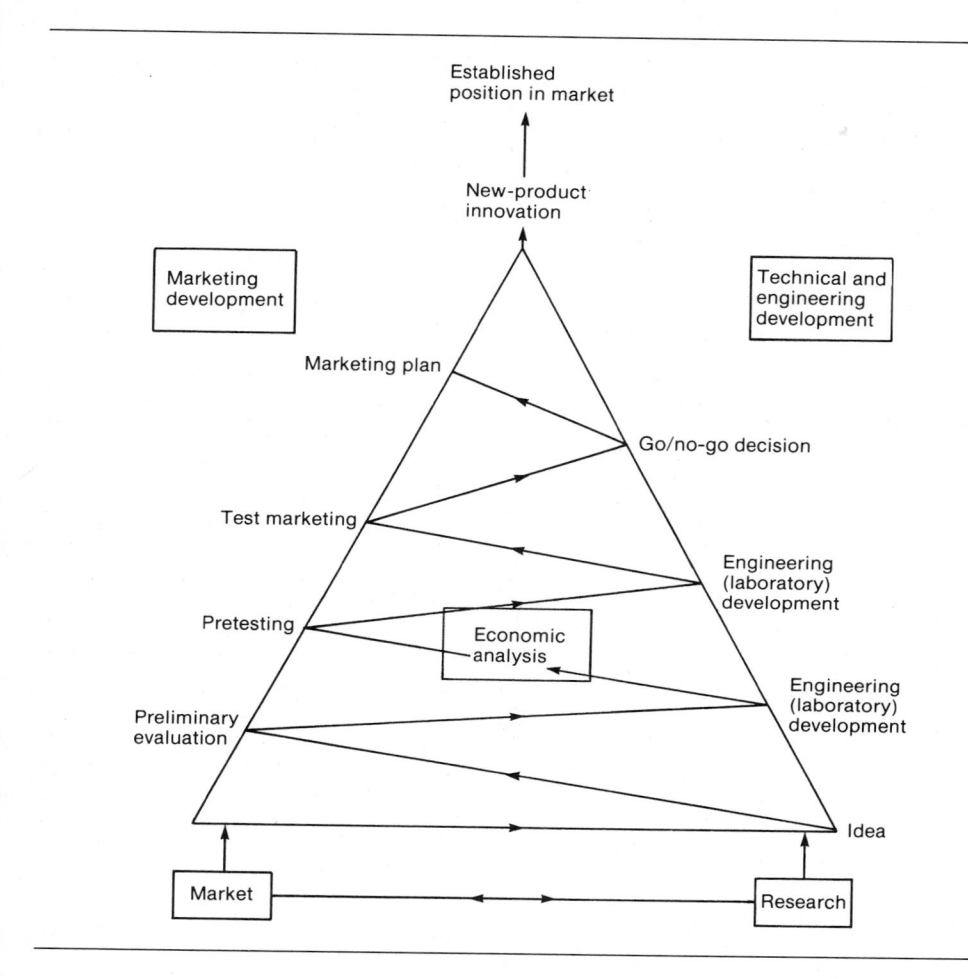

tion been accomplished, until that product has been accepted in the market. This achievement marks the adaptation of the new product to the market in an overt, profit-making sense. It is the point at which the basic objective of new-product development, maximization of profits, begins to be realized. In fact, it can be argued that product development does not end even here, that it is necessary to continue to change and improve products throughout the total life cycle if profits are to be maximized. However, this process is more commonly referred to as product improvement.

Concurrent marketing and production development.   As discussed above, product development involves all the operations of a business. Figure 7–2 stresses the concurrence of marketing and technical and engineering development. Technical and engineering development must be geared to marketing requirements as closely as possible. Production must provide the product the market wants, in the right quantities, at the right time. Marketing strategy, on the other hand, must reflect certain realities of the production process. For example, offering many varieties of size, color, and style may maximize sales, but only at prohibitive production costs. Profit is a function of the efficiency of the total firm, not maximum efficiency in one part or another.

Certain economies are offered by the concurrent development both the marketing and the engineering of a new product. Test marketing, for example, provides an opportunity to experiment with production processes so as to eliminate bugs before full-scale production is required.

Interdependence of marketing and engineering development.   In Figure 7–2 each of the steps in product development on the technical and engineering development side is related to a step on the marketing side, in the sense that each depends on the other. Perhaps this interdependence is most clearly seen in the case of laboratory research and marketing research. Laboratory research without accompanying marketing research can easily be misdirected and sterile. In a market-directed economy, the standards employed in laboratory research should reflect what people want from the product. High quality reflected, say, in durability is not a reasonable standard if consumers prefer low price and are willing to sacrifice quality in order to get it.

Before laboratory testing can be meaningfully undertaken, marketing research is usually necessary. The extent to which this is true, however, varies by products and by the type of standards involved. In many cases, important market standards for a product are already well known (for example, safety and durability of tires, efficacy of drugs, and purity of food). Some laboratory testing is often possible without market testing: *complete* laboratory testing usually is not.

The same type of interdependence exists among the other steps in production and marketing development. Essentially, the market testing activities provide feedback that allows engineering development to accurately reflect marketing requirements. The triangular shape of Figure 7–2 is intended to illustrate that product development is a process of merging marketing requirements with technical and engineering requirements through a step-by-step process. Only when such a merger has been completed is a successful product innovation possible.

Product development is a cautious process.   It is a step-by-step feeling out of the market as the process evolves. Each step taken is intended to reduce further the uncertainty inherent in the product development process by increasing the information available about marketing re-

quirements for the new product. Implicit in the taking of each step, therefore, is the need to decide how much additional market information is worth—in research expenditures, in time, and in relation to the cost of assuming more risk. The cost of reducing risk to zero, if this were possible, would usually be prohibitive. In carrying through this cautious approach, another objective is to retain as long as possible the option of *not* introducing the new product, with a minimal investment loss should this decision be made.

Product development involves the "total" product.   The need to develop such things as distribution strategy, promotional appeals, service policy, and warranty policy is as great as the need to develop the physical product. In reality, they too are a part of each of the steps in production and marketing development. For example, marketing research done on the new product is equally relevant to such matters as service, warranty, and so on. In fact, the physical product may even be changed to adapt to such things as distribution strategy and promotional appeals.

STEPS IN PRODUCT DEVELOPMENT

The preceding section considered some characteristics of product development as a total process. This section will take a closer look at what is involved in carrying out the specific steps in product development.

New-Product Ideas

Ideas for new products come from many sources—from the market, from production, from home office and research personnel, from salespeople, from other companies, and even from independent inventors. No one knows just where a good idea for a profitable new product might come from. Some sources are more likely to be productive than others, but no company wants to close off any of them.

Most firms claim to be receptive to new-product ideas, but few make an overt attempt to stimulate them or to ferret them out. Rather, this important process is left more or less to chance. That is a mistake. Some sort of organization seeking out and handling new ideas is required; what form this organization takes is of secondary importance. Unless responsibility is centered somewhere, both the search and the processing will be neglected. Both line and staff personnel are usually fully busy with current operations, and they neither welcome nor pursue added burdens.

The search for new-product ideas can go on in many ways, the most appropriate approach depending on the industry involved. Primarily

for industrial goods, but to some extent for consumer goods, call reports of salespeople may be so constructed and analyzed that they reveal consumer problems with present products, comparisons with competing products, unmet needs, and so on. Basic research may turn up many ideas that can be followed up profitably. Even brainstorming sessions may be worthwhile. Most important is that ideas be actively sought, whatever the methods used.

Preliminary Evaluation

The next step in Figure 7–2, preliminary evaluation of new-product ideas, is in essence the product choice decision discussed in the preceding chapter. However, it is usually not feasible to subject every new idea to complete and rigorous analysis. Most new-product ideas are not worthy of extensive consideration. Therefore, some sort of preliminary screening method is usually employed. It is quite customary to have a screening committee, made up of representatives from different functional areas of the business (marketing, production, research and development, finance, and so on), look over and discuss new-product ideas. On the basis of the breadth and background of the committee members' experience, these ideas are reviewed. Usually, most of the ideas are rejected. Those that look most promising are turned over to some sort of new-product task force for detailed study. This study might well follow the procedures outlined in the preceding chapter. This group then reports back to the preliminary screening committee, which reports, in turn, to top management.

Economic Analysis

An economic analysis of a new-product venture should begin at an early date. At that point, the inputs to the analysis will be rough. As the product development process continues, these inputs can be continuously refined. The economic analysis is necessary to achieve an estimate of the potential profitability of a product addition and the probability that this profit will be attained. The more common things that the economic analysis is expected to reveal are such things as:

1. The market potential for the product class of which the proposed product is a part.
2. Cost estimates.
   a. Variable costs.
   b. Fixed costs.
3. The expected price at which the product will be sold to consumers.
4. The margins required for middlemen.
5. The net selling price of the manufacturer.

6. The break-even volume (fixed costs divided by the difference between net selling price and variable costs).
7. The break-even volume given an expected return on investment.
8. The market share required to achieve the expected return on investment.

Such an analysis might reveal at an early date that the project is not feasible, thus preventing the waste of development funds that would have occurred if lack of feasibility had been discovered much later.

Engineering Development

Those new-product ideas which have survived preliminary screening and have produced a favorable economic analysis can now be subjected to engineering (laboratory) development to determine whether they are feasible from a technical standpoint. Perhaps the idea is "beyond the state of the art" from the standpoint of production capability. If a proposed product cannot possibly be produced, there is no point in going to the market to find out whether consumers would purchase it. Also, a more precise concept of what the product might be like and what it is intended to do is usually necessary before a logical pretesting program can be set up. Engineering development, at this stage, is unlikely to be complete, because more market information is required before it can proceed that far.

Pretesting

The fundamental purpose of pretesting is to acquire knowledge useful in assuring that the new product properly reflects demand factors. The "pre" in pretesting can mean preproduct, preproduction, premarketing program, and so on. Of necessity, it is a step that must come early in order to provide proper guidance. Because it must come early, the testing is usually done under circumstances that are somewhat artificial and are difficult in other ways.

The methods used in pretesting products are numerous and varied. This is an area with much room for ingenuity. A few of the more common methods are: (1) *Consumer panels and juries:* Groups of various sorts and sizes (women's clubs, company visitors, etc.) are asked their opinion of various proposed product features (styling, color, etc.). (2) *Consumer surveys:* Representative samples of consumers may be asked to view and comment on proposed new products. (3) *Field tests:* Tentative versions of new products may be presented to consumers for use in the home, and consumers' reactions ascertained. Pillsbury Mills asked housewives to bake two different formulas of cake mix, to serve them to their families, and then to record their preferences. Chrysler Corporation gave con-

sumers new turbine cars to drive for several weeks and then interviewed them to learn their reactions. (4) *Trade shows:* Products are often displayed at trade shows, and visitors are asked to fill out questionnaires to gauge their reactions.

Many other methods of pretesting are in use. All of them involve certain dangers. It is both difficult and costly to choose representative samples. The consumer's possible inability to indicate a true preference under artificial conditions always casts some doubt on the results. Even if consumers are able to express their true preferences, it is difficult to conclude what this means in terms of actual sales in the real marketplace.

Further Engineering Development

After pretesting, further engineering development is usually necessary. The product can now be refined to more fully reflect consumer tastes and wants. The feasibility and cost of alternative production processes can be compared. Some units of the product must be produced for distribution before the next step in marketing development—test marketing—can be taken.

Test Marketing

Test marketing involves the sale of a proposed new product under conditions as near normal as possible in a test market that is as representative as possible of the target market. Sales performance of the product in test markets is observed and measured in order to ascertain what sales performance can be expected in the total market.

The need for preliminary market testing of new products stems from the inherent limitations of pretesting. Pretesting is, as mentioned above, artificial in varying degrees as far as market conditions are concerned. Also, pretesting usually involves only some, and not all, aspects of the new product. A pretesting of Pillsbury cake mix, for example, was limited to taste preference between two alternative formulas. It revealed no information on such matters as package design, price, promotional appeals, comparisons with competing products, and so on. Consequently, it left a large measure of uncertainty about future market performance.

Test marketing, too, has limitations. The basic problem of sampling error is an important one. Cost limitations usually prevent the use of a truly representative sample of the total market. Usually only one or a few cities are chosen. Also, the cost of arranging for the gathering of maximum information in the test market is high. Expensive store audits and consumer surveys may be necessary to do this. Some companies set up their own test markets and do their own data collection. Others use the test markets of such market research organizations as the A. C. Nielsen Company, which have elaborate facilities for data gathering.

Because of cost, as well as for other reasons, the time that can be devoted to test marketing is usually limited. It is questionable whether sales in a short time period are fully representative of longer-term sales experience. The difference between initial sales and repeat sales is particularly critical: Initial sales may indicate a high consumer interest in a new product, but only repeat sales indicate the presence of the sort of consumer satisfaction on which long-term success must be built.

Market testing runs the risk of loss of secrecy for a firm's new-product plans. This may take away the promotional advantage associated with a dramatic, nationwide introduction. Also, it divulges a company's plans to competitors and may lessen the time it takes for them to retaliate. For such products as automobiles, these two limitations are deemed highly important.

Test marketing of new products provides an opportunity for further experimentation on the production side. The manufacture of limited quantities allows development of production processes and techniques so as to minimize production cost.

The Go/No-Go Decision

The process of product development up to this point has been one of gradual and continuous improvement in the information available for product decisions. Information seeking can vary greatly in extent, time consumed, and cost incurred. Throughout this process, management would normally attempt to retain as long as possible the option of going ahead or not going ahead with the introduction of the new product. At some point it becomes uneconomic to continue to seek information, and a decision must be made to "go" or "not go" with the product in question. The success of the new product at this point is always uncertain, sometimes highly so. It is a question of weighting carefully the probability of success and deciding whether or not to proceed.

The go/no-go decision is a difficult one. Information is never complete. Furthermore, the decision makers have a vested interest in a favorable decision in order to justify the substantial investment that has been made in bringing the product to this point. A no-go decision is, in a sense, a tacit admission that previous expenditures should not have been made. This is a difficult psychological barrier to overcome. An objective approach to this decision would, of course, ignore costs already incurred. These are "sunk" costs. The only relevant decision variables are future revenues in relation to future costs. This relationship determines the expected controllable profit that is associated with the new product.

The go/no-go decision involves, in essence, a careful review and correction of the several variables in the profitability formula developed in

the previous chapter.[5] Hopefully, as a result of pretesting and preliminary market testing, demand can now be more accurately defined both qualitatively and quantitatively. Expectations of price behavior, likewise, can now be refined. A recalculation of production and marketing fit, based on expanded knowledge of marketing and production requirements, should allow a refinement of earlier cost calculations. Expected life will usually still be a major uncertainty, but perhaps some estimating improvements are possible here. Effects on these same variables for existing products should now also be better known.

These refinements of the component variables in the profitability formula will now permit a more precise estimate of the expected profits associated with adding the new product. A comparison with alternatives available for investment will then allow the go/no-go decision to be made.

The Marketing Plan

The final step in this process, before actual introduction of the new product into the market, is the formulation of a detailed marketing plan. The purpose of such a plan is to give form, direction, and control to the market-introduction process. The new-product marketing plan must, of course, be integrated with, and fully consistent with, the overall marketing plan of the company.

Actually, the development of a marketing plan does not start from scratch at this point. Previous steps in the development process are as relevant to this activity as they are to the go/no-go decision. The evolution of the marketing plan began with the new-product idea and grew with each succeeding step. In fact, *some* marketing plan had to be used in test marketing. Further development of this plan, however, may now be in order.

The essential parts of a marketing plan for a new-product introduction are the same as those for the company's overall marketing plan: a situation analysis can be based on information gathered in the earlier steps in production and marketing development. If these steps were well handled, the requisite information will be available. The problems and opportunities that this situation provides should now also be known. What remains is refining the marketing strategy.

ANCILLARY PRODUCT DECISIONS

The term *product* is used in this text to refer to everything that the consumer receives when making a purchase. Consequently, product de-

---

[5] $P = [D \times (R-C) \times L] \pm [d \times (r-c) \times l]_1 \pm [d \times (r-c) \times l]_2 \cdots \pm [d \times (r-c) \times l]_n.$

cisions cover a wide spectrum. This has been recognized in the discussion up to this point, but emphasis has been placed on the physical product and little has been said about some of the special problems associated with such functions as packaging, branding, warranty policy, and service policy. A closer look at these areas is now in order.

Packaging

A package has two major functions: containment and promotion. Containment is essential to efficiency in physical distribution, while the promotional aspects of packaging operate to influence demand. The problems of containment tend to be technical and reasonably objective, such as requirements of strength, size, and resistance to moisture. Promotional requirements concern such things as the package's ability to attract attention, its comparison with competing packages, its adaptability to advertising and point-of-sale promotion, and its reflection on product quality. The development of a package that will serve such functions well is a more subjective process. Although the technical problems of containment are very difficult ones for some products, for most products the promotional aspects of packaging pose the more difficult decision requirements.

The role played by the package in the marketing mix, and hence the importance of the package development function, depends on many things. Packaging is usually a more critical element for convenience goods than for shopping or specialty goods. Within the convenience goods category, its importance varies with differences in the buying behavior of consumers; for example, consumers wish to see and touch fresh vegetables and will buy detergents sight unseen. Self-service enhances the role of the package. Product-use requirements of consumers (for example, frequent reseal and reuse) may make the package a major sales influence factor. For some products (for example, cosmetics, table salt), package differences among brands may be more important than anything else. In some cases, promotional requirements (use of television, for example) may strongly influence package decisions.

Diverse effects of package decisions.   Package decisions are complicated by the fact that they may have many indirect, and often unanticipated, effects on both the production and marketing functions. Such "side effects" are often difficult to foresee and even more difficult to evaluate. Take, for example, the decision of many soft drink manufacturers to package their products in cans as well as in returnable bottles.[6]

In the 1950s, soft drink companies began experimenting with the sale of soft drinks in cans. Cans were thought to have several distinct advantages: (1) They did not need to be returned and thus relieved consumers

---

[6]The following illustration is based on Orange Crush Company (*Michigan Business Cases*, Marketing Series, no. 21).

of an inconvenience and removed a major problem for supermarkets, which objected to handling bottle returns. (2) They substantially reduced product weight. A case of 24 six-ounce bottles weighs 50 pounds, while a case of 48 six-ounce cans weighs about 25 pounds and takes one third less space. (3) Bottles are hard to stack and take a great deal of room in storage. Cans can be stacked in displays and on shelves just like any other canned goods.

Among the side effects associated with this product change are the following: (1) *Taste*. It was feared that consumers might object to the slight metallic flavor picked up by carbonated beverages in cans. (2) *Price*. Although cans cost less per unit than bottles, the average returnable bottle made about 25 round trips. Thus, canned drinks would have to sell for 3½ to 4½ cents more per unit. (3) *Channels of distribution*. Present distribution was through bottlers who purchased syrup from soft drink firms. These bottlers were not equipped to can soft drinks. (4) *In-store promotion*. Present promotion strategy relied heavily on bottlers, who made frequent deliveries to retail stores, set up displays, and so on. The soft drink manufacturer was not equipped to do this. (5) *Present distribution through bottlers*. If canned soft drink distribution bypassed bottlers, yet cut into their sales of bottled beverages, their profit position might be endangered. This might lead them to dilute their sales efforts by adding other soft drinks or, in extreme cases, to relinquish their franchise. As bottled soft drinks were expected to continue to account for at least 90 percent of sales, this would seriously hurt the soft drink firms.

In the 1960s, canned soft drinks grew from 2 percent to 10 percent of total soft drink sales. This, along with other package changes in the industry, changed the entire distribution structure. Only high-volume bottling plants could justify the expense of installing canning lines. This probably played no small part in the reduction in the number of bottling plants in the United States from 4,300 in 1962 to 3,600 in 1968.[7] Parent companies took on the job of supplying smaller bottlers with canned soft drinks. What started as a "simple" package change revolutionized the whole industry.

In the 1970s new forces were set in motion which again influenced packaging decisions in the beverage industry. First, technological improvements in formulating plastic for bottles made these containers safer to use and to some extent biodegradable. It appeared that plastic bottles would further displace glass bottles as containers for beer and soft drinks. By the mid-1970s, however, legislation had been passed in four states (Michigan, Oregon, South Dakota, and Vermont) which discouraged the use of one-way containers for beer and soft drinks by requiring deposits on all containers. As of the early 1980s, glass bottles

---

[7]*Marketing Insights,* March 4, 1968, p. 15.

appear to be increasing their share of the beverage container market in those states.

Legal constraints on packaging. In addition to the state laws mentioned above, the principal legal constraints upon packaging decisions are those contained in the Food, Drug, and Cosmetic Act of 1938. The provisions of this act relating to packaging have two basic purposes: (1) to protect health and (2) to prevent deception. Information appearing on or within the package is controlled by the Food, Drug, and Cosmetic Act as well as by the Wool Products Labeling Act of 1939, the Fur Products Labeling Act of 1951, and the Textile Fibers Products Identification Act of 1958. For foods, Section 401 of the Food, Drug, and Cosmetic Act requires the establishment of definitions and standards for foods whenever such action will "promote honesty and fair dealing in the interest of consumers." The provisions for the labeling of drug products have long been very exacting, and in 1964 they were further strengthened by an amendment to the act. The other three acts mentioned above are primarily designed to prevent deception by requiring on the label an accurate and clear description of the product's composition.

Government-imposed standards of packaging and labeling have long been a subject of controversy. Some consumer groups and government agencies recommend more rigid controls. Extensive hearings were held by the antitrust subcommittee of the U.S. Senate, chaired by Senator Philip A. Hart, in 1961. Witnesses contended that the use of odd weights and sizes by competing brands made price comparison difficult, that net contents were often obscurely stated in small print, and that illustrations, descriptions, and terms such as *giant half-pound* and *jumbo quart* were misleading. Many other charges of consumer abuse through packaging were also strongly pressed.

The outgrowth of these and subsequent hearings and congressional debate, spread over five years, was the passage in 1966 of the so-called Truth-in-Packaging Act.[8] A brief summary of the act follows:

Mandatory labeling provisions. A primary objective of the act is to promote uniformity and simplification of labeling. The bill provides that:

1. The identity of the commodity shall be specified on the label.
2. The net quantity of the contents shall be stated in a uniform and prominent location on the package.
3. The net quantity of the contents shall be clearly expressed in ounces (only) and, if applicable, pounds (only) or, in the case of liquid measures, in the largest whole unit of quarts or pints.
4. The net quantity of a "serving" must be stated if the package bears a representation concerning servings.

---

[8]Public Law 89–755, 89th Cong., S 985 (November 1966).

Discretionary labeling provisions. The act authorizes the administering agencies to promulgate regulations when necessary to prevent consumer deception or to facilitate value comparisons:

1. To determine what size packages may be represented by such descriptions as small, medium, and large.
2. To regulate the use of such promotions as "cents off" or "economy size" on any package.
3. To require the listing of ingredients in the order of decreasing predominance.
4. To prevent nonfunctional slack fill.

Packaging provisions. The act provides for the voluntary adoption of packaging standards. It authorizes the secretary of commerce to call upon manufacturers, packers, and distributors to develop voluntary standards whenever undue proliferation of weights, measures, or quantities impairs the ability of consumers to make value comparisons. If voluntary standards are not adopted, the secretary of commerce shall report this fact to Congress together with a legislative recommendation.

Enforcement. Responsibility for enforcing the provisions of the act is divided between the Food and Drug Administration (FDA), which has jurisdiction over food and cosmetics, and the Federal Trade Commission (FTC), which is supposed to regulate the labeling of all other consumer commodities. The Truth-in-Packaging Act does not provide for criminal penalties.

Branding

Another integral part of almost every product is a brand. Selection of an appropriate product brand, one which produces maximum acceptability of a product, is an important part of the product development process. The term *brand* is a business term; the term *trademark* is its legal counterpart. A brand name is that part of the brand which can be vocalized. It should be remembered, however, that *brand* refers to *anything* which serves to distinguish one product from another. Brands owned by manufacturers are known either as "manufacturers' brands" or as "national brands," regardless of the scope of the area served. Brands controlled by wholesalers or retailers are known either as "distributors' brands" or as "private brands."

Basic objective of branding. The basic objective of branding is market control. A brand is essential to the promotional activities of the firm. Through promotion, acceptance or preference for a product can be established among consumers. If the product bears a manufacturer's brand and is available through many retail outlets, the goodwill of consumers is directed toward the manufacturer. Retailers will find it difficult to substitute other products for the branded one that consumers prefer.

On the other hand, if the wholesaler or retailer places his own brand on a product, the goodwill of consumers attaches to the wholesaler or retailer, and the manufacturer loses much control over the market for the product.

Brand selection.   Selection of a brand for a new product is an extremely important and often treacherous operation. New-product names such as Chrysler's Omni, Du Pont's Corfam, and Cities Service's Citgo grow out of meticulously planned campaigns involving computers, psychological tests, opinion surveys, and other scientific procedures. Too much is at stake to leave the choice to flashes of inspiration.

A good brand must meet two important requirements: (1) maximum promotability and (2) minimum risk of loss of ownership rights. Promotability is the result of a combination of factors, and no absolute criteria can safely be established. Normally, however, those brands are considered best which are short; easily pronounced, spelled, and remembered; distinctive; appealing; and adaptable to various promotional media. A hidden nuance in a name can do a lot of damage, undermining the consumer's image of the product. For this reason, some companies insist on "nonsense" words for brand names, and rely on computers to find them. Among these is Du Pont, which reasons that a nonsense word is likely to have fewer connotations than a word familiar to consumers.[9]

Ownership rights to a brand can be lost in many ways, of which the two most common are by infringing upon another brand and by becoming a generic term. The danger of inadvertent infringement is great. More than 300,000 brands are registered with the U.S. Patent Office, and at least that many more are registered with state bureaus; and according to the U.S. Trademark Association, there are probably a million more brands that are not registered but could lead to lawsuits if copied.

A brand name becomes generic when the public adopts it as a word to describe a general class of products. The courts may then rule that it is a part of the American language and cannot be appropriated for the exclusive use of one firm. Until 1921, "Aspirin" was a brand name of the Bayer Company. Then it became a generic name. In the same way, Du Pont lost "Cellophane," the Haughton Elevator Company lost "Escalator," and American Thermos Product Company lost "Thermos."[10]

Unfortunately, there is a conflict between the twin objectives of promotability and protection for brands. The factors that make a brand promotable are also the ones which might tend to cause it to be infringed by others or to become generic. There is need in brand administration to reconcile these two objectives, to achieve the optimum level of each without jeopardizing the other. Registration of a brand under the Lan-

---

[9]Max Gunther, "We've Got to Call It Something," *Saturday Evening Post,* September 11, 1965, pp. 60–61.

[10]Ibid., p. 61.

ham Act (Trade Mark Law of 1946) is a partial aid in accomplishing this goal.

Registration of brands. Under the common law, ownership rights in a brand are based on priority of use; whoever first used a particular brand in commerce is the "owner" of that brand. Registration of a brand is not essential to the protection of fundamental rights in that brand, but registration under the Lanham Act modifies and extends basic ownership rights. Among the important benefits which are gained by registering a brand under the Lanham Act are the following:

1. *Registration is prima facie evidence of ownership.* This means that in case of conflict over ownership rights in a brand, the burden of proof is on the owner of the unregistered brand. Because use of a particular brand by both parties may have begun many years ago, and evidence of the exact date of use is often skimpy, this can be a very important advantage.

2. *Registration is constructive notice of the registrant's ownership claim.* Under the common law an infringer can often gain ownership rights to a brand if the infringement was innocent, made without knowledge of the existence of the infringed brand. If a brand is registered, all parties are *presumed* to know of its existence, whether or not they do in fact and cannot claim innocent infringement.

3. *Registration permits cases of infringement to be tried in the federal courts.* This is important to protection of a brand because the federal courts will interpret cases in light of the relatively clear provisions of the Lanham Act rather than under the common law, which is far from clear and is the basis for adjudication in state courts.

4. *Possible collection of triple damages.* In cases of brand infringement, the courts normally award damages to the owner of the infringed brand. Under the Lanham Act, the federal courts are authorized to assess up to three times the actual damages. This serves as an obvious deterrent to infringement.

5. *Protection against imports which infringe registered brands.* Brands recorded on the Principal Register are filed in the U.S. Treasury Department and are checked against brands on imported goods to discover and halt cases of possible infringement.

6. *Achievement of incontestability.* After five years of registration on the Principal Register, a brand becomes "incontestable." As defined in the Lanham Act, this means that ownership rights cannot be lost to someone else on the grounds of priority of use. This limits to five years a risk which is eternal under the common law.

Warranty Policy

Decisions on warranty policies are also a part of the product development process. The assurance provided by a warranty that the consumer will actually receive the utility anticipated is a part of the value of

a purchase. Warranties may be either express or implied. An *express* warranty is stated by the seller in written or spoken words. A warranty is *implied* if, from the nature of the sale and the circumstances of the parties, the law believes it reasonable to surmise that a warranty was intended, although none was actually mentioned. Implied warranties have been codified and incorporated into the Uniform Commercial Code.

Warranties and consumer protection. Until recent years, warranties offered less protection to consumers than they usually believed. A typical warranty usually restricted the buyer's right to redress to claims approved by the seller, and at the same time disclaimed all other liabilities, express or implied. Such a warranty actually protected the seller more than the buyer. Most consumers did not realize how little protection most warranties provided because (1) consumers usually do not read warranties and (2) warranties were usually couched in ambiguous phrases that only a lawyer could understand.

Under new legislation that Congress passed in late 1974 and that became effective on July 4, 1975,[11] if a company wishes to offer a written warranty it must state clearly whether the warranty is "full" or "limited." There is no in-between ground, and minimum federal standards for each category must be met. Congress left it to the Federal Trade Commission to work out many of the detailed regulations, including the rules that a seller must follow in setting up an informal dispute settlement procedure. If unable to reach a settlement directly with the seller, a consumer may take his or her warranty case to court. In addition to providing for class action suits, the new law provides for reimbursement of the attorney's fees of any consumer successful in his or her case. At the time of this writing, companies are trying to decide whether they should offer full or limited warranties, or discontinue offering warranties altogether.[12]

Consumer Product Safety Act. The Consumer Product Safety Act of 1972 provides protection in addition to the protection provided consumers by warranties. The act does not concern warranties as such, but it supplements them. The act established the Consumer Product Safety Commission, one of the nation's powerful regulatory agencies. It has jurisdiction over every consumer product except automobiles, food, and a few others that are regulated by older agencies of government. At its discretion it can ban, order the redesign of, or publicize the dangers associated with any product that it determines poses an unreasonable risk of injury. It has the power to inspect facilities and to demand access to company files. It can even try to send offending executives to jail.[13]

---

[11]The "Magnuson-Moss Warranty Act," Public Law 93–637, 15 U.S.C. 2301–2310.

[12]"The Guesswork on Warranties," *Business Week,* July 14, 1975, p. 51.

[13]"The Hazards of Trying to Make Consumer Products Safer," *Fortune,* July 1975, p. 133.

Product Service

The term *service* is used loosely in marketing: it is employed in reference to promptness of delivery, returned-goods privileges, treatment of customers by retail salesclerks, and so on. *Product service* refers to service work intimately associated with the physical product itself—its adjustment, maintenance, and repair so as to assure the consumer the utility reasonably expected as a consequence of the purchase. Such service is sometimes referred to as *technical service,* although the amount of technical expertise involved varies widely. In the industrial market the adaptation of products to individualized needs of the buyers may call for a high order of engineering knowledge, whereas the repair of some consumer durables may be essentially a task of exchanging a new part for one that has proven defective.

Product service is today a major problem area for manufacturers of many products.[14] The increased complexity of products and the rapid growth of markets have outstripped the development of service facilities. As a consequence there is widespread dissatisfaction among consumers with the general quality of product service, and widespread concern among manufacturers because of their inability to cope satisfactorily with the situation.

Manufacturers are uncertain of the role that product service should play in marketing strategy. For example, should a manufacturer stress his service program in his promotion, or will this have a negative effect on the consumer's purchase decision because it brings to mind service problems that he has previously experienced? Product service, to the consumer, is something like a toothache; she does not look forward to it, wants immediate attention when her need arises, and wishes to forget about the matter as quickly as possible. Perhaps the greatest need for a manufacturer concerning service is to develop a rationale concerning the role of service in the total operation—what its objectives should be and how it should "fit in" with other elements in the marketing program.

Product service strategies. Manufacturers follow many different strategies with regard to product service. Their strategies are, in part, an outgrowth of the ways in which they view product service—the philosophies and attitudes concerning it which shape their thinking about its role in marketing strategy. Among the more common approaches to product service among companies are the following:[15]

The negative view. This view holds that product failures are clearly mistakes, and that product service is a kind of fire-fighting operation; the cost of performing it is a penalty paid for shortcomings in engineer-

---

[14]See "The American Repairman: A Vanishing Breed?" *U.S. News & World Report,* September 13, 1965, pp. 88–90.

[15]The views of product service presented here are not necessarily mutually exclusive. Approaches to product service often reflect a combination of these views.

ing and manufacturing performance. Product service is not seen as an activity that adds value to a product but as an unfortunate expense which should be kept at an absolute minimum until the deficiencies that cause it can be removed. Automobile manufacturers have been accused of adhering to this view in servicing automobiles that have been involved in recall campaigns.[16]

The quality policeman view.   This view of product service is an extension of the negative view and places primary emphasis upon the information-gathering role. Product defects are clues to needed product improvements. Careful records must be kept of the nature and incidence of defects so that the extent of the problem, as well as the need for corrective action, can be assessed. Primary allocation of product service resources should be to such information gathering, and only secondary consideration should be given to the correction of defects in products now in the hands of consumers. Product service is basically an adjunct of technical research rather than a means of building consumer goodwill in the short run.

The service-is-a-business view.   Service can be looked at as a business in itself, as a profit-making opportunity that should be exploited. When service is inevitable and the out-of-warranty product population is large, the opportunity is present to employ this approach profitably. Automobile manufacturers, among others, cultivate service business at a profit by manufacturing and selling replacement parts and by providing service facilities through their dealers. A basic problem associated with this approach is the possibility of conflict between the service end and the manufacturing end of the business; product improvement can cut directly into service profits by reducing the incidence of repair. An attempt to achieve a compromise between these two profit goals may lead to confusion of purpose.

The natural agent view.   This view holds that the dealer, rather than the manufacturer, has primary responsibility for product service. Nearest to the customer, the dealer has a higher capacity to act quickly and economically. Also, the dealer is the one to whom the customer will naturally turn when a service problem occurs. Acceptance of this view by the manufacturer limits the obligation to see that the dealer is properly supplied with the parts, service manuals, and so on, which the dealer needs to perform the service function. The dealer becomes the prime service factor, with the manufacturer assuming a facilitating role.

The factory service view.   Diametrically opposed to the natural agent view is the factory service view. It is argued that the manufacturer has most at stake, that his brand appears on the product, and hence that the consumer will blame him if the product is faulty. It is also pointed out that dealers have defaulted on the service function, that the manufac-

---

[16]*Time*, May 8, 1972, p. 79.

turer is more competent than the dealers, and that consumers have more confidence in service provided by the manufacturer. In recent years, automobile manufacturers have experimented with factory service centers in metropolitan areas. Appliance manufacturers have moved heavily in this direction.

The limited obligation view. This view holds that the manufacturer's product service responsibility is limited to the length of the warranty, that this is all that was promised when the consumer made the purchase. After expiration of the warranty, service is the function of independent repair shops, which can and do provide such service at a profit on a wide array of products. It can be argued that the reduction in the manufacturer's service cost which might be associated with this approach may lead to reduced product prices, thereby compensating the consumer for an increase in the cost of out-of-warranty service.

The competitive weapon view. Product service is, of course, an effective marketing tool that can be used to influence product value, product acceptance, and brand reputation to a significant degree. To achieve this objective, the service organization and its policies and functions should be designed around a concept of customer needs and wants in relation to product service. The promotion of Zippo lighters is a good case in point. This company has long advertised that "No one has ever had to pay for repairs on a Zippo lighter." The effect of such promotion on sales is, of course, difficult to measure.

The competitive weapon approach is not limited to small and inexpensive products, although the risks inherent in it are least for such products. In the case of automobiles, some foreign makes have had disappointing sales in the United States because of consumers' concern about adequacy of service. Volkswagen has placed heavy stress on the quality and availability of its service, perhaps thus gaining a competitive advantage over other imports.

The optimum quality view. This view of product service holds that product service can be useful in permitting an optimum level of quality to be attained. Product failure patterns are studied carefully and continuously to discover areas where too much money is spent on quality as well as those in which quality improvement is needed. Cost dollars can then be shifted away from areas that indicate little complaint activity to areas having high complaint ratios and service costs, thus achieving the optimum relationship between product quality and service requirements.

The socioeconomic view. Product service presents excellent opportunities to influence a firm's public image. Product service provides opportunity for the "personal touch," the chance to demonstrate that the large, impersonal corporation is concerned about the individual consumer's problems. Conversely, the failure to provide competent and responsible service may be considered the manifestation of a "public be

damned" attitude. Some public utilities seem to have learned this lesson well. Through extensive services reflected in their rate structures, they have gained widespread support among consumers. Others, often with lower rates but fewer services, have very unenviable reputations. Organizations whose activities are extensively controlled by public boards, which, in turn, are responsive to public opinion, can ill afford such adverse public reactions.

Quality–service interrelationships. The complementarity of product quality and product service and the trade-offs possible between the two are not always clearly recognized. Critics of business are fond of pointing out that the quality of many products is below the quality level possible. Vance Packard, in *The Wastemakers,* makes much of this charge. What such critics often fail to recognize is that the highest quality is not necessarily the "right" quality in terms of demand and cost considerations. Sellers must offer consumers what they want, and consumers often prefer lower quality to higher prices.

This suggests that there is an optimum relationship between product quality and product service, although the point at which that relationship exists might be hard to locate. The optimum relationship depends on many things, among them such factors as: (1) consumer attitudes toward the inconveniences associated with product service; (2) consumer purchase behavior—for example, whether consumers weigh service requirements heavily or lightly in purchase decisions; (3) the capabilities of a company's service organization; and (4) a company's ability to control quality.

Some of the criticism of business embodied in charges of "planned obsolescence" seems to involve a lack of recognition of the relationship between product quality and service cost. In a competitive economy, it is unlikely that business does not build products of as good quality as it is able to build, given the price at which these products must be offered. Business does, however, control quality and accept certain product service costs in order to provide consumers with the products that best meet their needs and buying patterns.

Service versus exchange. A basic trend affecting the service task has recently emerged and already seems rather well established. Increasingly, exchange of products and parts is replacing field service. General Electric was the first company to begin a policy of exchange rather than repair of electric blankets during the warranty period. This practice has now spread to many other small appliances. Automotive repair increasingly consists of installing new or rebuilt parts rather than attempting field repair of defective units.

There are several reasons for this trend. Foremost among them are the rapidly rising field repair costs that have resulted from increasing wage rates. The cost of repairing is rising much faster than the per unit manufacturing costs of new or rebuilt parts, the production of which

can benefit from economies of scale. Compounding this problem is the growing technical complexity of many products, which complicates the repair function. In addition, there is the failure of service personnel and facilities to grow apace with the expanding economy.

Special service problems for industrial goods. Service often plays an even larger role for industrial goods than for consumer goods because of the specialized nature of the products and because of the industrial user's need for continuous operations. It is not unknown for the cost of service to exceed the cost of the physical product itself.

One simple classification of industrial service is based on the time at which the service is performed: pre-sale, time-of-sale, or post-sale. In each of these cases the amount of service rendered may greatly exceed the amount that is normal for consumer goods. For time-of-sale and post-sale service, the problems differ from those associated with consumer goods primarily in degree, not in kind; pre-sale service causes the greatest perplexities.

Pre-sale service may consist of extensive and expensive engineering studies that are necessary to adapt a seller's offering to the specific requirements of the potential buyer. It may involve detailed cost studies that are essential to the buyer's purchase decision. These studies, or others like them, may utilize high-priced talent and consume much time.

The purpose of such pre-sale service is, in large part, to convince the buyer to purchase. It is a particularly expensive form of promotion. If the service is rendered and no sale is made, a substantial loss may be suffered. If an attempt is made to charge separately for pre-sale service, its promotional value is reduced. By attempting to recoup losses in higher prices to those who do purchase, the seller's competitive position is threatened. The seller faces a real dilemma from which there is no easy escape.

Approaches to the solution of this problem vary widely. In most cases they involve an uncomfortable effort to reconcile these various considerations to arrive at a viable approach to the market. Firm policies are hard to establish, and a normal result is to "play it by ear," compromising as necessary with regard to each potential sale.

CONCLUSION

In the past, the approach of many companies to new-product development has been casual. It has often been thought of as a one-shot activity to be engaged in when necessary and then forgotten until the need for additional new products can no longer be ignored. Such an approach is not adequate to today's dynamic market. One of the strongest assets that a company can have in a world of rapidly changing consumer wants is an effective product development capability.

QUESTIONS

1. Explain the concept of product positioning.

2. What steps are involved in determining the product portfolio of a firm?

3. The introduction of a new product into the market is a treacherous business, with the chances of failure greater than the chances of success. In light of this situation, is it ever desirable for a firm to undertake the sale of a new product without extensive market testing?

4. The Tosca Company, manufacturers of automotive electrical equipment, recently introduced a new automotive battery into the market. Sales have been very disappointing to date. This puzzles the company's executives because they are convinced that this is a very superior battery. It is carefully made, and its quality has been carefully checked in the laboratory. Although it is higher priced than other batteries on the market, it carries a five-year warranty in contrast to the typical two- or three-year warranty. Thus, its cost per year of use to the consumer is less.

   The president of the company believes that the fault may lie in the standards used in the laboratory to check quality. He has, therefore, called on you, a management consultant, to advise him on: (*a*) how laboratory standards should be determined, and (*b*) once those standards have been determined, how much reliance can be placed on conformance to them as an indicator of market success. What do you advise?

5. A leading manufacturer of cigarettes originally offered its king-size and filter cigarettes in packages virtually identical with the packages containing its regular-size cigarettes. Both the king-size and the filter cigarettes failed to sell in the volume anticipated. In order to improve their sales performance, the company undertook to differentiate the packages of both its king-size and filter cigarettes.
   a. How might this package similarity be at least in part responsible for the unsatisfactory sales of the two types of cigarettes?
   b. What steps should the company have taken in developing new packages for its products?

6. A brand, to be of value to its owner, must have some meaning and significance to consumers. Under what circumstances is a brand most likely to possess such meaning and significance?

7. How might it be argued that there is a basic conflict between the promotional requirements of a brand name and the protection of ownership rights in a brand name?

8. Contrast the warranty policies that you consider appropriate to (*a*) a manufacturer of cigarette lighters and (*b*) a manufacturer of air conditioners.

9. Discuss the role of warranties in marketing strategy for small appliances. What are the implications of this role for a decision on whether or not to liberalize warranties on small appliances?

10. Some manufacturers of consumer durables argue that the retail dealer is the "natural agent" to provide product service to consumers; others

endorse the view that the manufacturer has the prime responsibility for product service.

a. What is the rationale behind each of these positions?

b. To what extent are the views in conflict?

c. What major problems would you expect to be associated with each of these policies?

11. Many of the service problems now faced by consumer goods manufacturers would be eliminated if manufacturers built into their products the highest quality of which they are capable. Are they shortsighted not to do so?

BOWMAN AND COMPANY*

Mass marketing program for ethical pharmaceuticals

Bowman & Company built its business by promoting and distributing prescription pharmaceutical products in an environment characterized by a close relationship between private physicians and their patients. All Bowman's marketing operations were oriented toward promoting trademarked, originally created specialty products to private physicians so that they, in turn, would prescribe them for their patients. For many years this marketing approach was highly successful; in fact, the same approach was followed by most major marketers of prescription drug products.

In recent years many changes had taken place in the way health care was provided, and the private physician–private patient relationship was gradually being eroded. Most important, government was becoming an increasingly significant factor in the provision of health care. This trend, combined with other forces affecting the health care market, was drastically altering the market situation for prescription drugs. One of the results of these changes had been a decline in market share for specialties and an increase in the market share of multisource, or generic, drugs—those products offered by a number of suppliers and purporting to be duplications of existing trademarked specialty items but generally

*Written by Stewart H. Rewoldt, late Professor of Marketing, Graduate School of Business Administration, The University of Michigan.

sold under the generic name of the principal active ingredient and at lower prices. Some latecomers to this market also used distinctive trademarks as the names of products purporting to duplicate the originals—such products often being termed "branded generics." In reality, both trademarked and generic named products are branded—the package of each bears the name (the brand) of the marketer.

William Garner, vice president for marketing, was concerned about this shift toward a larger market share for generic drugs because he saw in it a threat to the continued profitability of Bowman & Company. The company was not geared to, or experienced in, serving the different type of market that the increased market share for generics would produce. It was urgent, Garner believed, that the causes of the growth of this market share be carefully studied so that a program could be devised to enable Bowman & Company to adapt in order to maintain or increase its profitability. Consequently, he appointed Howard Deziel as special projects manager to study the market trends for generic versus trademarked specialty drug products and to recommend a plan of action.

THE COMPANY

Bowman & Company, producer of ethical pharmaceuticals, was established in 1891 in Minneapolis, where it still maintains its headquarters and manufacturing plants. The company gained a reputation for outstanding original or innovative research, high-quality products, and aggressive merchandising. As an ethical prescription drug house, it aimed its promotional efforts at the health care professional (the physician, pharmacist, and institutional purchasing agent) rather than at the ultimate consumer. Bowman had, in contrast to many other ethical drug firms, followed a policy of selling directly to retail pharmacies rather than going through wholesalers. Bowman sales personnel concentrated on "detailing" physicians (i.e., describing to doctors the uses, contraindications, and side effects of Bowman products) and convincing the retail pharmacist to stock Bowman products in order to fill area doctors' prescriptions. Physical distribution was effected through company-owned sales offices and distribution centers located near population concentrations around the country.

THE CHANGING MARKETPLACE

Historical Leadership of Trademarked Specialties

The ethical drug market had long been led by trademarked specialties. A trademarked specialty is a drug product created and developed,

sometimes patented, and usually sold under a distinctive trademark by a particular pharmaceutical manufacturer. With a patent, the developer could be the sole source of a particular drug for the life of the patent. Upon expiration of the patent, any manufacturer could produce and market the product under the generic name but not under the originator's trademark. If a drug product was not patented, which was often the case, any manufacturer could at any time sell the product under its own trademark or under the generic name. (Any generic drug with more than one manufacturer is also known as a multisource drug.)

The long-term market leadership of trademarked specialties was attributed to two primary factors: (1) extensive drug research and (2) the better reputations of such products and their sources for safety and quality (effectiveness, purity, etc.). The 1950s and early 1960s were a boom period for the introduction of new trademarked specialties, but by the late 1960s research productivity tended to decline because of increasing difficulty in finding new, safe, and effective compounds and because of growing governmental delays in granting new-product approvals. Pressure for lower prices tended to reduce the credence accorded the quality distinction between the original trademarked products and so-called generic equivalents that tended to duplicate the original chemical compounds. These factors, and others to be discussed later, produced a rise in market share for generic drugs—from 6 percent in 1966 to 10.9 percent in 1975.[1] Simple extrapolation of this trend suggested that the market share for generics would be more than 20 percent by 1985. Other factors indicated that the trend would accelerate and make the 20 percent estimate a conservative one.

The Generic versus Trademark Controversy

A controversy had existed for many years as to the relative merits of trademarked drug products created by original innovative research and development, and copies of those products sold under the generic names. Trademarks had long been used to indicate a particular source of goods and to signify the uniform quality of products emanating from that source. The central issue in the controversy was whether generic drugs supplied by a multitude of sources with varying reputations for quality were indeed equivalent in safety and efficacy to their counterparts bearing trademarks that stood for the recognized quality of particular sources. All drug products passing in interstate commerce, trademarked and generic alike, were theoretically required to meet certain standards of production and quality control established by federal regulations and by the limited specifications for purity, potency, and content uniformity established by the *United States Pharmacopeia* and the *National Formulary*.

---

[1]"Generic Pharmaceuticals," *Wall Street Transcript*, Feburary 2, 1976, pp. 42, 778.

In fact, however, the federal government had long been regularly seizing adulterated and misbranded drug products not in compliance with the law, regulations, and the compendiums. Moreover, it had long been known that drug products bearing the same generic name, produced by different companies, and offered as meeting the above standards, were not necessarily equivalent in their therapeutic (or biological) activity. They might vary markedly in DEM characteristics,[2] identity of ingredients, method of manufacture, levels of drug produced in the body, and clinical response. In some instances this had led the U.S. Food and Drug Administration (FDA) to issue standards for the determination of drug bioavailability and to use those standards to help assure the therapeutic equivalence of drugs represented to contain the same chemical base. Many members of the medical community had come to believe that there were few differences, if any, between products sold under an originator's trademark and those produced by several suppliers and sold under the generic name, if they had indeed been shown to have the same bioavailability.

The Trend toward Generics

Of the nearly 750 million new prescriptions written in 1974, 82 million were written by physicians specifying the generic name. The growing importance of generically written prescriptions is depicted in Exhibit 1. While total new prescriptions increased 57 percent between 1966 and 1974, generic prescriptions advanced 175 percent during the same period.

Also noteworthy is the fact that products sold under both trademarks and generic names accounted for 16 of the 200 most-prescribed drugs in 1974. Ampicillin, an antibiotic which accounted for nearly 15 million prescriptions, was the leading generic product, with another antibiotic, tetracycline, a close second, with just under 13 million prescriptions written.

Reasons for the Growth of Generics

Many factors had a bearing on the trend toward a larger market share for generics in the ethical drug market. Among them, the four primary factors were: the increasing efforts of government to reduce health care costs, patent expirations, pricing pressures, and moves to repeal and amendment of antisubstitution regulations and laws.

Increasing role of government in health care. Government-financed drug programs were responsible for 28 percent of all drug purchases in 1975. The government was a major purchaser of drugs in its own right for use in military and Veterans Administration hospitals.

---

[2]Absorption–Distribution–Metabolism–Excretion of the drug in the body.

EXHIBIT 1　　New prescriptions (millions)

Year	New generic prescriptions	Total new prescriptions	Generic/new prescriptions
1966	29.7	475.9	6.4%
1967	34.5	492.2	7.0
1968	43.3	533.5	8.2
1969	48.4	561.7	8.8
1970	53.6	603.4	9.0
1971	58.6	645.6	9.2
1972	66.7	687.1	9.7
1973	76.2	728.8	10.5
1974	81.7	749.3	10.9

Source: Report by Halsey, Stuart & Co., Inc., affiliate of Bache & Co., Incorporated. Reprinted in *Wall Street Transcript*, February 2, 1976.

It also purchased many drugs for distribution under foreign aid programs. Since the mid-to-late 1950s, the government had moved heavily toward the purchase of generics, frequently limiting such purchases to those in which the products were subjected to and passed specific departmental tests. In some cases the federal government purchased drugs overseas if the prices of foreign suppliers were lower.

Medicare and medicaid legislation was passed in 1965. With the inception of these programs, the government began to exert strong pressure on physicians, hospitals, and other health care providers to prescribe generics in order to control costs. As the cost of administering these programs grew, far outstripping original cost representations, the pressure to prescribe generics increased even though the cost of drugs was low in proportion to the other health care costs. In 1976 the federal government instituted the Maximum Allowable Cost (MAC) program. This program effectively forced the prescribing of the lowest-priced generics generally available. If trademarked specialties were prescribed, reimbursement would still be only for the cost of the lowest-priced generic product generally available—a provision aimed at forcing generic prescribing.

Patent expirations.　　The expiration of ethical drug patents could be expected to accelerate in number and in the sales dollars they represented over the next decade. This was a direct result of the fruitful years of research in the late 1950s and early 1960s, which accounted for many of the 200 leading products currently being marketed. Of a total domestic pharmaceutical sales volume of $6.7 billion in 1975, $1.3 billion was attributable to multisource products for which there was no patent coverage or for which the patent had expired.

Exhibit 2 indicates the current sales volume of ethical pharmaceuticals losing patent protection during the indicated year.

Thus, by 1981 an amount of almost half of 1975 sales volume would be derived from products which would be in the generic realm. Only a resurgence in drug research productivity could lessen the impact of this changing situation.

The decline in the introduction of new drug products to the market was worldwide, but it was sharpest in the United States, which had been the leading innovator; it was less pronounced in other developed countries. The cause of this appeared to be directly linked to the increased difficulty in finding safe and effective new compounds, increasingly stringent rules governing the clinical studies of new drugs, and the increased time needed to satisfy the FDA that such new drugs were safe and effective. Contributing factors were woven into the fabric of research itself: scientific breakthroughs come unexpectedly and irregularly, and all branches of science go through periods during which fundamental insights are gathered, followed by periods in which those insights are applied to practical uses.

The 1962 amendments to the federal Food, Drug, and Cosmetic Act had added requirements of proof of effectiveness to the previously required proof of clinical safety. Thus, since 1962 the FDA had been able to specify the testing procedure a manufacturer had to use in order to produce acceptable information in support of its New Drug Application

---

EXHIBIT 2   Sales volume of products no longer patent-protected ($ millions)

	Total sales
Prior patent expirations:	
1975	$1,255
Future patent expirations:	
1976	211
1977	123
1978	103
1979	275
1980	387
1981	933
	$3,287

Source: Halsey, Stuart & Co., Inc., affiliate of Bache & Co., Incorporated. Reprinted in *Wall Street Transcript,* February 2, 1976.

(NDA). A result of this was a tremendous increase in the amount of testing and paperwork involved in submitting NDAs for approval. The cost of obtaining FDA approval for a new drug rose rapidly to an estimated range of $2.5 million to $15 million.[3]

Pricing pressures.   The increased pressure for lower prices which had led to the increased use of generics was a result of a number of factors, including:

1. The competitive aspect of the market.
2. Third-party influences.
3. A desire on the part of the hospital, the patient, and the physician to lower the costs of drug treatment.

As patents expired, formerly exclusive trademarked products—whose profits supported new research —could no longer maintain their previously high prices because of the introduction of products offered as equivalents by other pharmaceutical firms. An often overlooked factor affecting prices was the introduction of products which produced similar therapeutic effects but were not identical to and did not infringe upon the patent of the pioneering product. For example, the price of tetracyclines declined substantially before patent expiration because other antibacterials were introduced that offered the physician a greater choice of products in treating some of the same diseases. Also, there was price competition between suppliers of trademarked specialties.

Third-party influences (government, Blue Cross/Blue Shield and other health insurance underwriters, consumer activist groups, etc.) had had a major impact on drug prices. All of these third parties worked to lower the cost of health care. Although the really high-cost items in health care were complicated hospital costs, and although the costs of drugs for patients were frequently among the lower-cost elements, drug prices were relatively easy for third parties to isolate and attack. Some groups exercised their powers to promote an eventual move toward national health insurance; others to slow or halt the move toward national health insurance. In many foreign countries drug prices declined because local governments placed price ceilings on reimbursed or supplied drugs used for health care. This price ceiling concept could also be expected in the United States as medical health care delivery continued to become more social welfare-oriented. The previously mentioned Maximum Allowable Cost regulations were the first major effort of government to formally control drug prices by encouraging the use of lower-priced generic products.

Finally, pressure from the customer, as well as from the physician, tended to force prices down by encouraging the use of lower-priced

---

[3]Ibid., pp. 42, 778.

generic products. These pressures had been increasingly amplified through the efforts of consumer activist groups and through frequent commentary in the news media.

Repeal and amendment of antisubstitution regulations and laws in the filling of prescriptions. State legislatures in many states had, in the past, enacted regulations to help assure that patients received the drug products their physicians prescribed for them. Numerous suppliers had copied well-known products. The formulations were represented on the labels to be the same as the originals. The nonfunctional characteristics of size, shape, and color of the products were copies. The copying suppliers promoted the copies to retailers for use in filling prescriptions, the substitution to consist of palming off the copies on the customers as the genuine articles. Numerous retailers bought the copies, covertly filled the prescriptions with them, and pocketed the larger profits resulting from the use of the cheaper copies. The retail customers thought that they had received what their physicians had prescribed; they had paid for the genuine articles, but they received something else. Inspections of generic copies sometimes showed that the ingredients were not the same as those in the prescribed products. Some retailers charged more for the generics than their nearby competitors charged for the genuine articles. In addition, in some states antisubstitution laws were enacted to prevent this deception. Courts enjoined suppliers from offering these counterfeits to retailers for the purpose of palming them off on unsuspecting customers. Retailers, too, were enjoined from making these substitutions. Money damages were awarded by the courts against substituting retailers. State pharmacy boards suspended licenses for substitution.

At first, organized pharmacy supported these sanctions against substitution. Decades later it changed its position and supported repeal of the state regulations and laws on the theory that pharmacists should play a greater role in selecting the products to be dispensed. In fact, however, most pharmacists lacked the ability to select among brands other than by relying on manufacturers' reputations, reading the labels, and comparing prices. They lacked the equipment for ascertaining the quality and purity of the products dispensed. As it became clearer that the generic copy products could be furnished at lower prices in the face of medicare and medicaid expenditures for enormous numbers of people, governmental agencies sponsored their use. As a result, state regulations and laws designed to prohibit the interchange of products were changed with increasing frequency to authorize substitution under a number of different preconditions. In some cases substitution was allowed if the retail pharmacist informed the customer that he or she was receiving a product different from that prescribed by the physician. In other cases it was allowed if the physician gave up the right to choose so long as all of the savings accrued by the pharmacist's choice were passed along to

the customer. In most cases substitution required the pharmacist to maintain detailed records to indicate the specific products dispensed to the patient. By 1977, 22 states had repealed or amended their antisubstitution laws as indicated, with similar legislation pending in most of the remaining 28 states.

RECOMMENDATION FOR A MASS MARKETING PROGRAM

Having reviewed the present and emerging trends toward growing demand for the generic class of ethical drugs, Deziel submitted the following report to Garner.

MEMORANDUM

To: William Garner, Vice President for Marketing
From: Howard Deziel, Special Projects Manager
Subject: Establishing a Mass Marketing Program
Date: January 26, 1975

I. Introduction.

We all agree on the wisdom and necessity of Bowman's involvement in the area of the pharmaceutical market relating to generic drugs and mass marketing.

Group purchasing and the growth of retail chain stores, physician group practice, and prepaid insurance, along with governmental pressures to reduce health care costs, to institute a national health system, to require compulsory patent licensing, and to reduce the life of drug patents, make such a move vital to our corporate growth. *The question is not, "Should we enter the market?" but "How soon can we do so, and by what method?"*

However, before any meaningful planning and setting of objectives can be attempted, it is important to define what is meant by mass marketing and to set dimensions as to size of market, type of customer, anticipated financial investment, profit, and desired promotional expenses. The following data relating to market and expenses are, however, estimates and subject to change upon further study.

A. Definition.

1. *Mass marketing.* The sale of generic drug products to mass market customers.

2. *Generic products.* Those products that are either pat-

ent-free or will soon become eligible for sale by more than one manufacturer.

3. *Mass market customers.* Those customers (chain stores in some instances, governments, hospitals) that are buying generic products on a bid or a group basis and that portion of the prescription market which purchases generic drugs.

B. Objective.

The objective of mass marketing is to establish Bowman & Company as a major supplier of high-quality generic products and to obtain a significant share of the growing bid and prescription market for generic drugs at an acceptable profit level by the early 1980s.

II. Strategy.

The strategy outlined below is based on the aforementioned definition of mass marketing and assumes the establishment of the organizational structure described in greater detail later.

Assignment of responsibility and authority to move quickly and aggressively in the mass markets is paramount. The strategy is based on the premise that an acceptable profit will be attained, and assumes the utilization of the Bowman name, label, and existing sales force.

As would be expected, there are changes to be made and needs to be met if we are to attain our objective. Not the least of these needs is *a corporate commitment to financial investment, people, and facilities.* Some of the major elements of our strategy are discussed below; however, it should be pointed out that to keep abreast of this changing market we must also be committed to further change as the marketplace dictates. Since the forces contributing to the growth in commodity products are multiple and varied, so must our strategy be many-faceted and directed to many areas.

Essential ingredients of the strategy are, among others, bioavailability (quality), production flexibility, price leadership, the element of educated risk, and the firm support of the existing sales force. This includes actively seeking bid business from all sources as well as aggressively pursuing that portion of the prescription market which results from commodity products.

A. Image.

The time is ideal for a major drug firm which possesses adequate production facilities, a sales force strong in the hospital–institutional market, leadership in quality control, and medical support to expedite New Drug Applications (NDAs) and assist in bioavailability studies to capture a major segment of the generic mar-

ket. *To do so, however, a company must first be identified as a supplier of high-quality, competitively priced generic products. Bowman, as of now, does not have this image.* At present, our image is one of a company which supplies high-quality specialty products that are often not competitively priced. *Seldom do physicians, pharmacists, and purchasing agents think of Bowman* when they are in the *market for generic drugs.* We must be known both as a supplier of specialty products and as a *provider of high-quality, competitively priced generic products* designed for the mass markets. As indicated, we are not so identified at present, and *one of our most immediate problems is to establish this image.* This, then, to establish the proper image, is one of the immediate tasks of our mass marketing strategy and is fundamental to the approach.

While our salespeople will play a role in building our new image, it will for the most part be established for cost reasons through nonsalesperson activities, and the following are to play an important part:

Journal and direct-mail promotion.

New packaging.

Price leadership.

Public relations activities, including news releases and announcements to target audiences.

B. Organization.

Perhaps the most immediate need is one of organization, and the first step has already been taken in this regard by assigning to one individual, the special projects manager, responsibility for putting together the diverse functions required for a coordinated business effort. To be successful, the position requires sufficient stature, corporate identification, responsibility, and authority for coordinating all of the various functions required to get the job done.

At least one additional permanent staff member is needed to assist in preparing product forecasts; gathering, tabulating and establishing pricing and cost data; preparing situation and progress reports; obtaining current bid information; and reviewing current product sales. Addition of this staff member will permit the special projects manager to devote full time to the other projects that are to be undertaken and in order to get the operation going.

Following this initial phase, however, a permanent organization, including specialists from other disci-

plines, should be considered. Such an organization should combine permanent, full-time staff with temporary full-time support to provide the needed input from essential and relevant disciplines. This support should be provided by a manager from each discipline with special responsibility for mass market needs. Initially, the *support personnel* should remain in their respective units, but as programs of product acquisition and bioavailability are developed, these support personnel should be melded into a permanent staff.

1. Permanent staff.
   Market manager.
   Product manager.
   Financial analyst.
   Advertising specialist.
   Public relations specialist.
2. Temporary full-time support staff.
   Control.
   Production—product development.
   Medical.

C. Quality—bioavailability.

Two very important elements of mass marketing, quality and bioavailability, will affect the ultimate strategy in a major way. We do not now have a program enabling us to determine bioavailability, and there is concern regarding the quality of our products. Basically, we are geared only to meeting compendium (USP, NF) and other minimum legal requirements, and we need data to demonstrate that our products are of higher quality than the products of other companies. Essentially, our rejection of product is based on compendium limits, which are by design broad and do not consider the aspect of "building in additional quality." Compendium standards, of course, are purported to be met by nearly all competitors, including so-called generic companies.

As we become involved in the sale of generic products to mass market customers, the time could come when our only real marketable commodity might well be our ability to produce a better product than others, and it is here that our decision becomes important to our strategy. We are at present producing products that essentially meet compendium requirements as indicated. Our strategy at this point could be one of at least two alternatives:

1. Produce and sell products which meet only the minimum compendium requirements and at the same time attempt to compete with a low price.
2. Produce and sell products which exceed compendium requirements and price them above the lowest.

It is my belief at this time, however, that quality is a marketable commodity and does command some premium. Therefore, we should begin now to *produce in accordance with standards and specifications that are higher than those required by USP, NF, and other compendiums.* This decision, however, along with present corporate policy relative to meeting only minimum requirements, is so important and will affect our strategy to such a great degree that it cannot be made hastily. I am, therefore, recommending that we address ourselves to the problem by establishing a Quality Review Committee (see Recommendations—item F).

D. Product.

When the market for generic products is analyzed, it is quite apparent that one of our problems is lack of products. Even though, as indicated earlier, our most immediate need with regard to this project is not one of product or price, *lack of products in this growing segment of the pharmaceutical market is of serious long-range concern.*

It may not be realistic to assume that we can fill this gap by acquiring products and settling for 5 percent of the existing market. Consequently, serious attention should be given to a product acquisition program directed at acquiring products outright; we should also consider trading present products or patent rights in order to get into these markets before the products concerned become generic. Pertinent to our product acquisition program is timing and cost. While there are a number of products still covered by patent that are of interest, licenses obviously cost money and reduce our overall profit structure. From a short-range viewpoint, we will take a close look at products whose patent has already expired—especially with regard to the bid segment of the mass market. Add to this the fact that we do have a sterile product and ointment capacity in Production, and we get more rapid dollars at a greater profit.

As can be seen from our market projections (see Section VI), a considerable portion of the mass market will

result from physicians' generic prescriptions. Consequently, acquired products will require additional sales force time and effort in order to create specification by the physician.

E. Use of sales force.

As indicated, Bowman's existing sales forces are to be used in the exploitation of the mass market; thus "cost of promotion" is a serious concern. Salesmen must be used carefully because their overuse can reduce profit substantially. While it is difficult at this time to determine precisely how much time and in what vein the salesman's time will be utilized, some generalizations can be made.

1. There is little doubt that when we first acquire products to broaden our line, they will have to be treated as new products in terms of the sales force time needed to create physician specification. The products would be treated as new products, however, for only two to four months, after which they would be promoted as part of a broad line of generic pharmaceuticals.

2. Important to our strategy from a profit standpoint is the promotion (both salesman and nonsalesman) of a group or line of generic products. In this regard and as part of the support needed from our sales forces, some conference time should be allocated.

An initial conference devoted to the mass marketing venture should be considered, not to cover products per se, but rather to explain our entrance into this market along with the relationship of quality, price, bioavailability, package, and so on, to our overall strategy. At the same time, mass marketing should be part of the Price Reporting Network (PRN) system, and time should be spent in the bid and special quote aspect of mass marketing, because rapid intelligence will be important.

III. Implementation.

Since it is not possible to implement all of the elements of our strategy simultaneously, it will be pursued from a short- and long-range viewpoint.

A. Short range.

1. Establish budget requirements and organizational structure.

2. Begin an immediate program to establish Bow-

man's image as a supplier of quality generic products to the mass markets.

3. Aggressively pursue additional sales of Bowman products on which patent rights have already been lost.

4. Actively seek additional chain store business, considering, if necessary, contract packaging and alternative methods of distribution.

5. Review present product costs, including possible adoption of direct-costing system.

6. Complete bioavailability studies on our existing generic products.

7. Establish short-range sales goals on existing products.

B. Long range.

1. Broaden product line through acquisition, especially in disease categories where we have no product entry.

2. Establish an ongoing bioavailability program for all generic products.

3. Review existing Bowman production capabilities and flexibility, including possible future needs.

4. Review pricing policy, and propose policies for pricing of commodity products to both bid and prescription segments of the mass market.

5. Establish long-range goals in terms of market share, return on investment, and so on, for the next 10 years.

6. Develop methods of accountability—including comprehensive financial analysis.

IV. Budget.

The following preliminary budget estimates are solely for the first year. Estimates are also included for those items relating to image, products, medical, and bioavailability.

A. Personnel.

Staff and secretaries	$200,000–$250,000

B. Image.

1. Journal promotion	$150,000–$200,000
2. Direct mail	$ 60,000–$ 70,000
3. New package	$300,000–$400,000
4. Detail material	$100,000–$150,000

C. Medical—control—product.

1. Quality control	$ 10,000–$ 15,000
2. Bioavailability	$ 40,000–$ 60,000
3. Product acquisition, including NDA and clinical	$150,000–$200,000

D. Miscellaneous direct expenses.
  1. Travel $ 10,000–$ 15,000
  2. Display—movies, conventions, etc. $ 40,000–$100,000

Estimated total direct expenses for the first year are $1,060,000 to $1,460,000.

Obviously, an item of expense that must be considered is that of salesmen; since, however, this item (salesmen's time) relates more to product, it has not been included in the budget estimates because meaningful data have not yet been developed. The expense of salesmen, however, will be considered in the overall analysis of the contribution to earnings of both individual products and mass marketing.

V. Recommendations.

In order to implement our program of mass marketing immediately, I recommend that management:

A. Adopt and approve the above definiton of mass marketing as a unique market segment of the domestic pharmaceutical market. During the initial phase of our program and until the organizational structure is completed, the strategy should be more toward "management of market" than toward specifically product management, and it is recommended that the involved products continue to be handled by the current product managers. There will be close liaison with the product managers on pricing, packaging, and so forth.

B. Adopt the proposed strategy.

C. Implement the proposed organization.

D. Approve and establish a direct expense budget as outlined.

E. Authorize development and adoption of a unique package as soon as possible.

F. Institute a Quality Review Committee (QRC) to initiate a bioavailability program and to recommend corporate policy relative to quality standards.

In order to properly determine corporate policy in this regard, it is recommended that the QRC be established as part of the bioavailability program. Its functions would be to:

1. Recommend corporate policy relative to quality standards.

2. Evaluate the costs of producing in accordance with higher standards.

3. On a continuing basis, establish quality guidelines, including general specifications and goals.

VI. Market forecast.

This is perhaps the most difficult area in which to obtain

meaningful data. While the data are estimates, they are based on generally firm trends and information as to the future of the drug market. Current market data show domestic ethical pharmaceutical sales in 1975 at the $6.7 billion level, broken down as shown in Exhibit 3.

EXHIBIT 3   Domestic ethical market—1975 ($ millions)

Federal government	$ 370	
City, county, state	310	
Psychiatric hospital	120	28%, or
Private hospital	1,100	$1.9 billion
All other Rx market	4,800	
Total	$6,700	

Of the 28 percent of the market controlled by government and institutions, it is estimated that 50 percent consists of generic products.

A *substantial portion of the Rx market is subject to price and economic pressures,* which places at least a portion of it in the mass market category. Reliable estimates suggest that today at least 15 percent of this portion of the market consists of nonpatented drugs and that this share is growing. The approximate mass market potential as of 1975 is depicted in Exhibit 4.

EXHIBIT 4   Mass market potential ($ millions)

Federal government	$ 185
City, county, state	155
Psychiatric hospital	60
Private hospital	550
Rx (generic drugs)	720
Total	$1,670

This is believed to be a conservative estimate because it does not present a true picture of chain store influence in the Rx market. For example, nearly 50 percent of all Rx's are filled at chain stores, which are extremely sensitive to price and economic pressures. Certainly more than 15 percent of chain store business would fall into this category.

Assuming that the above mass market estimates are reasonably accurate, what of the future? The best available data suggest that due to the economic and governmental pressures discussed earlier, *nonpatented products will account for a larger share of the market in the next decade.* Thus, in order to estimate future market size, the following assumptions have been made:

1. Government, institutions, and hospitals will be responsible for approximately 33 percent of the total market in 1980 and 40 percent in 1985, up from 28 percent in 1975, of which 70 percent will be on bid.
2. Generic products will grow in importance during the next 10 years, accounting for 60 percent of the governmental and institutional portion of the mass market purchases by 1980 and for 70 percent by 1985.
3. The market share of Rx (generic) portion of the mass market, 15 percent in 1975, will grow to 20 percent by 1980 and to 25 percent by 1985.[4]
4. The domestic ethical pharmaceutical market will grow to $9.5 billion in 1980 and to $15.5 billion in 1985.

Changes in patent laws, licensing restrictions, or introduction of a national health system, including reimbursement for out-of-hospital drugs, could move these percentages upward. The mass market reflecting these assumptions appears in Exhibit 5.

Assuming that our trademarked specialty products will share in the growth of the total market and grow at the same rate, our present trademarked specialty sales of approximately $40 million should reach $60 million by 1980 and more than $144 million by 1985. Based on projections of the total market, however, our total sales (trademarked specialties plus generics) should exceed $450 million by 1985.

---

[4]These are considered very conservative estimates. In an article entitled "It's Time That RPh's as Experts on Drugs Play a Fuller Role in Product Selection," *AM Druggist,* April 1976, states that "IMS America Research Organization has predicted that by 1980 from 40 percent to 60 percent of all new prescriptions will be written generically. . . . Today, it is estimated that 14 percent to 16 percent of all new prescriptions are written by generic prescription."

EXHIBIT 5   Mass market sales projections ($ millions)

	1975	1980	1985
Government, hospitals, institutions	$ 950	$ 1,900	$ 4,340
Rx (nonpatented)	720	1,267	2,325
Total generic drug sales	$1,670	$ 3,167	$ 6,665
Bowman share (5%)	$ 83.5	$158.35	$333.25

QUESTION

1. Should Garner recommend acceptance of Deziel's report to the board of directors of Bowman & Company?

JOHNSON AND DAVIS (A)*

Decision to make or buy a product

Johnson and Davis (J&D) was founded in the early 1900s as a manufacturer of printed forms for both government agencies and private businesses. It set up a plant in a small town in the Midwest and sold its forms directly to customers in the area. In the years that followed, J&D added three more retail outlets which sold the printed forms (still manufactured at the home plant) as well as furniture, office and school supplies, and file and record systems supplied by various other manufacturers.

By the early 1970s, J&D's retail sales had become the dominant factor in its total operations. A large part of J&D's growth in the retail market was attributable to its sales of file and record systems. As a "systems dealer," J&D used a new and creative selling technique in which its salesmen worked with each customer individually to design a record system that would best satisfy the customer's needs. J&D then ordered the necessary components of the system from its suppliers and received a retail markup for its services. Because J&D's sales representatives helped in the actual designing of the file system, the customer usually came back to J&D for future expansion and replacement needs.

*Written by Eric Blanchard, research assistant, under the supervision of Professor Martin R. Warshaw, Graduate School of Business Administration, The University of Michigan, Ann Arbor.

One of the primary features of all the file and record systems offered by J&D was the use of color coding. By 1974, color-coded file systems had gained widespread popularity at banks, hospitals, public record offices, and other organizations with large filing needs. The principal advantages of a color-coded file system over a noncolor-coded one are: (1) search and file time can be reduced up to 40 percent; (2) misfiling is minimized, and misplaced files are spotted more quickly; and (3) color coding can be used to file by year, department, or function, using alphabetical, numerical, or terminal digit formats. The only disadvantage of color coding is the higher cost involved, especially in making the transition from an existing, regular file system to a new, color-coded one. This disadvantage, however, can often be more than offset by the long-run savings in filing time.

Until 1973, J&D had bought its color-coding supplies from Record Systems Inc. (RSI). These supplies included plain manila folders, manila folders with color-code labels already glued on, and self-adhesive labels for customers who wished to attach the labels to their own folders. RSI was the first manufacturer to offer color-code labels, in 1927, and it was still the industry leader in 1973. J&D had always been given exclusive distribution of RSI's line of color-code labels in the state in which all of J&D's outlets were located.[1]

Then, late in 1973, J&D got word that RSI was in the process of closing out its traditional distribution channel through retail outlets such as J&D and of setting up its own branch sales offices. In other words, RSI's own salesmen would sell its entire product line directly to the customer. For J&D, this meant that it would no longer be able to rely upon RSI to supply it with labels and folders, since J&D would soon be one of RSI's competitors.

A few months earlier, Tom Peterson, a former sales executive at RSI, had been hired by J&D to manage its File and Record Systems Division. It was Tom's responsibility to find an alternative source of supply for color-code labels. He did not feel that this would be a difficult task, since 12 other manufacturers in the industry were offering similar label designs at comparable prices. The only problem was that all of these 12 manufacturers were already distributing their labels through other retail outlets in the area. Thus, the exclusive distribution that J&D had always enjoyed while selling the RSI label would be lost.

For this reason, Tom began to look at a second alternative, that of making rather than buying color-code labels. Although J&D was not in a particularly good financial position to take on a new investment, especially for a product that accounted for less than 1 percent of its total sales, Tom felt that the potential for even larger future sales of color-code labels might justify the risk. Since patents had never been obtaina-

---

[1] See Exhibit 1 for a black-and-white view of the color-code label line.

EXHIBIT 1   Color-code labels

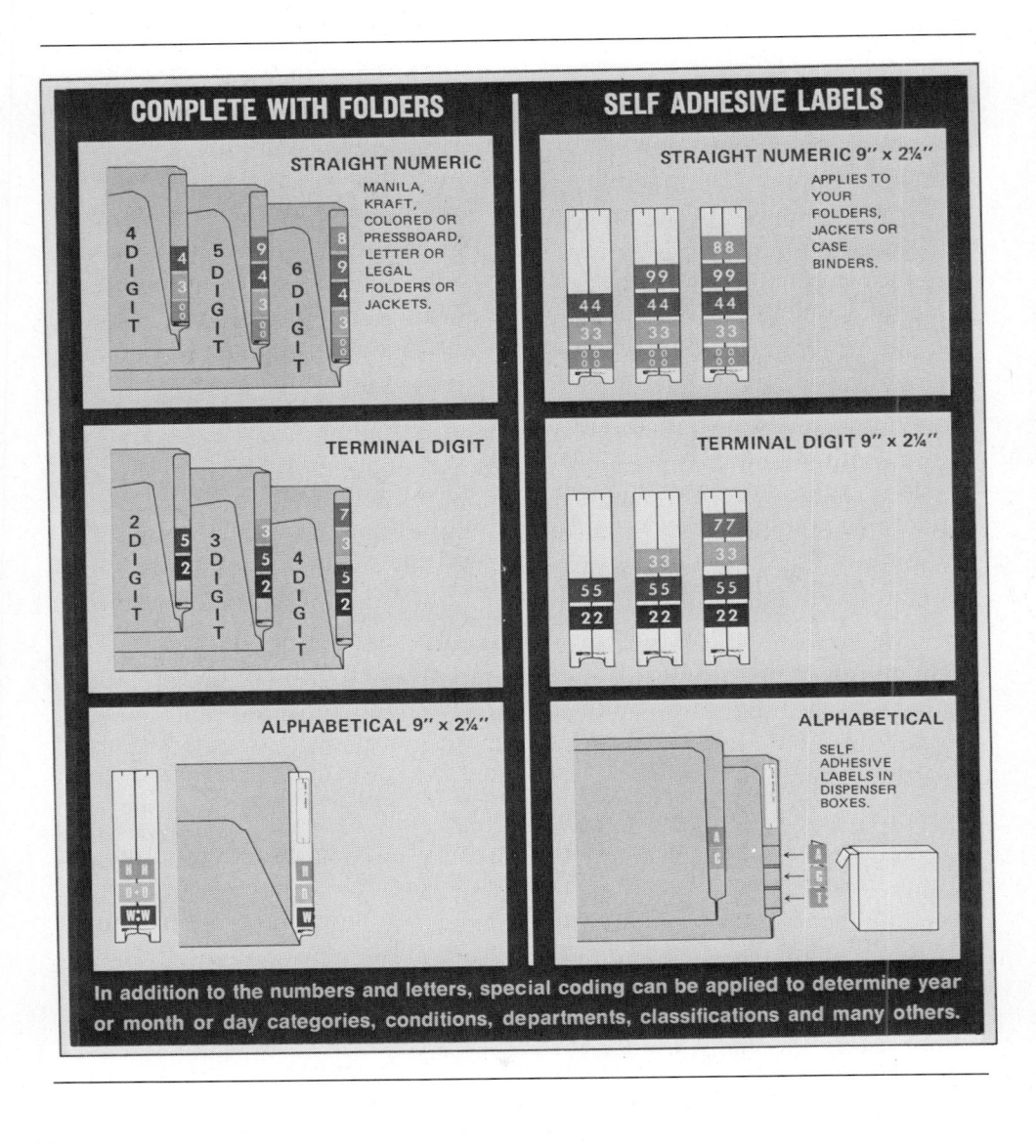

COMPLETE WITH FOLDERS

STRAIGHT NUMERIC

MANILA, KRAFT, COLORED OR PRESSBOARD, LETTER OR LEGAL FOLDERS OR JACKETS.

TERMINAL DIGIT

ALPHABETICAL 9" x 2¼"

SELF ADHESIVE LABELS

STRAIGHT NUMERIC 9" x 2¼"

APPLIES TO YOUR FOLDERS, JACKETS OR CASE BINDERS.

TERMINAL DIGIT 9" x 2¼"

ALPHABETICAL

SELF ADHESIVE LABELS IN DISPENSER BOXES.

In addition to the numbers and letters, special coding can be applied to determine year or month or day categories, conditions, departments, classifications and many others.

ble on any particular color-code label design, one possibility would be to manufacture labels identical to those produced by RSI. In this way, J&D could continue to satisfy the replacement and expansion needs of its past customers. Tom dismissed this idea, however, since he believed that there was more to be gained in the long run by avoiding direct competition with a systems firm as well known as RSI.

Instead, J&D might manufacture a new label that Tom had designed, which resembled RSI's label in all respects except the width of the color bands. The RSI label had been able to accommodate six 1½-inch color bands, each band containing a designated digit, 0–9. Tom's label had 1¼-inch color bands, and thus could accommodate seven bands or digits. Of greater importance, this difference would make concurrent use of J&D's label and RSI's (or any other manufacturer's) label virtually impossible. Although J&D would thus forfeit expansion and replacement sales to its old customers, it would avoid losing exclusive distribution of a color-code label.

But before presenting his superiors with this alternative and the alternative of buying from another supplier, Tom knew that he would need to find out the expenses and the profit potential associated with each alternative. First of all, J&D had already invested in some letterpresses and other lithographic machinery for its printing operations. In fact, Tom knew that there was an idle letterpress in the plant that could produce, at a cost of $54 an hour, all of the color-code labels demanded by J&D's customers. Its printing staff would then have to make image plates for the labels, and Tom estimated that this would cost $7,500. The plates were estimated to have a depreciable life of 15 years.

The major fixed cost of the project would be the production of a base stock inventory of color-code labels, each label containing just two color bands. This base stock would then be drawn from, and more color bands added to the labels, as specified by customer orders. Inventorying a base stock was a common, cost-efficient practice of all manufacturers in the industry. Tom estimated that the base stock inventory would amount to a $25,000 fixed investment for J&D.

Tom arrived at this figure by taking the total manufacturing cost per label—$25 per 1,000 glue-on manila tags and $50 per 1,000 self-adhesive adapter tags—and multiplying this cost by the size of the base stock needed. Using past sales as an indicator, 75 percent of which had been for the manila tags and 25 percent for the self-adhesive tags, Tom concluded that a base stock inventory of 600,000 manila tags and 200,000 self-adhesive tags would be sufficient. One other fixed cost that would be incurred in manufacturing the new label, as opposed to buying another supplier's label, was a $6,000 promotional appropriation to print and mail out introductory brochures.

Turning his attention to the profit potential involved, Tom realized that his options were severely limited by competitive pressures. Due to

the nature of the product, both dealer net prices and suggested retail prices were determined by the industry, with dealer net set at approximately 50 percent of suggested retail. Industry prices varied directly with the number of bands on the label, and quantity discounts were given for larger order sizes. Tom had manufacturing cost estimates only for the four-band labels ($40 per 1,000 manila tags and $70 per 1,000 self-adhesive labels), but he felt that he could compare these costs to the corresponding dealer net prices and come up with a general estimate of the manufacturer's margin involved in the sale of all the types of labels.[2] (See Exhibit 2.)

Tom now needed to make only a few more calculations before making a recommendation to management.

EXHIBIT 2   Price list for four-band labels (1974)

| | | | Range of Order Sizes | | | |
	A	B	C	D	E	F
Manila tag						
Dealer net	$120	$110	$100	$ 90	$ 85	$ 80
Suggested retail	240	220	200	180	170	160
Self-adhesive						
Dealer net	155	130	115	105	100	95
Suggested retail	310	260	230	210	200	190
Percent of total sales	10%	15%	30%	20%	15%	10%

Total sales in 1973 were $50,000 at retail, $25,000 at dealer net. Of these sales, 75 percent were for manila tag, 25 percent for self-adhesive.

Questions

1   What alternatives is Tom considering? What are the advantages and the disadvantages of each alternative? Can you think of any alternatives that Tom might have missed?

2   Why do you think color-code label prices are determined by the industry? How does this fact affect J&D's decision to manufacture the labels? How does it affect J&D's overall marketing strategy for the product?

3   What is the break-even point in units, retail dollars, and years for manufacturing the labels?

4   What advantages would accrue to J&D if they made their own labels?

---

[2]The $40 and $70 figures included the initial $25 and $50 cost, respectively, to produce the two-band base stock, plus an additional cost for printing on two more bands.

BURCH PHARMACEUTICAL COMPANY

Addition of a new product

HISTORICAL BACKGROUND

The Burch Pharmaceutical Company, a medium-sized producer of a variety of drug items, has earned a high reputation for its integrity and fair dealings. The firm was founded in 1925 by Dr. Fred Burch, a practicing physician, for the purpose of manufacturing and distributing better medication.

When Burch entered the pharmaceutical business, most drugs were dispensed by physicians. However, with the growth of drugstores and with the willingness of physicians to relinquish their dispensing of medicines, prescriptions began to be filled by the drugstore pharmacists.

The Burch Pharmaceutical Company adjusted to this distribution change by selling their products directly to drug retailers and drug wholesalers. The firm also divided its product mix into two groups, ethical and proprietary. The former are those that can only be dispensed with a doctor's prescription. The latter group, until five years ago, con-

This case was prepared by Professor Paul E. Arney of Bradley University. The name was changed to protect the confidentiality of the firm. Copyright © 1982.

Presented at the Midwest Case Writers Workshop and distributed by the Intercollegiate Case Clearing House, Soldiers Field, Boston, Mass. 02163. All rights reserved to the contributors. Printed in the U.S.A.

sisted of those products which are sold over the counter, e.g., vitamins, cough medicine, and aspirin. At that time the firm decided to introduce nonmedical products. The first was a line of toiletries, then chewing gum, and finally last year, toothpaste.

Since these nonmedical products are distributed with the same marketing strategy and to the same outlets as proprietaries, top management considers these products as part of the proprietary product line, and they are listed as proprietary products in the company's records. However, the marketing division keeps an unofficial record of these nonmedical items and refers to them as sundries. Historically 55 percent of Burch's sales have been proprietary drugs; only about one third of these carry the Burch label, and the balance have been sold as private labels to drug wholesalers and retailers.

ORGANIZING OF FIRM

The company is organized into three functional areas: manufacturing, finance, and marketing. The executives of these divisions are vice presidents and report directly to the corporate president, Fred Burch, Jr., son of the founder.

The marketing division is headed up by Ken Vogel and is subdivided into two basic groups, marketing operations and marketing planning. Lee March, who started with the firm seven years ago to manage the purchasing department, is the director of marketing operations. Dick Jetter, director of marketing planning, who launched his marketing career with a leading soap manufacturer, has been employed with Burch for five years. The advertising manager, general sales manager, and physical distribution manager report to March, while Bill Thomas (manager of product development), Ron Venture (manager of marketing research), and the manager of cost and price analysis report to Jetter. Both March and Jetter are responsible to Ken Vogel, vice president of marketing.

Every year of the firm's existence, Burch has experienced modest growth. This expansion can be attributed to the following five factors.

1. The development of exclusive contracts with an increasing number of druggists.
2. The expansion of the distribution area.
3. An increased number of products in both the ethical and proprietary product lines.
4. The production of private brands in the proprietary line.
5. The addition to the proprietaries of a new group of nonmedical products.

SPECIAL PROBLEMS

Fred Burch, Jr., was concerned for some time about the decreasing rate of growth during the past seven years. Although the dollar sales had increased during these years, the upward volume resulted from the increased prices of inflation. The young president was further concerned after reading two reports prepared jointly by Bill Thomas, Ron Venture, and Willard Wagner, general sales manager. The first report dealt with an analysis of last year's sales and the second with foreign competition.

In the analysis of sales, the three executives pointed out that the ethical drug sales for the past year accounted for 38 percent of the firm's business. Although ethical drugs showed a 10 percent increase, sales for ethical drug industries in the United States increased by 15 percent. The proprietary line accounted for 62 percent of Burch's sales. The sales in the industry of proprietaries were up 10 percent, while Burch's proprietary sales increased by 25 percent. However, when the sundries were shown separately, the proprietary sales represented 47 percent of total sales and sundries 15 percent. When the two types of products were separated, proprietary sales showed an increase of only 5 percent over the previous year. However, sundries increased over 80 percent. This large increase in sales was due to the introduction of dental hygiene products.

The second report, a projection of expected foreign competition in the pharmaceutical industry during the 1980s, represented a summation of several articles in trade papers. This report pointed out that foreign competition has already made inroads in the U.S. market in several industries (automobiles, steel, and electronics). The report predicted that in the 1980s this competition would extend into the ethical drug and over the counter drugs. Furthermore, several foreign drug companies have already developed new cardiovascular and antibiotic drugs and have made plans to introduce these items in the U.S. market. These foreign firms have been motivated to extend their markets into the United States by the vastness of this market, by the pricing freedom in this country, and by the high profit margins of pharmaceutical business.

Although drug laws in this country require foreign firms to meet certain manufacturing standards and to develop "in-country" medical data, and although differences exist in the marketing and distribution of pharmaceutical goods in the United States, the report pointed out that it is possible for a foreign firm to develop marketing strategy which would solve these problems. American firms are faced with potentially stiff competition from foreign enterprises during the next 10 years.

After careful consideration, Fred Burch distributed copies of these reports to the firm's vice presidents. He instructed these division execu-

tives to study the reports prior to a special executive meeting at which time the reports would be discussed. He also invited the marketing team to attend the meeting to answer questions that were bound to arise during the discussion. Burch also asked Ron Venture to prepare a report on the test market results of a new nonmedical product.

EXECUTIVE MEETING

Two weeks later at the special meeting, several of those present indicated that in their opinion the predicted competition from abroad would not and could not happen. Dick Jetter pointed out that this insight was no longer a prediction but a reality. In fact one foreign firm had entered into a joint-venture contract, and another was in the process of procuring a small American firm in which drugs would be produced.

Fred Burch asked Bill Warner to explain the "sundries" in the sales report. Warner explained that sundries included the nonmedical products such as toothpaste, chewing gum, and toiletries, and since the pharmaceutical industry report of proprietaries does not include these products, the sales of these nonmedicals should not be included in a comparative analysis with the industry's sales. George Heinzen, vice president of manufacturing, asked Lee March the cause of the ethical drug change from 55 percent to 38 percent of the firm's business. Lee answered that the cause was due to the increasing sales of the sundries. Lee added that in his opinion the future of Burch depended upon the success of the sundries.

After a lengthy discussion on the pros and cons of developing sundries, Burch asked Ron Venture for a report on the test market of Kissables. Burch reminded Ron that some of the persons present had only a limited knowledge of this new item.

Ron distributed to each executive a sample package of the new product, Kissables. After the sampling of the new product, George Heinzen asked Venture and Vogel to explain what happened to the original brand name, Contact, and the red-colored package. Ken Vogel told the executive committee that Contact was only a proposed brand name, and because another company was currently using that name for one of its products, Burch's legal department recommended changing the name of Burch's mouth mint. He continued to explain that the new-product department recommended the name Kissables, which would suggest that sweet breath is one result of using the product.

Ken further explained that the color of lettering on the package was changed from red to green since the color red is often used to denote danger and/or heat. Green color lettering with a white background was finally selected because green suggests freshness which is one of the

product's benefits and because green is the same color as the color of the product.

Next, Ron distributed and read the fact sheet for the product to the group. See Exhibit 1. He then handed out the Marketing Strategy plan (Exhibit 2) which was used in the test marketing of the product.

EXHIBIT 1   Kissables fact sheet

Kissables	An oral antiseptic designed to sweeten breath.
Brand name	Kissables suggests that having sweet breath is an advantage of using the product.
Product description	Green-colored tablet. Flat and round shape. Diameter slightly smaller than Life Savers. Thickness about half of Life Saver.
Package	Cylinder-shaped about length of Life Saver package. Color—white background with green lettering. (Originally planned red lettering. Changed to avoid perception of danger or heat. Green projects coolness and matches color of product.)
Product idea and concept	Laboratory tested two years ago. Burch board of directors green-lighted limited production for test marketing.
Product features	1. Tablets small enough to be unnoticed in use. 2. Convenient to use. 3. Small package easy to carry as routinely as cigarettes or gum. 4. Cool and refreshing flavor. 5. Good antiseptic results. 6. Low calories (2 calories per tablet).

Paul Stevens, vice president of finance, asked for the sales results of the test market. Warner volunteered to answer the sales volume inquiry. He reported to the committee that sales were 17 percent higher than anticipated. He added that sales could have been even higher, but the limited production of Kissables prevented Burch from filling reorders from many of the dealers who depleted their complete inventory.

Fred Burch asked for a report on the test market. While Jetter and Venture distributed the research plan (Exhibit 3) and the findings of the research (Exhibits 4, 5, 6, and 7) Vogel commented that the marketing

EXHIBIT 2   Marketing strategy for Kissables test market

Product	Kissables, an oral antiseptic. Available in single packages. See fact sheet for other product details.
Place	Test markets to be used—Kansas City, Cincinnati, and Peoria, for one month. Outlets: Supermarkets, drugstores, liquor stores, and restaurants.
Promotion	Advertising (all ads scheduled throughout the marketing test period).

	Media	Daily newspapers	2 column x 10 inches. Food section on Thursdays Sports section on Sundays and Fridays Morning and evening editions
		Radio stations	30-second spots 3 times daily (ROS)
		Television	30-second spots 3 times daily (ROS)
		Other promotion	Point of purchase displays Samples of product distributed

Price	Priced competitively to Certs and Clorets.

team was able to operate within its budget including the advertising expenditures which had been set at 10 percent of sales. Stevens remarked that 10 percent of sales is the normal advertising expenditure for a new product, although five percent of sales is the company's norm for advertising.

Ron Venture used the tabulation of the research to point out that hypotheses numbered 1, 2, and 4 were proven. Of all female respondents who bought Kissables, 46 percent were between 18 and 26 years old, and 37 percent of the male respondents were in the same age bracket. Almost all respondents were in occupations (including students) which bring them into close contact with other people. The study also indicates that 37 percent of the respondents repurchase the product weekly. Ron pointed out that 27 percent of the respondents were making their initial purchase when the interview took place.

Both male and female users compared the product to Certs and Clorets rather than as a mouthwash as had been hypothesized. Only 13 percent of the respondents considered the product to be a mouthwash.

The fifth hypothesis, that purchasers would have heard about the product through the medium of radio, was not proven. Word of mouth dominated as the number one source of information for both men and women purchasers. The other male respondents chose television, radio, and point of purchase displays almost equally as their sources of infor-

EXHIBIT 3   Research plan for Kissables in test market

Purpose	To gather information in five general areas: 1. Demographic characteristics of purchasers. 2. Facts concerning purchase behavior. 3. Motives for purchasing Kissables. 4. Opinions about product from users. 5. Data to determine the marketability of Kissables.
Hypotheses	1. The purchasers of the product will be between 18–25 years of age. 2. The users will be persons whose occupations bring them in close contact with other people. 3. Users will consider product as a "mouth wash" to remedy a breath problem. 4. Users will repurchase a tube of Kissables once a week. 5. Purchasers will have heard about the product through the medium of radio.
Sample design and technique	Sample to include only purchasers of Kissables during the one-month test period. Point of purchase interviewing technique to be used in supermarkets.

mation. The balance of female respondents rated television higher than radio for information. None of this latter group claimed point of purchase displays as the medium of information.

Dick Jetter commented briefly on the other parts of the test market results. Although 31 percent of the female respondents claimed the outstanding product feature to be taste, only 10 percent recommended taste to be used as a product feature in future advertising. It appeared from the data gathered that future ads should point out the convenience qualities of the product. A high percentage of the respondents rated this product feature to be outstanding, as well as recommending that it be used in future advertising.

During the discussion which followed the research report, the focal point tended to be on the best way to advertise the product. Finally, Fred Burch interrupted the discussion and asked Ken Vogel if he had a sales forecast and a proposed advertising budget for Kissables.

Ken replied, "I thought you'd never ask. We forecast $6 million in sales for the last three quarters of this year and $10 million next year. This will bring our total company sales this year to $300 million. Our advertising budget for this year includes $3.2 million for new-product advertising which has not been touched—except for the test market. You may recall we started our advertising budget with $14.8 million with $.5 million for newspaper advertising, $3 million for magazines, $5.4

EXHIBIT 4   Kissables test market research results in percentages female respondents (FR) according to age groups (represents 57 percent of sample)

	18–25	26–35	36–45	46–50	Over 50	Total FR	Percent of sample
Initial purchase respondents	9	7	8	2	2	28	16
Repurchase respondents	37	18	7	11	2	72	41
Product information source:							
Word of mouth	17	15	7	7	2	48	27
Television	9		1		2	12	8
Radio	7					7	4
Newspaper				4		4	2
Free sample	13	7	7	2		29	16
Frequency of purchase:							
Weekly	24	7		2		33	19
More frequently	2	2		2		6	4
Every 2 weeks	11	7	7	7	2	33	19
Initial purchase	9	6	8	2	2	28	15
Quantity of each purchase:							
1 package	43	22	15	10	4	94	55
2 packages	3			3		6	2
More than 2 packages							
Outstanding product feature:							
Taste	13	6	4	6	2	31	19
Convenience	13	10	4	2		29	16
Price	6	2				8	5
Effectiveness			4	2	2	8	5
Attractiveness of package	2					2	1
Brand name	2					2	1
No opinion	10	4	3	3		20	10
Comparable products:							
Life Savers	2	2				4	2
Clorets	11	4			2	17	10
Certs	19	7	4	2		32	19
Chewing gum			4			4	2
Mouthwash	4	2		7		13	8
Don't know/no opinion	10	7	7	4	2	30	16
Recommended product features for future advertising:							
Mouthwash	2			2		4	2
Effectiveness	10			2		12	6
Flavor	2		2			4	2
Price		2	2			4	2
Convenience	16	9	2	2	2	31	19
Breath purifier			2			2	1
Taste	10					10	5
Product uniqueness				2		2	1
Product package		2				2	1
No opinion	6	9	7	5	2	29	18

EXHIBIT 5   Kissables test market research results in percentages female respondents (FR) demographics by age groups (represents 57 percent of sample)

	18–25	*26–35*	*36–45*	*46–50*	*Over 50*	*Total FR*	*Percent of sample*
Marital status:							
Single	26	2	7	5		40	22
Married	20	20	8	8	4	60	35
Occupation:							
Office worker	22	11	2	4	2	41	23
Retail employee	5		2		2	9	5
Professional		4	2	7		13	8
Blue collar	2					2	1
Student	13					13	8
Housewife	4	7	9	2		22	12
Total age group	46	22	15	13	4	100	57

million for spot television, $1.6 million for radio, $.1 million for outdoor, $1 million for point of purchase, and $3.2 for new products."

Paul Stevens stated, "This firm should worry about future growth. There are two primary ways to expand: internal growth and by acquisition. In recent years the only internal growth of any significance has been the result of adding the nonmedical products. In view of the reports we heard at the beginning of this meeting, I suggest we show these nonmedical products as sundries as does the marketing department. It also appears to me that it's high time we concentrate on these items."

Stevens continued, "Kissables appears to be a possible new successful product. I suggest that the marketing team prepare a plan of marketing strategy including an advertising budget to be presented to this committee for approval prior to the commercialization of Kissables."

Fred asked if there were any other questions or any further discussion. Since there were none, he instructed the marketing team to prepare their strategy plan and budgets by the following Tuesday when the executive committee would again meet.

EXHIBIT 6 Kissables test market research results in percentages male respondents (MR) according to age groups (represents 43 percent of sample)

	18–25	26–35	36–45	46–50	Over 50	Total MR	Percent of sample
Initial purchase respondents	11	3	9		6	29	12
Repurchase respondents	26	23	11	11		71	31
Product information source:							
Word of mouth	26	14	9			52	23
Television	3	3	3	3		12	5
Radio			3	5		11	5
Newspaper		6				6	2
Store display	5		3		3	11	5
Free sample	3					3	1
Not certain			2	3		5	2
Frequency of purchase:							
Weekly	11	20	5	3		39	18
More frequently			3			3	1
Every 2 weeks	15	3	3	8		29	12
Initial purchase	11	3	9		6	29	12
Quantity of each purchase:							
1 package	34	23	17	11	6	91	39
2 packages	3	3	3			9	4
More than 2 packages							
Outstanding product feature:							
Taste	3	3	5		3	14	6
Convenience	15	3	3	3		24	10
Price	3	3				6	2
Effectiveness	9	14	9	5		37	16
Attractiveness of package					3	3	1
Brand name							
No opinion	7	3	3	3		16	8
Comparable products:							
Life Savers							
Clorets	9	6	5			20	9
Certs	15	8	9	3	3	38	16
Chewing gum		6				6	2
Mouthwash	3	3	3	3		12	5
Don't know/no opinion	10	3	3	5	3	24	11
Recommended product features for future advertising:							
Mouthwash	9	3				12	5
Effectiveness	9	11	5	5		30	14
Flavor							
Price					3	6	2
Convenience	11	3	3			17	7
Breath purifier	3					3	1
Taste	2	3	3			8	4
Product uniqueness		6				6	2
Product package							
No opinion			9	3	6	18	8

EXHIBIT 7   Kissables test market research results in percentages male respondents (MR) demographics by age groups (represents 43 percent of sample)

	18–25	26–35	36–45	46–50	Over 50	Total MR	Percent of sample
Marital status:							
Single	37	15	5			57	25
Married		11	15	11	6	43	18
Occupation:							
Office worker		6		3		9	4
Retail employee			5		3	8	4
Professional		8	10	8	3	29	12
Blue collar		3	5			8	4
Student	37	9				46	19
Total age group	37	26	20	11	6	100	43

QUESTIONS

1. What target market should be identified in planning a marketing program for Kissables (a breath-sweetener tablet)?

2. What marketing mix would you recommend for the introduction of this new product?

3. Would you recommend that the new product be marketed on a full scale? Why or why not?

HIGH-TECH*

In August of 1983, Mr. Robert Baird, president of High-Tech, Incorporated, was faced with planning the future of his small company. Heavy investment in R&D over the past three years had developed several promising products for High-Tech but had pushed the company into the red for fiscal year 1983. Baird was now under pressure from his board of directors to take the company public, a move which would protect their investments, if it was successful. Although he had personal reservations about going public, Mr. Baird realized that he had to come up with a marketing plan that would put the company quickly on its feet.

BACKGROUND

History

High-Tech was formed in 1969 as a corporation based in Ann Arbor, Michigan, to develop and manufacture a mini computer-based process

---

*Written by Brad Barbeau under the direction of James R. Taylor, Sebastian S. Kresge Distinguished Professor of Marketing at The University of Michigan. Copyright © 1983 by the Regents of The University of Michigan.

control system. Process control systems are found in a wide variety of manufacturing applications, such as chemical production, metal production, and assembly (e.g., auto assembly). They require the ability to interface with many varied devices to measure and control pressure, humidity, temperature, flow, etc. Over the past 14 years, High-Tech had developed process control systems for the manufacture of fiber optics, assembly monitoring, energy management, aluminum strip mill control, and boiler control.

Sales had grown slowly for High-Tech, reaching $3 million in 1982 but falling back to $2.8 million in 1983. (See Exhibits 1 through 3 for financial statements.) Profits had suffered in the past two years; after reaching a peak of $270,000 in 1981, they fell to $164,000 in 1982 and then to a loss of $54,000 in 1983. Baird attributed the fall in profits to High-Tech's increased expenditures for research and development, the fruit of which he hoped would provide a base of strong products from which the company would grow rapidly over the next several years.

High-Tech was in various stages of marketing five product lines: en-

---

EXHIBIT 1

HIGH-TECH, INCORPORATED
Statement of Operations and Accumulated Deficit
for the Year Ended June 30,

	1983*	1982	1981
Net sales	$2,812,489	$3,000,770	$2,369,381
Cost of sales	1,353,868	1,700,417	1,381,248
Gross margin	1,458,621	1,300,353	988,133
Selling, administration, and research and development expenses†	1,527,205	1,172,320	731,037
Income (loss) from operations	(68,584)	128,033	257,096
Other income (expense)—net	14,369	36,093	11,772
Income (loss) before income taxes	(54,215)	164,126	268,868
Income taxes	—	57,700	100,508
Income (loss) before extraordinary item	(54,215)	106,426	168,360
Extraordinary item—tax carryforward realized	—	57,700	100,508
Net income	$ (54,215)	$ 164,126	$ 268,868

*Preliminary unaudited balances.
†High-Tech had incurred the following research and development expenses for the past three years: 1981—$249,000; 1982—$383,500; 1983—$469,000.
Included in these figures are the research and development expenses required to develop the following: Offline Data Terminal—$91,000; General-Tools Assembly Control—$210,000; Energy Saver—$227,000.
Source: High-Tech Business Plan, August 25, 1983.

EXHIBIT 2

HIGH-TECH, INCORPORATED
Balance Sheet
June 30

Assets	1983*	1982	1981
Current assets:			
Cash and certificates of deposit	$ 206,022	$ 690,914	$ 759,111
Accounts receivable—trade†	631,225	258,726	356,779
Notes receivable	158,240	151,050	6,000
Inventories‡	788,401	819,732	784,065
Other current assets	72,398	51,104	70,348
Total current assets	1,856,286	1,971,526	1,976,303
Equipment:			
Equipment	476,062	426,554	296,037
Furniture and fixtures	79,362	74,065	68,157
Total	555,424	500,619	364,194
Less accumulated depreciation and amortization	365,881	283,231	209,039
Equipment, net	189,543	217,388	155,155
Notes receivable	237,361	129,672	12,500
Total	2,283,190	2,318,586	2,143,958
Liabilities			
Current liabilities:			
Capitalized lease obligations	10,238	10,238	16,529
Trade account payable	97,289	65,606	48,140
Accrued expenses	130,584	133,284	128,231
Total current liabilities	238,111	209,128	192,900
Long-term debt	1,007,637	1,017,963	1,023,970
Total liabilities	1,245,748	1,227,091	1,216,870
Stockholders' Equity			
Common stock, no par value	3,859,901	3,859,739	3,859,458
Accumulated deficit	(2,821,459)	(2,767,244)	(2,931,370)
Less treasury stock at cost	(1,000)	(1,000)	(1,000)
Total stockholders' equity	1,037,442	1,091,495	927,088
	$2,283,190	$2,318,586	$2,143,958

*Preliminary unaudited balances.
†The increase in accounts receivable in 1983 was largely due to a jump in sales during June. These sales were made on terms net 30 days.
‡During the fiscal year 1983, High-Tech wrote down inventory approximately $56,000 due to an error not found at the time of the year-end physical inventory.
Source: High-Tech Business Plan, August 25, 1983

EXHIBIT 3

HIGH-TECH, INCORPORATED
Statement of Changes in Financial Position
for the Year Ended June 30,

	1983*	1982	1981
Sources of working capital:			
Income before extraordinary item	$ (54,215)	$106,426	$168,360
Changes to operations not affecting working capital (depreciation and amortization)	82,650	74,192	49,581
Total provided from operations	28,435	180,618	217,941
Extraordinary item	—	57,700	100,508
Total	28,435	238,318	318,449
Proceeds from long-term borrowing	—	—	657,375
Decrease in notes receivable—officer	2,812	6,000	7,500
Proceeds from stock options exercised	162	281	2,687
Total	31,409	244,599	986,011
Application of working capital:			
Additions to equipment	54,805	136,425	45,373
Increase in notes receivable—trade	110,501	123,172	7,376
Loan to officer	—	—	20,000
Reduction of capital lease obligation	10,326	6,077	13,851
Total	175,632	265,604	86,600
Increase (decrease) in working capital	(144,223)	(21,005)	899,411
Increase (decrease) in working capital components:			
Cash and certificates of deposit	(484,892)	(68,197)	591,417
Accounts and notes receivable	379,689	52,232	70,485
Inventories	(31,331)	35,667	95,793
Prepaid expenses and other assets	21,294	(24,479)	39,680
Capitalized lease obligations	0	6,291	8,771
Trade accounts payable	(31,683)	(17,466)	63,664
Accrued expenses	2,700	(5,053)	29,601
Increase (decrease) in working capital	$(144,223)	$ (21,005)	$899,411

*Preliminary unaudited balances.
Source: High-Tech Business Plan, August 25, 1983.

ergy management systems, assembly control systems, a fiber-optics process control system, a new data collection terminal, and a credit/debit card system which was still under development (see Exhibit 4). Baird felt that, while each of these product lines had the potential to grow into a stand-alone company, High-Tech should find a way to exploit all of these opportunities, plus other products he hoped his company would develop.

EXHIBIT 4   High-Tech sales by product line

	1983	1982
Energy management systems		
Models 400 and 18	$1,009,000	$ 878,000
Enercon 5 and 50	277,000	168,000
Torque control systems	870,000	712,000
Fiber-optics process control	223,000	1,113,000
		129,000
Other		
Parts	207,000	
Service	59,000	
Engineering, programming, and R&D	143,000	
Miscellaneous	25,000	
Total	$2,813,000	$3,000,000

Source: Internal High-Tech documents.

Energy Management Systems

Energy management systems had been a major product line for High-Tech since 1975, when the first system was sold. These microprocessor-based systems are capable of managing the entire energy system for an office building or manufacturing plant. An energy management system controls the amount of energy being used at all times in order to avoid creating costly new, high peak power demands. In performing this task, as demand increases, the energy management system automatically turns off other devices consuming energy in order to maintain level demand, known as "load shedding." It also shuts off all devices which are not required at various times during the day or night. The system controls electrical power usage and temperature, monitors humidity, smoke and fire, plus many other functions—for several locations at the same time. It can provide monitoring functions in such a manner that maintenance problems can be identified by the computer when they occur. The system also accounts for the amount of energy used for various functions and analyzes where the major cost savings are being generated. Security-monitoring functions can also be performed.

The energy management system was sold by the company under the trademark "Energy Saver." The Energy Saver was available in several different models, depending on a customer's need for a large or small number of control and feedback points. The design of the system was modular, so it could be adapted and expanded to meet changing customer requirements. These systems could be used by any customer who uses relatively significant amounts of energy at different times or for

different purposes, such as office buildings, supermarkets, retail stores, industrial plants, warehouses, or hospitals.

The energy management product line consisted of the Model 400 and the new Model 18, which were sold directly through the company's sales force, and the Enercon 5 and Enercon 50, which were sold through the U.S. Heating Company. The Enercon 50 and the Model 400 were the same system. The Model 18 was a new development which was expected to partially replace the Model 400.

Model 400.   The Model 400 was designed for medium to large-size facilities (30,000 square feet and up) and was able to control 16 to 120 points,[1] or up to 94 points in a more complex facility. It could also monitor up to 96 inputs.

The Model 400 contained energy management and power demand software programs, including night set-back, optimum start, and temperature-based cycling. The Model 400 could use either front-panel keypad data entry or a CRT data entry and display terminal. Also available were printout programs, cassette-reloading capability, data transmission over telephone lines, and a variety of user-oriented software packages designed to increase user convenience and cost savings.

Hardware costs for the Model 400 ranged between $9,500 and $17,000, depending on the number of points.

Model 18.   The Model 18 was designed to accommodate small to medium-size facilities and was capable of handling 18 to 35 control points and monitor 28 inputs. However, the Model 18 could accommodate the large-facility market, being expandable to 64 points with 30 analog inputs or 32 points with 60 analog inputs.

The Model 18 represented state-of-the-art energy management system technology. While somewhat smaller in capacity than the Model 400, it had all of the capabilities of the Model 400 plus some added features. One of these allowed for interaction between temperature control and power demand, allowing temperature override of load shedding to ensure a comfortable environment. Hardware costs for the Model 18 ranged from $7,100 to $10,000.

The Energy Management Market

The market for energy management systems (EMS) had developed as a reaction to the rapid escalation in energy costs, combined with the rapid development of microprocessor technology. Despite the recent decline in energy prices, the EMS market had continued to grow as the technology for energy savings had been increasingly accepted. As it was unlikely that energy prices would continue to fall, and very likely that they would resume their upward climb, the EMS market was expected

---

[1]A "point" refers to a particular control point, such as a thermostat, light switch, or fan motor.

to continue strong through the 1980s. In 1982, the EMS market had been estimated to be $1.2 billion, and growth was estimated at 20 percent through the end of the decade. However, differential growth rates were expected to occur in the various segments within the EMS market. In the new-construction segment, market growth would be subject to fluctuation in the construction industry and would probably be below the market growth rate. Retrofit of large existing buildings, estimated to be nearly half completed, would also likely grow at a slower rate than the total market. The greatest opportunity existed in the retrofit of small to medium-size buildings of 20,000 to 100,000 square feet. A recent estimate was that only 10 percent of these buildings had been retrofitted with EMSs, and the ability of the EMS to substantially lower energy costs in these buildings was increasingly being recognized. The growth of this market was expected to substantially outperform the total market for at least the next three to four years. It was estimated that there were 1.2 million such buildings.

At the time, High-Tech was marketing its EMS systems to three types of customers. Systems were sold to large companies who installed and maintained their own systems, smaller companies who required installation and maintenance by High-Tech, and to the U.S. Heating Company, who installed the systems for other end users. The sales to smaller businesses comprised the largest and fastest growing part of High-Tech's EMS business. The company's plans called for rapid expansion of the smaller-business market, targeting auto dealerships and retail stores. The company had been successful with both groups of customers and believed that they represented the greatest immediate potential for High-Tech's EMS systems. In addition, the company was negotiating with several state governments to install the systems in government buildings. These states included Michigan, Ohio, West Virginia, Florida, and Indiana, and High-Tech had received favorable responses from these states.

MARKETING STRATEGY FOR THE SMALL AND MEDIUM BUSINESS EMS SEGMENTS

The company had segmented the small-business market by type of business and had singled out auto dealerships, retail stores, and food stores as target segments. Each of these segments had buildings which were suited to benefit from the EMS.

Product

The company had developed the Model 18 EMS specifically for the small- and medium-business market. In some ways more powerful than the Model 400, the Model 18 also had the advantage of much lower cost,

greatly increasing the benefit to the customer. The system was a micro-processor-based, on-premises EMS with the capability of load shedding, cycling and scheduling, manual override, hard copy printout, load status indication, power outage time update, and remote display and operation. This last feature allowed High-Tech to communicate with the EMS from High-Tech headquarters to monitor performance, update the program, and perform system malfunction diagnosis remotely.

Price

The Model 18 EMS, while more expensive than some less powerful systems on the market, was considerably less expensive than systems of similar capability. The company offered the system through three purchase plans: outright purchase, the no-investment plan (NIP), and the lease/shared savings (LSS). Under the NIP, High-Tech installed the system for the customer, who then paid for the system out of the savings it generated. High-Tech received the full value of the energy savings until the system was paid for, along with finance charges. This period averaged three years. Under the LSS, High-Tech installed and maintained the system and received as payment a share of the energy savings, usually 50 percent, for a period of seven years. Both the NIP and LSS plans allowed the customer to have the system installed without having to make a cash investment, while the LSS program had the added benefit to the customer of providing an incentive for High-Tech to ensure that the optimal savings are obtained from the system. Outright purchases were discounted 10 percent from the "equivalent case sales price" of the system, while the NIP were increased 10 percent over the "equivalent cash sales price." This ECSP averaged $30,000 per system installed.

Promotion and Distribution

The company had found that the EMS systems were sold most effectively by a High-Tech direct sales force. Attempts at sales through distributors had been unsuccessful, primarily due to the complexity of the product. The company had five full-time salespeople selling energy management systems and expected to double the number of salespeople in the next year. The company used little advertising and depended upon the ability of its sales people to develop the interest of the customers in the product.

In small companies, it was usually the president or chief financial officer who made the purchase decision on the EMS. The president and/or chief financial officer, in most small companies, didn't have the training to evaluate the technical aspects of an EMS purchase, which led High-Tech to develop a sales approach emphasizing the financial benefits associated with the purchase of an EMS.

Competitors in the EMS Market

The tremendous potential of the EMS market had attracted many firms to the market, firms of varying sizes and capabilities with several different market strategies. Present competitors ranged in size from giants such as IBM, American Bell, Honeywell, and Johnson Controls to many small, undercapitalized firms with sales of only a few hundred thousand dollars a year.

Large, established companies had entered the EMS market by extending their existing core product lines. HVAC (heating, ventilating, and air conditioning) companies, such as the U.S. Heating Company, had entered the new-construction portion of the business by adding an EMS to their HVAC package. These companies were also able to retrofit the EMS, along with other modifications, to existing HVAC systems to improve system efficiency. Computer and control companies, such as Honeywell and Johnson Controls, had used their capabilities to produce large, complex EMSs and had combined these with fire and security systems. Both of these companies, as well as American Bell, were developing complete building automation systems that included the EMS, fire and security systems, climate control, and telecommunications. These systems, however, would be applicable only to very large buildings.

While High-Tech could not compete directly against the ability of these firms, the markets that they were in were very different from that of High-Tech. While some of the larger firms such as Honeywell were entering the medium-size building retrofit market, the company believed that its capabilities were sufficient to defend its share of the market. Honeywell's share of the small and medium-size building market was about 20 percent, while no other competitor had more than 1 percent.

On the smaller end of the competitor scale, many small and/or newly established firms had entered the EMS market in the past two years. These firms had created a highly fragmented market for EMSs in the lower end of the retrofit market. Many of these companies lacked a sufficiently powerful product, experience in surveying and installing systems, and the ability to efficiently service them. However, some of these firms did have these capabilities and presented increasingly strong competition for the small-building EMS retrofit market.

Baird believed that, in order to be viable in this market, a firm would have to be able to build, install, and service the EMS itself. Most of the businesses that comprised the target market had limited technical capability and were concerned with the reliability of the systems. Due to the complexity of the EMS, a company which had full control over quality assurance in production, software development, installation, and servicing the system would be in the strongest position to ensure reliability and maximize the benefits of the system.

Problems in the EMS Market

With nearly all of High-Tech sales in the EMS market being through the NIP and LSS programs, the profitability of the EMS product line was highly dependent upon the company estimating both installation costs and system savings correctly for each job. Both of these were subjective estimates, based upon the characteristics of the individual building, and were highly dependent upon the skill of the energy management specialists trained by High-Tech for these jobs. While High-Tech felt that it had the savings estimates down to a fairly accurate science, installation cost overruns continued to plague the company. On a typical $30,000 (cash sales price) system, hardware cost accounted for approximately 40 percent of the selling price, and installation for another 10 percent. However, installation overruns of 100 to 200 percent had occurred, and overruns of 50 percent were not uncommon.

Under the LSS plan, High-Tech's return was also affected by weather conditions. An abnormally cool summer or warm winter can result in energy savings considerably less than those projected.

High-Tech Off-Line Data Terminal (ODT)

In response to the increased concern of companies for cost control through automation and improved cost control systems, High-Tech developed a microprocessor-based time clock and data storage device called the "Off-Line Data Terminal (ODT)." The basic function of the device was to accept, store, and transmit data, and several applications existed for the product. As an automated time clock, the device could interface with the IBM personal computer to greatly reduce clerical time involved in payroll calculations. As a job cost device, the ODT allowed a company to quickly and accurately track time and material spent on multiple jobs as they move through different stages of manufacturing. The ease and rapidity with which the ODT allowed this to be done made it suitable for use not only in custom job-shops, but also by lawyers and other professionals who had to keep track of time spent on multiple projects for individual billing. The ODT was also highly suited for applications in material forecasting and inventory control, work-in-process, and final goods inventory control.

While the basic device was completed and in the process of being demonstrated, some optional features were still being developed. Software had been written that allowed the device to interface with the IBM PC, as well as a software package for the IBM PC which allows the user to configure the data in a manner best suited to his/her purpose. Other options which were still under development included hard copy capability, a down-load operator interface program, telecommunications capability, and a bar code or magnetic card reader. These options were expected to be available in late fall of 1984.

High-Tech had begun some exploratory marketing of the ODT to find the best marketing program for the new product. Efforts of Baird had resulted in an agreement with Ron McInerny, a distributor of microcomputers and computer peripherals, to market the ODT for High-Tech. McInerny had placed a tentative order for 2,000 ODTs over the following 16 months, with 25 to be delivered over the next 5 months, 50 in the sixth month, 100 in the seventh, and 200 each month after that. However, only five ODTs had been firmly ordered by the company so far for demonstration purposes. Tom Scanlon, a young salesman for High-Tech, had been assigned to explore other opportunities for the ODTs. A tentative price schedule for the ODT called for a steeply sliding scale according to the volume of purchases. The scale began at $2,999 for purchases of 1–10 ODTs and fell to a low of $1,250 for purchases of 2,000+. Thus far, the company had only manufactured a few prototypes, but estimates were that volume production would result in a cost of approximately $1,000 per unit. See Exhibit 5 for the price schedule.

EXHIBIT 5   ODT price schedule

Order quantity	Price per unit
1–10	$2,999
11–50	$2,499
51–100	$1,999
101–500	$1,799
501–1,000	$1,599
1,001–2,000	$1,399
>2,000	$1,250

Source: Internal High-Tech documents.

A preliminary market study by the company had shown that many companies were interested in the ODTs but were concerned about the $3,000 price. A typical reaction, "I don't see why that little thing should cost more than $1,000," was heard from businesses that were presently using the old electromechanical time clocks.

Competitors' automated time clocks were generally priced in the $1,000–$1,500 range, although these clocks did not have the flexibility or internal processing capability of the High-Tech ODT. The only data collector on the market that could perform the multiple function of the ODT was priced at $12,000, although it performed the complete payroll process internally, including printing the checks.

The ODT market in 1982 was estimated to be $10 million, with rapid growth expected over the next several years as companies moved to replace their electromechanical time clocks and manual job-costing systems.

Assembly Control Systems

The company had developed a microcomputer-based system which controlled the amount of torque applied to a bolt during assembly. The system had been developed for General Tools, who used it to control the assembly systems which GT sold to the automotive companies. The assembly control system (ACS) had been a long-standing product for High-Tech, with the first version developed in 1974. Improved capabilities had been developed over the years, with the latest version representing the state-of-the-art in assembly control systems. This advanced digital system monitored the nut-driving process by measuring the stretch of the metal in the bolt, in real time, as the fastener was being tightened. This system allowed the use of techniques on the production line that were formally only available in laboratory test facilities.

The ACS systems were sold exclusively to General Tools, with no plans to locate other manufacturers who would be interested in it. General Tools had contracted a blanket order for the ACS system with High-Tech, which called for the purchase of at least 48 spindles[2] per quarter from High-Tech, plus any above that number that GT might order. Baird was informed in August by the GT vice president who had responsibility for GT's assembly systems that the company would be purchasing 2,000 spindles between then and December of 1984, although no firm orders above the blanket order had been received. In the past, GT had taken only a few units above the blanket order. High growth was expected in the auto assembly machinery market, in which GT held a 30 percent share. In all assembly systems GT was dominant, with over 60 percent of the market.

Revenue to High-Tech for the ACS systems was $2,000 per spindle, with manufacturing costs of $1,100 per spindle, on average. No salespersons were involved in the transaction; however, Baird would typically spend a few hours each month maintaining contact with GT. Also, Charles Feldt, the vice president of R&D, and another project engineer spend most of their time on the engineering of the ACS system.

Credit/Debit Card Processor

In summer 1981, High-Tech contracted with Imperial Oil Limited (70 percent owned by Exxon) to develop a prototype credit card proces-

---

[2]Each spindle controls a single drive and is the basis of measuring the number of ACS systems produced. Up to 10 spindles may be housed in a single ACS machine.

sor (CCP), plus field test units based on that prototype. In February 1982, High-Tech further contracted to develop a data concentrator to communicate with these credit card processors. A prototype CCP was delivered in spring 1982. Field test units were built shortly thereafter. A set of program enhancements was developed and delivered in late summer 1982, along with a number of other small hardware and software changes which were retrofitted into the field test machines.

In late summer 1983, High-Tech demonstrated a new CCP unit for Imperial Oil and was awaiting Imperial Oil's response. At stake was a contract to build 2,000 CCPs at an expected price of about $1,000 each. The contract, if obtained, would establish High-Tech as the pioneer in the field, although some other companies were also developing CCPs. It was estimated that by 1990 nearly all 181,000 gasoline stations in the United States would be outfitted with CCPs.

Fiber-Optics Process Control System

The production of the glass fibers used for fiber-optics requires glass of extremely high purity to be drawn into very thin and, most important, flawless strands. In addition, the fibers are of great length for communications applications, as light is lost wherever a joint occurs in the fiber-optics system. This places great demands upon the production process, and transferring the process from the laboratory to the manufacturing plant proved a formidable task. It was accomplished partly due to the development by High-Tech of a process control system which could maintain the manufacturing process within the required tolerances.

High-Tech developed the system for Federal Electric, who had been the sole purchaser of it. Federal Electric had purchased approximately 100 systems over the past several years. Fiber-optics control systems demand from Federal Electric had been estimated by Baird at 40 systems over the next five years. He estimated the system prices at $35,000 each, with a 50 percent gross profit margin.

MANUFACTURING

All of the products developed and manufactured by High-Tech consisted of electronic components and printed circuit boards mounted inside sheet metal and plastic enclosures. Electronic components and printed circuit boards were purchased from various vendors and assembled by High-Tech; the sheet metal and plastic enclosures were custom-made by local fabricators. The assembled parts were mounted into the enclosures by High-Tech. While some automation of the assembly process had been undertaken, the task of assembling parts onto the

printed circuit boards ("stuffing"), which required 25 percent of the assembly time, was still largely a labor-intensive process.

The printed circuit boards were common to all of the High-Tech products, although each product required a different type of board. The boards thus served as the basic yardstick of production. High-Tech was producing 100 printed circuit boards per month. Semi-automatic insertion equipment, which would lower the cost of stuffing the boards by approximately 30 percent, would become effective when volumes reached 500 boards per month. Automatic insertion equipment, which would lower stuffing costs to 50 percent of the present cost, would become feasible when volumes reached 10,000 boards per month.

At present production levels, a problem facing manufacturing was that there were very short assembly runs of each type of board. While setup costs were not a factor, increasing the number of boards of a single type that a worker assembled shortened the time necessary via a learning curve effect, so that a five-fold increase in the length of the runs would result in a 15 percent decrease in costs.

Another volume-related problem for manufacturing costs was that present production levels did not always allow for parts orders to receive large-lot discounts. This resulted in High-Tech paying approximately 20 percent more for its parts than it would if volumes were tripled. Inventory control at the larger volumes, however, would require the purchase of a new computer system, expected to cost about $100,000. Other manufacturing equipment which would need to be purchased are listed in Appendix B. Despite the present low volumes, High-Tech had experienced difficulties in getting orders "out the back door," i.e., built and shipped. Many of the recent delays had been due to an attempt to cut back inventory, which had sometimes resulted in parts shortages when vendors were not able to supply parts rapidly enough. Also related to the inventory–manufacturing scheduling problem was the inadequacy of the present computer system.

SALES

In the past, most of the sales of High-Tech products had been through the efforts of Baird, who also developed the core idea for the products. A typical scenario would be that Baird would identify a need of a business contact of his, develop a product to satisfy that need, and then sell it to that business contact's company. While this had been the mainstay of the company for 13 years, the past year had seen the development of a company sales force under the direction of Tom Baird. This sales force had been developed specifically to market the energy management systems to the small-business market. At the same time, the

company had worked to develop a strong marketing program for the EMSs, which had resulted in the development of the leased/shared savings (LSS) approach.

High-Tech had also sold its products through other companies, both through distributors and through original equipment manufacturer (OEM) agreements. Both the torque control system and the energy management systems (under the Unitrac brand name) were sold to OEMs who incorporate the systems into their own products. Sales growth to OEMs had been very slow, although both U.S. Heating and GT had consistently projected faster sales growth. High-Tech's experience with distributors had not resulted in satisfactory relationships. An attempt to market the EMS through Graybar Electric failed due to the inability of the Graybar salespeople to understand and sell the EMS. The arrangement with McInerny for the marketing of the ODTs had not resulted in any significant orders; however, the agreement was signed only in early August.

The products made by High-Tech had all been developed through the entrepreneurship of Robert Baird. A man of many ideas, Baird wanted to pursue all of those ideas—building each into a separate company spun off from High-Tech. Consistent with this, Baird felt that all of the current product lines were good products, and that they should all be pursued.

CONCLUSION

Faced with falling profits and a need for outside financing, Baird was being pressured by his board of directors to take the company public. Baird had reservations about making that move; he was wary of the "New York types" and believed that selling shares in a company that was losing money would be less than principled behavior. But keeping his company alive would clearly require that he choose his products and markets carefully.

One solution that Baird was considering was to spin off the individual product lines as individual marketing companies, in which High-Tech would hold a majority share. This would enable High-Tech to obtain financing for each product line. Baird hoped to use this arrangement to attract top marketing managers to head each subsidiary, by allowing them to own a part of their company.

To aid in planning the future of his company, Baird asked a team of students from a well-known, midwestern business school to write a business plan for the company. This plan, if accepted, would be presented by Baird to a venture capital firm to obtain financing. In drafting the plan, the team of students would have to consider carefully its financial, strategic, and managerial soundness for High-Tech, along with its fit with Baird's objectives.

APPENDIX A

Statement by Robert Baird about the energy management systems (contained in the 1983 High-Tech business plan)

The trend in energy management systems, as a result of technological advances, has been for these devices to become smaller and cheaper but more capable in the size of the task performed. The result, if traditional sales channels were followed, would be a lower return per unit. The company therefore embarked on a radical departure from existing marketing channels to develop a "shared savings program." This program required the development of the following:

1. High-Tech direct-sales personnel.
2. Installation personnel.
3. Installation management.
4. Energy management specialists.
5. Software for proposal generation and post-installation evaluation to calculate savings.

High-Tech has accomplished this difficult task. The goal of this program is to install systems at *no* cost to the building owner and to share the savings, usually on a 50–50 basis, over a period of five to seven years. Obviously, a program of this nature, never having been attempted before, requires a certain amount of learning. Some of the early installations would not be accepted under our current methodology, but we consider the effort a wise investment. Under today's contract, shared savings is an excellent financial arrangement for both the building owner and High-Tech. The concept of a shared savings program is gaining more acceptance; in fact, Time Energy Systems, Inc. of Houston went public in February 1983 with a program quite similar to that of High-Tech, with the exception that Time Energy purchases their computers, while High-Tech manufactures theirs. The acceptance of the sharing program is further demonstrated by the fact that the sales personnel are receiving signatures on contracts on the first call. The High-Tech contract, which is the essential part of the arrangement, gives the company the right to refuse the contract if it is not deemed to be profitable in the view of High-Tech. The company is therefore in control of its growth. This growth will be determined by the cash and personnel available to meet the overall company objectives.

The State High-Tech Program

The company has discussed the establishment of an office in each of 10 states with their economic department chiefs. The funding for such an office is to be generated by the placement, on a sharing basis, of High-Tech energy management systems in 100 or more state-owned buildings over a seven-year period, at *no* cost to the state. The results of such a program would be:

1. For High-Tech: the funding of an office in each state to be generated by High-Tech sharing the savings, from which it is planned to generate a capability that utilizes other product developments of the company.

2. For the state:
   a. Fifty percent of the savings generated from the sharing program.
   b. Development of a High-Tech office.

APPENDIX B

Description of Facilities and Planned Capital Improvements

High-Tech presently leases a modern, 24,000-square-foot facility situated in an industrial and technological center located in Ann Arbor, Michigan. Located one-half mile from Interstate 94, and only 30 minutes from Detroit Metropolitan Airport, this location affords High-Tech easy accessibility to predominant modes of transportation.

The present design of the floor plan is such that 9,000 square feet are devoted to office space, and 15,000 square feet for production and a research and development laboratory. If required, there are an additional 24,000 square feet available under the same roof; therefore, if High-Tech finds it necessary to acquire additional space, it will not necessitate a major move. Keeping its offices centrally located with its manufacturing facilities affords High-Tech direct lines of communication within the entire organization, thus

Sales level	Administrative improvements	Cost	Production improvements	Cost
Current	Computer system	120K	Upgraded flow solder equipment	30K
	Additional office space	5K	Test facilities	4K
	Additional office equipment	10K	Upgrade wire-cutting and stripping equipment	5K
			Production work space	3K
			Diagnostic equipment	10K
			Upgrade of prog equipment	20K
6M	Off-site office space for sales, customer service, and some administrative personnel	100K	Semi-auto insertion equipment	30K
			Integrated circuit tester	10K
			Production work areas	2K
	Company van	15K	Test equipment: curve tracer for QA department	10K
	Additional office equipment	10K	Additional warehouse	5K
			R&D equipment	8K
			Additional upgrade—prog equipment	16K
12M	Company van	15K	Board test equipment	30K
	Computer enhancement (CAD)	50K	Production work areas	8K
			R&D equipment	8K
	Additional office equipment	10K		
20M	Additional office equipment/ space	50K	Diagnostic equipment	20K
			R&D equipment	8K
			Network software development system	50K

Source: High-Tech Business Plan, August 25, 1983.

facilitating the overseeing of the entire operation—which allows High-Tech to fulfill the needs of its customers most efficiently and productively.

For the purpose of discussion, the timing of all capital improvements will be considered a function of sales volume and, indirectly, the personnel force required to support that level of sales. To simplify matters, capital improvement will be condensed into two components—administrative and production—corresponding to the current facility use.

APPENDIX C

Management Organization and Key Personnel

The company employs approximately 65 persons and is functionally organized into three divisions: Production, Sales, and Research and Development. Resumes for the President, Robert A. Baird, the three division directors, and the controller follow:

Robert A. Baird, the principal organizer of the company, has substantial experience in the field of computers. He has been the president of the company since its inception. After his discharge from the U.S. Navy in 1946, Mr. Baird received his bachelor of arts degree from the University of Western Ontario, in London, Ontario, Canada. From 1951 to 1963, he was employed as a sales representative for the Univac Division of Sperry Rand Corporation. In 1963, Mr. Baird joined the Collins Radio Company to market a new communications-oriented computer system. He remained at Collins until 1965, when he became an self-employed entrepreneur. He organized High-Tech in 1969. Mr. Baird has been a member of the Michigan Technology Council.

Thomas W. Baird, Director of Sales, joined High-Tech in 1972. Mr. Baird initially worked in the Production area and later became involved in the design and specification of hardware and software for the company's line of ENERGY OPTIMIZER systems. He was responsible for the company's first sales of energy management equipment to companies such as New York Telephone, First National Stores, AT&T Longlines, and Burroughs. More recently, Mr. Baird has been responsible for initiating a direct sales program including the hiring and training of the company's sales force. This program included the development of computer programs which generate proposals and evaluates savings for the purpose of billing customers involved in a shared savings program, which was developed under his direction.

Charles Feldt, Director of Research and Development, joined High-Tech in 1969 to develop a process control computer system. He has been responsible for the development of several of the company's major products. From 1959 to 1969, Mr. Feldt was employed as a senior engineer in the research laboratory of Bendix Corporation. From 1958 to 1959, he participated in a one-year engineer training program for the Chrysler Missile Operations. Mr. Feldt is a graduate of the University of Illinois, where he received a bachelor of science degree in electrical engineering. He has done graduate work in the fields of mathematics, feedback control, and digital computers at The University of Michigan and Wayne State University. He is a member of the Institute of Electrical and Electronic Engineers. He is a past instructor of Semiconductor Circuit Design and Integrated Circuits at Wayne State University, Applied Management and Technology Center.

Michael R. Baird joined High-Tech in 1982 as the Director of Manufacturing. His energies have been focused on increasing production through a thorough analysis of our manufacturing processes. Mr. Baird came to High-Tech from the Comprehensive Health Planning Council of Southeastern Michigan. As a senior planner, Mr. Baird prepared the agency's forecasts of needed health care resources, based upon analysis of demographic, utilization and health care status information. From 1976 to 1978, Mr. Baird was a researcher for the Commission on Professional and Hospital Activities in Ann Arbor, Michigan. In this capacity, he contributed numerous articles to various health care publications. Mr. Baird has a bachelor of science degree from Wayne State University and a masters degree from The University of Michigan.

Thomas M. McDougall, CPA, joined High-Tech as Controller in 1983. His emphasis at High-Tech will be in the development of a more efficient accounting and financial information reporting system. Mr. McDougall came to the company from Fox & Company, a national public accounting firm, where he had worked since 1976. As a supervisor on the audit staff of Fox & Company, he assisted clients in financial planning, development of accounting and financial information systems, and the reporting of financial information. Mr. McDougall received his bachelor of business administration degree from Eastern Michigan University in 1976 and received his CPA certificate from the State of Michigan in 1979. He is affiliated with the American Institute of Certified Public Accountants and the Michigan Association of Certified Public Accountants.

Consultants Used by High-Tech

Clarence C. Cadieux, former Vice President of Finance of National Twist Drill & Tool Company (a division of Lear Siegler), and the Chairman of High-Tech.

Dr. David Artzel, University of Michigan, Professor of Electrical and Computer Engineering.

Dr. Donald Reiss, University of Michigan, Professor of Electrical and Computer Engineering.

Dr. Keith Dumas, University of Michigan, Associate Professor of Electrical and Computer Engineering.

Ray Howard, Partner, Deloitte Haskins & Sells.

William L. Edwards, former General Manager, Westinghouse NUMA, Logic Division.

QUESTIONS

1. What are the strengths and weaknesses of High-Tech? What is its market share position in each of its product markets?

2. Suggest strategies for overcoming High-Tech's weaknesses.

3. What product strategy would you recommend to High-Tech?

Source: High-Tech Business Plan, August 25, 1983.

Part four

DISTRIBUTION STRATEGY

Distribution strategy is concerned with making goods available to potential customers. It involves the selection of paths or channels through the maze of marketing middlemen who constitute the distribution structure. In the first phase of distribution strategy, the producers attempt to identify those channels of distribution that will most effectively reach the markets they wish to serve. Producers then try to gain the support of those intermediaries in the desired channels so that they will take on the line and move it to market.

Another distribution strategy decision area deals with the number of middlemen to use at each level in the channel. Here the producer must weigh the benefits of intensive coverage of the market gained by using large numbers of middlemen versus the benefits derived from using fewer middlemen, each of whom can give the line more concentrated promotional support.

Finally, decisions have to be made as to how the goods are to be distributed physically once the channel or ownership paths have been decided. The firm must specify a level of customer service which is consistent with its overall marketing strategy. Then different physical distribution systems can be analyzed to find the one that meets the required service level most efficiently.

THE DISTRIBUTION STRUCTURE

8

Few products are sold by producers directly to consumers. More commonly, products pass through one, several, or many market intermediaries—institutions which exist for the distribution, rather than the manufacture, of goods. In contrast to manufacturers, who provide products with form utility, these institutions create time, place, and possession utility. It is not sufficient that products capable of satisfying human wants exist. These products do not truly serve a purpose unless consumers are able to obtain them when and where they are needed. The sum total of the agent middlemen, wholesalers, and retailers who bring the products to consumers constitutes the *distribution structure* through which manufacturers must work in marketing their products.

The course through this structure which a manufacturer has a product follow on its way to the consumer is referred to as a "channel of distribution." In selecting a channel of distribution, any manufacturer would usually choose to sell through only a very small percentage of the institutions that make up the distribution structure. If the channel of distribution is chosen wisely, the manufacturer will be in a position to obtain adequate market coverage and sales volume for the product. Choosing unwisely will deal a crushing blow to the manufacturer's chances for marketing success.

EXCHANGE AND MARKET INTERMEDIARIES

The existence of the complex of marketing institutions that form our distribution structure, and whose result is that products often pass through many hands on the way to consumers, causes much criticism of marketing and distribution costs. One of the suggestions commonly made for reducing the cost of distribution is to "cut out the middleman." It is a popular belief that costs are least when producers sell directly to consumers, as in the case of door-to-door sales of vacuum cleaners and cosmetics. Quite the contrary is true. This is a very high-cost channel of distribution. Sometimes manufacturers who use such a direct channel attempt to capitalize on this misunderstanding by claiming an ability to charge lower prices because they have circumvented the middlemen who make up the distribution structure. This helps to perpetuate the misunderstanding. To overcome this misconception, a better under-standing of the nature of the exchange process and of the role played therein by marketing institutions is necessary.

Exchange without Intermediaries

Why have so many market intermediaries arisen to carry out the exchange process? Why do producers and consumers not deal directly with each other to a greater extent than they do? To illustrate the basic, and perhaps obvious but still ignored, principle underlying the existence of market intermediaries, let us assume a primitive society consisting of but five families. Initially these families were self-sufficient, each pro-ducing all of the things it needed for its own existence. Soon it was discovered, however, that each family produced some things better than others. It would be to the advantage of all if a family concentrated on producing the product it could produce best, and then the families exchanged products with each other. Because of the commonly recog-nized advantages of division of labor, this would give a larger total prod-uct. As illustrated in Figure 8–1, one family concentrated on the production of shovels, one on cloth, one on meat, one on vegetables, and one on baskets. By trading among themselves, the families each acquired a supply of all the items.

Let us now focus on the exchange process involved in Figure 8–1. For each family to acquire all five products, 10 exchanges must take place. The number of exchanges required can be expressed by the formula

$$\frac{n(n-1)}{2}$$

where n is the number of consuming units involved.[1] The number of exchanges (10) in relation to the number of products (5) is high. Each exchange, of course, involves a cost in time and effort.

---

[1] Each family (n) must contact all other families ($n-1$), and when such contact is made, two (2) products change hands.

FIGURE 8–1   Exchange without market intermediary

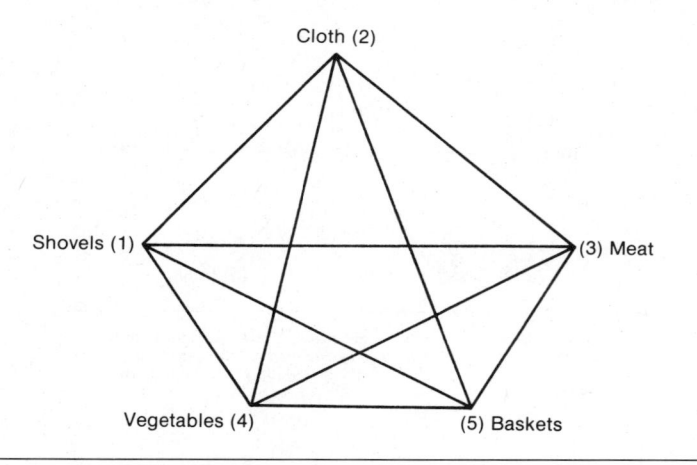

Source: Adapted from Wroe Alderson. "Factors Governing the Development of
Marketing Channels," in *Marketing Channels for Manufactured Products,* ed.
Richard M. Clewett (Homewood, Ill.: Richard D. Irwin, 1954), p. 7.

In Figure 8–2 we assume that some sort of market intermediary is
established to facilitate the exchange process. Each family now brings
the amount of the product it has produced in excess of its own needs to
a trading post and there exchanges it for the other four items that it
requires. In this case, only 5 transactions are necessary in contrast to the
10 required when no market intermediary was present. The time and
effort (cost) involved in the exchange process has been greatly reduced.

The ratio of advantage from use of a market intermediary in our
illustration is small (2:1) because the number of consuming units is
small.[2] In the real world, the number of producing and/or consuming
units would be far larger. If there were 25 such units, the ratio of advantage would be 12 to 1. If there were 100, it would be 49.5 to 1; if 500,
the ratio would be 249.5 to 1; and if 1,000 the ratio of advantage would
be 499.5 to 1. These are not large numbers in the real world of exchange. It is apparent, therefore, that use of market intermediaries
greatly expedites the exchange process.

---

[2]The ratio of advantage is

$$\frac{n(n-1)}{2} \big/ n$$

FIGURE 8–2 Exchange with market intermediary

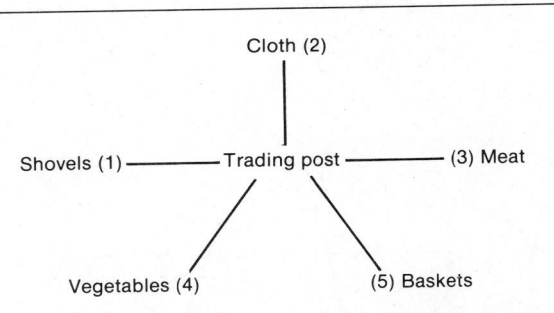

The Wholesaler and Exchange

To make more realistic the role played by middlemen in our real-world distribution structure, let us apply the above reasoning to the presence of a wholesaler who distributes the products of several manufacturers to a number of retailers. Figure 8–3, which is grossly oversimplified, contains five manufacturers and five retailers. Each manufacturer produces one of many products carried by each of the five retailers. If each manufacturer sold directly to each of the five retailers, a total of 25 transactions would be involved.[3] However, if each manufacturer sold only to the wholesaler, and then the wholesaler combined these five products and sold them to the retailers, a total of only 10 transactions would be required. In even this simple illustration, involving a mere handful of manufacturers and retailers, the use of a wholesaler reduces the number of transactions by 60 percent. If our illustration were more realistic, containing hundreds of manufacturers and perhaps thousands of retailers, the ratio of advantage from use of a wholesaler would be far greater. The ability of wholesalers to reduce transactions in this manner is the fundamental explanation for their existence.

---

[3]Because we are now assuming that the manufacturers in our illustration sell only to retailers, and not to each other, the formula for calculating the number of transactions used in our previous illustrations must be modified to:

$$\frac{n(n-1)}{2} - \frac{n}{2}\left(\frac{n}{2} - 1\right)$$

FIGURE 8–3   Role of the wholesaler

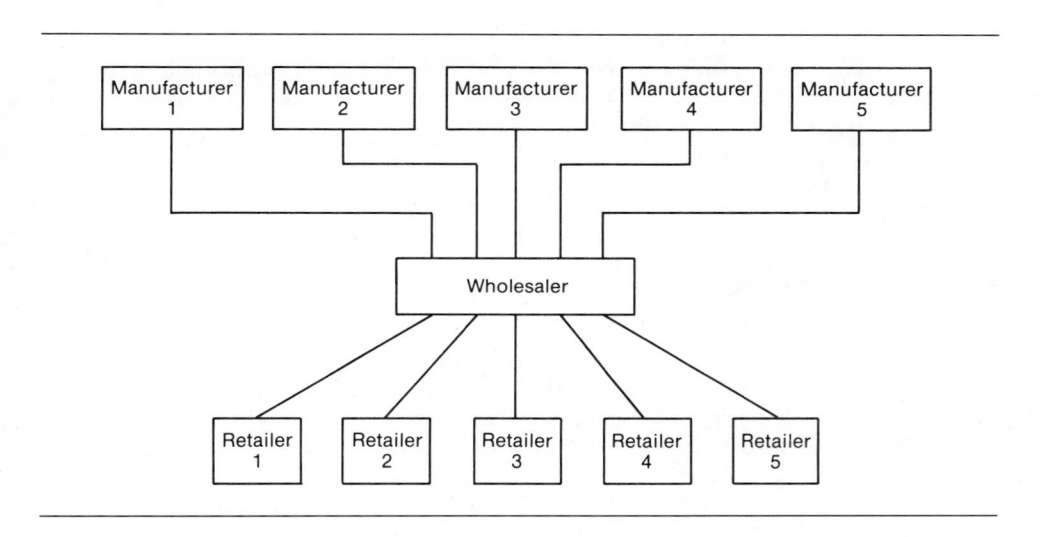

Principle of Minimum Total Transactions

By now it should be clear that the existence of a distribution structure made up of various types of middlemen serves to reduce the number of transactions involved in getting goods from producer to consumer. It has been implied that this increases the efficiency of distribution and thus reduces marketing costs. But we have not really explained why this is so. The answer lies in the fact that distribution costs tend to be *relatively fixed per transaction.*

Consider some of the activities involved in the sale of goods to a retailer, regardless of whether this sale is made by a manufacturer or by a wholesaler. Some sort of contact must be made with the retailer, probably by a salesperson. This involves travel and the costs associated therewith, plus the time spent in talking with the retailer. If this is a new account, a credit investigation should be made. Assuming that an order is received, it must be processed. The goods must be delivered, and, finally, the retailer must be billed for the price of the order.

The cost of a sales call on a retailer will be approximately the same whether the salesperson is selling one product or many products. The many costs of getting the salesperson to the account do not vary on this basis. The time spent on the sales call itself may vary somewhat with the number of products, but not proportionately. The cost of a credit check will be the same in either case. Order-processing costs will not increase

proportionately with the number of products, nor will delivery costs. Billing costs, surely, will be the same. The wholesaler, representing many manufacturers, has a far broader line of products than a typical manufacturer. Thus, the cost of distribution *per product, or per dollar of sales* (assuming equal sales effectiveness), tends to be less.

To restate concisely: (1) The use of middlemen reduces the number of transactions involved in the distribution of goods. (2) Distribution costs tend to be relatively fixed per transaction. (3) Therefore, a reduction in the number of transactions reduces distribution costs. This is sometimes known as the "principle of minimum total transactions."

CHANNELS OF DISTRIBUTION

The number of specific channels of distribution utilized by manufacturers is so large that all channel alternatives cannot possibly be described. It is possible, however, to point out certain basic types of channels and to compare them with each other. In doing so, we shall speak in general terms and not distinguish between types of institutions at either the wholesale or retail level. (That will be done later in this chapter.) Rather, emphasis is placed here on whether a particular *institutional level* in the available distribution structure is or is not included in the channel appropriate to certain types of goods.

Major Channels—Consumer Goods

The major basic types of channels used for manufactured consumer goods are the following:

Manufacturer ... Consumer
Manufacturer ... Retailer ...... Consumer
Manufacturer ... Wholesaler ... Retailer ...... Consumer
Manufacturer ... Agent .... Wholesaler ... Retailer ... Consumer

Although there are many examples of the sale of consumer goods by manufacturers directly to consumers, this is a relatively unimportant channel from the standpoint of both number of products and sales volume. It is a most significant channel for perishables and specialty products. Eggs, fresh fruits and vegetables, and other perishables are sometimes sold in this manner. The appeal of freshness is strong and will compensate for other inefficiencies attached to the use of this channel. Such specialty products as encyclopedias, cookware, and high-priced vacuum cleaners employ this channel because it permits use of highly aggressive selling. Usually these are products for which consum-

ers do not feel a great need until they are demonstrated. Under such circumstances, aggressive and high-cost selling can have a substantial "payout." The greater sales volume realized may well offset the high costs that use of this channel involves. Because this is true for relatively few products, the channel is quite unimportant.

Sale by manufacturers directly to retailers is a more important channel of distribution. Its use is, however, almost always associated with restricted retail distribution. Products which need to be sold through only a limited number of retail outlets can be distributed directly to retailers at reasonable cost if retail outlets buy in sufficiently large quantities. Although the number of transactions is larger than it would be if a wholesaler were employed, the ratio of advantage from use of a wholesaler is limited because of the restricted number of retail accounts. One of the major products sold through this type of channel is clothing, for which style considerations are important. This places a premium on close contact with the consumer market, in order to keep abreast of style trends, as well as on speed of delivery so that the product will be available at the particular time it is in demand. The fact that a direct channel is more effective on these two counts is a significant offset to the higher costs stemming from the larger number of transactions.

Sale by manufacturers to wholesalers, who in turn sell the retail trade, is the channel commonly employed for products requiring widespread distribution, such as groceries, drugs, hardware, and automotive parts. Because of the large number of retailers involved, each accounting for but a very small fraction of total sales, direct contact between manufacturer and retailer would be prohibitively expensive. The number of transactions would be very high in relation to sales, and there would be insufficient offsetting benefits derived from the direct contact. Of course, where sales are to large retail units, such as grocery chains and large department stores, this same reasoning does not apply, and a direct channel is normally employed.

When the manufacturer is very small, has a narrow product line, and sells to a widely dispersed or sparse market, it is common to interpose an agent middleman between the manufacturer and the wholesaler. This reduces the number of transactions that would otherwise be involved in sales to a large number of wholesalers. Canned vegetables are a good case in point. The typical food canner is small and has a narrow line because it usually processes only products native to the region in which it is located. Yet the market served is widespread and is reached by a very large number of wholesale and retail accounts. Another complicating factor is the seasonality of production. For all these reasons, canned foods are normally sold through food brokers. This is more economical than having the canner deal directly with the wholesalers. (See Figure 8–4 for a more extensive diagram of the alternative channels available to manufacturers.)

FIGURE 8–4   Manufacturers alternative marketing channels

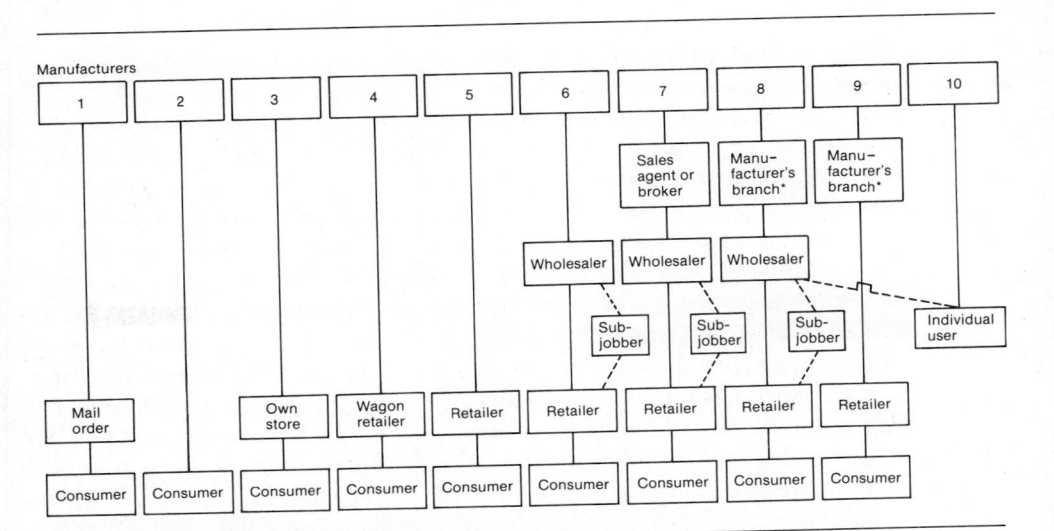

*A manufacturer's branch is owned by the manufacturer.
Source: Adapted from John R. Brothell, *Primary Channels of Distribution for Manufacturers*. Business Information Service, U.S. Department of Commerce.

Major Channels—Industrial Goods

The major channels of distribution employed for manufactured industrial goods are:

Manufacturer . . . Industrial user
Manufacturer . . . Manufacturer's agent . . . . . Industrial user
Manufacturer . . . Industrial supply house . . . Industrial user

In contrast to the situation for consumer goods, the most important channel of distribution for industrial goods is a direct one, involving no middlemen between the manufacturer and the industrial user. In light of our previous discussion of exchange and the role of middlemen in the exchange process, this should not be surprising. Unlike the consumer market, the industrial market is made up of a smaller number of relatively large buyers. In addition, these buyers are often concentrated geographically. Thus, the ratio of advantage stemming from the use of middlemen tends to be far lower for industrial goods than for consumer goods. Also, industrial goods are often technically complex and require

skilled selling. The gain in sales from more skillful selling can more than offset the higher costs brought about by the large number of transactions that result from not using middlemen. Where conditions such as those mentioned are not present, and the industrial market is more like the consumer market, indirect channels again tend to predominate.

Manufacturer's agents are used in the marketing of some industrial goods for the same reasons that agent middlemen are used in the marketing of consumer goods—the manufacturer is small, has a narrow line, and sells in a dispersed market. The use of a manufacturer's agent reduces the number of transactions and provides for a reasonable cost level, but not to the same degree as would the use of a wholesaler. This limitation is offset, however, by the more aggressive selling effort that the agent provides as compared to the wholesaler. The employment of a manufacturer's agent is a sort of "in-between" choice between selling directly and going through wholesalers. The agent provides some of the advantages of direct sale to a greater degree than does the wholesaler, while at the same time providing some reduction in the number of transactions.

The industrial supply house—the wholesaler of industrial goods—is used primarily for supply and maintenance items and for low-cost, fairly standardized industrial equipment. These products have highly dispersed markets, yet must be readily available when needed. Also, such products require no high degree of sales ability. They could be described as the "convenience goods" of the industrial market. As with convenience goods in the consumer goods category, a very great reduction in the number of transactions, and therefore in distribution costs, is effected by use of a wholesaler.

Use of Higher-Cost Channels

Two seemingly contradictory facts have now been established: (1) Indirect channels tend to be lower in cost, as a percentage of sales, than direct channels. This is due, of course, to the reduction in the required number of transactions that the use of market intermediaries makes possible. (2) In spite of the fact that more direct channels tend to be higher-cost channels, they are extensively used in the distribution of goods. This situation suggests an obvious question: *Why does a manufacturer choose to use a higher-cost channel when lower-cost ones are available?*

The answer to this seeming paradox is, in general terms, quite simple. Low distribution cost as a percentage of sales is not necessarily a reasonable objective for a manufacturer. The objective, rather, is to maximize profit on investment. Frequently this goal can be better achieved through higher-cost channels than through lower-cost channels. This is true because these higher-cost channels may produce sales that would not otherwise be realized. If sales are increased more than costs, profits

will be greater. A 10 percent return on sales of $1 million, for example, may provide a far better return on investment than a 20 percent return on sales of $100,000. The favorable effect on sales explains the use of shorter channels.

Use of Multiple Channels

Some manufacturers choose to follow only one path through the distribution structure, while others elect to use multiple channels of distribution. There is a basic difference on this score among manufacturers of different types of products, and frequently different manufacturers of the same product choose to follow different policies. Higher-priced consumer specialty products often move to market through a single channel, while most convenience goods, such as food products, move through several channels. For a given product, such as appliances, one manufacturer will choose to sell only to franchised retail outlets, while another will sell to any retailer wishing to buy—including discount houses.

For certain products a single channel of distribution may be capable of reaching a substantial part of the available market. This tends to be true of specialty products for which a strong brand preference exists. Automobiles are a case in point. Although a given automobile make can normally be acquired by the consumer through one channel only, sales are not unduly handicapped because the consumer will make substantial efforts to acquire this particular product. The market for many other products, however, is such that restricting distribution to any one channel means a severe reduction in market coverage. A grocery manufacturer, for example, who elects to sell only through independent wholesalers is cut off from the market represented by retail grocery chains. Electing to sell only directly to chains the grocery manufacturer loses the market made up of independent grocery retailers who normally buy from independent wholesalers. In the case of products for which, because of consumer buying patterns, broad availability is important, use of only one channel can restrict sales unduly. Because most products are in this category, the use of multiple distribution channels is common.

One product for which broad availability is extremely important is oil filter cartridges for automobiles. Every car owner must change oil filter cartridges at intervals, and he or she wishes to have this done along with other normal maintenance services. There is little brand preference, and the car owner will normally accept any cartridge that the service person chooses to install. Under these circumstances, broad market availability is essential to maximizing sales and profits. Figure 8–5 illustrates how this broad availability is achieved through the use of multiple channels of distribution. Filter manufacturers sell their product through vehicle

FIGURE 8–5   Major channels of distribution—Oil filter cartridges

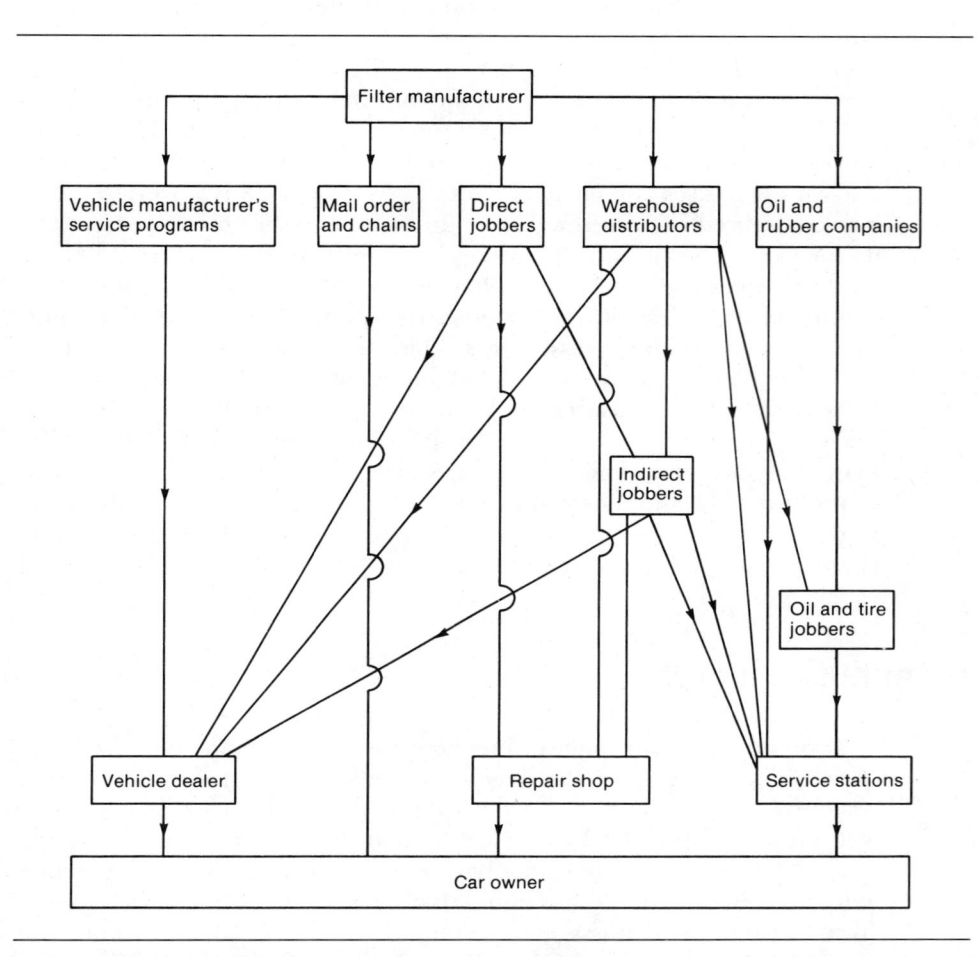

Source: C. N. Davisson, *The Marketing of Automotive Parts,* Michigan Business Studies, vol. 12. no. 1 (Ann Arbor: Bureau of Business Research, The University of Michigan), p. 652.

manufacturers to car dealers. Car dealers, however, account for a very small part of the filter cartridge replacement business, so the manufacturer also sells to mail-order houses and chains in order to reach the self-repair market, through direct jobbers and warehouse distributors to reach the general repair trade, and through the parts programs of oil and rubber companies in order to gain access to the retail trade they control. The net result of using these various channels is achievement of a higher probability that the car owner will find a particular brand of oil

filter cartridge in whatever type of outlet he or she chooses for maintenance services.

The use of multiple channels of distribution creates many marketing problems. Those involving promotional strategy and pricing we shall ignore until later chapters. The most basic and important problem is the creation of interchannel rivalry. Note in Figure 8–5 that four different types of middlemen compete for the oil filter cartridge business of the vehicle dealer, three compete in sales to the repair shop, and five sell to service stations. All of these retail service shops, in turn, compete with mail-order houses and chains in sales to consumers. Such overlap in the markets served by different distribution channels is commonplace, but it can cause ill will and difficulties for the manufacturer. Middlemen tend to resent the competition that such a channel policy creates. As a result, they are less willing to push the manufacturer's product, and sales effort is low in aggressiveness. This pushes back onto the manufacturer the job of doing whatever demand creation is necessary.

When electing to use multiple channels of distribution, a manufacturer is usually sacrificing "sales push" in order to gain availability. For many products this choice must necessarily be made, because sales push cannot possibly compensate for not having the product readily available in the market. Therefore, the problems which go with use of multiple channels are very often unavoidable.

THE RETAIL STRUCTURE

Everyone is a consumer and makes purchases in many types of retail stores. Therefore, everyone has some knowledge of the general retail structure and of the types of institutions that make it up. What is less well known and understood, even by marketing managers, is why the retail structure is as it is, and what forces cause it to change. Everyone who has traveled abroad has noted that the retail structure varies greatly from country to country. The retail structures of Great Britain, the continental Europe, the Middle East, and the Far East all differ in important respects from the retail structure of the United States. This suggests that there are different forces in different countries shaping the retail structure in different ways.

In order to make sound distribution decisions, a marketing manager must have a better knowledge of the retail structure than that gained by casual observation as a consumer. The marketing manager must also understand the change agents that cause that structure to change, in order to anticipate those changes and be ready to adapt to them. Therefore, a brief overview of the present retail structure will first be presented. Then, the forces that produce change will be discussed. Finally,

a brief look will be taken at possible future changes in the retail structure.

Classification of Retail Establishments

Retailing en masse in big business. Total retail sales passed the $1 trillion mark in the early 1980s. This grand total, however, was achieved through many diverse types of retailing establishments. Traditionally, the retail institutions that make up the total retailing structure have been classified on the following bases: (1) size, (2) extent of product lines carried, (3) form of ownership, (4) franchising, and (5) geographic location. A brief look at each of these bases of classification follows.

Size of retail establishment. Although retailing in the aggregate is a high-volume operation, most retail establishments are relatively small. Recent census data indicates that 46 percent of all retail stores had annual sales volumes under $100,000. Those stores with volumes under $20,000 a year make up 16 percent of the total number of stores but account for less than 0.3 of 1 percent of total sales. Assuming that these small stores have an average gross margin of 30 percent, even those at the upper end of the category have only $6,000 a year to cover all expenses, including salaries, and to provide a profit. In contrast, only 1 percent of stores had sales of over $5,000,000 annually, but these stores accounted for 32 percent of all retail sales. On the basis of size alone, retail establishments are clearly a highly varied lot.[4]

Extent of product lines carried. On the basis of the product lines they carry, retail establishments are usually classified as: (1) general merchandise stores, (2) single-line stores, and (3) specialty stores. Each of these general classifications can, in turn, be broken down into categories with designations very familiar to all consumers—drugstores, hardware stores, bakeries, and so on.

General merchandise stores offer a wide variety of products. They include such stores as department stores and variety stores. Department stores have significantly increased their share of total retail sales. This is explained not so much by the growth of the long-established, full-line department store as by the rise of a new type of department store, an illustration of which might be the K mart stores operated by S. S. Kresge. The growth of this type of store is due not only to the changes in methods of operation that it brought to retailing but also to the increasing appeal to consumers of one-stop shopping.

Single-line stores stick essentially to one basic line of products. Typical examples are clothing stores, hardware stores, gift shops, and jewelry stores. The definition of a single line, however, is gradually being broadened. Drugstores and supermarkets are still considered single-line

---

[4]Percentage of retail stores by volume classes from *1977 Census of Retail Trade, Establishment Size.*

stores, but they have added to their lines many products that they did not carry in the past. The whole concept of "single line" in classifying stores may soon have to be abandoned.

Specialty stores are those stores that specialize in carrying only part of a total line of products. Examples are bakeries, furriers, and shoe stores. Such stores typically carry a fuller assortment of the products in which they specialize than do single-line and general-line stores.

Form of ownership. In terms of ownership, retail establishments can be broadly classified as independent stores, corporate chains, and voluntary associations of independents, which include franchise operations. Independent stores make up the vast majority of all stores. They are to be found in every field of retailing, but their relative importance varies greatly by field. Usually they are small and serve limited markets. They have several advantages. They have a better opportunity to provide a personal touch. Perhaps this is why they are so important in clothing retailing. They often offer location convenience, which explains why neighborhood grocery stores continue to exist, in spite of their substantially higher prices. They are more flexible than chains in adjusting to changed conditions.

Corporate chains are organizations consisting of two or more stores which are centrally owned and managed. They are far fewer in number than independents, but they tend to have much larger sales. Their importance varies tremendously among different types of stores. Chains of 11 or more stores account for 81 percent of the sales of variety stores, 89 percent of the sales of department stores, but only 39 percent of drugstore sales and 25 percent of the sales of tire, battery, and accessory stores.[5]

Corporate chains have many advantages. Because of their much larger volume, they offer many economies of scale. Because division of labor is possible for them, they gain in efficiency of operation. They usually have much better, more professional management than do independent stores. They are able to spread risks and also to spread promotional costs over many outlets.

Voluntary associations of independents are of several types. In the grocery field, for example, there are so-called voluntary chains and retailer-cooperative chains. The voluntary chain is sponsored by a wholesaler who enters into contractual relations with a number of retailers. Each party agrees to do certain things. The wholesaler may agree to deal with all sources of supply, to provide certain management services, to make private brands available to retail members, to advertise jointly for all stores, and so on. The retailer may agree to identify the store in a prescribed manner, carry the private brands, participate in all sales events, and so on. The retailer-cooperative chain is similar, as far as operations are concerned, but has no wholesaler sponsor.

[5]U.S. Department of Commerce, Bureau of Census, 1977.

Franchising.   Operations such as Kentucky Fried Chicken, Mc-Donald's, and General Motors' dealer network all have one thing in common. They are part of the distribution form known as franchising. According to Hackett, franchising as a marketing strategy has been booming for the past 20 years and its future appears bright. Franchising is a continuing relationship between two independent parties based on contractual arrangements whereby a franchisor (producer) grants and provides tangible and nontangible assets as well as managerial guidance, training, and expertise to the franchisee for a fee. Generally, franchising comprises marketing activities pertaining to wholesaling or retailing and involves geographic and contractual restrictions. Licensing, on the other hand, is based to a greater extent on the granting of patents, trademarks, and technological processes by one firm to another and seems to be associated particularly with the manufacture of goods.[6]

Franchising is distinctly different from other distribution forms because of the independence from each other of the parties to the contract and the sharing of a common trademark. After emerging early in this century as a viable distribution form in the automobile, petroleum, and soft drink industries, franchising slowly increased in popularity before its rapid growth in the 1950s and 1960s. Total sales by 463,482 franchising establishments in 1977 amounted to $238 billion. As a percentage of total sales volume, the various kinds of franchised business rank as follows: automobile and truck dealers, 53 percent; gasoline service stations, 22 percent; fast-food restaurants, 6.7 percent; automotive products and services, 2.4 percent; hotels and motels, 2.2 percent; convenience stores, 2.0 percent; business aids and services, 0.8 percent; and rental services (auto, truck, aircraft, boats), 0.7 percent. Other types accounting for a small share of the total are laundry and dry-cleaning services; recreation, entertainment, and travel; and educational products and services.

Geographic location.   This classification of retail stores is simple and obvious and will not be discussed, only mentioned. Stores can be classified as downtown, suburban, or rural. They can also be classified on the basis of whether they are located in shopping centers or are freestanding. A basic trend in recent years has been the decline of downtown stores and the rise of suburban stores, often located in shopping centers.

Forces Influencing the Retail Structure

The retail structure is highly dynamic and constantly changing in form. The retail structure of today is substantially different, for example, from the one that existed just 10 years ago. Existing institutions change their nature, new institutions become part of the structure, and

---

[6]Donald W. Hackett, *Franchising: The State of the Art,* American Marketing Association Monograph Series no. 9 (Chicago: American Marketing Association, 1977), passim. This source provides background on the managerial aspects of franchising as well as trends in the field.

some institutions drop out of the structure. Because marketing managers must adapt marketing strategy to reflect these changes, they must understand the forces that produce change and how they do so. They must be able to anticipate changes to be ready for the changes when they occur.

In a general sense, all of the factors present in our environment have some impact on the retail structure. The retail structure is a reflection of the total environment in which we live. Emphasis will be placed here on a few of the most basic social and environmental factors that influence the retail structure with special attention paid to the effect of competition.

Social and environmental factors. Among the most basic factors shaping the retail structure are: (1) population density, (2) population mobility, (3) standards of living, and (4) social custom. Each of these will be discussed briefly before the effects of competition are considered.

Everyone is familiar with the general store of yesteryear as a result of watching Westerns on television. It was a store that sold a highly varied line, including foods, hardware, clothing, and farm supplies. The reason this type of store existed is very obvious. Population density was so low that a store handling only a single line of products could not achieve a sufficient sales volume to be economically viable. As population density gradually increased through the years, the trend in retailing was toward more specialization. Single-line stores became the most common type, and the general store became a rarity. The trend toward single-line stores, however, did not continue indefinitely. In recent years the trend has been in the opposite direction, toward again carrying a multiplicity of lines. When population density reaches a certain point, with the accompanying traffic congestion and shortage of parking spaces, one-stop shopping offers great appeal. Today we call this "scrambled merchandising," but in terms of breadth of lines carried, many of today's stores resemble the general store. Of course, there are many differences too, in types of products, depth of stock, merchandising methods, and so on. However, in terms of basic structure we have come full circle.

An increase in population mobility has effects similar to an increase in population density. It enables stores to serve a much larger trading area and thus permits more specialization. There are other effects on the retail structure. In the past, when consumers were heavily dependent on public transportation, stores in central business districts flourished because they were readily accessible by rail or bus. The rise in automobile ownership has changed that. Today, stores in outlying areas are more easily reached than those downtown, and parking is far easier. Outlying stores are increasing rapidly in number, and the share of the market served by downtown stores has declined sharply. At one time, mail-order houses served a primarily rural market, in which they had great popularity because of the isolation of rural residents and the difficulty of traveling to cities to shop. Today, most mail-order sales are

made in urban areas. Because of the automobile, rural residents no longer find it difficult to shop in stores. On the other hand, urban residents, because of traffic congestion and parking problems, find buying by mail relatively more attractive.

The living standard that a people possesses has many effects on the retail structure. A low living standard reduces mobility because it limits car ownership. It also restricts the number of in-home appliances. Where refrigerators are few in number and/or small, food buying must be done frequently and in small quantities. This favors smaller, conveniently located stores. Freezer compartments in refrigerators are common only in the United States. This, too, affects how consumers buy and where they buy. In Europe, where refrigerators are small and often do not have freezer compartments, mobile vendors who come to the home to sell groceries, baked goods, and even beer are commonplace. In the United States, they are rare. Living standards also affect the relative demand for different types of products. This, in turn, affects the assortment of goods that retailers offer, the size of retail establishments, and so on.

Social custom affects the retail structure in subtle ways. In many countries, shopping is a major social event for housewives. It is a way to meet one's friends, exchange gossip, and find out what is going on in the neighborhood. People are very much creatures of habit, and changes in the retail structure are often impeded by this.

Competition.   Although very much an environmental factor in the same category as those discussed above, competition is treated separately here because of its very special, and often unrecognized, effect on the retail structure. Two kinds of competition act as change agents. One is competition between retail institutions of different kinds; for example between supermarkets and single-line independent grocery stores. Another form of competition that affects the retail structure is that among retail institutions of the same kind, such as the competition of supermarkets with one another. The effect on the retail structure of competition between different types of retail institutions is readily understood. Some retail institutions, for any of many reasons, are more successful than others in attracting patronage. Therefore, they grow in numbers and importance while the less successful decline. The effect on the retail structure of competition among retail institutions of like kind is not as clearly perceived. The nature of this effect can best be explained by an illustration.

The "wheel of retailing."   In an attempt to explain the patterns of evolution among retail organizations, the "wheel of retailing" concept was advanced by Malcolm P. McNair.[7] In McNair's view, new retailing

---

[7]See M. P. McNair, "Significant Trends and Developments in the Postwar Period," in *Competitive Distribution in a Free, High-Level Economy and Its Implications for the University,* ed. A. B. Smith (Pittsburgh: University of Pittsburgh Press, 1958), pp. 1–25. Also, Stanley C. Hollander, "The Wheel of Retailing," *Journal of Marketing,* July 1960, pp. 37–42.

concepts are at first oriented toward low costs and prices. Over time, the retail institution gradually trades up in terms of store decor, services, and merchandise. Eventually the institution becomes vulnerable to a newer form of retailing operating with lower costs and prices.

The Retail Life Cycle

While the wheel of retailing hypothesis helps explain the evolution of retail institutions, it is not entirely sufficient as an explanation of certain contemporary retail developments.[8] Accordingly, the life-cycle concept has been advanced as an expansion of the wheel of retailing hypothesis to explain and predict the actions of retail institutions. This theory argues that retailing institutions, like the products they distribute, pass through an identifiable life cycle.

The retail life cycle is divided into four distinct stages.

1. *Innovation.* This stage is characterized by the emergence of a new, usually entrepreneurial, retail institution. As a result, it tends to enjoy a significant advantage, such as a tightly controlled cost structure that results in a favorable price position, or to offer a unique feature, such as a distinctive product assortment, ease of shopping, or a locational advantage. This produces a level of customer acceptance that causes sales to rise sharply. Profits may lag, however, because of operating problems, inability to secure economies of scale, or relatively large levels of start-up costs. Toward the end of the innovation stage, sales volume begins to increase even more rapidly—and profits also grow—as the initial operating problems are overcome.

Two examples illustrate the retail innovation phase. The supermarkets of the 1930s are a classic example of a retail innovation based primarily on cost and price advantage. By eliminating services, the supermarkets were able to operate on a gross margin of only 12 percent as compared with the 20 percent margin of the more conventional food outlets. Yet their net profit was 50 percent above that of the conventional outlets, and some supermarkets generated as much sales volume in two weeks as conventional food stores did in a year.

In contrast, the home improvement center focuses primarily on the "offer" of better combinations of related merchandise and services. Specializing in the sale of home repair items and related do-it-yourself items, the home improvement center brings together at one place the tools, the application products, and the information necessary to do an entire home improvement job. Price in this total offer is a factor but a relatively minor one.

The home improvement centers have been almost as spectacular a success as the supermarkets. There were only a handful of these outlets

---

[8]Adapted from William R. Davidson, Albert D. Bates, and Stephen J. Bass, "The Retail Life Cycle," *Harvard Business Review,* November–December 1976, pp. 89–96.

in the mid-1960s, but home improvement centers now account for more than 20 percent of total home improvement product sales, and they can be expected to increase that percentage steadily in future years.

2. *Accelerated development.* Both sales and profits experience rapid rates of growth. The market share of the innovating stores increases steadily, and conventional outlets get hurt. As a result, companies that had at first ignored the innovation begin to develop retaliatory programs.

During the early part of the accelerated development stage there is normally a favorable impact on profits. Toward the end of the period, however, both market share and profitability tend to approach their maximum level.

3. *Maturity.* This stage witnesses a dissipation of the earlier vitality of retailers. Market share levels off. There is a severe reduction in profitability.

4. *Decline.* This stage is often avoided or greatly postponed by re-positioning. By modifying its marketing concepts, management pro-longs maturity and avoids decline. When decline occurs, the consequences are traumatic. Major losses of market share occur; profits are marginal at best; and a fatal inability to compete becomes apparent to investors and competitors.

There is ample evidence to suggest that the duration of the retail life cycle is contracting. For a summary of the life-cycle characteristics of five retail institutions, see Figure 8–6. Note that the number of years required to reach maturity has declined as follows: downtown department store, 80 years; variety store, 45 years; supermarket, 35 years; discount department store, 20 years; and home improvement center, 15 years.

Retailing of the Future

Observers foresee a number of significant retail innovations. Man-agers making decisions on channels of distribution would be well advised to ask themselves what impact such developments may have upon the effectiveness of their marketing efforts. Some of the more significant trends and developments are discussed below. How fast these will occur is problematic, but it has been demonstrated that retailing institutions are changing more rapidly today than they ever have in the past. The references given in footnotes 9 to 14 provide more information on the changes that are taking place. (See also Figure 8–7.)

1. *Emergence of the superstore.*[9] Today's supermarket is designed to meet the consumer's total needs for food, laundry, and household main-

---

[9]Reprinted by permission from Walter J. Salmon, Robert D. Buzzell, and Stanton G. Cort, "Today the Shopping Center, Tomorrow the Superstore," *Harvard Business Review,* January–February 1974, p. 103 ff. Copyright © 1974 by the President and Fellows of Harvard College; all rights reserved.

FIGURE 8–6   Life-cycle characteristics of five retail institutions

Institution	Approximate date of innovation	Approximate date of maximum market share	Approximate number of years required to reach maturity	Estimated maximum market share	Estimated 1975 market share
Downtown department store	1860	1940	80	8.5% of total retail sales	1.1%
Variety store	1910	1955	45	16.5% of general merchandise sales	9.5%
Supermarket	1930	1965	35	70.0% of grocery store sales	64.5%
Discount department store	1950	1970	20	6.5% of total retail sales	5.7%
Home improvement center	1965	1980 (estimate)	15	35.0% of hardware and building material sales	25.3%

Sources: National Bureau of Economic Research, U.S. Department of Commerce, *Progressive Grocer, Discount Merchandiser,* National Retail Hardware Association, and Management Horizons, Inc.
Source: Reprinted by permission of the *Harvard Business Review.* Adapted/exhibit from "The Retail Life Cycle" by William R. Davidson, Albert D. Bates and Stephen J. Bass (November–December 1976). Copyright © 1976 by the President and Fellows of Harvard College; all rights reserved.

tenance products. The superstore of tomorrow is designed to meet all of the consumer's routine needs, including those now met by the supermarket as well as an extensive range of other products and services. The superstore is a natural evolutionary development in the marketing environment which was noted by Salmon, Buzzell, and Cort in 1974 as they were looking toward the 1980s. As this trend develops, it will have significant implications for current and future suppliers of food stores who market many of the items which serve "routine needs."

2. *Three recent evolutionary grocery retailing concepts.*[10]

a. *The modern warehouse store.* This type of store is a no-frills, reduced-service operation. The number of items carried is limited to from 1,000 to 8,000, as compared with 15,000 for the typical supermarket.

---

[10]"Continuing Evolution in Grocery Retailing," *Nielsen Researcher,* no. 2, 1980, p. 2 ff. Copyright A. C. Nielsen Co.

FIGURE 8–7   Retail trends and retail innovations forecast for the future

Nature of trend/innovation	When noticed or commented upon by observer	Time frame of forecast
1. Emergence of the "superstore"[1]	Salmon, Buzzell, and Cort (1974)	A natural competitive development as we move through the 1980s.
2. Three recent evolutionary grocery retailing concepts:[2] a. Modern warehouse store: No-frills, reduced-service operation. Number of items limited (1,000 to 8,000 versus 15,000 for supermarket). Number of outlets in United States estimated at 400–500. Account for 2 percent of all commodity sales.	Willard Bishop (1980); quoted in *Nielsen Researcher #2* 1980	These three types of stores are experiencing notable growth.
b. Limited-item stores: Introduced in 1976. Carry only 1,000 grocery items. Number of stores estimated at 700 in 1980. Account for a little under 1 percent of United States all commodity sales.		Lowered costs result in prices low enough to make some shoppers willing to trade conventional supermarket variety, name-brand quality, service, and atmosphere for these lower prices. Whether or not large proportions of the population will make these trade-offs remains to be seen.
c. Combination stores: Offer extensive one-stop shopping and reduced consumer cost in terms of time spent and miles traveled, while offering the service, extras, and variety eliminated by warehouse and limited-item stores.		Originated in the late 60s and early 70s. Have grown at a slow but steady pace. It is unlikely that combination stores will rapidly replace conventional stores in large numbers. They will, however, become an increasingly important segment of the industry.
3. Modernized door-to-door selling, handling perfumes, books, and other products by improved methods.[3]	*U.S. News & World Report* (1978)	Door-to-door sales industry has become a booming $6-billion-a-year business—up from $2 billion in 1956.
4. Nonstore retailers are appearing in new forms, proliferating in number, and gaining market share from store-based retailers.[4]	Rosenberg and Hirschman (1980)	Nonstore sales have been expanding from three to five times as fast as those of traditional store outlets. Examples: telephone and mail-generated orders received by store retailers; experimental use of two-way interactive cable TV to order

FIGURE 8–7 (concluded)

Nature of trend/innovation	When noticed or commented upon by observer	Time frame of forecast
		goods; merchandise offerings to credit card customers; in-flight shopping catalogs of major airlines; televised offerings for records and popular music.
5. In-home telecommunications[5]	Doody and Davidson (1967)	Will become commonplace during the 1970s.
	McNair and May (1978)	Doody and Davidson scenario OK, but timetable has run out. Telecommunications may be commonplace by end of 20th century.
6. Since 1940s, conventional retailing gradually eclipsed by *vertical marketing system.* Telecommunication merchandiser is part of a new system called an *offering system.*[4]	Rosenberg and Hirschman (1980)	*Offering system* includes suppliers, communications media, banks, telecommunication merchandisers, and in-home consumers. It is a virtual certainty that the era of widespread telecommunication shopping is approaching.

Sources:
[1]Walter J. Salmon, Robert D. Buzzell, and Stanton G. Cort, "Today the Shopping Center, Tomorrow the Superstore," *Harvard Business Review,* January–February 1974, p. 103 ff.
[2]"Continuing Evolution in Grocery Retailing," *Nielsen Researcher,* no. 2, 1980, p. 2 ff. Copyright 1980 by A. C. Nielsen Co.
[3]"How the 'New Sell' Is Raking in Billions," *U.S. News & World Report,* May 8, 1978, p. 74 ff.
[4]Larry J. Rosenberg and Elizabeth C. Hirschman, "Retailing without Stores," *Harvard Business Review,* July–August 1980, p. 103 ff.
[5]Malcolm P. McNair and Eleanor G. May, "The Next Revolution of the Retailing Wheel," *Harvard Business Review,* September–October 1978, p. 81 ff.

The items most often not carried are refrigerated and other perishables. These stores achieve a gross margin of 11 to 12 percent and get a high turnover rate (e.g., five times the supermarket average). They use computerized checkout. In 1980 the number of warehouse stores in the United States was estimated at 400 to 500; they were estimated to account for 2 percent of all commodity sales.

b. Limited-item stores. These stores were introduced from West Germany in 1976. They carry only 1,000 grocery items; they do not offer fresh meat, produce, or frozen foods. This type of store saves consumers

10 to 50 percent on the prices of individual items. The number of limited-item stores in the United States grew to 154 in 1978, more than 325 in 1979, and 700 in 1980. These stores account for a little under 1 percent of U.S. all commodity sales.

c. Combination stores. This type of store represents a more long-term evolution. It offers extensive one-stop shopping and reduced consumer costs in terms of time spent and miles traveled, while providing the service, extras, and variety eliminated by warehouse and limited-item stores. It places greater emphasis on pharmacy items than is typical in the superstores and supermarkets that sell such items. The combination store is really two stores in one; it offers greater product selection than is available in the supermarket or the superstore. Combination stores originated in the late 60s and early 70s. They have grown at a slow but steady pace as a result of their one-stop characteristic. They are expected to become increasingly important in the future, as a larger percentage of wives work and gasoline costs escalate.

The warehouse store, the limited-item store, and the combination store were experiencing real growth as of 1980. Each type appealed to major—and yet distinctly different—segments of the buying public.

3. Modernized door-to-door selling. Old door-to-door selling has been revamping its image, peddling perfumes, books, and other products in a variety of ways.[11] This industry had become a booming $6-billion-a-year business as of 1978—up from $2 billion in 1956.

4. Nonstore retailing. A revolution is under way in the store-dominated world of retailing. Nonstore retailers are appearing in new forms, proliferating in numbers, and gaining market share from store-based retailers.[12] As of 1980, it was estimated that nonstore annual sales were expanding from three to five times as fast as those of traditional store outlets. Examples:

The increasing volume of telephone and mail-generated orders being received by traditional store retailers such as Bloomingdale's, J.C. Penney, and Sears, Roebuck.

The experimental use of interactive two-way cable TV to order merchandise (Qube Division, Warner Communications, Columbus, Ohio).

The expanding selection of merchandise offerings made to credit card customers by VISA, MasterCard, and American Express.

---

[11]"How the 'New Sell' Is Raking in Billions," *U.S. News & World Report,* May 8, 1978, p. 74 ff.

[12]Larry J. Rosenberg and Elizabeth C. Hirschman, "Retailing without Stores," *Harvard Business Review,* July–August 1980, p. 103 ff. For background on two-way interactive cable TV services, see James D. Scott, *Cable Television: Strategy for Penetrating Key Urban Markets,* Michigan Business Reports no. 58 (Ann Arbor: Graduate School of Business Administration, The University of Michigan, 1976), chap. 2. Note especially pp. 61–75.

The increased popularity of the in-flight shopping catalogs of the major airline companies.

The success of televised promotional offerings for records and tapes of popular music "not available in any store."

5. *In-home telecommunication shopping.*[13] In 1967 it was thought that this would be commonplace during the 1970s. Although this scenario is sound, the original timetable has run out. Observers now believe that telecommunication shopping will be commonplace by the end of the 20th century.

6. *The offering system.* With the advent of widespread in-home tele-communication shopping it is expected that the trend toward nonstore retailing will accelerate rapidly. What is emerging is a new concept in the distribution of goods labeled the "offering system."[14] Let us examine the changing concepts of retailing (see Figure 8–8).

a. The initial concept of *conventional retailing* entailed a channel of independent participants, with retailers sandwiched between suppliers (producers and one or more levels of wholesalers) and consumers. Store-based retailing dominated.

b. Since the late 1940s, conventional retailing has been gradually eclipsed by the *vertical marketing system,* in which distribution system participants are viewed as an interdependent set. Either retailers or suppliers take on the coordinator role, making decisions for the system and influencing its members. The store is still the scene of purchasing.

c. The telecommunication merchandiser is part of a system that creates and distributes a total product service offering to subscribing consumers. Such a system differs in kind as well as degree from the familiar vertical marketing system. Because of its different emphasis, it is called an *offering system.* The offering system includes suppliers, the communications media, banks, telecommunication merchandisers, and in-home consumers. It is a virtual certainty that the era of widespread telecommunication shopping is approaching, and with it significant changes in our distribution system.

THE WHOLESALE STRUCTURE

Basic Types of Wholesale Middlemen

Wholesale middlemen can be divided into two broad categories: agent middlemen, who do not take legal title to the goods they buy or sell, but rather perform these functions on behalf of others, and merchant

---

[13]Malcolm P. McNair and Eleanor G. May, "The Next Revolution of the Retailing Wheel," *Harvard Business Review,* September–October 1978, p. 81 ff.

[14]Rosenberg and Hirschman, "Retailing without Stores," p. 103 ff.

FIGURE 8–8   Changing concepts of retailing

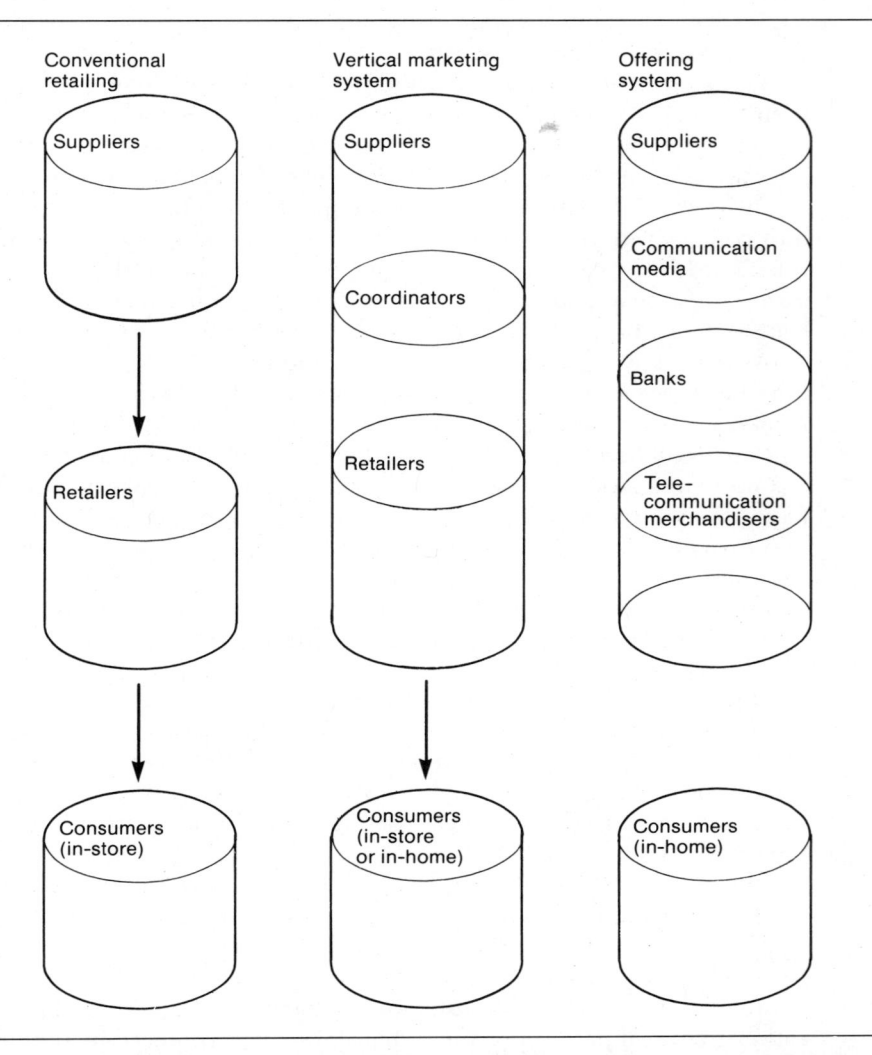

wholesalers, who do take title and sell primarily to retailers and industrial buyers. Within each of these general classes there are many variations, each variation reflecting some specialization of function. Also, some wholesaling institutions cut across the boundary lines of these classes. Combination wholesaler–retailers, for example, are common in the marketing of some products.

Agent middlemen. Agent middlemen are paid commissions for their services. They can be roughly divided into five classes: brokers, commission merchants, resident buyers, manufacturer's agents, and sales agents. The *broker* may represent either the buyer or the seller, and his or her basic function is to bring the party whom he or she represents into contact with another party. The broker negotiates the transfer of title. The broker cannot bind the principal, which means that each transaction must be approved by the broker's client before it is binding. The broker does not physically handle the goods that he or she buys or sells. Brokers usually represent many clients, and not necessarily on a continuing basis. Brokers offer a low-cost method of distribution because they represent many parties, provide minimum services, may be used when and as needed, and are compensated only if they produce results.

Commission merchants are in many ways similar to brokers, but differ from them in two essential respects. They can bind their principals, and they usually take physical possession of the goods. For these reasons, sale through a commission merchant is less time-consuming than sale through a broker. Commission merchants are common in the marketing of fresh fruits and vegetables because of the high degree of perishability of these products.

Resident buyers are of importance primarily in the marketing of style goods. They are located in various style and production centers, and they represent retailers throughout the country. They provide their clients with information on style and sales trends and buy merchandise for the account of their principals. They are particularly significant in the purchase of "fill-in" orders.

The *manufacturer's agent* (or manufacturer's representative) is one of the more ubiquitous types of agent middlemen. The manufacturer's agent serves, in effect, as the salesperson for several manufacturers who, for a variety of reasons, do not find it desirable to have their own salespeople in the market. Manufacturer's agents handle complementary rather than competing products. They are usually limited by the manufacturer to certain geographic areas, and they are quite carefully controlled in other ways as well. Narrow-line manufacturers may use manufacturer's agents in all of the markets in which they sell. Broader-line manufacturers may use them in sparse markets and employ their own salespeople in more concentrated areas.

The *sales agent* performs many more functions than the manufacturer's agent. He or she offers the manufacturer, in effect, a marketing department—often providing design services, marketing research, ad-

vertising and sales promotion, and so on, as well as field representation. The sales agent may take a manufacturer's entire output and handle its distribution in all markets. Because he or she represents a number of manufacturers, the sales agent can perform the marketing operation more cheaply than manufacturers can provide it for themselves.

Merchant wholesalers. In contrast to agent middlemen, merchant wholesalers take title to the goods they sell, and therefore assume the risks associated with product ownership. There are many types of wholesalers, and a complete classification of them will not be attempted at this point. One of the more basic distinctions is between *full-service* and *limited-function* wholesalers. Full-service wholesalers provide a wide range of traditional wholesaling services, such as carrying stocks, making delivery, extending credit, and maintaining a sales force. Limited-function wholesalers, in contrast, restrict in one way or another the functions they perform. Cash-and-carry wholesalers, as their name suggests, neither grant credit nor make delivery. Drop shippers do not physically handle the products they own and sell; hence, they perform none of the functions associated with physical handling. Wagon (or truck) jobbers limit the inventory-carrying function. Other limited-function wholesalers restrict their functions in other ways.

Typical wholesalers, whether full-service or limited-function, restrict themselves to all or a portion of the product line carried by a particular type of retailer. Thus, we have grocery wholesalers, drug wholesalers, auto-parts wholesalers, and so on. Wholesalers of consumer durables are generally known as "distributors." In the industrial goods field, wholesalers are referred to as "industrial supply houses." If they sell to the mining industry, they are "mine supply houses"; if they serve machine shops, they are "mill supply houses."

Wholesaling functions are often integrated into the operations of manufacturers and retailers. Manufacturers may operate wholesale establishments, known as *manufacturer's branches*. Large retailers, such as grocery chains, operate district and regional warehouses which perform for their retail units many of the same functions that independent wholesalers perform for independent retailers.

Forces Affecting the Wholesale Structure

Forces in motion for almost a century have threatened the continued existence of wholesaling. According to Bucklin these included, among others: (1) a small and declining share of the import–export trade held by wholesalers, (2) increasing vertical integration by manufacturers, and (3) the continued growth of corporate chain retail establishments which also engaged in vertical integration.[15]

---

[15]Louis P. Bucklin, *Competition and Evolution in the Distributive Trades* (Englewood Cliffs, N.J.: Prentice-Hall, Inc., © 1972) pp. 203, 208–9. Material adapted by permission of Prentice-Hall, Inc.

Since the close of World War II to the present, in spite of these ominous trends, the share of sales going through wholesalers has declined only slightly. Whereas in the past wholesalers accounted for slightly over half of all sales, they now handle slightly less than one half. In fact, during the past 20 years the growth of sales volume going through merchant wholesalers has kept up with the general growth of the economy.

Why this remarkable growth instead of the deterioration that some had predicted? (1) Not all of the credit can be given to a "new breed" of wholesalers, although these did account for a part of the growth. (2) Some of the credit—perhaps the lion's share—must go to manufacturers. In numerous commodity lines, manufacturers evaluated distribution alternatives, tried them out, and later abandoned these attempts to "eliminate the middleman." They learned that they could eliminate the middleman but that they could not eliminate the economic *function* of wholesaling.

According to Lopata, there are four good reasons why this is so:

1. The wholesaler has continuity in and intimacy with the market.
2. He has more acute understanding than do manufacturers of the costs of holding and handling inventory, in which, after all, he has a major capital commitment.
3. He can concentrate his managerial talent on localized marketing strategies without the distractions of manufacturing problems.
4. He has the important advantage of local entrepreneurship.[16]

In short, independent wholesalers remain a vital and significant part of the distribution system. Their future success will depend upon their response to the challenge of the manufacturers and the retail chains that want to absorb their function and on their ability to adapt and apply new concepts and techniques. Merchant wholesalers must change their strategies with changes in social, political, technological, and competitive developments, just as the manufacturer does.

Coming shifts in strategy.   Among the possible changes in marketing strategy that merchant wholesalers may adopt are the following.[17]

1. Shift to new commodities if existing lines show a declining trend.
2. Build regional or national networks of warehouses along single-commodity lines, as have the paper merchants, the electrical supply companies, and the automotive parts distributors.
3. Form tighter wholesale-retail franchised groups, as have Super Value, Ace Hardware, Butler Brothers, and Western Auto.

---

[16]Reprinted by permission from Richard S. Lopata, "Faster Pace in Wholesaling," *Harvard Business Review*, July–August 1969, p.132. Copyright © 1969 by the President and Fellows of Harvard College; all rights reserved.

[17]Ibid., pp. 134–35.

4. Become multicommodity supermarketing systems, with all the accoutrements of sophisticated marketing technology. (A prime example is Foremost-McKesson, whose sales of over $1 billion in 1967 included the wholesaling of drugs, grocery products, liquor, and health and beauty aids.

Change in attitude.[18]   Many wholesalers have stopped regarding themselves as strictly warehousing or break-bulk points in the distribution complex, and have begun to stimulate and respond to their markets on their own. This new marketing posture requires that the wholesaler dissect the available markets to determine which segments are potentially most profitable and exploitable. In some instances, the wholesaler has shifted selling emphasis from traditional markets to new ones. For example:

Many electrical and electronics distributors have directed a new sales effort in recent years to industrial and commercial markets, to supplement their established electrical contractor market.

The progressive plumbing house has expanded its market from nearly complete reliance on master plumbers and craftsmen to include industrial accounts as well.

Many grocery wholesalers, both the voluntary food groups and those independents who still exist, have added a sales effort geared to the growing institutional market, including hotels, airlines, restaurants, hospitals, and schools.

Basic trends.   Within the constant swirl of changing patterns we can distinguish several major trends that are likely to shape the future of wholesale distribution. These include:

1. *Increased integration, in which vertical and horizontal marketing systems are emerging.* In some of these systems the merchant wholesaler holds a pivotal position. For example, Midas International, which originated as an automotive warehouser-distributor, today both buys and manufactures items for its franchised network of Midas Muffler and Brake Shops.

2. *More "aggressive" service.* As newer technologies develop, new marketing systems evolve, and more sophisticated financial concepts come into use, the merchant wholesalers are adjusting their service emphasis. For example: (*a*) A number of wholesale druggists now handle the retail druggist's customer account records in order to tie the retailer more closely to them. (*b*) In the grocery field, credit extension used to be a prime function of the wholesaler. Today almost all wholesale grocery products flow into retail stores on a cash basis. Here service has shifted

---

[18]Ibid., pp. 135–36.

from credit extension to merchandising support, inventory management counseling, and profit analysis on behalf of the retailer.

3. *Pricing and credit.* The wholesaler has been critically reviewing pricing and credit policies and has changed them in such ways as (a) applying only direct costs to special sales, ignoring traditional gross-margin requirements, and (b) using control by importance and exception in credit operations.

4. *Regional coverage.* One of the new approaches is to set up subsidiary branches and "twigs" with limited, fast-moving inventories but with ready access to the central warehouse. (This pattern is well established among plumbing, heating, and cooling distributors.) Another new approach is a leapfrogging strategy of market penetration. This may involve reaching out as far as 1,000 miles from headquarters to establish operations which, hopefully, will spread back to the home base.

5. *Organizational form and size.* The trend toward larger corporate organizations through public financing, merger, and acqusition is particularly notable in the wholesaling area. According to Census Bureau reports, the following changes have taken place in the relative importance of different forms of merchant wholesaling organizations:

	1958	1963	1977
Sole proprietorships	31.0%	27.5%	15.5%
Partnerships	15.3	10.6	4.9
Corporations	52.6	61.3	78.0
Cooperatives and other forms	1.1	0.6	1.6
Total number of merchant wholesalers	190,000	209,000	307,264

CONCLUSION

If consumers are to have readily available the vast variety of products that they require in order to complete their demand assortments with reasonable effort and at reasonable cost, a complex distribution structure is a necessity, not a sign of waste in distribution. But it cannot be denied that this situation complicates the problem of channel choice for the manufacturer, who must choose the right path through this intricate maze of marketing institutions. In making this choice, many variables must be considered. In this chapter we have mentioned only the most basic variables. The following chapter, which considers at greater length the problem of channel selection, will focus attention on other things.

QUESTIONS

1. What is the basic difference between agent middlemen and merchant middlemen?

2. Compare and contrast (1) a manufacturer's agent with (2) a sales agent.

3. In general, the costs of distribution (as a percentage of sales) are less when use is made of an indirect channel rather than a direct channel. Why is this so?

4. If indirect channels are less costly than direct channels, why do so many sellers choose to sell (at a higher cost as a percentage of sales) through a direct channel?

5. A few years ago a major publisher of encyclopedias failed in an attempt to sell encyclopedias through department stores. An attempt by Sears, Roebuck to sell encyclopedias by mail also failed. What do you think caused these failures?

6. The X Company produces baking powder, baking soda, and other staple grocery products, with total sales of roughly $100 million per year. The company has long been dissatisfied with the failure of wholesalers to sell its products aggressively, and it is considering distribution directly to retail stores. Would you recommend that this change be made? Justify your answer in terms of (1) the relative costs of the two channels and (2) the difference in the attainable sales volumes for the two channels.

7. A reduction in transactions that is a result of using indirect channels of distribution is a function of the discrepancy in the assortment of goods at various levels of distribution. Explain.

8. How might it be argued that the choice of a channel of distribution depends largely on the nature of buyer behavior?

9. Refer to Figure 8–5. Explain why manufacturers of oil filter cartridges use multiple channels of distribution. Discuss the problems that this causes.

10. How might a manufacturer adjust marketing strategy so as to minimize the problems inherent in the use of multiple distribution channels?

11. Explain the effect of competition among stores of like kind on the evolution of the retail structure.

12. Why do wholesalers' sales continue to rise, although an increasing percentage of manufacturers elect to sell directly to retailers?

DISTRIBUTION POLICY DECISIONS

9

Marketing managers of individual manufacturing firms must develop and execute plans that will achieve a profitable flow of their products to the ultimate consumer or to industrial users. This planning process begins with a determination of market targets and a setting of objectives for channel strategy in reaching consumers in each target segment. For example, if a decision has been made to reach a target segment whose members seek health and beauty aids in supermarkets, then the channel objective might be to obtain shelf space in 80 percent of all major supermarket chains within one year after product introduction. To achieve this goal the channel strategy might be to utilize independent brokers to reach the buying centers of the supermarket organizations.

In the above example the channel objective is to gain availability in the end market. Other channel objectives might include gaining a certain degree of control over the way in which a product is resold, achieving a desired level of customer service, minimizing unit distribution costs, or even improving company image by being associated with prestigious resellers.

Because objectives may vary from segment to segment or over time and there are many channel configurations which may be used to reach these objectives, the marketing manager is faced with many distribution policy decisions. Among the most important of these are the following:

1. Should the manufacturer sell direct to the final buyer, or should middlemen be used?
2. If middlemen are to be used, what specific types should be utilized?
3. What degree of selectivity is desirable at the several levels of the distribution structure?
4. How much control should be sought over the institutions in the channel, and how does this affect the channel problem?

DEGREE OF DIRECTNESS

Marketing channels can be of varying lengths or degrees of directness. When the manufacturer sells directly to a final user, no intermediaries are utilized and the channel may be designated as being zero-level. As seen in Figure 9–1, as more intermediaries are utilized channel levels increase and degree of directness is lowered.

FIGURE 9–1   Channel level alternatives

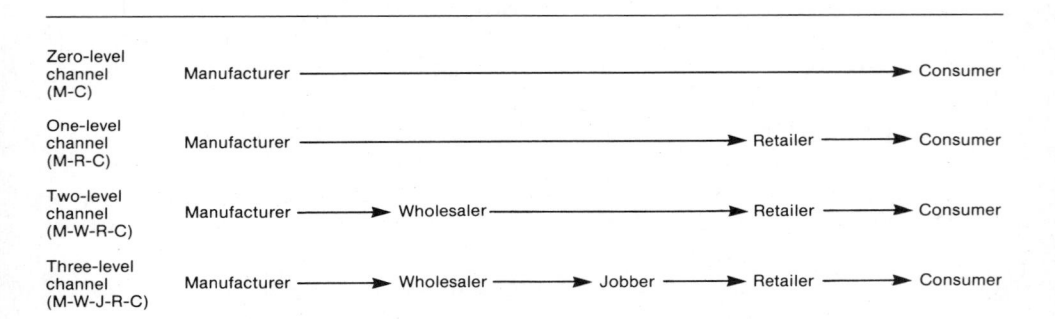

Source: Philip Kotler, *Marketing Management—Analysis, Planning, and Control,* 5th ed. (Englewood Cliffs, N.J.: Prentice-Hall, 1984), p. 542

The degree of directness that can appropriately be used in a channel of distribution is influenced by many specific factors. For purposes of simplicity we shall organize these specific considerations under the major headings of (1) nature of the product or product line, (2) characteristics of the market, (3) nature and availability of middlemen, and (4) characteristics of the manufacturer. Where possible, the relationship of these major considerations to sales volume, costs of distribution, and profit contribution will be traced.

Nature of the Product

The selling effort required to maximize sales volume depends upon the nature of the product and the needs of the prospective buyer. Technical complexity in a product, for example, increases the amount of skill and knowledge necessary on the part of the salesperson. Likewise, prospects are likely to devote more time and attention to the purchase of an item of high unit value than would be true where a product is not regarded as an important purchase. Executives considering the purchase of a computer, for example, might be expected to devote considerable attention to this matter. Considerable knowledge and skill would also be required on the part of the salesperson to explain the benefits of owning such equipment and to point out the merits of his or her own particular brand as compared with alternative makes.

In resolving the issue of directness under such circumstances, it is pertinent to inquire whether the available middlemen have the requisite order of skill and knowledge to sell the product effectively. The average industrial distributor, for example, handles a large number of items and represents a considerable number of manufacturers. The distributor's salespeople are not in a position to devote much selling time to the product of an individual firm. Instead, their approach is to take orders for whatever products the industrial user needs. For the same reason, it is likely to be difficult to get industrial distributors to undertake promotional work for a firm's product. If the manufacturer's product needs aggressive sales support, industrial distributors are not likely to provide it. These considerations help to account for the fact that most complex products tend to be sold directly to industrial users.

The service requirements associated with the product should also be considered in deciding whether to sell directly or to distribute through middlemen. Where the buyer requires highly technical service, this requirement favors the use of direct distribution. Middlemen are not likely to have the interest, the training, and the equipment to provide such high-quality service. On the other hand, the need for relatively simple but readily available service may favor the use of middlemen. Where ready availability of service close to the user is important, and available middlemen are able to maintain service facilities of the desired quality, there is an advantage in distributing through them. An example of these conditions is found in the case of manufacturers of relatively simple, standardized industrial machine tools. One of the factors which might lead such firms to favor distribution through industrial supply houses is that these middlemen maintain service departments.

Another product characteristic that should be considered in analyzing the issue of directness is bulk. Handling, transportation, and storage costs tend to be relatively high for bulky products. The distribution costs

tend to be less if the product is sold directly to the final buyer. Producers of sand and gravel would find the loading and unloading costs associated with an indirect channel prohibitively high. Consequently, sand and gravel are typically sold by the producer directly to the ultimate buyer. The same reasoning would apply to bulky manufactured products which involve high storage costs. There is a tendency to use a direct channel to minimize such costs.

Still other products are perishable in either a style or a physical sense. Style perishability places a premium upon the producer maintaining close contact with the ever-changing market. Speed in distribution is also essential. Both of these factors tend to favor direct sale by the manufacturer to the retail middleman. Products that are physically perishable, such as milk, eggs, and bakery products, require speed in distribution. As a consequence, such products tend to be either distributed directly to the consumer or through specialized middlemen who are geared to the tasks of providing the necessary refrigeration, storage, and rapid-transportation facilities.

In analyzing the issue of whether to use middlemen or sell directly to the buyer, it is helpful to consider the unit value and/or the unit sale of the product. Contrast, for example, how this factor might influence the analysis in deciding upon the degree of directness desirable in the distribution of $300 watches and table salt priced at 15 cents. In both cases it may be assumed that direct sale to retailers would be more costly than distribution through wholesalers. Let us also assume that the sale of fine watches directly to retailers would add $1 to the distribution costs of each watch. This would have a relatively minor effect on the demand for such watches, since an increase of $1 in the costs of distribution would add only 0.33 percent to the final retail price. In contrast, if $1 were added to the distribution costs of each package of table salt, the effect upon demand would be catastrophic.

In addition to unit value of the product, it is necessary to consider the average size of order that may be expected. If the typical order were for 10-case lots of table salt, then the dollar value of the order might be large enough to absorb the higher costs of direct sale. For some low-unit-value products this is the case. The significance of the unit value of the product in the analysis, therefore, is to provide a floor below which the dollar value of the order cannot fall.

Characteristics of the Market

In analyzing the wisdom of direct sale versus the use of middlemen, we now move to questions dealing with the influence upon our decision of the size and characteristics of the market. What types of prospects might purchase the product? Where are they located? How many good

prospects exist? What are their buying habits? Research may help determine the size of the potential demand and define market characteristics that will tend to influence the cost of alternative distribution approaches.

Extent of demand.   The size of the market for the product is a key factor in determining whether or not it is feasible to sell directly to either retailers or final buyers. If the total demand for the product in each market area is large enough, it may be more profitable to use a direct channel and gain the benefits of more aggressive representation and better control. Since the distribution costs involved in a direct channel tend to be relatively fixed in total, there is a minimum sales volume below which sales should not fall if direct sale is to be advantageous.

Assume, for example, that a manufacturer of complex technical equipment is currently selling to industrial distributors who receive a discount of 16 percent of the final price to compensate them for their services and whose total sales amount to $48,125,000. Since the manufacturer believes that her product would benefit from the increased aggressiveness of direct sale, she has worked out some cost estimates for setting up a sales force that would give her approximately equal market coverage. Let us assume that she plans to pay her salespeople on a salary basis and that the total additional costs of the necessary sales force, supervisors, warehouse and office space, order-handling clerks, warehouse staff, and shippers would amount to $7.7 million. A large portion of these costs would tend to be fixed in total, regardless of sales volume.

Under these circumstances, the elimination of the industrial distributors would provide the manufacturer with additional income equal to the 16 percent gross margin on the combined sales, or $7.7 million, which these firms now receive. If the proposed plan of selling directly to users is to *add* to the firm's profits, the market for the product must be large enough so that sales can be increased to more than the distributors' current sales volume of $48,125,000. At this figure, the industrial distributors' margin of 16 percent, or $7.7 million, is just equal to the additional costs involved in performing the distributors' functions, as estimated above. If the market is large enough so that direct sale will increase sales volume to $75 million, the new plan will clearly increase profits. Now the distributors' margins saved would amount to $12 million while the additional costs of direct sale would only be $7.7 million—a gain of $4.3 million. If there is no possibility of expanding sales above their current level, there would be no profit advantage in switching to the more direct method of distribution.

Anticipated fluctuations in the demand for the product in the future also have a bearing on the wisdom of direct distribution. In the above case, assume that a recession sets in and that sales of only $25 million are achieved. Since the costs of direct distribution tend to be fixed, they would remain at approximately $7.7 million. Had industrial distributors been handling the product, their discounts would have only amounted

to 16 percent of $25 million, or $4 million. Accordingly, the firm's profits would suffer to the extent of $3.7 million as a result of the decision to adopt direct distribution.

Concentration or dispersion of demand. An important factor influencing the cost of distribution is the extent of geographic concentration or dispersion of demand. In the sale of industrial goods, localization of industry tends to produce geographic concentration of prospective buyers for many products. This favors direct sale to the user, since the cost of maintaining a sales force tends to be low in relation to realized sales. If prospects are dispersed widely throughout the entire United States, salespeople will have to travel more extensively to reach them and achieve a similar sales volume. Fewer calls per working day and higher travel expenses would tend to make direct sale less attractive than the use of middlemen even if the size of the average order were the same.

If there is only a limited number of prospects and they may be expected to place large orders, this type of concentration of demand would also tend to favor direct sale. Tire manufacturers selling to automobile firms for original installation provide an example of such a situation. In contrast, the demand for replacement tires by ultimate consumers generally involves relatively small purchases (one to four tires) by buyers located throughout the entire United States. Where the average purchase is small and there are large numbers of prospects scattered throughout a large area, direct sale to consumers is clearly out of the question, and the use of retail middlemen is commonplace. In selling to retailers, the concentration or dispersion of demand is still an important consideration. Because tires should be available in each of the communities in which motorists live, sale through a relatively large number of retail outlets is desirable. The costs of direct sale to independent retailers tend to be high under these conditions, and if the average size of order is small, circumstances favor the use of wholesalers.

Buying patterns. Not only are the total yearly requirements of the final buyer or the retailer middleman important in determining directness, but also the frequency of purchase, the regularity with which orders are placed, and thus the average size of order which may be anticipated. If buyers anticipate their needs for a product, buy in substantial quantities, and carry an inventory from which their recurring needs can be met, such behavior may result in an average size of order large enough to favor direct distribution. On the other hand, if they follow a hand-to-mouth buying policy, maintain small inventories, and expect quick deliveries, then the average size of order will be substantially smaller and the costs of distribution higher, thus making direct distribution less feasible.

To take an extreme illustration, if consumers anticipated their requirements for cigarettes for 10 years in advance and, being heavy smokers, purchased a carload quantity of cigarettes at one time, it would

be economically feasible for the manufacturer to sell directly to consumers. If, instead, consumers wished to purchase one package of cigarettes per day throughout the 10-year period, the costs of selling directly to them would be prohibitive. When consumers purchase in the latter manner, market availability of the product becomes of prime importance. It is then necessary to have small stocks of the product available in many retail outlets that are scattered widely over the market.

The extent to which purchase of a product can be postponed determines the need for stocks located near to consumers and thus has an important bearing on the costs of direct distribution. Consumers can postpone the purchase of a new automobile for a period of time, but they cannot defer the purchase of gasoline if they use their cars to commute back and forth to work each day. Automobiles would thus require a lower degree of availability in each market area than gasoline, and fewer retail outlets would be required. A small number of automobile dealers than service stations per market area tends to make it less costly to reach automobile dealers through direct sale than to distribute to gasoline dealers in this way.

Characteristics of the Manufacturer

Two companies with similar products appealing to the same market may reach different decisions as to the use of a direct versus an indirect channel of distribution. This does not mean that if one firm is correct in its decision, the other must necessarily be wrong. Instead, manufacturers themselves may differ in important respects that have a bearing on the channel selection problem.

Size and resources. One of these differences is in size and financial resources. Assume, for example, that a firm has developed an improved food product that requires widespread availability in grocery outlets throughout the United States if sales are to be maximized. While the product is superior, it needs to be promoted aggressively to consumers through advertising and to grocery stores through personal selling in order to get the grocery stores to add it to their stocks. Under these circumstances, direct sale to chain stores, supermarkets, and independent stores would achieve the desired exposure to purchase. A new firm with limited financial resources, however, would find it prohibitive to organize and train the necessary sales force for direct sale to retailers, set up branch warehouses, purchase a fleet of trucks, undertake necessary advertising and promotion to create consumer demand, and do the other things required to achieve a profitable level of sales. Instead, such an organization might find it necessary to rely primarily upon wholesalers to sell its new product to retailers because of the smaller financial resources required in using this channel.

In contrast, a large, well-financed manufacturer distributing an estab-

lished line through wholesalers would be in a position to provide the sales force necessary to sell the product directly to retail stores throughout the entire market area during the introductory period, undertake extensive consumer advertising, and perform other tasks essential to securing national distribution of the new product within the desired time period. Even though two or three years of effort might be required before a break-even volume was achieved, the large firm could afford to make the necessary investment.

Width of product line. The choice between a direct and an indirect channel is influenced by the width of the product line that the manufacturer is already marketing. The broader the line of products a manufacturer is selling to a given market, the higher the average order that salespeople can secure, and therefore, the more feasible the use of a direct distribution channel. As the line of products broadens, the manufacturer takes on more and more of the characteristics of a wholesaler in that distribution costs are spread over a greater array of products, thus lowering distribution costs per unit. In contrast, manufacturers of narrow product lines may find it difficult to secure an average size of order that will cover the costs of direct sale. For them, indirect distribution channels may be more feasible.

Stage of development. The stage of a company's development is a factor that has a bearing on the issue of directness. An unknown company introducing a new product may have to be very aggressive in order to establish a foothold in the market. Direct sale to final buyers in the industrial field, or to retail middlemen in the consumer market, offers greater aggressiveness in the introduction of the new product than does the use of less direct channels. Whether the firm can utilize the direct channel depends, of course, upon the anticipated sales volume that might be achieved in relation to the estimated costs of the more direct approach.

Experience of executives. A direct channel is, in a sense, a "do-it-yourself" project. Successful use of this approach requires that company executives have the know-how and experience to deal with the various problems that may be encountered. Executives lacking such background may regard this as a good reason for selling through middlemen. In this manner, they may be able to take advantage of the marketing experience and customer contacts that the middlemen possess.

NATURE AND AVAILABILITY OF MIDDLEMEN

In analyzing the issue of directness, an important consideration is the nature of the middlemen who are available to perform the necessary distribution functions. In this analysis, one side of the coin is to define the distribution tasks that must be performed, and this we approached

through an analysis of the characteristics of the product, the market, and the manufacturer. The other side of the coin is to ask what types of middlemen the firm might seek to perform these tasks and whether these types of organizations are likely to function as effectively as the manufacturer's own direct-selling organization might be able to. How aggressively is the selling function likely to be performed by the middlemen, and would this degree of support make a substantial amount of difference in the sales volume that might result? Where do prospective buyers customarily purchase the product, and are middlemen likely to conform better to these buying habits than our own direct-sales organization? How important is widespread availability of our product, and can we achieve the desired coverage more economically through middlemen than through direct sale? Is the contribution to profits likely to be larger if the firm distributes through middlemen than through its own marketing organization? Answers to such questions involve a thorough understanding of the nature of the middlemen who serve the industry.

Although the foregoing analysis may indicate that indirect channels including certain types of middlemen should ideally be used, it may not be possible to get these firms to order the product. This difficulty is commonly faced by the manufacturers of new products and may force a more direct channel than is theoretically desirable. The producer of a new type of deodorant, for example, did not attempt to get distribution through drug wholesalers and retailers originally, although this would have been a desirable channel. Instead, the sales manager of this company decided to try to get initial distribution by selling directly to Chicago department stores. Although he offered to pay for advertisements over the retailers' names if they would place an initial order for a specific quantity, he was rebuffed by several cosmetic buyers before he finally secured initial orders from three department stores. When advertising produced an unusual sales response, the sales manager was able to use this experience to help him get distribution through department stores in other cities. Only after the product had proved to be profitable in department stores was the firm able to get distribution through drug wholesalers and retailers.

The firm considering new channels will generally find that preferred types of outlets are already handling competing products. Such middlemen tend to be reluctant to add another brand to the variety they now offer unless the prospective dollar gross margin is sufficient to outweigh increased inventory and other costs of adding the line. The problem of overcoming the reluctance of middlemen to stock new brands may be solved if the firm has developed an attractive product and has the resources to work out an effective strategy for getting distribution. The difficulty of getting middlemen to accept a new brand should not be underestimated, however, in the process of arriving at a decision on whether to use direct or indirect channels.

Trends in Wholesale and Retail Institutions

In choosing the middlemen to be included in a channel of distribution, it is desirable to consider the trends in both wholesale and retail institutions. Changes are taking place in the character and marketing strategies of familiar types of wholesalers, as was noted in the previous chapter. It is especially important to note the direction of these trends and the effect they may have upon the ability of a given type of middleman to perform the tasks desired by the manufacturer. So, too, the turn of the wheel of retailing and the movement of the retail life cycle should be considered in choosing the types of retailers to include in the channel. Producers of grocery staples, for example, would do well to recognize the development of telecommunication marketing, since future growth in this type of distribution may have a significant impact upon the way consumers buy products in their category.

Channel Member Behavior

Effective performance of necessary tasks by the middlemen included in a product's channel of distribution is the manufacturer's goal. Accordingly, it is helpful for the decision maker to view a distribution channel as a social system. From this perspective it is recognized that both economic and behavioral variables should be taken into account.[1] Building on this concept, Robicheaux and El-Ansary have developed a model designed to explain channel member behavior.[2] Channel performance constitutes the focal point of the model. In the model, channel performance depends on the effectiveness of the control exercised and on the satisfaction or dissatisfaction of the channel members with the channel relationship. Channel control depends on such factors as the channel members' power base and resources, dependence, tolerance for control, and leadership effectiveness. Channel member satisfaction or dissatisfaction depends on organizational performance. Poor performance will result in dissatisfaction, whereas good performance may bring about even better performance.

The model comprises the following five sets of variables: (1) position-role variables, (2) power-leadership-control variables, (3) conflict-cooperation variables, (4) performance-satisfaction/dissatisfaction variables, and (5) communication bargaining variables. (For an explanation of these variables and their relationships, see the article referenced in footnote 3.)

According to Shooshtari and Walker, this model represents a step

---

[1]Louis W. Stern, ed., *Distribution Channels: Behavioral Dimensions* (Englewood Cliffs, N.J: Prentice-Hall, 1966).

[2]Robert A. Robicheaux and Adel I. El-Ansary, "A General Model for Understanding Channel Member Behavior," *Journal of Retailing,* Winter 1975–76, pp. 13–30 ff.

toward the development of a major theory in the area of distribution channels.[3] It needs further testing and improvement. Nevertheless, it has the potential of becoming a highly valuable theory of channel performance. As such, it merits the attention of channel decision makers. It tends to broaden the scope of analysis in considering how to plan and manage in such a way as to achieve the desired level of channel member performance.

SELECTIVITY IN CHANNEL SELECTION

A basic policy decision concerns the number of outlets at each of the several levels in the distribution structure that the manufacturer will strive to obtain in the marketing of a product. A sound decision on this issue is important, since both cost and effectiveness in distribution can be vitally affected by the action taken. When a firm attempts to gain distribution through any and all outlets of good credit risk which are willing to carry a product, it is following a policy of *intensive distribution*. When a firm limits the sale of its product to chosen middlemen who meet certain criteria, it is following a policy of *selective distribution*. If this policy of restricting distribution is carried to the extreme of selling the product through only one reseller in a given geographic area, the policy is commonly referred to as *exclusive agency distribution*. Figure 9–2 illustrates these three policies and provides examples of goods which are currently distributed under each policy. The following section will discuss selectivity of distribution in some detail.

Illustration of the Above Policies

Intensive distribution. While the goal of intensive distribution is sale through all of the chosen types of middlemen with good credit standing who will stock and sell the product, actually the density of distribution attained will vary among companies and products. One study indicated, for example, that 12 firms producing toothpaste secured retail coverage of from 71 to 98 percent of the drugstores surveyed, while 7 firms producing tooth powder had retail coverage of from 51 to 97 percent of the stores.[4] While all these firms aimed at intensive distribution, they had achieved varying degrees of success in executing their policy.

---

[3]The foregoing discussion is indebted to Nader Shooshtari and Bruce Walker, "In Search of a Theory of Channel Behavior," presented at the *AMA's 1980 Special Educators' Conference*, February 1980, pp. 2–6, 13.

[4]J. D. Scott, *Advertising Programs for Products with Selected Distribution*, Business Research Studies no. 26 (Boston: Bureau of Business Research, Harvard Business School), p. 5.

FIGURE 9–2.   Exclusive, selective, and intensive distribution

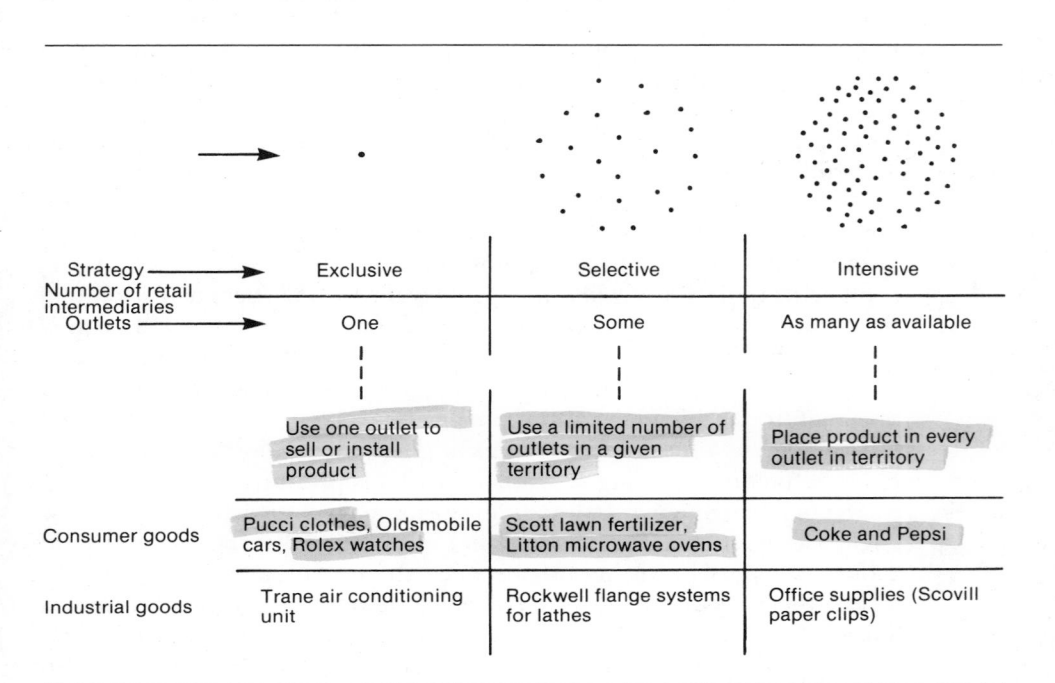

Strategy →	Exclusive	Selective	Intensive
Number of retail intermediaries Outlets →	One	Some	As many as available
	Use one outlet to sell or install product	Use a limited number of outlets in a given territory	Place product in every outlet in territory
Consumer goods	Pucci clothes, Oldsmobile cars, Rolex watches	Scott lawn fertilizer, Litton microwave ovens	Coke and Pepsi
Industrial goods	Trane air conditioning unit	Rockwell flange systems for lathes	Office supplies (Scovill paper clips)

Source: Thomas C. Kinnear and Kenneth L. Bernhardt, *Principles of Marketing* (Glenview, Ill.: Scott, Foresman, 1983), p. 348.

Selective distribution.   If a firm restricts distribution to chosen retailers according to specified criteria, then a selective distribution policy
is being followed. The degree of restriction will tend to be a compromise
between the desire to have the product on sale whenever prospective
buyers might expect to look for it and the desire to limit the number of
middlemen in each market area as a means of encouraging reseller sales
support, adequate inventories, and suitable service facilities (if needed),
among others. The number of outlets per market area resulting from a
policy of selective distribution commonly varies, depending upon the
size of the area, the total number of outlets serving it, and the share of
market that the firm has in mind as a goal. One manufacturer of automobile tires, for example, reported that the firm had an average of 5
retailers in cities of 100,000, an average of 12 retailers in cities of 1
million, 25 retailers in Chicago, and 35 retailers in New York City. Likewise, a manufacturer of shoes had an average of 2 retailers in cities of
10,000, 25 retailers in cities of 100,000, and 150 retailers in cities of 1
million; 300 retailers in Chicago; and 77 retailers in New York City. The

extent to which representative firms restricted distribution was determined by dividing the number of dealers used in New York City by the number commonly selling the product, as reported in the census. The percentage of possible outlets used by companies varied as follows: automobile tires, 0.7 percent; mechanical refrigerators, 3.9 percent; men's suits, 5.5 percent; shoes, 6.4 percent; radios, 10.4 percent; and ladies' hosiery, 14.2 percent.[5]

Theoretically, the percentage of outlets used could be much larger and still constitute selective distribution, as long as the firm selects less than the total potential number that might be available. Competition among sellers for distribution, together with the desire of resellers to limit the number of competing brands carried, tends to reduce the percentage of outlets that will sell a given brand in a particular market to a figure considerably less than the total number of outlets in that area stocking the type of product under consideration. It is conceivable, however, that a policy involving a limited degree of restriction on the part of one manufacturer might approximate the degree of coverage secured by another manufacturer who aims at intensive distribution but experiences difficulty in getting retailers to stock his product.

Exclusive agency.   Although exclusive agency distribution might be regarded as simply an extreme policy of selective distribution, the common practice is to distinguish between them. An exclusive agency restricts the sale of the manufacturer's brand to one reseller within a specified market area. When more than one reseller is used per market area, but the number of outlets is restricted as a matter of policy, then selective distribution is being practiced.

Even under an exclusive agency policy there is some opportunity for variations in the extent to which distribution is restricted. One source of difference is the size of the geographic area within which the reseller has exclusive sales rights. The area may be relatively small, such as a community of 5,000 population, or it may include a market as large as the metropolitan New York City trading area. An illustration of a highly restrictive policy of exclusive agency distribution is provided by a manufacturer of high-grade pianos who appointed only one retail outlet within a community and its trading area. Even in markets the size of Chicago and New York City, the brand was sold through only one retailer.

An important feature of the exclusive agency agreement is the designation of the brand to which exclusive selling rights apply. Some manufacturers may find that an exclusive agency policy tends to limit sales unduly in large-city markets, but may be reluctant to modify the arrangement because of the strong preference of dealers for it. One way of achieving a more satisfactory share of market in a large city is to add

---

[5] Ibid., p. 13.

a second or a third brand to the line and appoint a different exclusive outlet for each new brand.

Although the policies of selective and exclusive agency distribution have been discussed separately, they are commonly combined in actual practice as a means of adjusting the degree of product exposure to potential market areas of different sizes. A manufacturer of women's shoes, for example, had only one outlet, on the average, in communities of 10,000 population—an exclusive agency. In cities of 100,000 population, two dealers were usually selected, while in cities of 1 million population the number of outlets averaged four or five. In Chicago the firm had 20 dealers, and in New York City it had 30.[6]

Wisdom of Restricting Distribution

Obviously, a policy that restricts distribution limits the market availability of a product. For some products, such a limitation may be offset by benefits that justify the policy in terms of contribution to profits. For other items, the opposite may be true. Policies of selective and exclusive agency distribution should, therefore, be adopted only after discriminating analysis. Let us turn, therefore, to a consideration of the merits and limitations of restricted distribution.[7]

Benefits of restricted distribution. The more restricted the distribution of a particular product, the more the interest of the middleman comes to parallel the interest of the manufacturer. Restriction of distribution makes the product more valuable to the retail and wholesale outlets that sell it. They must share the market with fewer competitors; hence they have greater market opportunity. A policy of restricted distribution, therefore, tends to stimulate resellers to be more aggressive in their selling and promotional efforts than they would be under a policy of intensive distribution.

For what types of products is aggressive selling and promotion by resellers important? Clearly, aggressive sales effort is especially beneficial for mechanical or technical products that require explanation and demonstration. New-model automobiles and household appliances would certainly fall in this category. Where sales resistance must be overcome because the product is an important purchase (high unit price) and is purchased infrequently, aggressiveness by the reseller is required to offset the natural tendency of prospects to procrastinate in making a purchase decision. The task of getting retail dealers to stock and push a new product also requires aggressiveness on the part of the middlemen charged with this assignment. A beverage wholesaler secured aggressive sales support for a new chocolate drink, for example, by granting exclusive agencies to retail milk distributors.

---

[6]Ibid., p. 11.

[7]Portions of the discussion that follows are adapted from ibid., pp. 14–15.

For products such as shoes and paint, retailers are required to make a large investment in order to provide an adequate stock. If the retailer's competitors are selling the same brand, the available sales volume may be too small to justify the investment necessary to provide an adequate inventory of the item. The retailer may then carry an inadequate stock, with the result that sales will suffer.

For products such as household appliances, whose manufacturers often produce a complete line of items, the market protection that retailers receive through restricted distribution would tend to encourage them to carry the full line of products, including the less desirable along with the more desirable items.

There are products that require repair and maintenance service if they are to operate satisfactorily. To maintain a properly equipped service department with adequately trained personnel, however, involves the reseller in considerable expense. If the manufacturer sells products through as many dealers in a given community as will stock the item, and still expects them to provide the necessary service facilities, the result is almost certain to be an inferior grade of service or no service at all. By restricting distribution, the manufacturer makes it worthwhile for the dealer to provide the desired quality of service.

Consideration must be given to the size of the market area that is required to provide resellers with a profitable sales volume. The characteristics of expensiveness, high unit price, low incidence of the need for the product among consumers, and infrequent purchase tend to limit the potential sales volume for certain products to a relatively small amount per 1,000 population. Where the potential market is thin per 1,000 population, the policy of intensive distribution tends to make the line unprofitable for the dealer.

The benefits of restricted distribution are not necessarily limited to high-priced specialty goods. This is illustrated by the example of a manufacturer who was following a policy of intensive distribution and was selling to about 90 percent of all the U.S. retail stores handling that type of merchandise.[8] Many of the customers were small stores, and many of the orders were ridiculously small. Yet the firm's salespeople called upon these stores on an average of once a week. A study was made of the cost of serving customers in two of the firm's branches. It was found that two thirds of the company's orders and almost half of its accounts were costing more in marketing expense than they were worth in terms of gross profit. As a result, the firm increased the size of the minimum order sixfold, drastically reduced the number of contacts the salespeople had to make, and dropped unprofitable customers. Sales increased 82 percent; marketing expenses were reduced from 31.8 percent to 18.2 percent; and operating profit rose from 4.7 percent to 14.8 percent.

---

[8]C. H. Sevin, *How Manufacturers Reduce Their Distribution Costs* (Washington, D.C.: U.S. Government Printing Office, 1948), p. 17.

A policy of restricted distribution may help a manufacturer deal with the problem of predatory price cutting at the retail level. When the aim is intensive distribution, competition among a number of retailers in the same community may tend to result in price cutting, which makes the brand unprofitable for the retailers who handle it, so that desirable types of retailers refuse to stock the item. The manufacturer may also feel that price cutting damages the reputation of his or her brand. The policy of exclusive agency distribution eliminates competition among retailers in the same community and tends to prevent price cutting.

The above discussion serves to call attention to the fact that the "control" exercised by a manufacturer over the members of the channel of distribution is based primarily upon achieving cooperation through policies that recognize and appeal to the reseller's point of view and self-interest. The degree of control that can be exercised by the manufacturer depends upon the value of the franchise to sell the product. If it is a valuable right highly regarded by resellers, the manufacturer is in a favorable position to gain cooperation from them (or to exert control over them). Automobile manufacturers, for example, exert a large measure of control over the marketing policies of their retail dealers. They are able to do this because the right to sell a particular brand of automobile can be very valuable to the dealer. In contrast, manufacturers of chewing gum or cigarettes are able to exercise virtually no control over the retail outlets handling their product. The policies of intensive distribution that such firms follow mean that the right to sell an individual brand of such products tends to be of very limited value to the individual retailer.

Limitations of restricted distribution. In considering the wisdom of restricting the distribution of a product, the manufacturer should count not only the potential benefits that he or she may receive but also the limitations (or "costs") that may result. A key question is: In light of consumer buying habits, what will be the effect of restricted distribution upon sales? If a firm produces convenience goods, the sacrifices involved in gaining the benefits of restricted distribution will be too great. Consumers insist on buying these items with a minimum amount of effort. Consequently, ready availability is the single most important factor influencing sales volume. Examples of products in this category are cigarettes, razor blades, staple food products, and candy bars. These products tend to be purchased frequently and usually have relatively low unit value.

In contrast, the manufacturer of specialty goods is likely to find the benefits of restricted distribution substantial indeed. Such products characteristically have achieved brand preference among consumers, who are willing to make considerable effort to seek out the retail outlet that stocks them. Accordingly, the limitation in exposure to sale involved in a policy of restricted distribution is of little consequence when compared with the benefits that such a policy can bring.

A policy of restricted distribution creates another difficulty that is not encountered under intensive distribution. Because the number of outlets appointed per community is limited, it is necessary for the manufacturer to make certain that the local source of supply is identified through signs, window displays, and advertising over the retailer's name. Unless this identification is made, the demand created by the manufacturer's general advertising may be dissipated because of the consumers' lack of knowledge of where to buy the product. Failure to recognize the importance of this problem may result in ineffective advertising.

Finally, restricted distribution may tend to promote substitution. Dealers who cannot get the agency for a given brand may double their efforts to take business away from that brand by offering substitutes. The seriousness of this problem will depend upon the strength of the brand preference that the manufacturer can create.

LEGAL ASPECTS OF RESTRICTED DISTRIBUTION

At present, there are no legal restraints on the practice of restricted distribution *as such*. The courts have long upheld the right of a seller to choose his or her customers even when this extends to the practice of choosing to sell to only one customer in a certain market. From time to time, so-called right-to-buy laws have been proposed, but they have not been enacted, and at present there is no great prospect that they will be. The intent of these laws is to force a seller to make a product available to anyone who wishes to purchase it. This would, of course, make impossible the practice of effective restricted distribution.

Certain practices that have often been associated with restricted distribution, particularly with exclusive distribution, are of doubtful legality. The most important and most controversial of these are: (1) exclusive dealing and (2) territorial protection. Exclusive dealing is the practice of not allowing the dealer to carry competing products. Not all exclusive agency contracts involve exclusive dealing. The manufacturer may agree to sell through no competing dealers in a particular market but still allow the dealer to carry competing products. On the other hand, many manufacturers have sought to restrict dealers to their own products under exclusive agency contracts.

The major reason why manufacturers might wish to practice exclusive dealing is to encourage more aggressive selling and promotion on the part of their dealers. Retailers who handle only one brand of a particular product have no alternative items to push in competition with it. They must succeed in the sale of this one brand, or they will find their sales of the generic product unsatisfactory. For this reason, they are likely to be more aggressive than they would be if they carried compet-

ing brands. They are also likely to be more cooperative in maintaining necessary inventories of the line, in providing repair service of satisfactory quality where necessary, and in maintaining resale prices if manufacturers request such action.

Territorial protection clauses in exclusive agency agreements were common practice prior to the late 1940s. The essence of such agreements is that the manufacturer will attempt to prevent the sale of his or her product by any other party in a territory assigned to an exclusive outlet. The request for such clauses in exclusive agency agreements is likely to come from the dealer rather than from the manufacturer. Dealers wish to protect themselves against direct competition from other retailers who are handling the same brand. Various ways of enforcing such clauses have been utilized. For example, the dealer who has made a forbidden sale may be required to make a penalty payment to the dealer whose territory has been invaded. If such violations are continued, they may, of course, lead to cancellation of the franchise of the invading dealer.

Legal Status of Exclusive Dealing

Section 3 of the Clayton Act prohibits exclusive-dealing contracts where the effect of such agreement "may be to substantially lessen competition or tend to create a monopoly in any line of commerce." Note that exclusive-dealing contracts are not illegal as such, but rather that their legality depends upon how they affect competition.

The benchmark court case on exclusive dealing involved the Standard Oil Company of California and was decided in 1949. In this case the Department of Justice charged that the company, in its exclusive agency contracts, had violated Section 1 of the Sherman Act and Section 3 of the Clayton Act. The specific complaint was that the company's practice of entering into agreements with its 6,000-plus dealers for exclusive handling of its petroleum products and automotive accessories substantially lessened competition and tended to create a monopoly. At that time, this kind of contract was common in the petroleum industry as well as in many other industries. The Standard Oil Company of California then accounted for 23 percent of gasoline sales in the Pacific area; its products were sold through 10 percent of the available independent retail outlets. The stations with which it had exclusive-dealing contracts pumped only 6.7 percent of the gasoline in this area. An additional 6.8 percent of gasoline sales in the area were made through stations owned and operated by Standard. The firm attempted to demonstrate that its exclusive-dealing contracts did not substantially lessen competition. It cited its small share of the total market, the still smaller share of the gasoline sales that were made through outlets with which exclusive-dealing contracts had been arranged, and the fact that its share of the

market had not increased during the time that these contracts were in force.

In spite of this defense, the district court ruled against the Standard Oil Company of California, and its decision was upheld by the U.S. Supreme Court in 1949.[9] The Supreme Court made two main points. First, it held that the exclusive-dealing contracts violated Section 3 of the Clayton Act because they covered a substantial number of outlets and a substantial volume of sales. When this is true, said the Court, a substantial lessening of competition is a natural result and an actual reduction in competition need not be proved. This is the per se or "quantitative substantiality" doctrine. Second, the Court called attention to the fact that there had been widespread adoption of exclusive-dealing contracts by other major competitors in the area, with the result that independent producers were foreclosed from distributing through outlets serving a substantial share of the market in the area. Thus, when the exclusive-dealing contracts of a particular firm involve a substantial volume of trade, and when there is widespread use of such contracts by the firm's competitors, there is serious danger that such arrangements will be regarded by the courts as a violation of Section 3 of the Clayton Act.

Under different conditions, however, a manufacturer may make use of exclusive-dealing contracts without violating Section 3 of the Clayton Act. The J. I. Case Company, for example, followed a policy of exclusive dealing in the distribution of its farm implements. Where the market in an area justified it, the firm made a serious effort to get dealers who would carry the full line and devote the major part of their activity to Case implements. The handling of two full lines (Case plus a competing brand) was consistently discouraged. Dealers handling competitive lines to the detriment of Case were dropped. Because of these practices, the firm was charged with a violation of Section 3 of the Clayton Act. In a 1951 ruling, however, the district court found the evidence insufficient to establish an adverse effect upon competition.[10] During the trial no farm implement manufacturers presented evidence that their outlets had been restricted by Case's policy, and further, there was no indication that the available outlets had been narrowed in any way thereby. Because of the nature of the market, strategic location for dealers in farm machinery was not essential. Apparently, competitors had found no difficulty in obtaining dealers. An adequate number of full-line and short-line manufacturers were represented in most markets in agricultural areas.

As was pointed out in a 1961 Supreme Court decision, Section 3 of the Clayton Act was not intended to reach every remote lessening of competition—only those that were substantial—but earlier Court deci-

---

[9]*Standard Oil Co. of California v. U.S.*, 337 U.S. 293 (1949).

[10]*U.S. v. J. I. Case Company*, 101 F. Supp. 856 (1951).

sions had not drawn a line to indicate where "remote" ended and "substantial" began. The case involved was that of the Tampa Electric Company, in which the district court had ruled that an exclusive contract violated Section 3 of the Clayton Act but the Supreme Court had reversed the judgment.[11] In reviewing this case, the Court indicated that an exclusive-dealing arrangement does not violate Section 3 unless the Court believes it probable that execution of the policy will foreclose competition to a substantial extent. In determining the probable effect upon competition, the Court outlined the following considerations that must be taken into account: (1) the line of commerce—that is, the type of goods; (2) the geographic area of the affected competition; and (3) whether the competition foreclosed constitutes a substantial share of the affected market (the relative strength of the competing firms and the percentage of the total volume of the business involved). Applying these guidelines, the Court reasoned that the exclusive-dealing contract in this instance did not foreclose competitors from a substantial share of the business in the relevant market area. In effect, this approach applies the "rule of reason" in evaluating the effects of exclusive-dealing contracts. The central issue is the ease with which rival suppliers can secure access to customers in alternative ways.

It should be borne in mind, however, that Section 5 of the Federal Trade Commission Act has also been used by the commission in attacking exclusive-dealing contracts. Here the approach has been to charge that such contracts may constitute an unfair method of competition that may subtantially lessen competition. In the *Brown Shoe Company* case, for example, retailers who promised not to sell shoes made by competitors received a combination of benefits ranging from architectural plans and display materials to sales training and group-rate insurance. The FTC issued a complaint against this exclusive-dealing arrangement on the ground that it denied Brown's competitors the opportunity of selling to a substantial number of dealers. Brown argued that dealers were not coerced to join the plan, that the FTC had not shown any harmful effect upon competition, that only 650 out of 6,000 dealers participated, and that the outlets in question bought only 75 percent of their shoe stocks from Brown. The court of appeals set aside the FTC decision on the ground that the commission had failed to prove the system an "unfair method of competition."

In 1966, however, the Supreme Court reversed this ruling in an opinion written by Justice Black. If the attack had been brought under the Sherman or Clayton acts, Justice Black said, such injury to competitors would have had to be proved. But, he added, the purpose of the FTC Act was to stop unfair competitive practices before they become monopolistic. This case showed beyond doubt, he wrote, that Brown, the coun-

---

[11]*Tampa Electric Co. v. Nashville Coal Co.*, 365 U.S. 320, 327–29 (1961).

try's second largest manufacturer of shoes, had a program that required shoe retailers to substantially limit their trade with Brown's competitors. This obviously conflicted with the central policy of both the Sherman Act and the Clayton Act. In rejecting the argument that the commission need prove injury to competition, Justice Black said that the commission had power under the FTC Act to arrest trade restraints "in their incipiency" without proof that they amounted to an outright violation of the other provisions of the antitrust laws.

While the decision does not mean that all exclusive-dealing systems are illegal, it does suggest that large companies are especially susceptible to attack if such a system is used to help a firm gain a more dominant position in its industry. The ability to challenge potential restraints of trade in their incipiency tends to make such plans more vulnerable to attack than in the past.

Legal Status of Territorial Protection

In addition to the questions raised concerning exclusive dealing, the legality of other aspects of exclusive agency arrangements are very much in doubt. In granting an exclusive agency to a dealer, the manufacturer agrees to limit distribution in a specified geographic area to this outlet. In effect, this protects the dealer against neighboring retailers who might otherwise be competitors. In return for this protection, the manufacturer hopes to gain better cooperation from the dealer in maintaining inventories, giving service, and providing aggressive promotional support for the brand. The granting of exclusive distributorships in a specified territory is not covered by Section 3 of the Clayton Act as long as there is absence of restrictions on the sale of competitive products. Indeed, certain consent decrees have permitted such firms as the Wurlitzer Company and Philco to designate geographic areas as areas of primary responsibility for specific distributors.[12]

Manufacturers may, however, go one step further and require their dealers to confine sales activities to a described geographic territory— that is, prohibit them from invading the territories of other exclusive agents handling the firm's brand. While such territorial security clauses have never been ruled illegal in a higher court of law, much has occurred to raise serious doubts as to their legality. In 1949, for example, General Motors consented to the entry of a judgment that restrained the firm from incorporating into any contract a provision excluding dealers from any designated territory.[13] Later, all automobile manufacturers dropped the so-called territorial security and antibootlegging clauses from their

---

[12]*U.S.* v. *Wurlitzer Co.*, D.C., New York (1958); and *U.S.* v. *Philco*, D.C., Penn. (1956).
[13]"G.M. Precaution," *Business Week*, October 1, 1949, p. 52.

dealer contracts. Philco Corporation also signed a cease and desist order of the FTC, which prohibited such clauses in dealer contracts.[14]

Even though the territorial security provisions tend to be suspect, in a 1963 decision on the *White Motor Company* case the Supreme Court refused to support a district court decision declaring vertical territorial limitations illegal per se.[15] The White Motor Company had allocated exclusive territories to distributors but had reserved government, fleet, and large national accounts to itself—a vertical territorial limitation. In presenting the case in the district court, the Justice Department had merely presented evidence establishing the company's use of exclusive territories and the accompanying vertical territorial limitations, without attempting to prove that these practices unlawfully restricted competition. Accordingly, the district court handed down a summary judgment without full trial. The Supreme Court held that whether vertical territorial limitations violated antitrust laws could not be determined on motion by summary judgment in the absence of evidence which would enable the Court to determine whether the arrangement had the effect of stifling competition or had some redeeming virtue. The Court explained that it was reluctant to declare vertical territorial arrangements illegal per se because this was the first case involving such a restriction in vertical arrangements and too little was known about the "economic and business stuff" out of which such arrangements emerged.

The Justice Department is reported to have interpreted this decision as a mandate to bring up more cases and to try them more exhaustively. Federal judges, on the other hand, have accepted the companies' argument that competition is sometimes best served by letting companies contain the struggle for business among their own distributors in order to concentrate on "the real enemy"—that is, their competitors.[16]

In the *Schwinn* case (1966), the Supreme Court abandoned the cautious approach taken in the *White Motor* case and adopted a per se rule for evaluating the legality of exclusive territorial restraints. Instead of analyzing the actual impact of these arrangements on competition, the Court disregarded the economic arguments put forward on both sides and based its per se rule on an entirely different element of antitrust law—the concern for freedom of independent business units to sell their goods according to their best business judgment.[17]

The *Schwinn* decision provoked criticism which continued for 10 years. During that time lower courts carved out exceptions and qualifi-

---

[14]*U.S.* v. *Philco Corp.*, D.C., Penn. (1956).

[15]*The White Motor Co.* v. *U.S.*, 83 Sup. Ct. 696 (1963).

[16]"Is the Franchise System Legal?" *Business Week*, April 3, 1965, p. 66.

[17]*United States* v. *Arnold, Schwinn and Company.* (1966), 388 U.S. 365.

cations that allowed them to avoid the strict applications of the Schwinn rule of per se illegality.

In 1977 the Supreme Court considered distributor restrictions in *Continental TV, Inc.* v. *GTE Sylvania*. The Court expressly overturned the *Schwinn* decision and required distributor restraints to be judged under the "rule of reason."[18]

The rule of reason is not a clear-cut legal standard but rather an invitation for a thorough study of the situation to determine if the practice in question is important to the effective distribution of the product or service and if it is reasonable in the context of the competitive environment. Therefore, outcomes at best are unpredictable.

When applied to situations in which vertical restrictions on distributors are at issue, the rule of reason requires the courts to "weigh the reduction in intrabrand competition [rivalry among sellers of the same brand] against any increase in interbrand competition [rivalry among sellers of different brands] and to determine whether or not the restraints are necessary to facilitate an efficient or effective system of distribution.[19]

Given such formlessness, it is not surprising that the first case decided under the Sylvania approach resulted in a decision which seems at odds with the generally favorable attitude toward vertical restraints on distribution expressed in *Sylvania*. In deciding on the legality of territorial restrictions in the soft drink industry, the FTC ruled that restraints were illegal except for beverages sold in returnable bottles. The commission held that the suppression of intrabrand competition could not be offset by redeeming virtues. In the case of returnable bottles, the commission allowed the restrictions to remain because there was no distribution alternative that would assure bottlers a steady supply of their own bottles.[20]

Justification of Legal Restraints

Any restraints on distribution policies imposed either by legislation or by court interpretation are likely to cause substantial controversy among those parties who have a stake in the distribution of goods. The legislation and court rulings concerning territorial security, the franchise system, and exclusive dealing are no exception. Are such restraints in distribution policies warranted?

Business is, in a sense, like an athletic contest. Various parties compete with one another and vie for the attainment of a specified goal. Everyone would agree that ground rules are necessary in an athletic contest. The

---

[18]*Continental TV, Inc.* v. *GTE Sylvania, Inc.* (1977), 443 U.S. 33.

[19]John F. Cady, "Reasonable Rules and Rules of Reason: Vertical Restrictions on Distributors," *Journal of Marketing* 46, no. 3 (Summer 1982), pp. 27–37.

[20]*In the Matter of Coca-Cola Company et al.* (1978), Docket Number 8855.

same is true of business. Rules are necessary and desirable in order to channel the competitive efforts of business along lines that best serve the interest of the entire economy. The real question is not whether rules and regulations are necessary, but rather whether those rules are sound and whether they are properly administered.

It would seem that the prohibition of territorial security clauses in exclusive franchise agreements is sound and serves a major social purpose, namely, the enhancing of competition. To permit such clauses would give dealers a degree of monopoly in the territories in which they are located. By removing them from various competitive pressures, this might reduce the quality of the service which they render to consumers and could be a factor causing higher prices for consumers. Manufacturers, however, must be realistic if they hope to gain the benefit of aggressive selling by their dealers. To accomplish this objective they must offer the dealer a franchise which has value to him or her. Appointing too many "exclusive dealers" would be tantamount to a policy of nonexclusive distribution, would give minimum benefits to dealers, and would deny the manufacturer the benefits sought when he or she embarked on a policy of exclusive distribution. Recognition of this point should prevent harm to dealers by the absence of territorial security clauses.

Whether it is socially desirable to limit the action that manufacturers may take to prevent their dealers from selling through unauthorized discount outlets is a debatable question. An automobile manufacturer may claim that dealers are already in vigorous competition with one another in view of the limitations on territorial protection which now exist. Also, they are certainly competing aggressively with dealers handling other makes of automobiles in the same territory. In addition, legal limitations on action which may be taken to prevent dealers from selling through discount outlets may serve to erode the franchise system, which depends upon the strategic location of dealerships to make sales and service facilities and parts conveniently available to consumers. To permit dealers to sell through discount outlets might negate the manufacturer's attempts to build strong dealers through the use of the exclusive agency system. Moreover, the manufacturer would have no control over the amount and quality of the service offered by discounters, who in practice provide little or no service.

On the other hand, we should bear in mind that the prevention of sales through discounters may serve to protect dealers from the keen price competition of outlets capable of operating on a low markup. The spur of meeting such competition might stimulate innovation in the character and methods of operation of automobile dealers, which would tend to benefit consumers in the long run. Also, prohibition of sales through discount outlets prevents dealers from exercising their freedom to dispose of surplus inventory at a low markup when they find themselves overstocked because of sudden changes in the rate of consumer

buying, miscalculation, or the establishment of unrealistic sales quotas. Finally, choking off automobile sales through discount outlets denies consumers the benefits of low-markup discount selling which have been available in the purchase of household appliances, jewelry, and many other types of goods.

On balance, it is probably unwise to impose legal restrictions so strict as to prevent manufacturers from taking any action to limit sales by their dealers through discount outlets. Both consumers and dealers benefit from the maintenance of a franchise system which makes sales, parts, and service readily available through reputable firms. It might be wise, however, for automobile manufacturers to encourage certain of their dealers to experiment with types of operations that permit low costs of distribution and hence low markups and prices. It may be that certain dealers in large metropolitan areas could specialize in low-cost sales operations at the same time that others in the same areas provide necessary parts and service facilities. It is also evident, however, that better market intelligence, sales forecasting by dealer areas, and closer control over physical distribution need to be practiced as a means of preventing the accumulation of excess inventories, which tend to encourage dealers to turn to discount outlets for relief.

The legislative and court rulings concerning exclusive dealing have the same laudable objective as those applying to territorial security, that is, the maintenance of competition. However, a good case can be made for the fact that they have not served this objective very well. The per se doctrine does not clearly recognize the effect upon competition of exclusive-dealing practices. The mere fact that a substantial volume of trade is involved is not the equivalent of a substantial lessening of competition by any stretch of the imagination. Indeed, exclusive-dealing contracts could serve to enhance the degree of rivalry practiced by the dealers who must devote all of their efforts to the sale of one brand of a particular product because they have no others to distract their attention. This gives such dealers the same stake in the sale of the manufacturer's product within their territories as the manufacturer has.

Yet when the firm practicing exclusive dealing is a large manufacturer, and other leading competitors follow the same policy, the result may be to foreclose a substantial segment of the retail outlets from use by smaller firms seeking distribution for their products in that market. Under these circumstances, such potential competitors might be injured by the exclusive-dealing policies of dominant firms in the industry. Whether competition within the industry suffers, however, depends upon how vigorous the established firms are in vying with one another for market position and on whether smaller firms can develop a strategy which will enable them to develop a profitable business in spite of the limitations imposed by the exclusive-dealing practices of leading companies.

CONTROL AND COOPERATION IN MARKETING CHANNELS

As a product moves through a marketing channel from the manufacturer/producer to the ultimate consumer/industrial user, two or more independent channel members are involved in the flow. For maximization of channel profits and consumer satisfaction these channel members must act as a unit. Yet within the channel there exists a dynamic field of conflicting and cooperating objectives. If the conflicting objectives outweigh the cooperating objectives, the effectiveness of the channel will be reduced and efficient distribution impeded. The challenge to the manufacturer/producer is to identify and follow those methods of cooperation that will lead to increased channel efficiency.[21]

Three forms of distributive conflict may be identified:

1. Horizontal competition—this is competition between middlemen of the same type; for example, discount store versus discount store.
2. Intertype competition—this is competition between middlemen of different types in the same channel sector; for example, discount store versus department store.
3. Vertical conflict—this is conflict between channel members of different levels; for example, discount store versus manufacturer.

The basic source of conflict is the exchange act in which one channel member is the seller and the other is a buyer. Naturally, the seller wants a higher price than the buyer wishes to pay. The conflict is subdued through persuasion, or force by one member over the other, or refusal to buy, or finally, it is eliminated if the transaction takes place at a point of mutual satisfaction.

The channel can adjust to its conflicting–cooperating environment in three distinct ways: (1) It can have a leader (one of the channel members) who "forces" members to cooperate; this is an autocratic relationship. (2) It can have a leader who "helps" members to cooperate, creating a democratic relationship. (3) It can do nothing, and so have an anarchistic relationship. If anarchy exists, the chances are great that conflict will destroy the channel. If autocracy exists, there is less chance of this happening. However, the autocratic method creates a state of cooperation based on power and control. This controlled cooperation is really subdued conflict and makes for a more unstable equilibrium than does voluntary democratic cooperation.

The usual pattern in the establishment of channel relationships is that there is a leader. The manufacturer may be the leader, as with Chevrolet, but this is not always so. Large retailers such as K mart may challenge

---

[21]The following discussion is indebted to Bruce Mallen, "Conflict and Cooperation in Marketing Channels," in *Reflections on Progress in Marketing,* ed. L. George Smith (Chicago: American Marketing Association, 1964) pp. 65–85.

the manufacturer for channel leadership. Authorities differ as to which channel member should be the channel leader. Some argue that large retailers such as Sears, Roebuck should occupy this role on the ground that these firms serve as the purchasing agents of the consumer. If a manufacturer follows a consumer-oriented marketing program, then it may be argued that the manufacturer should take the channel leadership position. The marketing manager of such a manufacturer should choose and manage a distribution channel for the product which will function as a unified whole in the most effective possible manner. In effect, the channel may be regarded as an extension of the manufacturer's organization.

In following this philosophy, the manufacturer recognizes that the common interests of channel members are usually more significant than their conflicting interests. All channel members have a common interest in selling the product; only in the division of total channel profits are channel members in conflict. The task of the manufacturer in serving as the channel leader is to follow policies and procedures which will minimize conflict and strengthen the tendency toward voluntary cooperation.

Methods available to encourage cooperation may include using missionary salespeople, providing dealers with assistance in planning their promotional efforts, and making available to dealers various sales and promotional aids that are designed from the reseller's point of view. This topic will be explored more fully in Chapter 10, Promotional Strategy Decisions.

DISTRIBUTION CHANNEL CONTROL POLICIES

How much control should the manufacturers seek over the channel members who distribute their products? Before this question can be answered, it is helpful to consider what role reseller promotional activities should have in the basic promotional strategy for maximizing sales and profits. Once this is understood, the decision maker can return to the question of how much control is necessary to achieve the desired objectives.

As will be demonstrated in Chapter 10, the importance of reseller promotional efforts varies considerably among different products. Consider the Oldsmobile Division of General Motors, for example. In marketing the Cutlass Diesel automobile, it is essential that the product be stocked and sold by dealers who will carry adequate inventories; that an aggressive sales force be maintained to develop leads, demonstrate, and sell the Cutlass; and that local advertising be placed over the dealer's name which will reinforce Oldsmobile's general advertising of the Cutlass Diesel, identify the location of the local dealer, and provide pros-

pects with an incentive to visit the dealer's showroom. Efficient repair service at a reasonable cost should also be provided. The task of the general advertising for the Cutlass Diesel is to inform prospective buyers of its fuel economy as well as its other benefits, such as its safety, comfort, and dependability. While the general advertising performs an important function, the sales and promotional efforts of the local dealer are essential if sales and profits are to be maximized.

Revlon Formula 2 skin-responsive makeup provides a contrasting example. Here is an individualized product which appeals to strong basic desires and has a relatively large potential market among girls and women who wish a beautiful skin. The margin per unit and the potential unit sales are enough to support an aggressive advertising campaign. Clearly, then, the main burden of promotion should be on consumer advertising to arouse a desire for the product and create a selective demand for Revlon Formula 2. In planning distribution, Revlon would want dense coverage in stores where prospects would normally buy toilet articles. The firm would probably want the retailers who stock the product to display it attractively and, possibly, to include it in store advertising. But the main burden of selling the product would be on consumer advertising to stimulate consumer demand.

Once the decision maker has determined how much support he or she would like to have resellers give to the brand, then what strategy should be followed in order to get this degree of channel member support? In the good old days, according to Bucklin, a manufacturer would use trade discount policy to influence the amount of reseller support for the brand. If more push were wanted from the channel, a more liberal set of discounts from list price would be provided. If the manufacturer planned to do most of the marketing job by self, a smaller discount was allowed.[22]

This is no longer possible. Gone is the value of the list price to indicate what a customer should pay. Gone is the capacity of the manufacturer to control the margins that the trade channel members retain for their services. Gone is much of the distinction between the retailer and the wholesaler. There has been a shift to channel policies based on net prices instead of discounts. When pricing is done in this manner, no signals are sent to the channel members about their expected role within the distribution system. To preserve some semblance of a unified marketing program to the consumer, manufacturers must therefore turn to one of two strategies, or to some combination of the two: They must take over the performance of the channel support functions that they wish to have accomplished, or they must buy such services separately from the trade.

---

[22]This section is based on Louis P. Bucklin, "The New Math of Distribution Channel Control," in *Review of Marketing, 1978,* ed. Gerald Zaltman and Thomas V. Bonoma (Chicago: American Marketing Association, 1978), pp. 453–70.

Distribution channel services have become increasingly "unbundled" from the basic cost of the product itself.

Under this new situation each component of the channel support program carries a price tag, regardless of whether the manufacturer does the job or provides an explicit subsidy to the trade for that purpose. Incentives to perform these tasks efficiently should therefore increase under the new system.

Yet this is exactly what has *not* happened. Money often appears to be poorly spent. Too often, "deals" fall short of their objectives. Only a portion of the promotions offered to retailers by suppliers may actually be used to support the brand. Cooperative advertising programs may receive disappointing use unless they are carefully planned and supervised.

Bucklin lists the following suggestions for dealing with the problem of getting desired support from channel members.[23]

1. Develop clear and reasonable objectives for the channel support or control desired.
2. Understand the special needs and characteristics of the trade channel members whose behavior is to be influenced.
3. Construct integrated, precise, and timely programs that logically associate the use of specific promotional tools with given ends.
4. Develop tight controls for the administration of such programs.
5. Record the results carefully, and review them to evaluate the reasons for success or failure.[24]

PHYSICAL DISTRIBUTION

After channel-of-distribution strategy has been determined and policies have been established for its implementation, management must consider a closely related set of matters dealing with the physical distribution of goods. These matters include the location of fixed facilities, the size of inventories to be held in those facilities, and the modes of transportation to be used to move stock from factories to warehouses and thence to resellers or to direct-buying customers.

The ways in which these and similar matters are to be handled must be incorporated into policies which govern the performance of the physical distribution function. Effective management here is doubly impor-

---

[23]Ibid., p. 462. For a survey of sales promotion which documents ineffective management and suggests a practical step-by-step guide that companies can use to improve their management of promotional activities, see Roger A. Strang, "Sales Promotion— Fast Growth, Faulty Management," *Harvard Business Review,* July–August 1976, pp. 115–24.

[24]For additional background on how to gain greater support from dealers and distributors, see Benson P. Shapiro, "Improve Distribution with Your Promotional Mix," *Harvard Business Review,* March–April 1977, pp. 115–23.

tant not only because physical distribution accounts for a considerable portion of a firm's outlay for marketing but also because it provides a level of service for customers, which is increasingly becoming a prime weapon in the firm's struggle for competitive advantage.

Physical distribution has been called "the other half of marketing" because it accounts for approximately one half of the total outlay for marketing effort by American business firms.[25] While the promotional processes of seeking out buyers and persuading them to buy are relatively well known by businesses and consumers alike, that portion of the marketing task which is responsible for the distribution of goods after they have been produced has been shrouded in mystery. Indeed, only during the past 20 years has a real effort been made to reexamine that portion of the marketing task which provides time and place utilities in goods by moving and storing them. The reasons for this revived interest in physical distribution (or PD, as we shall sometimes refer to it) are varied. Three basic reasons are noted below.

Rising Costs

First, the costs of performing the functions of physical distribution have been rising steadily since the close of World War II. These costs have been incurred for labor, equipment, storage facilities, inventory holding, and transportation. Although cost behavior in this area has not been appreciably different from that in other sectors of business activity, the increased outlays needed for physical distribution have attracted the attention of management. The costs of physical distribution have also increased rapidly because of changes in overall product line strategy. Lines have been expanded in both depth and breadth, and this activity has resulted in a sizable increase in the costs of handling and holding inventory.

Cost-Saving Potential

A second reason for the increased attention that is being paid to the area of physical distribution is that although costs have been rising throughout all segments of business, there appears to be a greater opportunity to achieve cost reductions in the logistic area then elsewhere. For example, physical distribution activities offer opportunities for organization and systematization which are not available in the promotional area.

Promotional Potential

Last, but far from least, management has discovered that effective physical distribution is a potent promotional weapon. Prompt deliveries,

---

[25]Paul D. Converse, "The Other Half of Marketing," in *Twenty-Sixth Boston Conference on Distribution* (Boston: Boston Trade Board, 1954), pp. 22–25.

a minimum of back orders, infrequent customer need to file damage claims, and so forth, can give the seller a considerable advantage over rivals who do not provide equivalent levels of service. Of special interest to management is the fact that the cost of providing a given level of service to customers can be calculated and compared with the costs of both price and nonprice promotional alternatives.

Implications

Because of the reasons stated above, managers in many firms have ceased to view physical distribution as a peripheral area supporting production and promotional activities. Instead, these managers are treating physical distribution as a major functional area responsible for the movement of goods to customers and for the coordination of supply with demand as stimulated by the firm's promotional activities. By bringing the two halves of marketing—promotion and physical distribution—closer together, by coordinating efforts in both areas, and by giving physical distribution more attention than it has received in the past, these managers hope to achieve a synergistic effect. Their goal is a more desirable combination of cost savings and competitive advantage than would be achieved if promotion and physical distribution were treated as separate and unrelated functions.

Increasing costs are the prime motivating force behind a managerial review of how the firm is performing its physical distribution job. These costs may be the outlays required to sustain a given level of functional performance, or they may be profits foregone because of lost sales due to ineffective logistics. Regardless of specific causation, management action is usually aimed at reducing both outlay and opportunity costs from present levels. After such reductions have been achieved, then attention can be given to increasing the extent of customer service provided by a given expenditure.

A Physical Distribution System

Let us look at a simple distribution system. In Figure 9–3 we see a system in which the order is the input, transport is the component providing the delivery function, and actual delivery of an order is the output. It is a closed system in that delivery of the order in a satisfactory or unsatisfactory manner might provide feedback that, in turn, would trigger a new or replacement order. Because people are involved in most physical distribution systems, these systems are semistructured. Thus, output per given input is less predictable than it would be in a structured system.

As additional components are added to a simple physical distribution system, the interaction among these components becomes more complex. The more complicated the system, the more difficult system anal-

FIGURE 9–3   A simple distribution system

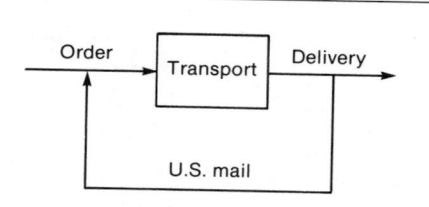

ysis, operation, or alteration becomes. Before we discuss the components, however, it is necessary to make a few generalized statements about the inputs and outputs associated with a physical distribution system.

System output.   The level of service provided to customers is generally the measurement variable for the output of a PD system. Called CSL (customer service level) in the trade, this variable is a complex combination of several factors. Three of the more important factors which go to make up the CLS are the length of the order cycle (the time between submission of an order and receipt of goods), the percentage of orders received in which some goods are back-ordered because the supplier was out of stock, and the physical condition of the goods when they are received.

System input.   The most widely used input variable for a PD system is the cost, measured in dollars, of the labor and materials utilized in the operation of the system. The determination of the costs associated with the performance of the physical distribution function is very difficult because traditional accounting practices do not usually identify a firm's cost elements in terms of whether or not they have been expended to create time and place utilities.[26] In fact, the commonly used methods of accounting may distort the cost consequences of a PD decision. Figures 9–4 and 9–5 illustrate such a situation.

Figure 9–4 compares the costs per hundred pounds (cwt.) of shipping goods rail-direct with the costs of shipping by a rail-barge combination. By reducing the costs of preparing and storing goods for shipment within the plant, by reducing transportation costs, and by assuming increased terminal expense, total costs are lowered from $3.15 to $2.50

---

[26]George G. Smith, "Know Your PD Costs," *Distribution Age,* January 1966, pp. 21–27.

FIGURE 9–4   Comparison of rail-direct and barge-rail

	Cost per cwt.	
	Rail-direct	**Barge-rail**
Plant production cost		
Packaging	$1.00	$0.00
Storage and handling	0.30	0.10
Financial costs inventory	0.10	0.25
Administrative	0.15	0.05
Subtotal	$1.55	$0.40
Transportation cost		
To customer	1.60	0.20
To terminal	—	0.30
Subtotal	$1.60	$0.50
Terminal expense		
Packaging	0.00	1.00
Storage and handling	0.00	0.30
Financial costs inventory	0.00	0.15
Administrative	0.00	0.15
Subtotal	$0.00	$1.60
Total cost per cwt.	$3.15	$2.50
Total cost 20 million lbs. per year	$630,000	$500,000

Source: H. G. Miller, "Accounting for Physical Distribution," *Transportation and Distribution Management,* December 1961, p. 10.

per cwt. Annual savings of $130,000 accrue on an annual volume of 20 million pounds.

Figure 9–5 illustrates the change in accounts resulting from the change in distribution methods. In-plant physical distribution cost reductions show up as lowered production costs, while decreases in transportation costs appear as increases in net sales. The terminal expenses that are assumed to make the other cost savings possible result in an accounting effect that indicates a substantial increase in field warehousing costs.

Unless care is taken to dig behind the traditional accounts or, preferably, until accounting procedures are changed to reflect better the true costs of physical distribution, the calculation of a PD system's input costs will be a difficult undertaking.[27]

[27]An attempt to improve accounting procedures for PD management has been sponsored by an industry trade association. See Michael Schiff, *Accounting and Control in Physical Distribution Management* (Chicago: National Council of Physical Distribution Management, Inc., 1972).

FIGURE 9–5   Change in accounts resulting from change in distribution method

	Cost per cwt.	
	Rail-direct	*Barge-rail*
Plant production costs		
All costs except PD	$10.00	$10.00
Physical distribution	1.55	0.40
Total production cost	$11.55	$10.40
Accounting effect—apparent reduction in plant production cost		
Transportation cost		
Gross sales price	$15.00	$15.00
Net freight cost	1.60	0.50
Net sales	$13.40	$14.50
Accounting effect—net sales dollars increase		
Warehousing and storage	$ 0.00	$ 1.60
Accounting effect—field warehousing cost substantially increased		

Source: H. G. Miller, "Accounting for Physical Distribution," *Transportation and Distribution Management,* December 1961, p. 10.

System linkages.   When the physical distribution system is viewed in terms of its elements, it becomes apparent that decisions in the area of physical distribution impinge upon production as well as upon the nonPD portion of the marketing function. Thus PD, itself a system, must be viewed as a subsystem of the master system, which is the firm. As such, the PD system is linked to the other subsystems within the firm. In addition, the PD system is linked to other systems that are external to the firm.

Figure 9–6 illustrates a PD system that has been defined to include the storage and handling of raw materials and parts prior to assembly. Our definition of PD in this chapter is a narrower one in which PD is concerned with the distribution of finished goods. Nevertheless, the figure illustrates the connections that exist among subsystems within the firm prior to its shipment of finished goods. In addition, the figure shows how the PD system of the firm must be interlinked with the PD systems of resellers.

System components and their interrelationships.   A physical distribution system may be thought of as being composed of three principal components: (1) a set of fixed facilities at which goods are produced or inventories are stored; (2) a set of inventories of goods; and (3) a trans-

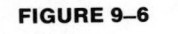

FIGURE 9–6 A physical distribution system for a consumer appliance manufacturer

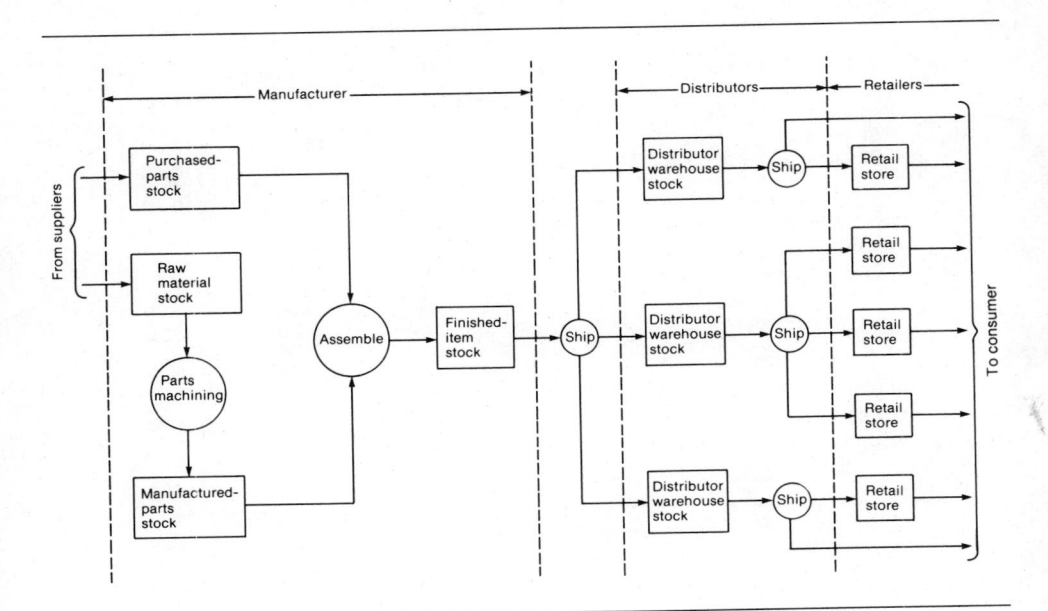

Source: John F. Magee, *Physical Distribution Systems*, p. 11. Copyright 1967, McGraw-Hill Book Company. Used with permission of McGraw-Hill Book Company.

portation network connecting the fixed facilities, one with another, as well as with customer receiving points. It is over this network that goods flow from producing points to intermediate holding points and thence to resellers or end users.

These components are linked together in a functional sense and are highly time dependent. Stewart's concept of the PD system as being made up of various activity cogs is useful in seeing the true nature of these linkages. It is illustrated in Figure 9–7.

Stewart holds that the inventory component is the key to total system management. He views inventory as the buffer between customers' orders and manufacturing activities. The filling of orders reduces the level of inventory held by the firm, while production activity increases the level. As the manufacturing process uses up raw materials, the flow of such materials into the firm must be increased. Finished goods leaving the assembly line require the multiple activities illustrated in the figure. The completion of each activity takes time, and the activities are linked sequentially in that certain of them cannot be started until others are completed.

FIGURE 9–7   Activity cogs in a physical distribution system

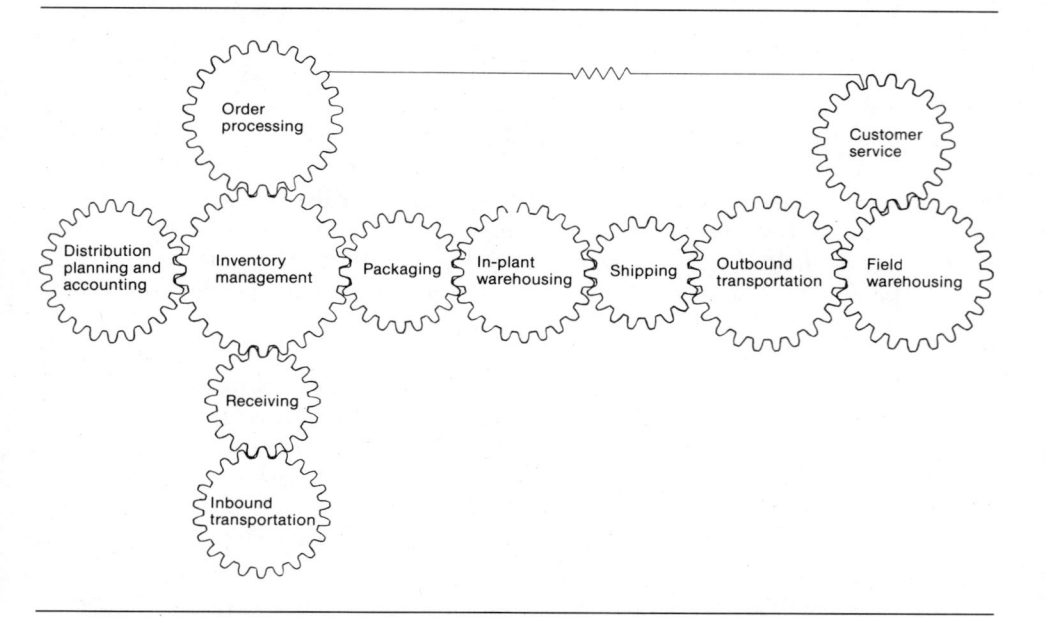

Source: Wendell M. Stewart, "Physical Distribution: Key to Improved Volume and Profits." Reprinted from *Journal of Marketing*, January 1965, p. 66. Published by the American Marketing Association.

The components of a PD system are also linked spatially. It is evident that no facility should be considered fixed in the sense that it would not be moved if cost or demand conditions so warranted. Indeed, a major option open to distribution system planners is to change the location of facilities. Such changes, however, cannot be considered in isolation, but must also be examined in terms of their effects on inventory-holding costs, transport costs, and the level of service provided to customers.

MANAGING THE PHYSICAL DISTRIBUTION FUNCTION

The discussion that preceded this section should by now have clearly indicated that effective management of PD function requires coordination among the diverse activities of the business enterprise. A PD system must be tuned to receive inputs from the production process as well as to furnish output as required by the marketing department. Even within the heart of the system the problems of managing the functions of

transport, warehousing, and inventory holding must be considered as interrelated issues.

Unfortunately, the typical firm is not organized to fully facilitate such coordination. Traffic seeks to route goods as economically as possible. Sales promises prompt delivery of goods. Warehouse managers try to run their show as efficiently as they can. But in all too many instances, there is no one person or group of persons to manage the cost trade-offs that are available among diverse functional areas and thus to optimize the performance of the total distribution system.

Some of the nation's more progressive firms have sensed that great opportunities for gains in performance and reductions in costs might be exploited if the systems approach were applied to PD and if the components of the PD system were viewed as pieces of the whole. These companies have attempted to provide the management structure needed to implement the systems approach.

In certain companies, for example, committees have been formed to set service-level goals and to coordinate the activities necessary for the attainment of these goals. The authority of such committees cuts across traditional functional lines and is exercised to prevent what is called suboptimization, or the seeking of higher levels of performance by components at the expense of total system performance. Other companies have gone still further by establishing a separate department for physical distribution. The status of this department may be equivalent to that granted to production and marketing. The more usual procedure, however, is to recognize the PD function and to place it under the control of an established function, such as production, control, or marketing. Those firms which are cost-conscious and do not have service-level problems generally choose to place PD under production or control. Those firms which are concerned with the levels of customer service provided for a given input of resources generally place the function within the marketing area.

The exact location of responsibility for PD management within the firm is not the major issue. Rather, what is vitally important is the recognition by top management that, wherever management responsibility is located, the people involved must have the authority to effect the coordination of activities both within and without the firm which is essential if distribution efficiency is to be maximized.

CONCLUSION

Distribution policy decisions are among the most basic and important decisions that marketing executives must make in planning their marketing strategy. They must decide whether to sell direct to the final buyer or through middlemen. If an indirect channel is decided upon,

they must select the types of middlemen to use, determine the desirable degree of selectivity to employ, and establish methods of control over channel institutions. These decisions in turn, will profoundly affect physical distribution requirements, promotional strategy, and pricing strategy. The influence of distribution policy decisions on other aspects of marketing strategy will be seen in subsequent chapters.

QUESTIONS

1. Approximately 37 percent of machine tools are sold directly to industrial users, while 45 percent are sold to the industrial market through manufacturer's agents. The remainder is sold through industrial supply houses. *Why* are some machine tools sold directly to users, while others go through manufacturer's agents and industrial supply houses?

2. The H. J. Heinz Company and Standard Brands, Inc., both broad-line manufacturers of grocery products, previously sold direct to small independent grocery stores. Since World War II, both have switched to selling through grocery wholesalers. What sort of changes in the situation surrounding the sale of grocery products probably explain this change in distribution channels?

3. Distinguish between intensive, selective, and exclusive agency distribution.

4. Manufacturers of major brands of household appliances usually follow a policy of selective retail distribution. What is the explanation for this choice?

5. As products move through their life cycles from the innovation stage to maturity, their distribution often becomes less selective. What explains this?

6. Distinguish between exclusive agency distribution and the practice of exclusive dealing. Is one ever found without the other?

7. Discuss the effect of exclusive dealing on competition. Under what circumstances might it reduce competition? Might it sometimes increase competition?

8. Do territorial protection clauses in franchise agreements tend to reduce competition? Explain.

9. What are some of the reasons for the renewed interest in the area of physical distribution?

10. What is systems analysis, and why is it so useful an approach for managing the functions of physical distribution?

11. What is the output of a physical distribution system? What is the input? How would you measure the efficiency of the system?

12. What are some of the difficulties that you might expect in the management of a physical distribution system in a typically organized firm?

Cases for part four

JOHNSON AND DAVIS (B)*

Distribution strategy alternatives

Johnson and Davis, a Midwest office supply dealer, began producing its own line of color-code labels in mid-1974. Its salesmen continued to sell labels supplied by Record Systems Inc. (RSI) until a base stock inventory of J&D's own labels could be completed. The salesmen then had little difficulty in switching over to the new label, incorporating it into the file and record systems that they sold. Over the next quarter, J&D's retail outlets reported that sales of color-code labels were slightly lower than normal, but this decline was expected as a result of the loss in expansion and replacement sales to customers to whom J&D had previously sold the RSI label design.

FROM 1974 TO 1977

In late 1974, Tom Peterson, the new manager of the File and Record Systems Division at J&D, began to receive inquiries about J&D's new labels from record systems dealers in various parts of the United States

---

*Written by Eric Blanchard, research assistant, under the supervision of Professor Martin R. Warshaw, Graduate School of Business Administration, The University of Michigan, Ann Arbor.

395

and Canada. Before joining J&D in 1973, Tom had been a salesman for RSI and had sold its labels to many of the same dealers. With no out-of-state salesmen to line up dealers for J&D, Tom had not intended at this time to expand distribution of J&D's labels beyond its four in-state retail outlets. But later Tom decided that as long as these dealers ordered in large enough quantities to make an acceptable contribution to profit, he would extend distribution to them as well.

As more and more dealers expressed an interest in J&D's new labels, Tom realized that with a little promotional work he might be able to line up permanent sales contracts with systems dealers across the nation. His first step was to attend the annual conventions of the American Associ-ation of Systems Dealers (AASD), a new association whose membership included about 200 of the nearly 1,200 systems dealers in the United States. At these conventions he exhibited J&D's full line of color-code labels. He then followed up the exhibits with direct mailings of introduc-tory brochures.

Tom chose to direct his efforts toward systems dealers rather than toward all office supply dealers for two reasons. First, he felt that only systems dealers, accounting for about 75 percent of the $10 million color-code label industry, could guarantee a large enough volume of sales to warrant permanent sales contracts. Second, being specialists in file and record systems, these dealers would require a less extensive initial training program than would regular office supply dealers.

Although sales were growing rapidly in the out-of-state wholesale market, Tom continued to devote much of his time to helping J&D's 38 salesmen in the in-state retail market. These salesmen, while very expe-rienced in selling regular office supplies, were required to have Tom approve the final design and sale of each new color-coded file system that they sold.

Tom also attended as many court, hospital, and medical conventions in the state as possible in order to demonstrate J&D's products directly to large potential customers. This in-state retail market was still very important to J&D's total sales of color-code labels, since the retail markup generated per unit profits nearly three times as large as those generated by out-of-state wholesale market. Furthermore, each in-state sale of color-code labels generated orders for other office supplies and equipment retailed by J&D.

As a result of Tom's three-year promotional campaign, sales of color-code labels rose from $50,000 in 1974 to $200,000 in 1977. About two thirds of this increase was attributable to the out-of-state market, which now included sales contracts with 27 dealers throughout the United States. J&D's market share of the color-code label industry rose from 0.625 percent to 2 percent, while total company sales nearly doubled and two new retail outlets were added.

AASD PROPOSAL

Early in 1977, the president of AASD offered Tom a contract to supply all the dealers in the association with either the existing J&D labels or with new labels to be designed and manufactured by J&D. In either case, AASD would put its own brand name on the product and receive a 10 percent commission on each label sold by its member dealers. AASD could not guarantee that all of its dealers would switch over to the J&D label, since AASD had no direct control over them. However, after examining AASD's record with other products, Tom estimated that about 75 percent of the members could be expected to make the switch within three years. This would bring J&D almost $1 million in business, or nearly one fifth of the wholesale market.

AASD would give no guarantees as to how much promotional work the association or its dealers would do for the product. Tom felt, however, that the 10 percent commission and the retail markup would give both association and its dealers an ample incentive to do at least as much promotional work as J&D had done. Of course, without its own name on the product, J&D could derive only limited long-term benefits from the promotion. Tom saw this venture chiefly as an attempt to gain high sales in a very short period.

The last plank of AASD's proposal stated that once J&D began distributing its labels to AASD dealers, it could not sell them to any non-member systems dealers. This presented no problem for J&D's out-of-state sales, since most of the dealers to whom J&D was making these sales were already members of the association. As for J&D's in-state sales, however, if J&D allowed AASD dealers to sell its original labels, the AASD dealers located in the same state as J&D's retail outlets would soon be in direct competition with them.

As Tom considered these two alternatives, he noted the cost estimates to be assigned to each. First of all, whether or not new labels were designed and manufactured, accepting the AASD proposal would necessitate buying another letterpress, an investment of about $30,000, and arranging initial regional training sessions for the AASD dealers at a cost of around $18,000. If J&D decided on the alternative of manufacturing new labels, it would also incur three additional costs, similar to those incurred when it first produced the old labels: $30,000 for production of a base stock inventory, $12,000 for introductory brochures, and $8,000 plus $500 annually for new image plates.

The costs involved in manufacturing new labels would thus be far greater than those associated with simply turning over the out-of-state distribution of the original labels to AASD. On the other hand, by manufacturing new labels, J&D could avoid direct in-state competition between AASD dealers and its own salesmen, could avoid losing the 10

percent commission on its current sales to AASD dealers until after these dealers had switched over to the new label, and, most important, could leave open the possibility of lining up new, non-AASD dealers on its own to handle distribution of the old labels.

This last idea brought Tom to consider yet a third alternative, that of rejecting AASD's offer altogether and instead expanding distribution of J&D's labels nationwide without AASD's help. To do this, J&D would need to hire and train salesmen to contact systems dealers around the country. Of course, If J&D rejected AASD's proposal, it could expect the association to find another manufacturer to furnish labels. Thus, one fifth of the market, including the 27 dealers J&D now supplied, would be lost to a competitor from the start.

This would still leave nearly 1,000 dealers, however, and Tom felt that a minimum of four salesmen (at least $40,000 per year each, including expenses) would be needed to reach them all. The costs for training sessions and promotional literature would vary according to the number of dealers contacted and obtained by the salesmen. But the key question for Tom was how much of that $10 million color-code label industry J&D could capture on its own and how quickly it could be done. With only 2 percent of the market, J&D's labels were not well known among dealers or end users. On the other hand, a venture of this sort could provide a means by which J&D could better promote the company name nationally and possibly even pave the way toward future expansion of its retail operations. Since AASD demanded that its own brand name be put on the product, it could not provide these opportunities to J&D.

Tom knew that J&D was in a much better financial position to expand its operations than it had been three years earlier when it began to manufacture color-code labels. Yet so much business had been gained simply by way of referrals from satisfied dealers and customers that Tom felt that he should not rule out the possibility of leaving the marketing strategy unchanged. This, then, was a fourth alternative that Tom could present to management before a final decision was made.

QUESTIONS

1. Which of the four alternative distribution strategies should J&D follow? Why?

2. How should J&D's success in the out-of-state wholesale market affect its selection of a distribution strategy?

CLEVELAND PLASTIC PRODUCTS, INC.*

*Manufacturer's sales representatives
versus use of own sales force*

In the years since its founding in 1966, Cleveland Plastic Products, Inc. (CPP), located in Cleveland, Ohio, had grown steadily and rapidly. However, its product lines, its markets, and the conditions under which it did business had changed dramatically through the years. As a consequence of these changes, Frank Sweet, president of CPP, had undertaken a project of rethinking the company's goals, policies, and procedures. Sweet was especially interested in deciding whether the company should continue to sell its HVAC (heating, ventilating, and air conditioning) line through manufacturer's sales representatives in all the markets it served or whether it should establish its own sales force in some or all of those markets.

COMPANY HISTORY

Before founding Cleveland Plastic Products, Inc., Frank Sweet, a chemical engineer, had worked for another flexible duct firm. This firm had specialized in the manufacture of high-technology flexible rubber

---

*Written by Stewart H. Rewoldt, late Professor of Marketing, Graduate School of Business Administration, The University of Michigan.

duct with tight specifications. The product was largely supplied to big U.S. aerospace defense contractors. Due to a cutback in aerospace contract appropriations, the firm suffered various financial setbacks and eventually went bankrupt. Frank Sweet suddenly found himself unemployed.

At this point, he founded Cleveland Plastic Products, Inc. For the first year or two after organizing his own firm, he served as a problem-solving consultant to companies manufacturing or using flexible rubber hose and parts. When necessary, CPP also manufactured rubber hose and parts on a job-lot basis.

A manufacturer's representative approached CPP about the possibility of its producing flexible plastic hose (unavailable from any other source) that was needed to fill an order from a recreational vehicle manufacturer. After some thought, Sweet decided that he could produce the plastic hose called for if the proper machinery were obtained.

After some negotiation, the recreational vehicle manufacturer agreed to purchase and make available to CPP the machine required to produce the flexible plastic hose. The capacity of the machine greatly exceeded the requirements of this one account. Further negotiations led to an agreement that CPP could utilize the machine to produce flexible plastic hose for sale to other users but that it would not sell the hose to any other manufacturer of recreational vehicles. The capacity of the machine would allow CPP to turn out close to $500,000 of flexible plastic hose per year in addition to meeting the needs of the recreational vehicle manufacturer. The most immediately obvious market for this excess supply was in the production of flexible vacuum cleaner hose for use on larger cannister-type units made for the consumer market. These low-cost utility units were becoming very popular for such uses as cleaning up after working on do-it-yourself projects, cleaning up in hobby shops, and so on.

THE VACUUM HOSE MARKET

Historically, commercial vacuum sweepers had used heavy-duty rubber and fabric vacuum sweeper hose. This type of hose accounted for the bulk of the sales to this industry. CPP decided to offer a light-weight plastic hose as an alternative. Sweet had only a $30,000–$50,000 investment of his own in the company at this time.

Rubber vacuum hose was purchased by the manufacturers of the vacuum sweepers. These sweepers were sold to wholesalers, who, in turn, sold a variety of products to dealers.

When CPP first entered the vacuum hose market, rubber and fabric hose sold at an average price of 37 cents per foot. By working to improve

the technology of flexible plastic hose manufacturing, CPP was able to reduce production costs and offer flexible plastic hose for sale at a significantly lower price than rubber hose. The packaging and freight costs for flexible plastic hose were substantially lower than those for rubber hose. Therefore, when all cost components were taken into account, flexible plastic hose enjoyed a distinct cost advantage. As a result, by 1977, 90 percent of all vacuum sweepers employed flexible plastic hose.

Originally, CPP sold flexible plastic hose to manufacturers through manufacturer's representatives who operated on a straight 5 percent commission. This channel of distribution soon proved to be uneconomic. Twelve OEMs accounted for most of the usage of vacuum sweeper hose. Sales through manufacturer's representatives were large, and their commissions were excessive in relation to the services they performed. The first step taken by CPP to control these excessive commissions was to adopt a sliding commission scale. As sales increased, the commission rate per dollar of sales declined. Sales continued to increase, and the commissions of the manufacturer's agents continued to be excessive, considering the services they rendered. It became evident that, given the small number of OEM accounts, each buying in relatively large quantities, it would be more economical to sell directly to the OEMs. Sales through manufacturer's representatives were discontinued, and sales to OEMs were henceforth made on a direct basis. In 1977, CPP had more than half of the vacuum sweeper hose market. Its channel of distribution for vacuum hose was as shown in Exhibit 1.

EXHIBIT 1

CPP—OEMs—Wholesalers—Dealers

THE MOBILE HOME MARKET

Air conditioning units are not customarily installed in mobile homes at the factory in which they are produced. They are usually an add-on item that is installed after the mobile home has been placed in a permanent or semipermanent location in a mobile home park. With the growth of the mobile home market, manufacturers of hot-air furnaces for mobile homes began to enter the mobile home air conditioning market. The installation of hot-air furnaces and air conditioners for mobile

homes required the use of insulated duct, and insulated flexible duct (large-diameter flexible hose) was the lowest-cost duct for these purposes.

CPP entered this market in 1969. The market grew very rapidly, and CPP's annual sales ranged between $1 million and $2 million between 1969 and 1973. As the market became saturated and the United States entered a period of recession, these sales declined. Between 1973 and 1977, CPP sales to the mobile home market were in the $1 million to $1.5 million range.

As it had done in the vacuum hose market, CPP originally sold to air conditioner OEMs through manufacturer's representatives. For reasons similar to those that applied in the vacuum hose situation (high commissions and large sales to a small number of customers), it soon switched to direct sale to OEMs. Today all such sales are handled by the assistant sales manager.

The channel of distribution for reaching the mobile home market is therefore as shown in Exhibit 2.

EXHIBIT 2

CPP—OEMs—Wholesalers—Dealers (installers)

THE HVAC MARKET

CPP first introduced its flexible ducts to the heating, ventilating, and air conditioning (HVAC) market in 1972. The HVAC market rapidly became the largest market served by CPP. Sales in 1977 were expected to range between $6 million and $8 million. CPP produced flexible plastic duct that would perform in low-, medium-, and high-pressure applications. Its duct was intended for residential, light commercial, and major commercial applications.

When CPP first entered the HVAC market, remembering its previous experience with manufacturer's reps in the dryer hose and mobile home markets, it began by selling directly to wholesalers, concentrating on those that were large enough to buy in truckload lots.

However, selling directly to wholesalers proved to be too big, complex, and costly a job. At that time, CPP did not have the staff to handle it (see Exhibit 3.) All sales were being made by the sales manager. There

was no established sales force to handle the task. Establishing a sales force for this purpose was not feasible because then the volume of business did not justify having company salesmen in most markets. The HVAC market was just beginning to develop, and sales to that market were being made in relatively small quantities scattered over a nationwide area. For these reasons, it was decided to establish distribution through manufacturer's representatives.

EXHIBIT 3   CPP's sales organization chart

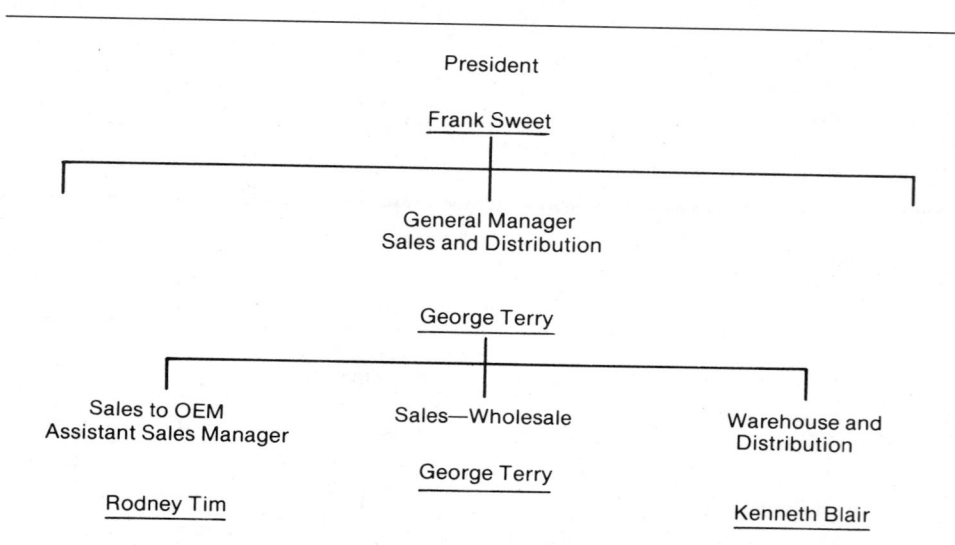

Therefore, in 1973 CPP decided to establish distribution in the HVAC market through manufacturer's reps. There was no such thing as a directory of the reps who would be suitable to carry its line. To solve the problem of lining up an acceptable group of reps, the sales manager visited each market area. He called on wholesalers who handled metal duct systems and/or associated products and gathered information from them about the reps with whom they were familiar. When the names of certain reps kept coming up again and again as good performers, the sales manager approached those reps to discuss with them the possibility of handling the CPP flexible plastic duct line. By this means, a group of nine of the best reps available was put together in 1974 to handle the HVAC line. These reps provided a total of 11 salespeople and offered

complete coverage of the United States with the exception of North Dakota and Montana. Because the HVAC line consisted of products relatively new to the market, only one of these reps already carried a line of flexible plastic duct. He switched to CPP because of the completeness of its line, the high quality of service that could be expected from it, and the superiority of its product.

The typical rep carrying CPP's HVAC line handled a total of four lines. By 1977, after only three years' experience with the CPP line, flexible plastic duct was often the best-selling and most profitable line that the rep carried. The rep was compensated by a straight 5 percent commission on all sales. The orders he wrote were usually called in to CPP directly by the wholesaler, though some wholesalers relied on the rep to transmit these orders. CPP's contract with the rep was the standard one for the industry, providing for cancellation by either party on 30 days' notice.

The channel of distribution for CPP's HVAC line was therefore as shown in Exhibit 4.

EXHIBIT 4

CPP—Manufacturer's reps—Wholesalers—Dealers (installers)

CPP more or less pioneered the sale of flexible plastic duct for heating, ventilating, and air conditioning. It continued to be one of the largest manufacturers in this market in 1977, but competition was developing rapidly. Although large fiberglass insulation manufacturers who produced similar ducts for HVAC installations were dropping out of the market, they were purchasing flexible plastic duct from manufacturers other than CPP and were selling in this growth market. CPP was not anxious to sell to fiberglass manufacturers because it would have to compete head-on with them at the wholesale level.

THE SITUATION IN 1977

CPP had established a strong position in the vacuum hose market, the mobile home market, and in the market for light-, medium-, and high-pressure flexible plastic hose for general heating, ventilating, and air

conditioning. The vacuum hose and mobile home markets did not have strong growth prospects, but the HVAC market had grown rapidly and was expected to continue to grow at a rate of about 25 percent a year.[1] CPP was doing $6 million to $8 million of business in the HVAC market in 1977, and it expected to reach $13 million by 1980.

The issue of continued sale through manufacturer's representatives had now arisen in the HVAC market, but the situation was very different from the one which had existed in the vacuum hose and mobile home markets. In the vacuum hose and air conditioning markets, the market intermediaries (the OEMs) were very few in number, and CPP could sell them directly in an economical manner. In the HVAC market, the intermediaries were wholesalers and their number was comparatively large.

In the Ohio territory, sales through a manufacturer's rep had had to be discontinued recently. The rep had been doing an unsatisfactory job of opening new accounts and a poor job of servicing existing accounts. Sales were switched directly to a large wholesaler who operated a fairly large number of branches. This provided reasonable coverage of the Ohio territory. In many other territories, however, wholesalers with extensive branch networks did not exist.

CPP's reps were compensated by being paid a flat 5 percent commission. As CPP sales rose, the reps' commission earnings rose along with them. The commission earnings per rep ranged from $2,500 per year to $75,000 per year. The highest-paid rep employed one outside salesman besides himself. If CPP HVAC sales rose to $13 million by 1980, the commissions would more than double for 8 reps (10 salespeople in total) through which CPP reached about 300 wholesalers.

Frank Sweet estimated that it would cost from $30,000 to $40,000 in salary plus expenses to maintain a CPP salesman in the field, the cost varying with the territory. A rough average might be $35,000. In some territories the point was bound to be reached in the near future at which having its own salesmen would be less costly for CPP than would continuing to sell through reps. Sweet was wondering what his policy should be with regard to this issue.

QUESTIONS

1. What are the pros and cons for CPP of continuing to sell the HVAC market through manufacturer's representatives?

2. What sort of distribution policy should CPP adopt, and how should that policy be implemented?

---

[1] *Air Conditioning and Refrigeration News,* January 1975.

THE UPJOHN COMPANY*

*Decision on channels of distribution
for new veterinary product*

The research and development division of The Upjohn Company had discovered a new product for the treatment of mastitis in dairy cattle. If established distribution and sales policies were followed in the marketing of this discovery, it was anticipated that sales would be limited to a fraction of the potential market. As a means of capitalizing to the maximum possible extent on research findings, therefore, company officials were considering the possibility of opening new distribution channels and of deviating from customary promotional policy. They did not want to act without giving the matter careful consideration, however, because of the likelihood that such innovations would meet with disfavor by veterinarians, who provided the traditional outlet for such products. There was also concern over the possible reaction of physicians and laymen, either users or potential users of the company's main product line of human-use pharmaceuticals.

HISTORY

The Upjohn Company, producer of ethical drugs and pharmaceuticals, was established in 1886 in Kalamazoo, Michigan, and its headquar-

---

*Written by Donald Mattison, Marketing Research Department, The Upjohn Company.

ters and manufacturing plants are still located there. The company was founded by Dr. W. E. Upjohn, at the time a practicing physician, for the purpose of manufacturing better pills, which were the most common form of medication at that time. After pills declined in popularity, the company began to move toward its present line of ethical drugs and pharmaceuticals. Outstanding research, high-quality products, and aggressive merchandising have all contributed toward making The Upjohn Company one of the largest ethical drug firms in the industry.

DISTRIBUTION AND SALES POLICIES

Ethical pharmaceutical houses are distinguished from proprietary drug firms by the fact that their promotional efforts are aimed at the professional (physician, druggist, hospital buyer) rather than at the ultimate consumer. Over the years, The Upjohn Company has followed the basic distribution policy of selling directly to retail druggists. In accordance with the "ethical" formula, the Upjohn sales force has been responsible for "creating" a demand for the firm's prescription drugs by "dealing" the physician (i.e., by doing missionary saleswork with doctors) and by selling the retail druggist on stocking Upjohn products. Heavy sales of nonprescription items such as vitamins, however, have resulted from the direct sales and promotional efforts of the retail druggist.

Physical distribution of Upjohn products was handled through 18 company-owned sales branches and warehouses located throughout the country. No account was farther than two days' delivery service from any branch warehouse. Most major trading centers received either same-day or following-day service.

While the company's main line of products was human pharmaceuticals, over the years ambitious salesmen had started calling on veterinarians to obtain additional sales on certain items of their line which also had applications in the DVM's practice. Examples of such products were antibiotics, sulfa drugs, cortisone, vitamins, antidiarrheal preparations, and cough suppressants. The basic policy of selling direct to retail professional outlets (drugstores, hospitals, etc.) made it possible to open new accounts in such allied field as the animal-health market.

Company officials had recognized this segment of business by establishing a separate research unit and sales force to give specific attention to its development. Ten salesmen had been added recently to call upon DVMs at an estimated annual cost of $150,000 for salaries and travel expenses. These men did not call upon druggists, farm-supply stores, cooperatives, or hatcheries. The regular Upjohn sales force did call upon druggists, however, and took orders for pharmaceuticals which the druggist dispensed for the treatment of both humans and animals.

In addition to the establishment of the separate sales force, a special

line of products was being developed for veterinarians. In the year prior to the discovery of the new product, the sales of products in the animal-health market amounted to approximately $250,000.

BACKGROUND FOR PROBLEM

In the animal-health goods market, according to an Upjohn official, the veterinarian's role is somewhat different from that of the physician in the human-health goods market. In the human-health field, the physician and druggist act as a team, with the physician "creating" the demand by writing a prescription to be filled by the druggist. In the animal-health field, prescription writing is at a minimum, with the exception of a few small-animal hospitals. The DVM usually considers the druggist as a competitor. Different types of outlets, accordingly, serve the animal-health goods market. These are: (1) the veterinarians, (2) drugstores, (3) farm-supply stores and cooperatives, (4) hatcheries, and (5) all other types (door-to-door, mail order, etc.).

As of the year of the new-product discovery, the relative importance of each type of outlet in the sale of pharmaceuticals was as shown in Exhibit 1.

EXHIBIT 1   Estimated annual sales by type of outlet, all animal-health pharmaceuticals (at manufacturer's level)

Type of outlet	Estimated sales ($000)	Percent of total sales
Veterinarian	$ 28,000	25
Drugstore	31,000	28
Farm-supply stores and cooperatives	35,000	32
Hatcheries	9,000	8
All other	8,000	7
	$111,000	100

Source: Company studies.

Among the more important pharmaceuticals included in the sales figures shown in Exhibit 1 are antibiotics, sulfa drugs, and anthelmintics.[1] The most important types of outlets for these three kinds of pharmaceuticals vary considerably, as is indicated in Exhibit 2.

---

[1]Anthelmintic—an agent to expel or destroy intestinal worms, thereby improving growth.

EXHIBIT 2

Pharmaceutical	Types of outlets listed in order of importance
Antibiotics	1st—DVMs; 2d—farm-supply stores; 3d—drugstores
Sulfa drugs	1st—drugstores; 2d—DVMs; 3d—farm-supply stores
Anthelmintics	1st—farm-supply stores; 2d—drugstores; 3d—DVMs

According to a company official, the proportion of pharmaceuticals administered to animals without diagnosis by a DVM varies widely by class of livestock and poultry and by disease being treated. The farmer can administer any and all pharmaceuticals to his animals if he so desires. If he believes he knows what the illness is, he may secure and administer what he thinks is the proper drug. His choice of what drug to give may be based on previous treatment of the same illness by a DVM, his own background in veterinary medicine, on the advice of his neighbors, or on information obtained from literature, advertising, and so on. If the animal does not readily respond, a DVM is normally called. Also, if the farmer does not have confidence in his own ability to diagnose a particular illness, he would usually call in the DVM to examine the animal and supervise the treatment. Since only 25 percent of the sales of animal-health pharmaceuticals are made through veterinarians, there is a strong implication that a large proportion of the drugs are administered by the farmer without the benefit of professional help.

Unless the advice of a DVM is required in the treatment of an animal, the buying habits of farmers do *not* differ in purchasing remedies for specific illnesses like mastitis, as opposed to vitamins, food supplements, and similar items.

STATEMENT OF PROBLEM

The research and development division of The Upjohn Company developed a new product called Corbiot for the treatment of mastitis in dairy cattle. Mastitis is a disease of milk cattle that renders the milk useless until the disease is cured. This results in a serious economic loss to the farmer. In most cases the farmer diagnoses mastitis without the services of a DVM. If he knows of a suitable remedy, he can administer it without the aid of a DVM. Where a case does not respond, however, a DVM is normally called.

Corbiot was proven to have definite advantages over any product on the market at that time. However, it was suspected that competitors would, in a relatively short time, have a similar product on the market. It was believed that six months to a year would be the maximum time in which Upjohn could hope to maintain its competitive advantage.

The estimated market for mastitis products at that time was in the neighborhood of $5 million at manufacturers' level or close to $10 million at retail level. While good estimates of the breakdown of this market, by types of outlet, were not available, it was assumed that it approximated the breakdown of all animal-health pharmaceuticals as shown in Exhibit 1.

Under the company's basic sales and distribution policies, the product, if announced, would be placed with and actively promoted to veterinarians, who accounted for 25 percent of the market. However, without active promotion to farmers it was doubtful whether Upjohn could expect active introductory sales support from druggists. If Upjohn actively promoted the new product to farmers, it was feared that serious objection would be raised by the veterinarians, possibly to the point where they would not only refuse to accept the new product but would also discontinue use of other Upjohn products.

The key question facing Upjohn management, therefore, was that of determining what marketing strategy would maximize the returns from the new-product discovery. The effect of its decision upon the existing sales of other products to veterinarians, as well as its effect upon sales of human-health products, was also a major part of this problem.

The importance of establishing sound distribution and sales policies for this new product was underscored by the fact that two other products were nearing the end of the development period and would soon be ready for marketing. It was also anticipated that other products would be forthcoming in the future as Upjohn's research and development work gathered impetus.

ALTERNATIVES

In evaluating the problem, Upjohn's management listed and considered the following alternatives:

1. Announce this product only to the veterinarian. It was realized that under this alternative the company would be competing in only 25 percent of the potential market for the product.

2. Follow the basic company policy of announcing the product both to the DVM and the drugstore, with no direct consumer advertising (i.e., advertising to the farmer). Without promotion to the farmer, the druggist could be expected to provide little active support for the product,

even though he accounted for 28 percent of the animal-health products market.

3.   Announce the new product both to the DVM and the drugstore, but also back the druggist with heavy consumer advertising (i.e., advertising directed to farmers). Here the company would be actively competing in 53 percent of the market (25 percent for DVM + 28 percent for drugstore). However, Upjohn would be taking the risk of the veterinarian's disfavor, a reaction that might possibly affect the entire line. In the past, other pharmaceutical companies had tried to simultaneously promote their products to farmers and sell DVMs. In these cases, the reaction of the DVMs had been negative, but the degree of the resulting buying resistance had not been measured. It was the observation of this experience that led Upjohn officials to anticipate unfavorable reactions from DVMs if Corbiot were heavily promoted to farmers. Some of the drugs distributed by competitors through channels other than DVMs were advertised to farmers; others were not.

4.   Follow alternative 3, reaching DVMs and drugstores by direct sale, but also add jobbers to obtain distribution in other farm outlets (i.e., farm-supply stores, co-ops, hatcheries, and so on). It was thought that jobbers would have to be allowed a 20 percent margin to get them to handle the line. From the standpoint of the farmer, purchase of Corbiot through outlets other than the DVM would offer the advantages of (1) convenience, (2) availability of credit, and (3) possibly a lower price. This plan would provide active competition in 100 percent of the market, but might result in a stronger DVM reaction than that anticipated in reaction to alternative 3.

5.   Sell under one trade name for the veterinarian market, and select a second trade name for sales to all other outlets. The product having the second name would then be advertised to farmers. It was not known what the DVMs' reaction would be to such a plan, but it was suspected that there would be at least some objection.

6.   Announce the new product to the veterinarian under the Upjohn label, and also either sell the product to another company for distribution to other outlets under its label or have Upjohn produce for marketing under private labels for feed companies and/or distribution. It was recognized that by giving up the marketing of the new product to all outlets except the veterinarians, Upjohn would have to share the profit from the research discovery with others.

7.   Form a subsidiary company or acquire another company with established distribution in outlets other than the DVMs. This alternative would give distribution under a different brand name in the missing type of outlets and might overcome the DVMs' objections to alternatives 3 and 4. However, this alternative raised the serious question of whether one or two products, plus future expectations which could not be fairly evaluated at the time, were enough to warrant such a drastic step.

QUESTIONS

1. Assuming no change in brand policy, which of the first four alternatives should the company choose? Why? (Disregard alternatives 5 through 7 in this phase of the analysis.)

2. Next broaden your analysis to take into consideration the possible changes in brand policy outlined in alternatives 5, 6, and 7. Which line of action would you now recommend? Why?

ROSSMOOR ELECTRIC, INC. (A)*

Subscription cable television service for Leisure World

Early in 1977, Ivan Foley, president, Rossmoor Electric, Inc., had become aware of a growing interest in pay-television entertainment in the communities surrounding Leisure World, Laguna Hills, California. Several pay television program distributors had contacted Foley as well as officials of Golden Rain Foundation, owner of Leisure World Cable Television System. Since Rossmoor Electric was operating and maintaining this cable system under contract with Golden Rain Foundation, Foley wondered whether there might be a potential market for pay television entertainment in Leisure World. If so, how might Rossmoor Electric capitalize upon this opportunity? Foley set about investigating the various alternatives available.

LEISURE WORLD COMMUNITY

Leisure World is an adult community located in Laguna Hills, California. As of 1978, it was a successful, self-contained private community with 12,541 residences. At that time the developer, Rossmoor Corpora-

---

*Written by James D. Scott, Professor Emeritus of Marketing, Graduate School of Business Administration, The University of Michigan, a resident of Leisure World.

tion, planned to build another 452 units during 1978–79. If these plans materialized, the community would consist of 12,993 residences and a population of about 23,000 people.

Since development of Leisure World began in 1964, the Rossmoor Corporation has followed the practice of constructing a group of residences in a specified area, or "village," and offering them for sale to individuals. Each "village" is then organized into a mutual corporation which manages the performance of specified maintenance, landscaping, and service functions for the benefit of all its residents. Then Rossmoor Corporation moves its construction activity into an adjacent area and the process is repeated with the creation of another mutual corporation. In this manner, necessary community functions and services are extended step by step as the population grows.

As of 1978, there were seven mutual corporations. One, United Laguna Hills Mutual, consists entirely of cooperative manors; the other six consist of condominiums. Each mutual elects its own board of directors. They in turn elect the directors of Golden Rain Foundation, a nonprofit corporation which owns and operates community facilities for the benefit of all members. These facilities include clubhouses, streets, recreation areas, minibus service, security, and a community cable television system.

The individual boards of directors of the mutual corporations and Golden Rain Foundation set the policies for their respective geographic areas and for the community at large. The Golden Rain Foundation and each mutual contract with Professional Community Management, Inc., an independent management firm, to manage the operations of the community.

ROSSMOOR ELECTRIC, INC.

Rossmoor Electric, Inc., located in Laguna Hills, California, is an electrical contractor that is independent of Rossmoor Corporation, developer of Leisure World. Under contract with the developer, the firm has engineered and constructed Leisure World Cable Television System step by step as the community has grown. This cable system consists of a community antenna which receives, processes, amplifies, and distributes television and FM programs through an underground coaxial cable to the homes of Leisure World residents. It cost $1,083,000 to build the system, which had an estimated replacement value of $2,231,400 as of early 1977. The Leisure World cable system provides residents with excellent reception of 10 Los Angeles TV stations, and two San Diego TV stations, and 13 FM stations in the area.

In addition, Rossmoor Electric has operated and maintained the cable system under contract with Golden Rain Foundation since 1966. The

firm also took over the operation and maintenance of the Leisure World closed-circuit television station, Channel 6, in January 1970. In order to maintain and operate both the cable system and Channel 6, Rossmoor Electric finds it desirable to invest in certain equipment and to provide adequate working capital. The amount of these investments, as of June 1976, was reported as follows:

	Equipment inventory	Operating capital	Total capital investment
To supply and maintain the Leisure World cable system	$133,143		
Less depreciation	61,913		
	$71,230	$50,000	$121,230
To support Channel 6 productions	$179,380		
Less depreciation	70,124		
	$109,256	24,000	133,256
Total capital investment			$254,486

Further insight into the operations of Rossmoor Electric is revealed by the statement it provided to Golden Rain Foundation on its estimated operating costs and profits for the year 1977. This information follows:

	LW cable system	Channel 6 productions
Estimated cost of operation	$352,677	$134,819
7½ percent profit	26,451	10,111
Total	$379,128	$144,930
Less estimated advertising revenue		25,000
		$119,930

Payment for the maintenance and operation of the Leisure World cable system and Channel 6 is determined by a contract that is negotiated periodically between Golden Rain Foundation and Rossmoor Electric. The total per manor per month was reported as follows in the *Leisure World News,* November 2, 1978:

1977	$3.51
1978	3.54
1979	3.75

By comparison, as of December 31, 1977, the average charge per month for television service provided by all cable systems in the United States was $7.[1] In Leisure World, PCM, Inc., collected the monthly charge for cable television system each month along with other charges levied to cover the cost of services and function performed by the mutuals and by Golden Rain Foundation. For 1978, the total charge per month per manor was $70.37; for 1979, it was set at $93.17.[2] As of early 1977,

---

[1] Paul Kagan Associates, Inc., *Census as of Dec. 31, 1977 of Pay-Cable Systems,* p. 12.

[2] *Leisure World News,* November 2, 1978, p. 1.

11,400 manors were connected to the Leisure World cable system. At that time it was estimated that 85 percent of Leisure World residents had two color television sets.

Ivan Foley had observed the introduction of pay cable entertainment service in several nearby communities. The spread of this entertainment service appeared to be explained, in part, by the fact that such programs were broadcast without the intrusion of commercials and by the fact that they made available movies in their original form—unedited and uncut. Foley wondered whether the subscribers to the Leisure World cable television system might like such entertainment and whether it might be profitable to propose its introduction to the Golden Rain Foundation.

After a meeting with the directors of Golden Rain Foundation in mid-February, 1977, Foley asked M. H. Waterman, president, GRF, Inc., whether he knew anything about pay cable entertainment. Waterman said that he did not but that he was acquainted with a new resident of Leisure World—J. D. Scott—who was interested in the subject. Scott, a recently retired professor of marketing, was doing research on pay TV entertainment under a grant from the Graduate School of Business Administration of the University of Michigan, Ann Arbor. Foley telephoned Scott shortly thereafter, and the two met to discuss pay television on February 28. On that occasion, Scott furnished Foley with a copy of his recently completed manuscript, "Bringing Premium Entertainment into the Home via Pay Cable TV."[3] He also provided copies of a recent census of pay cable systems showing when such service had begun, the rate per month charged to subscribers, and the penetration achieved. The introduction and growth of pay television in the Leisure World area is demonstrated by the selected data from the census provided in Exhibit 1.

From the *Pay TV Newsletter*, published by Paul Kagan Associates, Inc., Foley also noted information on the growth of pay television throughout the United States. Thus, as of December 31, 1976, pay cable entertainment was operating in 364 cable systems throughout the United States. The service had been offered to 4.37 million cable subscribers in areas in which the cable passed 9.19 million homes, or about one third of the cable television industry, which had an estimated 13 million subscribers as of that date. As of December 31, 1976, pay cable service had been accepted by 977,809 subscribers, or 10.6 percent of the homes passed by cable and 22.4 percent of the basic cable subscribers. The average pay cable monthly rate (estimated pay cable revenue divided by number of subscribers) was $7.87.[4] The average monthly rate for basic cable system

---

[3]James D. Scott, *Bringing Premium Entertainment into the Home via Pay Cable TV*, Michigan Business Reports no. 61 (Ann Arbor: Division of Research, Graduate School of Business Administration, The University of Michigan, 60 pp.). Copyright © 1977.

[4]Paul Kagan Associates, Inc., *Pay TV Newsletter,* February 16, 1977, p. 1.

EXHIBIT 1 Pay-television entertainment in southern California: Introduction and growth as of December 31, 1976

Cable system	Date pay began	Program distributor	Rate per month			Penetration (Pay subs ÷ Basic cable subs)
			Pay	Basic	Com-bined	
San Diego	March 1973	Cox Channel 100	$11.00	$6.50	$17.50	11.6%
Long Beach	March 1973	Showtime	8.50	7.00	15.50	53.5
Los Angeles	April 1974	Telenation				
		Program Services	8.95	8.45	17.40	46.2
Oxnard	June 1975	Pay TV Services	3.75	6.95	10.70	45.0
Burbank	May 1976	Telenation				
		Program Services	9.95	6.50	16.45	18.2
Lompoc	Aug. 1976	Home Box Office	9.95	7.00	16.95	7.6
San Bernardino	Oct. 1976	Home Box Office	9.95	7.50	17.45	10.4

Source: Paul Kagan Associates, Inc., *Census as of Dec. 31, 1976 of Pay-Cable Systems Operational on Sept. 30, 1976.* Estimates of Paul Kagan Associates, Inc., Rockville Centre, New York, published with the *Pay TV Newsletter,* February 16, 1977, passim.

was $6.72; thus the combined rate for both pay cable and the basic cable system was $14.59.

During March 1977 and the first half of April, Foley was busy supervising the expansion of the Leisure World cable system into a new village that was being developed by Rossmoor Corporation in the community, and so he did not meet with Scott again until April 19. On that occasion Foley explained that Rossmoor Electric, Inc., had reached an agreement with Golden Rain Foundation concerning the terms of the contract to maintain and operate both the Leisure World cable system and the community's closed-circuit television station, Channel 6. The combined total for the performance of these services was set at $3.54 for 1978 and $3.75 for 1979. This contract covered a five-year term, beginning on January 1, 1977. Accordingly, Rossmoor Electric was assured of continuity in its business arrangements with Golden Rain Foundation.

Since one aspect of Scott's research concerned the introduction of two-way interactive cable services in order to provide home security (burglar alarm monitoring, medical alert), the initial topic of discussion concerned the feasibility of supplying such service via the Leisure World cable system.[5] (CATV firms use coaxial cable to transmit commercial television programs "downstream" from subscribers to the head end of the system. This ability has encouraged cable operators to consider the possibility of offering a variety of two-way interactive cable services to consumers, institutions, and businesses. In 1977, such services were still in the experimental and testing stages.)

Foley was well informed on the technical aspects of two-way interactive services and called attention to a June 1976 report in the *Los Angeles Times* concerning a recent decision by the Newport Beach City Council to offer residents an opportunity to have home alarms wired into a computerized police dispatch system for the quickest possible response.[6] The City Council gave the go-ahead by budgeting $89,000 for the computerized alarm system. It was counting on receiving $72,000 in fees from persons who plugged into the system. Newport Beach residents would also be able to use their home alarms to report burglaries, fires, and medical emergencies. They would be tied to the police station either by telephone or cable television. The city's alarm dispatch system was expected to be in operation by October or November 1976.

According to Foley, it would be simpler to provide for a computerized home security system as new manors were constructed than to install the

---

[5]For background on two-way interactive services, see James D. Scott, *Cable Television: Strategy for Penetrating Key Urban Markets*, Michigan Business Reports no. 58 (Ann Arbor: Division of Research, Graduate School of Business Administration, The University of Michigan), chap. 2, "Two-way Interactive Cable Services," pp. 32–86. Copyright 1976.

[6]Thomas Fortune, "Computerized Home Alarm System OK'd, Direct Link with Police," *Los Angeles Times*, June 9, 1976, pp. 1, 6.

necessary equipment in the older homes in Leisure World. In the spring of 1977, there were 1,032 manors in the newer villages of Leisure World to which the service could be added with little cost—say, $100,000. The older manors in the community, however, would require a higher cost per unit to add the two-way interactive capacity to the existing cable equipment—in total, such a project would probably cost $500,000. Given the prevailing cost consciousness among Leisure World residents, Foley doubted there would be any widespread desire in the community to emulate Newport Beach and install a two-way interactive alarm system. Nevertheless, it was recognized that Leisure World residents had manifested a degree of interest in security in choosing a home in a community with gate guards and protective walls.

PAY TELEVISION ENTERTAINMENT

The discussion then turned to the potential for pay television entertainment in Leisure World. The growth of pay entertainment in various communities in southern California and the acceptance of such service by cable television subscribers had led Foley to think that there might be a profitable demand for such service if it were offered to Leisure World cable subscribers. He had noted two alternative ways of charging for pay television service: (1) per program, as introduced on the Mission Cable television system in San Diego; and (2) per channel, in which the subscriber pays a flat charge per month, regardless of how many programs he or she views during that period. The per channel approach is a simpler method of billing than the per program approach.

In March 1973, for example, Mission Cable TV, Inc., of San Diego, leased one of its channels to Optical Systems Channel 100, which offered subscription entertainment on a per program basis. Channel 100 paid Mission Cable 10 percent of pay entertainment revenue for the use of the channel. Under the Channel 100 per program plan, the subscriber was required to deposit $20–$25 for the per program converter. He then bought keypunched plastic tickets at a price of $2.25 for seven days of unlimited use for any movies shown on the pay cable channel, of $6.50 for a monthly pass, or of $7.50 for a package of tickets for five basketball games.

The pay entertainment was converted to Channel 13, transmitted in "scrambled" form, and then had to be decoded before the subscriber could view it. Each converter had an individual code which identified the subscriber; the plastic tickets had this code number stamped upon them; when a ticket was inserted into the converter, the computer at the head end recorded the program choice and the subscriber so that his bill could be computed and mailed at the end of the month.

The Optical Systems Channel 100 service was a very sophisticated pay

entertainment approach. Within three months after its introduction, Channel 100 had secured 5,000 subscribers, but as time went by, it experienced difficulty with "piracy" of programs. In 1977, American Television & Communications (ATC), Mission Cable's parent company, canceled its lease contract with Optical Systems. According to Paul Kagan's *TV Newsletter,* one of the reasons for the cancellation was piracy, which "had had a material adverse effect on subscriber penetration." ATC said, "Conservative estimates, with which we believe Optical agrees, are that there are over 7,000 illegal subscribers to the Optical System's [Channel 100]. Since Optical has reported 13,800 subscribers, illegals are apparently 50 percent of legals."[7]

Subsequent developments illustrate the use of the per channel method of billing. In February 1975, San Diego made a second pay channel available to Home Box Office, which offered its programs on a flat charge per month. One channel on the cable system was already tied up with Optical Systems Channel 100, and the cable management apparently wished to try the competing Home Box Office service. By December 31, 1977, the HBO pay service had achieved pay penetration of basic cable subscribers of 33.7 percent with a monthly charge of $9.95 in addition to an $8.25 price for basic cable service, or a combined rate of $18.20.

Observation of these developments had led Foley to believe that at the outset any pay television service offered in Leisure World should be on a monthly subscription basis. Later, when equipment which would prevent program piracy had been perfected, it might be advantageous to switch to a per program format.

Some observers believed that the per program approach was the technical system to which many cable operators would turn in the future. With the per program approach, the subscriber pays only for programs actually viewed, not for the entire month's programs, many of which would not interest certain viewers. In a community in which everyone is 52 years of age or older, and in which there are a large number of widows—and no children—only some of the items offered during a typical week's programming might appeal to the potential audience. If pay entertainment were offered on a per program basis, then the subscriber could pick and choose, and pay only for what was viewed.

From the point of view of the cable operator, per program equipment makes it possible to get immediate feedback on the relative popularity of each entertainment feature. Such information makes it possible to improve program appeal by offering the kind of material that subscribers "buy" and by avoiding the scheduling of items that have proved unpopular in the past.

While these are real benefits, the experience of Optical Systems Chan-

---

[7]Paul Kagan Associates, Inc., *Pay TV Newsletter,* August 1, 1977, p. 4.

nel 100 with program piracy makes it clear that designing per program converters is a difficult task. While it had been reported that such converters had been developed—one by Oak Industries—they were costlier than those used in the per channel approach.

In his contacts with pay TV program distributors, Foley had learned that there were four basic ways in which such entertainment was made available: (1) by stand-alone, in which programs were supplied on videotape, and accordingly might be custom-made to meet the interests of the individual community served; (2) by microwave and coaxial cable transmission from some central studio; (3) by satellite transmissions which were received by "dishes," or ground stations, near the head end of the cable system; (4) by scrambled over-the-air broadcasts which were picked up by homeowners' antennas and descrambled for viewing. These different methods of program transmission involved such differences as varying amounts of capital investment, varying ability to meet community entertainment interests, and variations in the character of the program mix.

In considering whether to suggest the addition of pay television service to the programs currently being offered over the Leisure World cable system, Foley had to analyze these alternatives and reach a decision on which of them to propose to Golden Rain Foundation as a means of providing local pay television entertainment. This was the type of analysis in which Scott had a research interest. Since there appeared to be an opportunity for mutually advantageous cooperation, it was agreed that Scott should work informally with Foley as he explored the possibility of proposing pay cable television service for the Leisure World Cable Television System. Foley expected to be working actively on this analysis during the next three or four months.

SATELLITE TRANSMISSION—HOME BOX OFFICE

Early in June 1977, Lisa Forrestal Connor, Western regional manager, Home Box Office, called on Foley to explain the HBO program service. HBO, a subsidiary of Time Inc., supplied pay entertainment service to 234 cable systems with 585,981 subscribers as of December 31, 1976, thus reaching 59.9 percent of the pay cable market (see Exhibit 2).[8] HBO was, accordingly, the largest pay television program distributor. TeleMation Program Services, an HBO subsidiary, ranked second, with a 21.2 percent market share; Self-booked Systems ranked third, with 6.4 percent of the market; Optical Systems Channel 100 fourth, with 4.5 percent; and Showtime fifth, with 2.6 percent.

Originally HBO had distributed pay entertainment via microwave

---

[8]Paul Kagan Associates, Inc., *Pay TV Newsletter*, February 16, 1977, p. 2.

EXHIBIT 2   Pay cable distributor/bookers, with market shares

Distributor	Number of systems booked		Number of subscribers		Percent share of pay cable market	
	6/30/76	12/31/76	6/30/76	12/31/76	6/30/76	12/31/76
Home Box Office	156	234	474,759	585,981	62.0%	59.9%
TeleMation Program Services*	41	40	178,173	207,705	23.3	21.2
Self-booked systems	19	23	43,902	62,618	5.7	6.4
Optical Systems Channel 100	16	15	48,636	44,308	6.4	4.5
Showtime	—	10	—	25,213	—	2.6
Hollywood Home Theatre	—	4	—	17,493	—	1.8
Pay TV Services	6	10	12,753	17,364	1.7	1.7
BestVision	12	23	4,636	9,733	0.6	1.0
Cineamerica	3	5	2,519	7,394	0.3	0.7
	253	364	766,100	977,809	100.0%	100.0%

*TeleMation figures include three systems booked by TPS, distributed by National Professional Services. TeleMation also supplies films for 26,150 apartment pay subscribers; HBO for 12,000 apartments.

Source: Paul Kagan Associates, Inc., *Pay TV Newsletter*, February 16, 1977, p. 2.

and coaxial cable primarily to four states in the northeastern United States. The firm added distribution via the RCA-Americom satellite communications network in the fall of 1975, thus making its program service available nationwide to any cable system willing to invest in an earth station receiver. The growth in pay subscribers resulting from the move to satellite distribution of programs is demonstrated by the following record of subscriber homes served by HBO: December 1974, 57,000 (before satellite distribution); 1975, 250,000; and 1976, 600,000.[9] The HBO network rose to 350 cable and Multiple Distribution Point (MDP) systems with June–early July start-ups. As of July 1977, it had 108 operating earth stations (32 systems being fed by satellite in Florida alone) and 95 systems getting terrestrial feeds from earth stations.[10]

HBO operated as a programming/marketing company. It provided a balanced mixture of current first-run feature movies, live sports events from around the country, and special interest programs for both children and adults—approximately 12 hours a day. The HBO program schedule for April 22–28, 1977, is presented in Exhibit 3 as an indication of the type of entertainment provided by this program source, A description of HBO program plans for the fall season 1977 is provided in Appendix B, a letter from the vice president—affiliate relations, HBO, to cable system managers.

Connor inspected the Leisure World Cable Television System in Foley's company and also toured Leisure World in order to become acquainted with the lifestyle and the demographic breakdown of the residents. She learned that Leisure World was conceived, designed, and built by Rossmoor Corporation to appeal to adults 52 years of age and older. A successful, self-contained private community, it had 12,541 residences and a population of about 20,000 as of 1977. Another 452 units were to be constructed during 1980–82 according to the Rossmoor Corporation's master plan for the development of the area. At the conclusion of the final phase of construction, therefore, there would be about 13,000 residences and about 23,000 people in Leisure World.

In discussing the HBO program distribution plan with Foley, Connor explained that an investment of $40,800 would be required in order to bring in the HBO program service, which was transmitted via satellite. Installation of a small earth station receiver plus an encoder would be required. Connor offered to make a five-year pro forma cash flow projection of revenues and expenses, an estimate of the time required to break even on the investment, as well as the interval rate of return on the investment required to introduce pay television and build up a market for the service. She and Foley agreed upon the business and financial

---

[9] "Home Box Office, Nation's Pay Cable Television Pioneer, Notes Fifth Year in Operation November 8," HBO press release, New York, New York, 1977.

[10] Paul Kagan Associates, Inc., *Pay TV Newsletter,* July 15, 1977, p. 2.

EXHIBIT 3   HBO *Program Schedule:* Typical week—April 22–28, 1977

SCHEDULE

APRIL 22-28

● SYMBOL INDICATES PROGRAM MAY BE PRE-EMPTED BY A PLAYOFF

THURSDAY, Apr. 22
12:30 MAN IN THE GLASS BOOTH (1:57)
2:30 MEMORY OF US (PG—1:34)
4:30 MARTHA'S ATTIC: BE A BUILDER
5:00 THE GOALKEEPER LIVES ON OUR STREET (0:51)
6:00 PERFORMING ARTS SERIES BLACK MUSIC IN AMERICA
● 6:30 MEMORY OF US (PG—1:34)
● 8:30 FRAMED (R—1:46)
● 10:30 BEYOND THE DOOR (R—1:38)

FRIDAY, Apr. 23
12:30 SPOTS (G—1:26)
2:00 AMERICAN FILM THEATRE MAN IN THE GLASS BOOTH (1:57)
4:00 FAMILY FEATURE SPOTS (G—1:26)
5:30 NANOOK OF THE NORTH
● 6:30 THE PALLISERS: EPISODE 24
● 7:30 THE PALLISERS: EPISODE 25
● 8:30 LES FOLIES BERGERES
● 10:30 FREEBIE AND THE BEAN (R—1:53)

SATURDAY, Apr. 24
12:30 MASTERS OF BALLANTRAE PARTS 1 AND 2
3:30 ANIMATED SPECIAL THE SEVEN RAVENS
4:00 THE GOALKEEPER LIVES ON OUR STREET (0:51)
5:00 MAN AND BOY (G—1:38)
● 7:00 BREAKOUT (PG—1:36)
● 9:00 ON LOCATION RODNEY DANGERFIELD
● 10:00 LES FOLIES BERGERES

SUNDAY, Apr. 25
12:30 PERFORMING ARTS SERIES BLACK MUSIC IN AMERICA
1:00 TWO ENGLISH GIRLS (1:48)
3:00 PERFORMING ARTS SERIES MIME OF MARCEL MARCEAU
3:30 PAPER TIGER (G—1:41)
5:30 THE PALLISERS: EPISODE 25
● 6:30 FAMILY FEATURE PAPER TIGER (G—1:41)
● 8:30 OPEN SEASON (R—1:43)
● 10:30 TWO ENGLISH GIRLS (1:48)

Royal Flash. Malcolm McDowell stars as a 19th century swashbuckling rascally rogue accidentally thrust into valor. This ribald adaptation of George MacDonald Fraser's bestselling scoundrel casts Florinda Bolkan as famed courtesan Lola Montez and Oliver Reed as the scheming Otto von Bismarck and Britt Ekland as McDowell's fiancée. *Premieres April 26.* (PG—1:39)

Les Folies Bergeres. The real star is the spectacle as sensational costumes, semi-nude, long-legged show-girls and vaudeville acts highlight a musical revue of the 107-year-old history of the music hall. Las Vegas' leading floor show comes to you from the Tropicana Hotel April 23, 24 and 27.

The Wind and the Lion. Sean Connery is featured as a Berber chieftain in this lavish story book adventure of the international repercussions that erupt when he kidnaps American Candice Bergen and her two children. Brian Keith co-stars as the outraged President Teddy Roosevelt, while John Huston portrays Secretary of State John Hay. *Premieres April 26.* (PG—1:59)

Jules and Jim. Director François Truffaut's charming thesis studies the delicate interplay between love, companionship and social climate. The film casts Oskar Werner and Henri Serre as best friends in love with Jeanne Moreau. This subtitled cinematic classic is based on a novel by Henri-Pierre Roché. *Premieres April 28.* (1:44)

The Space Explorers. An astronaut's son stows away on a rocket launched to rescue his father from outer space in this cartoon feature. "The finest film of its kind I have ever seen,"

says Dr. Franklyn Branley, Associate Astronomer of the Hayden Planetarium. *Premieres April 27.* (1:00)

Beyond the Door. Faustian pact buys a man ten more years of life, but at a devilish rate of exchange. (R—1:38)

Freebie and the Bean. James Caan and Alan Arkin are a pair of off-beat cops in San Francisco. (R—1:53)

Juggernaut. Madman plants bombs on a luxury liner and demands $1.5 million. Richard Harris stars. (PG—1:50)

The Pallisers: Episode 26. Plantagenet, now alone, must resolve his children's problems as the series ends.

ABA Playoffs. Denver has David Thompson, New York has Julius Erving. Both score, rebound, block, dominate. Dan Issel and playmaker Ralph Simpson will also bolster the Nuggets. Guards John Williamson and Brian Taylor should also aid the Nets. But there are other teams to contend with, especially San Antonio with George Gervin and Bill Paultz, and Kentucky with Artis Gilmore and Bird Averitt.

MONDAY, Apr. 26
12:30 ROYAL FLASH (PG—1:39)
2:30 MEMORY OF US (PG—1:34)
4:30 CHILDREN'S SPECIAL SKINNY AND FATTY
5:30 MONDAY NIGHT MOVIE ROYAL FLASH (PG—1:39)
7:30 PROFESSIONAL WRESTLING Direct from Madison Square Garden in New York City
● 10:00 MONDAY NIGHT MOVIE THE WIND AND THE LION (PG—1:59)

TUESDAY, Apr. 27
12:30 THE VOYAGE (PG—1:43)
2:30 JUGGERNAUT (PG—1:50)
4:30 MARTHA'S ATTIC: BOTTLENOSE?
5:00 YOUNG PEOPLE'S FEATURE THE SPACE EXPLORERS (1:00)
6:00 PERFORMING ARTS SERIES THE ART OF THE IMPOSSIBLE
● 6:30 JUGGERNAUT (PG—1:50)
● 8:30 LES FOLIES BERGERES Direct from Las Vegas
● 10:30 THE VOYAGE (PG—1:43)

WEDNESDAY, Apr. 28
12:30 PERFORMING ARTS SERIES MIME OF MARCEL MARCEAU
1:00 JULES AND JIM (SUB—1:44)
3:00 YOUNG PEOPLE'S SPECIAL THE VIOLIN
3:30 THE WIND AND THE LION (PG—1:59)
5:30 THE PALLISERS: EPISODE 26
● 6:30 THE WIND AND THE LION (PG—1:59)
● 8:30 FOREIGN FEATURES JULES AND JIM (SUB—1:44)
● 10:30 TWO ENGLISH GIRLS (1:48)

assumptions that were required in order to work out the projections. She then returned to the HBO regional office and used the HBO computer to work out the pro forma projections. The results were transmitted to Foley by letter on June 27, 1977. (See Appendix C for the HBO presentation.)

The highlights of the HBO analysis were as follows:

1. HBO suggested a retail price to subscribers of $8 per month, although the price could vary from $7 to $10 according to local option. Of this amount, 50 percent, or $4, would go to HBO for program service. HBO would bring subscribers eight motion pictures per month, top-notch sports events, and entertainment specials.

2. The time required to cover the necessary capital investment in pay television equipment, and to cover interest at 10 percent on that investment, would be a little over three years:

Capital required:

Terminal equipment	$ 72,000	
Earth station, encoder	40,800	$112,800

Cash flows, years 1-3	
($31,377 + $39,616 + $38,901)	109,894
Balance	$ (2,906)
Cash flow, years 4 and 5	
($38,115 + $37,250)	75,365
Balance after recovery of capital	$ 72,459

3. The return on capital invested in the pay television project was shown as follows:

Capital needed	$112,800
Plus interest	12,612
Total	$125,412
Cash flow, five years	185,259
Cash flow after capital and interest	$ 59,847

Return on investment: $59,847 ÷ $112,800 = 53 percent

4. Connor concluded her presentation with the following comment: "Ivan, even at 15 percent penetration the projections look excellent. At a 10 percent discount rate, you would enjoy an interval rate of return of 78.2 percent over a five-year period, and your cash flow becomes positive early in the third year."

In discussing Connor's five-year projections with Scott, Ivan Foley commented that he believed the HBO program service could get 10 percent of Leisure World cable viewers to subscribe during the first year of operation. Connor of HBO would provide assistance and advice in planning the marketing effort during the start-up period. Rossmoor Electric would have to hire a marketing executive who would plan and execute the actual marketing effort. While HBO suggestions might be helpful, some of them would have to be modified to meet the special conditions of the Leisure World community. For example, HBO favored the use of personal solicitation for the pay entertainment introductory period. Since Golden Rain policies did not permit house-to-house solicitation, the message would have to be disseminated through other channels. Among the available possibilities were advertisements in the *Leisure World News,* promotional announcements over Leisure World Channel 6 television, and direct mail. HBO would provide advertising aids, program guides, and newsletters concerning future programs—all at a relatively low cost to Rossmoor Electric.

In short, a skillfully planned and executed marketing effort designed to introduce and sustain the HBO program service could be expected to achieve 10 percent penetration of Leisure World cable subscribers by

the end of the first year; in five years continued marketing effort plus word-of-mouth comment could result in 20 percent penetration.

Foley believed that acquisition of an earth station for Leisure World would be a real asset for purposes other than affiliation with HBO. Quite aside from pay entertainment, a number of firms had announced a variety of nonpay programs which were to be distributed via satellite. If the Leisure World cable system owned a ground receiver, such programs could easily be made available to cable subscribers.

In the summer of 1977, Scott was undertaking research on "Marketing CATV: Key Problems—Suggested Approaches to Their Solution." One important problem under investigation was that of increasing the penetration of cable systems in large metropolitan markets; the percentage of cable subscribers to total television homes was substantially smaller in the major television markets than in medium-sized communities, small towns, and rural areas. Among several alternative possibilities for making cable television more attractive to the target group, recent developments in satellite transmission of program material to cable systems throughout the United States had opened up the possibility of making attractive program material from distant sources available to cable subscribers.

As one means of gathering background material on this topic, Scott attended a seminar sponsored by the Cable Television Administration and Marketing Society, Inc., held in Los Angeles on July 25–27, 1977.[11] One of the important sessions of the seminar carried the title "Update on New Program Services," and this topic dominated the meetings. Among the nonpay entertainment program announcements made during the seminar were the following:

1.   Southern Satellite Systems, Inc., had leased channel space from RCA's Satcom II for resale to Channel 17, a strong independent over-the-air television station located in Atlanta, Georgia. Southern Satellite Systems offered WTCG to all cable systems for a flat 10 cents per subscriber per month, with a $3,000 monthly limit on what any single system paid. Systems paying in advance for the year could take advantage of a 20 percent discount.

Cable operators had found WTCG's program package attractive to their subscribers. As a result, by July 1977 SSS had signed 50 cable systems with approximately 500,000 subscribers to receive WTCG's Channel 17 via satellite. It was estimated that WTCG's potential cable television audience could be expanded to include another 1.5 to 2 million homes; two thirds of these would probably be in the South and Southwest, with the remaining third in other sections of the country.

In July 1977, Southern Satellite Systems announced plans for satellite

---

[11]See Paul Kagan Associates, Inc., *Pay TV Newsletter*, August 1, 1977, p. 3, for a brief report of the seminar.

distribution of KTVU-TV, Channel 2, in San Francisco, to cable television companies in the United States. This second independent television station was chosen for satellite distribution not only because of its outstanding audience appeal in the San Francisco market, but also in CATV systems then receiving Channel 2 via microwave as far away as Oregon and Utah. KTVU, which reached a million homes in four states in July 1977, was expected to gain more than a million additional homes via satellite.

It was reported that KTVU had one of the finest movie libraries in the entire country. It was also the outstanding sports station in the northwestern United States. It had pioneered in specials—many of which were first runs. Satellite delivery of KTVU was scheduled to begin on August 1, 1978.

2.   A nonpay option that would become available in September 1977 was Madison Square Garden Sports, produced by Hughes Sports Network, which included 115 sports events that would be cablecast from the Garden in 1977–78. UA-Columbia Cablevision, Inc., national distributor of these events, planned to make satellite transmission available via RCA Satcom II Satellite. This package was described by one cable operator as "one of the best buys, economically speaking, that's available to the industry today."

3.   A representative of the Christian Broadcasting Network announced that its specialty religious programming had been made available to cable systems via satellite in May 1977. CBN was supplying 16 hours of religious programming via satellite to some 30 cable systems. Its offerings were made available to cable systems without cost. Cable operators might either carry the entire program schedule or select individual elements to fit the interests of their audiences. Certain cable operators had found that religious programs had considerable appeal among their viewers. Might not the Leisure World audience react in a similar way?

4.   Roy Mehlman of United Press International reported in July 1977 that his firm had installed and tested a complete system for the delivery of news via satellite. These tests promised large savings in the telephone toll charges incurred by UPI. In time, he said, it was likely that the UPI Newswire service would be delivered via satellite. He also announced that his firm would demonstrate a news picture service with an audio background during the fall of 1977. He claimed that the service would be entirely different from those currently available with audio news.

5.   John Goberman, Lincoln Center, New York City, noted that his organization had staged 220 separate cultural productions during the past year. The organization would like its program distributor to increase coverage, but the Lincoln Center needed additional funds to do so. How solve the problem of greater distribution of the center's pro-

grams? Under consideration in July 1977 was the organization of a network to deliver cultural programs—possibly via satellite. Such an arrangement would permit cable operators to achieve true diversity in their programming mix.

Scott reported these developments to Foley with the comment that they suggested the value of having an earth station in Leisure World. This reinforced Foley's own views on the matter.

APPOINTMENT OF PAY TV TASK FORCE

Several days prior to July 1, 1977, Morris J. Tobias, director of marketing, The TeleMine Company, Inc., a program distributor located in New York City, telephoned the following individuals in order to introduce the services of his firm and lay plans for a meeting in Laguna Hills during the week of July 11: M. H. Waterman, president, Golden Rain Foundation; Ivan Foley, president, Rossmoor Electric, Inc.; James D. Scott, resident of Leisure World; and Max Weingarten, PCM Inc. His telephone conversation with Tobias, together with the Tobias's request for a group meeting of the individuals named above, led Waterman to appoint a Task Force on Pay Television. His instructions to the task force were: (1) to determine whether it was desirable to add subscription (pay cable) entertainment to the programs currently being offered by the Leisure World Cable Television System; and if so, (2) to analyze the offers being made by alternative pay cable program distributors and suggest an approach to choosing a supplier of such programs. The members of the task force were: Robert L. Price, director of special projects, PCM Inc., chairman; Ivan Foley, owner of Rossmoor Electric, Inc.; and James D. Scott, resident, professor emeritus of marketing, The University of Michigan.

Membership on the task force provided Foley with an opportunity to participate in the fact-gathering process concerning the alternative program distributors that should be considered if pay entertainment were to be added to the Leisure World Cable Television System. Participation in the analysis of the task force findings also helped him to crystallize his own ideas about the opportunities and challenges in the pay cable business.

STAND-ALONE PROGRAM DISTRIBUTORS—BESTVISION, INC.

BestVision Inc. is a program distributor that specializes in serving cable television systems which wish to operate on a stand-alone basis. The firm has its headquarters in Glendale, Arizona, and in 1977 70 percent of its affiliated systems were located in western states. At that

time it served cable television systems with over 90,000 basic subscribers. By offering high-quality programs designed to meet the special interests of the community served, BestVision had helped its affiliates achieve relatively good acceptance of pay television by basic cable subscribers.

When Ivan Bigelow, vice president/marketing, BestVision Inc., called on Foley late in June 1977, the discussion focused on the possibility of supplying a pay television service to the residents of Leisure World at the minimum possible cost. Foley reasoned that the most economical approach to supplying pay service would be an arrangement in which all Leisure World cable subscribers would be required to take the pay entertainment programs. This, of course, would require the approval of Golden Rain Foundation's board of directors and would have to be viewed by the board as a service that most residences would want.

Accordingly, Foley asked Bigelow for a program price quotation and cost estimates on a proposed service at the lowest possible feasible figures. Bigelow gave the matter careful study and reported back on July 5, 1977. Excerpts from his letter follow:

> The attached proposal supports our discussion and your preference for a flat rate increase.
>
> Assuming you can get a $1.50 increase, your net revenue would be $3,200 per month. BestVision needs $1.20 for the services described. We do not dictate what the ultimate subscriber rate should be, but if a higher rate than $1.50 were available, we could adjust the program format to give you a heavier schedule.
>
> Please consider the proposal, and I will contact you shortly for discussion.
>
> *Programming format:* (a) Four premiere motion pictures per month, G & PG only. (b) One classic motion picture or children's program, etc.
>
> *System operator costs:* (a) $390 per month cassette fee. (b) $1.20 per month per subscriber to cover all royalty, booking, scheduling, marketing, and administrative costs.

STAND-ALONE DISTRIBUTORS—TELEMINE CO., INC., NEW YORK

Following up on his telephone conversations of late June 1977, Morris J. Tobias, director of marketing, TeleMine, Inc., made an appointment to meet with Leisure World representatives on July 12, 1977. Those present were: M. H. Waterman, president, Golden Rain Foundation; James D. Scott, professor emeritus of marketing, The University of Michigan; and Richard Morton, licensee, TeleMine of San Diego, Inc. Ivan Foley had a conflict and could not attend; Tobias planned to meet with him the following day.

TeleMine was a new entry in the pay cable stand-alone booking field; the firm had been franchising stand-alone cassette-apartment pay sys-

tems prior to 1977. As of May 1977, TeleMine had an estimated 1,500 subscribers out of 5,000 potential units. As a means of expanding into the pay cable field, the firm had appointed seven franchisees in various key markets throughout the United States. TeleMine of San Diego, Inc., was the licensee nearest to Leisure World; Richard Morton of that organization would provide day-by-day contact should TeleMine be chosen as Leisure World's program distributor.

The highlights of the TeleMine presentation are summarized below:

> TeleMine does not require heavy equipment investment in the form of cable, microwave, or earth station connections. Rather, TeleMine is a stand-alone service that connects directly to the cable system, with no need for capital investment on the part of the Leisure World cable system. Equipment in the form of automated programming devices, encoders, and modulators will be installed at Leisure World at no expense to Golden Rain Foundation or Rossmoor Electric, Inc.
>
> The encoder and modulator will be placed at the community system's head end. The automated programming device will fit comfortably into the existing studio facility without disrupting operations.
>
> TeleMine employs a stand-alone system that is adaptable to local needs. Each month, the programming delivered will be *selected exclusively* for Leisure World. Based on research of the Leisure World demographics, specialized entertainment programming will be developed. In addition, resident attitudes toward the TeleMine programming will be monitored regularly to keep a flow of information between our programming department and the Leisure World residents.
>
> Each month, TeleMine will provide eight currrent films to Leisure World. These films are not repeated in the ensuing months, as with other packages. In addition to movies, we offer entertainment specials with well-known performers, cultural events, plays, and educational programming. Most important, the nature of our system enables us to program our entertainment package directly to the tastes of the Leisure World residents.
>
> Two alternative marketing programs are proposed for you to choose between. Our first proposal is to lease both time and videotape equipment from Channel 6 and provide our service directly to those residents interested. TeleMine would maintain the master antenna system, promote the pay movie service, market the service, and install it. With the exception of providing the "vehicle," Rossmoor Electric would not be involved in the package. We would require four–six hours of time, seven days a week. TeleMine would supply its own personnel to operate equipment, promote, market, and install. We would lease the channel and equipment for $10,000 the first year, escalating to $12,000 annually by the end of our proposed five-year contract. In addition, we would pay Leisure World 10 percent of our gross subscriber revenue as a licensing fee, which should produce revenue in excess of $100,000 during our proposed five-year contract.
>
> The second possible approach is for TeleMine to sell its entertain-

ment package directly to Rossmoor Electric. Rossmoor would then, at its expense, promote, market, and install the system. TeleMine would only be the film supplier, though we would, of course, provide print material, marketing assistance, and the like, if requested. With this format, Rossmoor Electric has a different profit center.

Rather than receive lease channel and advertising revenue, Rossmoor would produce revenue through subscriber sales. Our charge to Rossmoor Electric would be $4.50 per month per subscriber, inclusive of all costs. However, with TeleMine it still has the advantage of a tailored product with no equipment costs.

No matter which program is decided upon, the entire package would be built around Leisure World rather than TeleMine. The cost to the subscriber is $8 per month, keeping a magic number of $1 per feature film.

In the discussion of the TeleMine proposal a question was raised as to whether the quality of the image on the viewer's screen would be as good with videotape projection as with programs received via satellite transmission and earth station reception. Tobias's response to this question follows:

> Let me point out, first, that no matter which pay television package is selected, all utilize first-generation videotape . . . whether supplied via satellite or done closed-circuit. No packager utilizes films directly. The major difference is that TeleMine supplies these first-generation tape cassettes directly to your location rather than broadcasting them regionally or nationwide via satellite or microwave distribution.
>
> It is just this difference that is critical to Leisure World. Because TeleMine supplies entertainment and educational products directly to the location, we are able to tailor our programming to fit Leisure World's particular demographics. TeleMine's unique programming service enables Leisure World residents to view a variety of films that they had a voice in selecting.

About a month later, Tobias wrote as follows:

> Just a brief note to describe a new TeleMine entertainment service. Beginning this fall, we shall videotape new Broadway shows, each to be viewed opening night throughout our network. This new package is owned exclusively by TeleMine.

Further discussion of the suggested lease arrangement, the first alternative described above, dealt with who would do the actual installation and maintenance work required. Since Rossmoor Electric had installed the cable television system and was currently responsible for maintaining it, the task force was reluctant to have another firm handle the installation work required by the TeleMine system. Tobias clarified this point by indicating that Rossmoor Electric would be contracted with to perform all of the service and installation work on an exclusive basis for the term of the agreement with Golden Rain. He suggested an installation

charge to subscribers of $19.95 to offset the costs of materials, labor, and equipment.

STAND-ALONE DISTRIBUTORS—TELEMATION PROGRAM SERVICES

TeleMation Program Services, a subsidiary of Home Box Office, served 40 cable systems early in 1977, accounting for 21.2 percent of the pay cable market. Accordingly, this firm ranked second in market share among the various pay cable distributors (see Exhibit 2). As a means of learning more about this firm's operations, Foley asked the HBO/ TeleMation Western regional manager to furnish a projected monthly profit and loss statement for a stand-alone operation in Leisure World. The statement is presented in Exhibit 4; the following explanatory notes relate to it.

EXHIBIT 4   Projected monthly operating statement: Stand-alone pay entertainment using TeleMation Program Services

Subscriber rate		$8.50
Number of pay subscribers (15 percent of 12,000)		1,800
Gross revenue (monthly)		$15,300
Expenses		
A. License fees at $2.31 per pay subscriber	$4,158	
1. Motion pictures (seven per month)		
2. Average cost of premieres at $0.33		
B. Cassettes—about $125 per title	875	
1. Mastering and duplicating: $110 per title		
2. Shipping (in and out): $15 per title		
C. TPS retainer	1,000	
Programming subtotal	$6,033	
D. Staff	1,200	
1. Operator/technician at $200 per week		
2. Clerical at $100 a week		
E. Marketing	2,700	
1. Program guides at $2,200		
a. Three-month format—total cost $6,600		
b. Four-color glossy paper, typewritten		
c. 12,000 copies, 16 pages		
2. Miscellaneous at $500		
F. Studio at $25,000		
1. 36-month depreciation	700	
Total cost		10,633
Operating profit (per month)		$ 4,667

Source: Correspondence, Western regional manager, HBO, Inc., September 2, 1977.

At a subscriber rate of $8.50 per month, assuming 15 percent penetration, 1,800 subscribers would provide $15,300 in gross monthly revenue. Programming expenses would total $6,033, or $3.35 per subscriber. Subtracting $3.35 from the subscriber rate of $8.50 leaves $5.15 per subscriber as a contribution to cover monthly staff costs of $1,200, monthly marketing expenses of $2,700, and a monthly depreciation charge of $700 on a studio equipment investment of $25,000 (36-month write-off). The total monthly expenses are thus estimated at $10,633. Revenue of $15,300 minus costs of $10,633 leaves an estimated profit of $4,667 per month.

In the September 2, 1977, letter accompanying these data, Lisa Connor, Western regional manager, commented as follows:

> Please note that your profit depends heavily on the types and amounts of programming you choose. For instance, an encore movie could cost $0.02 a subscriber; an excellent classic movie, $0.10; and a blockbuster movie, over $0.50.
>
> Also, in marketing, I assumed you gave a guide that we produce to every subscriber (this added to the cost). The guides can be produced more cheaply at lower quality or quantity.
>
> Please note also that installation costs and charges, disconnect costs, converter or trap costs, subscriber turnover, a contingency allowance, and other variables are not included in this HBO/TPS projection, as they were in the computer-generated HBO projection. The HBO projection was extremely conservative, to show you that even under the worst circumstances you would have a profitable business.
>
> We also know that HBO's movies, sports, and specials tend to attract more subscribers than a movies-only channel, and that with other satellite services going up on the bird, if you purchased an earth station, you could look forward to revenue and programming from more than just HBO.
>
> Nonetheless, HBO/TPS movies and technical quality are excellent, and if you decide to go stand-alone, you'll get top-notch service from us.

SUBSCRIPTION TELEVISION—OVER-THE-AIR

National Subscription Television, Glendale, California, began broadcasting pay entertainment programs over Channel 52 in April 1977. By August 1977, when NST officials visited Leisure World, the firm had 6,000 subscribers and was making 100 installations per day. Its programs were transmitted over the air in scrambled form. Descramblers were installed on subscribers' TV sets by NST crews. These men checked each subscriber's antenna carefully; if it was deficient, a new one was installed. NST provided pay TV service only if the set gave good reception over the air.

As of August 1977, NST's service was priced at $17 monthly. A charge of $29.95 was made for installation of a decoder; in addition, new subscribers were required to make a $25 refundable deposit on the equipment.

NST provided its service under the trademark "ON Subscription Television." The service included motion pictures—unedited and uninterrupted by commercial announcements; local sports—baseball, football, hockey, soccer, tennis, and championship boxing; and on one night a week, under the title "Dimension," stage productions, ballet, or opera.

If ON Subscription Television were brought to Leisure World residents the technical approach would be as follows. The ON programs would be broadcast scrambled over the air from the Channel 52 transmitter on Mount Wilson and brought in by the Leisure World community master antenna. If the service were made optional to the Leisure World cable subscribers, the scrambled signal would be converted to one of the mid-band channels between Channels 6 and 7—possibly Channel H or I. Converters would be supplied to pay subscribers who would be charged an installation fee (possibly $30); a refundable deposit of $25 might also be required of each subscriber. The monthly charge might then be $17 (or an amount agreed upon by Golden Rain Foundation and the management of National Subscription Television Channel 52).

According to NST executives, this technical approach would require the following investment:

Equipment at the head end plus labor to install it: $16,000.

One converter per subscriber at $60 per unit. These converters would have to be purchased in advance by the Leisure World Cable Television System prior to the beginning of ON Subscription TV service. The number to be purchased initially depended upon the estimated penetration for the first year.

If 2 percent penetration were achieved in the first year, this would amount to 12,000 homes × 0.02 = 240 × $60 = $14,400.

If 8 percent penetration were achieved in five years, then the total would be 12,000 × 0.08 = 960 × $60 = $57,600.

It would, of course, be necessary to undertake an introductory program of advertising and promotion as a means of getting Leisure World residents to subscribe to the ON Subscription TV service. NST would furnish a promotional videotape describing the service, emphasizing the benefits of subscribing, and previewing typical program features. Two or three subscription television programs might be transmitted free over Channel 6 to illustrate the character of the program material. These might include a full-length feature movie, a Broadway musical, and a sports program broadcast the day after the live event. NST marketing experts would provide advice and assistance in planning both the introductory and sustaining marketing efforts. The cost of these efforts would, of course, depend upon the media used and upon the number of advertisements scheduled.

Other anticipated expenses included the following:

NST program cost per subscriber (monthly)	$10.00
Cost of installation per subscriber	20.00*
Billing and collection (Golden Rain Foundation) (monthly)	0.50
Other costs, including computer, postage, and program guides (monthly)	2.00
Total monthly cost per subscriber	$12.50

*One-time cost

Revenues would include $17 per subscriber as a program fee. In addition, there would be an installation charge which might run $20 per new subscriber (the amount to be determined by Golden Rain Foundation in consultation with NST executives).

NST executives summarized the advantages of using Channel 52's ON television service as follows:

1. The Leisure World master antenna would bring in a strong Channel 52 signal.
2. The investment in equipment would be less than that required to bring in HBO programming via satellite.
3. Regional sports programs would probably appeal to Leisure World residents; these programs would not be available from competing program distributors.
4. The program director of ON Subscription TV service entertainment was an experienced and capable programmer with excellent connections in the motion-picture industry.
5. NST was associated with TAT Communications and Tandem Productions, organizations whose creative chief was Norman Lear, an outstanding producer of popular television programs.

NST executives stated that they expected the ON Subscription TV service to achieve between 35 and 40 percent penetration among Leisure World cable subscribers. They did not specify how much time would be required to reach this projection.

ROSSMOOR ELECTRIC'S ROLE IN SUPPLYING PAY TV ENTERTAINMENT

As the GRF Task Force on Pay Television investigated the desirability of adding pay TV entertainment to the Leisure World Cable Television System, Foley faced the question of what role Rossmoor Electric, Inc.,

should play in supplying such entertainment to the community. The following alternatives appeared to be open to his firm:

1. At a minimum, Rossmoor Electric's role would be limited to the installation of the necessary head-end equipment and the installation and maintenance of the converters that were likely to be required on each subscriber's TV set. For this work, Rossmoor Electric would charge for installation and for the repair and maintenance charges that were required subsequently. TeleMine's proposal to conduct a pay TV operation over leased Channel 6 facilities illustrates this approach.

2. Somewhat more involvement would be required under Tele-Mine's second plan of providing necessary capital equipment for pay TV service, furnishing the program package, but leaving the remainder of the pay TV operations in Rossmoor's hands. Under this approach, Rossmoor's compensation would be the profit from the pay TV business, if any.

3. Even greater responsibility would be required if Rossmoor were to make the necessary investment in the capital equipment required to provide pay TV, but secure program material from such distributors as HBO, BestVision, and National Subscription Television.

4. At a maximum, Rossmoor would operate an independent stand-alone pay TV business, providing the necessary capital, dealing directly with studios to obtain program material, and managing the pay TV function.

1. *Installation and repair service only.* During the period in which the Task Force of Pay Television was interviewing the various pay TV program distributors, Foley made it clear that he would like Rossmoor Electric, Inc., to handle the installation of pay TV equipment at the head end, the installation of converters on subscribers' sets, and any repair and maintenance work that might be required to insure proper operation of the premium entertainment service. He believed that this was necessary, regardless of which program distributor might be chosen to service Leisure World, in order to optimize the technical coordination of picture and sound quality, since Rossmoor Electric had installed the cable television system and handled all repairs and maintenance work on it. The task force agreed with him and incorporated these requirements into its November 23, 1977, progress report to H. H. Litten, general manager, Professional Community Management. It was thought that Rossmoor Electric might be paid from $2.00 to $3.25 per subscriber per month for this work, depending upon the functions it performed for the program distributor. In the final report of the task force, on January 30, 1978, it was also recognized that individual subscribers would be expected to pay a one-time charge of from $15 to $40 for installation of a "converter–descrambler unit," ownership of which would be retained by the pay TV contractor. Rossmoor Electric was to handle installation of the converter–descrambler for whichever pay TV program distributor was chosen to service Leisure World.

If Rossmoor Electric limited its role to these functions, then its profits would be the difference between the amount it charged for installation of the converter–descramblers and the costs it incurred in performing this function. For example, if, in line with the HBO estimates, Rossmoor Electric charged $15 for the installation service and the cost of performing this function ran $10 per unit, there would be a margin of $5 per installation. In addition, if each subscriber were charged $3.25 per month for subsequent repairs and maintenance of the pay TV equipment used in the system, then subtraction of the estimated costs of performing this maintenance service would give the estimated margin for this activity.

2. *Operator for HBO program service.* Since there appeared to be a prospect of future profitable business in furnishing pay TV to Leisure World, Foley decided to explore ways in which his firm might do more than furnish repair and installation service. One approach would be to accept the offer of Home Box Office and propose the introduction of this program service to Golden Rain Foundation. The following considerations came to mind as Foley analyzed this line of action.

a. It would be necessary for Rossmoor Electric, Inc., to invest about $112,800 in the equipment required to bring the HBO satellite program service to Leisure World; $40,000 for a small earth station, $800 for an encoder, and $72,000 for security equipment. Golden Rain Foundation would not provide the capital. HBO expected the investment to be made by the local operator. To participate in this business, therefore, Rossmoor Electric, Inc., would have to function as the local operator of the program service furnished by HBO. Would the anticipated revenue provide a prospect of profit that would justify a capital investment of $112,800?

b. In discussions with Lisa Connor, Western regional manager for HBO, pro forma projections of the anticipated cash flow for a five-year period had been developed. Assuming a 15 percent penetration of Leisure World cable subscribers, the time required to cover the necessary capital investment in pay TV equipment and to cover interest at 10 percent on that investment was estimated at a little over three years. The total cash flow in five years was estimated at $185,259; the capital needed, $112,800, plus interest of $12,612 totaled $125,412. The return on investment would then be $59,847, or 53 percent of $112,800. (See Appendix C for supporting data.)

c. As the Task Force on Pay Television had evaluated this cash flow projection, the assumption of a 15 percent penetration of Leisure World cable subscribers was examined carefully. As background, data from the Paul Kagan pay TV Census were studied (see Exhibit 2). The penetration achieved in the following cities appeared relevant:

(1)   In 3 years and 9 months Cox Channel 100 was purchased by 11.6 percent of the subscribers of the San Diego cable system who paid

$11.00 per month for pay entertainment in addition to $6.50 for the basic cable service, or a total of $17.50 per month.

(2)   In Long Beach, California, during the same period, Showtime penetrated 53.5 percent of the cable subscribers with service priced at $8.50 for pay entertainment plus $7.00 for the basic cable service, or a total of $15.50.

(3)   In 2 years and 8 months the Los Angeles cable system secured 46.2 percent penetration for the TeleMation Services, which cost $8.95 in addition to $8.45 for the basic cable service, or a total of $17.40.

(4)   In Oxnard, California, 45.0 percent penetration was achieved by Pay TV Services, which sold at $3.75 per month in addition to $6.95 for the basic service, or a total of $10.70.

It was recognized, of course, that the penetration achieved by pay TV entertainment in the above cable systems was influenced by such factors as the monthly charge for the service (which ranged from $3.75 to $11.00), the combined cost of the basic service and pay entertainment (which ranged from $10.70 to $17.50), the appeal of the program package to the cable subscribers, and the promotional and marketing skill demonstrated.

Foley's comments on HBO were as follows:

(1)   Judging from its program guides, HBO appeared to offer good programs. Its service would provide sports broadcasts that would probably appeal to Leisure World viewers. HBO was the "Cadillac of program distributors" and served 59.9 percent of the pay cable market as of December 31, 1976 (see Exhibit 2).

(2)   The marketing manager of HBO would provide assistance and advice in planning and marketing effort during the start-up period. Rossmoor Electric would have to provide a marketing executive to do the actual work in Leisure World. HBO would make available at low cost advertising aids, program guides, newsletters, and other promotional materials to help in marketing the pay service. Normally HBO favored personal solicitation for the introductory effort, but this was prohibited by GRF policy. Instead, Rossmoor Electric would have to rely on advertisements in the *Leisure World News*, announcements on Channel 6, and direct mail, but it was believed that such media would do the job.

(3)   It was anticipated that penetration for pay service would be achieved among 10 percent of the cable subscribers during the first year, followed by a gradual buildup to 20 percent in five years.

(4)   Installation of an earth station to receive HBO programs transmitted by satellite would also make available other attractive nonpay programs that were being transmitted by satellite from distant cities. The availability of such program material was expected to increase during the next five years.

3.   *Affiliation with TeleMine, Inc.* The necessity of investing $112,800

in equipment in order to affiliate with HBO led Foley to explore other alternatives requiring less capital. He recalled that TeleMine, Inc., had offered to furnish the necessary capital equipment to the Leisure World cable system under a plan in which the firm would also provide the program package, but Rossmoor Electric would then, at its own expense, promote, market, and install the pay TV system. Rossmoor Electric would pay $4.50 per month per subscriber for the TeleMine program package and, in turn, would sell the pay entertainment to Leisure World subscribers at $8.00 per month. Any profits would be taken, and losses borne, by Rossmoor Electric.

In discussing the TeleMine proposal with the Task Force on Pay Television, Foley said that while TeleMine would indeed furnish, without charge, the automated program devices, encoders, and modulators required to project the pay entertainment, it would, of course, be using all of the remaining necessary studio equipment (owned by Rossmoor Electric).

TeleMine programs would be selected for the Leisure World audience after research on their demographic characteristics and program preferences. Resident attitudes toward the programs would also be monitored regularly to maintain a flow of information between the community and the TeleMine programming department.

Foley examined the titles of the movies included in a typical TeleMine program schedule. He then contacted several motion-picture studios to see whether Rossmoor Electric could rent an equivalent schedule of movies directly instead of utilizing the services of pay TV program distributors. As a result of this check, he concluded that his firm could probably do as good a job of procuring movies as TeleMine was doing.

Foley had originally raised a question as to the quality of the picture that would be obtained by projecting from videotape furnished by TeleMine. Morris Tobias of TeleMine had responded that all pay television programs utilized videotape in projecting movies, that no program package utilized films directly. He said that TeleMine would supply first-generation tape cassettes directly to Leisure World. Foley concluded that Rossmoor Electric could also secure first-generation videotapes of feature movies and thus be able to project pictures of the same quality as the tape casssettes provided by TeleMine.

As Foley analyzed the TeleMine proposal, he recognized that Rossmoor would be expected to do all of the work involved in providing the pay TV service and of developing a market for it among Leisure World residents. In short, his firm would take the considerable risk involved in introducing the new concept of pay entertainment into the community and would be doing so on a margin of $3.50 per subscriber ($8.00 monthly fee less $4.50 to TeleMine for its service). This led him to wonder whether it might not be preferable for Rossmoor Electric to make the necessary investment in capital equipment and thus eliminate

the $4.50 per subscriber per month that the TeleMine proposal would involve. In this way, Rossmoor would stand to gain the entire profit which might result from pay television—a more adequate compensation for the substantial risks involved in such a new venture.

4. *Independent stand-alone versus program package service.* As a result of this line of thinking, Foley made the following analysis of the idea of Rossmoor Electric offering an independent stand-alone pay entertain-

---

INDEPENDENT STAND-ALONE VERSUS PROGRAM PACKAGE SERVICE

Advantages of stand-alone
1. Complete control over the selection of programming.
2. Wider selection of programming from which to choose.
3. Complete control of the advertising/promotion of the service.
4. Direct contact with programing source.

Advantages of program package service
1. Less involvement in booking, selection, and number of programs.
2. Less involvement in marketing and promotion.

Explanation

The greatest advantage of operating on an independent, stand-alone basis will be our complete control over programming.

Due to the explicit sexual depictions, use of "strong language," and excessive violence present in Hollywood films, our Leisure World movie channel should exhibit only G-rated and carefully selected PG-rated films.

By selecting our own programming, we would not have to exhibit any program that was not specifically chosen for our audience.

Despite the fact that Leisure World, Laguna Hills, is generally considered an affluent community, past experience has shown that the community, as a whole, spends money very conservatively.

According to the *Pay TV Newsletter,* August 23, 1977, the average pay cable monthly rate is $7.83. It is doubtful that the average Leisure World resident would be willing to pay that amount, over and above their monthly service charge, for a pay television service.

As a stand-alone operation with complete control over programming and related costs, we could safely broadcast our service to every home in Leisure World, Laguna Hills.

Thus, with a steady subscriber count, no hookup or disconnect fees, and no large additional equipment investment, our operational costs would be considerably less than those of the average pay cable system, and would therefore allow us to offer our movie programs at a very reasonable price.

As an added note, we found that all of the producers were more than willing to work with Rossmoor Electric, Inc., as a stand-alone operation. In fact, after explaining our audience limitations, we were encouraged and advised by the producers that we would best serve our own interests and the interests of the community by acting as a stand-alone operation. They also indicated that because of the size of the Leisure World community and legal requirements, there would be little, if any, difference between the price of programming to us and the price of programming a package programmer.

Considering that all of the major producers have their own pay TV package operations, we felt that this was a significant comment.

ment service in Leisure World as opposed to affiliating with a program package service such as TeleMine or Home Box Office.

5. *Movie program for Leisure World proposed by Rossmoor Electric, Inc.* As a result of the foregoing analysis, Rossmoor Electric executives decided to propose to Golden Rain Foundation a stand-alone movie program service designed specifically for Leisure World. The necessary investment in capital equipment would be provided by Rossmoor Electric which would also take over the functions normally performed by such program distributors as HBO and TeleMine, Inc. It was thought that this approach would maximize Rossmoor Electric's prospects for profit as compared with arrangements involving more limited involvement in the pay television enterprise. Accordingly, Foley hired a assistant to help him gather the information necessary to develop a proposal for submission to GRF. Data were collected on such matters as anticipated program costs, necessary capital investment, labor and studio expenses, and essential marketing and promotional costs.

In analyzing anticipated revenue and profit, Foley decided to propose that pay entertainment be provided to all subscribers of the Leisure World Cable Television System as an extension of existing cable television service. If this were done, the cost of the pay entertainment could be kept at a minimum level. In 1977, Leisure World residents paid $3.54 per month for the basic cable television service. Foley estimated that Rossmoor Electric could furnish a program consisting of one motion picture per week to subscribers at an additional charge of $1.97 per month.

Accordingly, on March 10, 1978, Foley finalized the Rossmoor Electric proposal for providing full-length, unedited movies by dealing directly with all major motion-picture producers and by handling all the functions of the program distributor. Since the Task Force on Pay Television had submitted its final report on January 30, 1978, before the Rossmoor proposal was completed, Foley transmitted his proposal directly to R. L. Disbro, acting general manager, Professional Community Management, Inc.

The Rossmoor Electric proposal for a stand-alone movie program service for Leisure World cable system subscribers is reproduced in Appendix A (on pages 442–45).

APPENDIX A

Rossmoor Electric Proposal for a Stand-Alone Movie Program Service for Leisure World Cable Subscribers at $1.97 per Month

INTRODUCTION

During the past several months Rossmoor Electric, Inc., has considered the feasibility of offering first-run movies as an extension of our present cable television service to the Leisure World, Laguna Hills, community.

Upon undertaking this study, it was necessary to consider the basic moral values, lifestyle, and economic conditions of the Leisure World audience.

Because of the community's uniqueness, it was felt that a custom-planned movie program might best suit the needs and preferences of the Leisure World community.

With that thought in mind, we contacted all of the major motion-picture studios and numerous independent companies that distribute special television programming. We discovered what product was available, the price, and under what terms the product could be exhibited. The information that was compiled is included in this report.

We have also examined the facts of operating a movie program, including a financial analysis, a programming format, and specific promotional considerations.

ASSUMPTIONS FOR A LEISURE WORLD, LAGUNA HILLS, MOVIE PROGRAM

The following assumed factors were the basis of our study on the feasibility of instituting a movie program for Leisure World, Laguna Hills.

1. Leisure World residents would enjoy viewing unedited current Hollywood movies without commercial interruption in the convenience and comfort of their own manors.
2. The movie program would be considered an additional service to the residents of Leisure World.
3. Rossmoor Electric could utilize existing equipment and personnel presently employed to perform present contract agreements.
4. The movie program would be received by every home in Leisure World, Laguna Hills.
5. The movie program would feature the exhibition of 52 films each year, featuring an average of 4.333 different movies each month, with movies being shown five days a week—Monday through Friday.

BENEFITS OF OPERATING A MOVIE SYSTEM AS AN EXTENSION OF THE EXISTING LEISURE WORLD, LAGUNA HILLS, CABLE TELEVISION SERVICE

Extremely reasonable cost due to utilization of existing broadcast facilities with minimal additional equipment investment.

A custom-planned selection of movies specifically chosen for the Leisure World audience.

Wider selection of movies because of independent status.

Direct contact with the studios providing movies.

EXPLANATION (excerpts)

The general philosophy of the Leisure World community has always involved sharing both the freedom to enjoy and the cost of the many Leisure World facilities and services. As the Leisure World community has continued to grow, so too have the quality and variety of the facilities available to the residents.

Rossmoor Electric is now proposing to offer the residents an additional source of entertainment that would be an extension of our existing cable television programming. The entire community would have the opportunity to enjoy the new service and at the same time keep the cost of the additional service at a minimal level.

The movies selected for exhibition would be carefully screened to insure their good taste. Every home in the community would receive the movie service, thus eliminating costly hookup and disconnect fees and *major* additional equipment investments that would accompany a typical subscription movie service. With lower operational investments and maintenance costs, the movie service could be offered to the residents at a very reasonable cost.

The major motion-picture distributors set the price of their product in direct relation to the monthly fees charged by the cable operator (i.e., the greater the monthly cable fees, the higher the costs for individual movies). Since Rossmoor Electric proposes to offer the movie service at a minimal cost, we would receive a considerable discount on the movie prices from the producers. If the same service were offered to the community on a subscription basis, operational costs would increase greatly, thus raising the resident's cost of receiving the service and finally resulting in a higher price being charged by the movie producers for an individual film.

PROGRAM PHILOSOPHY

Our overall statement clearly expresses our objectives in selecting material to be used on the Leisure World, Laguna Hills movie program:

1. To present good, quality entertainment at a reasonable cost, to every home in Leisure World, Laguna Hills.
2. To present a custom-planned selection of movie entertainment, pleasing to the largest possible majority of residents.

3. To present entertainment at a variety of times to accommodate numerous lifestyles and time preferences.
4. To offer an alternative to "free" television and not needless direct competition with "free" television.

MOVIE PROGRAM FACT SHEET

1. All movies and specials available to pay TV companies, with the exception of programs that they produce themselves, are also available to Rossmoor Electric.
2. In most cases, price per movie is based on a percentage of the subscriber cost. Our price structure will enable us to receive an impressive discount rate.
3. The new equipment required will cost approximately $17,500, with a four-year depreciation of $365 per month.
4. Maintenance costs of $250 will take care of the newly purchased equipment.
5. The introduction of a movie schedule in Leisure World by Rossmoor Electric will require the employment of two additional employees.
6. The two new employees will be needed in such areas as after-hours equipment operation, booking of films, dealing with the movie producers, ordering tapes from the various labs, programming the movie schedule, and publicity and public relations.
7. The cost of the new employees will be approximately $1,750 per month. Other labor costs: $315 per month. Total monthly labor costs: $2,065.
8. The cost of movies will average $0.35 each per manor per month.
9. Cost of tape transfer: $125 each.
10. Cost of screening: $15 each. Estimate 125 percent of total.
11. Cost of postage and insurance: $4.50 each.

Screening, 5.2 × 2	10.4
Movies	4.333
	14.733

Cost 15 × $4.50 = $67.50 per month

Cost per month

Equipment depreciation	$ 365 per month
Maintenance cost	250
Labor cost	1,750
Other labor cost	315
Tape transfer	542
Screening	81
Postage and insurance	68
Total other costs	$3,371 per month

$3,371/12,000 Manors = 0.2809

Movie cost	$1.52
Other costs	0.28
Movie price fluctuation	0.10
	$1.90
Profit margin	0.07
Total	$1.97 per month per manor
Possible additional costs:	
Monthly TV guide	$0.10?
LWN distribution	0.03?
	$2.10

EXHIBIT A–1   Hypothetical monthly program schedule

SUN	MON	TUE	WED	THU	FRI	SAT
						1
2	3 The Sting 8:00 PM	4 The Fortune 8:00 PM	5 The Sting 3:30 PM The Fortune 9:00 PM	6 The Sting 7:30 PM	7 The Fortune 3:30 PM The Sting 9:00 PM	8
9	10 Murder by Death 8:00 PM	11 Murder by Death 9:00 PM	12 Murder by Death 3:30 PM The Sting 9:00 PM	13 Murder by Death 7:00 PM The Fortune 9:00 PM	14 Murder by Death 9:00 PM	15
16	17 Bridge Too Far 8:00 PM	18 Bridge Too Far 9:00 PM	19 Bridge Too Far 3:30 PM Murder by Death 9:00 PM	20 Bridge Too Far 8:00 PM	21 The Sting 7:00 PM Bridge Too Far 9:00 PM	22
23	24 Gable & Lombard 8:00 PM	25 Gable & Lombard 3:30 PM The Sting 8:00 PM	26 Murder by Death 7:00 PM Gable & Lombard 9:00 PM	27 Bridge Too Far 3:30 PM Gable & Lombard 9:00 PM	28 Gable & Lombard 7:00 PM Murder by Death 9:00 PM	29

APPENDIX B

**Letter to CATV Systems Managers from Vice President–
Affiliate Relations, HBO**

HBO™

August 26, 1977

Dear Manager:

HBO will be moving into the fall 77 season with the strongest schedule of films and specials programming in its five-year history, augmented by sports programming that includes an exclusive weekly football series, "Inside the NFL," and beginning in late November, a series of top mid-week collegiate basketball games carried live from around the nation.

Our programming selections, as well as our expanded schedule (premiers on all three nights of the weekend, special "night owl" shows on Friday and Saturday), reflect HBO's extensive subscriber research over the past six months, as well as the lessons we've learned over our five years in pay TV. We are confident that the "fine tuning" that went into our fall schedule will make the HBO package more salable to new subscribers than ever before, and we invite you to read through the enclosed materials—especially the September issue of *Take One*—to get an idea of the titles, stars, and new promotional initiatives that will be creating a lot of excitement in HBO markets this fall.

We're excited about the months just ahead, but we see our fall schedule as just a beginning. The new range of movie products now available to us because of the landmark court decision in the HBO case, the enthusiastic response of HBO's viewers to our original "Standing Room Only" and "On Location" series, and our growing expertise in cost-efficient marketing techniques give us the highest expectations for 1978 and beyond.

Your HBO regional manager will be glad to answer any questions and provide more information on any aspect of HBO—from our rate card to our programming plans. You'll find all the regional managers' names and telephone numbers listed by region on the last page of *Take One*.

Best wishes for the fall!

Winston H. Cox
Vice President—Affiliate Relations

APPENDIX C

Home Box Office: Pro forma Projections of Cash Flow, HBO Program Service for Leisure World Cable Television System

---

HBO
Home Box Office from Time/Life

June 27, 1977

Mr. Ivan Foley, President
Rossmoor Electric Inc.
PO Box 2040
Laguna Hills, CA 92653

Dear Ivan:

Thanks again for lunch and my tour of Leisure World. I enjoyed it very much. Enclosed you will find an HBO Program Guide for July and a pro forma incorporating the assumptions we discussed in your office.

The following is a list of assumptions by line item:

Business assumptions

1.	Option 1 (converter)	Assumes Sylvania converter and TEST descrambler trap.
2.	CATV subs year-end	Assumes 12,000 CATVs with no increase years 2–5.
3.	Percent penetration	Assumes 15 percent.
4.	Turnover	Assumes 20 percent per year churn rate.
5.	HBO subs year-end	Constant level years 1–5. Note: Based on your commitment to perform maintenance marketing function.
6.	Average subscribers	Shows 75 percent of total subs first year due to start-up.

Financial assumptions

1.	HBO service rate	Assumes $8 a month (could probably charge $8.50).
2.	Installation charge	Assumes $15 charge per HBO subscriber connected.
3.	Installation cost	Assumes $10/unit (labor, etc.).
4.	Disconnect cost	Assumes $8/unit (no tuning necessary).
5.	Converter or trap cost	Assumes $32.50 for Sylvania converter and $7.50 for TEST descrambler trap.
6.	Program fees	Per sub payment to HBO; based on standard HBO Rate Card.
7.	Earth station	Assumes $40,000 small earth station plus $800 encoder cost.

Revenue

Self-explanatory.

Expenses

1. Program Fees — Sum of amount paid to HBO based on Rate Card.
2. Office staff — Assumes additional person for marketing and/or accounting at $13,000-a-year salary. Years 2–5 assume 10 percent annual salary increase.
3. Advertising and promotion — Assumes $10,000 launch marketing campaign first year, with $2,500/year (years 2–5) maintenance marketing. Also includes $0.10 per Program Guide, $0.15 computer cost, and $0.125 postage cost per bill and Guide mailed.
4. Installation maintenance — Previously explained under Financial Assumptions.
5. Disconnect cost — Same as above
6. Signal cost — Assumes earth station maintenance of $150/month.
7. Other expenses — Shows $1,000/year contingency.

Ivan, even at 15 percent penetration the projections look excellent. At a 10 percent discount rate, you would enjoy an interval rate of return of 78.2 percent over a five-year period, and your cash flow becomes positive early in the third year.

If you have any questions or would like me to do any more pro formas based on different assumptions, please let me know. I look forward to the possibility of your affiliation with HBO.

Regards,

Lisa Forrestal Connor
Western Regional Manager

Enc.
LFC/jl

Home Box Office, Inc./Subsidiary of Time Incorporated/100 Busch St./San Francisco, California/94104/(415) 982-0270

EXHIBIT C–2

ROSSMOOR ELECTRIC, INC.
Laguna Hills, California
Five-Year Projection

	Year 1	Year 2	Year 3	Year 4	Year 5	Total
Business assumptions						
Option 1 (converter) or 2 (trap)	1					
CATV subs year-end	12,000	12,000	12,000	12,000	12,000	
Percent penetration	15%	15%	15%	15%	15%	
Turnover	20	20	20	20	20	
HB subs year-end	1,800	1,800	1,800	1,800	1,800	
Average subs	1,350	1,800	1,800	1,800	1,800	
Financial assumptions						
HBO service rate	$ 8	$ 8	$ 8	$ 8	$ 8	
Installation charge	15	15	15	15	15	
Installation cost	10	10	10	10	10	
Disconnect cost	8	8	8	8	8	
Converter or trap cost	40	40	40	40	40	
Program fees	$ 4	4	4	4	4	
Earth station (10-year depreciation)	$ 40,800					
Revenue						
Subscription service revenue	$129,600	$172,800	$172,800	$172,800	$172,800	$820,000
Installation revenue	27,000	5,400	5,400	5,400	5,400	48,600
Gross	156,600	178,200	178,200	178,200	178,200	869,400
Expenses						
Programming fees	$ 64,800	$ 86,400	$ 86,400	$ 86,400	$ 86,400	$410,400
Office staff	13,000	14,300	15,730	17,303	19,033	79,366
Advertising and promotion	13,730	7,470	7,470	7,470	7,470	43,600
Installation and maintenance	18,000	3,600	3,600	3,600	3,600	32,400
Disconnect costs		2,880	2,880	2,880	2,880	11,520
Signal costs	1,800	1,800	1,800	1,800	1,800	9,000
Other expenses	1,000	1,000	1,000	1,000	1,000	5,000
Total	$112,330	$117,450	$118,880	$120,450	$122,180	$591,280
Operating income (loss)	$ 44,274	$ 60,752	$ 59,322	$ 57,749	$ 56,019	$278,116
Depreciation	18,480	18,480	18,480	18,480	18,480	92,400
Net income (loss) before tax	25,794	42,272	40,842	39,269	37,539	185,716

EXHIBIT C–3

	Year 1	Year 2	Year 3	Year 4	Year 5	Total
Net before tax	$ 25,794	$ 42,272	$40,842	$39,269	$37,539	$185,716
Taxes 50%	(50%)	(50%)	(50%)	(50%)	(50%)	(50%)
Net after taxes	$ 12,897	$ 21,136	$20,421	$19,634	$18,769	$ 92,858
Cash flow						
Operating income (loss)						
before taxes	$ 44,274	$ 60,752	$59,322	$57,749	$56,019	$278,116
Less taxes	(12,899)	(21,136)	(20,421)	(19,634)	(18,769)	(92,857)
Cash flow	$ 31,377	$ 39,616	$38,901	$38,115	$37,250	$185,259
Present value 10%	28,553	32,881	29,176	25,918	23,095	116,528
Terminal equipment	(72,000)					
Earth station	(40,800)					
	(81,423)*	(41,807)	(2 ,906)	(30,209)	(37,250)	(67,459)
Interest 10%	8,142	4,180	290	–0–	–0–	(12,612)
Capital needed after income	$(89,565)	$(45,987)	$ (3,196)			$ 54,847

*Terminal equipment $72,000 + earth station $40,800 = $112,800. $112,800 − cash flow year 1 of $31,377 = −81,423.

QUESTIONS

1. In view of the possible interest of cable subscribers in pay TV, how might Ivan Foley of Rossmoor Electric analyze the alternatives open to him? Consider these alternatives:

   a. Accept TeleMine's second plan of providing necessary capital equipment for pay TV service, furnishing the program package but leaving the remainder of the pay TV operations in Rossmoor's hands. Under this approach, Rossmoor's compensation would be the profit from the pay TV business, if any.

   b. Make the necessary investment in capital equipment required for providing pay TV, but secure program material from distributors such as HBO, BestVision, and National Subscription Television.

   c. Operate an independent, stand-alone pay TV business, providing the necessary capital, dealing directly with studios for program material, and managing the pay TV function.

2. a. What are the merits and limitations of Rossmoor's proposal to the Golden Rain Foundation board that the firm provide movie programs to all Leisure World residents a a monthly charge of $1.97 that would be added to the monthly GRF service charge paid by *all* residents?

b. If the mandatory charge of $1.97 were rejected by the GRF board, might Rossmoor be wise to propose the same plan, but at an optional monthly charge of $3 for pay TV service? Explain.

PROMOTIONAL STRATEGY

This part deals with the fundamental issue of how best to sell the firm's product. Decisions on other elements of the marketing mix (product, brand policy, distribution policy, and price) influence promotional strategy. The fundamental task is to determine what message to communicate to prospective buyers and then to decide through what channels to transmit this message. What to say will depend upon an understanding of consumer behavior gained through both research and experience. Once the message has been determined, the problem is to choose appropriate methods of communication from among available alternatives (advertising, personal selling, consumer promotions, reseller stimulation, and publicity) and to combine these methods into an effective promotional mix. These are the issues with which we shall be concerned in Chapter 10.

Closely intertwined with the decision on the character of the promotional mix is the decision on how much to appropriate for such activity. In Chapter 11, a theoretical solution to this problem is first developed, and then methods used by business firms are examined to see how closely they approximate this ideal. Problems to be resolved in reaching a sound decision include (1) how to separate long-run and short-run results of promotional effort and (2) how to measure the contribution to gross margin which may be expected from expenditures of various sizes

for advertising, consumer promotions, personal selling, reseller.stimu-lation, and publicity. Suggested research approaches for dealing with these questions will be evaluated.

Finally, Chapter 12 explores the promotional implications of brand strategy decisions. It is concerned with issues relating to family versus individual brands, brand–price–quality relationships, and the wisdom of manufacturing products to be sold under distributors' brands as op-posed to the firm's own brand.

PROMOTIONAL STRATEGY DECISIONS

10

Business success depends upon the firm being able to sell, at a profit, the merchandise it produces. Earlier discussions have demonstrated that the ability to sell a product depends upon sound action by executives on questions of product policy, branding, pricing, and the selection of effective channels of distribution. Yet these activities are wasted unless consumers or users are led to buy as the result of effective selling efforts.

What is the most effective way of selling a given product? This is the central issue with which we shall be concerned in the present chapter. Later we shall deal with the important related question of how much to appropriate to support the promotional program. We shall then turn to a consideration of the promotional aspects of brand strategy. In this discussion our point of view will be that of the marketing manager of a manufacturer or producer.

The development of an effective program of sales promotion involves both effective planning and skillful execution of plans. Because of the fundamental importance of sound sales-planning activities, we shall give emphasis to this phase of the problem in our discussions here. Questions of execution can best be considered in the specialized courses that customarily follow the basic marketing course.

DETERMINATION OF BASIC PROMOTIONAL STRATEGY

Promotion Involves Communication

The cutting edge of the marketing instrument is the message that is communicated to prospective buyers through the various elements in the promotional program. But the messages communicated by advertising, personal selling, publicity, and point-of-purchase promotion constitute only a portion of what the firm's marketing program tells prospective buyers. When the prospect perceives the firm's product, certain impressions are communicated—either positive or negative—and thus the product serves as a symbol of communication. Indeed, the product comes to have a "personality" or image in the prospect's mind as a result of its design, appearance, and who uses it, among other influences. So, too, the trademark and brand name are symbols that communicate messages to the prospective buyer. The package also communicates ideas that may enhance or detract from the product's image. The price communicates ideas as to quality, and the images which consumers have of the middlemen who display and sell the brand may add to or detract from the brand's image. Realization of the ways in which these aspects of the marketing program assist or detract from the image of the brand underscores the importance of recognizing the communication value of these factors and of shaping them to provide the desired impressions.[1]

Even so, the promotional program serves as the primary channel of communication to prospective buyers. It will help us in the planning of effective promotional programs if we review communication theory briefly and show its application to the development of promotional strategy.

How Communication Works[2]

The term *communication* comes from the Latin *communis*, common. When we communicate, therefore, we are trying to establish a "commonness" with someone. The marketer, for example, is attempting to share information about the features of a brand, the benefits it will provide users, and the desires its consumption will satisfy.

The basic elements of a communication system are the *source*, the *message*, and the *destination*. A *source* may be an individual (such as a

---

[1] For a discussion in which all marketing mix variables (product, price, place, and promotion) are treated as communication variables, see M. Wayne DeLozier, *The Marketing Communications Process* (New York: McGraw-Hill, 1976), chaps. 10–17.

[2] This section is adapted by permission from Wilbur Schram, "How Communication Works," in Wilbur Schram, ed., *The Process and Effects of Mass Communication* (Urbana: University of Illinois Press, 1955), pp. 3–26.

salesperson) or a communication organization (such as a television broadcasting system, a newspaper, or a magazine). The *message* may be in the form of printed words (as in a direct-mail letter), a spoken radio commercial, a picture, a symbol (such as the Chrysler Pentastar), or any other "signal" capable of being interpreted meaningfully. The *destination* may be an individual consumer listening, watching, or reading; the members of a group (such as housewives invited to the home of Mrs. Consumer to watch a demonstration of Tupperware), a football crowd (seeing a helicopter towing a sign promoting frankfurters), or an individual member of a mass television audience watching Johnny Carson on the "Tonight" show. Figure 10–1 is a diagram of this communication process that illustrates what has been said.

FIGURE 10–1   Diagram of a communication system

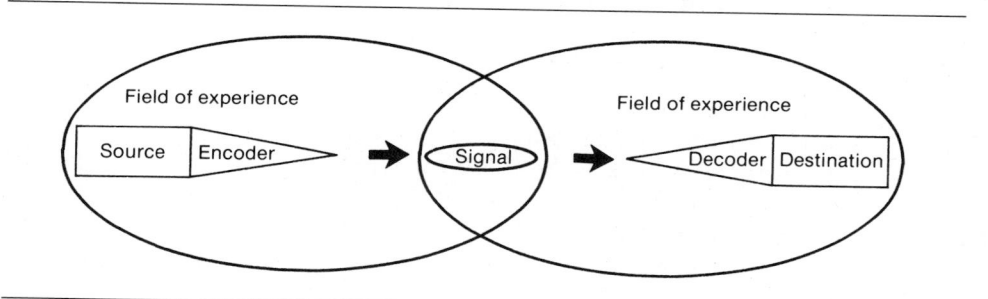

Source: Wilbur Schram, "How Communication Works," in Wilbur Schram, ed., *The Process and Effects of Mass Communication* (Urbana: University of Illinois Press, 1955), p. 6. Reprinted by permission.

If the consumer who receives the message understands its meaning, he or she may respond in various ways; that is, he or she may become a sender and encode some kind of message in return. If the commercial offers an attractive premium for a box top and 25 cents, the housewife who receives the message may buy the product and send the box top plus the money to the manufacturer. If the message urges the consumer to visit the Buick dealer and see the most recent model just put on display, he and his wife may decide to make such a visit within the next few days. If the commercial is designed to get the consumer to consider the brand the next time he or she is in the market, then no immediate action may result, but a favorable attitude may be created that will lead to examining the brand when the need for it arises. Of course, the consumer may also simply do nothing at all.

If communication is between a salesperson and a prospective buyer, we need to add the element of *feedback* in our conceptual scheme. As the prospect hears the sales message of the salesperson, he or she will decode it, interpret its meaning, and encode a response. The element of feedback enables the salesperson to determine whether the message is being understood and whether it is having the desired effect. The salesperson can then adjust subsequent messages accordingly. In mass communication such as a television broadcast, this direct type of feedback is impossible, and indirect responses must be substituted. Of course, interviews with television viewers may provide important feedback that will indicate whether the message is understood, believed, and has influenced attitudes toward the brand.[3]

In summary, if communication is to have effect it must (1) gain attention, (2) employ signs which refer to experience common to both the source and the destination to get the meaning across, (3) arouse personality needs in the destination and suggest some way to meet those needs, and (4) suggest a way to satisfy needs which is appropriate to the group situation in which the destination is at the time when he or she is moved to make the response desired by the source.

Determining the Promotional Mix

Let us now return to the point that the promotional program is the primary channel through which messages are communicated to prospective buyers. If this is to be done effectively, obviously the marketing executive must have a good understanding of who the prospective buyers of the product are, what desires may be satisfied through its use, what the prospects know about the brand, what attitudes they hold toward it, and what image it holds in their minds. Research is needed to gain this information, and the planning of this research is helped by an understanding of consumer behavior and appropriate models of the buying process, presented earlier in this book. Research to get feedback from prospective buyers on the impact of the messages communicated is also essential if weak links in the process are to be identified and communication is to be improved in the next campaign.

In determining how best to sell a given product, the basic decision that has to be made deals with the character of the promotional mix that is likely to be most effective. Specifically, how should advertising, personal selling, consumer promotions (contests, premiums, and combination offers), dealer promotional activities, and publicity be combined into an effective selling mix? The solution of this basic problem involves two subissues: (1) What promotional methods should be selected for use

---

[3]For additional background on the application of communication theory to promotional strategy, see J. F. Engel, M. R. Warshaw and Thomas C. Kinnear, *Promotional Strategy*, 5th ed. (Homewood, Ill.: Richard D. Irwin, 1983), chap. 2.

from among the alternatives available? (2) In what proportions should they be combined in order to get the best results?

Choice of Promotional Methods

The more important promotional tools (order-getting ingredients) which may be used in building an effective selling program are: (1) advertising; (2) personal selling; (3) consumer promotions ("forcing methods")—premiums, contests, and combination offers; (4) methods designed to stimulate dealer advertising and promotion—cooperative advertising, "merchandising the advertising," in-store promotions, and display and advertising aids; (5) publicity; (6) shows and exhibitions; (7) reciprocity; (8) warranty and service; and (9) competitive bidding.

In view of the wide variety of promotional methods from which to choose, this question naturally arises: How does the business executive approach the task of selecting those ingredients that will work most effectively for a particular product? Unfortunately, there is no generally accepted mix of promotional methods that will fit the wide variations in the circumstances which surround the marketing of the many different products produced and sold in our country today. Experience has demonstrated that different types of products require different mixtures of selling ingredients. This may be illustrated by contrasting the promotional strategies that might normally be used for an industrial product as opposed to a consumer good.

In the sale of diesel locomotives to railroads, for example, the Acme Corporation relies primarily upon personal selling because of the size of the investment, the technical nature of the product, the fact that the order will be placed by railroad executives, and the further fact that the number of prospective buyers is relatively limited (in number) while the size of the individual order is likely to be large. Along with personal selling, a supplementary campaign of advertising in trade journals read by railroad executives is also used.

In the sale of a patent medicine, however, the Mandell Company places its sole emphasis upon consumer advertising. This method is used because it offers the most economical way of reaching the large number of prospects who are scattered throughout the United States. The company has found that the demand stimulated through such advertising is strong enough to pull the product through wholesale and retail channels of distribution. Since the company has no sales force, orders from wholesalers and large retailers are received by mail. Thus, it is apparent that the patent medicine, a consumer good, requires an entirely different selling strategy from that needed for the diesel engine, an industrial product.

Even within the same industry, however, it may not be wise for all firms to use the same mix of promotional methods in the sale of their

various brands. Experience has shown that variations in the characteristics of competing brands, as well as differences in brand policy, distribution channels, and pricing policy, tend to require differences in the promotional mix if profitable results are to be achieved.

Suggested approach to the determination of promotional strategy. Since no single mixture of promotional methods is suitable for all products, or even for different brands of the same product, how should the business executive proceed in the selection and combination of selling ingredients? The most promising approach involves three steps. First, it is helpful to appraise the opportunity of making profitable use of advertising, personal selling, and other order-getting ingredients, in light of certain basic considerations that have been found, by experience, to influence the success of their application. Among the more important of these factors are:

1. The characteristics of the product and its stage in the life cycle.
2. The buying habits and buying motives of consumers or industrial users.
3. The point of view of middlemen.
4. The promotional strategy of competitors.
5. The probable size of promotional funds.

The significance of these considerations will be explained and illustrated at appropriate points in the following discussion of individual selling methods.

The preceding analysis will indicate in broad terms the relative emphasis which should be placed upon advertising, personal selling, and other order-getting ingredients in order to achieve desired promotional objectives. The second step, then, involves the use of this background in determining the total promotional appropriation and in working out its optimum allocation among the promotional methods to be used. In theoretical terms, the task is to set the total promotional appropriation at the point where the marginal revenue produced (output) equals or just exceeds the marginal cost of the last unit of input. Likewise, the amounts devoted to each promotional method (advertising, personal selling, dealer stimulation) should be set at the levels where the marginal gain per dollar cost among all promotional methods is equal. The practical adaptation of the marginal approach to the allocation of promotional dollars among alternative methods will receive consideration later in this discussion.

Third, whenever possible, it is desirable to check the decisions reached by this analytical process, through the use of research designed to measure the effectiveness of the promotional methods chosen as well as alternative combinations of promotional ingredients. Thus, if analysis indicates that there appears to be a good opportunity to make effective

use of advertising, it is wise to check this decision by utilizing suitable research techniques to measure the results of using the advertising method. If possible, research should also be used to verify decisions to include other methods in the promotional mix. Also, various combinations of advertising, personal selling, and dealer promotion should be tried out on an experimental basis as a means of identifying the most effective mix of these elements. Such research will serve to narrow the margin of error and will provide the facts needed to improve the quality of executive judgment.

At the same time, it should be recognized that the problem of measuring the results of using any given promotional method or combination of methods will often be a difficult one. Where the product has high unit value and is purchased at infrequent intervals, it may well be impossible to devise any small-scale test which will measure within a three- to six-month period the sales results of using advertising, personal selling, or other available promotional methods. Since many factors in the marketplace exert an influence upon sales, it may also prove to be very difficult for the manufacturer of such a product to isolate the influence of a single method, such as personal selling, where a given mix is subjected to appraisal by actual trial throughout the entire market. The point to keep in mind is that while, under certain conditions, research may provide helpful checks on management decisions on the choice of selling methods, there are other circumstances in which research has little to contribute because of the complexities of the problem. Where this is true, success depends upon the artistry and judgment of the executive as he or she attacks the problem of choosing the ingredients of the promotional plan. We may still conclude, however, that wherever possible it is wise to check decisions on the choice of promotional ingredients through the use of appropriate research methods.

Let us now turn to a discussion of some of the more important promotional methods available and the considerations which may guide the executive in the task of selecting the proper ingredients for the selling mix.

ADVERTISING

Advertising includes any paid form of nonpersonal presentation and promotion of ideas, goods, or services by an identified sponsor.[4] It is evident that advertising may be classified into two main types: (1) prod-

---

[4]*Marketing Definitions: A Glossary of Marketing Terms,* compiled by the Committee on Definitions of the American Marketing Association, Ralph S. Alexander, chairman (Chicago: American Marketing Association, 1960), p. 9.

uct advertising and (2) corporate advertising. Corporate advertising is designed to create favorable attitudes toward a company or an institution. Since our primary concern is with the use of advertising as a selling tool, the following discussion will deal with product advertising.

Such advertising may be directed to (1) the ultimate consumer or industrial user and (2) the middlemen involved in the distribution of the product. In our analysis, however, we shall be concerned with an appraisal of the opportunity of making profitable use of advertising addressed to ultimate consumers or industrial users for the purpose of promoting the sale of the manufacturer's or producer's brand.

If advertising campaigns were analyzed to determine their objectives, we would find that they could be classified into two basic types, depending upon the nature of the appeals used. On the one hand, there is advertising designed to stimulate a *primary demand,* which is a demand for a generic type of product. In order to accomplish this aim, primary appeals are used in the advertisements—appeals which may be expected to arouse a desire for a certain product category rather than for an individual brand. The other kind of advertising is that which aims to stimulate a *selective demand,* which is a demand for the brand of an individual manufacturer. Where such advertising is used, no attempt is made to increase the demand for the product category. Instead, the purpose is to secure for the brand which the manufacturer sells as large a percentage as possible of this demand. The method which is generally followed is to show that the advertiser's brand will satisfy a given desire more effectively than other brands. This is done by dwelling on the superior qualities or individualizing features of this brand which make it a better solution to the desire than other brands would be. Appeals of this sort are called selective appeals, since they aim to get the consumer to purchase only the advertiser's brand.

By far the greater proportion of the advertising of individual manufacturers and producers is designed to increase the share of the market secured by the seller's individual brand—that is, it is intended to stimulate a selective demand. The discussion which follows, accordingly, will deal with the problem of appraising the opportunity to make profitable use of consumer advertising in order to stimulate a selective demand.[5]

In deciding whether to choose advertising as a sales-making ingredient, the executive must do more than arrive at a judgment on whether the use of advertising will increase sales. He or she must estimate the cost of an adequate campaign of consumer advertising, and then determine whether that advertising will stimulate enough additional sales—at profitable prices—to cover advertising costs and leave a margin sufficient to increase profits.

---

[5]For a discussion of appraising the opportunity to stimulate primary demand, see N. H. Borden and M. V. Marshall, *Advertising Management: Text and Cases,* rev. ed. (Homewood, Ill.: Richard D. Irwin, 1959), chap. 4.

Appraising the Opportunity to Make Profitable Use of Consumer Advertising

In estimating the opportunity to stimulate selective demand profitably through advertising to consumers or users, the following leading considerations stand out:

First, advertising is likely to be more effective if a company is operating with a *favorable primary demand trend* than if it is operating with an adverse trend.

The second condition governing a concern's opportunity to influence its demand is the presence of a *large chance for product differentiation.* When products can be significantly differentiated, advertising is likely to be effective. Conversely, advertising is of smaller help when there is a marked tendency for the products of various producers to become closely similar.

A third condition is the relative importance to the consumer of the *hidden qualities of the product* as contrasted with the external qualities which can be seen and appreciated. When these hidden qualities are present, consumers tend to rely upon the brand, and advertising can be used to associate the presence of the qualities with the brand. Conversely, when the characteristics of a product which are significant to the consumer can be judged at the time of purchase, brand trends to lose some of its significance, and advertising is not needful in building mental associations regarding these characteristics.

A fourth condition is the *presence of powerful emotional buying motives* which can be employed in advertising appeals to consumers. Conversely, if such strong appeals cannot be used effectively, the advertising opportunity is not as great.

A fifth condition of importance is whether the concern's operations provide *substantial sums with which to advertise and promote* its products in the markets it seeks to reach. Advertising must be done on a scale large enough to make an effective impression upon its market. Consequently, the size of the advertising fund is an important consideration in an appraisal of advertising's opportunity. The matter of an advertising fund for any period depends upon the number of units of the product which can be sold during the period and upon the margin available for advertising. It should be stressed, [finally], that the opportunity to use advertising effectively generally depends not so much upon the presence of one of these conditions alone as upon the combination of these conditions which exists.[6]

When Should Advertising Receive the Main Emphasis in the Promotional Mix?

After having appraised the opportunity to make profitable use of consumer advertising, the executive is in a position to determine its relative importance in the selling mix. While in certain exceptional cases

---

[6]Adapted from ibid., pp. 162–65.

consumer advertising may be the only promotional method used, more commonly other selling ingredients, such as personal solicitation and dealer promotional efforts, are likely to be included in the mix. The combination of several promotional methods is often likely to be more effective in producing desired sales results than is exclusive reliance upon one method.

The process of determining whether the main burden of selling should be placed upon advertising, with other promotional ingredients occupying supplementary positions in the mix, begins with a careful estimate of the opportunity to make profitable use of each method which appears likely to make a useful contribution to the achievement of desired objectives. Consumer advertising is likely to receive the main emphasis under the following conditions: (1) when appraisal indicates that conditions are especially favorable for affecting consumer valuations and for the creation of quick buying action through the use of consumer advertising; (2) when analysis leads to the conclusion that retail personal selling is not important in the profitable marketing of the product; and (3) when dealer promotional efforts and other selling methods, if used alone, appear to offer less promise in consummating sales than does consumer advertising.

Examples of situations in which a firm might be wise to rely primarily upon the pull of consumer advertising to sell its products would include the following: (1) promotion of citrus fruits by the California Fruit Growers Exchange, (2) sales of proprietary medicines such as Geritol, (3) sale of highly individualized grocery specialties such as Maxim freeze-dried coffee, (4) promotion of cosmetics and beauty preparations such as Miss Clairol Shampoo Formula, and (5) sale of individualized dentifrices such as Mint Crest.

Other Problems of Advertising Management

If a careful appraisal indicates that there is a profitable opportunity to make effective use of advertising, the executive responsible for the management of the advertising force faces additional problems. (1) A decision must be reached on how much to spend on advertising. (2) Media to carry the advertising message must be selected. (3) Arrangements must be made for the preparation of effective advertisements. (4) Steps should be taken to measure the effectiveness of advertising, through pre-testing and post-testing, where appropriate, as a means of maximizing returns from the money spent. The task of preparing and placing effective advertisements is usually turned over to an advertising agency. The agency also assists in the selection of media, in recommending how much to spend, and in devising means of measuring the results of advertising.

Space does not permit detailed discussion of these problems of adver-

tising management. They constitute the subject matter of courses in promotional strategy and advertising management.[7]

PERSONAL SELLING

Personal selling is a second important order-getting ingredient available to the executive responsible for determining the promotional mix. It involves face-to-face contact between the seller or representative and the prospective buyer. The purposes of such personal contacts may include the following: (1) to get an order for the product, (2) to get retailers to actively promote and display the product at the point of purchase, (3) to get wholesalers to cooperate with the manufacturer by selling the product actively or by encouraging retailers to tie in at the point of purchase with the seller's advertising and promotional efforts, and (4) to educate those who may influence purchase to favor the company and its product.

Personal solicitation differs from advertising in that it delivers the selling message by personal contact as opposed to presentation through nonpersonal media such as newspapers, magazines, television, and industrial papers. For this reason, the salesperson may adapt the message to the needs, interests, and reactions of the prospect. The same advertising message, however, is delivered to all who see or hear the particular medium carrying the advertisement. Herein lies an important difference between advertising and personal selling.

Several different kinds of personal selling may be distinguished. The most familiar, perhaps, is retail selling as illustrated by the activities of the clothing salesperson in a men's shop. While the activities of the automobile salesperson also illustrate retail selling, they often involve contacts with prospects outside the dealer's place of business. House-to-house selling by the representatives of a manufacturer, such as the Avon Company, illustrates a third type of approach. A fourth would be personal contacts with industrial users by the salesperson of a firm manufacturing producer goods. The sale of electronic computers to manufacturers by the representatives of International Business Machines would illustrate this type of sales job. A fifth type would be the manufacturer's salesperson who calls upon wholesalers. This type is illustrated by the representatives of the R. J. Reynolds Tobacco Company who take orders for Winston filter cigarettes from tobacco, drug, and grocery wholesalers. The manufacturer's salesperson who calls directly upon retailers would illustrate a sixth kind of selling. Here an example would be the salespeople of Standard Brands, Inc., selling coffee, tea,

---

[7]For a discussion of these topics, see J. F. Engel, M. R. Warshaw, and T. C. Kinnear, *Promotional Strategy*, 5th ed. (Homewood, Ill.: Richard D. Irwin, 1983), part 4.

and yeast to grocery retailers. A seventh kind of selling job is that of the salesperson for a wholesaler whose function is to take orders from retailers. The salespeople of wholesale distributors representing the General Electric Company in calling upon dealers who retail color television sets would illustrate this type of selling.

In each of the above examples, the main function of the salesperson is to secure an order. Manufacturers distributing through wholesalers, who in turn sell to retailers, may also use missionary salespeople in carrying out their marketing plans. Missionary salespeople are sometimes used to extend distribution by getting orders from retailers and turning them over to wholesalers to be filled. Missionary salespeople may also call upon retailers for the purpose of encouraging them to promote and display the manufacturer's brand more actively. On such calls, the salesperson may help the dealer plan advertising and display activities featuring the company's brand, may set up window or floor displays, may train retail salesclerks to sell more effectively, or may simply encourage the dealer to tie in more aggressively with the manufacturer's promotional program.

In the sale of prescription drugs, manufacturers customarily use detail workers who perform missionary selling functions. In this field, however, the detail workers are generally assigned the task of calling upon physicians and pharmacists in order to inform them about new drugs that are being introduced or promoted. If appropriate, samples may be provided. The task of the detail worker is, thus, basically educational; he or she is generally not expected to seek orders. If the pharmacist does place an order, however, it is usually turned over to a drug wholesaler for handling, provided such a middleman is the customary source of supply.

The introduction of Pablum baby cereal, by Mead Johnson & Company, illustrates a situation in which the main burden of selling was placed upon detail workers. In keeping with Mead Johnson's status as a pharmaceutical house strongly identified with ethical drug specialties, Pablum was distributed through the drug trade. The product was promoted entirely through physicians by Mead Johnson sales representatives.[8]

Factors Influencing the Use of Personal Selling

Whether the manufacturer sets up a sales force to call upon ultimate consumers or industrial users is influenced by decisions on distribution policy of a type which have been discussed previously. Thus, if a decision is reached to distribute through middlemen instead of selling directly to

---

[8]L. L. Duke, *Packaging Problems in Redesigning a Product Line*, American Management Association Packaging Series, no. 42 (New York: American Management Association, Inc.), pp. 31–32.

the consumer or industrial user, then the manufacturer relies upon the dealers to furnish the kinds of amounts of the personal sales contact with prospects that appears to be essential. If personal contact is essential, the manufacturer may then seek types of dealers who have the necessary sales organizations to perform the desired task. To make sure that effective personal selling by middlemen supports the brand, the manufacturer may also assist dealers to do a better job of selecting and training salespeople.

Whether a manufacturer organizes a sales force to call upon retailers is likewise determined largely by decisions on distribution policy. The seller has the alternative of selling directly to retailers or of relying upon wholesalers to provide the necessary retail sales contacts. If a decision is reached to use wholesalers, the task of maintaining sales contact with dealers rests upon their shoulders. Under some conditions, however, the manufacturer may decide to set up a missionary sales force to supplement the work of the wholesalers' sales representatives. Whether a missionary sales organization is necessary will depend, in part, upon the kind of support that may be expected from the salespeople of the wholesalers. If the wholesalers' lines are wide and their salespeople are little more than order takers, occasions may arise in which the manufacturer feels that missionary salespeople would be desirable to provide more aggressive contact with retailers. If the company plans to introduce a new product, special effort will be needed in order to gain distribution through retail outlets. Missionary salespeople are often used temporarily to help build distribution for the new line. Where active dealer promotion and display are desired as a tie-in with the manufacturer's advertising effort, missionary salespeople may be used to encourage the necessary retail cooperation. Of course, the use of missionary salespeople is justified only where enough additional sales result from such effort to justify the additional expense incurred.

Where wholesalers are used, most manufacturers will set up a sales organization to maintain sales contacts with them. Except where advertising is strong enough to pull the brand through channels of distribution, the manufacturer is likely to rely upon personal selling to make sure that the brand is stocked and given the customary sales support by the wholesalers' sales organizations. Where consumer advertising is especially effective, as may be the case with individual brands of patent medicines, for example, firms have been known to operate without a sales organization and to rely upon securing orders from wholesalers by mail. Such cases are rare, however.

Even where distribution is achieved through middlemen, the manufacturer is still faced with the problem of determining whether personal selling to consumers or industrial users should be included in the marketing mix. If the best results appear to come through emphasis on personal contact with consumers at the point of purchase, the manufac-

turer will want to take active steps to influence dealers to provide the necessary personal sales effort to reap maximum returns. Experience indicates that it may be wise to include personal solicitation of ultimate consumers or industrial users in the selling mix under the following circumstances: (1) when the size of the purchase is relatively large, (2) if the product has features which require explanation and demonstration, (3) when the item is purchased at infrequent intervals, and (4) when prospects already own old models of the product upon which they will want a trade-in allowance.[9]

In the marketing of certain industrial goods, a survey of the prospect's needs is an essential preliminary to the making of a sale. Heavy installation equipment may sometimes need special adaptations in order to fit into the prospect's production line. Installation service may also need to be planned. In such cases, personal contact between the manufacturer's sales force and the industrial user is an essential element in the selling plan.

When Should Personal Selling Receive Main Emphasis?

Consideration of the factors outlined above enables the executive to make an estimate of the opportunity to make profitable use of personal solicitation in the selling program.[10] The question next arises as to when it is likely to be desirable to place the main burden upon personal solicitation in the selling mix. If the product is distributed through middlemen, such an approach involves getting the retailer or the industrial distributor to organize and maintain an effective personal selling organization. From what has already been said, it is clear that the policy of placing the main burden upon personal selling would tend to be desirable when two sets of conditions are present: (1) Circumstances would have to be unfavorable to the profitable use of consumer advertising to stimulate either primary or selective demand. Otherwise, a balanced program including both advertising and personal selling would seem to be indicated. (2) Conditions would have to be favorable to the profitable use of personal selling.

A situation in which the main burden should be placed upon personal selling is the marketing of electronic computers. Advertising to users tends to occupy a relatively minor role because of the high price of such equipment and the infrequency with which such installations are made. These factors, along with the need to explain how the computer can be used in different situations and to adapt the installation to individual

---

[9]For additional background on the role of personal selling, see Engel et al., *Promotional Strategy*, 5th ed., chap. 17.

[10]For the results of a landmark study of the personal selling function, see P. J. Robinson and Bent Stidsen, Marketing Science Institute, *Personal Selling in a Modern Perspective* (Boston: Allyn & Bacon, Inc., 1967).

circumstances, would indicate a need for heavy reliance on personal solicitation.

Other Problems of Sales Force Management

Once the decision has been made to include personal selling in the marketing mix, a number of important problems arise for consideration by the manager of the sales force. Among the more significant are: (1) how to recruit and select salespeople of the desired caliber, (2) how to train new salespeople so that they will perform their functions effectively, (3) what methods of compensation to use, (4) how to stimulate the salespeople to exert maximum effort on the job, (5) how to supervise the salespeople so that they will make the most of the opportunities existing in their territories, (6) how to determine the territories in which the salespeople are to operate, and (7) how to evaluate the salespeople's performance. Space does not permit the discussion of these problems of sales force management. Those interested will find these topics discussed in specialized sales management texts and in advanced courses in this field.[11]

DEALER PROMOTION

Dealer promotion is a third order-getting ingredient which many maunfacturers may want to include in the selling mix. Dealer promotion efforts may include various kinds of advertising, window and interior displays, demonstrations of the product, use of consumer contests, use of premiums, use of combination offers, distribution of free samples, and other activities designed to promote the sale of a given brand. Hence dealer promotion is a subclassification under the broader heading *sales promotion*. Let us clarify this distinction. Sales promotion is defined as those activities (other than personal selling, advertising, and publicity) that stimulate consumer purchasing and dealer effectiveness, such as displays, shows and exhibitions, demonstrations, and various nonrecurrent selling efforts not in the ordinary routine.[12] As a means of facilitating analysis, in this discussion the term *sales promotion* is divided into *dealer promotion,* including those tools involving action by the reseller, and those which the manufacturer initiates, including *consumer promotions* and *trade promotions.*

Regardless of how limited or how extensive the promotional efforts desired of the retail dealer in the promotion of a manufacturer's brand, it should be noted that the retailer's voluntary cooperation must be

---

[11]See Benson P. Shapiro, *Sales Program Management: Formulation and Implementation* (New York: McGraw-Hill, 1977).

[12]*Marketing Definitions,* p. 20.

enlisted if the project is to succeed. Before the dealer can be led to promote a manufacturer's brand, he or she must be convinced that it is advantageous to do so. Securing retail cooperation in promotional work, therefore, requires careful planning and execution on the part of the manufacturer. In considering whether to include dealer promotion in the selling mix, accordingly, the problems involved in getting the desired cooperation should be kept in mind.[13]

At the outset, it is obvious that only those manufacturers or producers who distribute through retail dealers or industrial distributors will be concerned with whether to include dealer promotion in the selling mix. Among those who would not use this selling method would be: (1) manufacturers selling by mail order to consumers or users, (2) firms whose salespeople call directly upon the consumer or user, and (3) producers who sell their products to chains or department stores to be marketed under the distributor's private brand.

It is also noteworthy that the need for identifying the retail middleman with the manufacturer's brand is related to the firm's distribution policy. Thus, where the policy of selective retail distribution is followed, it becomes essential for the manufacturer to take active steps to see to it that the local source of supply is identified with his or her brand.

Under the policy of selective distribution, a relatively small percentage of the available retail outlets will stock the manufacturer's brand; where exclusive agency representation is followed, only a single retailer in the community will do so. Unless the local source of supply is identified with the manufacturer's brand through signs, window displays, and advertising over own name, the demand created by the manufacturer's general advertising may be dissipated because of the consumer's lack of knowledge of where to go in order to buy the product. Failure to recognize the importance of this matter may result in ineffective general advertising.

Increasing Importance of Point-of-Purchase Promotion

Point-of-purchase communication vehicles constitute an important classification of dealer promotional activities. During the past 15 years they have taken on increasing significance to manufacturers of consumer goods who distribute through retailers. According to Quelch and Cannon-Bonventre, there are three reasons for this development.

> First, they often prove more productive than advertising and promotion expenditures. Second, the decline in sales support at the store level is stimulating interest among retailers in manufacturers' POP programs. Third, changes in consumers' shopping patterns and expecta-

---

[13]For further discussion of this topic, see Engel et al., *Promotional Strategy*, 5th ed., chap. 21.

tions, along with an upsurge in impulse buying, mean that the point of purchase is playing a more important role in consumers' decision making than ever before.[14]

Among those manufacturers who distribute through retail middlemen, two contrasting types of promotional strategy may be distinguished (see Figure 10–2). One approach involves pulling the product through channels of distribution by placing the main emphasis on a strong program of consumer advertising. Where this is the approach, dealer promotion is used in a supplementary role. A contrasting method is to rely upon dealer push to consummate sales. Here the manufacturer relies upon dealers to promote the brand locally through retail advertising, window and interior displays, or other promotional devices. Accordingly, the manufacturer's efforts are directed primarily at the dealer in order to encourage him or her to promote the brand aggressively. Dealer's sales and advertising helps may also be provided as a means of facilitating the dealer's promotional work. The manufacturer, however, undertakes little or no consumer advertising on behalf of the brand.

FIGURE 10–2   Push versus pull strategy

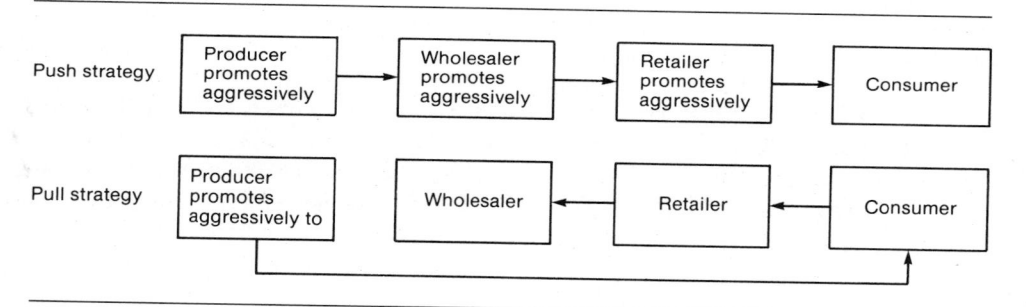

Source: Philip Kotler, *Principles of Marketing*, 2d ed. © 1983, p. 443. Reprinted by permission of Prentice Hall, Inc., Englewood Cliffs, N.J.

When Should Dealer Promotion Carry the Main Burden?

Under what conditions would it appear to be wise to place the main burden of selling upon dealer promotion? The first condition which

[14]Reprinted by permission of the Harvard Business Review. Excerpt from "Better Marketing at the Point of Purchase" by John R. Quelch and Kristina Cannon-Bonventre (November/December 1983). Copyright © 1983 by the President and Fellows of Harvard College; all rights reserved.

would encourage an executive to consider this strategy would be the lack of an opportunity to stimulate a profitable demand through consumer advertising. Since a poor consumer advertising opportunity may stem from several conditions, let us comment briefly upon some of the more important possibilities. At the same time, let us consider whether these conditions would tend to interfere with the possibility of getting effective dealer push.

Where the product is relatively standardized, the opportunity to make profitable use of consumer advertising tends to be limited. A standardized item such as cheesecloth, however, may be sold profitably by retailers provided it is displayed on aisle tables where there is considerable consumer traffic. Thus, the Claybon Company persuaded a department store to carry a special display of cheesecloth in handy-sized packages for one week. During this test period, the store sold 25,000 yards, which was 50 percent of its previous yearly sales. Dealer displays would therefore appear to offer a promising method of promoting the sales of a standardized item of this sort.

Again, when the important qualities of the product may easily be judged at the point of purchase, the possibility of stimulating brand discrimination through consumer advertising is very limited. This tends to be the situation in the sale of inexpensive children's toys, whose prospects tend to select the product on the basis of personal observation of the qualities of design, color, and motion represented in the individual items. These surface qualities lend themselves particularly well to effective retail advertising and to attention-getting window and interior displays. Dealer push would thus be an especially fruitful method of promoting the sale of children's toys.

Likewise, products likely to be purchased on impulse lend themselves especially well to sale through displays at points where a large number of consumers pass by. Items such as candy, neckties, inexpensive costume jewelry, and perfume fall into this category. Even though such products may not provide an opportunity for profitable use of consumer advertising, they may be sold effectively by getting retailers to display them in busy locations.

In contrast to the foregoing products, there are items with few important hidden qualities, in the purchase of which consumers are willing to exert more effort. Women's dresses are a good example. Qualities such as style, color, and type of material are surface characteristics which may be appraised by the consumer in the retail store. Yet women are willing to make a special trip into town and visit several stores in the process of buying a new dress. Products in this class may be sold very effectively through retail advertising as well as through window and store displays. Getting retailers to actively advertise and display such products is therefore sound strategy.

There are some products in the sale of which the retailer's name is

likely to be more important than the manufacturer's brand. Rayon cloth manufactured by Burlington Mills is a good example of such an item. Bedspreads, curtains, tablecloths, shower curtains, bath mats, fiber rugs, and window blinds are other examples of such products. Although the influence of fashion, the lack of hidden qualities, and the absence of individualizing features may tend to make the producer's brand unimportant, such items may be sold effectively through display. Manufacturers of such products might well aim at getting adequate dealer promotion as the key point in their selling strategy.

Finally, there are situations in which the product is distinctive and has hidden qualities but will not support an adequate expenditure for consumer advertising. A limited market, price resistance, or infrequency of purchase may prevent the early response needed to cover advertising costs. Or the firm may be handicapped by limited financial resources. Under these conditions, there is much to be said in favor of adopting the inexpensive strategy of encouraging active dealer display and promotion of the firm's brand.

When Advertising Is Emphasized, How Necessary Is Dealer Promotion?

The preceding section outlined the conditions under which a manufacturer would be wise to follow the strategy of placing primary emphasis upon getting retailers to actively advertise, display, and sell his or her brand. When the main selling burden should be placed upon consumer advertising, however, how necessary is dealer promotion? Carefully conducted sales tests demonstrate that window displays of nationally advertised brands tend to stimulate substantial sales increases in the store where the displays are located.

Similar tests of the use of interior displays appear to show conclusively that an advertised product would benefit considerably by being promoted in an appropriate manner within the retail store.

There are a number of conditions that tend to explain why window and interior displays increase the retail sales of even those brands that are most responsive to the pull of consumer advertising.

1. The effectiveness of advertising designed to stimulate a brand discrimination is enhanced by window and store displays, which reinforce the advertising message, serve as a reminder of a need, and encourage an immediate purchase.

2. Where a product is purchased infrequently, brand advertising is especially dependent upon window and store displays to recreate buying urges which have become dormant, to remind potential buyers of a need, and to encourage immediate action.

3. Where a substantial portion of customers shop for the generic product in a self-service store, prominent display at the point of purchase tends to stimulate sales.

4. Since a substantial portion of those who trade in self-service stores do not arrive with a shopping list, point-of-purchase displays serve to remind them of what they need.

5. Any brand that is purchased on impulse by a portion of the buyers will tend to benefit from point-of-purchase display.

Retail advertisements tend to enhance the effectiveness of a manufacturer's brand advertising. They provide the additional stimulus which may be needed to convert a brand preference into a buying urge. They add to the penetration of the advertising message within a local market. They serve as reminders of a need.

It is apparent from the foregoing discussion that with some expectations, even where the main selling burden is placed upon consumer advertising, the addition of retail advertising, display, and promotional efforts tends to enhance the effectiveness of the promotional program. Although dealer promotion would thus appear to be an essential part of the selling mix in the majority of these instances, we should not lose sight of the fact that its position is strictly supplementary to consumer advertising.

When Retail Personal Selling Is Emphasized, How Necessary Is Dealer Promotion?

In an earlier discussion, it was pointed out that retail personal selling tends to be effective when the size of the purchase is large, when the items purchased need explanation and demonstration, when purchase is infrequent, and when trade-in allowances are offered on old models. When the main emphasis is placed upon retail personal selling, how necessary is dealer advertising, display, and promotional effort?

If the manufacturer follows the policy of selective retail distribution, it is important to take active steps to make certain that dealers identify themselves as the local source of supply. Otherwise, the desire to examine the brand before making a buying decision may be frustrated by lack of knowledge of where to go for a demonstration. Although a diligent search might enable the prospect to uncover the name of a dealer, the manufacturer would be well advised to make it as easy as possible for the prospect to acquire the necessary information. Advertising over the dealer's name, store identification signs, and window displays thus serve a useful purpose in helping to bring prospects into contact with retail salespeople.

If the price of the product is relatively high, as in the case of a color TV set, the prospect has to sacrifice a substantial portion of the family's surplus for discretionary spending in order to make the purchase. If the product also has a relatively long life and thus is replaced infrequently, the natural resistance to the price may lead the prospect to postpone the purchase. Under these conditions, the manufacturer's brand advertising needs to be supplemented by strong direct-action stimuli designed to

get prospects to visit the dealer's store and examine the new model. Since dealers tend to favor advertising designed to bring an immediate response, the manufacturer may find it wise to encourage active dealer advertising and promotion.

If a product requires aggressive personal selling by the dealer's organization, this effort may be made most effective if it is supported by an active program of dealer promotion. The retail salespeople need to be assisted in making contact with likely prospects. Retail advertising, display, and promotion will tend to bring such prospects into the store or stimulate them to inquire by telephone or mail. With such assistance the salesperson can make the most effective use of time and persuasive talents.

Methods of Encouraging Dealer Promotion

After determining the role of dealer promotion in the selling mix, the manufacturer faces the problem of selecting suitable methods for encouraging the desired degree of dealer support. A common method is to provide retailers with dealer helps which will aid them in their display, promotional, and advertising work. Some firms offer dealers cooperative advertising allowances as a means of encouraging local advertising. Others rely upon the persuasive efforts of their salesforce to encourage dealers to tie in with the manufacturer's general advertising by using retail advertisements, window displays, counter displays, and other promotional methods. Factors to be considered in selecting the proper methods include: (1) how important active dealer promotion is believed to be, (2) whether distribution is selective or unselective, (3) competitive practice, and (4) the relative costs of alternative methods.

Gaining retail cooperation with POP programs. According to Quelch and Cannon-Bonventre:

> Retailers are becoming increasingly receptive to manufacturers' offers of POP merchandising programs. The delicate power balance between the manufacturer and the trade is such, however, that retailers will not give up control of the POP readily, particularly at a time when its importance is growing. Moreover, the pressure on retailers to carve out distinctive positionings to survive heightens their determination to control store layouts, space allocations, and POP merchandising.
>
> Hence, at the same time that their interest in manufacturers' POP programs is rising, retailers are becoming more selective than they once were and beginning to impose constraints [on what they will accept in the way of POP displays.]

* * * * *

How can consumer goods marketers address the different—and sometimes conflicting—interests of the manufacturer, the retailer, and the consumer at the point of purchase?

1. For one thing, they can use well-designed displays. They reduce

store labor costs by facilitating shelf stocking and inventory control, minimizing out-of-stock items, and lowering the required level of back-room inventory. For example, automatic feed displays such as 7up's single-can dispensers eliminate the need for store clerks to realign shelf stock.

2. Good displays are designed for a particular type of store and often for a specific store department. Good displays reflect the likely level of trade support. There is no point in offering the trade a perma-nent display for a seasonal product. Well-designed displays are versatile and can accommodate new products.

3. Innovative displays can be developed to supplement the efforts of salespeople. For example, Mannington Mills' Compu-Flor, a small computerized display placed in floor-covering retail outlets, is pro-grammed to use a potential consumer's answers to eight questions about room decor. The terminal then displays 3 to 10 appropriate Manning-ton styles for the customer to choose from. Mannington had placed the units in 700 stores by the end of 1982 at a cost of $8 million, an amount equal to the company's advertising budget.

Mannington found that Compu-Flor selected styles for customers more efficiently than salespeople, . . . encouraged salespeople to push Mannington products rather than those of its two larger competitors, . . . and boosted the number of sales closed on a customer's first store visit.[15]

The development of distinctive packaging is another way the manu-facturer can increase the likelihood of retailer cooperation at the point of purchase.

Appropriate packaging, of course, attracts attention at the point of purchase. Nabisco and Kellogg use the same package design for many items in their product lines to present a highly visible billboard of pack-ages to consumers at the point of purchase.

Standardized packaging also permits easy identification of brands, types, and sizes. Similarly, packaging communicates product benefits and identifies target groups. Contrast the packaging of Marlboro ciga-rettes, aimed at men, Virginia Slims, targeted at women, and Benson & Hedges DeLuxe Ultra Lights, with a silver package designed to appeal to elitists among both men and women.

* * * * *

Manufacturers are increasingly using consumer promotions to make shopping exciting [see the following section for a more complete discus-sion of this type of promotional effort]. These include premiums, cou-pons, samples, and refund offers in or on product packages to help them stand out and break through the visual clutter at the point of purchase. Package-delivered promotions have the further advantage of

---

[15]The material in this section is quoted from Quelch and Cannon-Bonventre, ibid., pp. 165–67.

being inexpensive in comparison with consumer promotions offered in magazine advertisements or direct-mail campaigns.

Manufacturers are also becoming aware that retailers favor manufacturers whose promotions bring consumers into the store. Retailers also like promotions that tie into store merchandising themes and cross-sell other products (promotions built around recipes or complete home decorating services, for instance).

Manufacturers can extend to retailers a number of innovative approaches for reinforcing brand awareness and delivering advertising messages at the point of purchase. These include:

Commercials broadcast over in-store sound systems.

Moving message displays units with changeable electronic messages.

Customer-activated videotapes and video discs that show merchandise such as furniture that is too bulky to be displayed on the department floor.

Television sets installed over cash registers to show waiting customers commercials for products that are usually available nearby.

Advertisements on cards used in supermarkets and other self-service stores.

Dangles and mobile displays that use available air space rather than limited floor space.

Not only is it important to choose appropriate methods to encourage the desired dealer support at the point of purchase, but also it is even more important to ensure that potentially effective programs are properly implemented at the store level. Only when this is done will retailers continue to support the manufacturers' plans and make effective use of the materials provided.[16]

CONSUMER PROMOTIONS

A fourth classification of order-getting ingredients includes various types of short-run consumer promotions designed to stimulate a quick buying response—contests, premiums, combination offers, coupons, and consumer price-offs, among others. Since these devices employ strong direct-action stimuli to force immediate purchasing action, they may also be termed "forcing methods." The basic appeal is to the desire for a bargain or the desire to get something for nothing. When these "forcing methods" are used by the retailer they may be classified under the "dealer promotion" category. If the same methods are used by the manufacturer then they may be labeled "consumer promotions." Closely related are various types of trade promotions, such as free goods, allow-

---

[16]For an excellent discussion of POP program development and practical ideas for effective program execution see Quelch and Cannon-Bonventre, ibid., pp. 168–69.

ances, and special discounts, which are designed to influence reseller cooperation. Such methods relate to the task of stimulating dealer promotion, discussed previously.

Consumer promotions are designed to achieve quick impact at the point of purchase, possibly along with one or more underlying goals. Specific objectives that are commonly identified include the following.

1. Getting prospects to try a new product (through "forced sampling").
2. Calling attention to improvements in established products.
3. Stopping the loss of old customers resulting from vigorous competition.
4. Encouraging active point-of-purchase display and promotion.
5. Helping and stimulating the firm's sales force.[17]

The use of consumer promotions is highly controversial. Some argue that their use is harmful, since they divert advertising and promotional effort away from the merits of the product and toward the contest, the premium, or the bargain which is being offered. Others say that consumer promotions are a useful way to stimulate "forced sampling" of a new product or to inject interest in an advertising campaign through the "change of pace" provided by a creative consumer promotion. Still others use them as a defensive measure in an attempt to nullify the effect of competitors' consumer promotions.

Obviously, the need for strong stimuli in the promotional program depends upon whether or not an early buying response may be expected to result from the combined impact of consumer advertising, personal selling, and dealer promotion. Quick buying action may be expected (1) if strong, dynamic appeals may be made to consumer buying motives, (2) if the price of the product is small and the potential market is relatively large, (3) if the promotion appears at a time when consumers' needs for the generic product are greatest, and (4) if the product is bought frequently. If these conditions are met, there is little need for using consumer promotions to force an early response. If these conditions do not exist, however, the use of consumer promotions may properly be considered.

Even where a strong stimulus appears to be necessary to achieve a desired degree of early buying response, the wisdom of including a consumer promotion in the mix is not a foregone conclusion.

In considering this possibility, it is wise to keep in mind that consumer promotions are short-run, tactical devices aimed at stimulating an early response at the point of purchase. Applied under proper circumstances, along with other elements in the promotional mix, short-run gains may

---

[17]From the Marketing Science Institute, *Promotional Decisions Using Mathematical Models*, p. 10. © Copyright 1967 by Allyn & Bacon, Inc., Boston.

result from their use. The long-run benefits of using promotions are more problematic, however. When they are used to promote forced sampling of a new product, long-run benefits may indeed result. When they are utilized in the promotion of well-known, established brands, increases in share of market are usually temporary.

Under what circumstances might we expect the use of a promotion to prove an exception to the common experience and achieve long-run gains? The following questions are suggestive: (1) Will consumers like the brand when they try it? (2) Are price, distribution methods, and advertising policies favorable to the improvement of the brand's competitive position? (3) Have successive and frequent uses been made of forcing methods so that smaller and smaller incremental gains may be expected?

While such considerations may help to identify the circumstances in which both short-run and long-run gains may be anticipated, a recent Marketing Science Institute study summarizes the limitations of our knowledge on this topic as follows:

> It is plain that promotion plays an important role in marketing, but our knowledge of its effectiveness is lacking. The unfortunate facts that many promotional efforts seem to be prosaic, that no distinct goals are set, that postaudits are unimaginative, and that brand profits are jeopardized by intrinsic risks or wrong decisions may be attributed primarily from our inability to effectively tailor promotional endeavors to particular products, markets, and circumstances. This problem of promotional selection is essentially the executive's responsibility, although effective research can assist in narrowing the areas for unaided judgment.[18]

As a means of improving decision making in this area, this MSI study emphasizes the following points: (1) the desirability of establishing explicit goals for consumer promotions, (2) the need for writing down such objectives so that all participants in the company's marketing effort will see what they are expected to do to achieve the desired objectives, (3) the wisdom of evaluating past performance to develop guidelines for the present and future, (4) the need for conducting scientifically designed tests or experiments to guide in decision making, and (5) the need for making carefully planned post-audits of both the short-run and long-run results of the consumer promotions used.

The primary purpose of the MSI study was to explain and demonstrate some applications of quantitative techniques, using real data, to measure and evaluate market response to promotions. While space does not permit a discussion of the quantitative methods used, those inter-

---

[18]Marketing Science Institute, *Promotional Decisions Using Mathematical Models*, p. 17. Reprinted by permission of the publisher.

ested will find it rewarding to examine the study itself for further information.

PUBLICITY

Another communication tool which may be included in the promotional mix is publicity. *Publicity* is defined as the activity for "securing editorial space, as divorced from paid space, in all media read, viewed, or heard by a company's customers and prospects, for the specific purpose of assisting in the meeting of sales goals."[19] While we are concerned with its use in promoting products or services, it may also be used to promote persons, places, ideas, or organizations, among others. Unlike advertising, publicity is not paid for by the sponsor.

Not only is publicity of potential use in product promotion, but also it is often an important communication tool in a firm's public relations program. Public relations "evaluate public attitudes, identifies the policies and procedures of an individual or an organization with the public interest, and executes a program of action to earn public understanding and acceptance."[20] The publics addressed may be consumers, employees, suppliers, stockholders, the investment community, government administrators, or the community at large. The methods of communication may be press relations, product publicity, personal appearances by executives, institutional advertising, and lobbying, among others.

Product publicity has certain advantages that make this tool worth considering in planning the promotional mix. A well-executed product publicity story that appears in a newspaper, magazine, or broadcast announcement has greater credibility than a paid advertisement presented in the same medium. The audience assumes that the medium is unbiased and hence the publicity message is more believable than an advertisement promoting the same product.

Then too, product publicity appearing in the media is not paid for by the manufacturer, while an advertisement must be paid for at rates depending upon the space used and the audience reached. According to Arthur Merims, an experienced executive involved in product publicity and public relations work, American Oil Company, for example, estimated the value of product publicity as follows:

> Media coverage included 3,500 column inches of news and photographs in 350 publications with a combined circulation of 79.4 million; 2,500 minutes of air time on 290 radio stations and an estimated audi-

---

[19]George Black, *Planned Industrial Publicity* (New York: G. P. Putnam's Sons, 1952), p. 3.

[20]Bertrand R. Canfield and Frazier Moore, *Public Relations: Principles, Cases, and Problems*, 6th ed. (Homewood, Ill.: Richard D. Irwin, 1973), p. 4.

ence of 65 million; and 660 minutes of air time on 160 television stations with an estimated audience of 91 million. If this time and space had been purchased at advertising rates, it would have amounted to $1,047,000.[21]

Although it is the least used of the major promotional tools, product publicity can play an important role in promotional programs under appropriate conditions. Accordingly, let us consider the circumstances in which there is an opportunity to make effective use of this promotional tool. Since information supplied to editors will only be printed or announced by broadcast media if it is of potential interest to media audiences, the proposed message must have potential news value. Introduction of new products or the announcement of new models (as with autos) would qualify. With food products, attractive recipes are often supplied to magazines or newspapers, which they may communicate as a service to their audiences. A significant reduction in prices may also qualify for a widely used product.

If there appears to be an opportunity to use product/service publicity in the promotional mix, how can it be integrated effectively with the remainder of the promotional program? A study of the effective and ineffective aspects of 17 publicity programs was made by Merims. His suggestions include the following:

> (1) Publicists, whether in-house or hired, are summoned at the start of the venture and given complete freedom to contribute in formulation of the marketing plan. (2) Marketing management and the publicists agree on specific goals that can be measured and evaluated. (3) These goals are targets for publicity alone, not merely a part of the overall marketing objectives. (4) Before the program is launched, members of the marketing team agree on criteria for comparing results with goals. (5) The publicity budget is separate from other budgets, and only the direct costs of the publicity program are included. (6) Like advertising and most products, publicity materials are pretested to improve quality and effectiveness. (7) The publicity campaign is launched before other promotional activities; to increase publicity's potency and measure its results, it is advantageous to conclude the publicity effort when other promotional efforts (such as advertising) commence. (8) Publicity materials are merchandised to the sales and distribution forces to boost their enthusiasm and enhance their selling efforts. (9) A dollar return on the publicity investment is calculated, if possible, using the contribution margin method or some other formulation satisfactory to management.[22]

---

[21]Reprinted by permission of the Harvard Business Review. Excerpts from "Marketing's Stepchild Product Publicity" by Arthur M. Merims (November/December 1972). Copyright © 1972 by the President and Fellows of Harvard College; all rights reserved.

[22]Ibid., pp. 57–63.

NEW WAYS TO REACH YOUR CUSTOMERS

In the preceding pages we have discussed the conditions under which personal selling, advertising, sales promotion, and publicity may be included in the promotional mix. According to Shapiro and Wyman, however, newer communication tools have evolved in recent years which should also be considered for possible combination with these traditional methods in order to more effectively sell a firm's products. In the paragraphs that follow, the approach suggested by Shapiro and Wyman is summarized.[23]

Important methods that help marketers communicate more effectively with potential and existing customers have come into wider use over the past decade. These techniques can assist marketers in two ways: first, they allow increased flexibility for devising marketing programs and, second, in an age of escalating selling and media costs, they enable marketers to hold down expenses.

*   *   *   *   *

The newer tools include *national account management, demonstration centers, industrial stores, telemarketing,* and new forms of *catalog selling.*

National account management. A few large accounts comprise a disproportionately large percentage of almost any company's sales (industrial as well as consumer goods and services). National account management can often be applied (*a*) if these large accounts are geographically or organizationally dispersed, (*b*) if the selling company has many interactions with the buying company's operating units, and (*c*) if the product and selling process are complex. National account management thus is an extension, improvement, and outgrowth of personal selling.

Demonstration centers. Specifically designed showrooms, or demonstration centers, allow customers to observe and usually to try out complex industrial equipment. The approach supplements personal selling and works best when the equipment being demonstrated is complex and not portable. Demonstration centers have been used in many industries including telecommunications, data processing, electronic test gear, and machine tools.

The demonstration center also supplements trade shows, with three major differences between them: (1) The demonstration center is permanent; trade shows are temporary. (2) The company can determine the location of the demonstration center, unlike trade shows. (3) Demonstration centers are designed to provide a competition-free environment for the selling process. Trade shows, of course, are filled with competitors.

---

[23]Reprinted by permission of the Harvard Business Review. Excerpt from "New Ways to Reach Your Customers" by Benson P. Shapiro and John Wyman (July/August 1981). Copyright © 1981 by the President and Fellows of Harvard College; all rights reserved.

But the primary benefit to the seller comes from demonstration—often to high-level executives who are unavailable for standard sales presentations. Demonstration centers in some situations, furthermore, replace months of regular field selling. Demonstrating equipment or processes often has more impact than describing them.

* * * * *

Industrial stores.   This approach also involves a demonstration of equipment or a process, with the emphasis generally on cost reduction not the creation of seller benefits. Stores are permanent. The idea is to bring the customer to the salesperson. The store approach works well when: (1) the sales are too small to justify sales calls, (2) the product or process is complex and lends itself to demonstration, or when (3) the company does not sell many products to the same customer.

The store approach has been successful in the small-business computer industry, where Digital Equipment has more than 20 stores in operation and development. Xerox has also made stores a major part of its marketing strategy. As selling and travel costs escalate, the use of stores will become even more popular.

Telemarketing.   Telephone marketing is an important emerging trend that companies can exploit in five ways—as a less costly substitute for personal selling, as a supplement to personal selling, as a higher-impact substitute for direct-mail and media advertising, as a supplement to direct mail and other media, and as a replacement for other slower, less convenient communications techniques.

Cost savings.   Telephone selling has traditionally provided a highly customized means of two-way communication. Greater sophistication in telecommunications equipment and services, new marketing approaches, and broader applications have turned telephone selling into telemarketing. It still does not provide the quality of a personal visit but is much cheaper.

Supplement to personal visits.   Some selling situations require periodic sales visits. Often the cost of the required call frequency is greater than the sales volume justifies and, in these cases, telephone calls can supplement personal visits.

Substitute for direct mail.   The telephone gives greater impact at an admittedly higher cost. Telemarketing has been successful in selling subscription renewals and could also aid sales of large consumer durables such as automobiles, swimming pools, and appliances.

As a supplement.   Telemarketing can add to as well as replace direct-mail and media advertising. Many companies have effectively used 800 telephone numbers in direct-mail, television, and print media advertising.

The combined media/telemarketing approach has been successful for a variety of products, including specialty coffees, smokeless tobacco, books, and records.

Customer–company coordination.   Finally, the telephone can be used as a part of a communications program to tie companies to their constituencies. The responsiveness and convenience of the telephone, com-

bined · with its two-way message content, make it particularly appropriate for this use. A dissatisfied customer, for example, can get a quick response to a problem.

Catalog selling. An old approach in the consumer goods market, catalog selling is an evolving method in industrial and commercial markets. Companies active in the office and computer supply businesses have found catalogs to be an efficient way of generating the relatively small dollar sales typical of their businesses.

Other industries have also used catalogs, particularly in conjunction with telephone order centers or telemarketing centers. Sigma Chemical Company, for example, uses a catalog to sell enzymes for laboratory use, although competitors generally use sales forces. Other catalog applications include electronic components and industrial supplies. The approach is highly cost-effective in transmitting a great deal of information to selected prospects and customers in a usable, inexpensive format.

Creating a program. The newer ways of selling, when combined with the traditional communications approaches, enable marketers to make precise choices in developing their communications programs. Four major steps are necessary for developing an effective program: (1) analyze the communications costs, (2) specify the communications needs, (3) formulate a coherent program, and (4) monitor the total system.[24]

DETERMINING THE PROMOTIONAL MIX

As you think back over the preceding discussion, it is apparent that the task of determining the promotional mix includes the following steps. (1) Decide which of the various available promotional methods to include in the mix. Factors to consider in appraising the opportunity to make effective use of consumer advertising, consumer promotions, personal selling, dealer promotion, and publicity have been outlined in the previous pages. (2) Determine whether it is likely to be most profitable to place the main burden of selling upon consumer advertising, personal selling, dealer promotion, or other selling methods. Estimates of the relative suitability of these methods will guide this decision. (3) Reach a decision on how supplementary promotional methods may be combined with the method to be emphasized in order to perform the necessary selling tasks and to achieve maximum effectiveness from the total mix. Most promotional programs are a combination of several methods. This fact highlights the need for careful integration of the methods chosen so that they constitute a well-coordinated, total program. This integration may be achieved through a careful definition of the necessary sales and promotional tasks and the intelligent choice of the various methods

---

[24]See ibid., pp. 107–10, for a full discussion of these four steps.

to be used in performing these tasks. Checklists showing the tasks to be performed and the methods selected to achieve desired goals may be helpful in achieving the proper integration of effort. Timing schedules listing the jobs to be done and those responsible for their performance may also assist in bringing about the necessary coordination.[25]

While the generalizations outlined above may be of assistance in the determination of an effective promotional mix, preliminary decisions based upon desk analyses should be checked by test campaigns in local areas wherever such campaigns are suitable and possible. Procedures should also be set up for measuring the results of the various promotional methods utilized. Such information will provide the basis for modification and improvement in subsequent campaigns.[26]

CONCLUSION

In this chapter we have turned from the basic questions of product policy and development, branding, pricing, and selecting channels of distribution to the all-important area of selling the product. To sell one must communicate, so we have described the nature of communication. The special theme of the chapter is the importance of sound promotional strategy and effective selection of appropriate communication methods in order to achieve the best promotional mix. The decisions that the marketing manager of a manufacturer or producer makes as to emphasis on advertising, personal selling, dealer promotion, consumer promotion, or publicity will be crucial to the success of the entire marketing program and of the business. It becomes clear that different products and different marketing situations call for different mixes of selling ingredients.

We now move on, in Chapter 11, to the decisions involved in determining the promotional appropriation.

QUESTIONS

1. Define *communication*. Explain and illustrate the basic elements in a communication system, using the following situations:

---

[25]The Program Evaluation and Review Technique (PERT) offers a promising solution to some of the difficulties encountered in the coordination of program elements. For an illustration of this approach, see Engel et al., *Promotional Strategy*, 5th ed., chap. 24.

[26]For a study ranking each of the promotional mix elements in terms of its importance for each of the stages of the product life cycle, see Ronald D. Taylor and John H. Summey, "The Promotional Mix and the Product Life Cycle: A Review of Their Interaction," in *Conceptual and Theoretical Developments in Marketing*, American Marketing Association's Special Educators' Conference, Phoenix, Arizona, February 10–13, 1980, in press. Note especially table 5.

a. A Ford Mustang salesperson talking with a lower-middle-class prospective buyer who has a three-year-old Pinto to trade in.

b. RCA-Victor advertising color television sets in The Netherlands.

How do these two situations differ? What implications do these differences have for marketing management?

2. What conditions must be present if communication is to be effective?

3. Distinguish between (a) product advertising and corporate advertising, (b) dealer promotions and consumer promotions, and (c) missionary salespeople and detail workers.

4. Appraise the advertisability of the following products (assuming that adequate funds are available to perform the necessary promotional tasks):

   a. Sugar.

   b. A patent remedy offering a sure cure for athlete's foot.

   c. Toys for three- to five-year-old children (colorful, offering movement and sound).

   d. Fine furniture in colonial styles sold nationally through 40 department stores, each with an exclusive agency for its market.

5. a. What considerations tend to determine the wisdom of using personal selling in the promotional mix?

   b. Would you place the main burden of promotion upon personal selling in the following situations?

      (1) A line of cosmetics.

      (2) A central home air conditioning system.

      (3) A new brand of freeze-dried coffee.

      (4) A line of apparel offering 200 different styles, including knit suits, dresses, slacks, sweaters, and blouses in casual designs aimed at the homemaker market and sold at modest prices.

6. a. Under what circumstances should dealer promotion carry the main burden of selling?

   b. Would you place the main emphasis upon dealer promotion in the sale of the following products?

      (1) Neckties.

      (2) Drapes for the living room.

      (3) A new soft drink with unusual thirst-quenching qualities.

      (4) Women's high-grade nylon hosiery.

      (5) Necklaces for men.

7. When advertising is emphasized in the promotional mix, is dealer promotion necessary? In answering, apply your analysis to the following products:

   a. Marlboro cigarettes.

   b. Toni hair coloring.

   c. Maxim freeze-dried coffee.

8. When retail personal selling is emphasized, is dealer promotion necessary? Answer by applying your analysis to the following products:

   a. Hickery Freeman high-grade men's suits.

     b.   Singer sewing machines.

     c.   Hi-fi sound systems.

     d.   Vacuum cleaners sold through department stores.

9. In the following cases, in which dealer promotion is essential, would you favor the use of dealer cooperative advertising allowances to encourage the desired effort, or would you emphasize "merchandising" the advertising to retail dealers to get their support?

     a.   High-grade men's shoes with selective retail distribution.

     b.   Medium-grade upholstered furniture.

10. Under what conditions is there likely to be an opportunity to make effective use of product publicity in a promotional program?

11. In what ways can an industrial marketer exploit telemarketing?

12. What are some of the innovative approaches that manufacturers may provide to retailers in order to encourage point-of-purchase promotion?

DETERMINING THE PROMOTIONAL APPROPRIATION

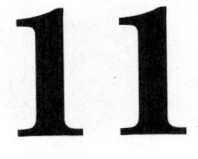

Closely related to the decision on the character of the promotional mix is the task of determining the size of the promotional appropriation. If analysis indicates that the main burden should be placed upon consumer advertising, the size of the promotional appropriation is likely to be larger than it would be if the primary emphasis were placed on dealer push. Conversely, the size of the expenditure that the product will support and that the company can finance is an important consideration in determining what promotional strategy is likely to be most effective for a given product and in deciding what combination of promotional methods to include in the selling mix.

The task of determining the promotional appropriation is of key importance, since this decision will have a significant influence upon the effectiveness of the promotional program and, hence, upon profits. Therefore, we have singled out that task for special consideration. Our primary purpose is to provide essential background on the approaches commonly used by executives in determining the appropriation for the total promotional effort in a given year, or, in the case of new products, for a period of several years. A secondary goal is to suggest some of the more important considerations that should be taken into account in reaching a decision on this important problem.

THEORETICAL ANALYSIS OF THE PROBLEM

The marginal approach to the determination of the promotional appropriation provides a useful theoretical framework against which we can later compare actual business practice. This approach is illustrated in Figure 11–1, which is a short-run analysis developed by Joel Dean based upon the following assumptions:[1] (1) Advertising cost is assumed to include all pure selling costs and is identified by the curve *SC*. Incremental advertising costs are the additional expenditures required to provide one additional unit of sales. (2) Incremental production costs are assumed to be constant at 20 cents per unit over the range of output covered in this example. In the short run, this tends to be true for firms whose production is mechanized. (3) Unit price is assumed to be constant at 70 cents over the range of volumes under consideration and does not change as a result of changes in selling costs. (4) The relationship between incremental advertising costs (*SC*) and sales volume is assumed to approximate a "U-shaped" curve which first declines as volume

FIGURE 11–1   Short-run determination of advertising outlay by marginal analysis

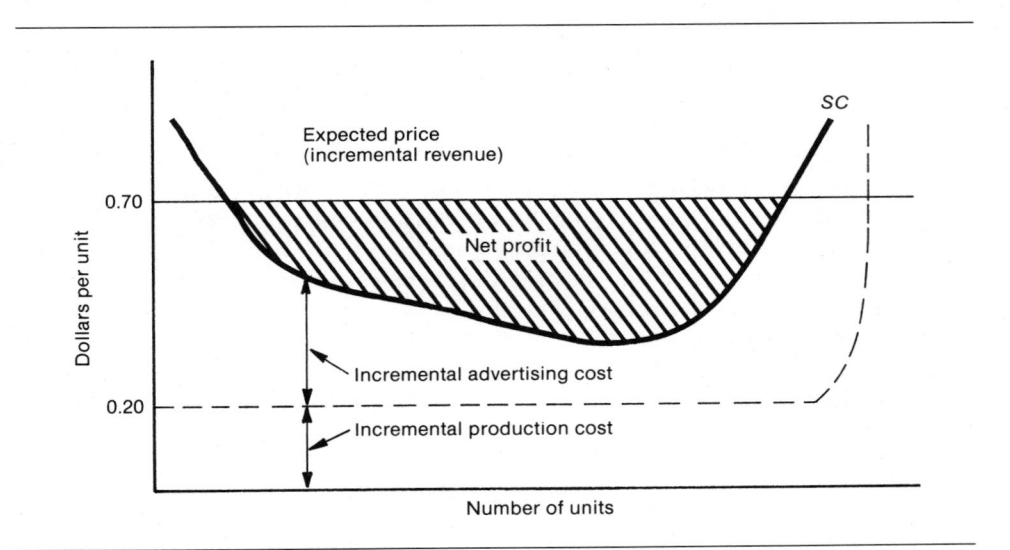

[1]Adapted from Joel Dean, *Managerial Economics*, pp. 356–61, © 1951. Reprinted by permission of Prentice-Hall, Inc., Englewood Cliffs, N.J.

increases, then is constant, and then rises at an accelerating rate. Incremental advertising costs (SC) may be determined from Figure 11-1 by identifying a given volume of sales and by running a vertical line to intersect curve SC. Then run a horizontal line from the point of intersection with SC to the vertical axis to read off the corresponding dollars-per-unit figure shown there—for example, 50 cents. From this figure, subtract incremental production costs of 20 cents per unit to get selling costs of 30 cents (50 cents − 20 cents = 30 cents). In this way, it may be determined that incremental advertising costs amount to $1 per unit at low volume, decline progressively as sales increase until a low point of 15 cents is reached, and then increase rapidly, as volume increases still more, until a figure of $1 is reached once again.

What is the rationale behind the U-shaped incremental advertising cost curve? The declining phase is explained in part by the economies of specialization: (1) As the appropriation increases in size, it becomes possible to make use of expert services. (2) Larger expenditures tend to make it possible to use more economical media. Even more important, however, are the economies that come from repetition of the advertising message and the learning that results. The increasing phase of the advertising cost curve results primarily because successively poorer prospects tend to be reached as advertising expenditures are increased. Then, too, increasing advertising expenditures may progressively exhaust the most vulnerable geographic areas or the most efficient advertising media.

Based on these assumptions, how should the advertising appropriation be determined? Clearly it would be profitable to increase advertising expenditures step by step until the incremental costs of advertising and production (as measured by the SC line) intersect the price line (i.e., until these costs are equal to the marginal revenue produced). In terms of the chart, if the incremental production cost equals 20 cents and the price amounts to 70 cents, then the gross margin is 50 cents. Accordingly, advertising costs per unit may be increased up to 50 cents per unit. Beyond this amount, the incremental revenues will be less than the incremental costs and thus the total profits will be reduced.

This analysis, of course, represents an ideal which most firms find difficult, if not impossible, to achieve. It assumes that the executive is able to make accurate estimates of the effect of advertising upon sales volume. Yet for most firms, the task of measuring the sales generated by advertising is a most challenging, if not impossible, research problem.

Part of the difficulty grows out of the fact that the sales volume achieved in any given year is the effect of both external environmental forces—such as general economic trends, changes in primary demand, and competitive activity—and internal influences, such as the marketing program. Within the marketing program itself, changes in sales volume may result not only from changes in the level of promotional expendi-

tures but also from changes in the impact of other elements in the marketing mix, such as product improvements, increased effectiveness of the distribution organization, and changes in prices. Even if it were possible to identify the portion of a sales increase that could be credited to the total promotional mix, there would still remain the task of determining what percentage of this amount resulted from advertising, as opposed to the shares which resulted from the personal selling efforts and the dealer promotional activities.

Again, this theoretical analysis does not recognize the cumulative effect of past advertising upon current or future sales. Many firms find that only a portion of the results of this year's advertising occur in the form of present sales, while the remaining results tend to carry over into future years. This problem is especially acute in the promotion of products of high unit value and infrequent purchase, such as automobiles. For firms making such products, a sizable proportion of this year's advertising expenditure is likely to pay off in terms of creating awareness, preference, or intent to buy which will tend to influence sales one, two, or more years into the future. At the same time, past advertising will have created attitudes that lead to current purchases. Since the advertising of many firms has such carry-over effects, the short-run marginal analysis outlined above tends to be of only limited value.

Despite its limitations, this theoretical analysis makes some conceptual contributions of practical importance. If the major part of the firm's advertising is designed to stimulate an immediate response, and if conditions are favorable to such a result, then the marginal approach provides a simple test of how much to spend and when to stop. The approach is also useful in providing management with guidelines as to the kind of information needed in deciding how much to spend on advertising. By the same token, it serves as a guide in designing research to evaluate the results of advertising and in gathering information that will help improve the quality of the appropriation decision.

COMMON APPROACHES TO DETERMINING THE APPROPRIATION

Now that we have outlined the theoretical approach to the determination of promotional expenditures, let us consider some of the more common approaches followed by business firms in actual practice. Four of the more important alternative methods will be discussed: (1) percentage of sales, (2) all available funds, (3) competitive parity, and (4) research objective. While our discussion will be in terms of determining the advertising appropriation, the analysis may be applied equally well to the determination of budgets for personal selling and sales promotional activities.

Some years ago, in making a survey of approaches to the determina-

tion of the advertising appropriation for the Association of National Advertisers, Richard Webster recommended that advertisers use a two-way classification originally suggested by C. M. Edwards and W. H. Howard: (1) the breakdown method and (2) the buildup method.[2] The breakdown method is described as providing a lump sum to be disbursed by the advertising department as it sees fit, and the buildup method is characterized as an appropriation that tells in detail exactly how the funds are to be expended. Since this classification will aid us in our analysis, let us take a moment to explain the principle upon which it is based.

In the breakdown method, the lump sum granted by management is the control. After the lump sum has been determined, advertising executives work out what they believe to be the most effective division of this amount by types of promotional efforts and advertising media. Under this approach, the primary emphasis is placed upon what the firm can afford. In the buildup method, the task to be accomplished by advertising is the control. Once the task has been defined, the budget is built up by determining the kinds and amounts of advertising and promotional efforts that are needed to achieve the desired goal and by estimating the cost of the necessary program. This emphasis upon estimating the costs of achieving desired goals is more consistent with the marginal approach than is the emphasis of the breakdown procedure.

Percentage of Sales[3]

A common approach falling under the breakdown classification is to arrive at a lump sum for advertising expenditures by multiplying dollar sales by a more or less arbitrarily chosen percentage. In making this computation, either past sales or estimated future sales may be used. The percentage applied may be either fixed (remaining the same over a period of years) or variable (changing from year to year). A variation of this approach is to substitute a specified number of dollars per unit for a percentage figure and to multiply that number by unit sales instead of dollar sales.

The variable percentage of estimated future sales is the most defensible variation of the breakdown method. The following conditions make the best possible case for using this approach: (1) the product is well established and has achieved a satisfactory share of market; (2) the

---

[2] Adapted by permission from Richard Webster, *Setting Advertising Appropriations* (New York: Association of National Advertisers, Inc., 1949), pp. 3–19.

[3] For a more complete discussion of all the methods commonly used in determining the advertising appropriation, see A. W. Frey, *How Many Dollars for Advertising* (New York: Ronald Press, 1955), pp. 48–82. See also David L. Hurwood and James K. Brown, *Some Guidelines for Advertising Budgeting* (New York: Conference Board, 1972).

external environment is relatively static during the period, so that the job to be done by advertising varies little from year to year; (3) management believes that a substantial change in advertising expenditures would be likely to stimulate strong, competitive retaliation; and (4) there is considerable uncertainty as to the effectiveness of advertising and thus some merit in giving considerable emphasis to what the firm can afford in determining the advertising appropriation.

The foregoing comments may suggest why 53 percent of leading consumer advertisers surveyed in 1983 reported that they used a percentage of anticipated sales in setting their advertising budgets.[4]

Since this approach treats advertising as an effect rather than a cause, however, it is still, in most instances, a questionable approach for management to use. Instead, it might be preferable to use an approach which makes the job to be done the guiding principle and then to check the firm's ability to finance the resulting appropriation by expressing it as a percentage of estimated sales.

All Available Funds

An extreme variation of the breakdown approach is one in which the firm allocates all available liquid resources and borrowable funds to support the advertising program. This variation was used by Brooks-Ledford Company in determining the initial advertising appropriation for Galaxy hairdressing and conditioner. Taking into account what portion of the sales dollar was needed to pay for direct production expenses, overhead, and amortization of bank loans, the firm allocated the remainder for selling and advertising expenditures. Salespeople were used in getting distribution and point-of-purchase promotion for Galaxy, while $75,000 was made available for cooperative advertising. This promotional program started Galaxy on its way to becoming a market leader in its field.

Under what circumstances might this method be defensible? (1) This method might be justified where there is an excellent opportunity to make use of consumer advertising in the introduction of a new product and where such promotional effort may be expected to produce an early, measurable sales response. Here, current profits may well be sacrificed in favor of attaining a sizable market share for the brand and, accordingly, a favorable rate of long-run profits. (2) Where the firm can estimate the marginal effectiveness of advertising, this method may result in reasonable satisfactory appropriations as long as the product is operating short of the point at which incremental advertising costs and

---

[4]Kent M. Lancaster and Judith A. Stern, "Computer-Based Advertising Budgeting Practices of Leading U.S. Consumer Advertisers," *Journal of Advertising*, 12, no. 4 (1983), p. 6.

incremental revenue are equal. Note that the use of such knowledge involves a combination of the marginal approach with the all-available-funds method.

At best, then, the all-available-funds approach is only a temporary expedient that may appear to meet the requirements of a new, inadequately financed firm or of a company that is short of working capital because of rapid growth. Circumstances may force a firm to give primary emphasis in setting the advertising appropriation to what the firm can afford. If this is the case, management should be impatient to shift to a more defensible approach as soon as circumstances permit.

Competitive Parity

The guiding principle of the competitive parity approach is to base the advertising appropriation in some systematic way upon what competitors are doing. One variation is to match competitors' advertising dollars. Another is to use the same percentage of sales for advertising as key competitors use or to use a ratio that is representative of the industry.

A more sophisticated variation of the competitive parity approach is to make the brand's share of total industry advertising expenditures equal to the desired share of market. Thus, if a 35 percent share of market were desired, the advertising appropriation would be set at a figure which represents 35 percent of the total estimated advertising expenditures for the industry.

This approach is an improvement over using the industry advertising ratio as the base, since consideration of the desired share of market for the brand involves an attempt to define the size of the job which must be performed by advertising during the coming year. The approach assumes, however, that the desired share of market, say, 25 percent, may be achieved by investing 25 percent of estimated industry advertising expenditures in the promotion of the company's brand. This may or may not be true.

Significant light is thrown on this matter by General Electric's extensive analysis designed to test the hypothesis that there is a direct and measurable relationship between share-of-industry advertising and share-of-industry sales.[5] The study extended over a period of four years and covered 16 products: 6 major-appliance product lines, 5 traffic-appliance lines, 1 consumer-supply line, and 4 industrial-component or -supply lines. G. A. Bradford summarized the results of this research:

---

[5] Adapted by permission from G. A. Bradford, "What General Electric Is Doing to Evaluate the Effect on Sales of Its Industrial and Consumer Advertising," a paper presented at the Association of National Advertisers, *Advertisers Evaluation Workshop,* January 27, 1960.

An objective summary of the study would have to state that the analysis did *not* prove the theory "that there is a direct relationship between share-of-industry advertising and share-of-industry sales." At the same time, it did not *disprove* the theory, but rather underlined the importance of other factors and influences in the selling situations.

The approach of making the brand's share-of-industry advertising equal the brand's market share also involves the problem of being forced to work with past data rather than with information on competitors' planned future advertising outlays. This version of the competitive parity approach likewise fails to consider whether the required share-of-industry advertising expenditure will be profitable. While anticipated advertising activity by competitors should obviously be considered by a firm in determining the appropriation for its product, strict adherence to the competitive parity approach would, therefore, be unwise.

Research Objective

The research objective approach (sometimes called the objective-and-task approach) is in direct contrast to the methods discussed up to this point.[6] It is a buildup method in which the job to be done receives primary emphasis, whereas the all-available-funds, percentage-of-sales, and competitive parity approaches emphasize the appropriation of a lump sum for advertising which is then broken down by specific types of promotional methods and media, as advertising executives see fit.

Under the research objective method, the firm first undertakes research to serve as a guide in setting reasonable objectives for the coming year's advertising. Guided by additional research, the firm then determines how much and what kind of advertising is necessary to achieve the stated objectives. The estimated cost of such advertising is the size of the appropriation to be recommended to top management. At this point, consideration is given to the question of whether the budget will permit the appropriation of the sum believed to be necessary to achieve the desired goals. If the initial sum appears to be excessive, then the firm will have to proceed more slowly and scale down the objectives until the estimated cost of their achievement comes within what the advertiser can afford.

The research objective approach, if properly applied, is clearly superior to the methods discussed previously. It encourages management to think in terms of realistic objectives for its promotional effort, to seek the most effective methods of achieving these goals, and then to recog-

---

[6]In his landmark study of advertising appropriation methods, A. W. Frey substitutes the label "research objective method" for the traditional title, "objective-and-task approach." This change in nomenclature appears desirable, since it emphasizes the reliance upon research which would characterize the approach. See Frey, *How Many Dollars for Advertising*, p. 51.

nize the necessary relationship between the costs of the resulting advertising program and the size of the job specified in the planning effort.
While ability to finance the recommended advertising effort is taken
into account, management is encouraged to think of advertising not just
as a cost but also as a method for producing income. Imaginative and
aggressive use of advertising is thus encouraged.

This approach also implies reliance upon research to provide management with facts upon which to base decisions as to appropriate goals,
proper methods, and necessary amounts of promotional effort to
achieve desired objectives. Intuition and guesswork in setting the appropriation should therefore be reduced and, hopefully, the quality of decision making improved.

The chief limitation of the research objective approach, as commonly
defined, is that it does not require the decision maker to determine
whether his or her stated objectives are likely to contribute enough incremental revenue to justify the costs involved in achieving them.

If the research objective approach is modified to eliminate this deficiency, it approximates the marginal approach, which was identified as
the theoretical ideal earlier in the discussion. Even then, executives who
attempt to use this modified method face challenging research problems
in (1) determining how much and what kind of advertising is required
to achieve stated objectives and (2) estimating the incremental sales
which may result from the achievement of specified communication
goals.

Nevertheless, there is evidence of a growing sophistication in the
budgeting practices of big advertisers. One recent study found that the
proportion of leading consumer advertisers using the objective-and-task
method had increased from 12 percent in 1975 to 90 percent in 1983.[7]

While the difficulties involved are challenging, the modified research
objective approach tends to direct analysis and research efforts into
promising channels. Even though we are still a long way from solving
the problems involved in developing an ideal approach to the determination of the advertising appropriation, several significant attacks have
been made on various aspects of the problem. In the following section
we shall review certain key developments.

Advertising as an Investment

In previous discussion it has been noted that advertising has two
effects: (1) it stimulates sales during the current year; and (2) it builds

---

[7]Lancaster and Stern, "Computer-Based Advertising," p. 6. For an illustration of
how the objective-and-task approach may be applied, see Jimmie D. Barnes, Brenda J.
Moscove, and Javad Rassouli, "An Objective and Task Media Selection Decision Model
and Advertising Cost Formula to Determine International Advertising Budgets," *Journal of Advertising* 13, no. 4 (1982), pp. 68–75. Note especially the flow model on p. 71.

awareness, preference, and favorable attitudes toward the firm which tend to produce sales in the future. Advertising which has an immediate effect may properly be treated as a current expense, whereas advertising which brings results in the future takes on the character of an investment and may justifiably be treated as such.

Consider, for example, the situation faced by Brooks-Ledford in planning to introduce a new aerosol shaving lather to the market under the brand name Jupiter. Jupiter shaving lather was a protein-based cream and thus was less irritating to the skin than the customary soap-based product. Because of this competitive edge, it was believed that the new brand could secure 7 percent of the market the first year, 10 percent the second, and 15 percent the third. To reach these objectives, the advertising agency believed that it would be necessary to outspend the market leader the first year. Advertising pressure might then be reduced somewhat during the second and third years as the new brand became established. Nevertheless, it was anticipated that it would take three years for the full effects of the introductory effort to be felt and for the brand to achieve break-even status.

Accordingly, the payout and spending plan for the first three years, shown in Figure 11–2, was worked out to guide decision making on the advertising appropriation. These estimates were based on a $1 retail price, a 40 percent discount for wholesalers and direct-buying chains, and a contribution to advertising and profits of 80 percent of the unit price the firm collected.

Note that the expenditure necessary to launch the product was expected to result in a loss of $1,600,000 the first year, no profit the second year, and a profit of $1,850,000 the third year. On a cumulative basis, therefore, it was anticipated that it would take three years for Jupiter

---

FIGURE 11–2   Payout and spending plan

	Year 1	Year 2	Year 3
Share objective (by percent)	7	10	15
Estimated sales ($000)	3,200	4,700	7,400
Contribution available ($000)	1,600	2,350	3,700
Advertising expense ($000)	3,200	2,350	1,850
Profit/loss ($000)	−1,600	—	+1,850
Cumulative P/L ($000)	−1,600	−1,600	+250
Advertising/sales ratio (by percent)	100	50	25

shaving lather to reach the desired market share objective of 15 percent and to achieve a break-even status on the investment made to introduce the new brand. In such a situation, management would clearly have to regard advertising as an investment in order to justify the heavy expenditures of the first year and the resulting substantial loss. Only if management were willing to treat advertising as an investment and wait three years or longer for the payoff, would the proposed advertising appropriation strategy be approved and steps be taken to develop the full potential of the new brand.[8]

In recognition of the fact that advertising often produces benefits that provide a payoff in the future, Joel Dean has suggested that such advertising be treated as a capital investment.[9] He argues that determination of the advertising appropriation then becomes a problem of capital expenditure budgeting. The profitability of capital invested in advertising would then be determined by the estimated amount and timing of added investment in comparison with added earnings, the duration of advertising effects, and the risks involved. Productivity of capital invested in this way should be measured by the discounted cash flow method in preference to the payback period approach. In short, advertising, which is expected to have long-run effects, should be placed in the capital budget. Promotional investments should then compete for funds on the basis of profitability, that is, discounted cash flow rate of return.

The chief deficiency of the return-on-investment approach is the difficulty of estimating the rate of return to be secured on advertising investments. The problems encountered involve (1) distinguishing investment advertising from advertising that is expected to have short-run effects, (2) estimating the evaporation of the cumulative effects of advertising, and (3) measuring the effect of advertising accumulation upon long-run sales volume and eventual price premiums. These measurement difficulties tend to rule out this approach as the sole criterion for decisions on investment-type advertising appropriations. Thinking about appropriations for institutional and cumulative advertising in this manner, however, would encourage research oriented toward providing the kinds of estimates that are relevant to the decision. Experimentation along these lines is therefore encouraged.[10]

---

[8]For additional discussion of the budgeting process for new products, see J. F. Engel, M. R. Warshaw, and T. C. Kinnear, *Promotional Strategy*, 5th ed., (Homewood, Ill.: Richard D. Irwin, 1983), pp. 203–8.

[9]The material in the two following paragraphs is based upon Dean, *Managerial Economics*, pp. 368–69; and Joel Dean, "Does Advertising Belong in the Capital Budget?" *Journal of Marketing*, October 1966, p. 21. Published by the American Marketing Association.

[10]For an explanation of capital-budgeting theory, see Harold Bierman, Jr. and Seymour Smith, *The Capital Budgeting Decision* (New York: Macmillan, 1960).

Research to Determine Expenditure Levels

A key problem in setting the advertising appropriation is to determine how much advertising is required to achieve a specified goal. Experimentation with different levels of advertising expenditures in different test markets is one way to attack this problem. An interesting example is the approach used by Sunoo and Lin in a field experiment to identify an optimal spending level for a nationally distributed commodity-type product with a mature product life cycle. In an annual marketing strategy meeting executives asked: "Should we increase or decrease our advertising dollars from the current level? If so, how much?"[11]

A field experiment method utilizing a dual-system CATV service was selected for the research project. Homes subscribing to CATV in a test city were wired to either Panel A or Panel B of the dual system. All variables (weather, product distribution, competitive advertising, trade and consumer promotion, and price) except those being tested were identical for both panels. The two panels of about 1,000 homes each were matched on demographics, TV viewing habits, and buying habits with regard to the product category. All panel members were asked to keep a weekly consumer diary of some food, drug, and other purchases. These diaries became the major source of data for the analysis of sales and market share. In this study, the Panel A homes received no advertising exposure to the product (a "zero-weight" level), while the Panel B homes received advertising exposure (a "heavy-up" level), for a total of 26 four-week periods.

The findings were as follows.

1. The relationship between advertising and consumer promotion for the product was a complex matter. (a) Daytime-TV advertising was more effective during the time when the consumer promotion activities were light. (b) Nighttime-TV advertising was more effective during the time when the consumer promotion activities were heavy. In other words, nighttime-TV advertising for the product tended to complement consumer promotion activities, whereas daytime advertising did not.

2. Determining the optimal advertising spending level for the product was also a complex matter. (a) A ceiling effect was noted for daytime advertising of the product beyond which daytime advertising was not effective in generating additional sales. The calculated maximum daytime advertising for the product was 421 GRPs in a four-week period. (b) A threshold effect was noted for nighttime advertising below which nighttime advertising was not effective. A total of 189 GRPs was calculated as the minimum nighttime advertising for the product in a four-

[11]D. H. Sunoo and Lynn Y. S. Lin, "A Search for Optimal Advertising Spending Level," *Journal of Advertising,* Summer 1979, pp. 25–28.

week period when the consumer promotion (deal) level was 3 on a scale of 0 to 4.[12]

3.   Two alternative plans for the product were presented to management. Plan I called for all-daytime advertising of 1,980 GRPs a year in three flights. These flights were time periods in which deal levels were relatively low. This plan called for a reduction of more than 60 percent from the current spending level of advertising. Plan II called for a mixture of both day and night advertising. This plan used the same number of daytime GRPs for the same flights schedule as that of Plan I, but it added 1,050 GRPs for nighttime television. The nighttime television allocation was for a flight covering three consecutive four-week periods during the time when consumer promotion activities were heavy. Plan II called for a reduction of more than 15 percent in the spending level of advertising. The estimated results from the alternative approaches were:

> Estimated sales volume (in percentage relative to Plan I): Plan 1—100; Plan II—117.
>
> Estimated profit (in percentage relative to Plan I): Plan I—100; Plan II—97.

Thus Plan I had a slight edge over Plan II on profit margin (3 points), while Plan II had a slight edge over Plan I on sales volume (17 points).

4.   The findings of the field experiment, coupled with analyses using a regression model and a marginal purchase equation, provided product management with useful quantitative bases for its decision making on advertising spending.[13]

Relation of Advertising Outlays to Market Share Objectives

Firms marketing nondurable goods in food stores and drugstores can make use of syndicated research services, such as those offered by the A. C. Nielsen Company, to measure the relationship between advertising expenditures and retail sales of their brands expressed in share-of-market terms. Here sales are determined by the retail inventory method based on audits of the operations of a scientifically selected sample of food and drug outlets. Through analysis of the actual results secured in the marketing of both new and established products, the firm may dis-

---

[12]GRP (gross rating points) is the product of reach times frequency. Reach is the number or percentage of homes exposed to the advertising schedule during a given period of time (usually four weeks). Frequency is the number of times that the average home reached was exposed to advertising during the same period. See Engel et al., *Promotional Strategy*, 5th ed., p. 284.

[13]For an interesting example of test marketing using the experimental crossover design, see J. C. Becknell, Jr. and R. W. McIsaac, "Test Marketing Cookware Coated with 'TEFLON,' " *Journal of Advertising Research*, September 1963, pp. 2–8.

cover useful guidelines as to the amount of advertising required to achieve market-share objectives.

A pioneering study of this type, covering 34 new brands of consumer nondurable goods, was made in 1966 by James O. Peckham, then executive vice president of the A. C. Nielsen Company. Each of these brands had achieved a "respectable market position" within the first two years from the decision to launch and actively market the brand nationally. The purpose was to determine whether useful guidelines could be developed from the analysis of past experience concerning the relationship between advertising outlays and share-of-market objectives.[14]

When the 34 new brands were considered as a whole, the relationship between average share of product category advertising and attained share of market over the initial two-year period was so consistent that it was possible to derive a "marketing experience curve" showing the approximate relationship between these two variables. This experience curve indicated that the relationship between share of category advertising for a brand and share of market was approximately 1.5 to 1.6—that is, the share of advertising devoted to the brand was about 1.6 times the share of market secured.

An update of this type of research appeared as the lead article in a recent issue of the *Nielsen Researcher*.[15] The article addressed the issue of how much to spend on advertising and analyzed advertising share versus market share for 74 national brands to provide a report on some significant relationships. A brief summary of this research follows.

> *How much advertising?* One manufacturer may simply spend every dollar he can manage, while another limits advertising expenditures to a certain percentage of sales. Some manufacturers examine competitors' outlays and match them. Others use advanced decision models designed specifically for their own marketing environments. But regardless of approach, the main objective remains the same: achieve the most efficient balance between apparent contribution to sales and cost of advertising.
>
> In order to examine the experience of manufacturers of consumer packaged goods in reaching this balance, a study of 25 food and drug store product categories was conducted. The product classes and measurement periods for the study were selected to avoid new products (or product failures) or other activities that might contribute to atypical conditions.
>
> *A caveat.* It must be realized . . . that advertising levels are not the sole determinant of market share performance. Two competing manu-

---

[14]Adapted by permission from James O. Peckham, executive vice president, A. C. Nielsen Company, "Can We Relate Advertising Dollars to Market Share Objectives?" *Proceedings, 12th Annual Conference, Advertising Research Foundation,* October 5, 1966, pp. 53–57. © Advertising Research Foundation, Inc., 1966.

[15]Advertising and Sales Relationships: A Current Appraisal," *Nielsen Researcher,* no. 1 (1980), pp. 2–9.

facturers might take identical advertising budgets and, through media selection, creative message, content, audience targeting, or through many other methods available, produce significantly different levels of consumer impact, retention and response. And, aside from advertising, other promotional techniques are normally at work, exerting their influence on market performance. Thus, the following assessment of advertising share versus market share should serve only as a benchmark and not as a set of hard-and-fast rules.

Leading brands. The most frequent targets of advertising effectiveness studies are brand leaders. These are the brands that have established and maintained a dominant share of a market through a harmonious program of consumer and trade appeal including the proper blend of trade promotion, consumer advertising, retail pricing, and other sales-influencing factors. The most critical of these factors, however, is often identified as advertising. It has been stated that in order to maintain brand leadership, one must maintain leadership in advertising spending.

As can be seen in Chart 1, this is not necessarily true. When the 25 product categories were evaluated in terms of the leading brand's share of advertising (plotted on the vertical axis in the chart) and share of market (plotted on the horizontal axis), it became apparent that a large market share does not necessarily carry with it a demand for a large advertising share. Eight of the leading brands maintained their position with advertising shares below their market shares. It will be noted, however, within the majority of product categories, that there was a strong correlation between brand share and advertising share leadership. In fact, the 25 leading brands studied had an average of 1.2 points of advertising share for each point of sales share.

Other brands. To some extent the advertising shares of leading brands have an impact upon the support activity and share levels of other brands in the product class. In order to examine the relationship between advertising expenditures of the primary brand and its leading competitors, advertising share and sales share data were assembled for the second ranking and—where significant—the third ranking brand in each product class under evaluation. The result was advertising share/sales share information covering 74 brands across the 25 categories. Because of the number of brands involved and potential differences between types of product, the information was broken down into five general categories for evaluation: Non-Perishable Edibles, Refrigerated Products, Non-Edibles, Personal Care/Beauty Aids, and Remedial Health Care Products.*

In conclusion. Stating precisely what advertising does is virtually impossible. Consequently, it cannot easily be said what dollar value should be committed to this activity.

Based upon the experience of the 74 national brands studied however, it does appear safe to state that if you expect to be first in market

---

*Note: Charts 2 to 6, together with analytical comments, omitted from this summary.

CHART 1   Advertising share versus market share of 25 leading brands

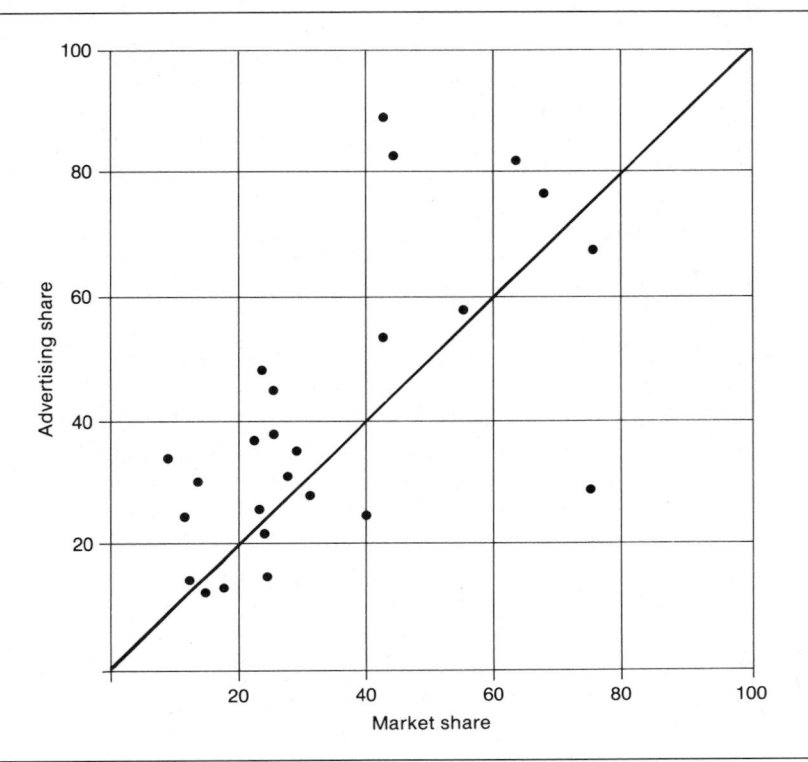

share you should plan to be first in share of advertising, too. For example, the average brand in this study had 1.3 points of advertising share for each point of sales share. For some brands, this rule does not hold true, *but in each case inspection reveals a strong compensating factor.* This factor might be price, or quality that assures brand loyalty, or a strong ethical connotation, for example.

What all this suggests is that advertising cannot be considered independently. More importantly, it implies that a proper mixture of advertising coupled with other promotion effort is essential to the well-being of a brand. And finally, that the blend of activity is dependent upon the unique skills of each and every marketer.

Is the approach illustrated above a satisfactory way to deal with the problem of determining the level of advertising expenditure required to achieve desired goals?

1. At the outset, it is wise to remind ourselves that the share of sales which may be achieved by a brand will be influenced by the entire marketing mix and not just by the amount spent on advertising.

2. Then, too, many of the brands studied were food, drug, and toiletry products with a demonstrable consumer-plus. As such, they would meet the criteria for advertisability, and consumer advertising was, therefore, probably the dominant sales-producing element in the promotional mix. Accordingly, application of the findings of the experience curve would have to be limited to products of equal superiority and for which primary reliance might likewise be placed upon consumer advertising.

3. It should also be recognized that the share-of-sales results would be influenced not only by the amount of advertising but also by the effectiveness of the media mix and the creative approach used. Research is recommended, therefore, to identify the most effective media mix and the best creative approach. Once this has been accomplished, then these factors may be held constant and attention directed to the amount of advertising required to achieve the desired market share.

4. These comments underscore the problems involved in separating the impact of advertising dollars from other marketing mix influences upon a brand's share of sales. They also serve as a reminder of the difficulty of using past results in making future plans. We can see that planning and executing research to measure the sales results of advertising is a difficult and challenging task.

5. While the Nielsen studies developed an experience curve by relating share of advertising and share of sales for nondurable products, it is significant to recall that General Electric failed to establish such a relationship in analyzing data covering experience with 16 product lines in the durable-goods classification—major appliances, traffic appliances, consumer electrical supplies, and industrial components and supplies. This may be due in part to the smaller influence of advertising in the selling mix for such items as and to the infrequency with which they are purchased. As General Electric suggests, the only way correlation studies will make a useful contribution for such products is to measure and correlate the effects of *several key* influences on share of market at one and the same time. Clearly the research approach must be determined in light of the nature of the product, the frequency with which it is purchased, and the role of advertising in the promotional mix.

Relation of Communication Objectives to Sales Results

As mentioned previously, manufacturers of infrequently purchased durable goods find it difficult, if not impossible, to measure advertising results in terms of sales. This leads them to adopt communication goals for their advertising instead of sales or share-of-industry goals. A problem then arises in deciding whether the desired objectives are worth the

costs involved in their achievement. Recognition of this problem has led to research designed to study the relationship between communication objectives (such as awareness, preference, and intent to buy) and actual sales results. This experimentation has led to the development of the "media-schedule" approach to setting the advertising appropriation, a method which falls within the research objective category and involves practical applications of the ideal incremental approach discussed previously.[16]

Of particular interest to us is the manner in which objectives are identified in following this approach. The basic idea involved is to recognize that advertising creates sales by making conscious impressions upon the minds of prospective buyers. Thus, the goal of the advertiser is to purchase an optimum number of conscious impressions with his or her dollars. It is recognized that the effectiveness of an advertisement scheduled a given number of times in any medium—a magazine, for example—results from a screening sequence somewhat as follows: (1) The magazine has a total circulation among people who are potential buyers or "influencers." (2) A larger number than this actually read the magazine. (3) A smaller number of individuals than the readers of the magazine are "exposed" to the page on which the advertisement appears. (4) A still smaller number actually pay attention to the advertisement. (5) A still smaller number receive a conscious impression. (6) The conscious impressions (*a*) make some readers *aware* of the product for the first time, (*b*) strengthen already present awareness in others, (*c*) move some people from mere awareness to a favorable *attitude*, and (*d*) move some people all the way to *purchase*.

In recognition of this screening sequence, research is then undertaken to establish the relationship among (1) conscious impressions, (2) awareness and favorable attitudes, and (3) purchases of the product. If such a relationship is established, then the next step is to determine the number of conscious impressions that may be secured through various combinations of media schedules. The advertiser is then in a position to determine the optimum advertising appropriation.

While this media schedule approach has conceptual value, the critical question is whether the individual advertiser will be able, through research, to establish a useful relationship among conscious impressions, awareness, favorable attitudes, and purchases. It is reported, however, that some advertisers have been able to establish this relationship to their own satisfaction.[17] Certainly an attempt should be made to do so, if at

---

[16]Reprinted by permission from A. W. Frey, "Approaches to Determining the Advertising Appropriation," in George L. Baker, Jr., ed., *Effective Marketing Coordination*, pp. 326–39. Published by the American Marketing Association, 1961.

[17]For a helpful discussion of the use of marketing experiments in determining the relationship between communication and sales, see Charles K. Ramond, "Must Advertising Communicate to Sell?" *Harvard Business Review*, September–October 1965, pp. 148–59.

all possible. If no satisfactory relationship can be found for certain types of products, however, the obvious answer is to disregard the goal of purchases and to select a certain goal of awareness and favorable attitudes as a guide. This is a better goal than is used by some advertisers in their decision making.

Decision Models for Setting Promotional Appropriations

The limitations of the various methods followed in determining the promotional appropriation have led several researchers to propose the use of decision models to assist in dealing with this complex task. Many of these models are not especially useful from a practical point of view, but progress is being made in their development and testing. According to Engel, Warshaw, and Kinnear, it is not yet clear that quantitative methods have remedied the deficiencies of traditional budgeting tools because there are some problems which have not yet been resolved: (1) The information required for the decision model is often virtually unobtainable at a reasonable cost. (2) Most of the models make budgetary recommendations based on the assumption that advertising is the only variable. Interdependencies within the marketing mix are ignored, and this causes the models to be highly unrealistic under most circumstances. (3) Many of the assumptions of the models tend to be arbitrary.[18]

Nevertheless, the development of these models represents an attempt to apply scientific method to a problem in which rule-of-thumb judgment is often used. Such experimentation serves to identify areas in which better data are required and thus may lead to improvement in data sources. Moreover, attempts to apply such models may also lead to their improvement.

Empirical Analyses of Why Promotional Costs Vary

While field experimental research and the application of quantitative models may have promise as means of arriving at sound promotional appropriations, these methods require money, time, and data that are often not available. Also, it is difficult to measure the effects of advertising and sales promotion accurately. For these and other reasons many businesses use rules of thumb to set promotional appropriations. A common approach is to take a percentage of sales to determine the advertising budget.

In an attempt to provide usable guidelines where the percentage-of-sales method is applied, empirical studies have been undertaken to de-

---

[18]For a brief introduction to the application of quantitative methods in setting the promotional budget, see Engel et al., *Promotional Strategy,* 5th ed., appendix to chap. 11, pp. 209–19. See also Philip Kotler, *Marketing Management,* 4th ed. (Englewood Cliffs, N.J.: Prentice-Hall, 1980), pp. 500–4.

termine why advertising and promotional costs vary. Thus, if data are available on industry or product category spending levels, the results of such empirical research might help a manager to determine whether his or her appropriation should be above or below the industry average, taking into account appropriate variables, such as the company's market share and contribution margin.

The ADVISOR study.   One such study was ADVISOR, a joint project of MIT and the Association of National Advertisers (1976). The data consisted of information on 66 products obtained from 12 companies selling to industrial and business markets. (In this study the term *advertising* was used to include marketing communications.)[19]

The median advertising/sales ratio was found to be 0.6 percent. The range, however, was wide, 0 percent to 68 percent, though most ratios were in the range of 0.1 percent to 1.8 percent.

The purpose of the ADVISOR project was to determine the key product and market factors that affect advertising expenditures. Analysis of the budget data established the preeminence of five factors in explaining budget variations:

1. Stage in life cycle. Early in the life cycle of a product, the advertising/sales ratio tends to be high; later, it tends to be low.
2. Frequency of purchase. The more often the product is purchased, the greater the advertising/sales ratio.
3. Product quality, uniqueness, and identification with company. If the composite index measuring these factors is high, then the A/S ratio is larger than when the composite index is low.
4. Market share. The higher the market share, the lower the A/S ratio.
5. Growth of customers. This factor is the percentage increase in the number of customers over the previous year. This was broken into high and low categories. Customer growth has a positive effect on the A/S ratio.

A 1984 paper reports on an interesting international study to determine whether the results of the ADVISOR project on the determinants of industrial marketing budgeting practices apply to European products. The findings show that the original ADVISOR results generally appear applicable: the overall relationship between strategic variables and spending levels is not significantly different between the original (U.S.) sample and the European sample.[20]

---

[19]Reprinted from "The ADVISOR Project: A Study of Industrial Marketing Budgets," by G. L. Lillien and John D. C. Little, *Sloan Management Review*, vol. 17, no. 3, pp. 17–31. Copyright © 1976 by the Sloan Management Review Association. All rights reserved.

[20]See Gary Lillien & David Weinstein, "An International Comparison of the Determinants of Industrial Marketing Expenditures," *Journal of Marketing* 48 (Winter 1984), pp. 46–53.

The Farris and Buzzell study.   A more extensive cross-sectional analysis of the variations in the ratio of advertising and promotion expenditures to sales of industrial products was reported by Farris and Buzzell. This study covered data provided by 789 businesses manufacturing industrial products which cooperated in the PIMS (Profit Impact of Marketing Strategy) project. An additional 281 businesses manufacturing consumer products were also included in order to make comparisons between these two types of products.[21]

The study focused on identifying factors that "explain" empirically the variations among business units in the ratio of advertising and promotion to sales. Its conclusions were as follows:

1.   Variations in the A&P/S ratio are quite systematic over a wide variety of businesses manufacturing both industrial and consumer products.

2.   We would expect the A&P/S ratio to be higher when:

The product is standardized rather than produced to order.

There are many end users (e.g., almost all households).

The typical purchase amount is small.

Auxiliary services are of some importance.

Sales are made through channel intermediaries rather than direct to users.

The product is premium-priced (and, probably, of premium quality).

The manufacturer has a relatively small market share and/or has surplus production capacity.

A high proportion of the manufacturer's sales come from new products.

3.   How might these results be utilized by a manager? The results might be helpful to a manager in determining whether his or her A&P/S ratio should be above or below the industry average, taking into account such factors as the own company's market share, contribution margin, and proportion of new products to total sales.

CONCLUSION

The task of determining the size of the promotional appropriation is important but difficult. The character of promotional strategy influences the size of the appropriation; simultaneously, the size of the funds available is an important consideration in deciding what type of promo-

---

[21]Reprinted from Paul W. Farris and Robert D. Buzzell, "Why Advertising and Promotional Costs Vary: Some Cross-Sectional Analyses," *Journal of Marketing*, published by the American Marketing Association, Fall 1979, pp. 112–22.

tional approach will be most effective. Ways of dealing with this problem which break this circularity are suggested in this chapter.

We have evaluated commonly used approaches, such as basing the appropriation decision on a percentage of sales, using "all available funds," considering competitive parity, and applying the research objective (or task) approach. We have concluded that a modified research objective approach, if properly applied, is clearly superior to the other approaches mentioned.

A key problem in setting the advertising appropriation is to determine how much advertising is required to achieve a specified goal. One way to deal with this problem is to make use of a syndicated research service to measure the relationship between advertising expenditures and retail sales expressed in share-of-market terms. Since market share is influenced by other elements in the marketing mix besides advertising, however, such correlations may provide only rough guidelines, and judgment must be exercised in their interpretation. Scientifically planned marketing experiments, in which the influence of factors other than advertising is either held constant or measured, promise to provide better information for decision-makers.

We shall now proceed to a discussion of brand strategy decisions.

ADDITIONAL READINGS

In planning the advertising appropriation a key question is how much advertising is required to reach desired goals—in terms of sales or share of market. Below are listed several interesting studies that address this question.

Paul Farris and Mark S. Albion, "Determinants of the Advertising-to-Sales Ratio," *Journal of Advertising Research* 21, no. 1 (February, 1981), pp. 19–28. A review of the findings of six empirical studies in which certain variables were found to be consistently related to industry A/S ratios: profit margins, market size, amount and frequency of purchase, product durability, number of brands, and surrogates for "product differentiability." Further differences in A/S ratios among firms in the same industry were explained by market share, relative price, and distribution strategies (p. 25).

Julian L. Simon and Johan Arndt, "The Shape of the Advertising Response Function," *Journal of Advertising Research* 20, no. 4 (August 1980), pp. 11–28. The question: What is the effect, for the firm and for society, of a larger rather than a smaller quantity of advertising? Findings: (1) Studies of the response function linking physical measures of sales impact to physical amounts of advertising consistently indicate diminishing returns to advertising. To put it differently, increasing returns have not been reliably observed in the laboratory

or in the field. (2) Studies of the function relating sales in dollars to dollars of advertising, which reflect the role of discounts, also show diminishing returns to advertising (with two exceptions). (3) Taken together, these studies add up to the conclusion that there are not increasing returns to advertising—that is, no S-shaped response function—over the normal operating range (p. 24).

David A. Aaker and James M. Carman, "Are You Overadvertising?" *Journal of Advertising Research* 22 (August–September 1982), pp. 57–70. A review of advertising–sales studies which concluded: (1) There are relatively few studies of this issue, and fewer yet that are persuasive. (2) Modeling the advertising–sales relationship is very difficult for many reasons. One is that the link between advertising and goodwill is elusive to model and measure. Another is that the important competitive response factor is not always observed and seldom modeled. (3) There is evidence that overadvertising has been empirically demonstrated. The 11 field experiments involving reduced weight, in which 10 implied that overadvertising existed, were the most impressive (p. 67).

QUESTIONS

1. *a.* Explain the essentials of the marginal method of determining the advertising appropriation.
   b. What difficulties are encountered in applying this approach in actual practice?

2. What are the basic principles behind (*a*) the breakdown and (*b*) the buildup methods of determining the promotional appropriation? Which approaches discussed in this chapter fall into each classification?

3. *a.* Under what conditions may a case be made for the use of a variable percentage of estimated future sales in determining the promotional appropriation?
   b. What criticisms may be made of this approach even under the best of circumstances?

4. Under what conditions can you defend the use of the all-available-funds approach to determining the promotional appropriation? What limitations does this method have?

5. *a.* Evaluate the plan for setting the advertising appropriation by making the brand's share of total industry advertising expenditures equal to the brand's desired share of market.
   b. Would this be an appropriate plan to follow in determining the appropriation for a new brand that is just being introduced? An established brand which rates number 3 in share of market? Number 1 in share of market?

6. *a.* What are the essentials of the research objective approach to setting

the promotional appropriation? What are the chief limitations of this approach?

b.   How might the approach be modified to eliminate these limitations?

7. a.   Under what circumstances might it be desirable to treat advertising as an investment?

b.   What difficulties are involved in following this approach? Does it appear likely that these difficulties will be overcome?

8. Does the Nielsen study of the relation between advertising outlays and market share objectives provide a helpful guide for setting the advertising appropriation:

a.   For a product like Simba, which is promoted as a means of quenching the "African thirst"?

b.   For a new portable color TV set?

c.   For Cessna aircraft marketed for pleasure and personal use?

9. What are the merits and limitations of field experiments involving the use of dual-system CATV to determine the optimum level of advertising expenditures?

10. The Farris and Buzzell study is an example of a cross-sectional analysis to determine why the ratio of advertising and promotion expenditures to sales varies among different products.

a.   Under what circumstances would you expect the ratio of A&P/S to be higher?

b.   How might the results of such studies be used by managers in determining the appropriate A&P/S ratio for their businesses?

11. a.   Under what circumstances would it appear to be desirable to base the advertising appropriation upon communication objectives rather than upon sales goals?

b.   What difficulties are encountered in following this approach (as illustrated in the media schedule method)?

c.   What attitude should management take toward the use of this method?

BRAND STRATEGY DECISIONS

12

In an earlier discussion, consideration was given to issues of brand policy related to product development decisions. We turn now to certain major questions concerning branding which arise in the process of working out the basic promotional strategy of a manufacturer. Of particular significance are the following issues: (1) What policies should be followed regarding the number and coverage of brands to be marketed by the firm? Specifically, should the manufacturer use one brand to identify many different products, as opposed to marketing each product under its own individual brand name? Where different qualities of the same product are produced, should all be sold under a single brand name, or should high-, medium-, and low-quality products be identified by separate trademarks? (2) Should the firm manufacture products to be sold under distributors' brands, or should it concentrate exclusively upon marketing products under its own brands? Each of these topics has important promotional strategy implications and will be analyzed on the pages that follow.

FAMILY BRANDS VERSUS INDIVIDUAL BRANDS

A producer following a manufacturer's brand policy faces the important question of whether to market his or her line under a family brand

or under individual brand names. A family brand policy is one in which two or more products are sold under the same brand name. Avon Products, Inc., is an example of a firm which follows this approach. In a recent year, the firm sold approximately 300 items under the Avon brand name, including fragrances, makeup articles, bath products, skin-care items, hair preparations, dental-care accessories, deodorants, and shaving products. Although products appealing to women were emphasized, items for children and men were also marketed.[1]

What advantages might Avon gain from this family brand policy? Since Avon products were sold house to house by company salespeople, a key advantage of family branding would be the possibility of gaining ready acceptance by regular customers of new products added to the company's line. The favorable brand image held by users of existing Avon products would tend to influence them to accept new items more readily if they carried the same brand than if new individual brand names were used. This, in turn, would tend to reduce the amount of introductory advertising required to create a demand for the new products and would also cut down the time and effort required by the salesperson to get orders for these new items.

While Avon management obviously believes that family branding is desirable, Lever Brothers Company made the opposite decision when it introduced a new beauty soap in test markets early in 1968. This new product, which was being tested in Albany, New York, and Columbus, Ohio, was identified by the brand name Caress. Rather than attempting to associate Caress with the firm's established brand, Lux Toilet Soap, Lever Brothers apparently intended to promote Caress separately as a means of more effectively exploiting this new entry into the competitive beauty soap market. While this approach may require a larger appropriation for advertising and promotion, such an investment is customarily made in the expectation that it will produce larger sales and profits than the decision to market under a family brand would yield. The contrast in brand policy illustrated by the Avon and Lever Brothers examples leads naturally to the question of what guidelines to use in making a decision concerning family versus individual branding when a new product is being added to an established product line. In considering this issue, it is helpful to approach the problem from the consumers' viewpoint. What is the psychological explanation of the tendency to develop generalized preferences for different types of products identified by a common family brand? What product characteristics tend to foster such generalization? What characteristics tend to discourage it? These questions will be considered in the following section.

---

[1]Seymour Freedgood, "Avon: The Sweet Smell of Success," *Fortune*, December 1964, pp. 111, 113.

Generalized Preferences for Family Brands[2]

The policy of family branding is based on the assumption that this practice leads to a "connection in consumers' minds" which generalizes consumer preferences to all product categories under a brand. A brand name linkage acts as a medium through which consumers spread or generalize preferences and loyalties from one category of products to another. The psychological theory that underlies this assumption deals with the effect of cognitive set on perception. The cognitive set influence important in this analysis is the "assimilation effect," the tendency of people to assimilate, or to shift the classification of set-related stimuli in the direction of their existing set.[3]

Generalized preferences for family brands are intervening variables that influence consumer brand choice. Since they are not directly observable, they are inferred from consumer buying behavior. Fry tested the hypothesis that consumers have generalized preferences by analyzing consumer purchasing behavior as reported by the *Chicago Tribune* consumer panel. Analyses were limited to frequently purchased packaged goods and covered about 600 households resident in metropolitan Chicago. Purchases of the following family brands of packaged goods were analyzed, among others:

1. Canned goods—Del Monte, Libby's, Hunt's, Heinz.
2. Frozen foods—Birds Eye.
3. Paper products—Scott, Kleenex.
4. Baking products—Pillsbury.

The degree of generalized preference for a given family brand was measured by analyzing the behavior of consumers in purchasing two different product categories (for example, canned peaches and canned corn) under a single family brand (for example, Del Monte). What percentage of the consumers who purchased Del Monte canned peaches also purchased Del Monte canned corn? How did this compare with the percentage of the consumers who purchased only Del Monte canned peaches or *only* Del Monte canned corn?

Analysis of the data for all of the family brands of frequently purchased packaged goods listed above led Fry to conclude that consumers do have generalized preferences for family brands.[4] The results were consistent with the hypothesis for a variety of brands, product categories, and purchase classifications indicating degree of brand loyalty.

---

[2]Reprinted by permission from Joseph N. Fry, "Family Branding and Consumer Brand Choice," *Journal of Marketing Research*, August 1967, pp. 237–47. Published by the American Marketing Association.

[3]Ibid., p. 238.

[4]See ibid., pp. 241–47, for a more complete discussion of the evidence resulting from this analysis.

Fry also inquired as to what factors contribute to the degree of generalized preference. He hypothesized that the degree of generalized preference for a family brand varies directly with (1) the degree of similarity in the competitive brand sets of two product categories identified by a family brand and (2) the degree of price similarity of the brand in two product categories.

Analysis of the data gave tentative confirmation to these secondary hypotheses. Accordingly, the findings of this study provide support for the common and important assumption that for frequently purchased packaged goods the promotion of one product under a family brand has beneficial effects for other products under that brand. The study does not, however, throw any light on the relative efficacy of family and individual branding.

In a study of semantic generalization as applied to family brands of eight household appliances, Kerby tested the hypothesis that meaning should be transferred between two or more physically dissimilar products if they share a common brand name. The results were negative. A large proportion of the respondents demonstrated either no tendency, or a weak tendency toward semantic generalization in evaluating the eight branded products. Why? Kerby suggests (1) that the physical characteristics of the major appliances varied too greatly to permit effective generalization or (2) that semantic generalization occurs only when the products are relatively unimportant, requiring a minimum of intellectual and emotional effort.[5]

Factors Influencing Choice of Family versus Individual Brands

The empirical evidence just cited points up the importance of careful analysis in reaching a decision on whether a new product should be marketed under a family brand or under an individual brand.

In this connection, the decision of Procter & Gamble brand managers to introduce their new mint-flavored stannous fluoride toothpaste under the established name Crest is interesting. The original Crest (with stannous fluoride) was flavored with wintergreen and had developed a significant market share. It faced direct competition from other fluoridated toothpastes, which were also available only in wintergreen flavor. There was no major stannous fluoride mint-flavored product. Research indicated that a segment of the market which wished the protection against tooth decay provided by a fluoridated brand did not like the wintergreen flavor of Crest but did like mint flavor in toothpaste. In recognition of this preference, P&G undertook the difficult task of developing an acceptable mint-flavored stannous fluoride toothpaste. After considerable

---

[5]For more information about this research, see J. K. Kerby, "Semantic Generalization in the Formation of Consumer Attitudes," *Journal of Marketing Research,* August 1967, pp. 314–17. Published by the American Marketing Association.

time and effort, the research team came up with a new product which received favorable responses in consumer taste tests. The new product, accordingly, differed from the original Crest primarily in flavor (mint instead of wintergreen). While its stannous fluoride formula may have differed from competing fluoridated brands in some respects, its chief distinction was its mint flavor. The new product might have been given an individual brand name, as is generally the policy when new products are added to the P&G line. The brand group, however, recommended marketing the new mint-flavored fluoridated toothpaste under the name Mint Crest. From this action it may be inferred that the P&G decision makers believed that the new product would gain substantial benefit from the reputation achieved by the original Crest brand. Here the benefits from generalization were apparently believed to be greater than any promotional advantages that might result from using an individual brand name. By calling the new product Mint Crest, however, the brand group obviously hoped to attract a new segment of consumers who may have tried wintergreeen-flavored Crest but had turned away from it to buy a less effective mint-flavored competing brand. It is noteworthy, however, that P&G introduced new Mint Crest with a heavy campaign of advertising and promotion. In that campaign new Mint Crest was associated with, but distinguished from, the original Crest (wintergreen).

Summary and Conclusions

In summary, the following factors would tend to favor marketing a new product under its own individual brand: (1) The new product is highly individualized, as compared with competing brands, and also meets other criteria that indicate a profitable opportunity to make use of consumer advertising. (2) It differs in product features, benefits, and hence selective appeals from the firm's own established brand and thus requires individual promotion. (3) It is either higher or lower in quality than other products sold under the existing brand. (4) It offers an opportunity to expand the company's market coverage by appealing to new segments of consumers. (5) It should be distributed through retail outlets different from those handling the existing brand.

In contrast, the following considerations would tend to favor selling the new product under an established family brand: (1) The new product is of the same type as the existing line. (2) It is similar in uses, wants satisfied, and appeals to buying motives. (3) It is of the same quality–price relation as the existing brand. (4) Its market is likely to be found in the same segments of the population as the present line. (5) It can be distributed through the same types of retail outlets as are now used. (6) It can be promoted jointly with established products sold under the family brand.

In the final analysis, what must be done is to estimate the sales volume, profit, and return on investment that may be achieved if the new product is introduced under the family brand, as compared to what might be expected if the new product were sold under its own individual brand, and to choose the alternative that offers significantly greater returns. Since the results of such analysis may not be clear-cut, judgment may be improved if market tests involving an introductory strategy based on an individual brand are compared with market tests making use of the family brand approach.

COMPANY NAME COMBINED WITH INDIVIDUAL BRAND

Some firms have found it desirable to establish an association between individual brands by tying them together with the company name. One example is the Kellogg Company, which consistently uses the company name along with individual brand names such as Corn Flakes, Rice Krispies, Sugar Corn Pops, and Pop-Tarts. Here the new products may be given individual promotional support and may develop individual brand images, yet they all gain from the association with the well-established Kellogg name. Another example is the Ford Motor Company, which gives strong emphasis to individual brands of automobiles such as Lincoln, Mercury, Thunderbird, Cougar, Torino, Tempo, and Mustang. Yet the entire line is tied together under the Ford name through such corporate advertising themes as: "Ford Has a Better Idea—We Listen Better" (1973–74); "Ford Wants to Be Your Car Company" (1975–77); "The Incredible World of Ford" (1978–80); "At Ford Quality Is Job 1" (1981–84) supported by a companion slogan, "There's a Ford in America's Future" (1982–83).

This strategy enables a firm to gain family recognition for its products at the same time that it achieves the benefits of individual branding.

BRAND EXTENSION STRATEGY

Brand extension strategy is an attempt to extend the use of a successful brand name to product modifications or additional product areas.[6] In the 1960s and early 70s, this was commonly referred to as "line extension." The new brands were usually simple variations of an existing brand. Management's objective was to broaden the existing brand's appeal and to satisfy an increased share of the user's requirements within

---

[6]See Theodore R. Gamble, "Brand Extension," in *Plotting Marketing Strategy,* ed. Lee Adler (New York: Simon & Schuster, 1967), pp. 170–71.

its product category. Flavor variations of a brand were the most frequently encountered approach. Consider Campbell's chicken soup, for example. Originally there was just Campbell's chicken rice soup. Today, besides chicken with rice, Campbell Soup Company makes chicken gumbo, chicken noodle, chicken noodle O's, curly noodle with chicken, cream of chicken, creamy chicken mushroom, chicken vegetable, chicken alphabet, chicken & stars, chick n' dumplings, and chicken broth.

The benefits from this line extension strategy might include: (1) low marketing investment required to establish awareness and trial, (2) low manufacturing investment (since the extension could usually be run on existing equipment), (3) low R&D expense, (4) increased retail shelf space, (and 5) cross-flavor promotional opportunities—all resulting in increased profits. The risks, on the other hand, are usually quite minimal. Usually the only major concern is that the line extension might cannibalize existing sales and not add new users.

Currently an increasing number of companies are considering a second type of brand extension: that is, broadening the profitability of their successful brand names by extending their use into additional product areas. For example, the makers of Levi jeans, slacks, shorts, and related items now also sell Levi shoes. Other market entries include Dunkin' Donuts coffee, Log Cabin pancake mix, Arm & Hammer deodorant, and Woolite rug cleaner.

When brand extension is under consideration, consumer research is desirable to determine the existing brand's assets relative to brands in different product categories and to directly competitive brands—to obtain a "relative brand profile." The purpose of such a profile is to identify the unique assets of the brand so that the transfer of these benefits to a new brand can be maximized. The second research step is to identify the product categories upon which marketing management might concentrate—that is, to understand the existing brand's "elasticity." Brand elasticity measures how applicable the existing brand is to a variety of product categories. The output of such research is a ranked list of product categories ranging from those most elastic (most suitable) to those least elastic (least suitable). If this approach were applied to a brand such as Minute Maid orangeade, lemonade, and limeade, the research output might appear as shown in Figure 12–1.[7]

In addition to determining the existing brand's elasticity, it would be wise to raise other analytical questions to determine how well the firm's marketing resources could be utilized by extending the brand to a different product category: Can the existing physical distribution facilities be utilized for the new product? The existing distribution channels? The

[7]Adapted from Ronald L. Dimbert and Howard W. Gibson, "Marketers Add Profitability by Making Existing Brands Work Harder," *Marketing News*, May 18, 1979, pp. 10–11.

FIGURE 12–1   Hypothetical Minute Maid elasticity profile

Most elastic (strongest)

+ + +	Jellies
+ +	Soups
+	Dinner rolls
0	Vegetables
0	Pie fillings
−	Cakes
− −	Peanut butter
− − −	Ice cream
− − −	Packaged meats

Least elastic (weakest)

Source: Reprinted from Ronald L. Dimbert and Howard W. Gibson, "Marketers Add Profitability by Making Existing Brands Work Harder," *Marketing News,* May 18, 1979, pp. 10–11.

existing sales force? Can the present production facilities be utilized? Plant capacity, labor skills, and technical know-how? Raw materials?

In short, while brand extension into entirely different product categories may offer some advantages, a careful analysis should be made to determine how well existing marketing and production resources would be utilized by such a move. The answer will differ from one product category to another. A balanced appraisal is important if a sound decision is to result.[8]

PROMOTIONAL IMPLICATIONS OF BRAND–QUALITY–PRICE RELATIONSHIPS

In the foregoing discussion, quality–price relationships were identified as an important consideration in deciding whether to seek generalization by using a family brand or to aim at distinctiveness by using an individual brand. In those instances in which the new product being

---

[8]Brand extension strategy has been widespread enough in recent years to attract the attention of newspaper feature writers who view the development from the consumerist angle. Of concern is whether brand extension tends to do such things as confuse the consumer, increase marketing costs, and raise prices. For example, the following articles, by A. Kent MacDougall, have appeared in the *Los Angeles Times:* "Battle of Brands: 70 percent of Those 'New' Items Really Aren't: Companies Use Product Cloning, Not Price, to Win Market Share," May 27, 1979, part 4, pp. 1–3, 18; and "Brand Proliferation: Public Pays," June 3, 1979, pp. 4–6.

introduced is of the same type as the existing line, for example, cameras, but is of either higher quality or lower quality than the present product, the question of whether to sell both products under the same brand assumes special importance. If the firm markets a high-quality line of men's shoes under a highly regarded brand name such as Status and then adds a medium-grade line under the same brand and promotes the new line aggressively, the sales of the medium-priced line will tend to increase at the expense of the higher-priced product. Consumers may tend to impute to the medium-priced line the high quality associated with the brand name Status and thus buy the medium-priced line in the belief that they are getting a bargain. This phenomenon is commonly identified as "trading down." Management should recognize the possibility of getting the trading-down effect when considering the wisdom of selling a lower-quality version of the product under a brand name already associated with a higher-quality level.

When a manufacturer wishes to add a lower- or higher-quality version of an existing product to the line and wishes to maintain sales of the original item, he or she would be well advised to give the new product a separate brand name in those cases where consumers are not likely to be able to discriminate between the two products at the point of purchase, where quality can be evaluated through usage, where consumers are likely to shop the different types of retailers who handle the different quality levels, and where salespeople are likely to switch too readily to the sale of the lower-quality item when sales resistance appears.

If the market for a higher-quality version is shrinking to unprofitable levels, however, a firm may wish to take advantage of the trading-down effect to help build up sales volume of a lower-quality line which will tap a new market segment. While we might question the ethics involved in deliberately setting out to confuse consumers, the above discussion indicates how the firm might proceed to achieve the desired result.

The reverse of the above situation occurs when a firm originally sells a low-quality product and then adds a higher-quality version of the same item to the line. If management wishes to reach a higher-income segment of the market through this action, the brand policy to follow will depend upon the same factors mentioned above. If consumers cannot distinguish between the two quality levels, are unable to judge quality through usage, and find both the higher- and lower-quality items in the same retail outlets, then management would be well advised to sell the higher-quality line under a separate brand name. If the objective of management is to get a trading-up effect, however, then the higher-quality version should be given the same brand name and should be promoted aggressively. The prestige associated with the higher-quality version will tend to rub off on the lower-quality item, and the sales of the lower-quality product will increase. Under this strategy the potential

of the higher-quality item will not be fully achieved, since it is being used as a means of stimulating the sales of the original lower-quality line. Again, we might question the ethics of a firm that relies upon confusion of the consumer to gain its objectives. Nevertheless, it is important to understand this phenomenon so that management will make its brand policy decision with a full realization of the probable consequences.

Finally, if consumers can discriminate between the two quality levels through inspection, and the two lines are distributed through different channels not customarily shopped by the same prospective buyers, then both higher- and lower-quality lines may be sold under the same brand name with little risk.

Another way to distinguish between quality levels, while still identifying the different items with the family name, is to follow the practice used by automobile manufacturers. Oldsmobile, for example, combines the family name with a model designation to distinguish between products with different price–quality levels within its line as follows: Cutlass, Delta 88, Ninety-Eight, and Toronado. Here there is little danger of confusion between quality levels, but the different lines all benefit from association with the Oldsmobile family name.

What has been said above relates to consumer goods. If the firm is selling industrial goods, however, there is little danger that the addition of a lower-priced line under the established brand will result in a shift of volume from the higher-quality to the lower-quality product. Industrial buyers are likely to specify the quality of product desired and to inspect the items delivered to make sure that they conform to specifications. Several persons are likely to influence the purchase. Industrial buying is likely to be more rational than consumer buying. Industrial purchasers are not likely to buy the wrong quality because the price is lower.

BRAND–QUALITY DECISIONS THROUGH TIME

When the quality specifications for a new brand are being defined, management may choose one of three levels: superior to competitors, equal to competitors, or inferior to competitors. In the PIMS study of the impact of marketing strategies on profit performance, the sample of businesses was divided into three equal groups on the basis of two factors: market share and product quality. The data for each of the nine subgroups shown in Figure 12–2 include between 40 and 70 businesses. It is significant that in each market share group, profitability increased with brand quality. For example, businesses with market shares of over 26 percent achieved the following returns on investment: inferior product quality—19.5 percent; average product quality—21.9 percent; and

FIGURE 12–2   Effect of market share and product quality on ROI

Market share	Product quality		
	Inferior	Average	Superior
Under 12%	4.5%	10.4%	17.4%
12%–26%	11.0	18.1	18.1
Over 26%	19.5	21.9	28.3

Source: Reprinted by permission of the *Harvard Business Review*. Exhibit from "Impact of Strategic Planning on Profit Performance" by Sidney Schoeffler, Robert D. Buzzell, and Donald F. Heany (March–April 1974). Copyright © 1974 by the President and Fellows of Harvard College; all rights reserved.

superior product quality—28.3 percent. This suggests that superior product quality tends to increase the effectiveness of marketing effort and hence return on investment.[9]

An issue related to the discussion of trading up and trading down is how to manage the brand's quality through time. There are three options: improve quality, maintain quality, or reduce quality. If a firm follows the practice of investing judiciously in research and development for the purpose of improving the quality of its brand in relation to that of competition, and is successful in such efforts, this provides a basis for a marketing program which may result in higher market share and hence higher return on investment. This has been the policy of Procter & Gamble, with the result that a number of its brands have achieved a leading position in their market categories.

An example of a brand that has maintained quality over a long period of time is Bon Ami Cleanser. Trademarked in 1886, the brand's main selling point was its formula. Feldspar, its principal ingredient, is softer and less abrasive, but also more expensive, than the silica or ground sand contained in many other cleansers. Thus, Bon Ami is less wearing on porcelain and other surfaces.

The Bon Ami trademark of a just-hatched chick above the slogan "Hasn't scratched yet" was familiar in almost every home in the early 1900s. When the brand was taken over by Faultless Starch Company in 1971, however, the cleanser had virtually disappeared from store shelves. Why? The former management had a poor reputation with retailers: it promised advertising but did not follow through. Also, the

---

[9]Adapted from Sidney Schoeffler, Robert D. Buzzell, and Donald F. Heany, "Impact of Strategic Planning on Profit Performance," *Harvard Business Review,* March–April 1974, pp. 141–42.

brand had encountered stiff competition from such industry giants as Procter & Gamble (Comet) and Colgate-Palmolive (Ajax).[10]

The strategy followed to revive the brand included the following:

1. Maintain the quality of the brand even though this meant that Bon Ami would cost more than the two leading competing brands.
2. Redesign the package.
3. Launch newspaper, magazine and network-TV advertising as a means of reestablishing Bon Ami's credibility with supermarkets.

As a result Bon Ami was stocked by 95 percent of U.S. supermarkets in 1980. Its share of market had increased from 1 percent in 1971 to 3 percent in 1980—moving into third place behind Comet (with 55 percent market share) and Ajax (with 30 percent).

The results of reducing quality are illustrated by the experience of Simmons Corporation. In 1971, the company used cheaper materials in its Beautyrest mattresses. Consumers and retailers soon noticed the difference. The firm also reduced inventories—upsetting delivery schedules to dealers. Within four years these and other deficiencies led sales to stagnate, share of market to fall, and profits to decrease.[11]

In 1975 the management began a series of sweeping changes designed to reverse the trend. Simmons restored the former specifications on its mattresses and corrected its inventory problem. But after three years the company's reputation lingered. The firm found that a turnaround was hard to bring off.

WHETHER TO MANUFACTURE UNDER DISTRIBUTORS' BRANDS[12]

This issue is of fundamental importance to manufacturers, since the decision made has an important bearing not only upon the promotional strategy followed by the firm but also upon product development, distribution policy, pricing, production, and finance. Reaching a wise decision may influence market share and profit performance for years to come. Recognition of this fact has led some of our largest corporations to set up special task forces to make a thorough study of the risks and opportunities of supplying large-scale distributors with products to be sold under their private brands.

While there has been a substantial resurgence of distributors' brands

---

[10]"Bon Ami Cleanser Tries Comeback," *Los Angeles Times,* December 11, 1979, part 4, p. 5.

[11]"Simmons: A Turnaround Proves Hard to Bring off," *Business Week,* June 5, 1978, pp. 146–50.

[12]Summarized from Victor J. Cook and Thomas F. Schutte, Marketing Science Institute, *Brand Policy Determination,* pp. 66–97. © 1967 by Allyn & Bacon, Inc., Boston. By permission of the publisher and the Marketing Science Institute.

during the years since World War II, the impact of private brands upon different industries varies considerably. In a recent study of brand policy by the Marketing Science Institute, it was found that the share of industry achieved by distributors' brands varied as follows: shoes, 52 percent; replacement tires, 36 percent; major appliances, 33 percent; gasoline, 16 percent; grocery products, 13 percent; and portable appliances, 7 percent. It is apparent that the opportunities for profiting from distributors' brand production, as well as the risks involved in following such a policy, vary widely in different product classifications.

There are three basic brand policy options available to the manufacturer. A company can elect to produce only its own brands and follow a "manufacturers' brand policy." Or a firm can follow a "distributors' brand policy," producing exclusively for sale under private labels and manufacturing nothing under its own brand. Between these extremes falls the "mixed-brand policy," in which both private and national brands are produced. Analysis indicates that each of these policy options may be appropriate under certain conditions. Reaching a wise decision therefore calls for careful analysis and discriminating judgment.

The executive faced with such a decision may get helpful guidance from the findings of the MSI study mentioned above.[13] This study was based upon intensive interviews with 112 different manufacturing organizations. Of these companies, 33 had a manufacturers' brand policy, 65 were committed to a mixed-brand policy, and 14 produced only private brands. The factors influencing management in following each of these alternative policies are outlined below.

Distributors' Brand Policy

Companies following a distributors' brand policy are essentially experts in the production of a given product line. The major marketing function is shifted to distributors. These manufacturers tend to have a limited sales force, limited capability in market research, restricted product development and consumer research activities, and limited warehousing and distribution facilities, and they undertake little promotion and advertising. Such firms tend to have low sales volume, often less than $50 million. Most of these companies share a common characteristic. At a crucial point in their histories, usually prior to World War II, they lacked the management resources or the financial backing to strengthen a dwindling market position and began producing distributors' brands as a means of increasing sales and profits. The distributors' brand policy was probably the best alternative open to them. Although the managements of some of these companies hope eventually to go into the production, distribution, and promotion of their own brands, most

---

[13]Ibid.

of these companies do not have the management capabilities or the financial strength necessary to compete effectively as producers of their own nationally advertised brands.

Manufacturers' Brand Policy

In contrast to the companies which follow a distributors' brand policy are the companies which are fully committed to the manufacture and marketing of their own brands—to a manufacturers' brand policy. These firms are often giants in their industries, with broad product lines, large brand shares, and established distribution systems. Such companies consider themselves to be specialists not only in production, but in marketing and distribution as well. They often have the required management and capital resources to keep their complex operations going at a highly profitable level. The managements of some of these firms do not view private brands as a serious threat, and the managements in other firms of this type do not even view private brands as serious competition. Accordingly, these firms do not produce distributors' brands because they feel that to do so would mean to give up more than they would gain.

Mixed-Brand Policy

There are other manufacturers, however, with marketing capabilities and sales volumes comparable to those of the top manufacturers' brand concerns, who choose to enter private-brand production under a mixed-brand policy. These firms are often large, well established, and experienced in marketing, and they often possess sufficient financial resources to stay near the top of their industries with their own brands. Nevertheless, they turn to the production of private brands. Indeed, in all the industries it studied, MSI found that an increasing number of manufacturers were turning to a mixed-brand policy. Moreover, a mixed-brand policy is probably the most common brand policy in existence today in most consumer product industries, both in terms of the number of companies involved and in terms of the proportion of industry volume that these companies represent. What rationale explains the adoption of a mixed-brand policy? Among the more important considerations are the following.

1. **Recognition of profit opportunities in the production of private brands.**

2. **An interest in reducing the average collection period and in improving the working-capital position.** Adoption of a mixed-brand policy enabled some firms to channel more sales into a few large-volume, quick-paying accounts (private-brand distributors) and proportionately less into many small-volume, slower-paying accounts.

3. Gains in production efficiency. Two production advantages were found to be extremely important in certain situations. First, long-term contracts with large distributors may provide a basis for plant expansion, resulting in a general reduction of unit costs on both national and private-brand volume through economies of scale. Second, even where private-brand volume does not justify large building programs, manufacturers may still experience a significant reduction in unit costs as a direct result of the distributors' brand business.

4. Marketing considerations. Gains in the marketing area are often important considerations in the adoption of a mixed-brand policy. Among the more important are the following:

a. Private-brand production provides a way of achieving rapid market information feedback. In the process of controlling their operations, large chain-store organizations collect valuable information on changes in consumer demand as they relate to such matters as product features, price lines, and new products. Regardless of whether this information is freely shared with the manufacturer or must be inferred from the character of private-brand orders, it is valuable feedback that could not be gained cheaply or quickly in any other way.

b. A mixed-brand policy enables the manufacturer to get detailed knowledge of the merchandising operations of the distributor (who is a major competitor) by supplying him or her with private-brand products.

c. The close working relationship between manufacturer and private-brand account may allow the manufacturer to exert some influence upon the product line and the merchandising programs of this distributor (who is also a competitor).

d. A mixed-brand policy may also provide a manufacturer with the opportunity of spreading marketing overhead to the added output generated by the private-brand contracts. Indeed, many companies interviewed in the MSI study found this advantage to be more important than the ability to spread manufacturing overhead.

e. Some manufacturers with broad product lines adopt a mixed-brand policy as a way of escaping the defensive, costly promotional competition encountered on certain of their products. Although the national brands of such firms may be market leaders in product categories accounting for most of their sales volume, the firms may be unable to maintain leadership in other categories, in which large advertising and sales promotion expenditures are made by competition. By manufacturing these products for private-brand distributors, such firms may recoup their volume at the same time that the burden of promotional competition is passed on to distributors.

f. One of the important reasons for adopting a mixed-brand policy is the high degree of pricing flexibility that may be achieved in this way. Under the Robinson-Patman Act, a seller is prohibited from discriminating in price between different purchasers of commodities of like grade

and quality where the effect of such discrimination may be to lessen competition substantially or may tend to create a monopoly. The difficulties of justifying price differences in the sale of the manufacturer's own brand tend to discourage the quoting of special discounts to large chain distributors. If a firm decides to adopt a mixed-brand policy, however, it may produce variations of its product to meet the specifications of large-scale distributors, who will then sell these items under their own private brands. Indeed, if these private brands differ enough from the manufacturer's own brand so that the manufacturer may justifiably claim that they are not of "like grade and quality," this will take the private brands out from under the restrictions of Section 2(a) of the Robinson-Patman Act and enable the firm to charge buyers of the private brands lower prices than the manufacturer's own national brand customarily brings. In this manner, greater pricing flexibility may indeed be gained, since the limitations imposed by the Robinson-Patman Act may be avoided.[14]

5. Risks of a mixed-brand policy.[15] It is recognized that certain risks are involved in the adoption of a mixed-brand policy. Accordingly, it is helpful to identify the risks that were anticipated by firms considering production under distributors' brands and to discover how serious these risks turned out to be in actual practice. The findings of the MSI study relating to these points are reviewed below.

a. Loss of trade support for the national brand. Manufacturers relying on franchise outlets for distribution of their national brand were fearful that the production of private-brand merchandise might result in a reduction of sales efforts by their dealers and even a loss in franchise outlets. For a few manufacturers, these fears were realized. Others found dealers less critical than they expected. Still others found it possible to minimize adverse dealer reactions by offering the wider margins made possible by private-brand business, or by handling the private-brand business through subsidiary companies that were not directly identified with the parent concern.

b. Recognition by consumers that products of the same manufacturer are available under both national and private brands. Manufacturers adopting a mixed-brand policy usually did all they could to minimize the recognition by consumers that their products were available under both national and private labels. Some took steps to make the appearance of the private brand different from that of the national brand.

---

[14]How much of a difference must be provided between a private brand and the manufacturer's own brand to escape from the restrictions of Section 2(*a*) of the Robinson-Patman Act would appear to depend upon the nature of the product. For helpful guidelines see *Federal Trade Commission v. Borden Company*, U.S. Court of Appeals for the Fifth Circuit, 381 F. 2d 175, No. 20463, July 14, 1967. Commerce Clearing House, *Trade Cases*, 1967, p. 84, 171–84, 176.

[15]Summarized from Cook and Schutte, *Brand Policy Determination*, pp. 93–96.

Others put provisions in contracts with distributors to prevent mention of the supplier's name in promotion. Yet for some companies, the problems of consumer-recognition were well known in advance and were accepted philosophically as a part of the private-brand business.

c. Loss of exclusive rights to new-product developments through adoption by private-brand customers. Where distributors work closely with manufacturers on research and development work, and contribute significant amounts to R&D activities, they may be expected to want equal access to the new-product developments which may result. Before the manufacturer enters into such an arrangement, of course, the gains and losses may be evaluated and cooperative R&D activities undertaken only if the net result is beneficial.

d. Disclosure of costs and operating data to a major competitor (the private-brand distributor) through known-cost contracts. This was recognized as an unavoidable problem of a mixed-brand policy, although few executives believed that the information would be used to their disadvantage by their private-brand customers.

e. Certain risks long associated with private-brand business were recognized by firms adopting a mixed-brand policy, but they were discounted as being of less concern than the risks discussed above. One was the risk that a mixed-brand policy might result in trading volume and dollars under the manufacturer's brand for volume and fewer dollars under the private label. Only a few firms following a mixed-brand policy actually experienced a drop in the sale of their own brands with private-brand production. On the contrary, the result was most often a substantial increase in total volume and at least maintenance of the previous sales levels that had been achieved under the manufacturer's brand.

Another commonly recognized risk was that of becoming unduly dependent upon giant private-brand distributors through gradual increases over time in the proportion of output going into the distributors' brands. While firms moving from complete reliance on national brands to a mixed-brand policy recognized this danger, many expressed a keen interest in increasing their private-brand sales—some even by 100 percent or 200 percent. Apparently they regarded this risk as one that was not of immediate concern in view of the magnitude of their current national-brand volume.

6. Relative profitability of different brand policies. According to the MSI study, firms following a mixed-brand policy were more profitable than firms entirely committed to private-brand production, but were less profitable than firms following a manufacturers' brand policy. Even so, examples of highly profitable mixed-brand organizations were found during the course of the study. According to MSI, "It cannot be concluded that a manufacturers' brand firm is likely to suffer a loss in profits by adopting a mixed-brand policy."[16] This finding led the researchers to

---

[16]Ibid., p. 83.

examine the characteristics of the more profitable mixed-brand manufacturers in an attempt to discover why these manufacturers had been unusually successful in their approach. The results of this analysis are outlined below.

   a. Such firms have formal policies that provide for the production of private brands on a continuing basis as an integral part of each company's operation, rather than for short-run, in-and-out tactics.

   b. They have a full-time private-brand administrator, reporting most often to the vice president of marketing.

   c. Most of these firms have specific criteria that they use in making a careful selection of private-label customers.

   d. Corporate resources—such as R&D staffs, marketing research data, and merchandising and promotional-planning experience—are made available to the private-brand administrator.

   e. The use of "known-cost" contracts—the type of contract which provides details on the manufacturer's cost structure—is another characteristic shared by the more profitable mixed-brand companies. The known-cost contract often appeared responsible for a close management contract between the supplier and the customer, another distinguishing characteristic of the more profitable firms.

   7. Summary. As indicated in the foregoing discussion, many well-established firms view private-brand production under a mixed-brand policy as a normal, profitable market opportunity. They often see production under private labels as a means of reaching a market segment not covered by their national-brand business. It is recognized that the adoption of a mixed-brand policy may entail serious risks. This indicates the wisdom of careful analysis of corporate, financial, production, and marketing considerations in evaluating the desirability of adopting a mixed-brand position. Judging from the MSI study, many firms believe that the advantages of a mixed-brand policy outweigh the risks associated with it. Then, too, the mixed-brand policy is viewed as the most flexible of the three policy options. It offers the opportunity to adapt quickly to basic changes in the market structure as large-scale distributors grow and capture an increasing market share for their private brands. It also opens up large amounts of volume that would remain unavailable under a policy of producing only manufacturer's brands. Companies included in the MSI study that integrated private-brand production into the mainstream of corporate activity by developing well-planned, long-term policies apparently found that this approach resulted in higher volume, greater overall market strength, and improved profits.

Generic Brands

   Generic products—also known as no-frills, no-name, and brandless items—appearing in plain white or brown wrappers have been making

inroads into the grocery marketing field.[17] This development is a challenge to producers of both manufacturers' brands and distributors' brands. Such firms face the question as to what action they should take either to combat the competition of generic brands or to supply the middlemen who are promoting these brands to consumers.

According to Willard Bishop, the Carrefour Group in France originated the "generic age" in 1976 with the introduction of *"produits libres."* Within 2½ years, these products had received widespread consumer acceptance and had obtained a sizable share of the French market. Jewel Tea Companies tested a limited line of generic products in selected Jewel stores and in several Star markets. By the beginning of 1978, strong consumer acceptance had prompted the expansion of generics to 70 of the larger Jewel food stores and 56 of the 58 Star markets. A survey of companies offering generics in the fourth quarter of 1978 revealed that some generic items were being offered in more than 8,000 supermarkets across the country. Entrants in the field in addition to Jewel Companies included Topco Associates, Pathmark Supermarkets, A&P, Safeway Stores, and Ralphs Grocery Company.

Ralphs Grocery Company offers Plain Wrap products in its 99 California supermarkets as "a new alternative" rather than as a replacement for national brands or private-label brands. "Instead, they are a third alternative, available only at Ralphs . . . an important new addition [of 200 items] to Ralphs super selection of up to 15,000 items."[18]

Plain Wrap products include canned food items, detergents, paper towels, napkins, toilet paper, and alcoholic beverages. According to an independent price survey conducted by Vector Enterprises, Inc., a leading research firm and authority on supermarket pricing, in March 1979 Plain Wrap was priced 28.7 percent lower than the national brands and 14.8 percent lower than the private-label brands carried in 16 major chains in Los Angeles. In making these comparisons, Vector Enterprises noted that "there will be some differences in sizing, color, texture and composition between 'Plain Wrap,' private-label brands and national brands."

In a brochure explaining why Plain Wrap products are priced lower than both national brands and private labels, Ralphs explains: (1) no fancy packaging—simple containers, plain labels; (2) no costly promotions—a minimum of promotion beyond their initial introduction; (3) no costly extras—for example, Plain Wrap peaches vary in size and are packed in light syrup instead of heavy syrup; and (4) no color or fancy designs—for example, paper products are available only in white.

---

[17]"Generic Groceries Keep Adding Market Share," *Marketing News,* February 23, 1979, p. 1 ff.

[18]*Ralph Introduces Plain Wrap,* brochure published by Ralphs Grocery Company together with supplementary information supplied by John Marasca, vice president–marketing, July 1, 1980.

According to the vice president–marketing of Ralphs, Plain Wrap items rank first in sales in all the product categories in which they compete.

Turning to Bishop's 1979 survey of generic products, these findings were reported: (1) There is a significant market for many generic products. (2) Generic sales vary greatly among stores and markets. (3) While the source of sales of generics is hard to identify, much of this business appears to be drawn from advertised brands. (4) Respected retailers have apparently concluded that generics will be profitable, at least in the short run. (5) It seems that there will be continued growth in the sales of generic products, the greatest increases occurring in nonfoods and perishables.[19]

In a later study of the market for generic brands, it was reported that 80 percent of all supermarkets in the United States were selling these items during 1982. Also, it was estimated that generic brand grocery products accounted for about $2.2 billion in retail sales during 1982, which represents over 2 percent of all supermarket sales.[20] Certainly this development represents a challenge of significant proportions to the manufacturers of advertised brands.

Accordingly, the executives of such firms might ask, What are the characteristics of the market for generic brand grocery products? Analysis of the purchase records of 1,442 households during an 18-month time period provides interesting information on this question. Of these households, 715 did not purchase any generic items, while the remaining 727 households were classified as "buyers." The results of discriminate analysis of these data indicate that, in comparison to the nonbuyer, the buyer of generic brand grocery products (1) shopped more frequently, (2) had a higher product-usage rate, (3) generally purchased lower-priced products, (4) exhibited a higher level of store loyalty, and (5) was less brand loyal for dry mix dinners, one of the four brand categories tested.

Implications. The findings of this research suggest several appropriate strategies for the marketers of generic brand products. (1) They should maintain the present price differential offered by generic brand grocery products. (2) Generic brand shoppers are not deal-prone. (3) Attempts to influence the product selection of generic brand-prone shoppers by advertising are not likely to be successful. (4) Many of these shoppers probably substituted the purchase of generics for their preferred store's private brands.[21]

---

[19]"Generic Groceries," p. 6.

[20]Adapted from Martha R. McEnally & Jon M. Hawes, "The Market for Generic Brand Grocery Products: A Review and Extension," *Journal of Marketing*, 48 (Winter 1984), pp. 76–83. See Table 1 of this article for an excellent summary of past research on the characteristics of the generic-prone shopper.

[21]For additional information about the characteristics of generic versus nongeneric brand shoppers and the influence of perceived risk upon their brand choice, see Beth

In summary, the trend toward offering generic products provides a "fourth alternative" for the manufacturer to consider in working out a brand policy. This approach should, however, be given especially careful analysis if the firm currently is marketing advertised brands. While it may be estimated that the unbranded generic merchandise sold at discount prices could add to short-run profits, the possibility that such items may cannibalize sales of advertised brands should be recognized. If this were to happen the combined profit showing of the manufacturer's brand and the generic line might be less than that of the manufacturer's brand alone.

If the firm following a manufacturer's brand policy decides *not* to sell unbranded generic products but to combat such competition, at least two possible approaches merit consideration. One is to take action to narrow the spread between the retail prices of the firm's advertised brand and the competing generic products through improvements in efficiency which result in cost reductions. A second is to undertake a systematic analysis of the existing marketing strategy for the purpose of improving the effectiveness with which the advertised brand is sold.[22]

If the manufacturer follows either a distributor's brand policy or a mixed-brand policy, then it is important to recognize the threat posed by generic brand products. It would be wise to check the research finding that generic-prone shoppers tend to substitute the purchase of generics for their preferred store's private brands. Does research indicate that this substitution occurs to a significant extent in the product classifications supplied to retailers for sale under their private brands? If so, then the firm must decide whether supplying retailers with generic brand products is more profitable than continuing to supply them with private brand merchandise. Or would it be more profitable to supply *both* private brand merchandise and generic brand products than to limit the business exclusively to one or the other of these alternatives?

Decision Theory Approach to Mixed-Brand Policy Choice

The foregoing discussion of the problem of whether a national-brand producer should seek private-brand and/or generic-label business makes

---

Axelrod, Bruce G. VanderBergh, and Dean A. Krugman, "Risk, Quality, and the Generic Grocery Item Phenomenon: Implications for Retail Advertising and Promotion," *Proceedings of the 1982 Conference of The American Academy of Advertising*, ed. Alan D. Fletcher (Knoxville, Tenn.: American Academy of Advertising, 1982), pp. 1–6.

[22]Improvement in the firm's marketing operations may result from a *marketing audit*. This is a comprehensive, systematic, independent, and periodic examination of a company's marketing environment, objectives, strategies, and activities with a view of determining problem areas and opportunities and recommending a plan of action to improve the company's marketing performance. See Philip Kotler, William Gregor, and William Rodgers, "The Marketing Audit Comes of Age," *Sloan Management Review*, Winter 1977, pp. 25–43.

it abundantly clear that the consequences of such action are not known with certainty. This suggests that management might well consider the possibility of analyzing this problem by means of the "decision theory" approach—that is, the method of *individual decision making under risk*.[23]

The decision theory approach may be summarized as follows:

1. Identification of alternative possibilities.
2. Identification of possible states of nature (i.e., conditions that cannot be predicted with certainty).
3. Exploration of further possibilities and outcomes. The analysis cannot stop realistically with a single "round" of actions and their outcomes. Instead it is necessary to explore the whole chain of effects and reactions that would follow a given decision by executives of the firm.
4. Estimation of payoffs. For each alternative decision and each outcome, the "payoff" to the decision maker should be estimated by tracing the effects of the decision and its outcome upon the firm's sales, costs, and profits.
5. Assessment of probabilities. Since the outcome of a given decision is uncertain, a key element in the analysis is to assign probabilities to the various possible "states of nature." These probabilities represent the decision maker's "betting odds" as to the probable responses of customers, competition, and so forth. This is a difficult step, but it is an essential element in decision theory.
6. Computation of a expected payoff. The expected payoff of an act is defined as the average of its net payoff under all possible states of nature, each weighted by its probability of occurrence.
7. Choice of optimal decision.[24]

Evaluation of Decision Theory Approach

Decision theory provides an approach for analyzing problems where the outcomes of possible alternative decisions involve considerable uncertainty (or risk). (The problem of whether to adopt a mixed-brand policy certainly falls into this category.) Such an approach encourages the identification and analysis of *all* the possible decisions that might be made (including doing nothing). Of particular significance is the emphasis on thinking through the possible consequences of the whole chain of events that may result from each possible action. Note that the process does not stop with a single "round" of actions and their outcomes. If possible, it should be carried through a second round and—if estimates

---

[23]The following discussion is reprinted by permission from Robert D. Buzzell and Charles C. Slater, "Decision Theory and Marketing Management," *Journal of Marketing* 26, no. 3 (July 1962), pp. 7–16. Published by the American Marketing Association.

[24]For an illustration of this approach as applied to a brand policy decision by a wholesale baker, see ibid., pp. 14–15.

of payoffs and probabilities can be made with satisfactory confidence—through a third and possibly even a fourth round. This aspect of the approach focuses attention on the critical issues involved in the various possible ways of dealing with the problem.

In most cases involving a mixed-brand policy decision, determination of the probabilities for the relevant "states of nature" (reactions of consumers, competitors, and so on) is difficult. A firm does not make such a decision often enough to gain experience which may guide future estimates. Nevertheless, even very crude approximations of the probabilities for the various states affecting the outcomes of the decision are better than none at all. Decision theory forces executives to recognize the subjective "betting odds" that lie behind their judgments and to put these odds into quantitative form as probability estimates.

Likewise, the task of estimating profit payoffs for each possible line of action several years into the future tends to encourage executives to be more careful in their analyses. The process of estimating payoffs and determining probabilities also tends to encourage management to examine the mixed-brand problem in concrete terms and provides a stimulus to more systematic thinking by those involved. Equally important, structuring the problem in formal terms helps to indicate the direction which future research should take if such analyses are to be improved.

It should be recognized, of course, that the application of decision theory to the mixed-brand policy problem will encourage estimates which may be based upon inadequate data and thus may represent only crude approximations of the information desired. It is necessary, therefore, to avoid imputing greater accuracy than they merit to the figures on estimated payoff, which represent the end results of the analysis. If the limitations of the data are kept in mind, however, the decision theory approach may aid management in the difficult task of making choices among alternative lines of action under conditions of uncertainty.

Perhaps the chief advantage of decision theory grows out of the fact that this approach requires the executive to *formalize* thinking about a problem—to structure judgment and write it down in black and white. It is self-evident that this is likely to improve the quality of executive judgment. Experimentation with this approach, therefore, would appear to be desirable.

CONCLUSION

Decisions on brand strategy have important promotional implications. In this chapter, we have focused on issues relating to family versus individual brands, brand–quality–price relationships, and the wisdom of manufacturing products to be sold under distributors' brands as opposed to the manufacturer's own brand. The competitive challenge that

generic products offer to producers of both manufacturer's brands and distributors' brands has also been discussed. Evidence has been cited that for frequently purchased package goods the promotion of one product under a family brand has beneficial effects for other products under that brand through the principle of generalization. In contrast, a study of semantic generalization, as applied to family brands of household appliances, raises some doubts as to the advantages of using a common brand name as a means of transferring attitudes between dissimilar products of high unit value.

On the question of distributors' brands versus manufacturers' brands, each of the three policy options open may be appropriate under certain conditions, but a Marketing Science Institute study indicates that a mixed-brand policy is probably the most common current posture in most consumer product industries. In our discussion we also noted that the outcomes of adopting any one of the three alternative policies as well as the generic products strategy involves considerable risk or uncertainty. Accordingly, the possibility of applying the decision theory approach was examined and its merits and limitations discussed.

QUESTIONS

1. Explain how the "assimilation effect" from psychological theory may be applied to family branding.

2. The text suggests several factors which tend to foster or retard the development of generalized preference for family brands through the process of assimilation. In the light of these factors, in which of the following situations would you recommend a policy of family branding?
    a. A new hair lightener for men to be introduced by Clairol, Inc., which formerly marketed hair preparations exclusively for women.
    b. A new snow blower added to its line by Yard-Man, Inc., a manufacturer of power lawn mowers.
    c. A stereo phonograph added to its line of sewing machines by Singer Company.
    d. A diaper-pail spray in an aerosol can introduced by the owners of the firm producing Lustur-Seal, an automobile paint conditioner.

3. Under what conditions might it be desirable to combine an individual brand name with the corporate name in identifying a product? When might it be undesirable?

4. Just after World War II, Levi Straus manufactured a short product line of basic blue jeans and related items mainly for the workingman. In the early 1950s, the firm added Levi's Lighter Blue, a line of faded blue demin jeans; still later, it added White Levi's and pastel jeans. Then the firm added Levi's shoes.
    a. What are the merits and limitations of brand extension into the shoe category?

b. Would you recommend marketing a 10-speed bicycle under the Levi brand? Why or why not?

5. Until 1965, Polaroid Land Cameras capable of producing color pictures in 60 seconds were priced at about $135 and $165. In 1965, Polaroid announced the addition of Model 103 to sell at about $90 and Model 104 priced at $60. Later that year, an economy model producing only black-and-white pictures was introduced at about $20. All of these models were sold under the Polaroid name. What is your analysis of the probability that these actions would result in trading down? If you believe that trading down would likely occur, would you regard this result as desirable or undesirable? Why?

6. In which of the following hypothetical situations would trading down be likely to occur?
   a. If Cadillac introduced a medium-priced car under the Cadillac name.
   b. If a manufacturer of high-grade women's dresses identified by the Smartset brand added a medium-grade line under the same brand name.
   c. If the manufacturer of the high-grade Hamilton watches were to offer a low-priced watch available only through mail-order houses.
   d. If a materials-handling company making industrial forklifts selling at $7,000 introduced an economy line priced at $1,500 under the same brand name.
   e. If the Kroehler Company, emphasizing medium- and low-priced upholstered furniture, were to add a high-grade line under the Kroehler brand name and sell it through retail outlets handling the original line.

7. According to the PIMS study, firms whose products are superior in quality tend to earn a higher ROI than is earned by firms with products of inferior quality. Assume that a firm which manufactures a household cleanser has a 3 percent market share, that its product is of average quality when compared with competition, and that it is getting an ROI of 10 percent on the line. Would you recommend that the firm increase its expenditures on R&D from 1 percent of sales to 4 percent of sales in the hope of improving the market share and ROI on its product? Why or why not?

8. Under what conditions are firms likely to concentrate their production on the manufacture and sale of products under distributors' brands? What are the risks of such a policy? How may these risks be minimized (if at all)?

9. Under what circumstances are firms likely to limit themselves to the manufacture and sale of their own brands? What drawbacks, if any, does this policy have?

10. List briefly the considerations which tend to lead a firm to adopt a mixed-brand policy.

11. Identify briefly the risks of following a mixed-brand policy.

12. In view of the risks which a mixed-brand policy involves, why have many well-established firms adopted this approach in the marketing of their products?

13. *a.* What are the merits of applying the decision theory approach to the question of whether to manufacture for sale under distributors' brands (assuming that the firm now concentrates on its own brands)?

　　 b. What conditions should exist if the decision theory approach is to be applied successfully?

Cases for part five

VERNORS INC. (B)*

Promotional strategy for Vernors' soft drinks

In his effort to increase sales by 10 percent over fiscal 1974, Leonard Heilman thought it important that Vernors resume the advertising program that it had suspended in January 1974. A small local advertising agency was hired in June, and it began work almost immediately. Although Heilman initially recommended that no more than $600,000 be spent on consumer promotional activity, he was open to alternative suggestions. Heilman expected that an equal amount would be spent on dealer promotions (Exhibit 1). Aside from his recommendations on the appropriate size for the total budget, Heilman recommended that other areas be given some thought. These included: the proper dollar allocation among the various media alternatives; at what time of day and at what time of the year advertisements should occur; which consumer segments should be targeted; which products and sizes should be promoted; and what creative themes could be employed.

---

*Written by Peter E. Robinson, research assistant under the direction of James D. Scott, Sebastian S. Kresge Professor of Marketing, Graduate School of Business Administration, The University of Michigan, Ann Arbor.

EXHIBIT 1   Preliminary Vernors advertising budget: Fiscal 1974–1975

Radio	$141,500	
Television	79,200	
Print	70,000	
Billboards	70,000	
Consumer promotions	24,000	
Total		$ 384,700
Merchandising		$ 120,000
Dealer promotions		650,000
Total		$ 770,000
Total		$1,154,000

Notes:
1. The advertising budget includes production costs which generally run 10–15 percent of budget.
2. The advertising coverage will include Detroit, Toledo, and the distributors' areas.
3. Approximately 90 percent of the advertising will be devoted to Vernors, 10 percent to 1-Cal.
4. Three different advertisements will be used on the billboards. All will advertise Vernors. A number 100 showing is the maximum showing possible. It guarantees that everyone who drives in the Detroit major market area will see the billboard at least three times.
5. Consumer promotions will be predominantly sponsorship of events in the Detroit area.
6. Print expenditures will be for newspapers.
7. Television advertising will be on Saturday mornings, aimed at children, and on prime time, targeted for the 25–40-year-old housewife.
8. Radio is targeted for teenagers at night, women during the day, and men during drive time.
9. Sales were estimated first, and then the advertising budget was computed.
10. Merchandising includes all point-of-purchase material.

DEALER PROMOTION

Promotions to dealers are considered essential by all soft drink bottlers. Vernors officials estimate that 20 percent of their yearly sales come during promotional periods. For instance, a chain such as Great Scott might order 6,000 cases during a normal week and 18,000 during a promotional week.

Almost every soft drink bottler in Detroit plans a dealer promotion around key holiday times, which include Easter, Memorial Day, July 4th, Labor Day, Thanksgiving, and Christmas. The participation of chain stores is highly sought after, and the competition for their acceptance of promotions is stiff. It is the responsibility of Vernors' key account man to convince the chain's central management to carry the promotion. If the central management accepts, every store in the chain is required to carry the promotion.

There are basically two kinds of dealer promotions, appropriately called the "cents off" and the "one with." The cents-off promotion offers a direct reduction in price from normal wholesale prices, whereas the one with offers one free case for every X number of cases that the retailer purchases (Exhibit 2). In both types, Vernors offers an additional 5- or 10-cent discount if the retailer agrees to advertise the product in print along with his other specials during the week.

In return for the discount, the bottler expects certain concessions. The retailer must offer a reduction from his regular retail price; he must advertise the special price in the local newspaper; and he must give the product an aisle display away from the soft drink area. The last requirement is essential for a successful promotion, with an end-of-aisle display producing the highest volume in the store.

The promotional schedules are planned in advance but are subject to change due to the competition's strategy and chain store acceptance. By law, a promotion must be offered to all stores that carry Vernors, chains and independents alike. Major chains serviced by the key account men with central offices in Detroit include A&P (103 stores), Farmer Jack (88), Chatham (41), Great Scott (51), Kroger (63), and Wrigley (84). Secondary chains are 7–11 (50), Quick Pic (60), Open Pantry (19), Cunningham (100), Arnold (31), Bi-Lo (9), Danny's (5), and Sentry Drugs (21). As a group, the chains are estimated to account for about 65 percent of all Vernors Inc. food store sales, with independent food outlets comprising 35 percent. Other chains in Vernors' distributor areas, but with central offices outside Detroit, are solicited by the area's distributor or the district manager.

An example of Vernors dealer promotions during fiscal 1974, all of which were for Vernors ginger ale and Vernors 1-Cal, is shown at the top of page 545.

ADVERTISING

Point of Purchase

Point of purchase is used in retail outlets to draw attention to the product on the shelf. A well-placed, eye-catching point-of-purchase piece can increase sales substantially. The four food items that are most often merchandised via point of purchase are: cookies and crackers, soft drinks, candy, and chip-type snacks. The point-of-purchase piece and the package are the final influences that a company has on its consuming public. Several kinds of printed pieces are used to provide in-store support at food stores and other retail outlets.

Shelf talker: The shelf talker attaches to the shelf and hangs directly below the product. It usually displays the product name, price, and

EXHIBIT 2

Vernors Inc.
4501 Woodward Ave.   Detroit, Michigan 48201   Phone (313) 833-8500

October 8, 1973

Mr. Gus Stevens
Great Scott! Super Market, Inc.
1111 E. Eight Mile Road
Ferndale, Michigan 48220

Dear Mr. Stevens:

The first of the Big "Vernor" holidays is just around the corner. To start this holiday season off with a big success, the following promotion will be available for any one-week period, beginning November 5th and running to November 24th.

Product	Size	Package	Price
Vernors Reg & 1-Cal	16-oz. NR	4/6-pks.	$3.57 89¢ 6-pk.

Promotion: one case free with six purchased at regular price with secondary off-shelf display and reduction in price, November 5th through November 24th.
Promo cost: 1W6 $3.06 case   77¢ 6-pk.   Discount 51¢ case

Product	Size	Package	Price
Vernors Reg & 1-Cal	28-oz. NR	12-btl. case 6-pk. or loose	$3.68

Promotion: Time—one week, November 19th through November 24th. One case free with six purchased at regular price with secondary off-shelf display and reduction in price.
Promo cost: 1W6 $3.15 case   26¢ btl.   Discount 53¢ case

Bonus promotion

If you would consider using this package as a feature, advertising in local newspaper or handbill, with a must display and reduction in price, we will extend this promotion as follows:
Promo cost: 1W5 $3.07 case   Discount 61¢ case

When considering the above promotions, we would like to ask for at least two weeks' advance notice so that proper plans can be made to insure sufficient inventories and distribution.

Sincerely,

Raymond H. Jonas
Sales Representative

Promotion period	Size	Partici- pating major chains	Promo- tion	Equiv- alent dis- count	Season
7/1–7/6	28-oz.	Farmer Jack Wrigley Great Scott Chatham	1W5 and 5¢ ad	51¢ off	July 4th
7/9–8/3	16-oz.	A&P Great Scott Kroger Farmer Jack Wrigley	1W5 and 5¢ ad	59¢	
7/20–9/3	12-oz. cans	Chatham Great Scott A&P	1W5 and 5¢ ad	55¢	Labor Day
8/6–8/30	10-oz. WM	Chatham Great Scott A&P Farmer Jack Wrigley	1W5 and 5¢ ad	51¢	One-week minimum introductory offer
11/5–11/24	16-oz.	Kroger Chatham Great Scott A&P	1W4 and 5¢ ad	69¢	Thanksgiving
12/10–12/29	28-oz.	All chains	1W5 and 5¢ ad	61¢	Christmas
1/14–2/15	28–oz.	Great Scott Kroger A&P	1W6		
3/25–4/14	28-oz.	All chains	1W5 and 5¢ ad	61¢	Easter
4/16–5/27	16-oz.	Great Scott	1W5 and 5¢ ad	59¢	
5/27–7/4	16-oz. cans	Farmer Jack A&P Great Scott Wrigley	1W5 and 5¢ ad	59¢	Summer July 4th

any special features. Shelf talkers usually remain for only a short period because they may fall off or be torn down.

Bottle hanger: This piece is usually hung over the top of a quart-type bottle. It might contain a recipe, a product promotion (for a Vernors lamp), and so forth. The hanger could also have a slogan to this effect: "Try me," "New," or "Improved."

Runners: These fit into the slots at the edge of the shelf. Made of plastic, they usually include the company logo and a place for a price.

Holiday posters: These pieces are usually 2' × 3' and are placed during the Easter, Christmas, Thanksgiving, Halloween, Fourth of July, and Labor Day periods. They are positioned at the end of the aisle above the Vernors display. Holiday recipes are included in the copy.

End-of-aisle display: When the retailer has a Vernors' promotion, end-of-aisle displays are customary. These are freestanding displays, and the company logo should be prominently in view. The product is held by the display, and usually a promotional piece is visible above the stacked product.

Window displays: These are frequently found in small food outlets or in area Dairy Queens. The food store piece features the company logo, together with an appropriate picture. The Dairy Queen pieces often display a picture of a Boston Cooler (Vernors and vanilla ice cream).

Menu boards: These are used in restaurants. The prices can be posted by inserting plastic numbers into slots. A promotional piece is attached to the top.

Historically, Vernors' point-of-purchase pieces have featured any combination of the company logo, the Vernors Gnome, an old oak barrel (Vernors is aged for four years in oak barrels), a picture of the product, and an attractive model.

Print

Print has never played a strong role in the Vernors media mix. In recent years, a full-page black-and-white *Detroit News* ad was placed to publicize the change in the can labels ("We changed our look but not our taste"). A one-half-page wide-mouth-bottle introduction in black and white was also utilized. In addition, the newspapers are used infrequently (one–two times a year at most) to advertise Vernors' recipes in conjunction with holiday promotions.

Although Vernors has done so only once in recent years, several soft drink manufacturers have been making regular use of newspapers to coupon the public for consumer promotions. With the coupon, the consumer can purchase the soft drink at a discount. The store sends all coupons to the soft drink manufacturer, who repays the store the face value of the coupon plus three cents per coupon for handling. A coupon promotion should be organized eight weeks in advance. The advantage of couponing is that it reaches almost everyone in one day and helps force distribution or gain display space.

The Vernors company philosophy is that newspaper advertising should be aimed at the housewife. Because most people go shopping on Thursdays, Saturday, Wednesday, and Thursday are considered the best days to advertise in newspapers. These are termed *best food days.*

Management is considering the possibility of advertising in magazines. To its knowledge, magazine advertising has not been used in recent memory.

Television

Although the company's emphasis changed in fiscal 1975, in the last decade Vernors' media emphasis has been on television. The television advertising for both Vernors and 1-Cal has been targeted to housewives. In 1973, Vernors television spots were placed predominantly during the late-night fringe time.

Company officials believe that television is best for reaching people immediately, but they consider it very expensive. Vernors avoids television advertising during the summer because at that time most people are outside rather than watching television; in addition, summer television is mainly rerun-type programming. The fall and winter months are preferred.

Radio

Radio is considered an ideal medium to reach the outdoor crowd during the summer. Vernors has used CKLW almost exclusively in recent years for teenage coverage and to reach its distributors' markets (Exhibit 3). During holiday periods, radio copy includes Vernors holiday recipes.

Vernors has found one advantage of radio to be that its rates are more flexible. Radio stations have approached Vernors to share in promotions in which the stations would have a contest and mention Vernors' name. Vernors, in turn, would provide its product as the prize. Vernors is constantly being approached for radio and other promotions in Detroit because of its long standing as a Detroit company. Such promotions have been held sparingly in recent years.

Billboards

Billboards have not been used in recent years by Vernors. But management believes that they could be an effective summertime advertising medium if used in conjunction with radio and television.

Consumer Promotions

Vernors' promotion program was moribund during the late 1960s and early 1970s, but it has come alive of late. In the years 1972–74, Vernors has had a name-the-Vernors-Gnome contest; has given away Vernors mugs and T-shirts; has sponsored a Detroit Loves Tennis clinic in conjunction with WXYZ and New Era potato chips; and has sponsored a national bicycle race in Pontiac, Michigan. The company once

EXHIBIT 3

Warren, Muller, Dolobowsky, Inc. 711 Third Ave., N.Y., N.Y. 10017, M01-4090

Copy (radio)   Date: 12/1/71   Job No.: VE-RR-722
Client: Vernors Inc.   "Teenage Problems—Breathe"

(Music throughout)

Girl: Some boyfriend I've got. Like we sit on the phone for *hours,* and you know what we do? *Breathe.* Yeah, *breathe.* Every once in a while you hear "cling cling" when he puts in the nickels. Cling cling, breathe breathe. Boy. My sister calls him Hot Breath. My father calls him The Dud. The drugstore man calls him Nickels. Sometimes I get tired of cling cling breathe breathe, and I just leave the phone there and go to the kitchen for a Vernors and come back, and he'll still be breathing. Finally, he'll say, "Watcha doin'?" and I'll say, "Drinking a Vernors," and he'll say, "Me too," and then we start breathing again. So he's not the strong, silent type. So he's just the silent type. I love him. He breathes real cute.

Announcer: This touching story comes from Vernors, the pop people. Vernors believes if you see the humor in your hang-ups, you'll obviously laugh more. If you laugh hard enough, your mouth will get dry. Which might make you feel like a good pop. Since Vernors is *really* good pop . . . gingery and smooth and good and sweet . . . maybe you'll buy Vernors. What makes it different is it's the *only* pop aged in oak barrels. Next time you laugh, remember Vernors.

(Music up and out)

Young Guy Talking: Was I fat. Sweet 16 and never been kissed. Precisely, I was 44 inches from kissing. Forty-four in the waist. Kids called me *Oval.* Yea, Oval. They'd say, "Hey Oval, wanna lose 40 pounds of ugly fat?" "Cut off your head." Corny. But if you're *fat,* you *laugh,* 'cause you're too slow to chase anybody. Finally I dieted. No pizza. No malteds. *Lotsa* yogurt and lettuce and yech. The only good thing was Vernors 1-Cal, 'cause it's sugarless. Now I weigh 140. And they *still* call me Oval. And still say, "Cut off your head and lose 40 pounds of ugly fat." Except now *I* think it's funny too. Oh. Also, now I've been kissed. Lose some, win some.

Announcer: This slender story comes from Vernors, the pop people. Vernors thinks fat jokes are only funny if you're not fat. So they have made Vernors 1-Cal, a diet pop that's smooth and good and *sweet. Without* sugar. It's really different because only Vernors is aged in oak barrels. To help lose ugly fat without chopping off your head, drink Vernors 1-Cal. To lose some. And win some.

maintained a soda fountain for the public in the bottling plant at its company headquarters. Vernors, Vernors floats, chocolate Vernors, and the like, were served, and the soda fountain became a major tourist attraction. Because of the deteriorating conditions in the neighborhood of the bottling plant, the operation was suspended in the mid-1960s.

Vernors plans to participate in a variety of promotions in which it can be associated with Detroit. Once again, its strong local image is desired by Detroit promoters.

MEDIA SLOGANS

A list of media slogans used in past years is:

	Radio	*Years*
1.	Va Va Voom—original—jingle	1961–62
2.	Va Va Voom—swing	1961–62
3.	Twist—jingle	1962–62
4.	Hootenanny	1963–64
5.	The Fun Ones—jingle (Al Hirt)	1964–65
6.	Vernors A-Go-Go	1965–66
7.	Adventure—interim spots	1966–67
8.	"No Slogan"	1967–68
9.	Jose and flavor gap jingle	1968–69
10.	Dana/no cyclamates	1969–70
11.	Flavor Gap jingle/Laugh Campaign	1970–71
12.	Do a Vernors pop	

	Television	
1.	Popcorn (Fun Ones)—60 sec.	1964–65
2.	Popcorn (Fun Ones)—30 sec.	1964–65
3.	Popcorn (1-Cal)—60 sec.	1964–65
4.	Popcorn (1-Cal)—30 sec.	1964–65
5.	Hot Vernors color—Winter 30 sec.	1965
6.	Flavor Gap—Bottle Drop	1968
7.	Jose spot	
8.	Dana spots/no cyclamates	1969
9.	Computer animation—1-Cal	1970–71
10.	Regular animation—Vernors regular	1970–71
11.	Different Thing	

APPENDIX

1973	$15,500,000
1972	14,200,000
1971	10,450,000 (8-mo. strike)
1970	15,000,000
1969	13,800,000
1968	12,100,000
1967	10,500,000

EXHIBIT A–2 Detroit sales—Vernors equivalent units (000 omitted)

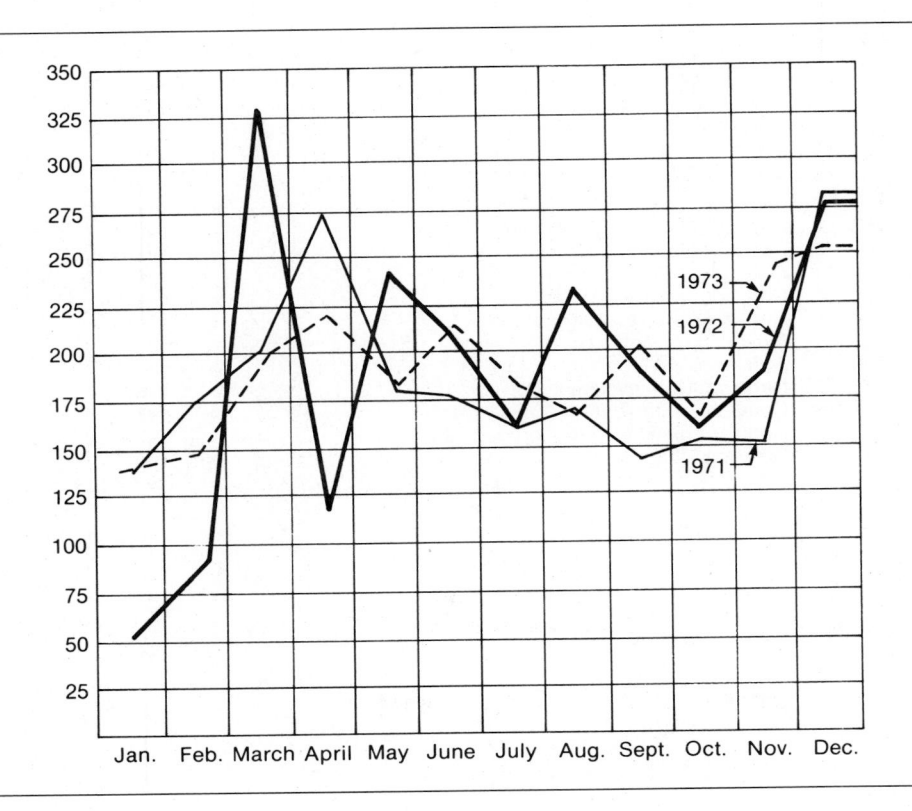

EXHIBIT A–3   Detroit sales—1-Cal equivalent units (000 omitted)

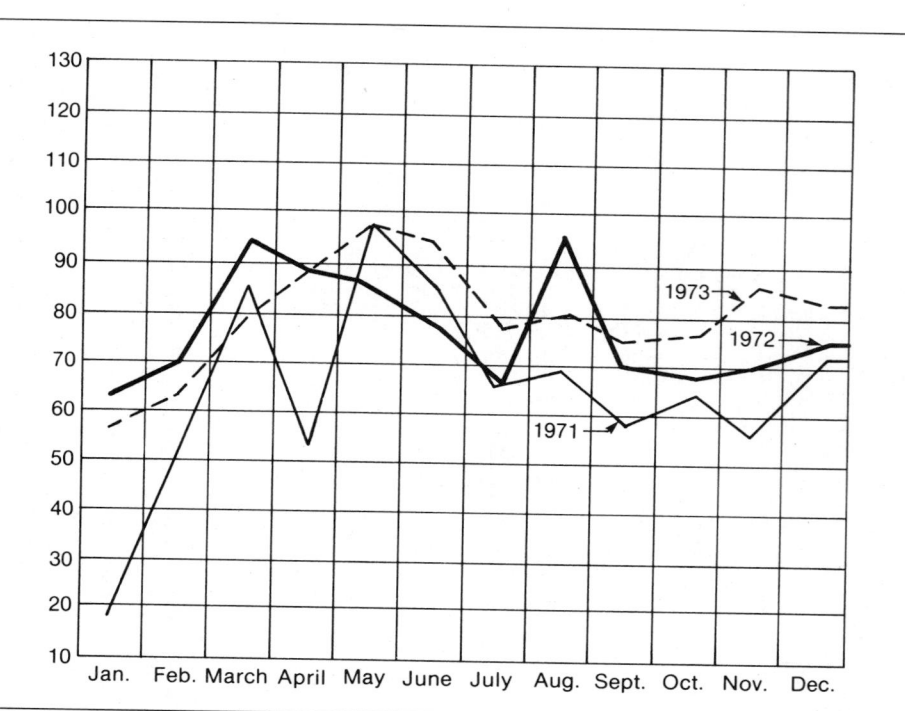

EXHIBIT A–4   Detroit major market area: Competitors' market share in food stores

	1970	1971	1972	1973
Pepsi	25.2	24.7	29.7	27.3
Diet-Pepsi	1.8	1.7	2.6	2.6
Coke	15.8	15.3	11.2	15.7
7up	6.5	6.5	6.9	6.7

EXHIBIT A–5   Vernors advertising expenditures, 1969–1974, by types of media

	Detroit 40	Toledo 41	Pontiac 47	Flint 48	Saginaw 49	Jackson 52
73-74						
Outdoor 43-130						
43-730						
TV 43-131	21,112.98	6,310.00		6,805.00		
43-731	27,528.13	3,070.00		3,520.00		
Print 43-132	4,254.44	1,097.17		500.00	500.00	250.00
43-732		22.11				
Radio 43-133	28,211.37	930.00		1,380.00		
43-733						
Promotion: Trade 43-150 and 151	216,746.94	19,326.79	24,993.98	20,340.51	12,818.13	5,881.35
43-750 and 751	50,759.11	1,445.70	11,058.64	5,095.79	3,386.34	2,042.37
Promotion: Consumer 43-152 and 153	9,980.63	363.82				
43-752 and 753	311.79	14.38				
72-73						
Outdoor 43-130	25.67					
43-730						
TV 43-131	14,745.00	6,365.00		2,478.55		
43-731	23,393.75	5,130.00		4,461.20		
Print 43-132	1,253.94	310.00				
43-732	1,115.75					173.13
Radio 43-133	24,690.25	3,868.50		2,920.29		53.13
43-733						
Promotion: Trade 43-150 and 151	239,034.64	(370.63)	21,251.79	20,686.95	17,204.05	3,655.65
43-750 and 751	70,144.35	335.80	8,487.16	4,483.09	7,581.40	1,414.53
Promotion: Consumer 43-152 and 153	17,228.06	277.67	49.28	18.21	3.32	3.00
43-752 and 753	4,771.82	77.99			1.55	
71-72						
Outdoor 43-130						
43-730						
TV 43-131	38,265.00					
43-731						
Print 43-132	133.25	27.85	383.50			410.40
43-732	6,857.10			820.80		25.00
Radio 43-133	23,177.50	1,890.00		1,482.30		
43-733						
Promotion: Trade 43-150 and 151	152,254.73	14,968.62	14,796.10	21,461.87	16,697.30	2,765.23
43-750 and 751	17,787.30		3,420.80	2,252.95	2,431.10	380.80
Promotion: Consumer 43-152 and 153	3,041.55	217.76	49.26	171.37		345.98
43-752 and 753						
70-71						
Outdoor 43-130						
43-730						
TV 43-131				(170.00)		
43-131						
Print 43-132	175.00	130.00			25.00	
43-732		(12.00)		(7.70)		
Radio 43-133						
43-733						
Promotion: Trade 43-150 and 151	214,754.79	16,658.77	19,586.94	13,978.51	10,969.70	5,077.24
43-750 and 751						
Promotion: Consumer 43-152 and 153	1,498.30	12.19	66.40	2.07		454.41
43-752 and 753						
69-70						
Outdoor 43-130						
43-730						
TV 43-131	60,519.42	8,851.00		10,375.00		
43-731						
Print 43-132	10,262.60	2,278.94	30.00	985.60		41.00
43-732						
Radio 43-133	18,071.60	8,540.30		2,151.80		495.72
43-733						
Promotion: Trade 43-150 and 151	94,466.35	9,277.35	8,805.45	19,042.59	11,621.30	2,541.85
43-750 and 751						
Promotion: Consumer 43-152 and 153	1,982.99	53.59	39.69	3.38	1.28	45.66
43-752 and 753						

	Ann Arbor 54	Lansing 59	Marys-ville 60	Central Office 99	Total year			
73-74								
Outdoor								
TV		5,190.00			39,417.98	Vernors	Vernors	77,983.41
		2,420.00			38,958.13	1-Cal	1-Cal	38,980.24
Print	250.00	460.00		153.68	7,465.29	Vernors		
					22.11	1-Cal		
Radio		566.25		12.52	31,100.14	Vernors		
Promotion: Trade	18,482.97	9,433.47	8,049.89		336,074.03	Vernors	Vernors	346,422.04
	470.76	3,210.19	1,657.89		83,363.64	1-Cal	1-Cal	83,689.81
Promotion: Consumer				3.56	10,348.01	Vernors		
					326.17	1-Cal		
72-73								
Outdoor					25.67	Vernors	Vernors	82,108.63
TV		1,919.00		14,294.87	39,202.42	Vernors	1-Cal	38,685.91
Print		3,529.25		837.83	37,352.03	1-Cal		
				3,388.50	4,952.44	Vernors		
Radio		1,107.60		165.00	1,280.75	1-Cal		
				5,168.33	37,928.10	Vernors		
Promotion: Trade	19,177.68	4,752.09	5,011.36	3.39	53.13	1-Cal		
	6,042.13	1,773.16	1,669.84		330,406.59	Vernors	Vernors	350,486.40
Promotion: Consumer		43.15	11.68		101,931.46	1-Cal	1-Cal	106,784.59
				2,445.44	20,079.81	Vernors		
				1.77	4,853.13	1-Cal		
71-72								
Outdoor								
TV					38,265.00	Vernors	Vernors	67,433.20
Print	410.40	752.40			544.60	Vernors	1-Cal	925.10
Radio		2,648.80			9,251.10	1-Cal		
					28,623.60	Vernors		
Promotion: Trade	10,947.25	3,698.60	4,423.39		242,013.09	Vernors	Vernors	246,185.27
	2,277.15	471.65	482.50		29,504.25	1-Cal	1-Cal	29,692.65
Promotion: Consumer	36.17	304.56	4.80		4,172.18	Vernors		
		181.40			188.40	1-Cal		
70-71								
Outdoor								
TV					(170.00)	Vernors		
Print					330.00	Vernors		
Radio					(19.70)	Vernors		
Promotion: Trade	11,447.65	4,316.61	3,955.80	105.00	300,851.01	Vernors		
Promotion: Consumer		9.89	8.27		2,051.53	Vernors	Vernors	303,042.84
69-70								
Outdoor								
TV					79,745.42	Vernors		
Print	480.00				14,078.14	Vernors		
Radio		1,768.65			31,029.07	Vernors		
Promotion: Trade	6,073.25	4,299.85	2,221.83	280.00	158,629.82	Vernors		
Promotion: Consumer		18.21			2,144.80	Vernors	Vernors	285,627.25

EXHIBIT A–6 Competitive soft drink advertising expenditures: 1969 versus 1970 (estimated)

Brand	Year	Television Network (prorated @ 2.28%)	Spot	Spot radio	News-paper	Out-door	Maga-zines (prorated @ 2.29%)	Local	Local + (prorated national)
Pepsi	1969	$119,522	$228,303	$181,308	—	$25,375	$ 25,228	$434,986	$579,736
	1970	119,522*	181,400	123,380	10,711	95,254	25,228*	410,745	555,405*
Coke	1969	51,161	204,555	67,274	29,248	61,421	64,687	362,499	478,347
	1970	51,161*	125,100	97,700	12,224	108,096	64,687*	345,120	460,958*
7up	1969	66,948	208,862	16,119	2,665	63,000	2,022	290,646	359,616
	1970	66,948*	192,400	—	2,100	67,536	2,022*	262,036	331,006*
Faygo	1969	—	167,091	34,495	—	—	—	201,586	201,586
	1970	—	113,350	24,800	—	—	—	138,150	138,150*
Canada Dry	1969	124,388	164,030	—	17,584	15,000	123,991	195,614	443,993
	1970	124,388*	101,900	32,800	14,905	21,834	123,991*	171,439	419,818*
Diet-Pepsi	1969	—	25,000	392	15,838	11,000	—	52,230	52,230
	1970	—	5,100	131,575	—	—	—	136,675	136,675

Squirt	1969	—	78,133	1,222	—	8,490	79,355	87,845
	1970	—	67,220	—	—	—	67,220	67,220
R.C. Cola	1969	22,387	—	16,000	—	—	16,000	38,387
	1970	—	16,000	—	—	—	—	—
Town Club	1969	—	6,000	6,264	—	—	12,264	12,264
	1970	—	23,000	17,968	—	—	40,968	40,968
Mountain Dew	1969	—	—	9,812	288	—	10,090	10,090
	1970	—	—	10,965	—	—	10,965	10,965
Dr. Pepper	1969	26,528	—	—	—	10,160	2,800	39,488
	1970	26,528*	—	2,800	—	10,160*	36,688*	36,688*
Nesbit Orange	1969	—	—	2,430	—	—	2,430	2,430
	1970	—	4,808	—	—	—	4,808	4,808
Carbonated beverage	1969	—	—	—	54,875	—	54,875	54,875
	1970	—	—	—	27,470	—	27,470	27,470
Hires Root Beer	1969	—	16,000	—	—	—	16,000	16,000
	1970	—	24,850	—	—	—	24,850	24,850

*Estimated—based on 1969 network TV and magazines.

QUESTIONS

1. What is your appraisal of the opportunity to make effective use of consumer advertising for Vernors soft drinks? Explain.

2. What emphasis should be placed upon dealer promotion versus consumer advertising in the promotional mix? Why?

3. What are your recommendations as to the objectives, creative theme, media, and appropriation for Vernors promotional activities for the coming year?

THE *ATLANTA JOURNAL* AND *CONSTITUTION**

Research to evaluate advertising media

Ferguson Rood, research and marketing director for the *Atlanta Journal* and the *Atlanta Constitution,* was still perspiring from the three-block walk in the hot August sun back to his office from the meeting he had just been to at Rich's Department Store. At the meeting he had been told that Rich's, the newspaper's largest advertiser, wanted to test the effectiveness of TV and radio advertising versus newspaper advertising for its upcoming Harvest Sale. He had promised to make his suggestions for the research plan in 48 hours and felt he had much to do in that short time. He wondered what recommendations he should make for the study and was concerned that the research design and questionnaire be developed so that the study would represent fairly the effectiveness of the *Atlanta Journal* and the *Atlanta Constitution.* As he began to review his notes from the meeting, he picked up the phone to call his wife and tell her he would be home very late that evening.

BACKGROUND

The *Atlanta Journal* and the *Atlanta Constitution* are a union of two of the largest-circulation newspapers in the South. The *Atlanta Constitution,*

---

*Written by Kenneth L. Bernhardt, Associate Professor of Marketing, Georgia State University. ©1976 by Kenneth L. Bernhardt. Reprinted by permission of the author.

EXHIBIT 1   Gross reader impressions, reach, and frequency of the *Atlanta Journal* and *Constitution*

Gross reader impressions delivered by the *Atlanta Journal* and *Constitution* in 15-county metro Atlanta:

During any five weekdays, 864,000 adults read the *Atlanta Journal* or *Constitution* an average of 3.5 times, for a total of 3,025,800 weekday gross reader impressions.

During any four Sundays, 907,600 adults read the *Atlanta Journal* and *Constitution* an average of 3.4 times, for a total of 3,085,800 Sunday gross reader impressions.

These newspapers deliver 3,933,400 adult gross reader impressions when one Sunday is added to five weekdays.

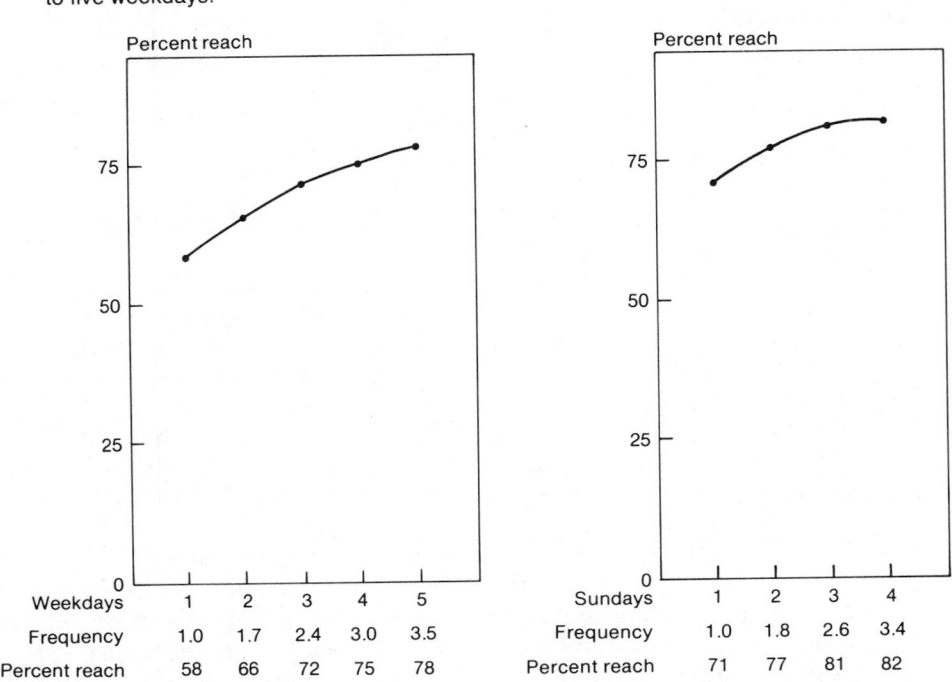

Weekdays	1	2	3	4	5
Frequency	1.0	1.7	2.4	3.0	3.5
Percent reach	58	66	72	75	78

Sundays	1	2	3	4
Frequency	1.0	1.8	2.6	3.4
Percent reach	71	77	81	82

winner of four Pulitzer prizes for its efforts in the area of social reform, was founded June 16, 1868. The *Atlanta Journal,* founded February 24, 1883, became the largest daily newspaper in Georgia by 1889. Also a winner of the Pulitzer prize, the *Journal* is the Southeast's largest afternoon newspaper.

In 1950, the *Atlanta Journal* and the *Atlanta Constitution* were com-

EXHIBIT 2   *Atlanta Journal* and *Consititution* readership information

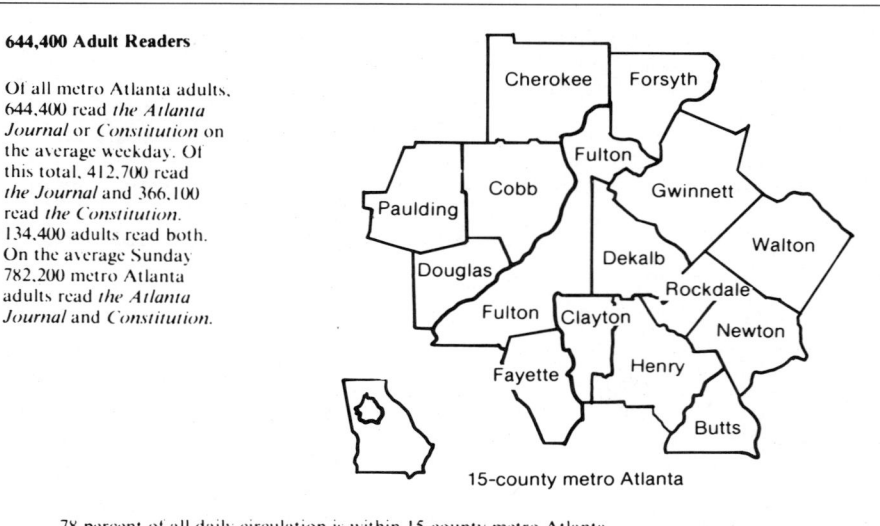

644,400 Adult Readers

Of all metro Atlanta adults, 644,400 read *the Atlanta Journal* or *Constitution* on the average weekday. Of this total, 412,700 read *the Journal* and 366,100 read *the Constitution*. 134,400 adults read both. On the average Sunday 782,200 metro Atlanta adults read *the Atlanta Journal* and *Constitution*.

15-county metro Atlanta

78 percent of all daily circulation is within 15-county metro Atlanta.
66 percent of all Sunday circulation is within 15-county metro Atlanta.

**Adult Readers of *the Atlanta Journal*
and *Constitution* in 15-County Metro Atlanta**

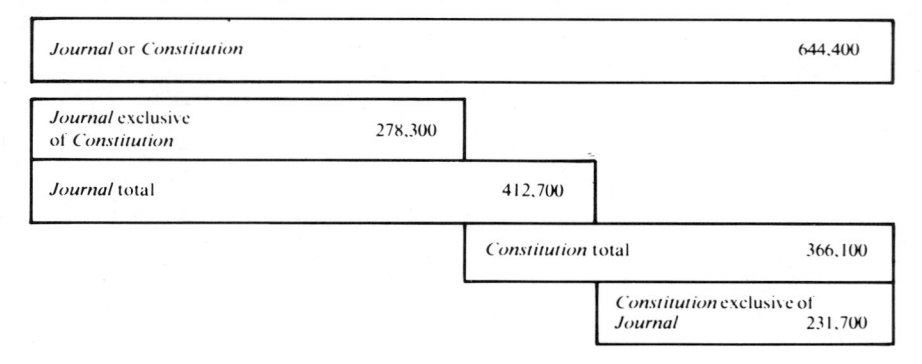

Journal or *Constitution*	644,400
Journal exclusive of *Constitution*	278,300
Journal total	412,700
Constitution total	366,100
Constitution exclusive of *Journal*	231,700

bined into Atlanta Newspapers, Inc., a privately held company. The two newspapers maintained independent editorial staffs, and there was little overlap of readers. Exhibits 1 through 4 present data from the newspapers' research department concerning the adult readership of the newspapers, reach and frequency, and readership over five weekdays and four Sundays.

EXHIBIT 3   Readership of the *Atlanta Journal* and *Constitution* over five weekdays

Of all metro Atlanta adults, 644,400, or 58 percent, read either the *Atlanta Journal* or *Constitution* on the average weekday. Over five weekdays these newspapers deliver 864,900, or 78 percent, of al metro area adults with an average frequency of 3.5 days.

	Total metro area adults	Average one-day readership		Cumulative five-weekday readership		Fre-quency
		Num-ber	Per-cent	Num-ber	Per-cent	
Total adults	1,105,500	644,400	58	864,900	78	3.5
Sex						
Female	588,500	331,700	56	447,600	76	3.5
Male	517,000	312,700	61	416,800	81	3.5
Household income						
$25,000 and over	104,200	85,900	82	102,700	99	4.2
$15,000–$24,999	195,300	146,400	75	181,900	93	4.0
$10,000–$14,999	241,900	152,800	63	203,900	84	3.7
$5,000–$9,999	334,200	170,600	51	241,800	72	3.5
Under $5,000	229,900	88,500	39	133,000	58	3.3
Age						
18–34	470,500	234,500	50	345,200	73	3.4
35–49	305,600	197,200	65	250,300	82	3.9
50–64	211,900	145,800	69	184,600	87	3.9
65 and over	116,500	66,700	57	84,700	73	3.9
Race						
White	872,800	528,800	61	685,100	78	3.9
Nonwhite	232,700	115,600	50	180,100	77	3.2
Education						
College graduate	173,500	138,000	80	172,600	99	4.0
Part college	194,700	137,600	71	174,100	89	4.0
High school graduate	360,500	225,000	62	302,900	84	3.7
Part high school or less	365,600	137,000	38	202,200	55	3.4

To provide advertisers and potential advertisers with information necessary to help them make their advertising media decisions, the newspapers do a considerable amount of research, often approaching $25,000 in cost per year. Most of the research is designed to be used in selling advertising to a wide range of advertisers and includes data on retail trading areas, shopping patterns, product usage, and newspaper coverage patterns. In addition to Rood, the research department had two other trained market researchers and one secretary.

Although there were nine daily newspapers in the Atlanta trading area, all but the *Journal* and the *Constitution* had very small circulations. The principal competition for large advertisers was with radio and TV stations. Exhibit 5 presents information on the circulation of the print

EXHIBIT 4   Readership of the *Atlanta Journal* and *Constitution* over four sundays

Of all metro Atlanta adults, 782,200, or 71 percent, read the *Atlanta Journal* and *Constitution* on the average Sunday. Over four Sundays these newspapers deliver 907,300 adults, or 82 percent of all metro area adults, with an average frequency of 3.4 Sundays.

	Total metro area adults	Average one-Sunday readership	Cumulative four-Sunday readership	Number of Sundays
Total adults	1,105,500	782,200	907,300	3.4
Sex				
Female	588,500	418,800	477,800	3.5
Male	517,000	363,400	429,500	3.4
Household income				
$25,000 and over	104,200	89,100	97,200	3.7
$15,000–$24,999	195,300	168,800	180,700	3.7
$10,000–$14,999	241,900	190,100	216,400	3.5
$5,000–$9,999	334,400	215,600	267,300	3.2
Under $5,000	229,900	118,500	145,600	3.3
Age				
18–34	470,500	313,000	390,000	3.2
35–49	305,600	221,300	248,500	3.6
50–64	211,900	167,000	179,900	3.7
65 and over	116,500	80,600	88,500	3.6
Race				
White	872,800	633,100	727,900	3.5
Nonwhite	232,700	149,100	179,100	3.3
Education				
College graduate	173,500	150,200	163,700	3.7
Part college	194,700	157,300	180,200	3.5
High school graduate	360,500	273,900	313,500	3.5
Part high school or less	365,600	192,300	240,000	3.2

media in the Atlanta area. Exhibit 6 contains information on the broadcast media in Atlanta. Although there were 40 radio stations, 28 AM and 12 FM, and 6 TV stations, WSB Radio and WSB-TV dominated the market. WSB Radio, for example, was consistently rated among the top six stations in the nation and had a greater Atlanta audience than the next four stations combined. WSB-TV and WSB Radio, both affiliated with the NBC network, were owned by Cox Broadcasting Corporation, which also owned television stations in Charlotte, Dayton, Pittsburgh, and San Francisco, and radio stations in Charlotte, Dayton, and Miami. Cox Broadcasting and the WSB TV and radio stations shared corporate headquarters in Atlanta.

WSB Radio was founded in 1922 by the *Atlanta Journal* paper. In

EXHIBIT 5   Circulation of print media in Atlanta

Metro Atlanta newspapers	Edition	*Total circula-tion*
Dailies		
Atlanta Constitution	Morning	216,624
Atlanta Journal	Evening	259,721
Journal-Constitution	Sunday	585,532
Gwinnett Daily News	Evening (except Sat.)	10,111
Gwinnett Daily News	Sunday	10,100
Marietta Daily Journal	Evening (except Sat.)	24,750
Marietta Daily Journal	Sunday	25,456
Fulton County Daily Report	Evening (Mon.–Fri.)	1,600
Atlanta Daily World	Morning	19,000
Atlanta Daily World	Sunday	22,000
Wall Street Journal	Morning (Mon.–Fri.)	16,180
Jonesboro News Daily	Evening (Mon.–Fri.)	9,100
North Fulton Today	Evening (Mon.–Fri.)	2,300
South Cobb Today	Evening (Mon.–Fri.)	2,400
New York Times	Morning (Mon.–Sat.)	500
New York Times	Sunday	3,100
Weekly newspapers		
Atlanta Inquirer		30000
Atlanta Voice		37500
DeKalb New Era		16400
Atlanta's Suburban Reporter		3900
Lithonia Observer		2765
Northside News		8000
Georgia Business News		4900
Southern Israelite		4300
Decatur-DeKalb News		73000
Southside Sun (East Point)		37700
Tucker Star		10000
Alpharetta, Roswell Neighbor		6800
Austell, Mableton, Powder Springs Neighbor		12123
Acworth, Kennesaw-Woodstock Neighbor		3242
Northside, Sandy Springs, Vinings Neighbor		20836
Smyrna Neighbor		6872
College Park, East Point, Hapeville, South Side, West End Neighbor		18813
Chamblee, Doraville, Dunwoody, North Atlanta Neighbor		14963
Clarkston, Stone Mountain, Tucker Neighbor		15074
Journal of Labor (Atlanta)		17500
Austell Enterprise		1911
Cherokee Tribune (Canton)		7100
Rockdale Citizen		6031
Covington News		6000
Forsyth County News		4800
Dallas New Era		4075
Douglas County Sentinel		7350
South Fulton Recorder (Fairburn)		4000
Fayette County News		4500
Jackson Progess Argus		2635
Weekly Advertiser (McDonough)		5650
Walton Tribune (Monroe)		5102

EXHIBIT 5 *(concluded)*

Metro Atlanta newspapers	Edition	Total circulation
Weekly newspapers (continued)		
Lilburn Recorder		5000
Lawrenceville Home Weekly		2000
Great Speckled Bird (Atlanta)		7925
Georgia Bulletin		14000
Covington News (Tues. and Thurs.)		6200
Creative Loafing in Atlanta		30000
Atlanta area newspapers		
Cobb		28000
North Fulton		36000
North DeKalb-Gwinnett		45000
South DeKalb		44000
South Fulton-Clayton		53000
Major magazines in Georgia		
American Home		70,485
Better Homes and Gardens		145,962
Good Housekeeping		114,045
McCall's		139,728
Ladies' Home Journal		128,331
Family Circle		106,245
Woman's Day		100,566
Redbook		86,354
National Geographic		103,941
Reader's Digest		331,240
Newsweek		41,070
Time		60,438
U.S. News & World Report		40,417
TV Guide		345,871
Playboy		98,389
Sports Illustrated		38,263
Outdoor Life		25,918
True		18,244
Southern Living		95,000
Progressive Farmer		70,000
Cosmopolitan		25,075
Calendar Atlanta		50,000

*These are supplements to the *Atlanta Journal,* and circulation is to *Atlanta Journal* subscribers only.
Source: WSB research department.

1939, James M. Cox, former Democratic presidential nominee and governor of Ohio, acquired the newspaper-radio combine. In 1948, WSB-TV was founded, and two years later the newspapers and broadcast media were separated when Atlanta Newspapers, Inc., was established. Today, there is no relationship between the newspapers and WSB-TV and Radio.

EXHIBIT 6   Broadcast media in Atlanta

Location	Station/network	Established	Frequency	Power	Channel	Network
Metro Atlanta						
AM radio stations						
Atlanta	WSB (NBC)	1922	750 khz	50 kw		
	WAOK	1954	1380 khz	5 kw		
	WGKA (ABC)	1955	1190 khz	1 kw day		
	WGST (ABC-E)	1922	920 khz	5 kw day 1 kw night		
	WIGO (ABC-C)	1946	1340 khz	1 kw day 250 w night		
	WIIN (MBS)	1949	970 khz	5 kw day		
	WPLO	1937	590 khz	5 kw		
	WQXI	1948	790 khz	5 kw day 1 kw night		
	WXAP	1948	860 khz	1 kw		
	WYZE (MBS)	1956	1480 khz	5 kw day		
Decatur	WAVO	1958	1420 khz	1 kw day		
	WGUN	1947	1010 khz	50 kw day		
	WQAK	1964	1310 khz	500 w		
North Atlanta	WRNG (CBS)	1967	680 khz	25 kw day		
Morrow	WSSA	1959	1570 khz	1 kw day		
East Point	WTJH	1949	1260 khz	5 kw day		
Smyrna	WYNX	1962	1550 khz	10 kw day		
Buford	WDYX	1956	1460 khz	5 kw day		
Austell	WACX	1968	1600 khz	1 kw		
Lawrenceville	WLAW	1959	1360 khz	1 kw		
Marietta	WCOB	1955	1080 khz	10 kw day		
	WFOM	1946	1230 khz	1 kw day 250 w night		
Canton	WCHK (GA)	1957	1290 khz	1 kw day		
Covington	WGFS	1953	1430 khz	1 kw day		
Cumming	WSNE	1961	1170 khz	1 kw		
Douglasville	WDGL	1964	1527 khz	1 kw		
Jackson	WJGA	1967	1540 khz	1 kw day		
Monroe	WMRE	1954	1490 khz	1 kw		
Metro Atlanta						
FM radio stations						
	WSB-FM	1934	98.5 mhz	100 kw		
	WPLO-FM	1948	103.3 mhz	50 kw		
	WZGC-FM	1955	92.9 mhz	100 kw		
	WKLS-FM	1960	96.1 mhz	100 kw		
	WQXI-FM	1962	94.1 mhz	100 kw		
	WBIE-FM	1959	101.5 mhz	100 kw		
	WLTA-FM	1963	99.7 mhz	100 kw		
	WJGA-FM	1968	92.1 mhz	3 kw		
	WCHK-FM	1964	105.5 mhz	3 kw		
	WGCO-FM	1969	102.3 mhz	100 kw		
	WABE-FM	1948	90.0 mhz	10.5 kw		
	WREK-FM	1968	91.1 mhz	40 w		

EXHIBIT 6 (concluded)

Location	Station/ network	Estab- lished	Fre- quency	Power	Chan- nel	Net- work
Metro Atlanta television stations						
	WSB-TV	1948			2	NBC
	WAGA-TV	1949			5	CBS
	WXIA-TV	1951			11	ABC
	WTCG-TV	1967			17	IND
	WETV	1958			30	NET
	WGTV	1960			8	NET

Source: WSB research department.

Rich's Department Store was the largest advertiser for the *Journal* and the *Constitution,* accounting for almost 5 percent of their advertising revenue, and was WSB's largest local advertiser. Founded in 1867, Rich's by 1970 had grown to a company with seven stores located throughout Atlanta, as shown in Exhibit 7. Its sales were approximately $200 million per year, with earnings after taxes of almost 5 percent of sales. The company was classified as a general merchandise retailer, and it carried a very wide line of products, including clothing, furniture, appliances, and housewares. Rich's dominated the Atlanta market, with close to 40 percent of department store sales and approximately 25 percent of all sales of general merchandise. The merchandising highlight of the year was its annual Harvest Sale, first held in October 1925. The sale typically ran for two weeks.

BACKGROUND ON THE MEDIA EFFECTIVENESS STUDY

Before preparing his proposal to Rich's for the media effectiveness study, Rood reflected upon the events of the past 24 hours. The day before, he had received a phone call from Rich's vice president and sales promotion director inviting him to the meeting at Rich's the next day. Having been told that Rich's research director and the research director of WSB-TV and Radio would also be there, Rood had been a little apprehensive before going. At the start of the meeting, he was asked whether the Atlanta newspapers would be interested in participating in a cooperative research study aimed at measuring the effectiveness of various advertising media during Rich's Harvest Sale, their largest annual sales event. It became immediately apparent to him that the re-

EXHIBIT 7   Map of Atlanta and seven Rich's stores

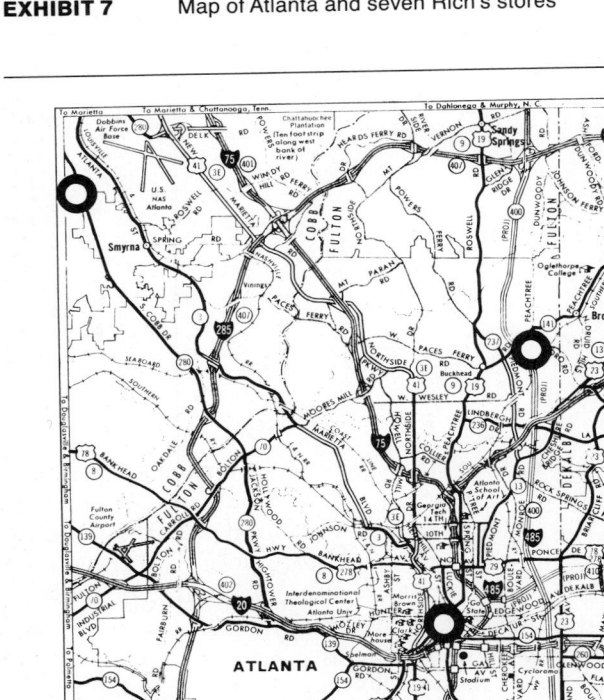

search director from WSB, Jim Land, had met with the Rich's people the week before and was probably the source of the idea to conduct a study. A document was then passed out that had been prepared by WSB and was entitled "Suggestions for Rich's Media Research." This document is included as an appendix to this case; it outlines the objectives of the study and presents a suggested methodology together with a questionnaire.

The suggested objectives for the project were: (1) to measure the ability of TV, radio, and newspapers to sell specific items of merchandise in Rich's seven Atlanta stores; (2) to determine how each advertising medium complements the others in terms of additional units sold to various segments of the customer population (age, sex, charge account ownership, etc.); and (3) to determine what each advertising medium contributed in regard to additional store traffic. Rood's broadcasting counterpart stated at the meeting that "if Rich's is interested in conducting research to measure the effectiveness of various advertising media, WSB-TV and WSB Radio will be happy to assist." Rood felt he had no choice, so he volunteered the support of the newspapers to the study.

Rich's research manager then asked whether the media would participate financially in the study. Rood suggested that each of the three media participate equally, and committed the newspapers to $500 for a study that he figured should cost between $2,500 and $3,000 for interviewing. Land indicated that Cox Broadcasting would be willing to put in $500 each for TV and radio.

They discussed how the research could be conducted. The WSB proposal suggested in-store surveys, with a separate survey conducted for each item of merchandise tested. The survey would be conducted by Rich's employees working overtime in appropriate store locations during the peak shopping hours. The tabulation of the results could be handled by the broadcast station's computer. Care was to be taken to insure that the TV, radio, or newspaper advertising for the individual items not be "stacked" in favor of one particular medium. The questions in the proposed questionnaire included queries on how the respondents happened to buy the merchandise at Rich's; whether they recalled seeing TV, newspaper, or radio advertising; and whether they bought anything else. Questions were also asked about age and about ownership of a Rich's charge account.

Land stated that WSB was not trying to take business away from the newspapers and that Rood had nothing to fear. He recommended that Rich's not take anything away from the newspaper advertising budget. He suggested that the amount of space purchased in the newspapers be the same as it was the previous year, with additional monies being committed to the broadcast media. Rich's sales promotions director then discussed some of his thoughts concerning the study. He indicated that Rich's had been sending 400,000 direct-mail pieces to announce the Harvest Sale; this year it would send 200,000, diverting the other money to broadcast. This would make $7,600 available for broadcast, and an additional $12,000 to $15,000 would also be made available to purchase broadcast time.

The Harvest Sale was to open with courtesy days on Monday and Tuesday, September 21–22, with the sale beginning the evening of the 22nd and running for 13 days. Although decisions concerning which

sales items were to be included in the study and the media schedules to be used were not yet available, some progress had been made. Approximately 10 items were to be researched, and the newspaper ads on Sunday, September 20, would include all or most of the 10 items. Newspaper ads for the items would be repeated Monday and Tuesday, with emphasis on the *Journal*. The interviews were to be conducted Monday through Wednesday.

On Sunday and Monday, with a possible spillover to Tuesday due to availability, Rich's would run 120 30-second TV commercials on all commercial stations except Channel 17 (the independent station). During the same time it would run 120 30-second radio commercials on a list of stations that had not yet been determined. With both TV and radio, WSB was to get the lion's share if availability could be arranged. Rood felt certain, in view of the client and the research, that WSB would manage to come up wth several prime-time commercial openings even if this meant bumping some high-paying national advertisers.

Eleven items were mentioned as possible subjects for the research. The 10 final items selected would come mostly from this list, although one or two other items might be chosen. The items mentioned included: (1) color TV consoles at $499, (2) custom-made draperies, (3) Sterns & Foster mattresses at $44, (4) carpeting at $6.99 per square yard, (5) Gant shirts at $5, (6) Van Heusen shirts and Arrow shirts at two for $11. (7) women's handbags at $9.99, (8) Johannsen's shoes, (9) pantsuits, (10) Hoover upright vaccuum cleaners, and (11) GE refrigerators.

Rood, who had not said very much at the meeting, then asked for 48 hours to review the proposal. Everyone agreed to this, and Rood promised to present a counterproposal at that time.

Even though it had been rather obvious to Rood who had initiated the idea for the study, and he at first had felt that newspapers were being "set up" by WSB, it had been basically a relaxed meeting among friends. Land and Rood had worked together in the Atlanta chapter of the American Marketing Association and had a great deal of respect for each other. Rood thought Land was a tough competitor, and understood that he had been successful in using awareness-type studies in Cox Broadcasting's other markets to gain additional advertising for broadcast.

When he returned to his office, Rood pulled out some of his files on Rich's. He noticed that the amount of newspaper advertising had been over 100 pages for the two-week period during the past three Harvest Sales and that basically the same products had been promoted. A typical Harvest Sale ad is included in Exhibit 8. He also pulled from the files rate schedules for the *Atlanta Journal* and *Constitution* and WSB (see Exhibits 9 and 10), even though he realized that the exact media schedule would be developed by Rich's advertising agency. Approximately

EXHIBIT 8   Typical Rich's Harvest Sale ad

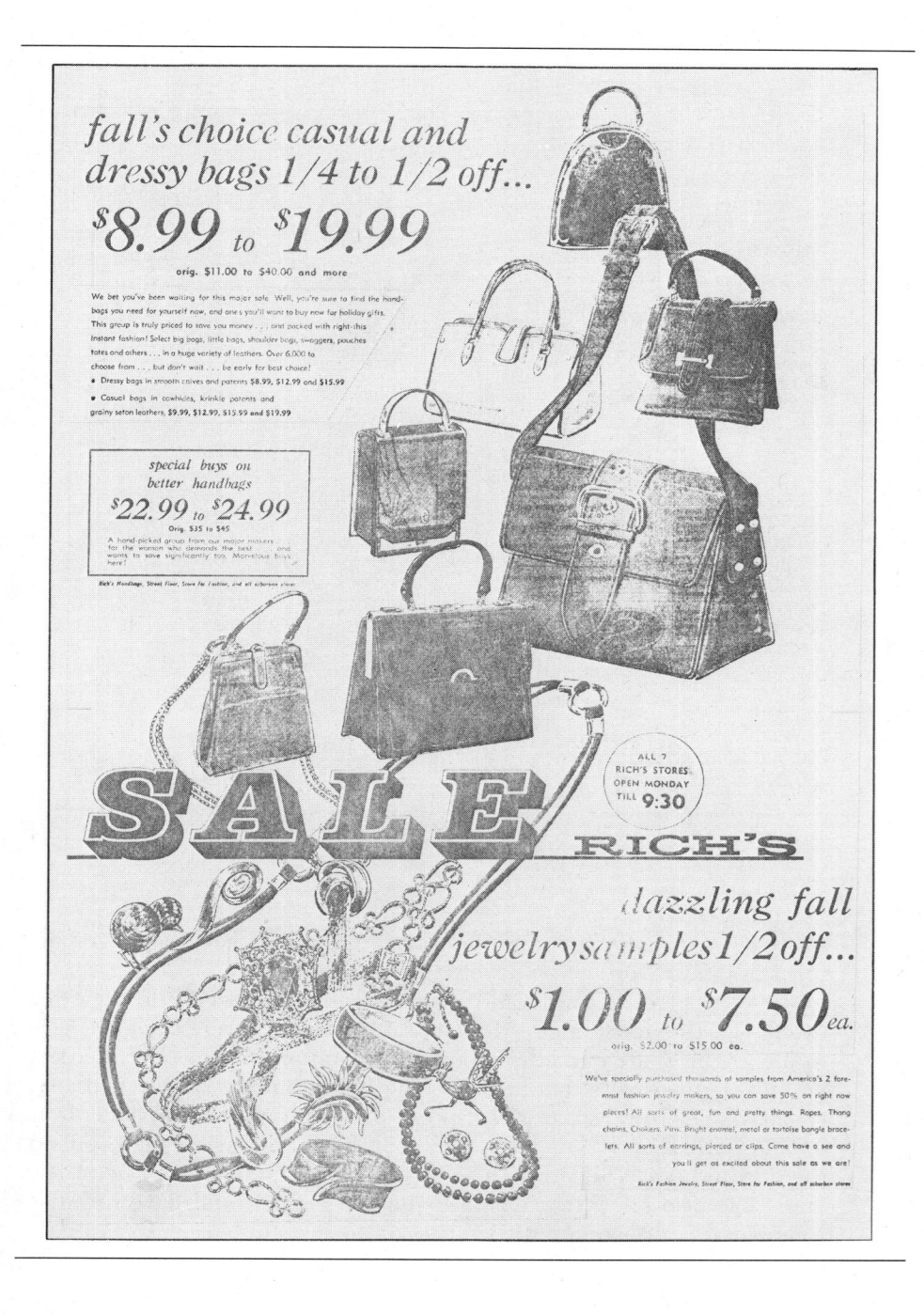

EXHIBIT 9   The *Atlanta Journal* and *Atlanta Constitution* retail display rates

Open rate per column inch:

Constitution	$8.15
Journal	$11.27
Combination	$14.83
Sunday	$15.56

Note: There are 8 columns by 21 inches, or 168 column inches, on a full page.

Yearly bulk space rates:

Inches per year per inch	*Constitution*	*Journal*	*Combined*	*Sunday*
100	$6.21	$8.43	$11.09	$11.65
250	6.16	8.35	11.00	11.55
500	6.10	8.28	10.90	11.45
1,000	6.05	8.21	10.81	11.35
2,500	5.99	8.13	10.70	11.24
5,000	5.93	8.05	10.59	11.12
7,500	5.90	8.01	10.54	11.07
10,000	5.87	7.97	10.48	11.01
12,500	5.85	7.93	10.43	10.96
15,000	5.82	7.89	10.38	10.90
25,000	5.70	7.73	10.17	10.68
50,000	5.61	7.69	10.05	10.61
75,000	5.51	7.65	9.93	10.53
100,000	5.41	7.61	9.81	10.46
150,000	5.21	7.51	9.56	10.31
200,000	5.01	7.41	9.32	10.15
250,000	4.81	7.31	9.08	9.99

$100,000 would be spent promoting the Harvest Sale, with over one third of this amount being devoted to the sale items.

Rood decided that he would have to assume confidence in the effectiveness of the newspapers. He felt that if the study were done right, he would get his share of media exposure and influence. The other decision he quickly made was that in preparing his comments on the proposed research, he would take Rich's point of view rather than that of the *Atlanta Journal* and *Constitution*. He then began to review the events of the day and the WSB proposal in light of what he felt Rich's needed to know. He also knew that whatever he proposed would have to be acceptable to Land. Noting the lateness of the hour, he began work on the counterproposal.

EXHIBIT 10   WSB TV and radio advertising rates

	One minute	20/30 seconds	10 seconds
WSB-AM radio: Spot announcements— package plans*			
12 per week	$40	$34	$24
18 per week	38	30	21
24 per week	32	26	19
30 per week	28	24	17
48 per week	26	20	15

WSB-FM radio: Package plan—52 weeks†
1 minute	$16
20/30 seconds	14

WSB-TV
Daytime rates
  60 seconds $75–235 depending on program
  30 seconds   40–140 depending on program
Prime-time rates
  60 seconds‡ $540–660 depending on program
  30 seconds   390–725 depending on program

*Available 5:00–6:00 A.M., 10:00 A.M.–3:30 P.M., and 7:30 P.M.–midnight, Monday–Saturday; and 5:00 A.M.–midnight, Sunday. Best available positions in applicable times—no guaranteed placement.
†Quantity discounts available. For example, 18 times per week for 52 weeks is one half of the above rates.
‡Very few available.

APPENDIX

Suggestions for Rich's Media Research

OBJECTIVES

If Rich's is interested in conducting research to measure the effectiveness of various advertising media, WSB-TV and WSB Radio will be happy to assist. As a basis for discussion, here are suggested objectives for this project:

1. Measure the ability of TV, radio, and newspapers to sell specific items of merchandise in Rich's seven Atlanta metro stores.
2. Determine how each advertising medium complements the others in terms of additional units sold to various segments of the customer population (age, sex, charge account ownership, etc.).
3. Determine what each advertising medium contributes in regard to additional store traffic.

HOW THE RESEARCH COULD BE CONDUCTED

The project could consist of a series of in-store surveys. A separate survey would be conducted for each item of merchandise tested. The more items tested, the more reliable the results of the overall research project would be.

If possible, all seven Rich's stores in the Atlanta metro area should participate in the research.

Each survey could be conducted by placing interviewers (Rich's personnel working overtime) in appropriate store locations during peak shopping hours with instructions to complete *brief* questionnaires with customers purchasing the item being tested. (See questionnaire attached.)

The interview could cover how the customer got the idea to buy the item, other planned purchases in the store during the same visit, charge account ownership, and any other pertinent data. Each interview would last less than a minute and would not bother the customer.

The sample size would vary, depending upon the number of stores participating, the type of merchandise and the sales volume. Interviewers would strive to include all customers purchasing the items during peak hours. Tabulation of the results could be handled by the WSB computer.

CAREFUL ATTENTION TO ITEMS AND MEDIA SCHEDULES

In order to make the research valid and meaningful, the items to be tested must be selected carefully. In addition, care should be taken to insure that the TV, radio, or newspaper advertising for these items is not "stacked" in favor of one particular medium. Close attention to the items being tested and the media schedule for each is necessary.

QUESTIONNAIRE

The proposed questionnaire follows:

Possible questionnaire for Rich's in-store survey (All customers purchasing the item advertised are interviewed.)

1. *How* did you happen to buy this merchandise at Rich's?
   Saw on TV .... (   )
   Heard on radio .... (   )
   Saw in newspaper .... (   )
   TV and radio .... (   )
   TV and newspaper................................ (   )
   Newspaper and radio............................. (   )
   TV, radio, and newspaper........................ (   )
   Saw on display .... (   )

   Other:_____(   )

Asked of customers not mentioning a medium (2, 3, 4):

2. Do you recall seeing this merchandise advertised on TV?
    Yes .... ( )
    No................................ ( )

3. Do you recall seeing this merchandise advertised in the newspaper?
    Yes .... ( )
    No................................ ( )

4. Do you recall hearing this merchandise advertised on the radio?
    Yes .... ( )
    No................................ ( )

5. Are you buying *anything else* at Rich's today?
    Yes .... ( )
    No.................................... ( )
    Maybe, don't know .... ( )

6. Do you have a charge account at Rich's?
    Yes .... ( )
    No................................ ( )

7. In which group does your age fall?
    Under 25............................. ( )
    25–34 .... ( )
    35–49 .... ( )
    50 + ... ( )

Store_____

Time of interview_____

QUESTIONS

1. Evaluate the research proposal prepared by Jim Land, research director of WSB, and entitled "Suggestions for Rich's Media Research" (see Appendix). Include in your analysis the suggested objectives, the proposed methodology, and the questionnaire, among other considerations.

2. In light of your analysis, what recommendations should Rood make to Rich's sales promotion director concerning the proposed media effectiveness study? Explain your reasoning.

S. S. KRESGE CO., INC.*

Promotional policies of the K mart Division

COMPANY HISTORY

As of January 27, 1971, the S. S. Kresge Co., Inc., headquartered in Troy, Michigan, had seen sales rise from $450,605,000 in 1961 to $2,558,712,000 in 1970. Per share earnings had risen from $0.28 to $1.86 per share over the same period. The tremendous success of the S. S. Kresge Company was caused by the K mart Division, which accounted for over 80 percent of all sales and profits. Since the first K mart was opened in Detroit on March 1, 1962, 410 K marts had been constructed and put into operation.

The development of the K mart organization began in 1958. In that year Harry B. Cunningham, who later became chairman of the Kresge board of directors, undertook a challenging task. For two years he was assigned the task of finding a means to increase the static sales and declining profits of the S. S. Kresge Variety Stores. From World War I to the early 1950s, these variety stores had been preeminently successful merchandisers. However, with the population move to the suburbs and the decay of central cities, their success had diminished (see Exhibit 1).

---

*Written by Darcy J. Running, research assistant, Bureau of Business Research, under the supevision of James D. Scott, Sebastian S. Kresge Professor of Marketing, Graduate School of Business Administration, The University of Michigan, Ann Arbor.

EXHIBIT 1   Landmarks in Kresge history

1897	Sebastian S. Kresge opens his first dime store.
1912	With 85 stores and sales of $10,325,000 Kresge's five-and-tens are the second largest dime store chain in America.
1929	The Kresge variety stores reach sales of over $156 million.
1946	696 Variety Stores reach sales of $251,453,000.
1952	Experimental Variety Stores are converted to checkout-type operations.
1956	The first Variety Store is opened in a Detroit shopping center.
1962	The first 18 revolutionary K marts are opened.
1966	The S. S. Kresge Co., Inc., achieves sales of over $1 billion in 915 stores, including 162 K mart outlets.
1969	Over 335 K mart outlets help generate over $2 billion in Kresge's sales.
1970	With over 410 K mart outlets, Kresge's sales rise to over $2.6 billion.

Cunningham's extensive study concentrated upon the analysis of environmental trends, especially in relation to alternative strategy changes. After much investigation, analysis, and thought, a strategy was tentatively accepted by management. Briefly, the strategy called for discount-priced department stores with reliance upon volume sales. Several changes were made from the discount store strategy developed by others during the 1950s. The stores were to be modern, effective (one floor only), large (up to 100,000 square feet), and pleasant, and they were to have convenient selection and checkout facilities. The merchandise selection ranged from apparel to hard goods—any item that the average consumer purchased *annually*. Only nationally known name brands were stocked, and "imperfects" were not allowed. The prices were to be as low as or lower than those of any competitors. Advertising was to be used extensively to build and maintain volume. The store manager had complete authority to make any changes he saw fit, with the exception of two areas:

1. He could not remove or add any department.
2. He could *never* raise prices, though he could lower them without even consulting the district manager.[1]

In 1972 these fundamental policies were still in effect. The S. S. Kresge Co., Inc., built its first 18 K mart stores in 1962, and by the end of the 1970 fiscal year had over 410 K marts, with 80 stores scheduled to open each succeeding year (including in Canada and Australia).

---

[1]A district manager only advised the store manager and was required to evaluate him annually.

SITUATION ANALYSIS

Demand

Accurate estimates of demand for the products featured in K mart stores were difficult to determine due to the full range of products offered. It was also difficult to correlate national economic fluctuations with sales forecasts. During growth cycles purchasing power increases were translated into sales growth, while during recessional periods buyers became more price-conscious and turned to K mart. Variations in regional sales growth occurred. In the Pacific Northwest, for example, when the aerospace industry was depressed, the sales growth rate declined, though the growth declines were never substantial. Thus demand throughout the nation and in each locale could only be optimized through experienced purchasing of merchandise and effective promotional strategy. Executive judgment was the sole basis used for merchandise decisions and promotional strategy. Studies of demand had never been undertaken. Key noncompetitive elements in site selection for a prospective store were area population and its trends, and as a function of population, the disposable income of the area. A market evaluation team was responsible for determining the basic demand requirements for a site.

In general, company management ranked the buyer decision variables as follows:

1. Price.
2. Product design and quality.
3. Advertising.
4. Store location.
5. Service personnel.
6. Credit availability.

History of the Discount Store Concept

The underlying causes of the tremendous success of the K mart Division and of discount store chains in general during the period up to 1972 were the intrinsic merits of the discount store system and the readiness of their managements to adjust their operations to changing environmental conditions.[2]

The strength the discount stores possessed was due to their ability to combine wholesaler and retailer functions. Thus they were able to present better values via lower prices to the consumer by featuring products in a wider selection.

The ability to advertise heavily allowed the discount stores to maintain their required volumes. The volumes of sales achieved forced them to use more scientific equipment and methods of management.[3] Thus they were able to operate on less profit per unit.

---

[2]G. M. Lebhar, ed., *Chain Stores in America: 1859–1962*, 3d ed. (New York: Chain Store Publishing Corp., 1963), p.79.

[3]Ibid., p. 83.

A discount store is defined as a concern which sells merchandise to the public at below-"retail" prices and has more than 10,000 square feet of floor space. Originally mills in depressed cloth-milling towns were acquired and with no refurbishing were converted to consumer outlets featuring apparel. By 1960, several companies independently discovered that these stores were not being driven out of business and struck upon the idea of opening similar facilities in reconverted shopping center supermarkets. Nearly all were successful, and soon chains were formed which sold wide lines of merchandise.

Competition

K mart Division viewed its major, direct competition as being other mass merchandisers such as Sears, Penney's, and Wards and including, as well, discount chains such as Woolco, Zayre, and Gibson (a large franchise operation in the South and Southwest). In general, any outlet which had lower prices due to direct, volume buying, a good basic assortment of merchandise, substantial freight savings, reliance on volume lines, and therefore lower operating costs was viewed as direct competition by the K mart Division.

Viewed as indirect competitors were local "Mom and Pop" stores and cooperatives, which generally incurred high labor costs due to their willingness to offer higher levels of personal shopper assistance.

During the decade beginning in 1972, the management of the K mart Division expected to open approximately 80 stores per year and sought a 20 percent annual sales growth. It anticipated that competition in the industry would become far more intense. Many of the choicest locations were already taken, and competitive chains were viewed as stronger than they had been a decade earlier.

Distribution

K mart Division maintained a large, efficient, and modern distribution center (DC) in Fort Wayne, Indiana. Approximately 20 percent of all merchandise purchased by S. S. Kresge Company buyers was shipped from the place of manufacture to DC or three other warehouses under DC control. Other merchandise was shipped directly to individual stores after instructions were received from the buyer's office. This pattern of distribution typified the industry.

Marketing Laws

The S. S. Kresge Company was very careful to observe all fair-trade laws (laws which stipulated that a manufacturer's suggested minimum price could not be broken) in order to avoid restraint-of-trade charges. In fact, this was one prime reason for an upswing in K mart-branded merchandise. Any violations of municipal, state (for example, Sunday

closing laws), or federal laws were strictly forbidden by management. Federal antitrust laws and restraint-of-trade regulations were not considered as impeding upon K mart operations.

Product Policy

The K mart policy, as originally conceived, was to operate a full-line, low-margin discount store. As of 1972, this policy had not been substantially modified. The merchandise offered was to be of the highest quality at the lowest possible prices. Therefore, three price–quality relationship tiers were created (the third was added in 1969). "Good" merchandise was sold, and because this tier was to be highly promoted in advertisements, it had to feature low prices. The second tier was merchandise tagged "better" by management. It was not highly promoted, and it carried a larger profit margin. Management hoped that customers would be drawn into a K mart by the "good" merchandise, and then would spot the "better" merchandise and purchase it. This strategy proved to be highly successful.

Annually, all products in all departments were studied for sales and profit positions. Products were sometimes also researched by testing sales in about 25 stores. Minor product changes also caused revisions in the products carried.

Inventory turnover and profit contributions were determined from purchases, not sales, and analyzed by computers for stores, districts, and regions by each of the four main departments. The failure rate of the new products offered was therefore quite low. For example, the computer assisted the buyers in the hardware department so that a failure rate of only 10–15 percent was achieved on products which had been on the market before.

Shopper "risk" was minimized by two policies. First, factory imperfects, freight-damaged merchandise, and the like, were *never* offered. Second, a satisfaction-always policy was offered which enabled the customer to be safe when shopping. For all merchandise returned, the customer was given cash (or the customer's account was credited) even if the customer only wanted to exchange the merchandise. The only requirement was that the merchandise had not been abused. Even merchandise purchased from another K mart was returnable. Courteous and *friendly* returned goods personnel was one of the store manager's prime responsibilities.

K mart buyers had to prove to management that new products and product groups, called "lines," were profitable. First, cost estimates of proposed product inclusion were made. Cost estimates from manufacturers of new products were judged as to whether they were reasonable by experienced buyers. Consideration was also given to other cost factors which added appreciably to costs, such as freight expense.

After cost estimates had been made, several price tiers were projected and demand estimates for each price were formulated. Demand estimates, including seasonal fluctuations, for one year into the future were made based on: (1) the experience of the buyers, (2) estimates of what competitors were pricing or would price the product, or (3) occasionally a test marketing in approximately 25 stores. The price competitors were using was usually accepted. When competitors were not dealing in the proposed merchandise, cost was combined with a "reasonable" gross margin, and then estimates of selling quantities were made. Calculations were made to determine whether gross margin requirements were satisfied.

K mart product policy specified the sale of manufacturer-branded merchandise. However, it also dictated a switch to K mart-branded merchandise when the prospective product offered superior value and superior selling merit. In certain instances, K mart was *forced* to stock private-brand merchandise. Manufacturers either could not supply requested quantities or required that the merchandise be fair-traded.

Store designs and department layouts were preset by the marketing staff. (A store manager could not move a counter or eliminate a department.) In-store displays and point-of-purchase materials were designed by the staff or provided by the manufacturer. Gondola layouts and signs sought to promote volume turnover. Displays had to be eye-catching and attractive and had to contain economic stock levels, correct assortments, information, and prices. The store manager and the department manager received photographs of a model display several months in advance. A clerk was instructed to set up the display exactly as in the photograph. The display (prices excepted) could only be modified with the change of seasons, stock shortages, or if a better way could be found.

Distribution

The four warehouses, controlled from the Fort Wayne main warehouse, were highly computerized and used sophisticated physical distribution techniques. The main functional areas—data transmission, inventory control, transportation, and warehousing—were analyzed and managed in order to optimize distribution.

Computer-readable order sheets along with recommended order quantities were periodically sent to managers. After being filled in, these were sent to DC, which decided the time and means of shipment. DC also forwarded direct shipments, 80 percent of all orders, to the respective suppliers.

If possible, stores were situated where they would be easily accessible to both suburban and urban customers. All stores featured wide selections, snack bars for shoppers, multiple checkouts, and a service desk.

Price Policy

The basic price policy of K mart, which had not been modified up to 1972, was: "As low as or lower than any competition." A store manager could lower but *not raise* prices. All store managers were instructed to actively determine the prices of competitors, lower prices, and change advertised prices. They were even instructed to meet competitors' loss leaders. These actions were especially important in regard to highly promotable merchandise.

When items were not price competitive, a "reasonable gross profit" was sought. Items for which quality differentials prevented direct consumer price comparison—about 90 percent of the many items stocked—were preferred. Loss leaders were used in store openings and in aiding the volume building of troubled stores. Approximately 10 percent of a normal store's sales contributed to costs but not profit.

Personal Selling Policy

The goal of the personal selling policy was friendly, courteous, and helpful service from all personnel. With the opening of the first 18 stores in 1962, the customer service concept was imposed. The premise was that the average customer did not want to be "bothered" by an attentive salesclerk and that most customers were willing to wait upon themselves. The concept stipulated that merchandise be displayed so that the customer could self-select the merchandise desired. Clerks were to set up, stock, tidy up, and generally maintain displays and were also to be unobtrusively available to customers in merchandise selection. They were not to psychologically force a purchase. Clerks received only in-store training. Reliance, therefore, was mainly upon good displays and selling aids which were provided to department managers. Economizing on personnel costs helped to make possible lower selling prices.

Before a store opening, the regional personnel staff aided the store and department managers in recruiting and training personnel.

Promotion Policy

All discount stores must have volume in order to survive. Their operating margins are always below 30 percent markup, far below those of conventional retailers. Thus, for discount stores to be profitable, volume sales are necessary. After low prices, advertising is the main means of building volume. Thus, advertising must be highly effective and its effectiveness must be measurable in sales terms.

In the past, 99 per cent of all K mart advertising had been placed in weekly newspaper ads. As of 1972, all media were used, with about 96 percent of the $60 million advertising budget being placed in newspapers. The basis for this policy, formed solely by executive judgment, was

the feeling that the only effective way to daily present selected items among the many types stocked was through newspapers.

All advertisements were drawn up completely—including merchandise featured, photographs, layouts, copy, and prices—by the central advertising staff. A high degree of coordination among the advertising, purchasing, and distribution functions was required. Photographs of merchandise, with descriptions and prices, were laid out and checked. The completed advertisements were then photographed and transposed into glossy or mat form. These were sent to the store manager about two weeks before the publication date. The manager would deliver them to the local newspaper, which would add location information. A "proof," an actual print of each advertisement, was then returned to the store manager, who had it checked for typographical errors and made price corrections. He also worked with his department managers to insure sufficient stock levels and correct prices. The corrected proof was then returned to the newspaper for printing.

Rotogravure supplements were also used heavily in conjunction with the newspaper media schedule. Heavy usage of rotogravure supplements accounted for 15–20 percent of K mart division's advertising budget. Rotogravure supplements are 8, 12, or 16 full-sized or tabloid-sized pages of four-color high-quality newspaper stock. K mart executives stated that the usage of the four-color process increased readership three- or four-fold. They also pointed out the tremendous success that had been achieved when rotogravure supplements were used. These rotogravure newspaper supplements were also liked because, unlike the recipients of direct mail, their readers paid for them and their circulation was therefore deemed to be more effective.

In 1972, 10 to 13 supplements were printed annually and timed to correspond with seasonal sales. Approximately 21 million copies were printed in 1971, when there were about 63 million U.S. households. Of course, in areas where there were no stores, there was no coverage. Supplements were printed by four printers on a bid basis with a five-month lead time, which increased coordination problems. All supplements were laid out by the corporate advertising staff.

Edward J. Kreitz, the advertising director of the S. S. Kresge Company, indicated that in the foreseeable future newspapers should continue to account for from 90 percent to 95 percent of the advertising budget. He also said that K mart was considering advertising in locally edited and published Sunday magazine sections of newspapers and would urge the printing of midweek newspaper magazines.

Television accounted for 3.5 percent of the advertising budget. Aside from the reasons outlined below, it was used for volume-building purposes in various locales as needed. Readily known and regularly purchased items that could be easily described were featured in 10- and 30-second spots. Sales results were found to be excellent means for mea-

suring advertisement effectiveness. All television creative work was done by K mart's advertising agency.

Kreitz also indicated that computers and other sophisticated techniques were used to forecast future advertising placements for each product. Store, district, region, national, and department information was inputted. Next, a running record of conformity to budget was kept for each level. The rates, open or contract, for each newspaper were also inputted. Then inventories were taken before and after the advertising of every item advertised in every store. Each store manager reported on computer-readable sheets the quantity of each item sold during the campaigns. Finally, orders by item by store were also inputted. Thus, known sales results were inputted. All of these variables then could be electronically manipulated to determine:

1. Average sales per item during the campaign.
2. The effectiveness of the campiagn.
3. The advertisability or promotability of any item.

Other sales influences were included in noncomputer analyses. They were:

1. The timing of the advertisement.
2. The weather during the campaign.
3. Competitors' actions.
4. Competitors' advertising patterns.
5. The influence of displays and point-of-purchase materials.
6. The in-store inventory level.
7. The quality of store management.

Store Opening Promotions

Typically, when a new K mart store is being opened in a city, television and radio are used in a supporting role. Their three intended purposes are to: (1) announce the opening of the new store; (2) build the image of the K mart organization; and (3) announce and explain K mart policies (e.g., the return goods policy). Newspaper advertisements comprise 94 percent of the typical opening budget. Newspapers are used for three purposes: first to advertise the thousands of items; second, to accomplish the above purposes; and finally, to accomplish public relations purposes.

Eighteen months before an intended store is to open, a real estate evaluation team, a market evaluation team, and a media evaluation team (evaluating available media and their quality and circulation) analyze the proposed area. All teams are required to concur before the site is approved for a lease.

Three months before the scheduled opening date, multimedia publicity is released to explain policies, build the K mart image, and stir interest.

Ten days before the grand opening, the campaign begins! Daily pre-opening institutional advertisements explain policies and build an image. Most of the budget is spent in newspapers, though radio, direct mail, and television are used in the support function.

The grand opening days are usually Thursday, Friday, Saturday, and Sunday. A Wednesday evening or Thursday morning 14–16-page newspaper advertisement is run. Every day of the opening week, at least a full-page advertisement appears in the local newspaper. Many loss leaders are used, based upon the store manager's estimate of how best to lure shoppers into the store. All regularly sold merchandise features extra-low prices to impress the K mart price-quality relationship on customers. Newspaper coupons are not used, though in-store unadvertised discounts and five-minute sales announced on the public address system are used. Most advertisements are aimed at the women who do most of the retail spending.[4]

The store manager learns about advertising techniques by acting as an assistant store manager, not through formal training or by occupying a staff advertising position. Once he becomes a store manager, he is able to change the preset advertising as he wishes, barring price raises. The district and regional advertising managers can suggest changes, which are usually heeded, but these suggestions are not binding upon the store manager.

Operating Store

An operating store's advertising budget is determined on a management by objectives basis. The corporate advertising staff, after determining the national objectives, annually evolves a "basic" advertising program. All stores modify it to attain their own and the national objectives. The basic A program is divided into 12 phases by the month. The corporate advertising staff sets up the number of inches allowed for each department each day. The preset ads are then made and sent to every store. Six to ten newspaper pages are used each week. A store budget is set as a function of local newspaper rates to accomplish the basic A program.

Advertising costs usually amounted to 1.5 percent of sales. However, if more than one store was covered by the media, the budget allocation was split among them and the savings were spent in other, extra advertising programs. Multiple-store areas usually had an advertising manager who could only recommend.

---

[4]K mart Division had found that young adults in the purchase cycle of their lifetimes, between the ages of 20 and 40, were easier to attract than older adults who had settled buying habits and purchased less. In either case, the woman's interest was aroused and K mart relied upon her to bring her husband in. Women were also found to rely more heavily than men upon word-of-mouth advertising. Thus, aiming advertisements at women served a dual purpose.

The basic B program was aimed at increasing Sunday volume. (Saturdays and Sundays had proved to be the largest sales days. Wives brought their impulsive husbands, who would usually authorize larger purchases.) All stores, even if they were not open on Sundays, were required to follow the two-page basic B program.

The basic S program was a program to promote volume in specialty departments, such as building materials. Any store featuring the specialty department concerned was required to run this program.

The K or key-city program promoted specialty departments in locales where more than one store existed. In this way, the advertising budgets of stores were fully utilized. Over 5,000 extra inches were used in some areas annually in this program. The average newspaper contained about 2,400 lines per page, while tabloids contained about 1,000 lines per page.

BRAND STRATEGY DECISION

The original policy of the K mart Division was to be a discount department store featuring low prices on several thousand nationally known and branded items. However, for one or more reasons:

1. The manufacturer did not have the production capacity required by K mart sales volume.
2. The manufacturer insisted upon having his own merchandise fair-traded.
3. The cost of national advertising that the manufacturer passed along to K mart was substantial.
4. A poor value to the K mart customer or a poor gross margin for K mart existed with a national brand.
5. The national brand's claims to "superior selling merit" proved unjustified.

K mart was forced into private branding of its merchandise.

During its early years of operation, in order to conserve funds for the expansion of K mart stores the K mart Division had contracted with the Fisk Tire Division of Uniroyal to provide auto centers near most K mart cities. A typical auto center, located in the same shopping center as a K mart, marketed automobile and small truck tires in a separate section of about 10 bays and approximately 5,000 square feet. The auto centers also featured at discount prices Fisk-branded batteries, shock absorbers, antifreeze, and most of the automobile services that could be acquired at gasoline stations and dealerships. Later, after the K mart automobile service concept had proved highly successful, the K mart Division directly managed the auto stores built, kept the basic operating strategies, and changed the brand used in its new tire centers to K mart. The

contract with Uniroyal prevented conversion of the other centers until 1974.

In the spring of 1972, a major promotional problem was under consideration: Having dual brands prevented the use of the customary K mart economics of scale in advertising to achieve a competitive posture in the tire centers market. This policy also made it necessary to create and execute two completely separate advertising programs. Edward J. Kreitz, advertising director, and Emory Larson, K mart sales manager, were in the process of considering long-range plans. The annual division planning meeting with the board of directors was 40 days away. Accordingly, Kreitz and Larson addressed themselves to the following important questions:

1. Should the Fisk-branded tire centers be converted to the K mart brand in 1974?
2. If so, what promotional strategy and advertising tactics should be formulated?

In the process of preparing recommendations on these questions, they undertook to review the present brand strategy.

Some members of the task group Kreitz had assembled to consider this issue felt that the brands should be converted and an entirely new promotional approach be developed. The goal of the approach was to build a national-brand image for K mart tires, auto products, and services, the tire centers, and K mart as quality automobile accessories merchandisers. It was decided to aim the program at men between the ages of 20 and 40, who were intuitively thought to be the principal purchasers. Second, it was determined through projections of 1974 sales that the budget was large enough for national media coverage. It was felt that substantial savings, with the ability to completely cover the tire market, would be possible if the dual brand policy were eliminated. Third, some K mart brand promotion should rub off to increase the sales of other K mart brands and K mart stores.

Several promotional tactics were open to Kreitz and Larson. The entire budget could be devoted to newspaper advertisements. Radio and television local spots or national time could be purchased. Or funds could be devoted to appropriate national magazines and direct-mail campaigns.

At an early staff meeting, one of Mr. Kreitz's assistants disagreed. He proposed that a national campaign be avoided. Advertisements, he maintained, should be placed in newspapers at appropriate times, such as during the fall to promote mud and snow tires. He reasoned that substantial savings (over 75 percent) could be achieved from not advertising, thus contributing to lower margins and greater profits. Second, word-of-mouth advertising would successfully and rapidly build consumer awareness, acceptance, and preference. Finally, it was possible to

instruct clerks to discretely mention the manufacturer of K mart-branded products if desired. Kreitz instructed the task group to study this alternative as well.

PROMOTIONAL STRATEGY FOR MURRAY, UTAH, STORE

Another problem that Kreitz faced was one that the Western regional advertising manager had brought to him: the promotional problem of the Murray, Utah, store. Volume is crucial for K mart outlets. From past experience, management knew what usual growth of sales an outlet should achieve. It was easy to determine that the Murray K mart was in serious trouble. Normally, the store manager had the responsibility for diagnosing the problem's source. Then he had to devise promotional alternatives and decide upon which course to take. If he was unable to solve the problem in the district, then the regional or corporate advertising staff was enlisted. Requests for higher-echelon support were highly encouraged and did not in any way reflect upon the store manager involved.

The normal solution was to reduce prices 3–4 percent on all merchandise and to raise the advertising budget to 3.5 or 5 percent of sales. This usually solved the volume problems. (In the case of the Murray store, however, the media used covered two other Salt Lake City K marts).

A crash program, C, had been developed to handle such situations. Realizing that the best sales days were Saturdays and Sundays, a crash program of additional newspaper advertisements on weekends was used. Loss leaders, blue lamp sales, and many other "gimmicks" were used to build up the habit of shopping K mart in the locale. Executive judgment determined the advertising level and the duration of such campaigns.

Advertisements were also reduced photographically to 77 percent of their original size. The resulting savings were then put into local radio/television spots which emphasized loss leaders.

During conferences in Salt Lake City, several possible reasons were brought to Kreitz's attention. First, a large, highly religious population segment existed. They frowned upon the use of coffee, tea, cigarettes, and other stimulants sold in K mart stores. Second, they were extremely loyal to their present place of purchase. K mart had been forced by competitors to remain open on Sundays.

Daytime and evening network time for television spots was found to be extremely expensive. Viewership was found to be the lowest in the nation, due to the large percentage of viewers who disapproved of much of the television content in the area.

The Salt Lake City morning and evening newspapers, owned by one concern, were the only print media available in Murray and the surrounding area. Unfortunately, its circulation in this area was remarkably low (see Exhibit 2).

EXHIBIT 2   ABC facts: The basic measures of circulation values

ABC Facts/The basic measures
of Circulation Values.

Salt Lake City, Utah
TRIBUNE, DESERET NEWS

audit report

For 12 months ending September 30, 1970

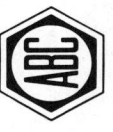

The Average Paid Circulation as
reported by publisher in statements
to the Bureau has been substantiated by this audit.

Audit Bureau of Circulations
Chicago, Illinois

Source: Audit Bureau of Circulations, ABC Report for the 12 months ending Sept. 30, 1970, covering the Salt Lake City, Utah, TRIBUNE, DESERET NEWS. Reprinted by permission.

EXHIBIT 2 *(continued)*

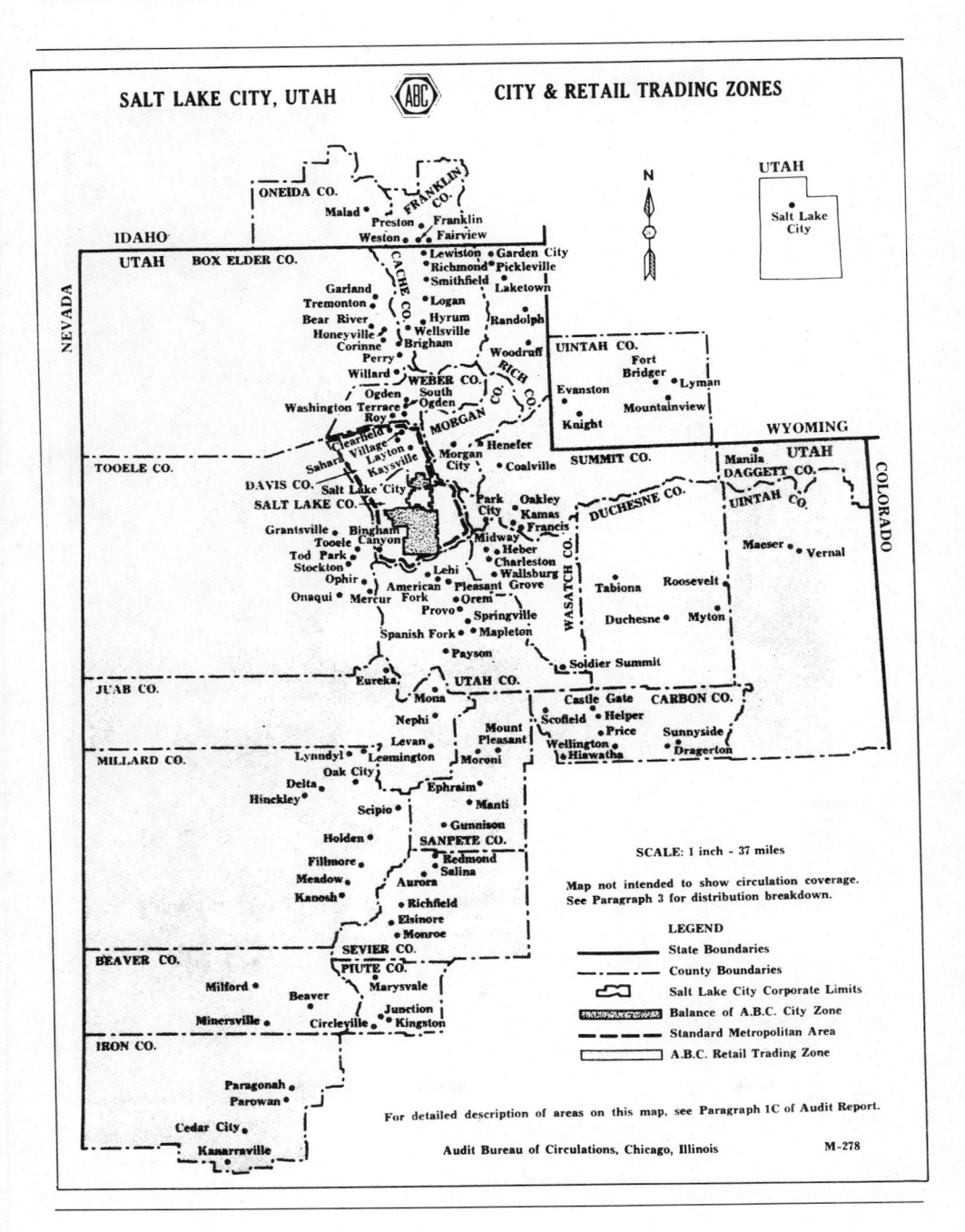

SALT LAKE CITY, UTAH   (ABC)   CITY & RETAIL TRADING ZONES

EXHIBIT 2 (*continued*)

For comparative purposes, the average paid circulation by quarters as shown in audits for the previous three years and for the period covered by this report is shown below:

	Combined daily	Morning	Evening	Sunday
4th quarter, 1966	200,391	110,289	90,102	191,648
1st quarter, 1967	199,849	109,512	90,337	190,876
2d quarter, 1967	198,144	109,062	89,082	190,400
3d quarter, 1967	190,508	108,077	82,431	186,034
4th quarter, 1967	191,955	107,771	84,184	187,811
1st quarter, 1968	191,465	107,441	84,024	188,533
2d quarter, 1968	193,530	108,138	84,392	189,054
3d quarter, 1968	192,728	108,401	84,327	188,344
4th quarter, 1968	195,044	109,152	85,892	180,917
1st quarter, 1969	192,441	107,725	84,716	189,051
2d quarter, 1969	188,620	105,730	82,890	184,988
3d quarter, 1969	188,713	107,212	81,501	184,103
4th quarter, 1969	190,667	107,505	83,162	187,131
1st quarter, 1970	192,193	107,494	84,699	188,196
2d quarter, 1970	192,171	107,902	84,269	188,038
3d quarter, 1970	190,957	108,166	82,791	186,907

The records maintained by the *Tribune* and the *Deseret News* pertaining to circulation data and other data reported for the period ending September 30, 1970, have been examined by the Audit Bureau of Circulations.

The examination was made in accordance with the bureau's bylaws, rules, and auditing standards and included such tests of the accounting records and such other auditing procedures as were considered necessary in the circumstances.

Based on this examination, the data shown in this report present fairly the information pertaining to the circulation data and other data of the *Tribune* and the *Deseret News* as verified by the bureau auditors.

DATE: November, 1970.

AUDIT BUREAU OF CIRCULATIONS

EXHIBIT 2 (continued)

State county town	Households 1960 census	Households 1969 ABC estimate	Morn- ing	Even- ing	Com- bined daily	Sunday
Utah						
Salt Lake City ABC City Zone as described in Paragraph 1C is the following:						
(MA) Salt Lake City						
Salt Lake County (ABC City Zone [part])	105,683	120,000	(Adjusted figure) 64,655 / 62,422	49,299 / 47,527	113,954 / 109,949	107,191 / 104,830
(MA) Davis County						
Salt Lake City (ABC City Zone [part])	4,763	7,050	(Adjusted figure) 3,689 / 3,562	4,567 / 4,403	8,256 / 7,965	8,249 / 8,067
Total Salt Lake City ABC City Zone	110,446	127,050	(Adjusted figure) 68,344 / 65,984	53,866 / 51,930	122,210 / 117,914	115,440 / 112,897
Metropolitan area Counties of Salt Lake and Davis only (Gross distribution one day only)	123,415	152,775	(Adjusted figure) 70,892 / 68,601	56,246 / 54,401	127,138 / 123,002	120,291 / 117,870
Total retail trading zone— average paid circulation						
Total city and retail trading zones—average paid circulation			26,967	24,792	51,759	51,807
All other—average paid circulation			92,951	76,722	169,673	164,704
Total average paid circulation			14,817 / 107,768	7,000 / 83,722	21,817 / 191,490	22,864 / 187,568

Beaver County	1,244	1,175	(Adjusted figure				
Adamsville				17	16	33	39
Beaver				163	195	358	331
Milford				293	53	346	336
Minersville				54	34	88	91
Total Beaver County				527	298	825	797
				541	310	851	817)
Box Elder County	6,610	5,925					
Brigham City	3,213	4,450		936	873	1,809	2,202
Corinne				24	18	42	19
Garland				57	104	161	62
Mantua				12	31	43	39
Tremonton				168	210	378	155
Willard				34	60	94	113
Balance in county				18	42	60	39
Total Box Elder County				1,249	1,338	2,587	2,629
				1,283	1,390	2,673	2,696
Cache County	9,892	11,875	(Adjusted figure				
Clarkston				15	25	40	43
Hyde Park				30	37	67	60
Hyrum				50	104	154	129

EXHIBIT 2 (continued)

AUDIT REPORT—NEWSPAPER

The *Salt Lake Tribune* (Morning and Sunday) and *Deseret News* (Evening), Salt Lake City, Utah

Year Estab: Morning 1871
Evening 1850
Sunday 1871

Published: Morning. Evening. (See Par. 4) Sunday.

Report for 12 months ending September 30, 1970.

			Average paid circulation		
		Combined daily	**Morning**	**Evening (see Par. 4)**	**Sunday**
1. TOTAL AVERAGE PAID CIRCULATION		191,490	107,768	83,722	187,568
1A. TOTAL AVERAGE PAID CIRCULATION BY ZONES: CITY ZONE					

	Popu-lation	**House-holds**				
1960 census	393,492	110,446				
1969 ABC estimate	457,775	127,050				
Dealers and carriers not filing lists with publisher			115,860	65,229	50,631	111,873
Street vendors			1,946	692	1,254	975
Publisher's counter sales			49	27	22	30
Mail subscriptions			59	36	23	19
Total city zone			117,914	65,984	51,930	112,897

RETAIL TRADING ZONE

	Popu-lation	House-holds				
1960 census	477,505	126,010				
1969 ABC estimate	572,875	150,700				
Dealers and carriers not filing lists with publisher			50,103	25,641	24,462	51,600
Mail subscriptions			1,656	1,326	330	207
Total retail trading zone			51,759	26,967	24,792	51,807
Total city and retail trading zones			169,673	92,951	76,722	164,704

	Popu-lation	House-holds				
1960 census	870,997	236,456				
1969 ABC estimate	1,030,650	277,750				
ALL OTHER						
Dealers and carriers			18,478	13,336	5,142	21,287
Mail subscriptions (See Par. 12a)			3,339	1,481	1,858	1,577
Total all other			21,817	14,817	7,000	22,864
TOTAL PAID excluding bulk			191,490	107,768	83,722 (a)	187,568
(For bulk sales, see Par. 5)						

(a) Includes Predate Edition. See Paragraphs 4 and 12c.

EXHIBIT 2 (concluded)

AVERAGE PAID

	Combined daily	Morning	Evening (see Par. 4)	Sunday
4th quarter, 1969	190,667	107,505	83,162	187,131
1st quarter, 1970	192,193	107,494	84,699	188,196
2d quarter, 1970	192,171	107,902	84,269	188,038
3d quarter, 1970	190,957	108,166	82,791	186,907

1B. STANDARD METROPOLITAN STATISTICAL AREA—COUNTY OF PUBLICATION:
Answer optional and not made.

1C. CITY AND RETAIL TRADING ZONES:
AREA INCLUDED IN CITY ZONE IN PARAGRAPH 1A is the corporate limits of Salt Lake City, Midvale, Murray, Riverton, Sandy City, South Salt Lake, South Jordan and West Jordan, census county divisions of Draper and Holladay, balance of Midvale and south Salt Lake divisions and in Magna Division area extending south and west of the corporate limits of Salt Lake City bounded by Riter Canal, southwest and northwest to State Highway 201, west to 92d Street West, south to the Utah and Salt Lake Canal, southeast to 72d Street West, south to 41st Street South, east to 56th Street West, south to 62d Street South, east to 32d Street West, south to the corporate limits to West Jordan, east to the division boundary and north to the corporate limits of Salt Lake City, including the delimited unincorporated communities of Kearns and Magna in Salt Lake County, Utah. In Davis County, Utah, city of Bountiful and towns of North Salt Lake and Woods Cross.
AREA INCLUDED IN RETAIL TRADING ZONE IN PARAGRAPH 1A is, with exception of city zone:

In UTAH—counties of Beaver, Box Elder, Cache, Carbon, Daggett, Davis, Duchesne, Iron, Juab, Millard, Morgan, Piute, Rich, Salt Lake, Sanpete, Sevier, Summit, Tooele, Uintah, Utah, Wasatch, and Weber.
In IDAHO—counties of Franklin and Oneida.
In WYOMING—Uinta County.

2. AVERAGE PAID CIRCULATION IN PUBLISHER'S PRIMARY MARKET AREA (complete abutting counties and/or selected abutting parts of county/ies [census units]):
Answer optional and not made.

Kreitz realized that store managment could also have been the crux of the problem. Perhaps display maintenance, point of purchase, or window signs were "untidy." The clerks and/or returns personnel may have been unhelpful or discourteous. Or, the department managers may not have had a feeling for local tastes and may have overstocked the wrong merchandise or apparel styles. In the past, the action of the store manager could affect sales up or down 20 percent. The national economy in 1971 was also causing erratic purchase behavior by some segments of the U.S. population. A major aerospace employer had recently left Murray, while other aerospace employers were contemplating layoffs. Kreitz was told that rumors of layoffs were rampant in the area. Finally, Murray was located immediately south of the rapidly growing Salt Lake City metropolitan area. The effect of and amount of shopping outside the community were not known.

After accumulating the foregoing information, Kreitz and his associates had to decide how these circumstances related to the promotional problem of the Murray store and what promotional plan to formulate.

QUESTIONS

1. Should the Fisk-branded tire centers be converted to the K mart brand? Why or why not?

2. If so, what promotional strategy and tactics should be formulated? Explain your reasoning.

3. What is your diagnosis of the source of the disappointing performance of the Murray store?

4. What action would you recommend to deal with the problem? Why?

SPORTSFAN MAGAZINE*

Promotional strategy alternatives

"When you pick up a marketing textbook, it will say that to introduce a new product or service you must have a niche. This is exactly what we have found—a specific void in the marketplace. It is classical—right out of the Marketing 101 textbook!" These were the thoughts of an excited Harry Moorhouse in early February 1980. With over a year of research, preparation, and organization behind him, Moorhouse felt that the market was ripe for the introduction of his new publication, *Sportsfan* magazine. *Sportsfan,* a monthly magazine, was designed to cover professional and amateur sports on a local basis, specifically the Detroit metropolitan area. Although Detroit was a very sports-conscious community, it had no publication which emphasized local sports action. Moorhouse had conducted extensive research regarding promotional strategy alternatives, and he was confident that spring was the best time to introduce the new magazine, due primarily to the high public interest in the forthcoming baseball season. Thus, he deemed it essential to make his marketing decisions immediately in order to meet this deadline. An "unbeatable idea" was now ready to put to the market test.

---

*Written by Greg M. Boll, research assistant, under the supervision of Professor Martin R. Warshaw, Graduate School of Business Administration, The University of Michigan, Ann Arbor.

HISTORY

Harry Moorhouse received his BA in history from Wayne State University in 1968. He began his career as a division sales manager for the National Chemsearch Corporation of Dallas, Texas. Since leaving this position in 1975, he had assumed the role of a young entrepreneur. At the time of this case, he was engaged in several endeavors in the Detroit area, the most significant being his work as a manufacturer's representative and vice president for Galtco, a maintenance hardware firm, and as a buyer for a dealer involved in the precious metal scrap business. Moorhouse noted that although these interests provided his current income, he planned to devote full time to *Sportsfan* when it became a full-grown, moneymaking venture.

Sportsfan magazine was conceived in January 1979 as the result of a personal observation by Moorhouse:

> The way this whole project really got started was this: In following local [Detroit] sports, I found that there wasn't anything to read, and I wondered why in a sports-minded area like Detroit there was no magazine emphasizing local sports action. I also wondered if you can make any money in the publication business, so I picked up a pencil, and off the top of my head came up with these wild figures. You can make a fortune at something like this if it is successful.

After these hunches were substantiated with further research, *Sportsfan* was off the ground.

The initial step was to gain exposure with the advertising and sporting communities. For example, in order to produce a good sports publication, it is essential to obtain field and locker room privileges from the target sports teams. This is the only avenue through which to acquire the interviews, photographs, and "inside scoops" necessary for a successful venture. Most major sports teams, however, want to see something in "black and white" before granting such press privileges. So "we were caught in a merry-go-round."

In order to resolve this problem, the *Sportsfan* staff assembled a preview issue in July 1979. Its purpose was to prove to these various constituencies that *Sportsfan* was for real. It was distributed to the major sports teams, the advertising community, and financing sources.

Although the quality of *Sportsfan Preview* was not as high as that planned for future issues, its impact was quite significant. By early fall, the *Sportsfan* staff had gained at least minimally acceptable press privileges from all Detroit professional teams as well as from local universities. Exhibit 1 lists these teams and provides a detailed summary of the privileges granted. Moorhouse noted that the ease in gaining press privileges was inversely proportional to the fame and standing of the team. "The upstart teams, such as the Express [professional soccer], are much

EXHIBIT 1   *Sportsfan* press privileges, Detroit area sports teams, December 31, 1979

Institution/franchise	Degree of press privileges
Detroit Tigers (professional baseball)	Full field and photo deck access. Limited access to locker room and press box.
Detroit Lions (professional football)	Press box access granted. Limited field privileges and no locker room privileges.
Detroit Red Wings (professional hockey)	Preferred seating and photo arrangements. No locker room privileges.
Detroit Pistons (professional basketball)	Preferred seating and photo arrangements. No locker room privileges.
Detroit Express (professional soccer)	Complete field, press box, and locker room privileges.
University of Michigan	Complete privileges for all sports except football and basketball, for which requests were handled individually.*
Michigan State University	Complete privileges for all sports except football and basketball, for which requests were handled individually.*
Wayne State University	Complete privileges for all sports.
Special events (golf and tennis tournaments, boxing matches, auto racing, horse racing, etc.)	Requests handled individually.

*The casewriter noted that *Sportsfan* photographers were on hand for several football and basketball games at the University of Michigan and Michigan State University in 1979.

easier to deal with because they need as much publicity as they can get." Overall, however, he was quite pleased with his success in this area, and he felt that *Sportsfan* would be granted complete press privileges for all area teams as a result of the first publicly circulated issue.

Another result of *Sportsfan Preview* was the interest it generated within the advertising and financial communities. Exhibit 2 lists the local businesses that had expressed an interest in advertising in *Sportsfan* as of February 1, 1980.

From a financial standpoint, progress was somewhat inhibited throughout 1979 but *Sportsfan Preview* stimulated the interest of several investors. Complete financial data are included in a later section.

EXHIBIT 2   *Sportsfan* magazine: Potential sources of advertising, February 1, 1980

Ford Motor Company
American Motors
Seymour Cadillac
Mirada Dodge
Detroit Oldsmobile dealers
Champion Spark Plugs
Monroe Shock Absorbers
Hughes and Hatcher (men's clothing)
Van Horn's (men's clothing)
Van Dyke's (men's clothing)
Pine Knob Manor Homes
K mart
Hiram Walker
National Bank of Detroit
WJR Radio
ON TV (subscription television)

Source: Company records.

Overall, Moorhouse felt that the progress to date had been quite acceptable, and he knew that with a solid marketing strategy he could capitalize on an ever-growing interest in local sports.

THE ENVIRONMENT

"The golden age of sports is now, and the American passion to participate, view, and bask in the glory of athletics has created a sports culture which generates billions of dollars annually."[1] More people of every age and culture are participating in and following sports than ever before. For example, 29 million people now call themselves tennis players, compared to 5.6 million just 16 years ago.[2] Similar trends are being exhibited in television ratings, attendance figures, and even jogging.

The Detroit area is certainly no exception to this trend. Historically, the Detroit sports fan has been highly loyal to hometown teams, even in "bad" or "rebuilding" years. Exhibit 3 shows attendance figures and records for the major area teams in 1975–79. Other current developments include the following:

1. The Pontiac Silverdome, home of the Lions (pro football), Pistons (pro basketball), and Express (pro soccer), was completed in 1978.

---

[1] Tony Velocci, "The Games People Play—and Pay to Watch," *Nation's Business,* March 1979, p. 29.

[2] Ibid.

EXHIBIT 3   Attendance figures and records of major sports teams in southeastern Michigan, 1975–1979

		Season ended				
		1975	**1976**	**1977**	**1978**	**1979**
Detroit Lions	Attendance	513,383	418,685	459,401	499,219	520,589
	Record (W–L)	7–7	6–8	6–8	7–9	2–14
	Home dates	7	7	7	8	8
Detroit Pistons	Attendance	307,180	251,352	303,792	223,382	389,936
	Record (W–L)	40–42*	36–46*	44–38*	38–44	30–52
	Home dates	41	41	41	41	41
Detroit Red Wings	Attendance	459,280	436,320	385,400	555,280	587,658
	Record (W–L–T)	23–45–12	26–44–10	16–55–9	32–34–14*	23–41–16
	Home dates	40	40	40	40	40
Detroit Tigers	Attendance	1,058,836	1,467,020	1,359,856	1,714,893	1,639,029
	Record (W–L)	57–102	74–87	74–88	86–76	85–76
	Home dates	78	77	78	78	78
University of Michigan (football)	Attendance	689,146	722,113	729,418	629,697	730,315
	Record (W–L–T)	8–1–2†	10–1–0†	10–1–0‡	10–1–0‡	8–3– 0§
	Home dates	7	7	7	6	7

*Indicates playoff participant.
†Indicates Orange Bowl participant.
‡Indicates Rose Bowl participant and Big Ten Conference champion.
§Indicates Gator Bowl participant.
Source: Public relations offices of respective franchise/insertion.

It is considered by many to be one of the finest sports complexes in the nation. It is a domed structure, seats approximately 80,000, and is maintained at a temperature of about 70 degreees F.

2. The Joe Louis Arena, completed in downtown Detroit in January 1980, provides a beautiful new home for the Detroit Red Wings (pro hockey).

3. Tiger Stadium, home of the Detroit Tigers (pro baseball), is currently being totally modernized and renovated.

According to Moorhouse, these and other indicators provide a highly favorable environment in which to embark on a venture such as *Sportsfan*.

THE MARKET

Southeastern Michigan contains a cluster of cities, each within 80 miles of the Detroit metropolitan area (see Exhibit 4 for a map of this

EXHIBIT 4   The Detroit metropolitan area and vicinity

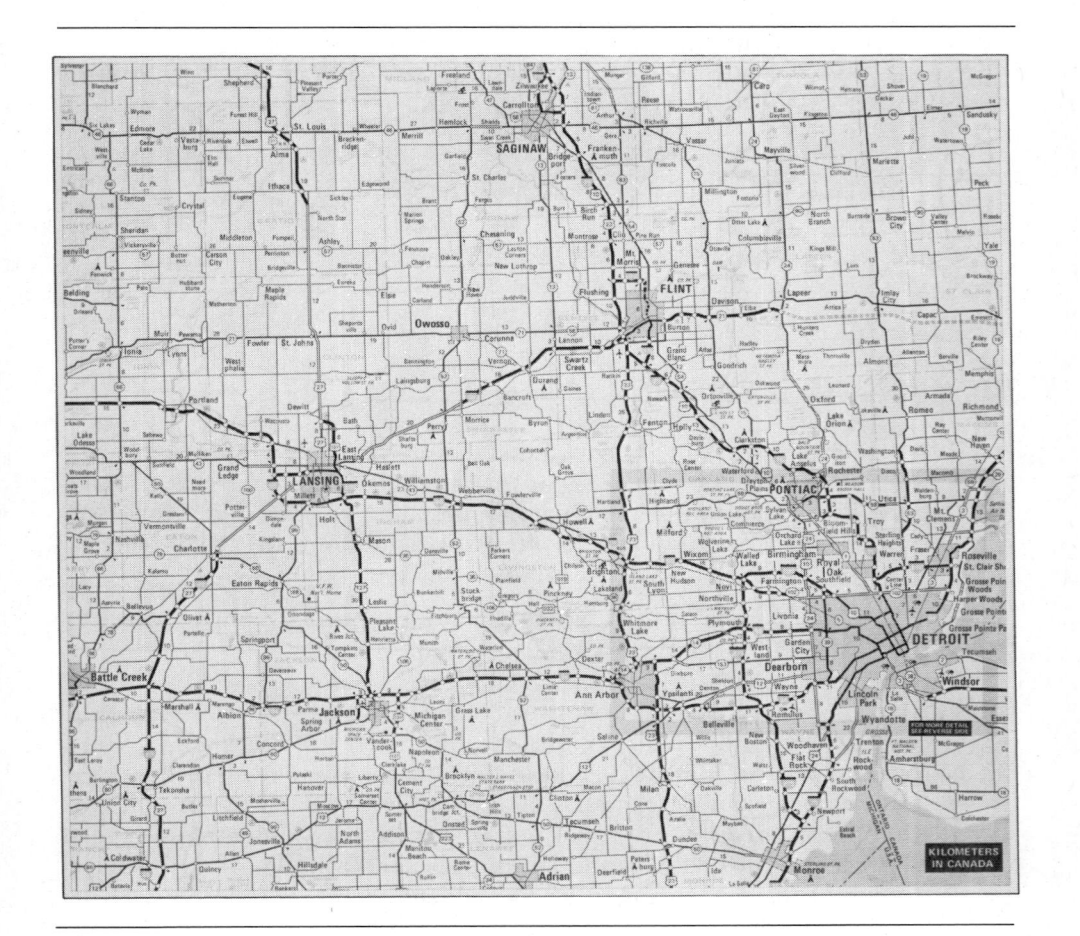

marketplace). The total population is about 6 million, nearly two thirds that of the entire state. (See Exhibit 5 for a detailed breakdown of the population and Exhibit 6 for the appropriate demographic trends. These figures were obtained from the 1970 census, as the 1980 figures have not yet been reported.)

In addition, the *Sportsfan* staff reported that the Detroit metropolitan area generated retail sales of $15 billion in 1979, fifth largest in the nation.

EXHIBIT 5   Population distribution by age category: *Sportsfan* market, 1970 census

	Michigan	Ann Arbor	Detroit	Flint	Jackson	Lansing	Saginaw
Under 5	804,463	19,841	378,586	50,215	12,577	35,444	22,418
5-14	1,903,083	39,600	893,102	116,881	30,301	75,798	51,176
15-24	1,575,366	68,104	705,022	85,190	24,004	90,482	36,975
25-44	2,084,685	58,659	1,008,185	125,003	35,210	89,341	51,636
45-64	1,754,531	34,288	874,640	86,257	28,067	61,630	40,654
65+	752,955	13,611	340,396	33,112	13,115	25,998	16,884
Total	8,875,083	234,103	4,199,931	496,568	143,274	378,423	219,743

THE MAGAZINE INDUSTRY

Each magazine has two potential sources of revenue: (1) magazine sales to the consumer and (2) advertising sales to the business community. It is important to note that emphasis can be placed in a variety of proportions between these two alternatives, but some degree of penetration in both areas is usually vital to the success of a magazine.

Magazine Sales

There are two primary avenues for distributing magazines to consumers—newsstand sales and direct mail. Countless newsstands exist at a variety of Detroit area locations, ranging from street corners to shopping centers and airports. Because of this complicated structure, most publications achieve newsstand distribution through the Ludington Company, a distributor specializing in this service. Ludington's range of services includes: (1) distribution of the current month's issues, (2) collection of the previous month's unsold issues, and (3) collection of sales revenue from the newsstand. In exchange for these services, the net receipt to the publisher is 50 percent of the cover price.

The second avenue of distribution, mailing the magazine directly to consumers, simply involves stamping the magazines with address labels and placing them in the mail. Postage for bulk mailings of 10,000 or more issues amounts to $0.03 per magazine.

Obtaining names and addresses is the biggest obstacle that must be overcome when the direct-mail option is used. One way to do this is to purchase a mailing list from an established publication. Although "purchase" is the term used here as well as in the industry, a better description of this transaction would be "rent." That is, a "purchase" of this kind permits only one use of each name; the names must be repurchased for

EXHIBIT 6   Percent changes in age groups: *Sportsfan market 1960–1970*

	Michigan	*Ann Arbor*	*Detroit*	*Flint*	*Jackson*	*Lansing*	*Saginaw*
Under 5	(17.0)%	(0.9)%	(19.0)%	(12.9)%	(19.3)%	(5.0)%	(13.3)%
5–14	17.3	33.3	16.2	31.1	14.3	24.9	22.4
15–24	55.8	88.4	59.1	55.8	42.9	83.1	51.5
25–44	0.4	24.5	(5.0)	10.1	(1.5)	17.7	5.4
45–64	16.6	24.1	16.3	16.6	10.5	17.4	17.2
65+	18.0	15.1	26.4	21.8	9.9	11.2	12.6
Total percent change	13.4%	35.8%	11.6%	19.3%	8.5%	26.6%	15.2%

Source: U.S. Department of Commerce, Bureau of the Census, *1970 Census of Population and Housing: General Demographic Trends for Metropolitan Areas, 1960 to 1970.*

subsequent use. Violators of this code are subject to criminal prosecution under the federal copyright laws. In order to "own" a name, an organization must receive a written request for a subscription directly from the consumer.

According to Moorhouse, *Sportsfan* has recently obtained the opportunity to purchase the southeastern Michigan mailing list of *Playboy* magazine, which has a circulation of 57,000 in that area. The cost of each name would be three cents per month, and the list must be purchased in three-month blocks. *Sports Illustrated* and *Sport* each refused *Sportsfan's* request to purchase such lists, but Mr. Moorhouse believed that he could obtain deals similar to that of *Playboy* from the following publications:

Publication	Circulation
Time	50,000
Business Week	50,000
Tennis	20,000
Golf Digest	20,000

Advertising Sales

The most significant source of revenue for most magazines is derived from sale of advertising space. This is considered to be a very tough kind of selling, as it is important to appease both the "target company" and its advertising agency. The first step is to go to the appropriate advertising agencies. These agencies are interested in various characteristics of the publication, such as circulation, cost, quality, and overall ability to draw readers. According to Moorhouse, it is also a real plus for a new publication to have the mailing list of a well-established magazine, especially one that corresponds with the potential advertiser's target market.

If the publication is recommended by the agency, the sales effort is then directed to the actual advertiser, as he is the one who makes the final decision. Likewise, if the agency does not grant a recommendation, the advertiser can be pushed to override this advice.

According to *Sportsfan* records, the company will incur variable selling expenses of approximately $250 per page of advertising in the first month, and $200 for each month thereafter. Competitive advertising rates are given in Exhibit 7.

Competition

Moorhouse believes that he has found a niche in the market, and thus he sees little direct competition. "There is no competition. I feel that increased sales of *Sports Illustrated,* for example, is a good sign for us. This is not an either/or situation. We fully expect a large percentage of the market to purchase several sports publications, *Sportsfan* being one of them."

EXHIBIT 7   Competitive market comparisons

	Publication			
	Sport	**Sports Illustrated**	**Sporting News**	**Monthly Detroit**
Frequency	Monthly	Weekly	Weekly	Monthly
Reader's median age	30	25	n.a.	38
Michigan circulation	49,700	86,000	13,198	40,000
Reader's median household income	$19,600	$15,000	n.a.	$28,000
Advertising rate (per black-and-white page)	$1,616	$1,700	$2,278	$1,050
Advertising rate (per color page)	$2,107	$2,651	$3,403	$1,475
Cover price	$1.50	$1.25	$2.00	$1.50

Source: Company records.

The Detroit metropolitan area, however, does possess many alternatives for the potential reader or advertiser. *Sports Illustrated, Sport,* and *Sporting News* are the three major sports publications. Although each of these is national in scope, they all offer several pages per issue for local advertising. This is possible because the magazines are printed in decentralized locations and in local batches. Therefore, Detroit companies have the option of advertising in each of these publications on a local basis.

Another possible source of competition is *Monthly Detroit* magazine. *Monthly Detroit* is local in scope, and it emphasizes news, human interest, and social events. (See Exhibit 7 for complete data on all of the above competitors.)

Last, the editors of *Newsweek* were currently developing a new national monthly publication called *Inside Sports*. This was slated to be introduced in April 1980, and it would have marketing characteristics very similar to those of other national sports magazines.

ADMINISTRATIVE AND PRODUCTION COSTS

In addition to Moorhouse, two other administrative managers are involved with *Sportsfan*. These men, the financial and marketing directors, were currently receiving no fixed income. Like Moorhouse, their compensation was deferred, pending the eventual success of the venture.

There were, however, many staff members who were to be paid di-

rectly for their work. These included 9 free-lance writers and about 20 photographers. These people were paid only if their work was used in a published issue.

Production was to take place at the Saffran Printing Company, one of the biggest printers in southeastern Michigan. The cost for this service was semivariable: $15,000 plus 25 cents per magazine (64 pages). A summary of these and all other production and administrative costs is given in Exhibit 8. According to Saffran, the printing of *Sportsfan* would be done in one batch and would require about three days.

EXHIBIT 8   Production and administrative costs

Fixed component, Saffran Printing	$15,000
Variable component, Saffran Printing	$0.25 (Volume)
Free-lance writing (estimated)	
(about 25,000 words/issue @ $0.075 per word)	$1,875
Photography (estimated)	
(about 30 pictures/issue @ $50 per picture)	$1,500
Art (estimated)	
(about 10 drawings/issue @ $50 per drawing)	$500
General and administrative	$2,875
Total cost	$21,750 + $0.25 (Volume)

Source: Company records.

Moorhouse called attention to the low risk that had been involved in this business to date. Each of the aforementioned costs is avoidable; that is, there is no expense unless an issue is actually produced. However, since production is in one batch, the number of magazines desired must be stated before the press starts rolling. Therefore, once an issue is committed to print, all production and administrative costs are fixed.

PROMOTIONAL ALTERNATIVES

The final hurdle for *Sportsfan* was to determine what promotional mix would be appropriate to adequately gain market penetration. Moorhouse knew that a general acceptance by the public would be necessary for the magazine to merit substantial advertising dollars. He also felt that the organization could afford no more than a $20,000 cash outlay for promotional requirements. A variety of alternatives were now being considered by him.

Television.   Moorhouse knew that television advertising would be a very effective tool since it has both audio and visual components. Also, television is the perfect medium with which to reach a target audience. For example, a spot during a televised sporting event would directly address the type of person interested in *Sportsfan*. The major disadvantage of television was its extremely high cost (complete cost data for this medium are given in Exhibit 9). Moorhouse noted that spots during sporting events would be considered "prime time" in terms of the rate structure. The cost to produce a television advertisement would be approximately $500.

EXHIBIT 9   Detroit metropolitan area television rates

	Cost per 30-second spot			
	WDIV TV-4 NBC	WJBK TV-2 CBS	WXYZ TV-7 ABC*	WXON† TV-20
7 A.M.–9 A.M.	$ 125	$ 130	$ 135	$ 55
9 A.M.–5 P.M.	240	300	310	70
5 P.M.–11:30 P.M. (prime time)	1,500	1,500	1,550	110‡

Notes:
1. A 5 percent reduction is granted for the purchase of 10 or more spots.
2. A 10 percent reduction is granted for the purchase of 20 or more spots.
3. Ten-second spots can be purchased for one half the 30-second rate.
*Estimated
†Local station. Primary programming includes nightly broadcasts of old television shows, such as "Get Smart," "Gomer Pyle," and "Superman."
‡Regular programming stops at 8:00 P.M. for subscription TV, which broadcasts no advertising.
Source: *Spot Broadcasting Rates and Data,* Standard Rate & Data Service, Inc., 1979. Data simplified for case.

Radio.   There are two big advantages to radio: (1) it has the ability to reach a large number of people (especially during traffic rush hours) and (2) each station has its own identifiable target segment. Radio advertising is also much less costly than television advertising (see Exhibit 10 for a listing of selected Detroit radio stations, their target markets, and comparative costs). However, Moorhouse knew that the rush hours and sports programming spots would be classified as AAA, or prime time.

One unusual radio alternative was provided by WJR Radio, which agreed to grant *Sportsfan* about $10,000 worth of spot ads on the J. P. McCarthy morning show in exchange for five full-page spreads on the back cover of the magazine. This was a very intriguing idea because J. P. McCarthy was one of the most widely heard morning voices in the nation.

EXHIBIT 10   Selected Detroit radio stations: Characteristics and rates

Sta-tion	Age target	Type of programming	Cost					
			AAA		AA		A	
			1 min.	30 sec.	1 min.	30 sec.	1 min.	30 sec.
WJR	Adults	Personalities, news, sports, classical music, voice of the Detroit Tigers and Pistons	$355	$284	$330	$264	$175	$140
CKLW	20–49	Adult contemporary music; popular current and past hits	300	225	160	120	120	90
WDRQ	18–44	Pure disco	160	150	150	140	n.a.	n.a.
WRIF	18–34	Adult-oriented rock	127	107	112	94	95	79
WWJ	Adults	News, sports, weather, college and pro football play-by-play, features	170	136	100	80	55	44

Legend:
AAA—prime time; rush hours and sporting events; also 2 P.M.-A.M. for rock stations.
AA—primarily late morning, mid afternoon, and late evening.
A—primarily late night (after 11:30 P.M.).
Source: *Spot Radio Rates and Data,* Standard Rate & Data Service, Inc., 1979. Data simplified for case.

The cost to produce a radio advertisement would be about $250.

Magazines. The cost structure of magazine advertising has been discussed in previous sections and is summarized in Exhibit 7. Moorhouse liked the idea of gaining exposure through a medium that addressed itself directly to the magazine reader. Also, he knew that he could include a subscription request form with a magazine ad. However, he was uncertain whether these advantages would justify the cost.

Newspapers. There are two newspapers in the area, the *Detroit Free Press* in the morning, and the *Detroit News* in the afternoon. Complete advertising cost data for these publications are given in Exhibit 11.

EXHIBIT 11   Advertising rates of Detroit newspapers

	Cost per line	
	Detroit Free Press	*Detroit News*
Under 500 lines	$4.10	$4.31
500 lines	n.a	4.20
1,000	3.99	4.16
2,500	3.97	4.11
5,000	3.87	4.04
10,000	3.85	3.90
25,000	3.80	3.94
35,000	3.77	3.92
50,000	3.75	3.90
75,000	3.71	3.86
100,000	3.70	3.84
150,000	3.69	3.82
200,000	3.62	3.80
Circulation:		
Monday–Sunday (except Saturday)	610,849	630,795
Saturday	558,986	606,021
Sunday	705,398	828,052

Note: One small advertisement (three column inches) is approximately 40 lines.
Source: *Newspaper Rates and Data,* Standard Rate & Data Service, Inc., 1979.

Billboards. The main advantage of billboards is that they can be strategically positioned in order to gain maximum exposure. If located along a main freeway, a billboard may well be seen by millions of eyes each day. The cost of renting a billboard is $1,550 per board per month, with a minimum contract length of four months.

Discount price/free subscriptions. This form of promotion minimizes out-of-pocket costs and can be very effective in gaining extensive

exposure. Mailing the magazine free of charge to the consumers on a purchased mailing list has two main benefits: (1) it provides a direct and widespread form of exposure and (2) it informs the business commmunity that the magazine is in public circulation and thus is more apt than other methods to result in advertising sales. Moorhouse believed that, at least in the short run, advertisers did not care whether the magazine was purchased—only that it was in public circulation.

DECISION POINT

On February 10, 1980, Moorhouse and *Sportsfan* had reached a critical point. Moorhouse had to make many crucial decisions immediately if the introduction of *Sportsfan* was to coincide with the rapidly approaching baseball season (about April 1). First, he had to decide the appropriate mix among distribution alternatives, and what prices to charge through newsstands and through subscriptions. Second, he had to make a firm decision on his advertising rates, as ads would have to be booked before March 1 to be included in an April issue. Third, a promotional mix had to be determined which would provide maximum exposure to both consumers and advertisers. Finally, Moorhouse had to decide how he was going to "package" *Sportsfan;* that is, what type of cover would be most likely to catch the consumer's eye—a bright drawing, a photograph, or another alternative.

In considering his potential courses of action, Moorhouse had one final consideration riding in his mind. By noon on the next day, he would have to advise the people at Saffran Printing Company of his intentions for April. He knew that if he gave them an affirmative answer, this would positively commit him to a specified volume and a cash outlay in excess of $25,000.

QUESTIONS

1. Should Mr. Moorhouse commit himself to production for April? Why or why not?

2. Assuming *Sportsfan* is committed to print:
   a. What should the target market be?
   b. What distribution alternative(s) should be employed?
   c. How many magazines should be produced?
   d. What price should be charged for advertising? Newsstand sales? Subscription sales?
   e. What promotional mix should be used?

3. Calculate a break-even point given the strategies proposed above. (Hint: hold newsstand and subscription sales constant, and calculate the break-even point in terms of pages of advertising.)

4. How sensitive is financial success to magazine sales as opposed to advertising sales?

5. If you won the state lottery, would you invest $10,000 in *Sportsfan* magazine?

■

Part six

PRICING STRATEGY

The selection of a level of price for a product is but one of several pricing decisions that must be made by marketing management. In many cases, freedom to price at levels different from the current competitive level is limited, and therefore the marketing strategy of the firm emphasizes nonprice methods of attracting patronage. In other instances, however, the decision as to level of price is of special importance. These include, for example, instances in which a price must be set for a new product, an established price must be changed, or a price must be chosen for an addition to an existing line of products.

Once a level of price has been determined, the question becomes one of how to select and administer the specific pricing policies. These policies may range from an immediate departure from the established level, by means of discounts and allowances, to an attempt to maintain a given level of price through resale price maintenance or geographic pricing systems.

The theme of this section is that pricing can be a potent promotional instrument. But successful pricing requires consideration of potential changes in competition, product development, and market acceptance. Thus, pricing decisions cannot be made without considering how these decisions are related to the other marketing strategy variables and to the overall marketing program of the firm.

PRICE DETERMINATION

13

Although the concept of the marketing mix describes a blending process in which management combines various controllable elements in an attempt to develop an integrated program to achieve stated objectives, there is nothing in the concept which requires that all of the elements be added to the mix at the same time. In fact, quite the opposite is true. Once market targets have been defined and environmental constraints considered, marketing management faces decisions in the areas of strategy dealing with the product, its distribution, and its nonprice promotion. Only after having made decisions in those areas which reflect the interrelationships among the variables concerned and which are consistent with the achievement of the specified marketing goals, can management devote its attention to the remaining element of the mix—that of pricing.

INTRODUCTION

In the decision area of pricing, many different types of questions must be answered, ranging from the determination of a price for a new product to the redetermination of a price for an established product. In addition, strategies must be formulated to gain the promotional advan-

tages of varying from an established level of price or, conversely, of preventing such variation by resellers.

Once the decisions have been made with respect to determining a level of price and whether or not to vary from that level, then, of course, those decisions must be integrated with the decisions previously made in the areas of product, distribution, and (nonprice) promotional strategy. Adjustments in all areas are likely to be necessary in order to create a marketing mix that is consistent, integrated, and capable of achieving predetermined goals.

This chapter will consider the first part of the pricing decision, that is, the determination of a level of price for a new product, an established product, or an addition to a line of products. The following chapter will cover those pricing decisions of an essentially promotional nature that enable the seller to adapt better to the diverse needs of customers or to competitive pressures. Although these chapters will illustrate the use of various tools borrowed from economics and accounting as aids to decision making, the point must be made at the outset that pricing is more an art than a science. In the process of making pricing decisions, analytic tools are most helpful, but when the chips are down, the judgments of intelligent, experienced, and highly intuitive human beings are vital.

Price versus Nonprice Competition

Because most marketing managers would be well advised to work out the nonprice aspects of the marketing mix before turning to the questions involving price determination and variation, some attention should be given to the relative emphasis placed by business firms on price versus nonprice means of competing. Although it would be wrong for an individual firm to bias its strategy to conform to the norm of its industry, it is important for the managers of an individual firm to recognize the relative emphasis that its major competitors are placing on price. Most firms making such an investigation in the decades of the 1950s and 1960s would have found that industry marketing mixes were heavily biased in favor of nonprice methods of competing for market acceptance. Product differentiation, broad market coverage to provide availability, and considerable personal selling and advertising effort to create selective demand seemed to be the favored means of attracting patronage. Recourse to frequent or drastic changes in price appeared to be a less popular strategy. Indeed, a study made in 1964 indicated that price was ranked in sixth place among those factors of competitive strategy for their firms.[1]

Given a decade of rising price levels, price has increased in importance. A study similar to the one made in the mid-1960s was replicated

---

[1]Jon G. Udell, "How Important Is Pricing in Competitive Strategy?" *Journal of Marketing,* January 1964, pp. 44–48.

a decade later. Price had moved to first position among these variables deemed to be of strategic importance by marketing executives.[2]

Special Importance of Pricing Decisions

There is considerable evidence that during periods of inflation the importance of the pricing variable increases relative to that of the other controllable elements of the marketing mix. During the decade of the 1980s only a return to a more stable price level will reduce the importance of the pricing decision in comparison with that of decisions on the product, distribution, and nonprice promotion.

Regardless of the behavior of the price level, the pricing area requires special attention in three situations. These are: (1) when a firm must set a price for a new product, (2) when a firm wants to initiate a price change for an established product, and (3) when a firm producing several products with interrelated demands or costs is faced with the problem of pricing an addition to the product line. Before considering these situations in greater detail, some additional attention must be paid to the influence of the competitive environment on the price-setting process.

PRICING AND THE COMPETITIVE ENVIRONMENT

In order to better understand the environment in which pricing decisions are made by managers of individual firms, it is helpful to rely on economic theory. Although instances in which economics provides a ready-made answer to the pricing problem are rare, in an ever-increasing number of applications economic theory has provided the insight necessary to improve the quality of the pricing decision.

If one examined the nature of the pricing decision faced by the manager of a small wheat farm, one would find it very simple indeed. All that this "manager" has to do is to check with the local grain elevator to see what the going prices are. These prices quoted by the elevator, in turn, reflect the interaction of industry supply and demand in the grain market at Chicago. The economist would draw the diagram shown in Figure 13–1 to explain the derivation of industry price as well as the price as viewed by the individual firm. In the situation pictured, the farmer would sell quantity $Q*$ at industry price $P*$ if his goal were that of maximizing profits in the short run. This is because at quantity $Q*$ the marginal cost of producing another unit is equal to the marginal revenue obtainable from its sale. At this output, total profits are maximized.

---

[2]Robert A. Robicheaux, "How Important Is Pricing in Competitive Strategy?" in *Proceedings: Southern Marketing Association,* ed. Henry W. Nash and Donald P. Robin, January 1976, pp. 55–57.

FIGURE 13–1   Price determination in purely competitive markets

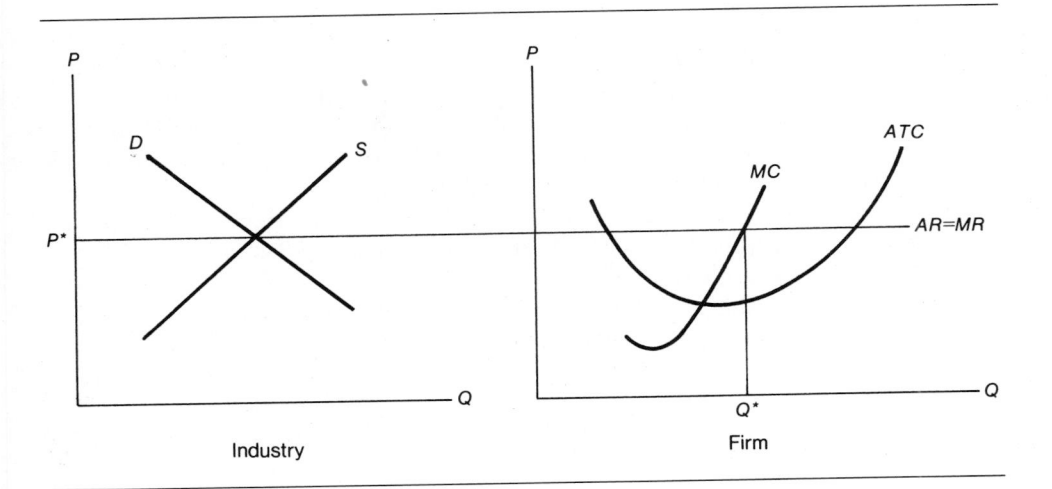

It is not our purpose to delve into price theory to any great extent, but it is important to recognize that the wheat farmer producing a homogeneous product and unable to influence the industry price by dumping wheat or withholding it from the market has no opportunity to set a price for his output. Economists characterize this type of market situation as being "purely competitive." The choices open to the farmer include the decision to sell or not to sell, the decision as to what quantity to sell, the decision to effect changes in his farm's cost structure, or the decision to go out of business if the industry price drops below his level of costs. In no event does the farmer have the opportunity to make a true pricing decision.

The other extreme in terms of market environment is illustrated by the situation faced by the owner of an isolated water source in the midst of the Arizona desert country. As far as she is concerned, she is the only firm in the industry, and her picture appears as shown in Figure 13–2.

Because she does not have to face competition from others, she takes the aggregate or industry demand schedule as her own. This schedule is simply a curve relating the number of gallons of water that can be sold to the local inhabitants at varying levels of price. Inasmuch as she has no competition, she simply adjusts her output so that she will sell quantity Q^* at price P^*. Given the nature of her cost structure, she maximizes profits at the Q^*, P^* combination. This is the classic monopoly situation in which a single seller can set his or her price to sell whatever output he or she wishes to dispose of.

FIGURE 13–2   Price determination by a monopolist

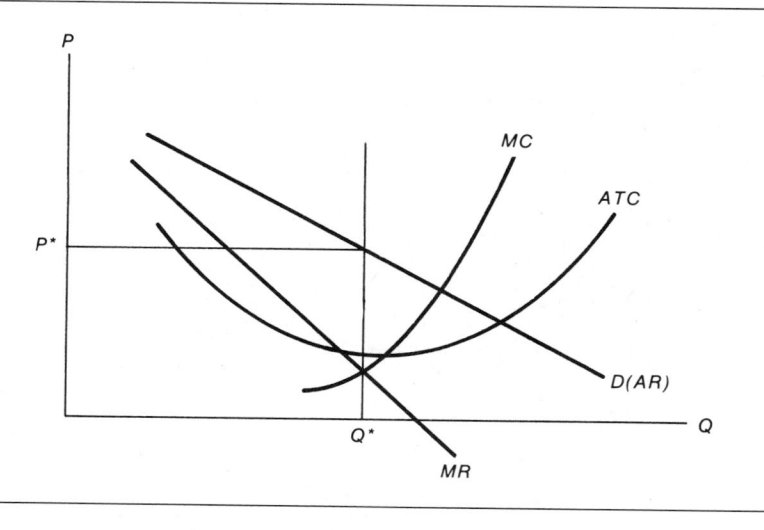

In the world of business we very rarely face either of the above types of market situations. Rather, most pricing decisions are made in market environments having characteristics of both pure competition and monopoly. Such market environments are described as being monopolistically or imperfectly competitive. In these types of markets, we find that the firm does not view the industry demand schedule as its own. Depending on the degree of selective demand developed for its output, the firm may view its demand schedule as being somewhat independent of the industry schedule. Of course, the industry demand schedule is still the aggregate of all the individual schedules of the member firms. The overall view, therefore, is of an industry schedule made up of many segments which may tilt or shift as competition or changes in buyer behavior cause changes in demand for the products of a given firm. Figure 13–3 illustrates some of these movements. Remember that this is a diagram of a firm and that, as such, it resembles the picture of the monopoly situation. The difference here is that this firm is not alone in its industry but is one firm among many. There is, in addition, relative freedom of entry or exit of firms to or from the industry.

Figure 13–3 indicates the theoretical short-run profit maximization combination of price and quantity that would result if this firm were able to calculate its marginal cost and marginal revenue data at any given instance of time. Profit is indicated by the shaded areas, and at this combination of P^* and Q^* it is at a maximum.

FIGURE 13–3 Price determination in monopolistically competitive markets

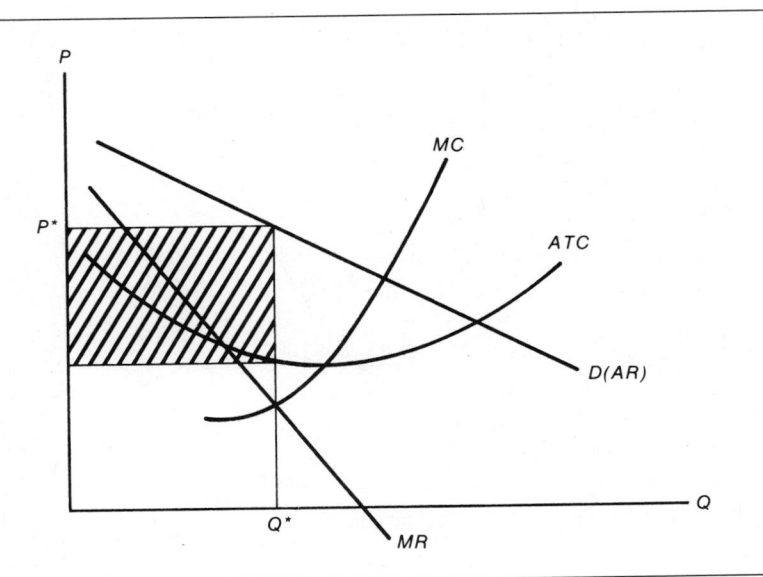

From this theoretical model can be gleaned several important insights which are helpful in considering actual problems of price determination. These include:

1. Both the industry demand schedule and the segment of the industry schedule faced by a firm are downward sloping to the right. For the industry, of course, this means that if larger and larger quantities of ouput are to be sold, the price of this output must be reduced. Shifts in the curve's position come about as a result of changes in consumer tastes for the industry's product or as a result of interindustry competition. Such shifts in the industry demand schedule may, however, be accelerated by the combined effect of the promotional activities of the individual firms in the industry.

2. Although the individual firm usually faces a demand schedule which is downward sloping to the right, it is not without recourse to certain moves which can improve its profit position. Unlike the farmer, managers of this type of firm can exercise some control over the prices they charge for their output. They can, for example, select some price other than the established industry price at which to sell their product. The extent to which they can exceed the competitive level of price is a function of the strength of the selective demand that they have been

able to create for their output. This demand is, in turn, a function of their product's value in use, distinctive features, and general availability. In addition, the ability to price above the market level is related to the effectiveness of the firm's nonprice promotional efforts and the degree of competition faced from producers of substitute products or services.

3.   The ability to price continually below the generally accepted industry level is also dependent upon the reaction of competitors. If pricing below the market level is a reflection of the firm's inferior position in terms of product features and/or market cultivation, then some price differential is probably sustainable. If the decision to price lower than competitors is the result of conscious strategy aimed at increasing market penetration, then competitive reactions of either a price or nonprice nature can be expected.

4.   The alternative of nonprice promotion has as its objective the shifting of the demand schedule to the right so that a greater quantity can be sold at a given price. Sellers would also like to get a greater slope ("tilt") in their schedule reflecting a lowered sensitivity of their demand to changes in price (especially upward changes).

In Figure 13–4 the firm is facing a demand schedule D. With price P, quantity of output Q can be sold. To sell output Q', three actions are possible:

1.   Price P can be reduced to price P'.
2.   Demand schedule D can be shifted to D' by vigorous nonprice promotion.

FIGURE 13–4   Price and nonprice moves in monopolistically competitive situations

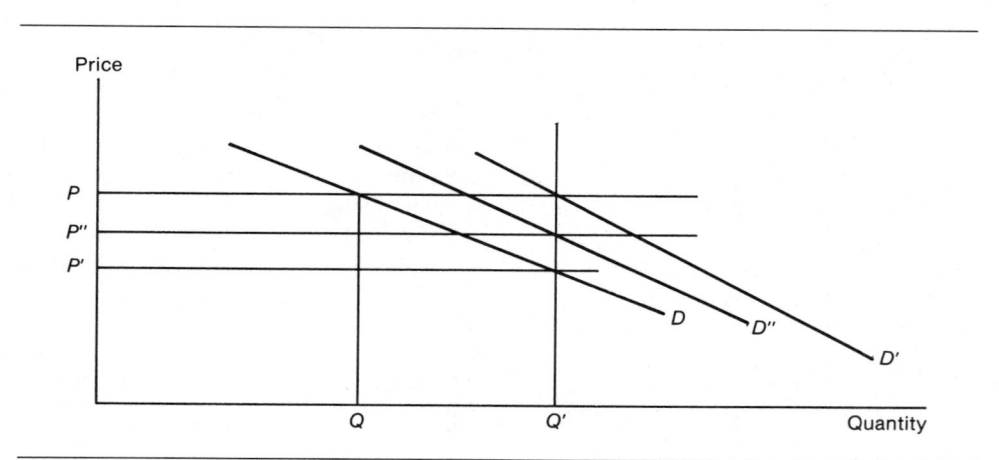

3. Some combination of lowered price and nonprice promotion can be selected, for example P'' and D''.

Note that in cases 2 and 3, which involve some shifting of the demand schedule, the "tilt" or slope increases, thus reflecting what economists call greater price inelasticity of demand or less sensitivity of demand to changes in price. (For example, a percentage change in price will cause a smaller associated percentage change in quantity demanded along schedule D' than along schedule D.)

Implications

Without becoming too involved in price theory, it becomes evident that the pricing decision is closely interrelated with several other areas, both external to the firm and internal to it. Certainly pricing managers must have a clear idea of the competitive environment in which they operate so that they can estimate the extent of pricing flexibility available to them. Although they will generally be operating under market conditions of monopolistic competition, in an ever-increasing number of situations the sellers in the industry are few in number. Then the reactions of rivals become especially important, and the pricing decision area becomes more limited. These problems of oligopoly pricing (pricing when sellers are few) will be discussed in another section of this chapter.

In addition to knowing about the competitive environment, one needs to recognize the legal restraints that limit freedom of pricing action. This area will be covered in the next chapter.

Finally, pricing decisions must be related to the overall objectives of the firm and the marketing strategy designed to reach these objectives. Pricing decisions cannot be made in a vacuum, for they involve one of "action parameters" by which the firm seeks to reach its goals in a given market environment.

PRICING OBJECTIVES

In addition to knowledge of the market environment in which prices are to be set, the marketing manager must define clearly those objectives of the firm whose attainment his or her pricing must further. As a result of a study by the Brookings Institution and an accompanying journal article by one of the principal investigators, some light has been shed on the major pricing objectives in selected large American business firms.[3]

---

[3]A. D. H. Kaplan, Joel B. Dirlam, and Robert F. Lanzillotti, *Pricing in Big Business* (Washington, D.C.: Brookings Institution, 1958); Robert F. Lanzillotti, "Pricing Objectives in Large Companies," *American Economic Review* 48, no. 5 (December 1958), pp. 921–40.

The major pricing goals pursued by the 20 firms in the sample studied were: (1) pricing to achieve a target return on investment, (2) stabilization of price and margin, (3) pricing to realize a target market share, (4) pricing to meet or prevent competition, and (5) pricing to maximize profits.[4] These and other pricing objectives classified in terms of whether they are profit, sales, or status quo oriented are illustrated in Figure 13–5.

FIGURE 13–5   Possible pricing objectives

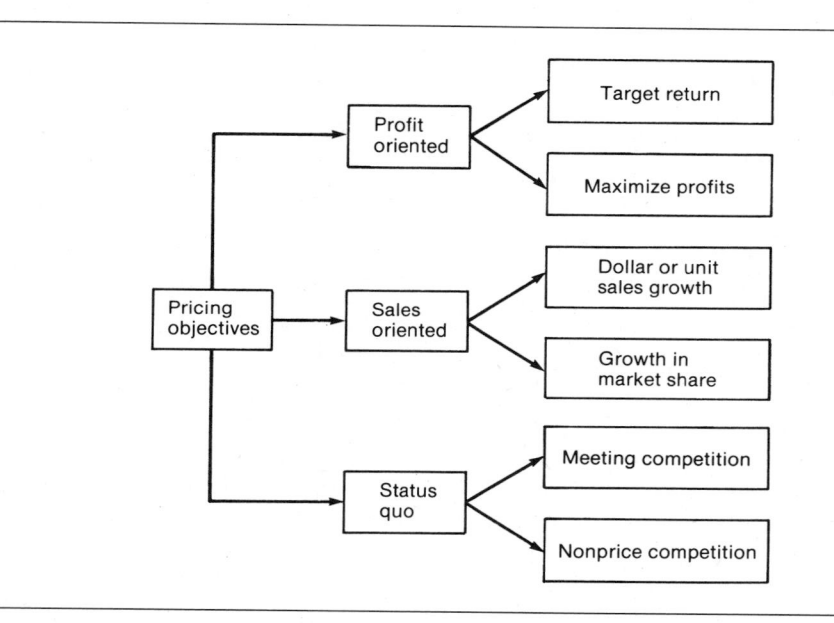

Source: E. Jerome McCarthy and William Perreault, Jr., *Basic Marketing—A Managerial Approach,* 8th ed. (Homewood, Ill.: Richard D. Irwin, 1984), p. 557.

It is not the purpose of this text to discuss these objectives in detail. It is important, however, to recognize that the major pricing decision, that of setting a basic price for a product, is related not only to the external market environment but also to the goals of the firm. Price determination is a means to an end and not an end in itself. Recognition must also be given to the fact that rarely does a firm seek only a single objective. In most cases, a combination of goals is sought. For example, a firm

---

[4]Ibid.

might seek maintenance or improvement of its market share while at the same time aiming for a target return on invested capital. This combination of goals may well describe the objectives of a large automobile manufacturing company such as General Motors or Ford.

The final goal of pricing, maximizing profits, does require some further discussion because it is rather ambiguous. Perhaps one might generalize by saying that all firms attempt to maximize profits in the long run. That is their basic objective, and all other goals, such as growth, control over markets, and freedom from excessive competition, are corollary objectives which are supportive of the goal of long-run profit maximization. In like manner, the goals of pricing are also supportive of the objective of long-run profit maximization. When, however, the pricing goal is short-run profit maximization, the situation is somewhat different. Here we have a goal which is consistent with one of the assumptions underlying the economic models discussed previously. In such a situation the economist's suggestion that short-run profits are maximized when marginal costs equal marginal revenues provides a good basic guide to price determination.

The first step in establishing a price system is to formulate an objective and state it clearly in writing. Once the price objective is agreed upon, the executives can move to the heart of price management—the actual determination of the base price of the products or services.

SETTING THE BASIC PRICE FOR A NEW PRODUCT

Assuming that the executives responsible for the pricing decision have a clear understanding of the competitive environment in which they must operate and that the pricing objectives of the firm have been specified, those executives can now begin to set the basic price for a new product.

Their first task is to find out what the demand schedule for the new product might be like in terms of its location, its slope, and its degree of shiftability. It is not necessary, however, to be concerned with the entire schedule but only with that portion of the schedule which is meaningful in terms of the specific pricing decision under consideration. Figure 13–6 might be helpful.

Price p'' is the ceiling price or estimate of the highest price that might be charged for the new product. This estimate is based on an appraisal of the new product's superiority or inferiority as compared to close substitutes as well as on the need to sell a minimum quantity of output to cover associated costs. Price p' is the minimum price at which the firm would be willing to sell, given the nature of its future costs. Such a level is generally set by the price of the lowest-priced substitute product, but

FIGURE 13–6   The zone of demand resulting from a range of prices and a shifting of the demand schedule for a new product

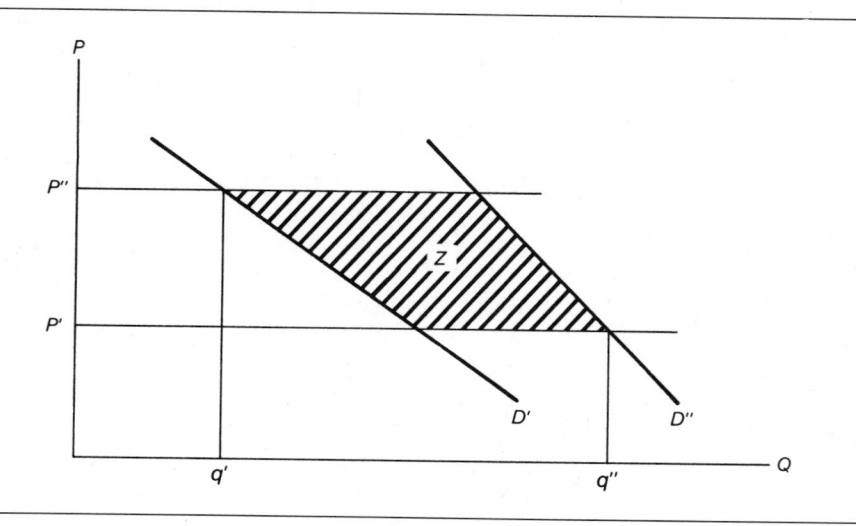

quite often strategy considerations will result in a price considerably below that of close substitutes.

D' is the demand schedule that reflects the most pessimistic estimate of consumer acceptance and/or competitive retaliation, assuming little or no nonprice promotion. D'', on the other hand, reflects the most optimistic view of consumer acceptance, considering planned nonprice promotional efforts and anticipated competitive response. The zone of demand relevant to the decision is, of course, Z, while the interval p''–p' is the range of prices under consideration and the interval q''–q' is the range of quantities that might be sold under all combinations of price and demand within their respective ranges.

Demand Estimation

Although the preceding discussion has conceptual value in terms of explaining why an estimation of demand, given a set of prices and assuming various combinations of promotional efforts (both by the firm and by its competitors), is vital to the process of price determination, it does little in the way or producing usable data. What is needed is a more concrete evaluation of product utility.

Comparison with close substitutes.   If the product is a new version of an established type of product, then, of course, some information is available as to the size of the present market for the generic product type. A careful evaluation of the relative ability of the new product to fill consumers' needs vis-à-vis available substitutes can give some idea of the share of total market that the new product might capture over time if it were priced at the current level at which close substitutes are being sold. Once this estimate has been made, consideration can be given to the effect upon sales and market share that prices slightly above or below the market level (say 10 percent) would have. This type of analysis would, of course, be highly subjective, but it would force management to estimate the new product's superiority (or inferiority) with respect to available substitutes. In addition, estimates as to the sensitivity of demand to prices slightly above or below current market levels would have to be made. By continuing to estimate possible sales at prices 15, 20, or even 25 percent over or under the current levels at which close substitutes are being sold, management can get some idea as to the location and slope of that portion of the demand schedule which is meaningful to the determination of the basic price for the new product.

Asking customers.   Estimation of demand by managers can often be improved by surveying the more astute members of the reseller organization. Wholesalers and retailers who are in closer contact with the market than are manufacturers develop an instinctive feel for what is a "right" price for a new product. They can evaluate the product's attributes from the buyer's point of view and reflect the buyer's appraisal of product utility. Such questioning of potential buyers need not stop at the reseller level but may well include the questioning of end users by means of consumer panels or of personal interviews with selected individuals. It has been suggested that the concept of the "barter equivalent" be applied in cases where the uniqueness of the new product rules out the use of a similar product as a basis of comparison.[5] In this approach the new product, surrounded by a diversity of other products whose uses and prices are well established, is placed in front of a consumer panel. The members of the panel are then requested to match up the new product with a product of roughly equivalent value. By such means, insight can be gained as to how the consumer might value a new product which cannot be compared with close generic substitutes.

Test marketing.   As the process of estimating demand at various prices proceeds, there comes a point at which an actual market test is required. Only in this way can consumer response to a price level (or a variety of price levels) be measured in a realistic manner. The market test allows demand response to be viewed under actual purchase condi-

---

[5]Joel Dean, "Pricing Policies for New Products," *Harvard Business Review,* November–December 1976, p. 145.

tions, with controlled nonprice promotional inputs, and in the face of real competition. The disadvantage of such testing is that it blunts the surprise effect of the new-product introduction upon rivals. However, in many situations in which a wrong pricing decision could be most costly, market testing is desirable even if it alerts competitors to the introduction of a new product.

Capitalization of cost savings. The steps in the process of estimating demand, which have been discussed briefly, have a very strong consumer product orientation. This is not to say that the producer of a new product for sale to the industrial market would not find comparison of the product with close substitutes useful in aiding setting a basic price. Moreover, the producer would also find the distributors most helpful in appraising the salability of the new product at a given price or over a given range of prices. What is important to note, however, is that the value in use of industrial products is easier to measure than is product utility in the consumer market. This is because industrial buyers can measure the cost savings that are likely to accrue from the use of a new product. These cost savings (which may differ by application), capitalized over the life of the new product, indicate the ceiling price which may be charged for a new product when it is used in a specific application. It is evident that if the cost savings associated with the use of a new industrial product have a present value of $1,000, the purchase price must be somewhere below this figure unless some other technical factors are involved.

Derived demand. Because the demand for industrial goods as inputs to an industrial process is derived from the demand for the output of the process, it is less sensitive to price changes than is consumer demand. When demand for the end product is stable or falling off, sales of capital equipment are limited to the replacement market and prices must reflect the cost savings which the new machine can offer over continued use of the old. In viewing the economics of replacement, it is found that a rather large price reduction would be required to cause a replacement sale to be made in the absence of technologically induced cost savings. On the other hand, when end-product sales are rising, the prices of new machinery can be raised above the level of capitalized cost savings with little effect on the quantity demanded.

Price sensitivity of demand for industrial goods varies with respect to the type of goods being considered. Moving from capital equipment to accessory equipment, component parts, and operating supplies, one finds increasing price elasticity of demand. But in almost all cases such sensitivity is less in the industrial market than in the consumer market. Derived demand and its influence have been discussed in greater detail in Chapter 5.

The purpose of demand analysis is to provide some estimates of the market's evaluation of product utility or value in use. In addition to

discovering the location of the demand schedule, some information as to its probable slope and shiftability is also needed. The end result of demand analysis, therefore, is the delineation of a range of prices acceptable to the market and the achievement of some idea of sensitivity of demand to various prices within this range. The top of this range is the demand "ceiling." The next step in the pricing process is to relate demand over the acceptable range of prices to the cost of producing output. As demand sets the ceiling on price, costs set the floor.

The Role of Costs

Although costs may be viewed as setting a floor to price, while demand constraints set the ceiling, those persons responsible for the pricing decision must recognize that there are several cost floors from which to choose. In any summation of costs for floor determination, questions arise as to the types and amounts of the costs that are to be included in the buildup. Should overhead costs, for example, be allocated on the basis of standard volume? Over how long a time should research and development costs be amortized? Should estimates of future costs be used rather than past or present costs?

In attempting to wend their way through the maze of costs and the various methods by which costs can be allocated to products, the pricing executives must keep two points in mind. First, in most cases, over the long run an individual product must bring in revenues which fully cover allocated costs and provide a reasonable profit. Second, because there is little or no causal relationship between cost and price in the short run, for the individual firm a price that fails initially to cover "full costs" may be a good price.

Cost-plus pricing.   Because of the confusion of short- and long-run goals, businesses often engage in the cost buildup process and add to the cost floor thus obtained some amount of "plus" in order to arrive at a price. The plus is either described as providing a certain percentage return on the invested capital associated with the introduction of the new product or, in a more general sense, as an attempt to guarantee that with each sale the firm will receive a predetermined margin of profit. In retrospect, however, such an approach is neither as easy as it appears to be, nor is it really safe. The question arises as to what costs are to be used for the base. Should the price setter consider past costs, present costs, or future costs? How large should the "plus" be?

Regardless of how sophisticated the approach, one thing is evident: cost-plus pricing which ignores the demand aspect of the pricing problem involves circular reasoning. Because price influences the volume that can be sold and volume affects unit costs, it is obvious that costs are determined factors in the pricing process rather than determining factors. Although the "plus" is management determined, it is often set

without a clear understanding of the consequences. Too large a "plus" can result in too high a price, too low a volume, and too high unit costs. Thus, a hefty "plus" aimed at improving gross profit per unit may prove very disappointing if the resulting price fails to fit in with the market's evaluation of product utility or fails to consider the alternatives that competitors offer potential customers.

The tier concept.   A clearer understanding of what a cost floor actually is and how its definition is relevant to the pricing decision may be gained by examining the tier concept. This is merely a way of looking at the full-cost floor in terms of its component layers, or "tiers." As illustrated in Figure 13–7, one writer has suggested that the full-cost floor may comprise as many as seven subfloors.

FIGURE 13–7   The cost components of price

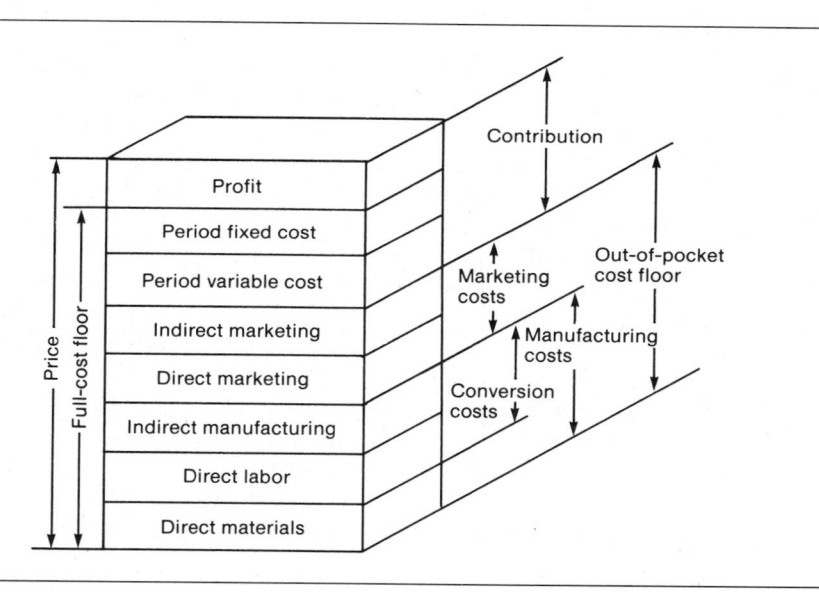

Source: Adapted from Phillip F. Ostwald, *Cost Estimating for Engineering and Management,* © 1974, p. 266. Reprinted by permission of Prentice-Hall, Inc., Englewood Cliffs, New Jersey.

In order to simplify the analysis, let us consider only three subfloors. These will be period fixed cost, period variable cost, and out-of-pocket costs. If the demand ceiling were high enough, the full-cost floor could be covered by price. This type of situation is illustrated by Figure 13–8.

FIGURE 13–8   Demand ceiling above full-cost floor

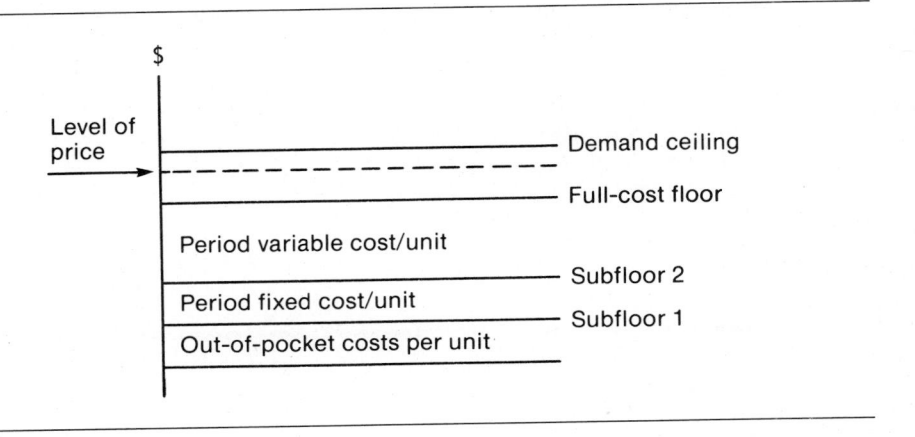

If the demand ceiling were below the full-cost floor, as illustrated in Figure 13–9, the price setter would have to consider whether or not he or she could set a price below the full-cost floor but above subfloor 1, which covers out-of-pocket costs per unit.

Such a decision to price below the full-cost floor would be feasible only if the firm produced other products which could be sold at prices high enough to make up for the lack of contribution to overhead resulting from pricing this product at less than the full-cost level. Another possible reason for initially pricing below full cost would be that such a price would, in time, bring in sufficient volume to cause a reduction in the full-cost level per unit, as illustrated in Figure 13–10.

Thus, the cost floor which the price setter uses may vary with the competitive situation faced, with the behavior of costs over time as volume changes, and with the need to have a full line or family of products. The revenues from all the products sold must, of course, cover the full costs in the long run. In the short run, however, when single products are being priced, the full-cost floor is not an absolute barrier to lower prices.

Costs and pricing strategy. In addition to setting the floor (or floors) to price, costs also enter into pricing strategy decisions. Knowledge of one's own costs, for example, provides insight into the nature of the cost structures of competitors and thus enables one to estimate better the reactions of rivals to pricing moves. Evaluation of costs also can help answer the question of whether a pricing proposal will invite competitors

FIGURE 13–9   Demand ceiling below full-cost floor

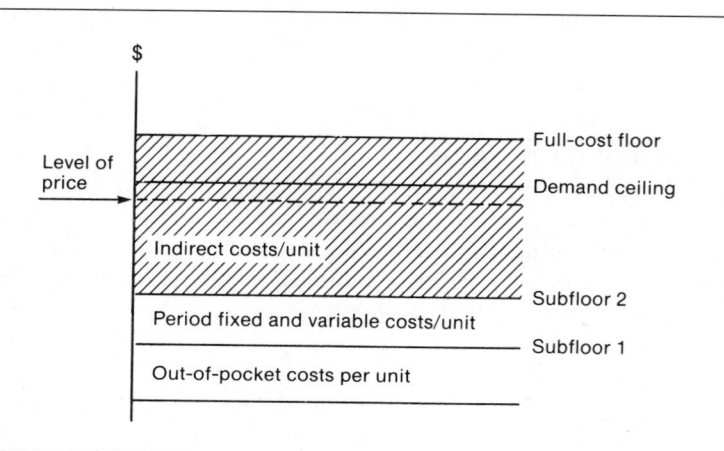

FIGURE 13–10   A dynamic view of the cost floor–demand ceiling relationship

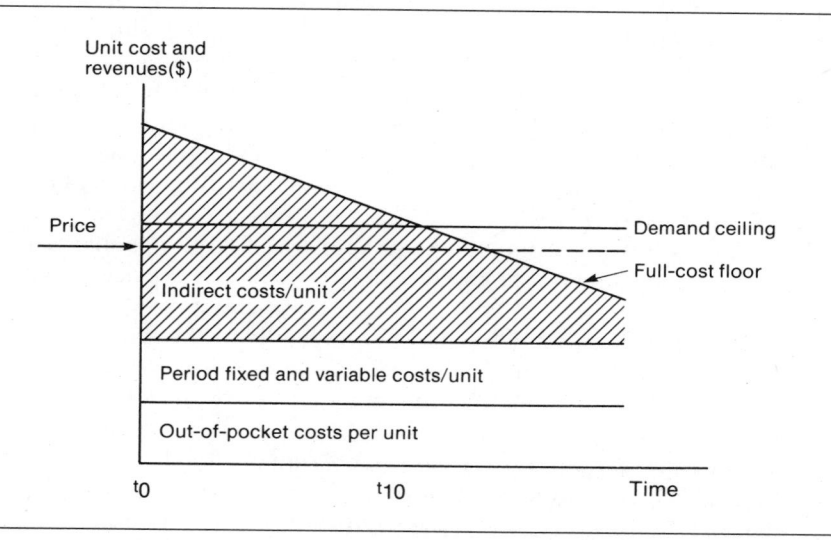

into the market or whether it will discourage their entry. Finally, knowledge of costs can help the firm decide whether to make a component or to buy it on the outside.

There will be a further discussion of pricing strategy a little later on. At this point, however, it is advisable to examine an approach in which demand and costs are considered together.

THE INTERACTIVE APPROACH

It is far safer to view the pricing process as the interaction of costs and demand rather than as a sole function of either. If the firm starts with costs and tests various cost buildups against demand, the dangers associated with a purely cost-plus approach may be averted. In like manner, starting with demand and working back to costs is a more desirable approach than straight cost-plus pricing. Of course, in recommending the interactive approach, it is assumed that the pricing decision is concerned with manufactured goods which, although new, are not totally unknown (in a generic sense) to the market. In those cases where the product being sold is a highly specialized custom-built item purchased by a single buyer, cost-plus may be the only feasible way in which a price can be set.

Break-Even Analysis

In using the interactive approach to price determination, some method of visualizing the relationships among fixed costs, variable costs, volume, and price, and the effects of these relationships on profit is almost a necessity. Break-even analysis is such a method. It calls attention to the various types of costs involved, such as those which are fixed over the range of output, those which vary with output, and those which vary with executive decisions. The analysis also allows management to visualize a series of preliminary prices which are then evaluated in terms of volume possibilities.

With known or estimated costs and a series of possible prices, the volume requirements to break even for any given price proposal are identified.

Break-even analysis also shows how rapidly profits can be increased if volume above the break-even level can be secured. In like manner, the analysis shows management the size of the loss at volumes below the break-even level.

In Figure 13–11 those costs which remain fixed over the range of outputs to be considered are estimated to be $10,000. Those costs which vary with output are zero at zero output and $10,000 at 500 units of output. They are $20 per unit in this illustration, where variable costs

FIGURE 13–11   A break-even chart

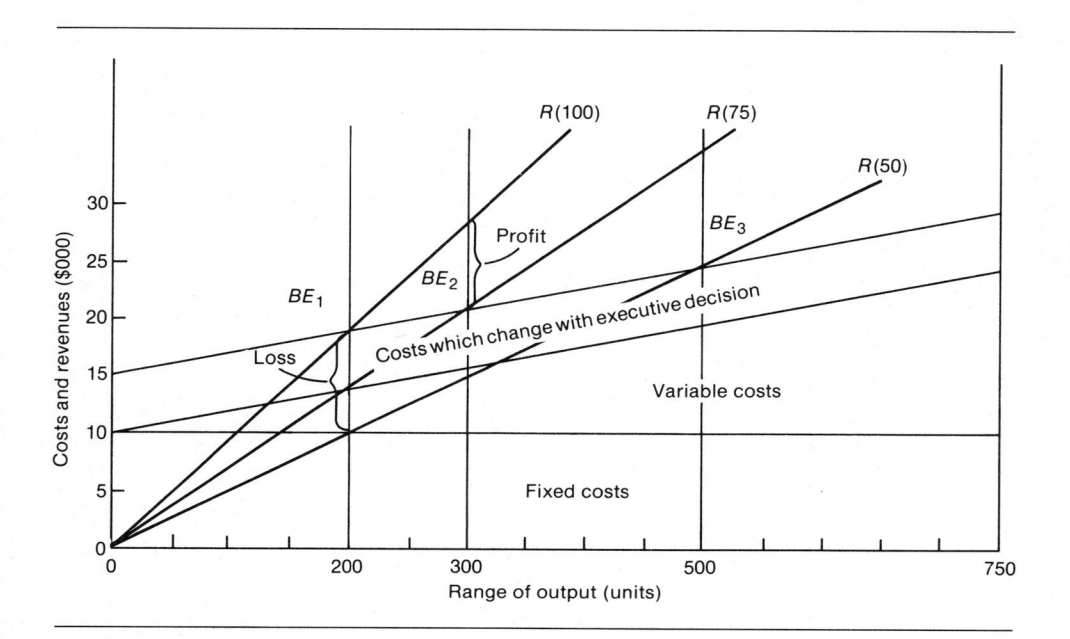

are assumed to vary directly with output. This assumption is not necessary for the analysis, as costs which vary with output on a nonlinear basis could be portrayed by an appropriate curved line. In similar manner, fixed costs which change abruptly at different levels of output could be illustrated by means of a step function.

The last element of the cost buildup is that which represents the costs associated with specific executive policies, for example, those relating to nonprice promotional efforts. In Figure 13–11 they are shown as being constant over the range of output and of the magnitude of $5,000. Thus, from zero to 750 units of output, total costs vary from $15,000 to $30,000.

Looking now at the revenue side of the picture, one sees three revenue lines, each associated with a price proposal. The first price suggested is $100 per unit; the second, $75 per unit; and the third, $50 per unit. Each revenue line indicates the extent of gross income (price times volume) forthcoming from the associated price proposal over the range of outputs.

The volume requirements needed to cover costs (or to break even) for each price proposal are clearly seen to be 200 units at $100, 300

units at $75, and 500 units at $50. Profits are shown by the vertical distances between the total costs and the revenue line to the right of the break-even point. For example, at a price of $100 per unit, break-even occurs when 200 units are sold. If 300 units are sold, profits would be about $8,000 as shown by the line segment labeled "profit." Losses are shown by vertical distances between the total costs and revenues to the left of a given break-even point. For example, at a price of $50, break-even occurs when 500 units are sold. If only 200 units are sold, the loss is approximately $8,000, as shown by the line segment labeled "loss."

The use of break-even analysis requires that levels of demand must be estimated for each price proposal. These estimates must take into account not only the impact of price but also the effects of the other elements of the associated marketing strategy mix and the likely reaction of competitors.

An approach to the problem of estimating the demand response to a given price proposal which has operational value has been suggested by Darden.[6] He recommends that a probability distribution of sales volumes be developed for each price proposal and that the expected value of the distribution then be related to the volume needed to break even, given the cost consequences of the proposal. Figure 13–12 illustrates such a linkage.

As can be seen, three estimates of sales volume must be made for each price proposal, with full consideration being given to the other strategy mix variables and to the environmental constraints. Thus, for any price proposal (P_n) three estimates of sales volume must be made: a most likely estimate (Q_m), a pessimistic estimate (Q_p), and an optimistic estimate (Q_o). By instructing the estimators to choose Q_m as the most likely value and Q_p and Q_o as values with a probability of occurrence of 0.01, a beta probability distribution can be used to approximate the distribution of sales volumes likely to occur, given a specific price proposal.

By using a beta distribution as an approximation of reality, the expected value of sales volume (Q_E) can be calculated for any Q_m, Q_p, and Q_o. The appropriate formula is as follows:

$$Q_E = \frac{Q_p + 4Q_m + Q_o}{6}$$

The use of the beta distribution allows the estimators to skew the distribution to the high side or the low side or to allow it to be symmetrical to the most likely value. In Figure 13–12 the beta distribution is skewed to the high, or optimistic, side so that it will be consistent with the following example.

Given a price proposal of $75 per unit, the estimators felt that the most likely sales volume (Q_m) would be 500 units, the pessimistic estimate

<hr>

[6]Bill R. Darden, "An Operational Approach to Product Pricing," *Journal of Marketing*, April 1968, pp. 29–33.

FIGURE 13–12   Use of three volume estimates to fit a beta distribution
at a given price of $75

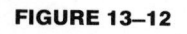

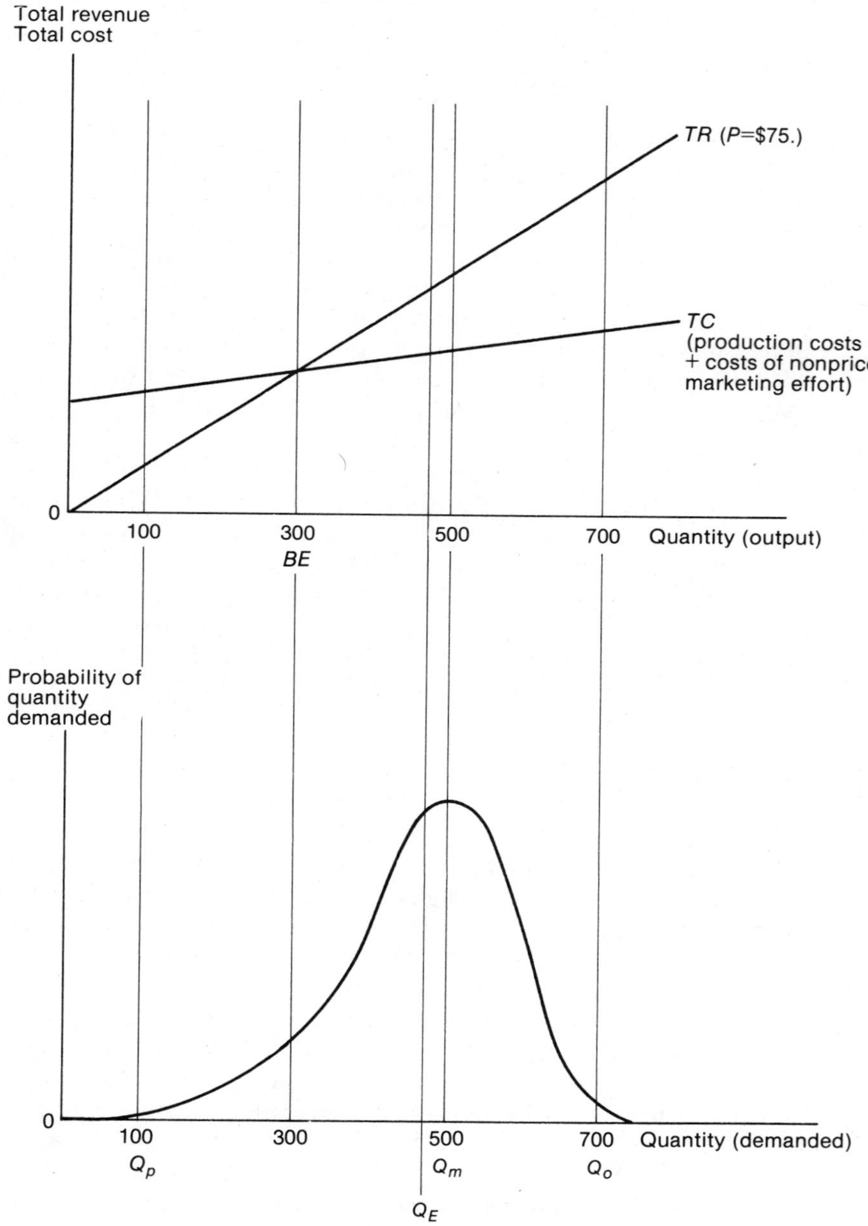

Total revenue
Total cost

TR (*P*=$75.)

TC
(production costs
+ costs of nonprice
marketing effort)

0

100   300   500   700   Quantity (output)

BE

Probability of
quantity
demanded

0

100   300   500   700   Quantity (demanded)

Q_p Q_m Q_o

Q_E

(Q_p) would be 100 units, and the optimistic estimate (Q_o) would be 700 units. Thus the expected sales volume can be calculated.

$$Q_E = \frac{100 + 4(500) + 700}{6} = 467$$

Returning to Figure 13–12 (which has been based on Figure 13–11), it can be seen that the expected value of 467 is above the break-even point of 300 units, and thus the proposal should be a profitable one. The estimators do not know, however, whether it is the optimal proposal. What is required now is the evaluation of a series of proposals to find out which one generates the largest difference (expected profit) between expected revenue and the associated costs.

An analysis of Figure 13–12 also indicates whether or not the downside risk for a given price proposal is large. In the example at hand, it can be seen that the bulk of the probability density lies above the 300-unit mark. Only if one of the more pessimistic estimates actually occurs will the sales volume be below break-even; and if the demand estimates are correct, the probability of such an occurrence is quite small.

Value and limitations of break-even analysis.   Break-even analysis is a useful technique in balancing demand and cost factors in the process of determining price. It requires of the pricing executive estimates of demand at different levels of price, and then it indicates the behavior of costs at the various levels of output associated with the different price proposals. Of course, the quality of the analysis can be no better than the quality of the cost-data and demand-data inputs, but the very nature of the approach forces a consideration of the interaction of demand and costs. As such, break-even analysis clearly indicates that neither cost nor volume is solely determinative of price.

PRICING STRATEGY

Having a clear understanding of how the pricing decision is related to the achievement of the objectives of the enterprise and being familiar with a range of possible prices given the demand and cost constraints, pricing executives can then consider those strategies that might be followed to attain the desired goals. In this area of decision, executives often share feelings held by military officers who are planning an assault on the enemy. In both the business and military environments, consideration must be given to the options available, the resources at one's disposal, the possible reactions of the enemy, and the consistency of one's moves with other elements of the overall program. Thus, pricing strategy, like military strategy, is uniquely associated with the available opportunities and the means on hand for their exploitation.

It is senseless to talk of strategy unless alternatives are available. As-

sume, for example, that pricing executives face a situation in which the price they can set is limited on the high side by competition and on the low side by the full-cost floor. If the distance between the floor and the ceiling is fairly large, the executives have some discretion as to whether to set the price near the ceiling or near the floor or somewhere in between the two extremes. If the floor and the ceiling are closer together, the discretionary range is smaller. It may even be nonexistent if the floor and the ceiling coincide or if the floor is above the ceiling.

Let us look at situations A, B, and C in order to see what strategies might be available in each case. In situation A, where the range of discretion is fairly wide, the price might be set up near the demand ceiling. This would be a "skim" type of strategy, in which a high initial price for a new product would be set to "skim the cream" off the market. Such a strategy could be expected to work over a period of time only if the product were protected from competition because of its technical or design uniqueness. If such were the case and the demand ceiling held at its original level over time, a skim-pricing strategy accompanied by heavy nonprice promotion would offer considerable advantage.

Certain other attributes of a situation might suggest a skim strategy. Limited production facilities, need to recoup research and development expenses, and unclear nature of demand would all indicate that a high-price, limited-volume strategy would be best at the beginning. Such a strategy would be even more effective if the market could be divided into segments and promotion could be directed to those segments where demand was relatively insensitive to price.

The advantages of a skim strategy are great when product uniqueness provides protection from competition, thus allowing a high initial price to provide for new-product introduction by means of generous trade margins and nonprice promotion. There are, however, situations in which a strategy of a low initial price might be called for. If, for example, the new product were of a type generally known to the consumer, if competition were a strong threat, if demand were estimated to be sensitive to price, and if sizable economies of production were associated with volume, then a low initial or "penetration" price might be superior to a higher one. It would allow the product to gain a mass market quickly, thus moving in ahead of competition. The low price would not allow for much nonprice promotion or for wide trade margins, but because of the sensitivity of demand to a low price, nonprice promotional efforts could be kept to a minimum. Finally, even if price were set at the full-cost floor, over time, as production economies took effect, the floor would be lowered, thus producing greater profits. Figure 13–13 illustrates in a more graphic way the criteria that might be applied to a skim versus penetration decision.

Situation B in Figure 13–14 is a variant of situation A. In this second example the floor and the ceiling are much closer together and the

FIGURE 13–13   Criteria for choosing between market penetration or skimming as pricing goals when pricing new products

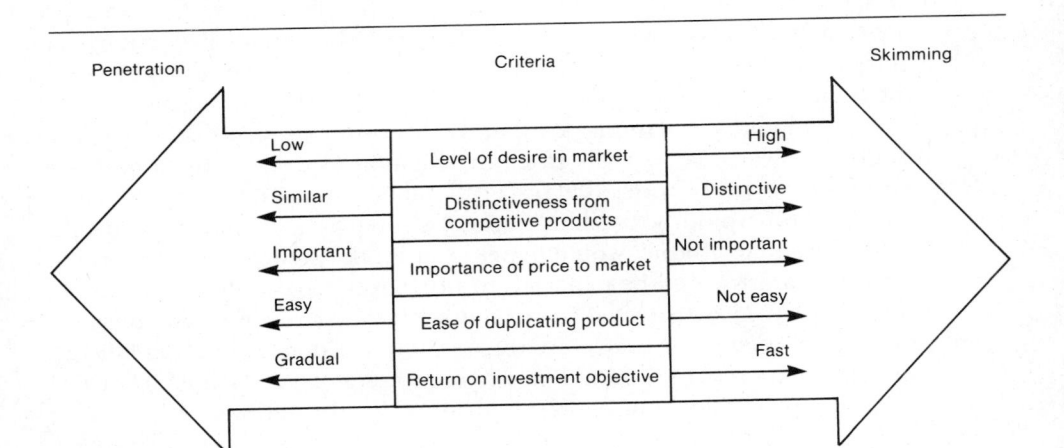

Source: Richard T. Hise, Peter L. Gillette, and John K. Ryans, Jr., *Basic Marketing: Concepts and Decisions* (Cambridge, Mass.: Winthrop Publishers, 1979).

FIGURE 13–14   Illustration of three floor–ceiling combinations

Demand ceiling ————— D

Range of discretion

Full-cost floor ————— C_f

A

Demand ceiling ————— D

Range of discretion

Full-cost floor ————— C_f

B

Full-cost floor ————— C_f

Demand ceiling ————— D

Out-of-pocket cost floor ————— C_o

C

range of discretion is more limited. In situation C the demand ceiling (D) is actually below the full-cost floor (C_f). This means that the product's value in use is less than the producer's full costs of manufacturing and marketing or that competitors offer close substitutes at prices lower than the producer's costs. In this type of situation, the manufacturer faces

the alternative of either not introducing the product or of placing it on the market at a price under the present full-cost floor but above a cost subfloor such as the one representing out-of-pocket costs. A strategy of pricing below full costs might be indicated when cost reductions are anticipated with volume or when the product is an essential part of a line and must be placed on the market even if its price will only cover part of its cost of production and marketing. If the price can cover out-of-pocket costs, some contribution to overhead may be forthcoming. Placing a new product on the market at a price below its present full costs may be a profitable move, especially when the new product is viewed as a member of a family of products, each making a different-sized contribution to overhead and profit.

Strategy over time.   The discussion of pricing strategy to this point has been essentially in static terms or at the very best has dealt with pricing in the short run. The concepts of demand ceilings or cost floors, although helpful in determining the range of discretion open to the price setter at the time of new-product introduction, can be dangerously misleading if it is not viewed in a dynamic context. Demand ceilings change over time, as do cost floors, and the price setter must be aware of these changes and anticipate them by changes in strategy.

We have already spoken of the case in which the price of a new product is set high to tap those segments of the market in which demand is relatively inelastic and in which the need is great to bring in revenues quickly. We have also looked at situations in which the initial price might be set close to the full-cost floor or even below it. There are strategies, however, in which future product and/or market changes are considered. One such strategy has been called "sliding down the demand curve."[7] The firm following such a strategy starts with a high initial price emphasizing value more than cost in an attempt to skim the cream from successive market segments. However, the firm anticipates competition and reduces price faster than is required by the market. Thus, potential competition is forestalled, and the firm becomes an established volume producer over time with a price approaching the level that a penetration-pricing strategy would have required initially.

Because new products age in that they lose their aura of uniqueness or face increasing competition from substitutes, pricing strategies suited to the introductory stage of the product's life cycle must be amended over time. As competition increases, prices are forced down and price becomes the dominant element in the promotional mix. When brand preference weakens and private brands enter in force, there is little left to do but reduce prices promptly to forestall private-brand competition.

---

[7]D. Maynard Phelps and J. Howard Westing, *Marketing Management,* 3d ed. (Homewood, Ill.: Richard D. Irwin, 1968), p. 326.

This is merely the acceptance of the fact that in the mature stage of the product life cycle, competition is largely on a price basis.

Strategy options and market situations. The market share held by a firm in a given market and the rate of growth of that market can have considerable influence on the range of options available to the pricing strategist. As is illustrated in Figure 13–15, when the share of market held by the firm is high and when markets are growing rapidly, a wide range of pricing strategies are available. Premium pricing, price leadership, price maintenance, or even penetration strategies are feasible. In contrast, firms with low shares of slowly growing markets can do little more than emphasize price and meet the competitive level.

FIGURE 13–15   Pricing options under different market situations

		Market Share	
		High	Low
Market Growth	High	Maintain price Price leadership Meet competitors' prices Penetration pricing Set high prices	Premium pricing Meet competitors' prices Follow the leader Skimming pricing
	Low	Hold steady Meet lower prices Protect market share Initiate lower prices if necessary	Price emphasis Meet competitors' prices

Source: William Lazer and James D. Cully, *Marketing Management Foundations and Practices* (Boston: Houghton Mifflin, 1983), p. 549.

PRICE REDETERMINATION

In addition to the problem of determining a price for a new product, marketing executives are often faced with the problem of changing the price of an established product. This process is called "price redetermination," and the problems arising from it differ somewhat from those associated with the determination of initial price. Essentially, these differences are an outgrowth of the aging of the product. The problems of pricing in the competitive or mature stages of product life are less involved with uncertainty than are those dealing with the pricing of a

product in the introductory stages of its development. In the competitive stage, for example, more is known about demand. The degree of sensitivity of demand to changes in the producer's promotional mix, to actions of competitors, and to variations in the overall economic environment is understood with greater clarity. In like manner, the producer has a clearer picture of his or her production and marketing costs with an established product than with a new one.

Motivation for Redetermination

Management may decide to change a price for several reasons. It may be necessary to raise or lower a price to reflect a modification in the market's valuation of a product. On the other hand, the change may be the result of variations in costs of production, distribution, or promotion. Or the price move may come about to increase market share or to gain some other competitive advantage. Finally, a defensive price change may be made to meet the price or nonprice moves of rivals.

Changes in market valuation.   If demand for a given product slackens over time and if there have been no overt changes in the producer's promotional mix or the actions of competitors, then it is quite obvious that changes have taken place in the market. Perhaps the market segment composed of prospects who placed a high value in use on the product has been saturated. Or perhaps the novelty aspects of the product have worn off, and consumers have turned elsewhere to spend their money. Regardless of causation, the producer must readjust the promotional mix to conform to the realities of the marketplace. Such a readjustment usually entails a reduction in price to enable the producer to tap segments of the market in which demand is more sensitive to a price reduction than to additional nonprice promotion.

Changes in costs.   Although demand is usually the controlling factor in the pricing of fabricated goods, cost changes can have a motivating or triggering effect on price redetermination. For example, cost reductions associated with volume production may allow price reductions that will either help maintain current volume levels or increase them. Price redetermination which is associated with a declining cost floor has several strategic implications which will be discussed shortly.

In contrast, product cost increases associated with (1) declining volume, (2) rising labor and/or material costs, or (3) both factors may force consideration of higher product prices. The decision to raise price is, of course, influenced by the general sensitivity of demand to price and by the possible reaction of competitors. Thus, it is quite evident that although cost changes might motivate price changes for established products, whether or not such changes are made depends on demand factors, that is, on how consumers value the product and what substitutes are available to them.

Changes in strategy.   Price redetermination, especially in the downward direction, may be used to implement a new marketing strategy. As was noted earlier, a desire to "slide down the demand curve" requires frequent evaluation of the competitive situation and correctly timed price reductions. Through these reductions the firm hopes to tap successive layers of demand which vary in price sensitivity. Timing is crucial, as the reductions must be made early enough to dissuade competitive entry or to catch off guard those rivals who are already in the market.

Price increases that are made as part of a process of redetermination also have strategic implications. For a firm with a highly differentiated product, a move to a higher level of price may reflect product superiority. The higher price may well bolster the quality image of the line. Such upward moves are, of course, easier to sustain when nonprice promotional efforts have created a strong selective demand for the product. Price redetermination on the upside may reflect a decision to pursue a high-price, limited-volume strategy by reblending the marketing mix to give price a lesser role in relation to the other elements.

Changes in competition.   Price changes, either upward or downward, after initial introduction of a product may be necessary to adjust to the actions of competitors. Such changes become especially necessary when there are only a few sellers.

Let us start with a market situation in which there are many sellers in the industry and selective demand for the products of individual sellers varies from weak to strong. In this type of environment, the firm that develops the strongest demand for its product would have the greatest degree of flexibility in dealing with competitive change of a price or nonprice variety. The firms with weak selective demand would find that demand for their products would be very much affected by the price or nonprice moves of rivals. Because of lack of product differentiation or other reasons which have denied them strong selective demand, the response of these "weak demand" firms is very much limited to changes in price. Thus, for a very large number of sellers in markets which are monopolistically competitive, price is the major vehicle by which adjustments are made to competitor-invoked change.

Price redetermination when sellers are few.   The problem of price redetermination becomes especially complex when the number of sellers in the industry is small and the degree of product differentiation is slight. The economist would call such a market situation an example of a nondifferentiated or pure oligopoly. In such an environment a firm would have to be very careful about redetermining its prices because such a redetermination could under certain conditions result in a redetermination of the *industry* price level and the industry marketing mix. As the degree of product differentiation increases when sellers are few, the extent of price differences among them may also increase. There still comes a point, however, when a price move by one firm will cause an industrywide reaction.

Perhaps some idea of the short-run price behavior of firms in oligopolistic industries may be gained by viewing the "kinked" oligopoly demand curve.

In Figure 13–16, p is the industry price or the modal value of the cluster of industry prices. If a firm in the industry raises its price to $p +$, one of two responses can be expected. If the rest of the firms in the industry feel that strength of demand or pressures of cost suggest an upward readjustment of industry price, they may follow the first firm up to price $p +$. In this case the operative demand schedule for the initiating firm would be the segment D'' above the intersection with D'. This segment is relatively inelastic because all suppliers of close substitutes have also raised their prices.

FIGURE 13–16   Kinked oligopoly demand curve

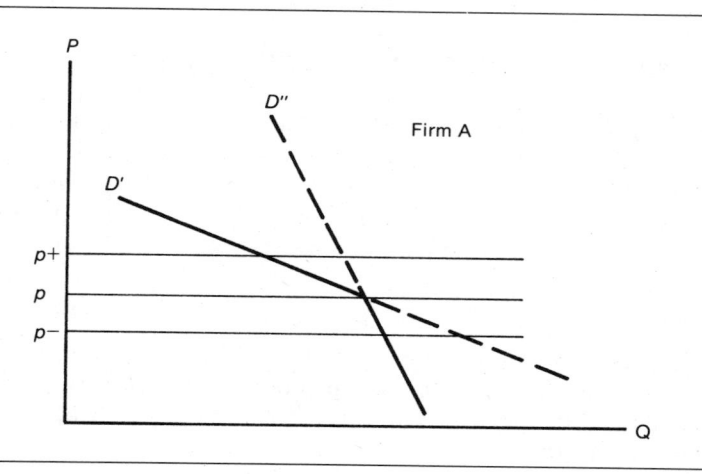

On the other hand, if the other firms do not follow the initiating firm, a great deal of the initiator's patronage will shift to the firms in the industry which offer lower prices. Thus, in this situation the demand curve which is operative for the initiating firm is the segment of D' above the intersection with D''. It is highly elastic, for demand falls off rapidly for the firm which raises its price above the industry level but does not have the degree of selective demand to support the differential in price.

Looking at the downside, we see a similar pattern of behavior. If the initiating firm drops its price to $p-$ and the rest of industry is forced to follow, schedule D'' downward from the intersection with D' becomes

operative. It is relatively inelastic for the initiating firm because all firms in the industry have matched the move. An important question to raise here, however, is, What effect will a lower industry price level have on industry demand?

If the initiating firm lowers its price and is not followed, then, of course, it will gain a great deal of patronage at the expense of its rivals. In this case the demand schedule D' downward from the intersection with D'' would be operative. Because rivals would react quickly, this highly elastic segment would not be operative for long, if at all.

It can be seen from this brief discussion that price redetermination when product differentiation is weak and/or sellers are few is quite a touchy task. This is because price moves by the firm are closely related to the reactions of rivals. In like manner, price moves by rivals have an important effect on the firm. In many situations, therefore, price redetermination by a firm is forced upon it by competition. When a firm itself initiates a price change, especially in an oligopolistic industry, it is actually proposing a readjustment of the relative importance of price in the *industry's* marketing mix.

PRICING A NEW ADDITION TO THE PRODUCT LINE

The problem of pricing a new product is compounded when the new product is to be part of an existing group or line of products. The products involved may be physically distinct, or they may be physically similar but sold under different demand conditions reflecting value-in-use, seasonal, or life-cycle variations.

Cost Interdependence

In many situations, prices for new additions to the product line are made on the basis of costs. Dean reports that common policies include setting price proportional to full cost, setting price proportional to incremental costs, or setting price to provide profit margins that are proportional to conversion costs.[8]

Using cost as the sole basis by which to set the price for a new addition to the line can be dangerous. Many of the costs of producing and marketing the new product are overhead costs or joint costs. Allocation or separation of these costs may be impossible, and therefore any attempt to determine the full-cost floor for the new addition will require that costs be applied on an arbitrary basis. Even if direct or incremental costs are used, too great an orientation to the cost side can cause management to lose sight of the reasons for the introduction of the new product. Cost

---

[8]Joel Dean, "Problems of Product Line Pricing," *Journal of Marketing*, January 1950, pp. 519–20.

pricing which ignores variations in demand or in competition may cause the firm to forego opportunities for market segmentation.[9]

Demand Interdependence

The main economic issue raised when a new product is added to the line is not usually concerned with costs. It is concerned, rather, with demand interdependence. Is the new product a complement or a substitute? Can the new product be used as an instrument for market segmentation and/or price discrimination? The answers to questions such as these, which have a strong demand orientation, are useful in finding the "right" price for a new addition to an established line.

The pricing of a new member of the product line, like the pricing of an individual new product, must be an outgrowth of overall strategy. Is the goal of the firm to increase its penetration of specific market segments? Does the firm wish to favor certain items in the line over others? Is the firm committed to a policy of "full-line" pricing whose goal is to set an array of prices for members of the line so that the total contribution of the line is maximized?

Given a clear understanding of the firm's goals for the longer run, the pricing decision in the short run assumes a strategic as well as a purely economic character. Perhaps a view of two diverse situations will offer a better view of the problem.

A substitute product.   A large manufacturer of industrial chemicals had developed a nontoxic solvent for degreasing metal parts. The basic chemical in this product was produced as a by-product of another process and thus carried a low cost burden. The new solvent was superior to carbon tetrachloride, the currently used chemical. The firm which made the new solvent was one of the largest producers of carbon tetrachloride. It sold about 20 percent of its output to the solvent market and 80 percent as a raw material for the subsequent manufacture of chlorinated hydrocarbons.

The new chemical was clearly a substitute for the established product in the solvent market. If the new product were priced somewhat higher than the old, it could displace carbon tetrachloride in applications where toxicity was a major problem. If the product were priced equal to, or slightly lower than, carbon tetrachloride (as the cost floor readily allowed), considerable displacement would occur. In fact, preliminary market research indicated that if priced at the level of carbon tetrachloride, the new product would almost completely take over the cold-cleaning solvent market.

The question which faced the manufacturer was whether or not a relatively low price on the new product and its subsequent penetration

[9]C. N. Davisson, "Pricing the Product Line," unpublished technical note, Business Administration Library, The University of Michigan.

of the cold-cleaning market would invite competitors to cut their prices on carbon tetrachloride. If this were to happen, the gains in revenues from an increased share of the solvent market would be more than counterbalanced by losses in revenues in those markets where carbon tetrachloride was purchased as a raw material.

Thus, the issue facing the manufacturer in pricing the new addition to the line concerned the cross-elasticity of demand not only between items in the line but also between the market segments served by the firm and its rivals.

A complementary product. In another situation a firm which produced home appliance appliances found that it was losing business to competitors because its line did not include a small portable mixer. To remedy this weakness the firm developed a new mixer which on the basis of cost estimates would have to be sold at a price 10 percent above the price of competing products in order to make an average contribution. Careful evaluation indicated that product superiority was not sufficient to warrant the price premium, and the decision was made to price the new product at a competitive level. It was felt that although the product was somewhat better than competing items, it would be sold at the price which would guarantee market acceptance, even if the revenues received barely covered the direct costs. The manufacturer reasoned that the new product would stimulate sales of the rest of the line and that total contribution was more important to the firm than was the contribution of any one item in the line.

Dual relationships.[10] In addition to being a substitute or a complement, a product well may be both. For example, in the case of the solvent manufacturer we viewed the new product as a substitute for the old. If, however, the addition of the new product enabled the manufacturer to attract new customers, to strengthen the distributor organization, or to gain fuller coverage for the line, the demand interrelationship between the new product and the rest of the line would be one of complementarity. In similar fashion, if the portable mixer that was developed to fill a gap in the line of the home appliance manufacturer shifted sales away from the standard mixer, then a substitute relationship would exist.

Implications

If a new product is added to a line to implement the firm's marketing strategy, as is usually the case, the demand factors must dominate the pricing decision. The degree of flexibility open to management is, however, limited by the extent of demand interdependence between the new product, existing products in the line, and the products of competitors.

As is the case with individual products, costs set the floor for the price of an addition to a product line. Management does have considerably

---

[10]Ibid.

more discretion in defining the cost floor when adding a product to an existing line than when introducing a single product. This flexibility arises from management's ability to apportion revenues received across the line to the coverage of direct and indirect costs.

While gaining some flexibility on the cost side, the firm probably loses some on the demand side, as has been noted above. As demand is probably the prime determinant of price, in most cases there is a net loss in flexibility when setting the price for a new addition to a line. This loss in flexibility, however, need not prevent a price setter from tapping specific market segments on the basis of price. Market opportunities are always present, and only a constant appraisal of demand will make their exploitation possible. A continuing process of demand appraisal is especially important when demand interrelationships change over the product's life cycle to such an extent that price redetermination may be necessary.

CONCLUSION

In this chapter we have considered the role of price in the marketing mix. In contrast to the other mix elements which absorb revenues while providing differential advantage, price is a competitive device which is also a revenue producer. While in the past price decisions were not accorded top importance by marketing managers, a decade marked by inflation and recession has caused these same executives to upgrade their estimates and move pricing into first position vis-à-vis the other mix elements.

The steps that are recommended in setting a price include making an estimate of the competitive environment in which the firm operates, setting clear objectives for the firm which the pricing decision can help to achieve, determining the constraints emanating from the supply as well as the demand side of the pricing equation, and developing a strategy for an initial price for a new-product introduction.

The chapter next covered the need to redetermine prices of established products when demand and/or cost situations change. Finally, attention was paid to a consideration of the complementary or substitute effects which might be engendered when a price is specified for a new addition to an existing line of products.

QUESTIONS

1. Why is it generally suggested that the nonprice aspects of marketing strategy be determined before the pricing decision is made?

2. What is the value, if any, to a pricing decision maker of the economist's models of price determination in diverse market situations?

3. Can a firm have differing pricing objectives in the short run as opposed to the long run? Can a firm have more than one pricing objective for the same time period? Explain.

4. Why is demand estimation so vital to the process of price determination? How might one go about estimating demand for a new consumer product? A new industrial product?

5. What is meant by "cost-plus" pricing? What are the advantages and limitations of this approach?

6. What is meant by a "cost floor"? What is the "tier concept," and what is the pertinence of this concept to pricing decisions?

7. "Break-even analysis cannot determine a price." Comment on the preceding statement, and if you agree, indicate the value, if any, of such analysis to the pricing decision maker.

8. Describe those characteristics of a situation which would indicate the use of an initial strategy of pricing near the demand ceiling; of pricing near the full-cost floor; of pricing below the full-cost floor.

9. Can cost floors change over time? Explain.

10. Why must prices be redetermined on a periodic basis?

11. Union Carbide Corporation is a large producer of ethylene glycol, a chemical used as an antifreeze. It supplies this product in bulk to private labelers and packagers. Union Carbide also sells large quantities of ethylene glycol under its well-known Prestone brand.

    Wyandotte Chemical Company, which supplies ethylene glycol antifreeze only in bulk to private branders, announced an increase in price from $1.24 per gallon in truckload lots to $1.345 per gallon.

    The Wall Street Journal reported that Union Carbide as well as Olin Mathieson and Allied Chemical Company, other producers of ethylene glycol, were studying Wyandotte's move.

    a. How should Union Carbide Corporation executives reason before deciding whether or not to raise ethylene glycol prices to the level set by Wyandotte?

    b. How should Union Carbide Corporation reason if, contrary to the above situation, Union Carbide contemplates assuming the role of price leader by initiating an increase in ethylene glycol prices with Wyandotte's reaction being uncertain?

12. How does the problem of pricing a new addition to a product line differ from the problem of pricing a single new product?

13. Does each product in a product line have to cover its full costs in the short run? In the long run? Explain.

PRICE POLICIES

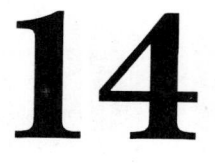

14

This chapter will discuss certain policy alternatives open to those in management who are responsible for the administration of prices. These alternatives range from immediate departure from the established price to the maintenance of the level of price over the longer run. The discussion, therefore, will cover such topics as price variation, discounts and discount policy, geographic pricing, and resale-price maintenance. In each of these areas attention will be focused on the marketing significance of the policy as well as those legal constraints which are likely to be encountered.

INTRODUCTION

A central theme of this chapter is that price policies, whether aimed at price variation or price maintenance, are promotional instruments and should be considered as means by which the firm attempts to implement its overall marketing strategy.

Basic Policies

The administration of a price or a set of prices may be guided by certain basic policies. These include (1) the single-price policy, (2) the nonvariable-price (one-price) policy, and (3) the variable-price policy.

Under a single-price policy, there is but one price for all buyers, regardless of the timing of the purchase, the quantity ordered, or other aspects of the transaction. Such a policy may be highly discriminatory in an economic sense yet, as will be discussed later, not illegal.

A nonvariable-price (one-price) policy is one under which the seller charges the same price to all buyers who purchase under similar conditions. This policy should not be confused with the single-price policy, under which there is one price for *all* buyers. Under the nonvariable-price policy, different prices are charged. These differences, however, reflect variations in quantities purchased, in timing, and in other pertinent conditions of purchase. Under a nonvariable-price policy, the terms of sale are known and are administered uniformly. Although utilizing price differentials, a nonvariable-price policy may be nondiscriminatory in both an economic and a legal sense.

A third type of basic policy is that of variable pricing. Under this policy the price arrangement between the seller and each buyer is the result of direct negotiation or other means of reflecting relative bargaining power based upon the buyer's evaluation of the product's value in use and the availability of alternative sources of supply.

The use of a single-price policy appeals to firms selling to small customers. The policy is easy to administer, and it permits the emphasis of nonprice appeals by salespeople and in advertisements. The policy is not likely to appeal to large buyers who believe that their volume purchases entitle them to a price reduction. The large buyers feel that a single-price policy discriminates against them, and unless the seller has built a very strong selective demand for the product, the buyers will seek a source which will vary price in their favor.[1]

Because the U.S. market is so large and diverse, and because a single-price policy usually limits patronage to small customers, most sellers vary their prices. The question is therefore not usually one of choosing between a single-price policy and a variable-price policy. It is, rather, deciding what kind of variable-price policy to follow.

Variable- versus Nonvariable-Price Policies

Under a variable-price policy, prices are changed when such adjustments are indicated by market conditions. These adjustments, either upward or downward, may reflect a change in competition, the differing elasticities of demand among potential buyers, and differing costs of production and/or marketing accruing to the seller.

The major advantage of a variable-price policy is its speed and flexibility. Competitive moves can be counteracted almost immediately. Desires for bargaining can be accommodated. The relative emphasis upon price versus nonprice promotion can be changed to suit the needs of a

---

[1]D. Maynard Phelps and J. Howard Westing, *Marketing Management*, 3d ed. (Homewood, Ill.: Richard D. Irwin, 1968), pp. 361–62.

particular situation. In all, a variable-price policy is a powerful promotional device.

The policy is not without its disadvantages. These include: (1) the need to delegate pricing authority to sales managers or salespeople, thus requiring them to be skilled in negotiation; (2) the increased cost of selling due to the time taken up by the bargaining process; (3) the loss of centralized control over prices; (4) the customer ill will caused by differences in prices even though the conditions of sale are similar; (5) the weakened sales effort caused by the substitution of price cutting for intensified personal selling; and (6) the legal complications growing out of the Robinson-Patman Act.[2]

The advantages of a nonvariable-price policy include ease of administration, simplification of the selling process, and a general recognition that such a policy is "fair to all buyers regardless of their ability to bargain or of the competitive situation surrounding the transaction."[3] In addition, a nonvariable-price policy avoids many of the previously noted disadvantages of a variable-price policy. Although a nonvariable-price policy has been found most often in the United States at the retail level, manufacturers appear to be recognizing the advantages of such a policy and "seem to be adopting a one-price (nonvariable-price) policy to a far greater extent in recent years than in the past, although considerable price negotiation between manufacturers and their customers still takes place."[4]

PRICE VARIATION

Regardless of whether the firm follows a nonvariable- or a variable-price policy, the set of charging different prices for essentially similar products or services is one of price variation. The reasons for such variation are generally, but not exclusively, to advance the promotional strategy of the firm. Individual companies may use differential pricing to achieve goals unique to themselves. There are, however, several commonly sought-after objectives, which are noted in the next section.

Goals of Price Variation[5]

Change of purchase patterns.   Sellers use differential prices to influence or change patterns of purchase. Lower prices may be granted to induce customers to buy in larger quantities, to buy in anticipation of future needs, or to concentrate their purchases among fewer sources of

---

[2]Donald V. Harper, *Price Policy and Procedure* (New York: Harcourt Brace Jovanovich, 1966), p. 174.

[3]Ibid., p. 175.

[4]Ibid.

[5]See Joel Dean, *Managerial Economics* (Englewood Cliffs, N.J.: Prentice-Hall, 1951), p. 515; and Phelps and Westing, *Marketing Management*, pp. 358–59.

supply. Higher prices may be charged certain customers to discourage them from carrying the line, thus reducing the intensity of competition in certain markets.

Market segmentation.   Price variation can be used to tap segments of a market which differ in price elasticity of demand. These differences in sensitivity to price may come about because of differing values in use among various classes of buyers and/or differing competitive situations facing the seller.

Market expansion.   By offering lower prices to customers who have lower values in use, the market for a given product or service may be expanded. Such expansion may also be accomplished by offering lower prices to present customers to gain new applications of the product or service where prior price levels made such applications uneconomic.

Utilization of excess capacity.   Differential prices which gain additional volume may utilize excess productive and/or marketing capacity. If such capacity exists, a price differential which makes a sale possible and which covers direct costs may contribute to the total profits of the firm.

Implementation of channel strategy.   Differential pricing is a major device by which a firm attempts to implement its marketing strategy with respect to channels of distribution. Price variations may reflect differences in the marketing tasks performed by various types of resellers or differences in the competitive environments in which they operate. Price differentials may encourage certain channels to engage in vigorous promotion of the line, or they may be used to gain representation of the line in diverse channels. On the other hand, differential pricing may discourage certain channels of distribution when such a policy is deemed useful in the furtherance of overall strategy.

To meet competition.   Price variation is, of course, a device which can be used to meet competition. As previously discussed, the price ceiling for a given product or service is set by the value in use or utility offered the buyer as well as by the alternatives open to the buyer with respect to other sources of supply. In many situations, although the utility offered is high, the options available to the potential customer are numerous. Under such circumstances, the varying of a price in favor of the buyer may induce him or her to become a customer. Where the seller is disadvantaged because production facilities are located far from the potential buyer, a price differential may be used to make the delivered price competitive with that of a seller located closer to the potential customer.

Implementation of Price Variations

A variation from the established price level may be the result of direct negotiation between the seller and the buyer. In many situations the

transaction may reflect economic costs to the seller and economic values to the buyer better than would be the case if the sale were made at established prices. On the other hand, where the economic power or bargaining skill of the buyer and the seller are markedly unequal, equity may be better served by an established price rather than by one which is negotiated.

When established price variations are used, a schedule may be developed showing the net prices charged to various customers or to all customers who buy in specified quantities or at special times. A more common approach, however, is to develop a schedule of discounts from the established level of price. These discounts reflect the extent of variation in the prices offered to those who represent a given class of customer or who buy under certain specified conditions.

Whether or not prices are stated as net, or gross less a discount, some variation from the established level must be specified. If discounts are used by sellers to implement their price-variation policies, they must not only offer the price concession needed to attract patronage, but they must also operate in a manner consistent with the overall marketing strategy of the firm.

DISCOUNT POLICY

The discounts most commonly used to implement a policy of nonvariable pricing include quantity discounts, trade-functional discounts, and promotional discounts and allowances. Cash discounts, although widely used for financial purposes or because they have become trade practices, will not be discussed here. Discounts in the other three categories will, however, be examined in some detail in terms of how they are used to achieve certain marketing goals and of the degree to which specific discounts reflect cost savings accruing to the seller. This latter point is especially important when the conformance of a particular discount to the Robinson-Patman Act is being considered.

Quantity Discounts

The quantity discount is the most widely used instrument for establishing price variations among customers. There are two types of quantity discounts: the cumulative and the noncumulative. Each has different purposes and different capacities to reflect seller cost differentials.

Noncumulative quantity discounts (NCQDs). This type of discount provides a reduction from the established or list price for customers buying in specified quantities. An NCQD is applied on a per order basis, and the principal goal of the user is to effect some change in the purchase pattern of the buyer. This change may be in the direction of

making larger but less frequent orders, buying in anticipation of demand, or purchasing the full line.

Larger, less frequent orders allow more efficient scheduling of production and provide economies of scale with respect to billing, physical distribution, and selling activities. Cost savings, therefore, do accrue to the seller who can gain such orders through the use of NCQDs. Whether these savings are sufficient to cover the revenues foregone by the discount is one question. Another question, and one which appears to be more important from the marketing point of view, is whether the discount offered is large enough to compensate buyers for the increase in inventory holding costs occasioned by purchasing in larger quantities. Given today's legal environment, the second question cannot be considered alone. Figure 14–1 graphically indicates how the two questions pertaining to the use of NCQDs are interrelated.

The shaded areas in the illustration show that in certain instances the discount required to induce buyers to purchase in larger quantities can reflect the seller's cost savings. In other instances (the unshaded areas) the seller's cost savings are insufficient to fully reflect the discounts needed to change buyer behavior.

FIGURE 14–1   Relationship between buyer and seller costs as order size increases

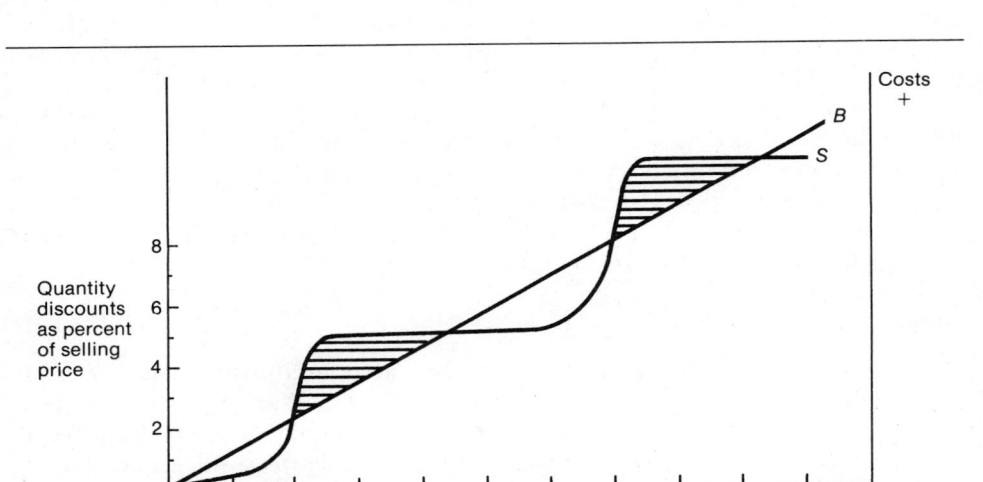

B represents increased buyer inventory holding costs with quantity purchases.
S represents seller's cost savings with quantity sales.
Source: Adapted from J. L. Heskett, Robert M. Ivie, and Nicholas A. Glaskowsky, Jr., *Business Logistics—Physical Distribution and Materials Management*, 2d ed. © 1973 The Ronald Press Co., New York.

Although NCQDs are used primarily to implement marketing strategy by getting customers to buy in larger quantities, they may have a secondary application. An NCQD can be used to satisfy the demands of large buyers for price concessions without the need to identify these customers by trade status, industry grouping, or other criteria. NCQDs can thus be used to reflect variations in price elasticity of demand among firms of varying size and bargaining power without regard to arbitrary and often difficult classification procedures. The discount approach essentially attempts to formalize price adjustments which might be brought about by interfirm bargaining and negotiation.

Cumulative quantity discounts (CQDs). This variant of the quantity discount is also used to change purchase patterns. The CQD differs from the NCQD, however, in that it is granted on the basis of total purchases over a specified period of time. For example, a discount of 2 percent might be granted a buyer purchasing at least 100 units per year.

The basic marketing goal of a CQD is to tie the customer more closely to the seller. By granting a price concession on the basis of total volume of sales per period of time, the seller can induce the buyer to concentrate purchases to as great an extent as is consistent with his or her needs to maintain multiple sources of supply. Although the CQD is used to "tie up patronage," it does a rather poor job of reflecting cost savings. There are, of course, some reductions in selling costs if sellers can count on continued patronage from their customers, but such savings are hard to quantify. Under a CQD policy, there is no penalty to the buyer who purchases frequently and in small quantities. If the buyer does this, the seller's costs of producing and distributing may well increase. Thus, in many instances, sellers use NCQDs and CQDs together to gain the advantages of each without the disadvantages that might arise from the use of a CQD by itself.

Regardless of the behavior of the seller's cost in any specific case, CDQs can never be easily defended on the basis of cost savings. This is what might well be expected, because the objective in using a CQD is not to save on per unit production and marketing costs but rather to hold on to customers. When the pressure for justification of discounts is great, the seller is on much firmer ground with a noncumulative rather than a cumulative quantity discount.

Trade Discounts

A reduction in price given to a buyer because of his or her position in a channel of distribution is called a trade discount. If the trade discount is granted to compensate customers who are resellers for their performance of certain marketing functions, perhaps a better name for the trade discount would be a "trade-functional" or "functional" discount. If the trade discount is granted to gain entry to a channel or to stimulate the resellers in the channel to provide promotional support for the product,

a better name for the trade discount would be a "competitive-functional" discount.

Trade-functional discounts.   As noted above, this type of discount compensates resellers for performing such marketing functions as holding inventory, engaging in sales promotion, and offering credit. Because so many resellers today have mixed trade status (e.g., wholesalers who engage in retailing, and vice versa), paying resellers on the basis of functional performance has become more meaningful than paying them on the basis of their trade classifications. If the seller's objective in using a trade-functional discount is to provide compensation for functions performed by channel intermediaries, variations in the discounts offered to customers in competition with one another may be defensible under the Robinson-Patman Act. This is especially true when variations in the discounts offered reflect variations in the cost savings accruing to the seller because of customer assumption of a greater part of the marketing task.

Competitive-functional discounts.[6]   When a seller wants to gain entry into a channel of distribution or wants a certain level of marketing effort from resellers in established channels, the seller finds that compensation for functional performance is not enough. The discounts which he or she offers must also take into account the competitive pressures under which the resellers operate. Their pressures include the rivalry faced from other sellers for channel support, the rivalry that resellers face from other resellers within their own channels, and the competition among all resellers for patronage in the end market. Thus, for a discount policy to be effective in gaining channel access or support, the payments made must be in excess of those required to compensate resellers for their functional performance. When such payments are made, the seller is said to be "buying distribution." Under such a discount policy, the payments made reflect the competitive as well as the functional needs of resellers, and thus the name "competitive-functional discounts." Unfortunately, the discounts which are used to buy distribution do not reflect variations in the seller's costs of serving different customers except by coincidence, and are therefore difficult to defend under current price-discrimination legislation.

Trade-Discount Strategy

The development of a trade-discount structure to implement marketing strategy is not a simple process. The objectives of the seller may vary, the needs of resellers are diverse, and competition impinges unequally on different parts of the distribution structure.

---

[6]For a more complete discussion of competitive-functional pricing, see Charles N. Davisson, *The Marketing of Automotive Parts* (Ann Arbor: Bureau of Business Research, Graduate School of Business Administration, The University of Michigan, 1954), pp. 910–17.

If the seller's objective in using trade discounts is to pay for functions performed by resellers, the discount structure must be oriented to the costs incurred by these resellers in providing a given level of functional performance. Discounts must be set high enough to gain the support of those marginal resellers whose costs are higher than average but who are needed in each geographic area to provide the intensity of distribution required by the seller. Finally, the discount schedule must reflect the seller's cost of using alternative channels of distribution (including the direct channel) to reach the market.

If the seller's strategy is aimed at buying distribution, the demand factors become more important. Questions to be considered include: (1) the discount structure of competitors, (2) the value of gaining entry to a new channel or of getting increased promotional support from an existing channel, and (3) the ability to sell to market segments of varying price elasticity of demand.

Trade-discount schedules set to implement overall marketing strategy are usually discriminatory in that they favor some customers over others. Yet these discounts are means of engaging in price competition, and, as such, they are of economic value to our society. From the seller's point of view the use of varying trade-discount schedules, although resulting in different net prices from customers in different channels, increases total revenues and, hopefully, total profits.

Promotional Discounts and Allowances

Price reductions or payments granted by sellers to buyers in return for promotional services rendered by the buyer are called promotional discounts or allowances. An example of such a discount is one in which a buyer is offered a 2 percent discount on his or her purchases if he or she will give prominent window display space to the seller's product for a specified period of time. An example of an allowance is a payment to a buyer for the services of an in-store demonstration program featuring the seller's product. Other types of promotional discounts or allowances may be made to support a cooperative advertising program or to furnish incentive payments to sales personnel.

The marketing objective of these discounts or payments is to gain the promotional cooperation of the reseller. Variations in these discounts or allowances among customers may represent differences in the seller's costs but, as will be noted later, a cost defense is not generally applicable when discrimination is charged on the basis of the seller's use of varying promotional discounts or payments. When promotional discounts or allowances exceed the costs of services performed by buyers, they may be considered to be disguised quantity discounts or just simple price variations.[7]

---

[7]Phelps and Westing, *Marketing Management,* p. 370.

PRICE VARIATION—LEGAL ISSUES

Whether implemented by negotiation or a discount policy, price variation is a form of price discrimination. The object of price variation is to adapt price to the requirements of a given market situation. In some cases, prices may be lowered to reflect a lower value in use in a specific application. In other cases, price may be raised to reflect the increased costs of serving a customer and/or the absence of a competitive source of supply. Regardless of why a price variation is used, it is almost inevitable that two or more customers will pay different prices for essentially similar products or services. When such a practice occurs, it is price discrimination, and the legal constraints relating to such discrimination must be noted by those responsible for pricing policy. Further consideration of the legality of specific price variations must await a brief discussion of the Robinson-Patman Act, which is the principal federal law relating to price discrimination.

The Robinson-Patman Act[8]

In 1936, Section 2 of the Clayton Antitrust Act of 1914 was amended by the Robinson-Patman Act. The amended section dealt with price discrimination, and the amendment sought to strengthen its provisions and extend its jurisdiction. At this time the Robinson-Patman Act has survived almost 50 years of administration by the Federal Trade Commission and continuous judicial review by the federal courts. To understand the act, which is the major legal constraint facing sellers who use differential prices, is not an easy task. This is because the Robinson-Patman Act is not in the form of a traditional antitrust law. It is, rather, a law which attempts to redress imbalances in economic power. It is a creature of the depression years of the 1930s—a politically motivated response to the growing power of the corporate chain stores in relation to the smaller and economically weaker independent wholesalers and retailers.[9]

The Robinson-Patman Act is composed of six sections. Because it amended Section 2 of the Clayton Act, these sections are denoted as 2(a) through 2(f). Sections 2(a) and 2(b) deal with price discrimination and certain defenses available to those charged with the offense. Section 2(c)

---

[8]This discussion is very much condensed, and the intent of its presentation here is to give the reader a general overview of the act and its marketing and legal implications. Three sources which explain the act in greater detail are: Brian Dixon, *Price Discrimination and Marketing Management* (Ann Arbor: Bureau of Business Research, Graduate School of Business Administration, The University of Michigan, 1960); Phelps and Westing, *Marketing Management,* pp. 386–400; and W. David Robbins, "A Marketing Appraisal of the Robinson-Patman Act," *Journal of Marketing,* July 1959.

[9]See Joseph C. Palamountain, *The Politics of Distribution* (Cambridge, Mass.: Harvard University Press, 1955).

deals with allowances in lieu of brokerage commissions; Sections 2(d) and 2(e) cover the granting of promotional services and allowances; and Section 2(f) holds that buyers accepting or inducing illegal price reductions are in violation of the act together with the grantor of the discriminatory price.

Injunctive or punitive action under the act may be initiated by either an FTC examiner or a private complainant. If the presumed violation is one of price discrimination under Section 2(a) a prima facie case must be shown to exist. The elements which must be present to make such a case should be fully understood by pricing executives. They include: (1) a sale at different prices, (2) by a seller engaged in interstate commerce, (3) to two or more competing customers, (4) of commodities of like grade or quality, (5) with a tendency to injure competition.

Faced with such a case, the respondent may avail himself or herself of several defenses. These include: (1) that not all of the elements of a prima facie case were actually present as charged, (2) that variations in prices charged competing customers reflected the seller's cost differentials in producing, selling, or delivering goods to these customers, (3) that a price reduction was granted to one customer "in good faith" to meet the lower price offered the customer by a competitor, and (4) that there was a change in market conditions or in the goods being sold which required a distress sale at lower prices.

Respondents may avail themselves of these defenses, and if they are not satisfied with the findings of the FTC in their case, they may appeal the commission's findings to the federal courts. If found guilty of a Robinson-Patman violation, a respondent may be required to cease and desist from current pricing activities, to pay a fine, or to be imprisoned for up to one year. Customers or competitors who claim injury by the respondent's price discrimination may sue him or her for treble damages in the federal courts.

Implications for Discount Administration

What types of price variations are allowed under the Robinson-Patman Act? What types are patently illegal? Which pricing policies appear safer than others? These are some of the questions for which pricing executives need answers.

First, the act allows price differentials to customers who are in competition to the extent that these differentials reflect the seller's cost differences in manufacturing, selling, and/or delivery to the specific customers.

Second, under the "good-faith" defense, a seller may lower the price to one customer while keeping the price at former levels to competing customers if the lower price is necessary to meet a price offered the customer by a competitor.

Third, price reductions may be granted to some customers and not to others in response to "changing market conditions," such as deterioration or obsolescence of the commodity being sold or a licensed discontinuance of business by the seller.

The wording of the act does not outlaw any specific type of discount or discount policy. It only says that price discrimination under certain specified conditions is illegal. A single-price policy, although discriminatory in that it penalizes customers who buy in large quantities, is not illegal under the act because a difference in price, which is the first element of a prima facie case, is missing. Likewise, a nonvariable-price policy under which the same discounts are received by all customers who are of a similar class or who buy under the same conditions of sale is easier to defend under the act than is a variable-price policy.

In terms of a cost defense, it is clear that noncumulative quantity discounts reflect seller cost savings better than do cumulative quantity discounts and that trade-functional discounts reflect variations in seller costs better than do competitive-functional discounts.

The good-faith defense as stated in section 2(b) was originally a procedural defense or a rebuttal to a prima facie case. A Supreme Court decision in 1951 in the *Detroit Gasoline* case held that the good-faith defense was an absolute defense.[10] To utilize this defense, the seller must be able to prove that a customer was actually offered a lower price by a competitor and that the meeting of said price was necessary to retain the customer. Any use of a lower price to gain a customer, to effect a partial meeting of a lower price, or to undercut a competitor's price will invalidate the defense.

Section 2(c) is concerned with the granting of price reductions to buyers who perform their own brokerage services. The law simply states that such payments or allowances are illegal. The political basis of this section of the act was the desire to keep the large integrated chains from gaining a price advantage over their smaller and nonintegrated competitors. There are no defenses to the charge that a seller gave a buyer an allowance to reflect nonuse of a broker except proof that such was not the case.

Sections 2(d) and 2(e) cover the granting of promotional allowances or the offering of promotional services. These sections were placed in the act to prevent discrimination in the disguised form of supplementary payments or services offered to selected buyers and not to others. Two guidelines govern the use of promotional allowances and services under current FTC rulings.

First, payments or services must be granted on a *proportionately equal* basis. This means that competing buyers can receive payments or services which are roughly proportional to their dollar purchases from the

---

[10]*Standard Oil Co.* v. *FTC*, 340 U.S. 231, 71 S.Ct. 240 (1951).

manufacturer. For example, a buyer of goods worth $100,000 may receive 10 times the dollar value of services and/or allowances received by a buyer of goods worth $10,000.

The second guideline is that all competing buyers must be able to *participate* in the manufacturer's program. The concept of participation covers both the manufacturer's informing of all buyers of the allowances and services available and the designing of a program sufficiently flexible so that all buyers can benefit from the involvement. In other words, the manufacturer's program must not be tailored to the needs of the larger buyers.

There are no absolute defenses to a Section 2(d) or 2(e) violation except proof that the allowances and services were properly offered and were distributed in a nondiscriminatory manner. Although in a very few isolated cases defenses available under Section 2(a) and 2(b) have been attempted, the results have been inconclusive.

Section 2(f), which holds a buyer who knowingly induces or receives a discriminatory price, allowance, or service equally guilty with the grantor, has no specific defense. The best course of action for a buyer charged with a 2(f) violation is to help the grantor prove that there was no illegal discrimination. Another and more difficult approach for buyers is to prove that they were unaware that the price, allowance, or service received was illegal.

GEOGRAPHIC PRICING POLICIES

In addition to developing price differentials that reflect variations in quantities purchased, the trade status of the buyer, and the extent of the marketing job performed by the buyer, the seller must consider price policies that concern the relative geographic location of the seller and the buyer. These policies range from those under which the seller absorbs the varying costs of transportation to arrive at a uniform delivered price for all customers to those under which the seller passes all freight costs on to the buyer. In between these extremes are policies which attempt to simplify the administration of price variations imposed by location or which seek to improve the position of sellers when they are faced with competition from rivals located nearer to customers.

FOB factory. The first policy to be considered is that of "free on board" at the seller's factory or warehouse. Under this arrangement the customer assumes title to the goods when they are turned over to a common carrier and in addition assumes the costs of transport and insurance. The delivered price varies in relation to the distance between the factory and the customer, while prices at the factory net of transport costs are constant for all customers served unless some other type of price variation is operative.

Uniform delivered price.   Under this policy the seller assumes all the costs of delivery so that all customers will pay a single delivered price. Such a policy is often called "FOB customer's place of business," "freight allowed," or "postage stamp" pricing. Although the delivered prices which customer pay are equal regardless of their location, the net prices received by the seller at the factory differ in relation to the location of the customer served.

Freight equalization.   Sellers engaged in FOB factory pricing often discover that their markets are limited geographically because competitors located closer to customers than they are have an advantage in that they can quote lower delivered prices. In order to extend their markets, sellers may absorb some of the freight costs, so that their delivered prices are equal to or less than those of rivals located closer to the customers. This practice, called freight equalization, involves the absorption of different amounts of freight costs, resulting in varying net receipts for the seller.

Zone pricing.   When the costs of freight are too high to allow a uniform delivered price over the entire market area, the seller may compromise by establishing a uniform delivered price for a given geographic area or zone. In so doing, a seller may gain some of the promotional and billing advantages of a uniform delivered price policy without having to assume all of the freight costs. A policy of zone pricing should not be undertaken lightly by management because certain associated results of such a policy may be illegal. Perhaps the following illustration will indicate the nature of price behavior under zone pricing.

Assume the following attributes for the zone system pictured in Figure 14–2: (1) firm A, located in Ann Arbor, sells a single product with a factory price of \$100; (2) the delivery costs are linear with distance and are \$0.10/mile; and (3) the zonal boundaries are 100 miles apart. The problem facing the seller in this system is how to set the price for each zone. If the price is determined on the basis of factory cost plus delivery cost to the leading edge of the zone (for example, x_1 in zone II), then the delivered price for all customers in zone II will be \$100 + \$0.10/ mile (50 miles) or \$105. If the seller sets the price to reflect costs to get to the far side of the zone (x_2 in zone II), then the zone price is \$100 + \$0.10/mile (150 miles), or \$115.

In the first case the seller is absorbing varying amounts of freight costs for customers in the zone located beyond the leading edge; in the second case the seller is charging customers located nearer to it than x_2 for freight costs that do not exist. This practice results in customers paying what has been called "phantom freight."

If the seller sets zone prices on the basis of the average cost of delivery to the zone, all customers located before the zonal midpoint will be charged phantom freight, and all customers located beyond the zonal

FIGURE 14–2   A zone pricing system (single firm)

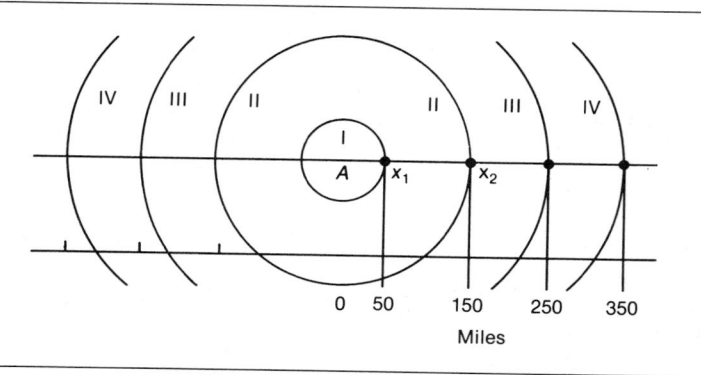

midpoint will have some of their freight charges absorbed by the seller. The legal implications of these happenings will be discussed at the end of this section.

Basing point pricing.   The last type of geographic pricing method to be discussed is one in which delivered prices are quoted by adding to the FOB factory price the delivery cost from a specific geographic location to that of the customer, whether or not the shipment was made from that point. The specific location so chosen is called a basing point.

If there is but one location from which all sellers quote delivered prices, the industry is said to use a single basing point system. The steel industry's "Pittsburgh Plus" was the prime example of the use of a single basing point from which to set prices.

When more than one geographic location is used from which to calculate delivered prices (either by a firm or a group of firms in an industry), a multiple basing point system is said to exist. These systems are not illegal per se, but certain attributes associated with their use may run afoul of the law.

In Figure 14–3 a situation is illustrated in which three selling points, S_1, S_2, and S_3, serve three customers, B_1, B_2, and B_3. The prices at S_1 and S_3 are $100 per unit. These locations are designated as basing points, while S_2 is a nonbase mill or point of origin. Distances between these points are as noted on the connecting lines.

From an examination of the behavior of individual transactions, it can be seen that when a seller is serving a customer located closer to a base mill than to the seller's mill, freight charges must be absorbed by the seller. Such absorption occurs when seller 1 ships to buyer 2. Al-

FIGURE 14–3   A multiple basing point system with two base mills

	Price at destination	−	Delivery cost	=	Factory net (price at origin)
Seller 1 (base mill) sells to					
Buyer 1	$103		$ 3		$100
Buyer 2	104		10		94
Buyer 3	107		7		100
Seller 2 (nonbase mill) sells to					
Buyer 1	103		5		98
Buyer 2	104		5		99
Buyer 3	107		6		101
Seller 3 (base mill) sells to					
Buyer 1	103		9		94
Buyer 2	104		4		100
Buyer 3	107		10		97

Price at base mill = $100 per unit

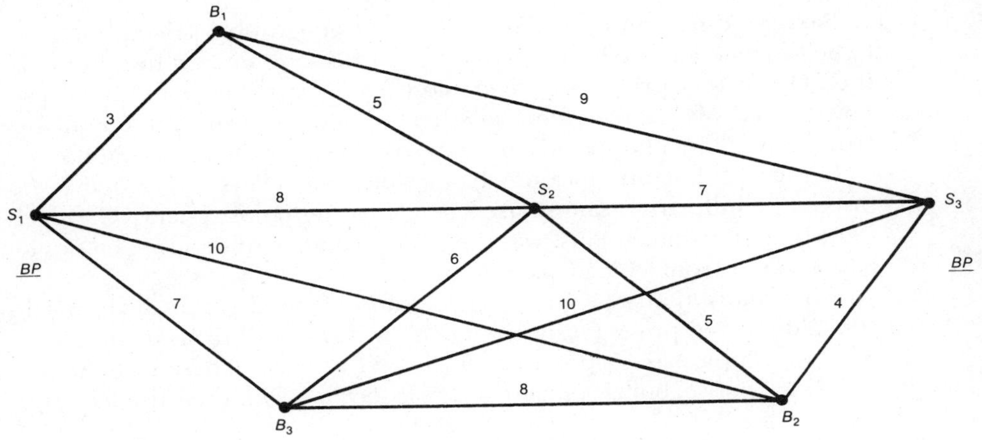

though the freight costs are $10, the customer is located sufficiently close to the basing point at S_3, so that the seller must absorb $6 in freight costs.

In other cases, the seller is forced to raise the price above that which would be expected based on actual cost of delivery. For example, seller 2 charges buyer 3 $107, although the actual freight costs are $6. The added charge of $1 is a phantom freight assessed because the price the

buyer pays is related not to the point of origin of the shipment but to the location of the buyer in relation to the nearest base mill. That mill in this case is S_1.

Geographic Pricing—Legal Constraints[11]

Many of the geographic pricing policies described above have run into legal difficulties over the past 60 years. In 1921, for example, the FTC complained that the single basing point system used by the steel industry discriminated in price in violation of Section 2 of the Clayton Act. The FTC claimed, in addition, that the "Pittsburgh Plus" method of quoting delivered prices violated Section 5 of the FTC Act. It held that the steel industry was engaged in a collusive attempt to fix prices and that such activity was deemed an "unfair method of competition" under the law. In 1924 the commission ordered the steel industry to cease using a single basing point system. The industry obeyed without going to court and changed to a multiple basing point system. For the ensuing 16 years all was relatively peaceful, but in 1940 the FTC opened a new attack on basing points which was to last a decade. The various rulings of the FTC and the subsequent support of the FTC by the courts resulted in a substantial limitation of the use of multiple basing points as a means of implementing a delivered-price policy.

The two major questions raised by the use of basing points are: (1) Is the system a method by which competing sellers attempt to fix prices? (2) Does the system discriminate in price to such an extent that competition is diminished among buyers? At present, it appears that if a basing point system does not result in price fixing through the systematic absorption of freight, if it does not contain nonbase mills which give rise to phantom freight, and if it does not result in different factory nets being received from competing buyers, then the user of the system has a good chance of avoiding legal difficulties. However, the design of such a system is so difficult, and the assurance that present FTC policy will hold for the future so tenuous, that most sellers who formerly used basing points have changed to straight FOB factory pricing.

Individual sellers who engage in freight equalization on an *ad hoc* basis have had very little trouble with the law. A policy of uniform delivered price also seems to be quite acceptable to the FTC because under this policy all delivered prices are equal. The irony of the situation is that in the case of basing points the FTC defines price as mill or factory net. Under a policy of uniform delivered price, the opposite definition prevails: that the price is the amount which is paid at the destination. Legislative change or judicial review is sorely needed to clarify the question of whether price is the amount which is received by the seller at the

---

[11]See Phelps and Westing, *Marketing Management*, pp. 400–7, for a most complete treatment of this subject.

point of shipment or the amount which is paid by the buyer at the point of receipt.

Zone pricing by members of an industry has run into legal difficulties when all members of the industry have used identical zonal boundaries and identical zonal price differentials. The charge has been violation of Section 5 of the FTC Act. The courts have held that in these cases evidence of collusion is not necessary if the results of a pricing system are the same as if there had been an actual meeting of the competitors or communication among them.

Section 5 is not violated by an individual firm's use of a zone system. Problems can arise, however, when customers who are located near zonal boundaries and are in competition pay different prices. In these situations the seller may be in violation of the Robinson-Patman Act.

RESALE PRICE MAINTENANCE

As stated in the introduction to this chapter, a seller may choose from pricing policy alternatives ranging from those which entail variations of price from an established level to those which are aimed at the maintenance of such a level. The latter policies are especially difficult to implement when the seller uses independent resellers in a pattern of distribution and when the title to the goods being sold passes to these middlemen.

When the seller decides to follow a policy of resale price maintenance, commonly called RPM, it is because the advantages of this course of action outweigh the disadvantages. These advantages are diverse, but like those sought by the user of a policy of price variation, they are essentially promotional. They arise out of the ability of a properly executed RPM policy to eliminate or control price rivalry among resellers in the channels of distribution. When price rivalry is diminished, certain benefits may accrue to the seller. These include the following.

Protection of product image. The reduction of price rivalry at the retail level may protect the consumer image of a product or a brand. The stabilization or control of the resale price is especially important when the buyer associates quality with price, as in the case of a luxury good or a prestige item. Stabilization or maintenance of retail price is also of value when consumers purchase the product as a gift item.

Reduce interchannel rivalry. The use of an RPM policy can restrict price competition among different channels of distribution, thus protecting the margins of resellers in high-cost channels. The promotional advantage sought is the added market coverage gained through the seller's ability to distribute through a variety of channels which differ in their average costs of operation.

Reduce intrachannel rivalry.   The use of RPM to reduce price competition among competing resellers in the same channel of distribution is aimed at protecting reseller margins from erosion. If RPM can preserve margins, the seller may be able to gain the support of the resellers in terms of higher levels of nonprice promotion and service to the consumer.

Implementing a Policy of Resale Price Maintenance

If the development of overall marketing strategy indicates that a price maintenance policy is desirable, there are several ways in which such a policy might be implemented. The seller might, for example, become sufficiently selective in distribution so that the line becomes important to the reseller. Then a franchise agreement might be negotiated with each reseller, specifying the price and discount schedule which would govern the resale of the product line. Failure to comply with this agreement would be grounds for its possible termination. Where the product line requires more intensive distribution to gain market coverage, the manufacturer's bargaining power is diminished. Selling to specific market segments which do not overlap at prices which reflect the elasticity of demand in each segment may keep prices stable both within the segment and among segments. Finally, the seller might consider reducing discounts so that margins are not so wide that they induce price cutting.

In some situations an option which appealed to the seller was to enter into a price-setting contract with the resellers. Because these contracts were "price-fixing" agreements, legislation at the state and federal level was necessary to remove them from conflict with existing antitrust laws. These enabling statutes were known as "fair-trade" laws and the policy of using the contract approach to RPM was termed "fair trading." Born in the 1930s and reaching its widest use in the 1940s and 1950s, fair trade declined as an option as state after state found that its enabling legislation was unconstitutional. Fair trade met its demise in early 1976 when an act of Congress terminated the federal enabling legislation.[12]

An analysis of the methods used to encourage stability of retail prices by manufacturers of consumer goods indicated that fair-trade laws, promotional allowances, and more suasion were relatively ineffective ways of attaining RPM goals. The author of the study suggests that restricting the intensity of distribution, market segmentation, and reductions in discounts and allowances are more effective and less controversial ways of gaining price stability at retail levels.[13]

---

[12]"Measure to End State 'Fair Trade' Laws Is Sent to Ford with Approval Certain," *The Wall Street Journal,* December 3, 1975, p. 3.

[13]See Louis W. Stern, "Approaches to Achieving Retail Stability," *Business Horizons,* Fall 1964, pp. 75–86.

Analysis suggests that a policy of RPM is too intimately related to product, channel, and promotional strategy to be applied by law. It appears that successful application of RPM is more dependent upon the overall program of the manufacturer (or other seller) than upon the legal environment in the existing market area.

Implications

The basic questions to be asked by a seller in attempting to decide whether or not to follow an RPM policy might include: (1) Will the revenue gains from an RPM policy cover the costs of policing the dealer organization? (2) Will most of the resellers stay loyal to the seller's policy in the face of a few recalcitrant price cutters? (3) Are stable and relatively high prices needed to support the prestige image of the product or product line? (4) Does the amount of aggressive selling required from resellers demand an RPM policy to protect their margins? If the answer to most of the above queries is positive, RPM becomes a viable policy alternative.

In contrast to a policy of price variation, RPM attempts to reduce the influence of price in the marketing mixes of the members of the reseller organization. Thus, if price variation aimed at gaining greater volume from various resellers results in a mix of both price channels and channels which do not emphasize price in their promotional strategies, the seller will have great difficulty in implementing an RPM policy. Price-variation and RPM policies appear to work in opposite directions, and wise manufacturers will decide in which direction they want to go and will develop a consistent policy which will enable them to go in that direction. Only if the market is clearly segmented can the seller use both policies with some hope of success. Here an RPM policy may be used in one market segment while a policy of price variation may be used to tap another and more price-sensitive market segment.

CONCLUSION

In the preceding chapter, the discussion centered on the problems of determining a price or a basic level of price. This chapter has attempted to illustrate how variations from the established level or maintenance of levels of price may be used for promotional purposes. The coverage of topics was highly selective and of necessity brief. The purpose of the two-chapter sequence has been to provide an overview of pricing in the context of the marketing mix.

Pricing in all of its various nuances is more an art than a science. But in the same manner in which an artist improves a work by studying the principles of composition, perspective, and color, the executive can im-

prove the quality of pricing decisions by understanding more thoroughly the economic, psychological, and legal forces which impinge upon price determination and administration.

QUESTION

1. Why do most American business firms follow a variable-price policy rather than a single-price policy?

2. How does price variation relate to the development of an overall marketing strategy? Specifically, how does price variation facilitate the achievement of product, channel, and nonprice promotional objectives?

3. "Discounts differ in terms of the marketing goals they seek to achieve as well as in their ability to reflect differences in sellers' costs." Explain the promotional and legal implications of this statement.

4. Compare and contrast trade-functional discounts and competitive-functional discounts.

5. What is the difference between a promotional discount and a simple price variation? Is this difference as clearly defined in practice as in theory?

6. What types of price variations are allowed by the Robinson-Patman Act? What types are illegal?

7. What is the "good faith" defense to a Robinson-Patman Act violation? Trace the evolvement of this defense from its initial interpretation to its present interpretation.

8. What is a basing point? A basing point system? Are all basing point systems illegal?

9. What are some ways in which sellers may implement a policy of resale price maintenance? What legal restrictions must the sellers be aware of in designing their programs?

Cases for part six

DUTCH FOOD INDUSTRIES COMPANY (A)*

In early September, Jan de Vries, product manager for Dutch Food Industries' new salad dressing product, was wondering what strategy to follow with respect to this new product. His assistant had prepared information concerning alternative promotional methods to use to introduce the new product, and he was concerned with exactly which of these he should recommend for the product's introduction. He also wondered what price the new product should retail for and when the company should introduce the new product. De Vries had to decide these issues in the next couple of days, as his report containing his recommendations on the introduction of the new salad dressing was due on the desk of the director of marketing the following Monday.

COMPANY BACKGROUND

The Netherlands Oil Factory of Delft, The Netherlands, was founded in 1884. This firm, which supplied edible oils to the growing margarine industry, merged in 1900 with a French milling company. The new firm then operated under the name Dutch Food Industries Company (DFI).

---

*Written by Kenneth L. Bernhardt, Associate Professor of Marketing, Georgia State University. Assisted by Jos Viehoff, graduate student, Netherlands School of Economics.

From this origin, the brand name DFI became increasingly strong and was eventually given to all of the company's branded products. More recently, the name was registered for use internationally.

In the course of the 1920s, DFI became an important factor in the margarine market. The company was a troublesome competitor for the Margarine Union, the company formed by the merger in 1927 of the two margarine giants, Van den Bergh and Jurgens. In 1928, an agreement was reached by which DFI joined the Margarine Union.

In 1930, the interests of the Margarine Union were merged with those of International Industries Corporation—a large, diversified, and international organization. In this way DFI became a part of the International Industries complex of companies.

International Industries Corporation (IIC) is a worldwide organization with major interests in the production of margarine, other edible fats and oils, soups, ice cream, frozen foods, meats, cheeses, soaps, and detergents.

The total sales of IIC were more than $1 billion.[1] Profits before taxes were $56 million.

Within IIC, DFI proceeded with its original activities after its margarine factory was closed, namely developing its exports of oils and fats, its trade in bakery products, as well as a number of branded food products. The following list indicates the range of consumer products which the company marketed: table oil, household fats, mayonnaise, salad dressing (several varieties), tomato ketchup, peanut butter, and peanuts.

DFI's total annual sales were between $14 million–$28 million. Profits before taxes were between $1.4 million–$2.8 million.

BACKGROUND ON THE DRESSING MARKET

A large and growing percentage of Holland's population eats lettuce, usually with salad dressing, with their meals. Estimates indicated that 82 percent of the people ate lettuce with salad dressing regularly. The salad dressing market has extreme seasonal demand, as shown in Exhibit 1. This seasonal pattern coincides with the periods of greatest production of lettuce in Holland. Thus, 50 percent of the total year's volume for the salad dressing market occurs in the four months beginning in April. During this period, lettuce is plentiful and sells for approximately $0.46 per head.

The total salad dressing market was growing at approximately 7 percent per year. DFI's share of the market had declined from 20.7 percent to 16.6 percent over the last five years. The total market for salad dressings at manufacturer's level was currently estimated at between $7 mil-

---

[1]All financial data in this case are presented in U.S. dollars.

EXHIBIT 1   Seasonal analysis of salad dressing market (percentage of annual total market sales—bimonthly periods)

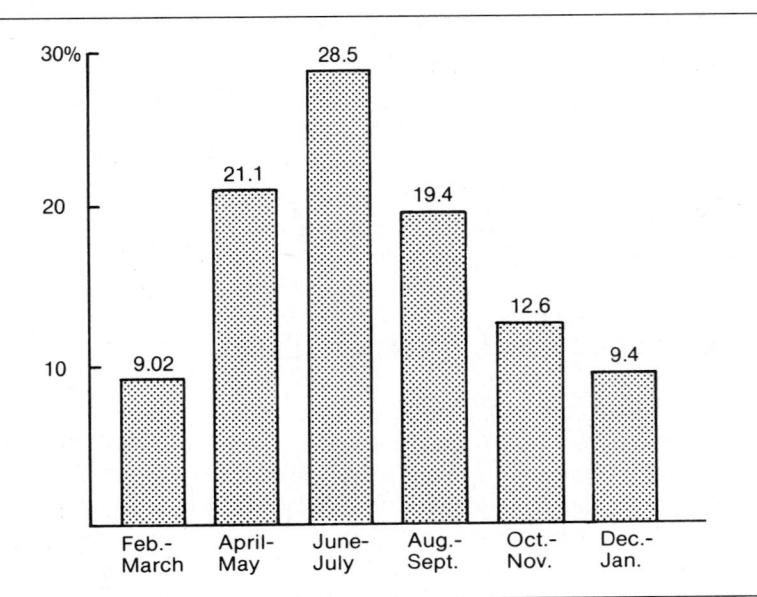

lion and $8.4 million. The company was looking for ways to halt the decline in market share and, in fact, increase DFI's share of the growing market.

Historically, the salad dressing market was composed of two segments. The first was a 25 percent oil-based salad dressing, which comprised 90 percent of the total market. The other 10 percent of the market consisted of 50 percent oil-based salad dressing, a slightly creamier product. Previously, DFI, in an effort to increase its market share, had introduced a new product which was 50 percent oil-based. Up to that time, DFI sold only 25 percent oil-based salad dressing. The product, called Delfine, was not successful in obtaining the desired volume and profit. While DFI still marketed Delfine, almost all of DFI's volume came from its 25 percent oil-based product, Slasaus.

A research study was conducted to help the DFI marketing executives determine why Delfine was not successful. Several reasons emerged:

1. The potential of the 50 percent oil-based market was much smaller than originally anticipated, and only a small percentage of the total population was even interested in this product.

2. The consumers could detect only a small difference between the 25 percent oil-based and the 50 percent oil-based varieties when blind-tested. The difference was not noticeable enough for the consumers to prefer the 50 percent oil-based product.
3. The 50 percent oil-based salad dressing was more expensive, and the consumer was not willing to pay the difference for an apparently almost imperceptible difference.

Because the Delfine sales were well below expectations, DFI removed the heavy promotion support it had been giving the product. The executives decided to wait for a significant breakthrough of a product with unique advantages. The Delfine experience indicated to them that it would take a totally new type of product for DFI to increase its market share significantly.

BACKGROUND AND DEVELOPMENT OF SLAMIX

Every two years, the company conducted a housewives' habits study in which a panel of 700 consumers was asked about their household and their food preparation habits. In August two years before, the company received the most recent study, called PMC-11. The housewives were asked how they prepared their lettuce and what ingredients they used. The results showed that an extremely large percentage of the housewives added not only salad dressing to lettuce, but also added other ingredients such as salt, pepper, eggs, onion, gherkins, and so on. Thus DFI executives got the idea that putting some of these ingredients in the salad dressing would result in a real convenience for the housewife, and DFI would have the significant new product for which they had been searching. The laboratory, in August of the same year, began developing a "dressed" salad dressing which included some of the ingredients which many housewives were accustomed to adding.

Early in the next year, a committee called the Slamix Committee,[2] was formed to make sure that every part of the company was involved in the development of this new product. The committee, which was headed up by the product manager, had representatives from various parts of the company, including development, production, and marketing. The commmittee studied production problems, laboratory findings, and in general, was charged with the responsibility of seeing that the development progressed as scheduled. The committee did not have decision-making powers but either invited decision makers to important meetings or wrote reports to the people who were in a position to make the required decisions.

---

[2]Literally translated, Slasaus means "lettuce sauce," and Slamix is literally "lettuce mix."

After several product tests concerned with taste and keeping properties were conducted at the factory, the company, one year after laboratory work began, undertook its first consumer test of the new "dressed" salad dressing. A panel of housewives was shown a bottle of the new product which was a salad dressing containing pieces of gherkins, onions, and paprika. Several conclusions emerged from this study:

1.   The "dressed" salad dressing was seen by the housewives as more than a salad dressing with ingredients. It was seen as a completely new product.
2.   There were two sides to this newness:
     a.   By looking at the product, they thought that it had a new taste.
     b.   The convenience aspect was strongly stressed by the housewives.
3.   The housewives thought that the new product would be good for decorating the lettuce. With its new color (light red with colorful ingredients), they thought that they could decorate the lettuce much better than with present salad dressings which were creme-colored and very similar to mayonnaise.
4.   When asked about the ingredients, one half of the housewives were favorable toward paprika, and half were against it. This apparently was a troublesome ingredient. However, because of the convenience aspect, gherkins and onions were favored by the housewives.

Later, a second consumer study was conducted by the Institute of Household Research in Rotterdam. A sample of 140 housewives who actually used salad dressing on lettuce was given a bottle of the new product to take home. Then, they were visited in their homes. Much useful information emerged from this study. After looking at the product, but before trying it, the housewives said that it looked like a fun product, it made them happy, and they thought that it would taste good. When asked what they thought the product contained, they said tomatoes, red paprika, celery, gherkins, and green paprika.

However, the company was disappointed with the housewives' overall evaluation of the product. Only 20 percent of the housewives said that they thought the product was very good, 11 percent did not like the product, and 69 percent of the housewives said that there were some favorable and some unfavorable aspects of the product. The main reason for the 80 percent unfavorable reaction was the consistency of the new salad dressing. It was too thin. The housewives could pour it too easily and it rapidly went to the bottom of the bowl. Because it fell to the bottom, the housewives said that it was much harder to decorate their salad. It was also uneconomical because they felt that they would put too much on if the product was that thin. There were also problems with taste. Many of the housewives thought it was too sour or too sharp. The paprika was the main reason for the dissatisfaction.

In spite of the above problems, there were several aspects of the study

which encouraged the company to proceed with the development of this new product. When asked how they would change the ingredients in the "dressed" salad dressing, only 47 percent of the housewives suggested changes. Most recommended that more onions be added. The housewives were asked for their preference between DFI's Slasaus and the new "dressed" salad dressing. As shown in Exhibit 2, the housewives preferred the new product, except for its consistency. Sixty percent of the housewives said that they would buy the product if it were possible to buy it in a store. Since this was a very high positive response, the company was very encouraged.

EXHIBIT 2   Preference test: Slasaus versus "dressed" salad dressing

Prefer	*Taste*	*Appear-ance*	*Decoration aspects*	*Con-sistency*	*Con-venience*
"Dressed" salad dressing	59%	73%	46%	48%	50%
Slasaus	38	20	44	65	20
No preference/no difference	3	7	10	17	30
	100%	100%	100%	100%	100%

The marketing, production, and development groups, coordinated by the Slamix Committee, began work on incorporating the required changes made evident by this consumer study. DFI's development group experimented with changes in the consistency, taste, and ingredients. The production group experimented with a new production process. DFI had intended to introduce the new "dressed" salad dressing in a few months. However, the top corporate executives decided that, before the new product could be introduced, an extensive test of its keeping properties (vulnerability to deterioration) would have to be conducted.

The keeping properties test showed that after several months the light red-colored product changed to a pink color. The difference in color was only slight, but DFI executives thought that the consumer reaction to this change should be tested. They decided that at the same time they would conduct a consumer test to find a name for this new product. A sample of 180 housewives from the Institute of Household Research was used to get at these questions. Only 2 out of the 180 housewives saw that there was a difference in color between the two bottles of the new product. When they were told that there was a slight difference and were shown the two bottles together, most of the house-

wives could not see the color change, and those that could were not unhappy about it.

The housewives were then asked what the name for this product should be. The phrase "mixed salad dressing" kept coming up. The housewives were then asked what they thought of two names which the company had screened, "Slamix" (lettuce mix) and "Spikkeltjessaus" (sauce with little spots). Eighty-one percent thought that Slamix was a very good name. Only 26 percent thought that Spikkeltjessaus was a good name. The name Slamix was chosen for the new product. Interestingly, that was the name that the company had used internally for the new product when it was first being developed.

A short time later, DFI had solved the color-change problem. The company now thought that it had a product ready to be marketed, so a final consumer test was undertaken to test the effect of all the changes that had been made during the previous year.

Two versions of Slamix, a white one and a pink one, were tested at the Institute for Household Research. One hundred eighty housewives were asked what they thought of the product and whether they would buy it or not. The negative reactions to the product were minimal. Almost no negative comments were voiced. The problems of consistency, color, taste, and ingredients had apparently been solved. When asked if they would buy the product, 76 percent of those shown the pink product, and 70 percent of those shown the white product responded in a positive manner. After tasting the two versions of Slamix, the housewives revealed a strong preference for the pink Slamix. The DFI executives felt that the product was now ready to be marketed.

DFI executives next reviewed the financial projections prepared by Mr. de Vries, the product manager. Almost no capital investment would be required as the Slamix would be produced by using present production facilities. Only a few machines, at a total cost of $11,000, would be required.

At an early stage in the development of the product, Slamix sales had been forecasted at 3.7 percent of the total market at the end of the first year. Encouraged by the results of the consumer tests, DFI executives revised their estimate of sales. The new forecast was for approximately 6.7 percent of the market. (See Exhibit 3.)

The directors of the company thought that they finally had the product for which they had been waiting. The consumer tests were complete, and the product had found very high favor with the consumers. There was significant technological development involved in the product, and DFI executives thought that it would take considerable time for the competition to duplicate the product. The product manager's projected sales seemed reasonable. De Vries was asked to prepare a comprehensive report concerning the introductory marketing strategy to be used to introduce the new product.

EXHIBIT 3 Forecast sales of Slamix

Year	Share of market (percent)
Original estimates	
Year 1	3.7%
Year 2	3.9
Year 3	4.4
Revised estimates	
Year 1	6.7
Year 2	11.7

PRICING STRATEGY

The first problem that the product manager had to resolve concerned the suggested retail price that the company should charge for Slamix. To help de Vries make his recommendation, his assistant product manager had made a list of the following considerations:

1. The company's total cost for a 0.30-liter-size bottle of Slamix was $0.20. This was 20 percent higher than DFI's regular salad dressing, Slasaus.

2. The gross margin for Slasaus was 22 percent. Because of the unique qualities of Slamix, large development costs, and possible substitution with Slasaus, a higher gross margin for Slamix might be considered.

3. DFI gave the wholesalers a 12.5 percent margin and retailers a 14.3 percent margin for Slasaus. Possibly these should be increased for Slamix to encourage greater acceptance and promotion by the trade channels of distribution.

4. The two leading salad dressings, Salata by Duyvis and Slasaus, both had a retail price of $0.28 for the 0.30-liter bottle. The retail price for the 0.60-liter bottle was $0.48. Private-label salad dressings were $0.22 for a 0.30-liter bottle. The average price for all salad dressings was approximately $0.26.

5. DFI had conducted some research on the optimal price of Slamix. After using a sample of the product, 140 housewives were asked what price they would be willing to pay for Slamix. Their responses, by percent, were:

	Percent
$0.31 or less	45%
Between $0.31 and $0.40	41
$0.40 or more	14
Total	100%

The average price mentioned was $0.34.

The assistant product manager also prepared the table shown in Exhibit 4. The first column shows the retail price and gives data that allows one to calculate trade margins and gross margin for Slasaus. The remaining six columns show alternative retail prices for Slamix, resulting from different trade margins and gross margins. De Vries wondered which of these prices he should recommend to the board of directors.

EXHIBIT 4   Alternative prices for Slamix*

		Slamix					
	Slasaus	1	2	3	4	5	6
Retail price	$0.28	$0.32	$0.34	$0.34	$0.36	$0.37	$0.38
Price to retailer	0.24	0.28	0.28	0.29	0.295	0.31	0.316
Price to wholesaler	0.21	0.25	0.25	0.26	0.26	0.28	0.28
Cost	0.165	0.20	0.20	0.20	0.20	0.20	0.20

*Selected figures in this table have been disguised.

PROMOTION ALTERNATIVES

The board of directors told the product manager that he had $203,000 for his promotion budget. Of this, $7,000 was to be allocated as Slamix's share of the general corporate advertising which aided all DFI products. The $203,000 was determined by using a percentage of the "expected gross profit of the first year" for Slamix.[3] DFI's policy was to break even in the third year of the new product, attaining a total

---

[3]It was possible that the percentage could be greater than 100 percent. This would mean that the company was willing to spend more than the first year's gross profit for initial promotion.

payback within five years. The company was generally willing to spend the gross profit for the first year as part of the total investment.

The company had already given considerable thought to the sales message and the brand image desired for Slamix. The information below was sent to the advertising agency to help in planning the promotional program of the company:

> *Sales message.* It is now possible, in a completely new way, to make delicious salad. Sla + Slamix = Sla Klaar. (Lettuce + Slamix = Lettuce ready)
>
> *Supporting message.* Slamix is a salad dressing with pieces of onion, gherkins, and paprika.
>
> *Desired brand image.* With Slamix you can make, very easily and very quickly, a delicious salad that also looks nice. Slamix is a complete, good, handy product. DFI is a modern firm with up-to-date ideas.

Thus, the company wanted to get across three principal points. They are (1) that Slamix is a completely new product, (2) that it is convenient, and (3) that it is a salad dressing with ingredients making it a complete salad dressing.

The product manager was undecided as to how to divide the $196,000 among the following alternatives:

1. Television.
2. Radio.
3. Newspaper advertising.
4. Magazines.
5. Sampling.
6. Coupons.
7. Price-off promotion.
8. Key chain premiums.
9. Trade allowances.

Television

The product manager thought that television would be advantageous because of the ability to show the product in actual use—a housewife pouring Slamix onto the lettuce. The cost of using the television medium is shown in Exhibit 5. The company did not have a choice among the seven blocks of time but had to take whatever was available. For planning, however, they figured an average cost of a 30-second ad would be $1,800. De Vries felt that at least 25 advertisements were necessary before the TV advertising would have maximum impact.

EXHIBIT 5   Data on Dutch television media

Station	Block number	Time	Cost of 30-second ad
Nederland 1	1	Before early news	$2,300
Nederland 1	2	After early news	2,300
Nederland 1	3	Before late news	2,950
Nederland 1	4	After late news	2,950
Nederland 2	5	After early news	500
Nederland 2	6	Before late news	840
Nederland 2	7	After late news	840
Average cost per 30-second TV ad			$1,800
Production cost for a TV ad			7,000

TV coverage per 1,000 households = 850 or 85 percent. Only about one half of the homes can receive Nederland 2.

Radio

The chief attraction of radio was its extremely low price. Each 30-second radio ad cost $126 on Radio Veronica, a popular station during the daytime. Production costs for a radio ad were approximately $840. Only 60 percent of the households could receive Radio Veronica, mainly in the western part of the country. De Vries felt that if radio were used, a minimum of 100 spots should be purchased.

Newspapers

De Vries thought the main advantage of newspapers would be the announcement effect and its influence with the local trade. Nationally, the cost of each half-page insertion would be $14,000.

Magazines

Magazines would be a desirable addition to the promotional program for several reasons. Due to the ability to use color, the company could show the product as it actually looked on the shelf. By using several women's magazines, the company could reach a select audience of people reading the magazine at its leisure. Data on selected Dutch magazines are shown in Exhibit 6. Mr. de Vries thought that if they were to use a magazine campaign, at least 10 insertions would be necessary before the advertising would be very effective. Of the possibilities in Exhibit 6, the agency thought that the combination of *Eva, Margriet,* and *AVRO-Televizier* would be the most effective for DFI, since the combination would reach a large number of people at a relatively low cost.

EXHIBIT 6   Data on selected Dutch magazines

Magazines	Type	Circulation	Frequency	Price for full-page ad Black and white	Color	Cost per 1,000 circulation*
Eva	Women's	375,000	Weekly	$ 770	$1,408	$3.75
Margriet	Women's	825,000	Weekly	2,100	3,440	4.15
Libelle	Women's	570,000	Weekly	1,416	2,340	4.10
Prinses	Women's	213,000	Weekly	660	1,175	5.55
Panorama	General	403,000	Weekly	1,300	2,150	5.40
Nieuwe Revu	General	261,000	Weekly	920	1,540	5.90
Spiegel	General	175,000	Weekly	710	1,325	7.55
Het Beste	Digest	325,000	Monthly	965	1,615	4.90
Studio	TV guide	575,000	Weekly	1,525	2,420	4.20
NCRV-gids	TV guide	482,000	Weekly	1,420	2,290	4.75
Vara-gids	TV guide	504,000	Weekly	1,500	2,370	4.70
AVRO-Televizier	TV guide	950,000	Weekly	2,600	3,870	4.05
Combination of Eva, Margriet, and AVRO-Televizier				4,900	7,785	3.65

*Cost of one-page color ad, divided by circulation in thousands. With Eva as an example, cost per 1,000 circulation = $1,408/375 = $3.75

Sampling

Although he realized that it was very expensive, Mr. de Vries considered the use of direct-mail sampling. A small 12 cm. by 18 cm. (approximately 5 × 7 inches) folder could be mailed to Holland's 3.7 million households for $20,000. The cost, however, would increase substantially if a small bottle of the product were to be included in the direct mailing. This cost would be 10 cents for handling, plus 16.5 cents for the actual sample. Thus, it would cost $980,000 to sample the whole country.

Coupon

De Vries was considering whether or not to include a coupon good for $0.04 off the purchase of Slamix with one of the other DFI products —mayonnaise, for example. He estimated that 900,000 coupons would be distributed. At a redemption rate of 5 percent, the cost would, thus, be approximately $1,700.

Price-off Promotion

DFI made use of a reduced retail price for most of its new-product introductions. Thus, the product manager thought it quite normal to consider the use of reducing the retail price by U.S. $0.07 per bottle and

identifying this price reduction on the label of the product. It was felt that this reduced price would encourage the housewives to try Slamix. It was also quite normal to follow up this sales promotion with a similar price reduction approximately five months after the product was introduced. This would encourage those who had still not tried the product to purchase a bottle and would encourage those who had already bought one bottle to continue purchasing the new product. The cost of this price-off promotion is shown in Exhibit 7.

EXHIBIT 7

Introduction
720,000 bottles at 25 cents (U.S. $0.07) off each	$50,400
Handling and display materials	2,800
Total	$53,200

Follow-up five months later
600,000 bottles at 25 cents (U.S. $0.07) off each	$42,000
Handling and display materials	2,800
Total	$44,800

Key Chain Premium

It was very unusual to use a free premium to introduce a new product, but de Vries was considering this alternative for several reasons. Many products in Holland at this time were using key chains as a premium. As shown in Exhibit 8, an extremely large percentage of people

---

EXHIBIT 8   Percentage of households collecting key chains

	June	July	September
Households with children	45	n.a	n.a.
Households without children	5	n.a	n.a.
Total (weighted average)	34	37	41

n.a. = not available.

in Holland were collecting key chains. The details of the research showed that mothers and daughters were more likely to collect key chains, especially if the children were between 8 and 11 years of age. Mr. de Vries felt that if he used key chains as premiums for the introduction of Slamix, he could have a follow-up promotion five months later using either key chains or price-off deals. Selected cost information on the key chain promotion is shown in Exhibit 9.

EXHIBIT 9

Introduction	
720,000 bottles = About 220 metric tons	
750,000 key chains at $0.056	$42,000
Handling costs and display materials	16,800
Total	$58,800
Follow-up five months later	
600,000 bottles = About 180 tons	
625,000 key chains at $0.056	$35,000
Handling costs and display materials	14,000
Total	$49,000

Trade Allowances

The product manager also considered the use of trade allowances to encourage the retailers to accept and promote the new product. The company traditionally offered $0.28 per case of 12 bottles. Thus, if it was decided that trade allowances were desirable, the cost would be $16,800 for the initial introduction and an additional $14,000 used during the follow-up promotion five months later. Trade allowances could be used together with either the price-off promotion or the key chain promotion. The product manager felt that trade allowances would not be very effective without one of the two consumer sales promotions.

DISTRIBUTION

Outside of the question of what trade margins to use and whether or not to use trade allowances during the consumer sales promotion discussed above, Mr. de Vries did not see any problems with distribution. DFI had a sales force of approximately 50 persons who regularly called on 10,000 outlets in Holland. It was felt that the sales force could handle the introduction of the new product with no problem.

The last problem the product manager faced concerned the timing of the introduction of Slamix. The product would be ready for introduction in October. De Vries wondered whether the seasonal nature of the demand for the product would make it more desirable to hold off the introduction until March of the next year.

QUESTIONS

1. Analyze the marketing situation faced by Dutch Food Industries, and identify the problems and the opportunities which it faces.

2. On which segment of the market should they concentrate? How should they define the target market for Slamix?

3. As the product manager for Slamix, send a report to the director of marketing outlining the complete marketing plan for the introduction of Slamix. Your report should include recommendations regarding price, promotion strategy, and timing of the introduction of the product.

GOLDEN RAIN FOUNDATION OF LAGUNA HILLS (A)*

*Addition of subscription entertainment
to cable TV services*

In spring 1978, R. L. Disbro, general manager of Professional Community Management, Inc., for Leisure World, Laguna Hills, California, received a report from a task force that had been set up to consider whether subscription television entertainment should be added to the services provided by the Leisure World Cable Television System to the 20,000 residents of the community. If such a service was to be added, the next step would be to choose among six program distributors who had proposed different combinations of programs and prices for the service.

LEISURE WORLD, LAGUNA HILLS—A RETIREMENT COMMUNITY

Leisure World is an adult community nestled on 2,465 acres of rolling hills overlooking Saddleback Mountain and the beautiful southern California countryside. It is located in Laguna Hills about seven miles inland from the Pacific Ocean midway between Los Angeles and San Diego.

---

*Written by James D. Scott, Professor Emeritus of Marketing, Graduate School of Business Administration, The University of Michigan, a resident of Leisure World.

Leisure World was conceived, designed, and built by Rossmoor Corporation to appeal to adults over 52 years of age. A successful, self-contained private community, it had 12,541 residences and a population of about 20,000 people as of 1978. Another 452 units were to be constructed during 1980–1982 according to the Rossmoor Corporation 's master plan for the development of the area. At the conclusion of the final phase of construction, therefore, there would be approximately 13,000 residences and a population of about 23,000 people in Leisure World.

According to the Rossmoor Corporation, Leisure World is a residential–recreational community that has been planned to provide a richly rewarding, serene, and secure way of life for active mature adults. Home ownership arrangements, community facilities, location, and climate have all been planned to make it possible for residents to achieve such a lifestyle.

Since the first housing units were completed and occupied in 1964, Rossmoor Corporation had followed the practice of constructing a group of residences in a specified area or village and offering them for sale to individuals. Each group was organized into a mutual corporation which managed the performance of specified maintenance, landscaping, and service functions for the benefit of all the residents in the mutual. Then Rossmoor Corporation moved its construction activity into an adjacent area, and the process was repeated with the creation of another mutual corporation. In this manner, necessary community functions and services were extended step by step as the population grew.

During the period from 1964 to early 1968 the villages were organized as cooperative mutuals in which the home purchaser becomes a coowner with other owners of manors within a prescribed area. The Federal Housing Administration guaranteed 40-year loans at 5¾ percent interest on most of the first 6,323 units, which were grouped into 21 cooperative mutuals. The function of each cooperative mutual was to operate and maintain on a nonprofit basis the housing units, or "manors," other buildings (such as laundries), and the grounds included in the area. The cooperative mutuals also held an undivided beneficial interest in all Leisure World community facilities held in trust for them by Golden Rain Foundation.

In accordance with FHA regulations, each cooperative mutual was governed by a board of directors composed of residents of the mutual. The property held by the mutuals, however, was managed by an independent, professional community management firm following policies determined by the boards of directors.

In an effort to gain economies in operation and simplify the community organizational structure, the 21 original cooperative associations were gradually combined into one corporation, United Laguna Hills Mutual. Ownership rights of the residents in the original 21 cooperatives

are evidenced by two membership certificates, one in United Laguna Hills Mutual, which provides an occupancy agreement entitling them to their residences or manors, and the other in Golden Rain Foundation of Laguna Hills, which permits them to use community recreational and social facilities.

Since early 1978 the mutual corporations created in the process of construction have been condominium associations in which the owner has a real estate title to his own manor and is coowner of the surrounding grounds, carports, laundry buildings, and other common areas within the geographic limits of the mutual. Boards of directors govern the areas owned in common on behalf of all the condominium association members. The boards establish all rules and regulations, approve operating budgets, and cooperate with Golden Rain Foundation and other mutuals in community matters.

As of 1978, 10 condominium mutuals were in operation. According to construction plans announced by Rossmoor Corporation in April 1978, four additional mutuals were planned for the final phase of Leisure World development. These would add 452 housing units to the current total of 12,541, for a grand total of 12,993 residences when the project was completed.[1]

Leisure World, Laguna Hills, is a community governed by resident members who elect their mutual directors by direct vote. In turn, the directors of the several mutual corporations elect the 15 directors of Golden Rain Foundation. (See Appendix A for a chart that pictures the organizational relationships mentioned above.) Golden Rain Foundation of Laguna Hills is a nonprofit corporation which owns and operates community facilities and services for the benefit of all its members, such as clubhouses, streets, recreational areas, minibus service, and security. It has also contracted with a local hospital for certain home care and emergency medical support services.

The individual boards of directors of the mutual corporations and Golden Rain Foundation set the policies for their respective geographic areas and for the community as a whole. Golden Rain and each mutual contract with Professional Community Management, Inc. (PCM), an independent professional management firm, to manage the operations of the community. The functions of PCM include: operation of all the official activities and services of the community, handling of all corporate fiscal affairs, employment of all personnel, procurement of all materials and equipment, and administration of contracts.

---

[1]As of 1978, the open and landscaped land owned by Rossmoor Corporation within Leisure World boundaries totaled about 40 acres, including 10 acres which were reserved for the undetermined route of the projected Oso Parkway extension. Should Orange County abandon the parkway plans, Rossmoor could build another 90 residences on the 10 acres of reserved land, bringing the total number of housing units to 13,083.

BENEFITS FEATURED IN MARKETING LEISURE WORLD HOUSING UNITS

The location, climate, and characteristics of the Leisure World development provide the basis for the benefits emphasized by Rossmoor Sales officials in their promotional efforts. (See Appendix B for excerpts from a recent sales brochure.) Purchase of a housing unit in Leisure World, according to this source, offers the buyer true resort living at its finest the year around. The warm California sunshine and mild sea breezes combine to give Laguna Hills a near-perfect climate.

Whether the home is located in a cooperative or condominium mutual, monthly payments are made to cover all exterior maintenance, repairs, and upkeep of manors or villas as well as all gardening and landscaping of common areas. Thus the resident is relieved of time-consuming chores of mowing, raking, watering, trimming, cutting, and painting. Time is available for whatever activities appeal to the individual.

In recognition of this fact, a wide variety of community recreational and social facilities have been made available for the use of all residents. Included in the price of each housing unit is an amount allotted for the development of community facilities. Golden Rain Foundation operates all community facilities for the benefit of the residents. The current expenses of operating these services and facilities are covered by Golden Rain Foundation and the mutual organizations.

As a result of this arrangement, the following facilities are available to all residents:

Five clubhouses complete with art, craft, and hobby shops; game rooms; billiard rooms; and an 834-seat theater.

Four large swimming pools and three jacuzzies.

Tennis courts, lawn bowling greens, and shuffleboard courts.

Three golf courses—an 18-hole course, and two 9-hole courses—which may be used for a nominal fee.

A riding stable with horses to rent at nominal fees.

Adult education classrooms.

A 14,000-volume library.

A master antenna cable television system serving each housing unit.

A no-fare minibus that provides easy access to all community facilities and local shopping areas.

Another important feature of Leisure World is the freedom from worry that is provided by a carefully planned security system. A protective wall surrounds all residential areas. Access to the community is through gated entrances manned by security officers 24 hours a day.

These arrangements restrict vehicular traffic, eliminate unexpected visitors and door-to-door salesmen, and reduce the risk of theft and violence.

According to Rossmoor Corporation, Laguna Hills offers Leisure World residents big-city facilities in a small-town atmosphere. The community offers several regional shopping and financial centers, including major department stores, financial institutions, specialty stores, service shops, and restaurants. Also available are service stations, a professional office building, a modern medical clinic, and the 160-bed Saddleback Community Hospital with a medical staff of 140 members.

COMMUNITY ANTENNA CABLE TELEVISION SYSTEM

Leisure World residents are served by a community cable television system which provides excellent reception of programs from 10 Los Angeles stations (7 VHF and 3 UHF) and 3 San Diego stations. This system also transmits its own closed-circuit television programs with entertainment and information for and about Leisure World people and activities. It uses a master community antenna to receive television programs for Los Angeles and San Diego. The television signals are then processed, amplified, and distributed by underground coaxial cable to all manors in the community.

The cable television system is owned by Golden Rain Foundation on behalf of the residents of the community. It was constructed under a contract between Rossmoor Corporation (the developer) and Rossmoor Electric, Inc., a privately owned firm not connected with the developer. When the system was completed, title was transferred from Rossmoor Corporation to Golden Rain Foundation. The cable system is operated and maintained by Rossmoor Electric under contract with GRF.

Rossmoor Electric, Inc., also maintains and operates Channel 6, the community closed-circuit channel under contract with Golden Rain Foundation. Channel 6 broadcasts an average of six hours a day, five days a week. Fifty percent of this is live, from the studio; the balance is tape relays or films.

Under the GRF/Rossmoor Electric contract the monthly charge per resident for maintaining the cable television system was $3.54 in 1978. At that rate, the owners of the 12,541 residences in Leisure World were getting cable television service at a relatively modest charge compared with charges made by privately owned CATV systems serving other communities. According to the census of pay cable systems conducted by Paul Kagan Associates, Inc., in December 1977 subscribers served by 3,350 operating systems throughout the United States paid an average monthly fee of $7, with a range of from $6 to $9.

PROPOSAL THAT CABLE SYSTEM ADD SUBSCRIPTION ENTERTAINMENT SERVICE

During the summer of 1977, several pay cable program distributors had contacted officials responsible for the management of Leisure World to suggest the addition of subscription entertainment to the weekly program offerings. These distributors provided various combinations of "premium entertainment" which could be transmitted to cable subscribers without the interruption of commercial announcements. The cost of such entertainment would be covered by payment of a monthly subscription fee ranging from $3.00 to $18.75 per month, depending on the amount and caliber of the program material.

M. H. Waterman, president, Golden Rain Foundation, knew that a number of cable television systems in the United States were increasing their revenues and profits by adding subscription television programs to their systems. Indeed, a number of cable systems in southern California had taken such action. He wondered whether there was an unmet desire for such television entertainment among Leisure World residents that might make it desirable to provide this additional service to the subscribers of the cable television system.

Accordingly, he requested that PCM appoint an ad hoc task force with instructions: (1) to investigate whether it was desirable to add subscription (pay cable) entertainment to the programs currently being offered by the Leisure World Cable Television System and (2) if so, to analyze offers being made by alternative distributors of pay cable programs and suggest an approach to choosing a supplier of such entertainment. The members of the task force were: Robert L. Price, director of special projects, PCM, Inc., chairman; Ivan Foley, owner of Rossmoor Electric, Inc.,; and James D. Scott, resident, professor emeritus of marketing, The University of Michigan, who was currently doing research on pay television under a grant from the University of Michigan Graduate School of Business Administration.[2]

DESIRABILITY OF ADDING PAY CABLE SERVICE

It was recognized that the Leisure World CATV system provided residents with excellent reception of programs from 10 Los Angeles stations and 3 San Diego stations. The first question considered by the task force, therefore, was whether sufficient benefits would be received

---

[2]For background information made available to the committee from this source, see James D. Scott, *Bringing Premium Entertainment into the Home via Pay-Cable TV* (Ann Arbor: Division of Research, Graduate School of Business Administration, The University of Michigan, 1977).

from subscription television by Leisure World residents to justify the anticipated cost of such service (expected to range between $3 and $18.75 per month). Pay TV distributors claimed the following benefits for their programs:

1.   A substantial portion of television viewers are annoyed by the number, frequency, and character of the commercial interruptions that they must tolerate in order to view the movies and other entertainment features on over-the-air programs.[3] Pay television programs have accordingly been developed to provide entertainment without the intrusion of commercial announcements.

2.   Since much "free television" programming is aimed at attracting viewers who will constitute a mass market for the products advertised, the entertainment interests of smaller segments of the public are too often neglected. It was considered possible that Leisure World residents, being 52 years of age or older and relatively affluent, might find the offerings of subscription entertainment distributors more appealing than the regular fare available over the Leisure World CATV system.

The types of entertainment offered by the various pay cable distributors included the following: unedited, uncensored, and uninterrupted programs consisting of current full-length feature movies; the best of foreign and classic films; special events such as ballet and theater performances; professional live sports events that were normally blacked out in the metropolitan areas surrounding home teams (including the Los Angeles Dodgers, Rams, and Angels); and such sports specials as horse races and boxing matches, among others.

3.   Of course, residents wishing to attend a movie could do so by driving or busing to Clubhouse III in Leisure World,[4] to nearby El Toro, Laguna Beach, or into Los Angeles. Travel was also necessary to see plays in Laguna Beach, musical comedies in Los Angeles, baseball games in Anaheim, and so on. Subscription entertainment might bring such entertainment features uncut and uninterrupted into the living room of the resident, thus eliminating the time and effort involved in driving and parking. Since a drive to central Los Angeles involved traveling about 1½ hours each way on the busy metropolitan freeways, and convenient parking is expensive and difficult to find, many Leisure World residents would probably prefer to avoid such trips.

Consumer benefits such as those outlined above were believed to explain in part, the growth of pay television service in the United States.

---

[3]Ibid., pp. 7, 8, 49.

[4]The PCM, Inc., Recreation Division sponsored regular entertainment programs each month in the auditorium in Clubhouse III. During the month of April, for example, the following movies were scheduled: *20,000 Leagues Under the Sea, Lawrence of Arabia,* and *The Other Side of the Mountain.* The price of admission was $1 per person. Programs were screened at 7:30 P.M. on weekdays and at 2:30 P.M. and 7:30 P.M. on Sundays.

According to the *Census of Pay-Cable Systems as of Dec. 31, 1977*, taken by Paul Kagan Associates, Inc., the growth in the pay TV population substantially exceeded expectations during the second half of 1977, reaching an estimated 1,733,611 on December 31, 1977.[5] This figure includes pay cable, multipoint distribution service (MDS/cassette) providing programs to viewers in hotels and apartment buildings, and subscription television (STV) offered over the air by broadcasting stations. Thus, total pay subscribers as of December 31, 1977, had increased by 69.7 percent over the December 31, 1976 figure.

According to Paul Kagan Associates, Inc., there were two primary reasons for the thrust: (1) 240 new pay cable systems were launched in 1977, a 66 percent increase over the 364 operating on December 31, 1976 and (2) there was considerable internal growth for the first time in the industry's history: pay cable systems whose growth had previously flattened out came back to life in 1977. As a result, the average penetration of homes passed had moved above 12 percent and the average penetration of basic cable subscribers was over 25 percent.

Selected penetration data from CATV systems located in California were then examined by the task force. These figures are given in Exhibit 1.[6]

The Irvine cable system was near Laguna Hills and had 14,712 subscribers who paid $6 per month for the basic service as of December 31, 1977. Pay cable service had been introduced in July 1976, and 3,818 persons had subscribed in 18 months at a charge of $9.95 per month. Thus, 25.9 percent of the basic cable subscribers, or 19 percent of the homes passed by the cable system, had signed for the pay cable entertainment. Subscribers taking both the basic service and the pay entertainment were paying a combined monthly rate of $15.95 for the two.

These results were then compared with the performance of all CATV systems offering pay entertainment in the United States as of December 31, 1977. There were 604 systems providing pay service. It had been accepted by 12.2 percent of the residents of homes passed by the cable system and by 25.3 percent of the basic cable subscribers. The Irvine system's performance was better than that of the average U.S. system: 19 percent of the homes passed had pay cable service at $9.95 per month as compared with the U.S. average of 12.2 percent at $7.92 per month; while 25.9 percent of basic cable subscribers, as compared with 25.3 percent, had added pay entertainment at $9.95 to the basic cable charge of $6.00 per month for a total of $15.95. (The U.S. combined rate was $14.92 per month.)

The Laguna Beach cable system performance was also given special

---

[5] Paul Kagan Associates, Inc., *Pay TV Newsletter,* March 8, 1978, p. 1.

[6] Paul Kagan Associates, Inc., *Census as of Dec. 31, 1977 of Pay-Cable Systems Operational on Sept. 30, 1977,* pp. 4, 5, 7.

EXHIBIT 1

Cable TV system and program source	Date pay 1st offered	Pay sub-scribers	Homes passed	Percent pay pene-tration	Pay rate	Cable sub-scribers	Percent pay pene-tration	Basic cable rate	Com-bined rate
Irvine, California (Cinemerica of Beverly Hills, California)	7/76	3,818	20,084	19.0%	$9.95	14,712	25.9%	$6.00	$15.95
Los Angeles, California (Hollywood Home Theater)	4/74	49,000	270,000	18.1	8.95	85,000	57.6	8.45	17.40
Orange County, California* (Showtime)	3/77	6,782	36,130	18.8	4.95	18,554	36.5	7.50	12.45
Laguna Beach, California	3/77	3,855	27,347	14.1	9.95	16,942	22.7	7.25	17.20
All systems: totals and averages		1.6 million	13.4 million	12.2	7.92	6.5	25.3	7.00	14.92

*Orange County consolidates Times Mirror Systems in Aegean Hills, Mission Viejo, San Clemente, and Tustin.

attention by the task force. Pay entertainment, supplied by Showtime, had been introduced in March 1977 and had been accepted by 22.7 percent of basic cable subscribers (U.S. average 25.3 percent) and by 14.1 percent of homes passed (versus U.S. average of 12.2 percent). Laguna Beach subscribers paid $9.95 for pay programs and $7.25 for basic cable service, or a total of $17.20.

The response to pay cable TV in other nearby communities in Orange County (Mission Viejo, San Clemente, Tustin, and Aegean Hills) was also of interest. Thus pay service on these systems was initiated in March 1977; by December 31, 1977, 36.5 percent of basic cable subscribers, or 18.8 percent of homes passed, had purchased the service (U.S. averages 25.3 percent and 12.2 percent, respectively). The Orange County subscribers paid $4.95 per month for pay cable programs in addition to $7.50 for basic cable service, or a total of $12.45 per month.

Finally, the Los Angeles experience was studied as a means of determining the results of marketing pay entertainment since April 1974—three years and eight months. In Los Angeles the basic cable service cost $8.45 per month and pay entertainment was provided by Hollywood Home Theater at a charge of $8.95, or a total of $17.40. It is noteworthy that 57.6 percent of basic cable subscribers, or 18.1 percent of homes passed, had contracted for pay entertainment (U.S. averages 25.3 percent and 12.2 percent, respectively).

In summarizing the data reviewed above, the task force noted that from 14 percent to 19 percent of cable subscribers located in nearby communities had bought pay entertainment within 9 to 18 months of its introduction. These subscribers were paying from $4.95 to $9.95 for the premium entertainment provided. When the charge for pay TV was added to the basic cable charge, the total price amounted to from $12.45 to $17.40 per month.

As the task force discussed the data reviewed above, the question was raised as to whether residents in Leisure World would respond to the offer of pay television to the same degree as the subscribers of cable systems in nearby communities had done. This question was based upon the following considerations: (1) The residents of Leisure World were all over 52 years of age; most of them were retired. (2) Most of the residents were living on Social Security pensions and other retirement income and hence had a tendency to be budget conscious. They paid only $3.54 for cable service, and they might be reluctant to add from $5 to $10 per month for the pay entertainment. (3) The Leisure World cable system provided excellent reception of 10 Los Angeles television stations (including 3 educational TV channels) and 3 San Diego stations. Accordingly, many residents might not feel a strong enough desire for premium entertainment to pay the monthly subscription fee.

These comments led to a discussion of whether there was any evidence of interest in pay TV among the Leisure World residents. Ivan

Foley, owner of Rossmoor Electric, reported that he had received several telephone calls indicating a desire for pay television. Some of these were from newcomers who had previously lived in other areas served by pay television. Others were the result of word-of-mouth comment heard by Leisure World residents from friends who were enjoying such service. Robert L. Price, director of special projects, after reviewing his own observations, concluded that there did not yet appear to be any clamor for pay TV in Leisure World, even though the idea was expanding rapidly throughout the nation.

Nevertheless, it was recognized that there might be an unrealized desire for premium television entertainment at a price if residents knew that such service could be provided and if the benefits of pay television were promoted. Discussion with pay TV distributors had indicated that the cost per subscriber might fall within the range of $5 to $9 per month. Taking into account the capital investment necessary and the direct costs of operation, it appeared that a minimum of 10 percent participation by residents, or 1,200 customers, would be needed for the cable operator to break even on the addition of pay television service. At this point the task force turned to a consideration of who might serve as the pay-television contractor, how the acquisition of programs might be handled, what capital investment would be required, what direct costs would be involved, what revenue per customer might be anticipated, and what the break-even point might be for the Leisure World operation.

What organization should serve as the pay TV operator? While Golden Rain Foundation owned the Leisure World Cable Television System, the maintenance and operation of the system was handled under contract by Rossmoor Electric, Inc. It was the opinion of the task force that if pay entertainment were to be introduced, Rossmoor Electric should be involved in the installation of the necessary pay equipment and in the maintenance of the system. This was believed to be essential so as to optimize the technical coordination of picture and sound quality.

The basic technical concept behind pay television is the scrambling of both picture and sound at the transmitter. Then, once provisions have been made for payment, a special device in each subscriber's home unscrambles the program and permits viewing.

How might the acquisition of programs be handled? Investigation by the task force indicated that pay television service was available from program distributors using four basic methods of transmission and reception: (1) Programs originating in a central studio were transmitted via microwave and coaxial cable to the head end of the cable television system, where they were "scrambled" and redistributed over the cable. Pay subscribers were provided with converters that unscrambled the signal and enabled them to view the program on their television sets. (2) An approach gaining widespread acceptance was to transmit the

program via satellite from a central point such as New York City. In order to receive this signal the cable system had to install an earth station. Here again, the program was scrambled at the head end of the cable system and unscrambled by converters on the pay subscribers' television sets. (3) Programs were placed on videotape by the distributor and sent to the cable system, where videotape projectors were used to distribute the entertainment to pay subscribers. Following this approach, the pay distributor developed a tailor-made program for individual cable systems. Accordingly, this method of operation was customarily referred to as "stand-alone," as opposed to the approach of distributing the same program material to all cable systems served by the pay distributor. (4) Subscription television programs were broadcast scrambled over the air. Subscribers received the program over their television antennas; a converter was provided to unscramble the signal. In Leisure World the subscription television programs could be received on the community antenna used by the cable system and distributed to pay subscribers provided with converters to unscramble the signal.

What television channel could be made available for pay service?   The Leisure World cable system offered residents 12 channels. Channel 6 was used as a medium for such features as community news, announcements, and programs produced by the Leisure World Studio. All other channels were currently filled; indeed Channel 3 was shared by the independent Los Angeles television station KWHY (Channel 22) and the Los Angeles public broadcasting system station, KOEC (Channel 50). The task force did not believe that it would be desirable to remove an existing channel in order to make room for pay entertainment. Each of the existing channels had faithful followers who would object to the loss of a valued source of entertainment. According to Foley, through the provision of a proper converter on the television sets of pay cable subscribers, it would be possible to use one of the nine mid-band channels that fell between Channel 6 (frequency range 82–88 MHz) and Channel 7 (frequency range 174–180 MHz). These were identified as mid-band channels A through I; Channels G, H, and I appeared to be logical candidates for the Leisure World pay program.

What capital investment would be required to provide pay-TV service?   In seeking information to facilitate an analysis of the cost and revenue aspects of introducing pay television, the task force interviewed representatives of six program distributors.[7] It soon became clear that there would be considerable variation in the investment required, costs, and revenues, depending upon which firm was chosen to provide pay service. As a means of developing a financial analysis to assist the Golden

---

[7]The information gathered from these six program distributors is presented in Case 4–4, Rossmoor Electric, Inc. (A).

Rain board of directors to reach a decision on the question of whether to add pay television service, however, the following hypothetical figures were developed as being roughly representative.

1. Customarily, program distributors would be looking to the owner of the local cable system for the initial capital outlay required for installation of the necessary pay television equipment. It was estimated that this equipment would cost $100,000 and would include the following items:

1,000 converter/descramblers installed in homes of subscribers at $40 each	$40,000
Central equipment at the head end	60,000
Total	$100,000

2. Individual subscribers would be expected to pay an installation charge of from $15 to $40 for the converter/descrambler unit, ownership of which would be retained by the Leisure World cable system. The initial investment in these 1,000 converter/descramblers would be made by the cable operator.

What expenses and revenues might be expected? The monthly charge to subscribers was expected to run between $5 and $9 per month, depending upon which program distributor was used. A hypothetical breakdown of the anticipated charges and cost elements follows:

	Per subscriber
Service charge to program distributor	$4.25
Services of Rossmoor Electric in installing and operating the system	3.25
Golden Rain Foundation for billing and collection expenses	0.50
Total	$8.00

The payment to the program distributor would cover the program fees. The amount varied, depending upon the monthly fee charged to subscribers, but a quantity discount was granted, depending upon the number of subscribers. The amount could vary from $3.00 to $4.40; for this illustration a program charge of $4.25 per subscriber has been assumed. It was customary, however, for the program distributor, assisted by the local cable operator, to take primary responsibility for the initial marketing program used to get subscribers for the pay entertainment. The local cable operator would be responsible for subsequent marketing efforts.

A second cost element listed above is payment for the services of Rossmoor Electric in installing, operating, and maintaining the pay television system. This firm was responsible for maintaining good cable

television service in Leisure World. It was important that converter/ descramblers be installed correctly so that high-quality transmission of picture and sound would be maintained. Operation of the pay television equipment at the head end also had to be coordinated with the day-to-day cable system operations. Proper maintenance of the pay cable equipment was also necessary. It was estimated that these services would cost $3.25 per subscriber.

The necessary billing and collection services could be provided by Professional Community Management, Inc., on behalf of Golden Rain Foundation. Since PCM was already handling such work in connection with other community services, it was believed that the charge of 50 cents per subscriber would be adequate.

Investigation suggested that space for pay television equipment was available at the head end or studio so that no additional building would have to be provided for this purpose.

If pay television were offered, should it be optional?   If the task force were to recommend adding pay television to the cable system, should it be offered to residents as an optional service? Or should the Golden Rain board of directors make it mandatory and add the price of the pay service to the monthly carrying charges assessed to all Leisure World homeowners? During 1978, for example, each homeowner was assessed $70.37 to cover operating expenses shared by Golden Rain Foundation and the mutuals. Of this amount, $3.54 was budgeted to cover the cost of the cable television system. The GRF board could add the cost of the pay entertainment to these monthly carrying charges and thus provide assured revenue for the pay television service.

Information supplied by the six program distributors indicated that programs of the desired quality would probably cost $6 per subscriber if 100 percent participation were required. On this basis, 12,000 subscribers would contribute $72,000 per month in revenue for pay entertainment, or $864,000 per year. By contrast, if pay service were made optional and 10 percent, or 1,200, subscribed a charge of $10 per month would bring in $12,000 in revenue, or $144,000 per year.

The plan of making pay service mandatory would be consistent with the present arrangement of requiring all homeowners to pay $3.54 per month for cable television. Clearly, it would simplify the task of marketing pay entertainment service. Such effort could be confined to providing information about the programs available, the benfits of having such a service, and the rationale of the Golden Rain board in making subscription to the service mandatory.

Price expressed concern about the mandatory approach, however. He reminded the task force that inflation had made members of the Leisure World community sensitive to any proposed increases in the monthly carrying charges. Also, there was some doubt about what percentage of the cable subscribers would choose pay entertainment if they were of-

fered the option of making their own decision on the service. If only 10 percent really wanted pay entertainment strongly enough to pay for it voluntarily, then the other 90 percent would certainly protest action by the Golden Rain board making the service mandatory. Under these circumstances he questioned the wisdom of adding $6.00 to the monthly carrying charges of $70.37—an increase of 8.5 percent.

Based on this discussion, the task force voted to make pay television optional should it be added to the Leisure World cable system.

What revenue per subscriber might be anticipated from pay television? In order to make it possible to compute the number of subscribers required to break even on an investment of $100,000, the task force turned to a discussion of anticipated revenue per customer. This would depend, of course, upon the monthly charge established for the Leisure World pay television service. Helpful information on the charges set by cable systems adding pay entertainment was found in *Census as of Dec. 31, 1977 of Pay-Cable Systems.* From this source, data were extracted on the rate per month charged for pay television, the acceptance of such service by basic cable subscribers, and the penetration achieved by pay television (see Exhibit 1). The task force noted especially the following information:

1. The average pay television rate per month was $7.92 while the average basic cable rate amounted to $7.00, or a total combined rate of $14.92 per month. Subscribers to the pay service amounted to 25.3 percent of basic cable customers, or 12.2 percent of the homes passed by the cable system.
2. The charges made for pay service by nearby cable systems ranged from $4.95 in Orange County (combined rate $12.45) to $9.95 in Laguna Beach (combined rate $17.20) and $9.95 in Irvine (combined rate $15.95). Pay penetration of basic cable subscribers was 36.5 percent in Orange County, 22.7 percent in Laguna Beach, and 25.9 percent in Irvine.

In order to get a rough idea of the anticipated revenue per subscriber from pay television, the task force made a preliminary calculation in which it assumed that the monthly charge for pay service was set at $10. This was approximately the same charge as that made in Laguna Beach and Irvine. The first step was to compute the monthly contribution per subscriber that would be available to cover the fixed capital cost of $100,000 necessary to set up the pay system.

The second step was to estimate what percentage of cable subscribers would probably subscribe to pay service during the first five years. By referring to the Paul Kagan census data for cable systems in which pay service had been offered for three months or less, it was found that the average penetration of cable subscribers was 21.6 percent. The average

Revenue per subscriber per month		$10.00
Less monthly expenses and charges:		
Service charge to program distributor	$4.25	
Services of Rossmoor Electric in installing and operating the system	3.25	
Golden Rain Foundation for billing and collection expense	0.50	
Total		8.00
Amount available to contribute toward coverage of capital costs		$2.00

penetration for all systems offering pay television was 25.3 pecent.[8] For the purpose of this analysis, therefore, it was assumed that the penetration at the end of the first year of pay service in Leisure World would be 22 percent. Since it would probably take at least three months to achieve this level, the average penetration for the first year would be approximately 20 percent.

On this basis the estimated revenue and the time required to break even would be as follows:

```
1st year
   12,000 subscribers × 20 percent
      purchasing pay service = 2,400 pay subscriptions
   2,400 × $2 contribution = $4,800 per month
   $4,800 × 12 = $57,600 contribution
2d year
   $100,000 fixed capital − $57,600 = $42,400 remainder
   Penetration = 22 percent
   12,000 cable subcriptions × 0.22 = 2,640 pay subscriptions
   2,640 × $2 contribution/month = $5,280 per month
   Remainder of capital costs to cover = $42,400
   $42,400 ÷ $5,280 per month = 8.03 months to cover
      capital costs
```

In short, it was estimated that the Leisure World cable system would break even on the $100,000 capital investment in pay service in approximately 12 + 8 = 20 months. Thereafter, the $2 contribution per subscriber per month, or $5,280 per month, would be profit on the operations. Thus, in five years the revenue from pay service might be expected to pay back the $100,000 invested to provide the service and, in addition, contribute the following amount to profit:

2d year, $5,280 × 12	63,360
Less capital cost	− 42,400
	20,960
3d, 4th, and 5th years, $63,360 × 3	
Contribution to profit, five years	+ 190,800
	211,760

---

[8]Paul Kagan Associates, Inc., *Census as of Dec. 31, 1977 of Pay-Cable Systems Operational as of Sept. 30, 1977*, pp. 11–12.

It was recognized that the foregoing calculation assumed a penetration of only 22 percent of cable subscribers during the third, fourth, and fifth years after the introduction of pay television service, whereas actual performance in those years might be higher. In Los Angeles, for example, pay television was first offered at $8.95 per month in April 1974. In 3½ years pay penetration had reached 58 percent of cable subscribers. In Irvine, where pay television had been introduced in July 1976 at $9.95 per month, penetration had reached 26 percent by December 31, 1977. In assuming a penetration of 22 percent of Leisure World cable subscribers in the third, fourth, and fifth years after introduction, the task force was making a conservative estimate.

Then, too, in analyzing the pay television census data, the task force realized that there was not a simple relationship between the rate charged for pay entertainment per month and the percentage of cable subscribers who bought the service. Clearly, the demographic characteristics of the area would influence the demand for pay entertainment. Likewise, the character of the programs delivered by different program distributors would be an important influence upon the acceptance of pay television by prospects. Also, the effectiveness of the marketing and sales promotional efforts of both the distributor and the cable operator would have considerable influence upon the acceptance of pay entertainment by the cable subscribers. And, of course, the alternative entertainment facilities easily available to the prospects (movies, athletic events, musicals, and plays, among others) would influence the decision of whether to subscribe for pay entertainment on the cable system.

In spite of these caveats, it was believed that the rough approximations resulting from the use of the census data and the necessary simplifying assumptions would be helpful to those who were required to make a decision on the question of whether to add pay TV service to the Leisure World cable system.

How would a lower or higher charge for pay service influence the results?   In the process of gathering information for use in the above calculations, the task force became interested in the results achieved by cable systems that set a monthly charge for pay service either substantially lower or higher than the average of $7.92 mentioned above (plus the average basic cable service rate of $7.00, or a total of $14.92). Attention was focused upon the relationship between the monthly charge and the percentage of penetration achieved by these systems (see Exhibit 2).

The highest rate for pay cable systems in 1977 was $11.95 per month. The penetration of homes passed by cable systems using this rate ranged from 2.1 percent in Toledo, Ohio, to 11.2 percent in Walnut Creek, California (U.S. average 12.2 percent). Acceptance of pay service by cable subscribers ranged from 5.9 percent in Toledo to 17.8 percent in Stockton, California (U.S. average 25.3 percent).

EXHIBIT 2 Selected data on pay cable rates and penetration, 1977

System/pay distributor	Date pay service started	Pay subscribers	Homes passed	Pay penetration of homes passed	Pay rate	Pay penetration of cable subscribers	Basic cable subscribers	Basic cable rate	Combined rate
Dayton, Ohio, suburbs (TPS)	9/77	3,011	9,100	33.1%	$3.95	88.9%	3,386	6.95	10.90
Dayton, Ohio (TPS)	3/77	2,809	10,100	27.8	3.95	64.9	4,328	7.25	11.20
Dover, N.H. (TPS)	5/77	2,137	11,300	18.9	3.95	25.1	8,510	6.25	10.20
Jackson, Mich. (TPS)	5/77	4,843	17,500	27.7	3.95	43.6	11,090	7.40	11.35
La Habra, Calif. (Best)	5/77	2,000	11,000	18.2	3.00	100.0	2,000	7.00	10.00
Lansing, Mich. (TPS)	5/76	18,378	51,300	35.8	3.95	72.7	25,265	6.95	10.90
New Haven, Conn. (TPS)	3/77	4,520	12,690	35.6	1.50	82.4	5,485	7.50	8.50
Orange County, Calif. (Show)	3/77	6,782	36,130	18.8	4.95	36.5	18,554	7.50	12.45
Oxnard, Calif. (PTV)	6/75	7,200	35,000	20.6	4.50	4.1	13,300	6.95	11.45
Redondo Beach, Calif. (Best)	5/77	3,500	19,000	18.4	3.00	100.0	3,500	7.00	10.00
San Jose, Calif. (TPS)	2/76	66,250	170,000	39.0	3.00	98.8	67,000	7.95	10.95
Relatively high rates									
Burbank, Calif. (TPS)	4/75	4,850	41,467	11.7	11.45	23.5	20,555	6.00	17.45
Concord, Calif. (OTP)	8/74	4,440	31,026	14.3	11.95	15.9	27,891	6.82	18.77
Monterey, Calif. (OTP)	7/75	1,178	18,448	6.4	11.95	8.7	13,407	6.95	18.90
Stockton, Calif. (OTP)	6/75	2,373	49,300	4.8	11.95	17.8	13,277	6.50	18.45
Stockton, Calif. (Best)	7/76	436	800	54.5	6.75	72.6	600	6.50	12.75
Toledo, Ohio (OPT)	9/73	3,000	146,000	2.1	11.95	5.9	50,500	7.50	19.45
Walnut Creek, Calif. (OPT)	8/74	1,567	13,935	11.2	11.95	10.9	14,374	6.65	18.60

Source: *Census as of Dec. 31, 1977 of Pay-Cable Systems*; estimates of Paul Kagan Associates, Inc., Rockville Center, New York; supplement to *Pay TV Newsletter*, March 8, 1978, pp. 1–10.

In contrast, relatively low rates per month were charged for pay service by the following cable systems:

San Jose, California (TPS)—rate/month $3.00—penetration 39 percent of homes passed, 98.8 percent of cable subscribers, achieved in two years.

Jackson, Michigan (TPS)—rate/month $3.95—penetration 28 percent of homes passed, 44 percent of cable subscribers; achieved in seven months.

Note that while pay penetration of homes passed for all U.S. systems was 12.2 percent, San Jose achieved 39 percent and Jackson achieved 28 percent. While penetration of cable subscribers for all U.S. cable systems was 25.3 percent, San Jose hit 98.8 percent and Jackson 44 percent.

It is also helpful to add the charge per month for pay service to that already being paid for basic cable service in order to check on the revenue per subscriber from both services.

Jackson, Michigan was charging $7.40 for basic cable service; pay was added for $3.95 per month; the combined rate was thus $11.35. Since 44 percent of cable subscribers signed up for pay, the total revenue per cable subscriber was $9.12.

San Jose, California, was charging $7.95 for basic cable service; pay entertainment was added at a cost of $3.00 per month; the combined charge was thus $10.95. Since 98.8 percent of cable subscribers bought pay service, the total revenue per cable subscriber amounted to $10.92.

In contrast, the two cable systems charging $11.95 for pay service achieved the following results:

Toledo, Ohio, was charging $7.50 for basic cable service; pay was added at $11.95; the combined charge was $19.45. Only 5.9 percent of the basic subscribers bought pay service; the total revenue per cable subscriber was thus $8.21 per month.

Walnut Creek, California, was charging $6.65 for basic service; pay was added at $11.95; the combined rate was thus $18.60. Since 11.2 percent of basic cable subscribers signed up for pay TV, the total revenue per month per cable subscriber was $7.95.

In short, the contrasting pricing strategies of the four cable systems mentioned above were associated with the following total revenue figures per cable subscriber:

	Pay TV $3.00 or $3.95 per month		Pay TV $11.95 per month
Total revenue per cable subscriber:			
San Jose	$10.92	Walnut Creek	$7.95
Jackson	9.12	Toledo	8.21

Break-even at a higher rate per month for pay TV.   With the above census data as background the task force calculated the time required to break even on a $100,000 capital investment, assuming that the pay television service were priced at $11.95 per month. Since Leisure World residents paid $3.54 per month for basic cable service, the addition of $11.95 for pay entertainment would make their total payment for television entertainment $15.94. (In Walnut Creek, California, the combined rate was $18.60 per month on December 31, 1977. In Toledo, Ohio, it was $19.45 per month.)

At a charge of $11.95 for pay entertainment, it was assumed that the Leisure World system would achieve a penetration of 11.8 percent of basic cable subscribers. (Five cable systems charging $11.95 per month for pay TV achieved an average of 11.8 percent penetration in 2½ to 4¼ years.) Calculations of the contribution per subscriber to cover capital costs and the time required to break even follow.

1. Calculation of contribution per subscriber to capital costs and profit:

Pay cable charge per month		$11.95
Less monthly expenses and charges:		
Program distributor	$4.25	
Rossmoor Electric for installation and maintenance	3.25	
Billing and collection (Golden Rain Foundation)	0.50	8.00
Contribution	$3.95	

2. Time required to break even:

Capital costs = $100,000
Penetration: 12,000 subscribers
  × 11.8 percent* = 1,416 pay-TV buyers
1,416 × $3.95 per month = $5,593 per month
$100,000 ÷ $5,593 = 17.8 months

*Average of penetration percentages achieved in the following cable systems charging $11.95 per month for pay TV; Concord (after 3½ years), 15.9 percent; Monterey (after 2½ years), 8.7 percent; Stockton (after 2½ years), 17.8 percent; Toledo (after 4¼ years), 5.9 percent; and Walnut Creek (after 3½ years), 10.9 percent.

After these calculations were completed it was noted that the time required to break even on the capital investment for pay TV would be 20 months if the service were sold at $10 per month. If the charge were increased to $11.95 per month, then it was estimated that it would probably take 18 months to break even—or 2 months sooner.

Break-even at a lower rate per month for pay TV.   When attention was turned to the possibility of charging a rate as low as $3 per month for pay TV, it was evident that this price would not cover the monthly charges and expenses estimated at $8 above (see p. 700 for an explanation of this estimate). The $8 figure, however, was based upon quotations received from program distributors transmitting material via microwave, coaxial cable, or satellite. Cable systems charging $3 per

month for pay TV were operating on a stand-alone basis; their programs were furnished in videotape form and consisted of "movies only" entertainment. Accordingly, the programs offered by the stand-alone pay TV operations provided less variety than was customarily provided by distributors transmitting via microwave, coaxial cable, or satellite.

Then, too, it was believed that videotape offered less assurance of delivering high-quality image and sound than did the alternatives mentioned above. Nevertheless, it was argued that Golden Rain might require stand-alone distributors to work with Rossmoor Electric as a means of getting the best possible technical quality in the television programs received by Leisure World subscribers. Accordingly, the task force approached stand-alone distributors for information upon which cost and break-even estimates might be made.

These distributors indicated that stand-alone operation would probably involve the following charges and expenses which tend to vary according to the number of subscribers served:

	Costs per subscriber
Programming costs: booking, scheduling, license fees (services performed by distributor)	$3.50
Maintenance of descramblers installed on subscribers' TV sets (to Rossmoor Electric)	0.50
Billing and collection (to Golden Rain)	0.50
Total	$4.50

In addition, the following costs were anticipated (these would be determined periodically by executive decision and contractual arrangement):

	Per month
Labor	$1,000
Cassette fee (to distributor)	550
Preview videotapes	35
Program guides at 5 cents each (assume 12,000 distributed per month)	600
Quarterly program guides at 50 cents each ($1,800 per quarter ÷ 3)	600
Total	$2,785

Finally, it was estimated that the following investment would have to be made in order to initiate the pay television service:

Programming equipment (automatic video cassette player/charger)	$15,000
Security equipment ($17 each; assume 2,640, or 22 percent of residents, subscribe first year). It is necessary to order this equipment in advance of marketing pay TV. If subscribers are charged $17 for installation of descramblers, this revenue will eventually offset the above investment	44,880
Marketing: four free movies; direct mail; first-month program guide; quarterly color brochure with survey questionnaire to determine program preferences—12,000 at 50 cents (prior to start-up)	12,000
Total	$71,880

When the task force examined these figures, it became clear that a charge for pay television of $3.00 per month was not feasible since the programming, maintenance, billing, and collection expenses were estimated at $4.50 per subscriber. Estimated programming costs of $3.50 per subscriber assumed seven movie titles of good quality at 50 cents each. This cost could be reduced somewhat by booking movies of lesser quality or by offering only one movie per week. Stand-alone distributors advised that high-quality movies be scheduled in Leisure World in order to build the subscriber penetration needed to make pay TV a profitable venture. It might be possible, however, to reduce programming costs by offering only five movies per month at 35 cents per movie, or a total of $1.75 per month. If maintenance costs of 50 cents and billing and collection expenses of 50 cents were added, the total would be $2.75 per month. At a charge for pay TV of $3 per month, this would leave only 25 cents per month to cover other necessary expenses. Since these expenses were estimated at $2,785 per month, it would take $2,785 ÷ 0.25 = 11,140 pay TV subscribers out of 12,000 cable customers, or 93 percent, to break even. Until this figure was exceeded, there would be no contribution to cover the capital costs and provide a profit.

Was it likely that pay cable would achieve 93 percent penetration in Leisure World if it cost $3 per month? The Paul Kagan census listed four cable systems that charged $3.00 to $3.95 per month for pay TV in 1977. The average rate of penetration of pay TV in these four systems amounted to 61.5 percent. This experience raised serious doubts about the possibility of achieving a 93 percent penetration. Indeed, the only cable systems in which virtually all subscribers had pay television were those of cities like San Jose, whose cable system received permission to raise its basic cable rates by $3 and provide pay entertainment to *all* cable subscribers. In short, basic cable service and pay TV were sold as a package for $10.95 ($7.95 for basic service plus $3.00 for pay TV). The basic service could *not* be purchased separately.

Since the task force had previously decided that it would not be wise to attempt to get the Golden Rain board to approve pay cable service as a mandatory charge to all Leisure World residents, attention was then turned to the examination of the probable results if the pay entertainment price were set at $6 per month. The following calculations were then made:

	1st month	Later months
Revenue per subscriber, per month	$ 6.00	$6.00
Installation charge per subscriber	17.00	—
	$23.00	
Programming, maintenance, billing, and collection costs per subscriber	4.50	4.50
Cost of descrambler + converter	17.00	—
	$21.50	

	1st month	Later months
Contribution to cover monthly expenses, $23.00 − 21.50	$ 1.50	$1.50

Monthly costs for labor, cassettes, preview
  videotapes, and program guides = $2,785
Subscribers required to break even on
  these monthly expenses: $2,785 ÷ $1.50 = 1,857 households
  1,857 ÷ 12,000 cable subscribers = 15.4 percent penetration

Of course, the more significant question was how many subscribers would be required in order to break even on both monthly expenses and the total capital costs? This calculation follows:

Over a period of 12 months a subscriber
  contributes $1.50 × 12 = $18 toward covering monthly
  expenses and capital investment.	

Yearly cost for labor, cassettes, preview
  videotapes, and program guides:
  $2,785 × 12
	$33,420

Capital investment: programming equip-
  ment, security equipment, and initial
  marketing effort
	71,880

Total	$105,300

Number of subscribers required to break even: $105,300
  divided by $35 (12-month contribution of 18 plus
  installation payment of 17)
Capital investment of $105,300 ÷ $35.00 = 3,009
  subscribers, or 25 percent of Leisure World cable
  subscribers

According to the above calculations, it would require 3,009 pay subscribers, or a penetration of 25 percent of cable users, for the Leisure World cable system to break even. This assumed an expenditure of $27,000 for programming equipment and the initial marketing effort. Since 2,640 descramblers would have to be purchased in advance of actual installation during the first year of pay TV, this would require additional capital of $44,880. Since each subscriber would pay an installation charge of $17, the investment of $44,880 would be liquidated by the time 22 percent of the residents (2,640) had bought the service.

How long would it take to get 3,009 pay subscribers? Reference to Paul Kagan's census of pay cable systems which introduced service at $6 per month during October, November, and December 1977 was helpful. The three systems which fell into this category achieved the following penetration of cable subscribers: (1) East Lansing, Michigan (Home Box Office programs), 35 percent of cable subscribers at charges of $5.95 for pay and $6.95 for basic cable service, combined rate $12.90; (2) Laceyville, Pennsylvania (Home Box Office), 8.5 percent of cable subscribers at charges of $6.00 for pay and $5.75 for basic cable service, combined rate $11.75; and (3) Marietta, Georgia (Telemation Program

Service), 75 percent penetration of cable subscribers at charges of $6.00 for pay and $6.95 for basic cable service, combined rate $12.95. The average penetration of cable subscribers achieved by the pay service of these three systems was 39.5 percent. Because the ratios varied from 8.5 percent to 75 percent, however, this average figure was not especially helpful. Based on the limited evidence available, however, it appeared that a charge of $6 per month for pay entertainment over the Leisure World cable system would stand a chance of reaching or exceeding 25 percent.

In summary, as a result of the above cost and revenue estimates the following was provided to the Golden Rain Foundation board for consideration in evaluating the wisdom of adding pay entertainment to the Leisure World Cable Television System:

1. At a $10 per month rate for pay television, the contribution toward covering the estimated capital investment of $100,000 would be $2 per month per pay subscriber. Assuming 22 percent penetration by the end of the first year, pay television would break even in 20 months. The profit contribution of pay television in its first five years would be $210,940.

2. At the higher monthly rate of $11.95 the contribution per pay subscriber toward covering the $100,000 capital would be $3.95 per month. At this price the time required to break even would be 18 months.

3. A lower monthly rate of $3 would be possible only by offering movies-only entertainment (as opposed to a wider variety of features assumed above), fewer movies (four or five compared with seven), and lower-quality features (averaging in cost 25 cents per picture instead of 50 cents). On this basis a $3.00 rate would involve programming and other variable costs of $2.75 per subscriber, so that only 25 cents per subscriber could be applied to monthly costs of $2,785 (for labor, cassettes, preview videotapes, and program guides). At this rate, 93 percent of cable subscribers would have to contract for pay service just to cover these monthly costs. Until more than 93 percent subscribed, there would be nothing to cover estimated capital costs of $27,000 for programming equipment and initial marketing effort. Since four cable systems charging $3 achieved a penetration of 61.5 percent on the average, it does not appear likely that Leisure World would hit the 93 percent necessary just to break even on monthly costs. Recovery of capital invested would be impossible.

4. At a $6.00 rate per month the contribution toward covering capital investment would be $1.50 per pay subscriber. Estimated capital costs would amount to $71,880. Break-even would require a penetration of 25 percent. Census data suggest that the Leisure World cable operator should be able to reach this goal in three months and contribute to profits thereafter.

5. Whether the rate for pay television is set at $6.00 or at $11.95, it appears probable that this service would break even on invested capital

of up to $100,000 within a period of 20 months or sooner. The break-even could probably be reached in 3 months at a rate of $6 offering a movies-only format; with a $10 per month charge and higher-quality program material, the break-even could be reached in 20 months; at a rate of $11.95, the break-even could occur in 18 months.

Need for a cable subscriber survey. At this stage in the analysis there remained an important unsettled question: Was there a desire for pay cable television service in Leisure World? This question was addressed in a progress report made by the task force on November 23, 1977, as follows: "There does not appear to be any clamor for pay TV in Leisure World yet, even though the idea is expanding rapidly throughout the nation." In the discussion on this question, however, it had been argued by one member of the task force that there might well be an "unfelt desire" for pay television (premium entertainment) that would surface if it were announced that the introduction of pay television was under consideration by the Golden Rain Foundation. Or if pay television were marketed effectively, this unfelt desire might come to the surface of the minds of enough residents to provide the basis for a profitable business. Finally, it was argued that one way to get information on the potential demand for pay television would be to conduct a survey of the subscribers of the Leisure World Cable Television System in an attempt to estimate the extent of their interest in such a service.

This idea received support from the task force, and a suggested questionnaire was drafted. The estimated costs of the survey are listed below:

Letter from Golden Rain Foundation explaining the purpose of the questionnaire and requesting cooperation—12,000 at 5 cents each	$ 600
Questionnaire, one page, 12,000 at 5 cents each	600
Mailing costs, 12,000 at 13 cents each (assumed that residents would pay the postage needed to return the completed questionnaires)	1,560
Tabulating and analyzing the returns (assumed that volunteers from the community would be used to perform this task)	—
Total	$2,760

RECOMMENDATIONS BY THE TASK FORCE

The task force submitted its report on subscription (pay) television on January 30, 1978, to R. L. Disbro, general manager, Professional Community Management, Laguna Hills. The recommendations contained in this report are summarized below.

1. If pay television is introduced in Leisure World, it should be offered on an optional basis. The possibility of making it available to all through a blanket assessment has been discussed. We estimated that the

probable cost of pay entertainment for all subscribers of the cable system would be $6 per month. Accordingly, this approach was not pursued.

Subsequent research by Mr. Foley, however, led him to believe that pay television could be made available to all Leisure World residents for as little as $3 per month if this amount were added to the monthly assessments collected from all homeowners. The shared expenses of Golden Rain Foundation and the mutuals amounted to $70.37 per month in 1978; the $3.00 would be added to this figure and collected by PCM, Inc., for Golden Rain and the mutuals.

Mr. Foley developed a proposal for a stand-alone pay television operation which would be run by Rossmoor Electric, Inc., and which would offer a movies-only program format to Leisure World residents at a charge per month of $2. [This proposal was presented along with those of five program distributors in Case 4–4, Rossmoor Electric, Inc. (A).]

2. Decisions as to program package and rate to charge per month should be made later after further research. The range from a stand-alone program package at $6.00 per month to a satellite-transmitted program at $11.95 might be considered.

a. A questionnaire should be mailed to all residents to determine their possible interest in pay entertainment (copy attached). Provision should be made for easy mailing response (postage-paid envelopes). The questionnaire should include questions on the types of program material preferred as well as the prices associated with each type of entertainment.

b. Technology in pay television is developing rapidly. Programs may be distributed via coaxial cable, microwave, videotape, and communication satellite. The approach chosen will influence the quality of the program material, the necessary capital costs, the choice of a program distributor, the ability to adapt programs to the tastes of the community, and so on. Much has been learned by the task force in contacts with program distributors; further study would be helpful in the choice of program distributors should the Golden Rain board decide to introduce pay television in Leisure World. Rapid technological advance encourages deliberate decision making in this area.

3. It is proposed that one of the mid-bands between Channels 6 and 7 be set aside for pay television. A converter is necessary on each television set on the cable in order to gain access to such a channel. (Channel 6 covers a frequency range of 82–88 MHz; Channel 7 includes 174–180 MHz. The mid-band is divided into nine segments identified as Channels A through I. Channel G, H, or I might be used for the Leisure World pay channel.)

4. The task force has solicited formal proposals from seven program distributors plus Rossmoor Electric, Inc. It is proposed that the PCM staff finalize all seven proposals, working with the present task force. At that point a final report should be made to the Golden Rain Foundation board, including a recommendation as to which program distributor best meets the selection criteria.

5. Further negotiations with the contractor should follow in the light of questions raised by GRF board members. Sample program showings should be provided for the board members, as well as examples of the trial offers that might be made in promoting the new pay television service.

6. There should then be a final review by the PCM staff. Preparation of the final contract should follow, utilizing legal counsel.

7. The contract with the program distributor should then be presented to the GRF board for final approval.

8. Implementation should then follow.

A work sheet attached to the task force report presented calculations dealing with estimated revenues, costs, and capital investment; possible pay television rates per month; anticipated penetration; break-even; and return on investment. This material was essentially the same as that included in the foregoing discussion.

ACTION TAKEN ON RECOMMENDATIONS

The task force report on pay television was referred to the Community Relations Committee of the Golden Rain Foundation by R. L. Disbro, general manager of PCM, Inc. Dorothy H. Novatney, chairman of the Community Relations Committee, appointed an ad hoc group to review and analyze the questionnaire suggested for use in connection with the pay television proposal. Included in the ad hoc group were: Ken Brouwer and Charles Bowes of the Community Relations Committee; James Scott of the Task Force on Pay Television; and T. J. Tandle, director, Government and Community Relations.

The ad hoc group met on March 16, 1978, and analyzed the questionnaire carefully. Suggestions originating in the Community Relations Committee were added to those generated by the group itself. On March 20, 1978, the following recommendations were made by Tandle as spokesman for the ad hoc group in a memorandum to Novatney:

1. Resulting from our lengthy discussion and the suggestions originated by the GRF Community Relations Committee, attached you will find what we consider to be the best possible questionnaire.

2. It is recognized and agreed that this document should go to the GRF board for review and final decision.

3. If sufficient returns indicate an interest in pay TV, only then would it be advisable to research the community on the all-reception option [proposed by Ivan Foley in a separate proposal].

4. It would appear to me that any suggestion worthy of a community participation and response should be sent to the resident membership by Golden Rain on appropriately addressed stationery, bulk mail. While it is known that newspaper surveys are cheaper, this community

has in the past responded much more completely to the direct-mail approach.

5. It would be expected that those who desire to participate in such a direct-mail survey would pay 13 cents to get their response back to Golden Rain.

6. It would also be very necessary, if mailing of this nature were to actually occur, that a group of volunteers be assembled and instructed on how to process the results. There is no way that the current Community Relations and general manager's staff could devote the necessary time to a project estimated to be sizable.

The memorandum from the ad hoc group was discussed at the April 1978 meeting of the Community Relations Committee. During the discussion it was mentioned that the cost of the pay television survey would probably run close to $3,000. Since the Golden Rain board of directors was making every effort to reduce or hold down expenses for 1978, it was wondered whether the information secured by the survey would be worth the $3,000 expense.

A committee member also expressed the opinion that there did not appear to be any strong interest in pay television in the Leisure World community. This opinion met with considerable agreement within the committee. Accordingly, the proposal to survey Leisure World residents to determine their interest in pay television was tabled. Should evidence of a demand for pay television become apparent, then the matter might be reopened for further consideration.

In line with this decision, the Community Relations Committee made no recommendations to the Golden Rain board on the proposal to undertake a survey to find out what interest existed in pay television among Leisure World residents.

The Rossmoor Electric proposal of a stand-alone pay television service to be made available to all Leisure World residents at a charge of $2 per month was also rejected by the Community Relations Committee. In view of the absence of evidence indicating any demand for pay television, there was extreme reluctance to make any recommendation that would increase the monthly assessment collected by PCM, Inc., on behalf of Golden Rain and the various mutuals.

APPENDIX A

Community Organization: Leisure World, Laguna Hills, California

EXHIBIT A–1   Your corporate interrelationship

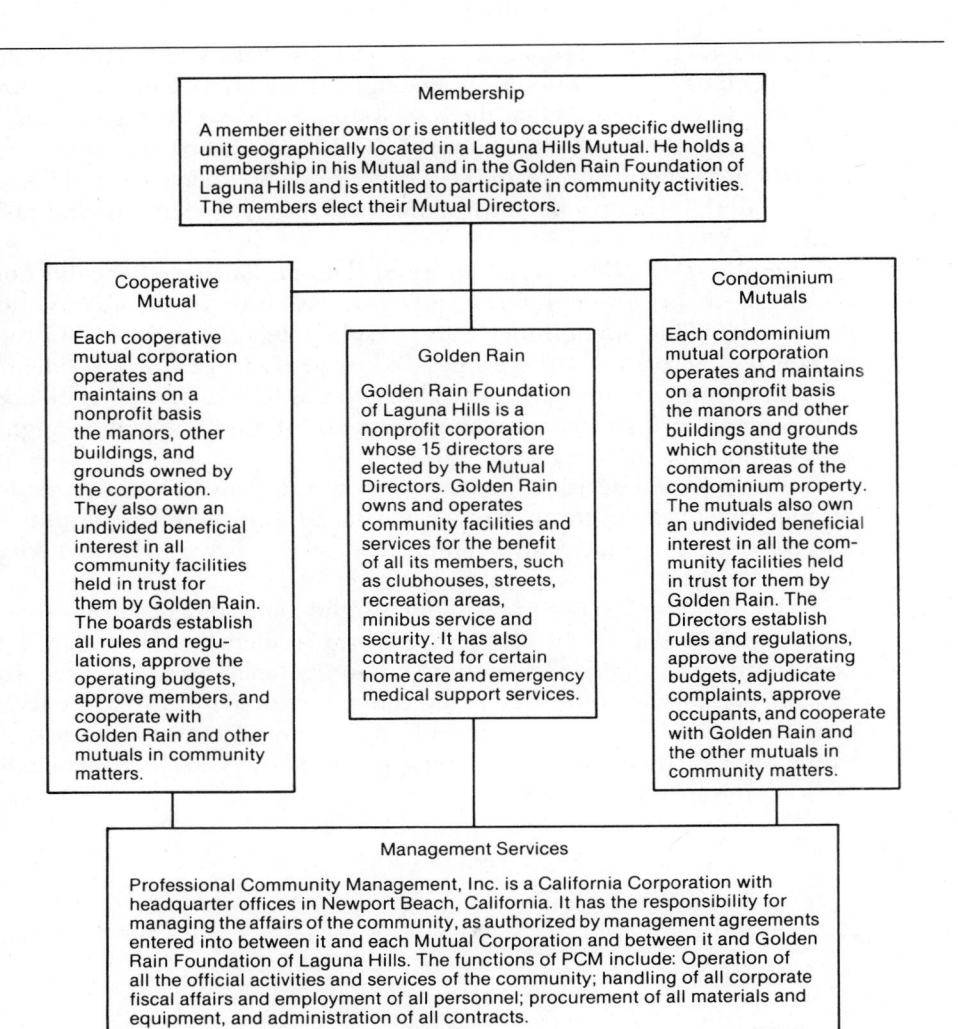

Membership

A member either owns or is entitled to occupy a specific dwelling unit geographically located in a Laguna Hills Mutual. He holds a membership in his Mutual and in the Golden Rain Foundation of Laguna Hills and is entitled to participate in community activities. The members elect their Mutual Directors.

Cooperative Mutual

Each cooperative mutual corporation operates and maintains on a nonprofit basis the manors, other buildings, and grounds owned by the corporation. They also own an undivided beneficial interest in all community facilities held in trust for them by Golden Rain. The boards establish all rules and regulations, approve the operating budgets, approve members, and cooperate with Golden Rain and other mutuals in community matters.

Golden Rain

Golden Rain Foundation of Laguna Hills is a nonprofit corporation whose 15 directors are elected by the Mutual Directors. Golden Rain owns and operates community facilities and services for the benefit of all its members, such as clubhouses, streets, recreation areas, minibus service and security. It has also contracted for certain home care and emergency medical support services.

Condominium Mutuals

Each condominium mutual corporation operates and maintains on a nonprofit basis the manors and other buildings and grounds which constitute the common areas of the condominium property. The mutuals also own an undivided beneficial interest in all the community facilities held in trust for them by Golden Rain. The Directors establish rules and regulations, approve the operating budgets, adjudicate complaints, approve occupants, and cooperate with Golden Rain and the other mutuals in community matters.

Management Services

Professional Community Management, Inc. is a California Corporation with headquarter offices in Newport Beach, California. It has the responsibility for managing the affairs of the community, as authorized by management agreements entered into between it and each Mutual Corporation and between it and Golden Rain Foundation of Laguna Hills. The functions of PCM include: Operation of all the official activities and services of the community; handling of all corporate fiscal affairs and employment of all personnel; procurement of all materials and equipment, and administration of all contracts.

Source: *Community Information Manual,* Rossmoor Leisure World, Laguna Hills, California, 1978, p. iv.

APPENDIX B

Benefits Featured in a Leisure World Sales Brochure

1. *Resort living all year 'round.*

Rossmoor Laguna Hills offers you true resort living at its finest all year 'round. The warm California sunshine and mild sea breezes combine to give Rossmoor Laguna Hills a near-perfect climate.

Inside Rossmoor you're surrounded by the beauty of lush, green foliage. Flowers, shrubs, trees, acres of manicured lawn, all part of your immediate environment. Outside is the town of Laguna Hills with its fine restaurants and modern shopping centers, nestled at the foot of gently rolling hills. The Pacific Ocean and coastal art colony of Laguna Beach are a mere seven miles away.

But you won't have to leave Rossmoor to find things to do. Whether you're the type who's always on the go or the one who prefers a more leisurely pace, Rossmoor has an activity you'll enjoy. Like 27 challenging holes of golf, tennis courts, swimming pools, riding stables, whirlpool baths, shuffleboard courts, lawn bowling, billiards, ping-pong, and four multimillion-dollar clubhouses where you can enjoy woodworking, lapidary, pottery, sewing, and much, much more.

2. *Your time is all yours.*

When you live at Rossmoor Laguna Hills, your time will be all yours. No more painting, trimming, cutting, mowing, or raking. Your lawn and garden, your home exterior, and those of your neighbors are all constantly maintained by teams of experts at Rossmoor.

3. *Peace of mind.*

Rossmoor provides you with one of today's most precious freedoms—freedom from worry. A protective wall surrounds all the residential areas. Courteous security attendants are on duty 24 hours a day at all the entrances. And a professional security patrol is always there to protect you, your possessions, your property.

4. *24-hour health watch.*

There's always someone watching out for you at Rossmoor Laguna Hills. Registered nurses are on duty 24 hours a day, ready to help whenever necessary. Armed with your medical history and backed by the doctor–nurse teams at the multimillion-dollar Medical Center, they're prepared for any type of emergency. In addition, the 160-bed Saddleback Community Hospital is adjacent to the Leisure World community.

5. *Getting around.*

Going shopping, out to lunch, to church, to one of the clubhouses, or to visit a friend? Just step on board one of the fare-free Rossmoor Laguna Hills minibuses.

Especially handy for those who don't drive or who like to get out from

behind the wheel once in a while, our friendly minibuses make their "round" on schedule.

6.   *Southern California: Land of variety.*

Rossmoor Laguna Hills is designed for your enjoyment *and* located for your enjoyment. Locally, you're just seven miles to the fine restaurants, fascinating art galleries, plus the surf and sand of Laguna Beach. The new marina at Dana Point is just south of Laguna Beach. East of Rossmoor Laguna Hills are the beautiful Santa Ana mountains with hiking and riding trails, parks, and picnic areas and the sometimes-snowcapped Saddleback Peak.

Rossmoor is almost midway between Los Angeles and San Diego, so you can enjoy the wonderful metropolitan attraction of both cities as well as all the nearby attractions Orange County has to offer.

Source: *Rossmoor Laguna Hills* (Rossmoor Corporation, 1978), 12 pp.

QUESTIONS

1. Drawing on data gathered by the Task Force on Pay Television, estimate the number of cable subscribers needed to break even, assuming a capital investment of $100,000. In making your analysis, consider the following possible alternative monthly charges for pay entertainment:
   a. $12.
   b. $8.
   c. $4.

2. The average charge for pay TV was approximately $8 per month. How responsive would you expect Leisure World cable subscribers to be to a lower price of $4—that is, would you expect total revenue to increase? If $12 were charged, would you expect total revenue to decline? Explain.

3. What monthly charge for pay TV would you recommend to the general manager for his consideration? Why?

4. Would you recommend an expenditure of $3,000 for research on potential demand for pay TV in Leisure World? Why or why not? Can you suggest a less costly research approach?

ROSSMOOR ELECTRIC, INC. (B)*

Decision on price/program package to propose for subscription television service

In March 1978, Ivan Foley, president of Rossmoor Electric, Inc., had submitted a proposal to the assistant general manager of Professional Community Management, Inc., indicating that his firm would be willing to provide a stand-alone pay television service to be made available to all Leisure World residents at a charge of $2 per month.[1] This proposal was forwarded to the Community Relations Committee of the Golden Rain Foundation for consideration along with other proposals from pay television distributors. The Rossmoor Electric proposal was rejected by the Community Relations Committee along with the six other proposals under consideration.

The following letter to Ivan Foley written by Kenneth J. Brouwer, vice chairman, Community Relations Committee, dated May 23, 1978, explains the committee's action:

> The Golden Rain Community Relations Committee has considered your proposal for paid television programming for the Leisure World community. There have been a number of such proposals. They all have

---

*Written by James D. Scott, Professor Emeritus of Marketing, Graduate School of Business Administration, The University of Michigan, a resident of Leisure World.

[1]See Rossmoor Electric, Inc. (A), for excerpts from this proposal and the rationale supporting it.

merit. However, the committee has decided not to recommend any of the proposals to the Golden Rain Foundation of Laguna Hills.

The committee's decision is based, in part, on the fact that the residents of Leisure World have not evidenced any interest in such programming.

This action was reported to the Golden Rain Foundation board at its May 1978 meeting. Notice of the decision was published in the *Leisure World News* on May 4, 1978.

REACTIONS OF RESIDENTS TO THE COMMITTEE'S REPORT

Following the article in the *Leisure World News* there was an immediate reaction from a resident which was published in the "Letters to the Editor" on May 11, 1978. Excerpts from this letter follow:

> I note that a member of the GRF committee has commented that, in regard to pay TV, "no one has requested it at all." I beg to differ with him as my husband and I are very much interested in pay TV and have twice called the Leisure World TV Cable System to inquire about pay TV, and both times we were told that a committee is working on it and so far nothing has been determined but she was pretty sure that it would be.
>
> Did GRF check to see how many other people might have called them? It would be nice if we had a choice.
>
> Dorothy Timelson
3379-C Punta Alta

During the period ending January 1979, five other letters were published in the *Leisure World News* expressing much the same sentiment. Numerous requests for pay TV service were also directed to Rossmoor Electric during this period. As a result of this reaction, Foley decided to approach the Golden Rain Foundation board once more with still another pay television proposal for Leisure World.

In considering the available alternatives, the concept of making pay TV mandatory for all Leisure World residents was rejected. In the discussion of this approach by the Task Force on Pay Television, Robert Price, chairman, had expressed the opinion that an attempt to make pay TV mandatory would probably run into serious opposition in the community. Residents of Mutual III, for example, were being assessed $70.37 per month per manor in 1977 to cover GRF and mutual shared operations. Of this amount, $3.54 per month was budgeted to cover the cost of the cable TV system. It was anticipated that the monthly carrying charges for 1978 would have to be increased by at least $32 to cover

inflationary cost increases and provision for anticipated reserves for maintenance and repairs of existing facilities. A suggestion that as little as $2 per month be added to this amount would probably meet with strong opposition from those who were not interested in pay TV. If pay TV service were made optional, this opposition would be eliminated. Accordingly, Foley reviewed the optional approaches available to his firm.

ALTERNATIVE PAY TV PLANS TO BE CONSIDERED

In reviewing pay TV plans for detailed analysis, Foley gave consideration to the price and program combination that would result from each alternative, the tasks that Rossmoor Electric would have to perform and the costs associated with such work, the capital investment required at the head end and in order to provide desired security from unauthorized reception of programs, and the penetration required to break even on the necessary costs and earn a profit on the investment.

1. Offer movie programs on an optional basis at $6 per month. The plan of offering a stand-alone operation featuring movie programs custom-built for the Leisure World audience on an optional basis had several advantages. (1) It was believed that such program offerings would have maximum appeal to the local residents as compared with those available through other distributors, and thus might provide a basis for achieving a favorable penetration of cable subscribers. (2) This plan would eliminate the middleman (program distributor) and his gross margin. (3) The investment in equipment at the head end was estimated at $17,500. To this figure it would be necessary to add the investment in security equipment (converter/descramblers) which would have to be purchased in advance of the introductory marketing program. If it is assumed that 1,650 Leisure World residents subscribed for pay TV during the first year and the converter/descramblers cost $17 each, the total investment would amount to $28,050.

(4) Since the pay TV service would be optional, it would be necessary to undertake an introductory marketing campaign to get customers, plus a continuing promotional effort to build the customer list up to the desired penetration level. In discussions with the Task Force on Pay Television, it had been estimated that the following marketing effort would be necessary:

> Four free movies; direct mail to 12,000 residents; a program guide for the first month of service; quarterly color brochures with survey questionnaire to determine program preferences; advertisements in *Leisure World News*. Estimated cost: $12,000. (Note: These estimates were based on information gathered during interviews with program distributors.)

(5)   In short, the capital investment required prior to start-up of the pay TV service when operated on a stand-alone basis was expected to be:

Equipment required at the head end	$17,500
Security equipment	28,050
Introductory marketing effort	12,000
Total	$57,550

(6) It was estimated that the following monthly out-of-pocket operating costs would also be incurred:

	Monthly costs
Maintenance cost	$250
Labor cost	1,750
Other labor cost	315
Tape transfer	542
Screening	81
Postage and insurance	68
Total	$3,006

$3,006 ÷ 12,000 manors = $0.2505 per month

(7)   If pay TV service were offered at $6 per month, the following results might be anticipated:

	1st month	*Later months*
Revenue per subscriber per month	$ 6.00	$6.00
Installation charge per subscriber	17.00	—
Total	$23.00	$6.00
Programming costs		
Movies	$ 1.52	
Other monthly costs (from above)	0.25	
Monthly TV guide	0.10	
Leisure World News distribution of TV guide	0.03	
Total	$ 1.90	1.90
Cost of converter/descrambler plus installation	17.00	—
Total costs	$18.90	1.90
Contribution to cover capital investment:		
1st month $23 − 18.90	$ 4.10	
2d month $6 − 1.90	$ 4.10	

(8)   How many subscribers would be required to break even on both the monthly expenses and the total capital costs? This calculation follows:

Over the period of a year a subscriber contributes $4.10 × 12 = $49.20 toward covering monthly expenses and capital investment.	
Yearly cost for labor, tape transfer, screening, postage, insurance, and maintenance amounts to $3,006 × 12	$36,072
Capital investment: programming equipment, security equipment, and introductory marketing	57,550
Total	$93,622

Number of subscribers required to break even
  12-month contribution per subscriber of $49.20
    plus installation payment per subscriber of $17.00 = $66.20
  Capital investment of $93,622 ÷ $66.20 = 1,414 subscribers,
    or 1,414 ÷ 12,000, or 11.8 percent of Leisure World cable
    subscribers

When this alternative was discussed with the Task Force on Pay Television, the following comments were made: (1) The key question, of course, was whether the movies-only format would be as satisfactory from the television viewer's standpoint as the program proposals of competing distributors such as Home Box Office or the ON Subscription Television service of Channel 52. Both of these distributors supplemented movies with other entertainment material, such as musical comedies and athletic events. (2) Also, would Rossmoor Electric be able to hire a programmer who would be as skilled in choosing program material and in conducting the necessary negotiations as were the programmers working for competing distributors?

(3) Along the same lines, it was noted that Rossmoor Electric's management and personnel had had no experience in handling the various functions involved in conducting a pay TV operation. Program distributors with which Rossmoor Electric might affiliate had worked out successful pay TV operations and could cite their track records. Rossmoor Electric might be well advised to limit its involvement to the installation and maintenance functions and to affiliate with an experienced program distributor in order to secure attractive program material and assistance in the marketing and management activities involved in pay TV.

2.   Recommend affiliation with the Home Box Office service at $8.50 per month.   Affiliation with HBO would relieve Rossmoor Electric from the management responsibility and work involved in handling the program distributor's functions and would also make it possible for Rossmoor Electric to take advantage of the management advice and assistance which HBO offered its affiliates. Since HBO was the leading program distributor in the United States, such guidance and support were believed to be of considerable value.

However, Rossmoor Electric would have to invest $112,800 in the capital equipment required to receive HBO programs distributed via satellite: $72,000 in terminal equipment and $40,800 in an earth station and an encoder. The cash flow projections made by Lisa Forrestal Connor, regional representative for HBO, estimated that it would require three years to cover this capital investment if subscribers paid $8.50 per month for the HBO service and 15 percent of the Leisure World cable subscribers became subscribers of the service. According to this estimate, the return on investment in five years would be 53 percent. (See Rossmoor Electric, Inc. (A), Appendix C, for the HBO pro forma projections of cash flow.)

Then, too, investment in an earth station would make it possible for

EXHIBIT 1 Comparison of programmers (based on affiliates operational as of June 30, 1977)

Rank by percentage of pay penetration of homes passed	Programmer	Total number of systems	Number in top 50 by percent of penetration		Percent penetration of homes passed	Percent penetration of basic subscribers	Average pay rate
			Homes passed	Basic subscribers			
1	BestVision	29	12%	10%	21.5%	39.8%	$ 5.62
2	Showtime	24	6	3	14.3	26.2	9.29
3	TPS	49	8	8	12.2	30.5	7.32
4	Prism	9	2	2	11.5	26.6	9.60
5	Home Box Office	271	25	29	10.8	23.3	8.47
6	Cinemerica	5	0	0	9.8	20.1	7.17
7	Independently programmed	25	1	0	9.6	16.9	7.77
8	Pay TV services	10	0	3	9.3	38.8	4.16
9	Channel 100	14	0	0	5.8	9.7	11.00
10	HHT	5	0	1	4.8	19.1	7.59
	Industry total/averages	441	54*	56*	11.0%	23.0%	$ 7.83

*Larger than 50 due to tied positions for some percentages.
Source: Paul Kagan Associates, Inc., *Pay TV Newsletter*, June 30, 1977.

Rossmoor Electric to receive a variety of nonpay programs being transmitted by satellite. This would enrich the program offerings of the Leisure World cable system at no additional cost to subscribers.

HBO offered its subscribers eight motion pictures a month, top-notch sports events, and entertainment specials. It was thought that this program mix would have greater appeal to viewers than a movies-only format. According to the Paul Kagan Associates June 30, 1977, census of U.S. pay TV systems, however, HBO affiliates nationwide reached only 10.8 percent of homes passed or 23.3 percent of basic cable subscribers (see Exhibit 1). Program distributors such as BestVision, which tailored their movie packages to meet local preferences, achieved higher penetration. As of June 30, 1977, for example, BestVision achieved 39 percent penetration of basic cable subscribers in the 29 stand-alone affiliated cable systems which the firm served. This evidence suggested that a custom-made selection of material would have a greater appeal to the Leisure World audience than would programs designed to serve a nationwide audience.

Propose affiliation with NST Channel 52 at $19.50 per month.   The probable reaction of Leisure World cable subscribers to alternative types of pay TV programming led Foley to review the information available about the over-the-air service offered by National Subscription Television via Channel 52, Los Angeles. NST Channel 52 offered current movies; special events such as nightclub acts, concerts, and theater ballet; and sports exclusive to NST, such as the home games of the Dodgers, Angels, Lakers, Kings, and Aztecs and the Santa Anita races. (See Exhibit 2 for the program schedule for a typical month.) While this program package was designed to serve the broad Los Angeles market, rather than specifically for Leisure World, it was believed that it would have more appeal than the HBO service or a movies-only format.

Channel 52 programs would be broadcast from Mount Wilson, received by the Leisure World community antenna system, and converted to a mid-band channel that would be an addition to the stations currently being received on the cable system. Equipment required at the head-end location would cost approximately $8,000. One converter–descrambler would be required for each subscriber at a cost of $60 each.

The monthly subscription fee would be approximately the same as NST charged its subscribers in the Los Angeles market, with the exception of hookups and returnable deposits.

	NST	Rossmoor
Hookup	$39.95	$30.00
Deposit	25.00	—
Tax on converter	0.48	—
Program fee	18.95	19.50
Monthly charge for service	$19.43	$19.50

EXHIBIT 2   Programs offered by NST Channel 52 during a typical month

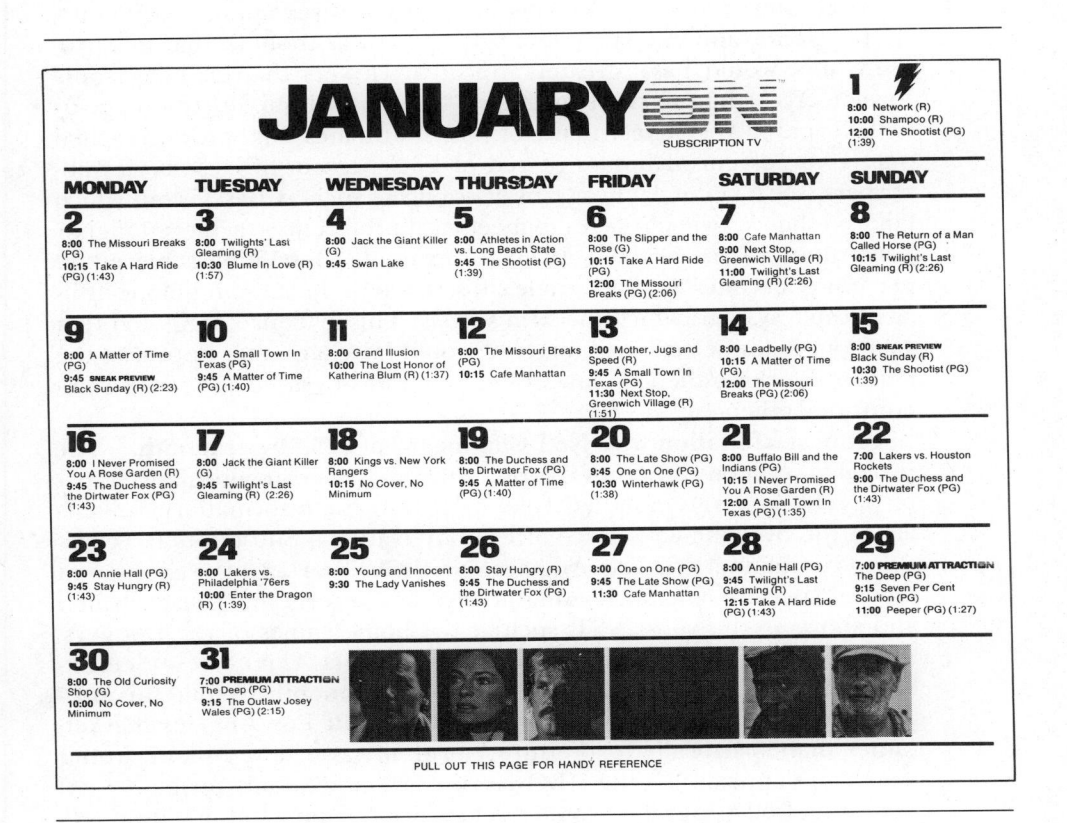

PULL OUT THIS PAGE FOR HANDY REFERENCE

The purchase price paid by Rossmoor Electric for the NST signal delivered to the head-end location would be $11.40 per subscriber per month. Rossmoor Electric would be responsible for all costs for financing, promotion, equipment purchase, maintenance, hookups, disconnects, billing, and collection and for any other unforeseen costs. There would be no financial liability to Golden Rain Foundation or to any mutual corporation at Leisure World, Laguna Hills.

With this information at hand, Foley undertook a five-year projection of revenues, investment, and costs to assist him in making the decision on the profit possibilities of NST affiliation. In projecting revenues, he assumed that there would be 12,500 manors in the cable system and that the following percentages of Leisure World cable subscribers would buy the NST subscription television service: first year, 2 percent; second year,

4 percent; third year, 6 percent; fourth year, 8 percent; and fifth year, 8 percent.

A number of other assumptions were also made: *(a)* One converter per subscriber at $60 each would be required. *(b)* There would be a 20 percent turnover in subscribers from one year to the next, and each "disconnect" would cost $20. *(c)* The installation cost per subscriber would be $20; the charge for installation would be $30. *(d)* The cost of equipment and labor to prepare for start-up of NST Channel 52 service would be $16,000. *(e)* Estimated investment in converters each year for four years would total $60,000, as follows: first year, $12,000; second year, $18,000; third year, $15,000; and fourth year, $15,000. *(f)* Depreciation on a $16,000 investment in equipment would be charged off in five years: hence the annual depreciation charge would be $3,200. *(g)* The total investment in converters in four years was estimated at $60,000. Assuming that each year's investment was to be charged off in five years, the annual charges would be: first year, $2,400; second year, $6,000; third year, $9,000; fourth year, $12,000; fifth year, $12,000; sixth year, $9,600; seventh year, $6,000; and eighth year, $3,000. Thus the annual charges would total $60,000.

On this basis, Foley estimated that NST subscription entertainment would show a loss of $11,760 in the first year but that thereafter the service would be profitable. In seven years the total profits would amount to $113,131 on an investment of $16,000 for head-end equipment and $60,000 for converters, or a total of $76,000. In short, pay TV would produce a cash flow of $113,131 in profit plus $76,000 in depreciation on head-end equipment and converters, or a total of $189,131, in a period of eight years. This total divided by eight years would give an average cash flow of $23,641 per year. An investment of $76,000 in head-end equipment and converters, therefore, was expected to produce a return of $23,641 per year, or 31 percent. (See Appendix A for five-year projections of the results on NST pay TV service.)

When the foregoing proposal was discussed with the Task Force on Pay Television, the suggested charge of $19.50 per month for NST Channel 52 service generated comment. It was noted that this charge was high when compared with the $8.50 per month price suggested by HBO or with the $6.00 per month figure included in the stand-alone proposal. NST executives had justified their charge of $19.43 for the Los Angeles market by noting that pay television competitors such as Theta Cable charged $8.45 for basic cable service plus $8.95 for pay entertainment (Channel Z), or a total of $17.40 for the combined package. The NST subscription entertainment charge of $19.43 did not appear to be out of line with the combined rate that viewers paid for Theta Cable's Channel Z.

When pressed to quote a lower price for NST Channel 52 service in Leisure World, the vice president in charge of operations said that his

firm was reluctant to cut the charge for pay TV service in Leisure World since the firm had over-the-air customers in nearby communities who would be paying the full $19.43 per month. He questioned the fairness of such a price difference.

Then, too, a member of the task force noted that Leisure World cable service in 1979 would be supported by a monthly assessment of $3.69— the amount included in the monthly charge for services and functions performed by the mutuals and the Golden Rain Foundation operation. Accordingly, the combined basic cable service charge of $3.69 and the proposed NST Channel 52 charge of $19.50 would total $23.19. It was argued that further consideration should be given to the probable impact of this charge upon the number of cable subscribers who would buy the subscription television service.

At this point, reference was made to the report of a discussion at the 1978 convention on the National Cable Television Association in New Orleans. Excerpts from this report follow:

> One question constantly asked by pay TV marketers is: how high is up or down for monthly rates? . . . Tele-Communications pres. John Malone ignited a marketing panel with this challenge: "HBO says it can't correlate price and penetration. We think they're honest, although there's some advantage in silence. What do you find?"
>
> One by one, ATC, United Cable, CPI and TCI itself reported efforts that had tried and failed to solve a major marketing mystery.
>
> One of the cable systems exploring this subject closely is Alda Communications. . . . Gen. Mgr. and CEO Barry Stigers . . . is a believer in systemwide (combined rate) pricing. In Bridgeport, CT—Alda's first venture—a $14 combo rate is promoted. It's $8.50 for basic and $5.50 for Hollywood Home Theater's movies. Says Stigers: "Pay penetration *is* price sensitive. The lower the price, the better."
>
> High penetration of pay/basic saves Alda from buying traps, but the real key is that it shares relatively less revenue per sub with program sources. One of the latter, though—Paramount's Alan Fields—sees a tradeoff: "We've always believed pay penetration would be much better at lower prices."

Since the Paul Kagan Associates census of pay television as of December 31, 1978, was available, a member of the Task Force on Pay Television tabulated the penetration ratios for pay TV achieved by cable television systems charging as little as $3.00 and as much as $17.42. These data are shown in Exhibit 3. Highlights from this tabulation are commented upon briefly below.

a. The penetration of basic cable subscribers achieved by three cable systems charging $3.00 per month (combined rates ranging from $10.00 to $11.75) amounted to one at 99 percent and two at 100 percent. In these cable systems, however, subscribers were required to take both the basic cable service and the pay TV service. Systems in which pay TV was

offered as an optional service, charging $3.95 per month, had sold the pay service to 24 percent, 40 percent, and 74 percent of the basic subscribers (average penetration 46 percent). All three cable systems were served by Telemation Program Service. The first two had received pay TV since May 1977; the third, since May 1976. (See Exhibit 5.) (The average penetration of five systems was 39.5 percent.) The range is so wide that computation of an average appears to be meaningless.

  b. Cable systems affiliated with BestVision also experienced wide variations in the penetration achieved by their pay TV service. At a charge of $6 per month the percentage of basic cable subscribers buying pay TV service ranged from 7.2 percent to 10.7 percent. The average penetration reached by eight systems amounted to 26.8 percent. (See Exhibit 5.)

  c. TeleMation Program Services served three systems, charging $3.95 per month for pay service. The penetration of pay service was as follows: 24.1 percent, 40.5 percent, and 73.8 percent. (In San Jose, subscribers were required to take pay service at $3.00 per month together with basic service at $8.75, or a combined cost of $11.75; 99 percent of the subscribers did so.) The average penetration of the pay service in the three systems where it was optional amounted to 46.1 percent.

  d. Showtime served three affiliates which charged $11.95 per month. Here the range in penetration was narrow: 27.3 percent to 30 percent. The average was 29.4 percent.

  e. Optical Systems had seven affiliates which charged $11.95 for the pay TV service. Penetration ratios ranged from 6.5 percent to 21.2 percent. The average was 15.3 percent. For a chart showing relationship between pay TV price and penetration, see Exhibit 4.

  Examination of these results led to the comment by a member of the task force that the variations in penetration among affiliates of the same program distributor might be explained, in part, by differences in the demographic characteristics of the different communities served. Although NST Channel 52 executives might claim that the high price of $19.50 would not restrict significantly the penetration of pay TV among Leisure World cable subscribers, the Leisure World community differed considerably from the broad Los Angeles market which NST Channel 52 served.

  Thus, the residents of Leisure World were all age 52 or older. Their average age in 1979 was 72.4 years. Among the owners of the 12,000 manors, there were estimated to be 4,000 widows. While the Leisure World residents were believed to be relatively affluent, a good proportion of the families were living on retirement pensions and, given the relatively high inflation rates of recent years, were required to watch their expenditures carefully. Indeed, it was estimated that 700 to 800 families were living primarily on Social Security payments.

  It was also estimated that the average wealth of Leisure World resi-

EXHIBIT 3   Selected data on pay cable rates and penetration as of December 31, 1978

System/pay distributor	Date pay service started	Pay subscribers	Homes passed	Pay penetration homes passed	Pay rate	Pay penetration of cable subscribers	Basic cable subscribers	Basic cable rate	Combined rate
A. Pay cable rates ranging from $3 to $4									
Dover, N.H. (TPS)	5/77	2,212	16,530	12.8%	$3.95	24.1%	8,813	$7.45	$11.40
Jackson, Mich. (TPS)	5/77	4,510	17,300	26.1	3.95	40.5	11,149	7.40	11.35
La Habra/Brea, Calif. (Best)	5/77	3,800	14,000	27.1	3.00	100.0	3,800	7.00	10.00
Lansing, Mich. (TPS)	5/76	21,213	60,617	35.0	3.95	73.8	28,742	6.95	10.90
Orange County, Calif.									
*1—Show	3/77	4,534	38,632	11.7	9.95	22.0	20,603	7.57	17.52
*2—Show	3/77	4,229	38,632	8.4	5.95	15.7	20,603	7.57	13.52
Redondo Beach, Calif. (Best)	5/77	4,000	15,000	26.7	3.00	100.0	4,000	8.00	11.00
San Jose, Calif. (TPS)	2/76	70,750	176,000	40.2	3.00	99.0	71,500	8.75	11.75
B. Pay cable rates approximating $6									
Atascadero, Calif. (Best)	7/76	491	9,774	5.0	5.95	7.2	6,868	7.20	13.15
Athens, Ga. (HBO)	1/78	1,177	19,986	5.9	6.10	11.4	10,314	6.50	12.60
Bridgeport, Conn. (HHT)	6/77	11,948	49,000	24.4	5.50	99.3	12,037	8.50	14.00
Bryan, Tex. (HBO)	1/76	400	16,500	2.4	6.00	2.9	14,000	4.00	10.00
Bryan, Tex.—MID (HBO)	2/76	2,500	16,000	15.6	6.00	21.7	11,500	4.00	10.00
Camarillo, Calif. (Best)	10/76	1,845	8,050	22.9	5.95	42.8	4,314	7.20	13.15
Casa Grande, Ariz. (HBO)	12/77	208	2,176	9.6	5.95	100.0	208	9.00	14.95
Charlotte, N.C. (HBO)	7/78	11,600	48,300	24.0	5.95	61.1	19,000	7.50	13.45
Cordova, Alaska (Best)	12/75	312	600	52.0	6.00	60.7	514	20.40	26.40
Edwards AFB, Calif. (Best)	11/76	452	2,275	19.9	5.75	22.5	2,010	5.25	11.00
Fort Wayne, Ind., suburbs (HBO)	3/77	5,406	12,600	49.9	5.95	80.1	6,750	7.00	12.95
Ithaca, N.Y. (HBO)	10/73	4,100	25,250	16.2	6.00	22.2	18,500	6.75	12.75

Los Angeles County, Calif. (Best)	9/76	1,488	22,179	6.7	6.00	10.5	14,174	7.95	13.95
Ridgecrest, Calif. (Cine)	8/74	404	4,800	8.4	5.95	28.9	1,400	6.25	12.20
Ventura, Calif. (Best)	7/77	1,006	8,400	12.0	5.95	15.8	6,350	6.50	12.45
Ventura-Century, Calif. (Best)	7/77	1,455	10,000	14.6	6.25	36.4	4,000	6.83	13.08
West Plains, Mo. (Best)	3/77	486	3,000	16.2	6.00	18.7	2,600	6.00	12.00

C. Pay cable rates approximately $12 or more

Burbank, Calif. (TPS)	5/76	5,536	52,743	10.5	11.45	22.7	24,376	6.25	17.70
Concord, Calif. (OTP)	8/74	4,255	33,560	12.7	11.95	13.5	31,584	7.50	19.45
Hemet, Calif. (HHT)	11/76	1,000	13,000	7.7	9.95	14.3	7,000	7.50	14.45
Hemet, Calif. (NSTV)	2/78	600	13,000	4.6	12.50	8.6	7,000	7.50	20.00
Juneau, Alaska (HBO)	9/77	1,200	5,500	21.8	14.95	29.3	4,100	18.00	32.95
Kodiak, Alaska (Show)	6/77	600	2,300	26.1	11.95	30.0	2,000	17.00	28.95
Martinez, Calif. (OTP)	9/75	3,025	29,862	10.1	11.95	12.2	24,851	5.25	17.20
Monterey, Calif. (NSTV)	7/75	1,090	18,500	5.9	11.95	8.0	13,618	6.95	18.90
Oxnard, Calif. (OPT)	6/78	290	35,000	0.8	17.42	2.0	14,663	6.95	24.37
Oxnard, Calif. (NSTV)	6/75	6,635	35,000	19.0	4.50	45.0	14,663	6.95	11.45
Oxnard, Calif. (PTV)	6/75	960	19,000	5.1	11.95	8.3	11,540	8.00	19.95
Pacific Grove, Calif. (OPT)	5/77	200	750	26.7	11.95	30.8	650	20.00	31.95
Petersburg, Alaska (Show)									
Stockton, Calif. (OPT)	6/75	3,106	50,517	6.2	11.95	21.2	14,679	7.00	18.95
Toledo, Ohio (OPT)	9/73	3,566	100,000	3.6	11.95	6.5	55,000	7.50	19.45
Toledo, Ohio (Show)	10/73	12,000	100,000	12.0	7.95	21.8	55,000	7.50	15.45
Walnut Creek, Calif. (OPT)	8/74	1,748	17,000	10.3	11.95	11.8	14,882	6.65	18.60
Wrangell, Alaska (Show)	4/77	150	650	23.1	11.95	27.3	550	20.00	31.95

*Note: Programs 1 and 2 differ in number of movies and content.

Legends of program distributors:

Best—BestVision
Cine—Cineamerica
HBO—Home Box Office
HHT—Hollywood Home Theater
IND—Independent (self books)
NSTV—National Subscription TV (over-the-air)
OPT—Optical Systems
PTV—Pay TV Services
Show—Showtime
TPS—TeleMation Program Services

Source: Paul Kagan Associates, Inc., *Census as of Dec. 31, 1978, of Pay-Cable Systems Operational as of Sept. 30, 1978,* passim.

EXHIBIT 4   Relationship between charge for pay TV and penetration of basic cable subscribers, December 31, 1978

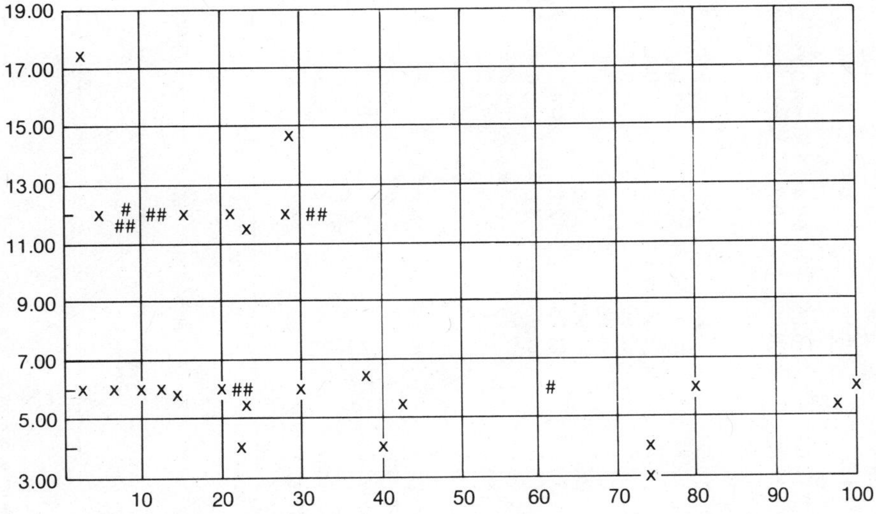

Source: Tabulated from Paul Kagan Associates, Inc., *Census as of Dec. 31, 1978, of Pay-Cable Systems Operational as of Sept. 30, 1978*, passim.

EXHIBIT 5   Selected data on pay cable rates and penetration as of December 31, 1978

System/pay distributor	Date pay service started	Pay penetra-tion of homes passed	Pay rate	Pay penetra-tion of cable sub-scribers	Basic cable rate	Com-bined rate
Home Box Office (HBO)						
Athens, Ga.	1/78	5.9%	$ 6.10	11.4%	$ 6.50	$12.60
Bryan, Tex.	1/76	2.4	6.00	2.9	4.00	10.00
Casa Grande, Ariz.	12/77	9.6	5.95	100.0	9.00	14.95
Charlotte, N.C.	7/78	24.0	5.95	61.1	7.50	13.45
Ithaca, N.Y.	10/73	16.2	6.00	22.0	6.75	12.75

$$\frac{197.4}{5} = 39.48\%$$

System/pay distributor	Date pay service started	Pay penetra-tion of homes passed	Pay rate	Pay penetra-tion of cable sub-scribers	Basic cable rate	Com-bined rate
Juneau, Alaska	9/77	21.8	14.95	29.3	18.00	32.95

EXHIBIT 5 *(continued)*

System/pay distributor	Date pay service started	Pay penetra- tion of homes passed	Pay rate	Pay penetra- tion of cable sub- scribers	Basic cable rate	Com- bined rate
BestVision (BV)						
La Habra, Calif.	5/77	27.1	3.00	100.0	7.00	10.00
Redondo Beach, Calif.	5/77	26.7	3.00	100.0	8.00	11.00
Atascadero, Calif.	7/76	5.0	5.95	7.2	7.20	13.15
Camarillo, Tex.	10/76	22.9	5.95	42.8	7.20	13.15
Cordova, Alaska	12/75	52.0	6.00	60.7	20.40	26.40
Edwards AFB, Calif.	11/76	19.9	5.75	22.5	5.25	11.00
Los Angeles County, Calif.	9/76	6.7	6.00	10.5	7.95	13.95
Ventura, Calif.	7/77	12.0	5.95	15.8	6.50	12.45
Ventura–Century Calif.	7/77	14.6	6.25	36.4	6.83	13.08
West Plains, Mo.	3/77	16.2	6.00	18.7	6.00	12.00

$$\frac{214.6}{8} = 26.8\%$$

System/pay distributor	Date pay service started	Pay penetra- tion of homes passed	Pay rate	Pay penetra- tion of cable sub- scribers	Basic cable rate	Com- bined rate
Telemation Program Services (TPS)						
Dover, N.H.	5/77	12.8	3.95	24.1	7.45	11.40
Jackson, Mich.	5/77	26.1	3.95	40.5	7.40	11.35
Lansing, Mich.	5/76	35.0	3.95	73.8	6.95	10.90
San Jose, Calif.	2/76	40.2	3.00	99.0	8.75	11.75
Burbank, Calif.	5/76	10.5	11.45	22.7	6.25	17.70

$$\frac{138.4}{3} = 46.1\%$$

System/pay distributor	Date pay service started	Pay penetra- tion of homes passed	Pay rate	Pay penetra- tion of cable sub- scribers	Basic cable rate	Com- bined rate
Showtime						
Orange County, Calif.–2	3/77	8.4	5.95	15.7	7.57	13.52
Orange County, Calif.–1	3/77	11.7	9.95	22.0	7.57	17.52
Kodiak, Alaska	6/77	26.1	11.95	30.0	17.00	28.95
Petersburg, Alaska	5/77	26.7	11.95	30.8	20.00	31.95
Toledo, Ohio	10/73	12.0	7.95	21.8	7.50	15.45
Wrangell, Alaska	4/77	23.1	11.95	27.3	20.00	31.95

$$3 @ 11.95 = \frac{88.1}{3} = 29.4\%$$

System/pay distributor	Date pay service started	Pay penetra- tion of homes passed	Pay rate	Pay penetra- tion of cable sub- scribers	Basic cable rate	Com- bined rate
Optical Systems						
Concord, Calif.	8/74	12.7	11.95	13.5	7.50	19.45
Martinez, Calif.	9/75	10.1	11.95	12.2	5.25	17.20

EXHIBIT 5 *(concluded)*

System/pay distributor	Date pay service started	Pay penetration of homes passed	Pay rate	Pay penetration of cable subscribers	Basic cable rate	Combined rate
Monterey, Calif.	7/75	5.9	11.95	8.0	6.95	18.90
Pacific Grove, Calif.	6/75	5.1	11.95	8.3	8.00	19.95
Stockton, Calif.	6/75	6.2	11.95	21.2	7.00	18.95
Toledo, Ohio	9/73	3.6	11.95	6.5	7.50	19.45
Walnut Creek, Calilf.	8/74	10.3	11.95	11.8	6.65	18.60

$$\frac{106.9}{7} = 15.3\%$$

Source: Basic data from Paul Kagan Associates, Inc., *Census as of Dec. 31, 1978, of Pay-Cable Systems Operational as of Sept. 30, 1978.*

dents in 1978 was $180,000. The inclusion of several millionaires in the group tended, however, to skew the average on the high side.

It was noted that a good many Leisure World residents were inclined to oppose any proposed increase in monthly maintenance charges, increases in green fees for golf, charges for horseback riding, or proposals involving higher contributions to the GRF to provide for the construction of an outdoor recreation area providing such facilities as additional tennis courts, handball courts, and racquetball courts. In short, it was difficult to anticipate how residents might respond to a $19.50 charge for NST Channel 52 subscription entertainment.

The Task Force on Pay Television had suggested that a questionnaire be distributed to Leisure World residents to get their reactions to alternative prices for pay TV as well as various types of program material. Preliminary estimates suggested that it might cost about $3,000 to prepare, administer, and analyze a mail questionnaire. The Community Relations Committee of the GRF board had rejected this suggestion on the ground that there was not enough interest in pay TV to justify such an expenditure. If Foley wished to get the information that such research might provide, he would have to absorb the cost in the investment required to get the pay TV project under way.

Check on pay TV prices commonly charged. In analyzing the Paul Kagan Associates census of pay cable systems as of December 31, 1978, it was decided to check on the number of operators charging various

possible prices for pay service. Exhibit 6 contains a summary of this tabulation.

Analysis of Exhibit 6 indicates that the price most commonly charged fell into the class $7.95 to $8.44 with 249 pay TV systems falling within this category. ($7.95 and $8.00 were the most common charges.) The median price also falls in this bracket. The lowest price charged was

---

EXHIBIT 6   Frequency distribution of pay cable rates charged December 31, 1978

Pay TV charge per month			Number of systems using charge
$ 1.45	to	$ 1.94	1 (Woodland 1—$3.50)
1.95	to	2.44	1 (Woodland 2—1.60; Rosemont—$2.00)
2.45	to	2.94	—
2.95	to	3.44	12
3.45	to	3.94	2
3.95	to	4.44	24
4.45	to	4.94	5
4.95	to	5.44	14
5.45	to	5.94	2
5.95	to	6.44	21
6.45	to	6.94	7
6.95	to	7.44	102
7.45	to	7.94	20
7.95	to	8.44	249 Median = 458
8.45	to	8.94	59
8.95	to	9.44	135
9.45	to	9.94	17
9.95	to	10.44	186
10.45	to	10.94	4
10.95	to	11.44	31
11.45	to	11.94	1
11.95	to	12.44	14
12.45	to	12.94	2
12.95	to	13.44	2
13.45	to	13.94	—
13.95	to	14.44	1
14.45	to	14.94	—
14.95	to	15.44	1
15.45	to	15.94	—
15.95	to	16.44	—
16.45	to	16.94	—
16.95	to	17.44	—
17.45	to	18.44	1 (Oxnard: $17.42; basic, $6.95; total, $24.37)

n = 914 systems

Source: Tabulated from Paul Kagan Associates, Inc., *Census as of Dec. 31, 1978, of Pay-Cable Systems Operational on Sept. 30, 1978,* passim.

$1.60, in Woodland, California, where the cable system offered two pay TV program packages supplied by BestVision. The Woodland cable system charged $8.50 for the basic cable service.

a.   One hundred percent of the 3,400 basic cable subscribers purchased program package 2 at $1.60 per month. The basic service plus program package 2 thus cost them $10.10 per month.

b.   In addition, 35.3 percent of the basic cable subscribers added program package 1 at $3.50 per month to the $10.10 they were already paying, or a total of $13.60 per month.

At the high end of the scale, the Oxnard, California, cable system charged $17.42 per month for NST Channel 52 pay TV service in addition to the $6.95 paid for the basic cable system, or a total of $24.37 for the combination. At these rates, the NST pay TV service, first offered in June 1978, had been bought by 2.0 percent of the 14,663 cable subscribers. (It had thus been available only six months.)

DECISION QUESTION FACING ROSSMOOR ELECTRIC

Late in January 1979, after reviewing the foregoing information, Foley was prepared to choose among three basic alternatives under which pay TV programs would be offered on an optional basis in Leisure World:

1.   Offer movie programs selected by Rossmoor Electric personnel on a stand-alone basis at a charge of $6 per month. This would involve eliminating program distributors and dealing directly with motion-picture producers.

2.   Recommend affiliation with the Home Box Office service at a price of $8.50 per month. This would involve the purchase of an earth station to receive programs broadcast by satellite.

3.   Propose affiliation with National Subscription Television's Channel 52 ON program service at a charge of $19.50 per month. The NST Channel 52 signal would be received over the air from Mount Wilson by the Leisure World Community antenna and distributed to those who subscribed via the local cable system.

In each instance, the investment in equipment required at the head end, as well as the converters required for security purposes, would be made by Rossmoor Electric, Inc. Likewise, all the costs of operation would be paid by Rossmoor Electric out of the revenue received from the sale of subscriptions to the pay TV service. The profit, or loss, would accrue to Rossmoor Electric.

Regardless of which alternative Foley chose, it would be necessary for his firm to obtain the approval of Golden Rain Foundation for any plan

that would make pay TV available on the Leisure World Cable Television System. Although Foley believed that the Community Relations Committee of the GRF board was more likely to give favorable consideration to his proposal than had been the case with earlier suggestions, he had no assurance that approval would be forthcoming. There had been enough requests for pay television service in the *Leisure World News*, through correspondence and by telephone, however, to lead him to believe that the Community Relations Committee would be willing to reopen the question. Foley planned to make his decision by the end of January 1979.

APPENDIX

Five-Year Projection of Net Income from NST Channel 52 Pay TV: Rossmoor Electric, Inc., January 1979

	Year 1	Year 2	Year 3	Year 4	Year 5
Monthly subscribers (estimated)	200	500	750	1,000	1,000
Turnover disconnects	40	100	150	200	200
Total hookups install	240	400	400	450	200
Revenue					
Subscriber revenue	$46,800	$117,000	$175,500	$234,000	$234,000
Installation revenue	7,200	12,000	12,000	13,500	6,000
Gross	$54,000	$129,000	$187,500	$247,500	$240,000
Expenses					
NST programming fee	$27,360	$ 68,400	$102,600	$136,800	$136,800
Office staff + 7 percent per year	12,000	12,840	13,739	14,700	15,730
Advertising and promotion	5,600	3,600	3,600	3,600	3,600
Installation cost	4,800	8,000	8,000	9,000	4,000
Disconnect cost	800	2,000	3,000	4,000	4,000
Maintenance cost	4,800	12,000	18,000	24,000	24,000
Other costs*	4,800	12,000	18,000	24,000	24,000
Total	$61,160	$118,840	$166,939	$216,100	$212,130
Operating income (loss)	$ (6,160)	$ 10,160	$ 20,561	$ 31,400	$ 27,860
Depreciation	5,600	(9,200)	(12,200)	(15,200)	(15,200)
Net Income (loss) before taxes	(11,760)	960	8,361	16,200	12,660
Taxes 50 percent	(11,760)	480	4,181	8,100	6,330

Assumptions

	Year 1	Year 2	Year 3	Year 4	Year 5
Business assumptions					
Converter: one per subscriber	60				
Total system manors	12,500	12,500	12,500	12,500	12,500
Percent penetration	2%	4%	6%	8%	8%

	Year 1	Year 2	Year 3	Year 4	Year 5
Turnovers	20%	20%	20%	20%	20%
Subscribers year-end	250	500	750	1,000	1,000
Average subscribers first year– 80 percent	200	500	750	1,000	1,000
Financial assumptions					
Subscriber rate	$ 19.50	$ 19.50	$ 19.50	$ 19.50	$ 19.50
Installation charge	30.00	30.00	30.00	30.00	30.00
Installation cost	20.00	20.00	20.00	20.00	20.00
Disconnect cost	20.00	20.00	20.00	20.00	20.00
Converter cost	60.00	60.00	60.00	60.00	60.00
NST fee	11.40	11.40	11.40	11.40	11.40
Equipment and labor cost to start	16,000				
Converter cost per year	12,000	18,000	15,000	15,000	—
Yearly depreciation on equipment	3,200	3,200	3,200	3,200	3,200
Yearly depreciation on converters	2,400	6,000	9,000	12,000	12,000
Total depreciation	5,600	9,200	12,200	15,200	15,200
Balance forward	22,400	31,200	34,000	33,800	18,600

Notes: Estimated Expenses—5-year projection

Labor and equipment cost				
Equipment at head end			$ 8,000	
Labor at head end	25 hours	$25 ea.	625	
Labor at system	300 hours	$25 ea.	7,500	$16,125
Year 1 converters	200	$60 ea.	$12,000	
Year 2 converters	300	60 ea.	18,000	
Year 3 converters	250	60 ea.	15,000	
Year 4 converters	250	60 ea.	15,000	60,000
Total				$76,125
Depreciation 20 percent per year				
Advertising and promotion				
Year 1	$2,000 + $300 per mo.			$ 5,600
Years 2–5	$200 per mo.			2,460
Installation charges			$30	
Installation cost			20	
Disconnect cost			20	
Maintenance cost			2	
Staff person				$12,000 + 7 percent years 2–5
Program fee NST	per subscriber		11.40	

*Other costs include computer, postage, bad debts, billing, program guide, reports for NST, and reports for GRF.

QUESTION

1. Which of the three alternative plans for pay TV service should Foley propose to the GRF board? Why?

UNITED TECHTRONICS*

In June 1977, United Techtronics faced a major pricing decision with respect to its new video screen television system. "We're really excited here at United Techtronics," exclaimed Mr. Roy Cowing, the founder and president of United Techtronics, "We've made a most significant technological breakthrough in large screen, video television systems." He went on to explain that the marketing plan for 1978 for this product was now his major area of concern, and that what price to charge was the marketing question giving him the most difficulty.

COMPANY HISTORY

United Techtronics (UT) was founded in Boston in 1959 by Mr. Cowing. Prior to that time Mr. Cowing had been an associate professor of electrical engineering at MIT. Mr. Cowing founded UT to manufacture and market products making use of some of the electronic inventions he had developed while at MIT. Sales were made mostly to the space program and the military. Sales grew from $100,000 in 1960 to $27 million in 1976. Profits in 1976 were $3.2 million.

*Written by Thomas C. Kinnear, Professor of Marketing, Graduate School of Business Administration, The University of Michigan. Used by permission.

THE VIDEO SCREEN PROJECT

For a number of years beginning in the late 1960s, Mr. Cowing had been trying to reduce the company's dependency on government sales. One of the diversification projects that he had committed research and development monies to was the so-called video screen project. The objective of this project was to develop a system whereby a television picture could be displayed on a screen as big as 8 to 10 feet diagonally. In late 1976, one of UT's engineers made the necessary breakthrough. The rest of 1976 and the first few months of 1977 were spent producing working prototypes. Up until June 1977, UT had invested $600,000 in the project.

VIDEO SCREEN TELEVISION

Extra-large screen television systems were not new. There were a number of companies who sold such systems both to the consumer and commercial (taverns, restaurants, and so on) markets. Most current systems made use of a special magnifying lens that projected a regular small-television picture onto a special screen. The result of this process is that the final picture lacked much of the brightness of the original small screen. As a result, the picture had to be viewed in a darkened room. There were some other video systems that did not use the magnifying process. These systems used special tubes but also suffered from a lack of brightness.

UT had developed a system that was bright enough to be viewed in regular daylight on a screen up to 10 feet diagonal. Mr. Cowing was unwilling to discuss how this was accomplished. He would only say that the process was protected by patent, and that he thought it would take at least two to three years for any competitor to duplicate the results of the system.

A number of large and small companies were active in this area. Admiral, General Electric, RCA, Zenith, and Sony were all thought to be working on developing large-screen systems directed at the consumer market. Sony was rumored to be ready to introduce a 60-inch diagonal screen system that would retail for about $2,500. A number of small companies were already producing systems. Advent Corporation, a small New England company, claimed to have sold 4,000, 84-inch diagonal units in two years at a $4,000 price. Muntz Manufacturing claimed one-year sales of 5,000, 50-inch diagonal units at prices from $1,500 to $2,500. Mr. Cowing was adamant that none of these systems gave as bright a picture as UT's. He estimated that about 10,000 large-screen systems were sold in 1976.

COST STRUCTURE

Mr. Cowing expected about 50 percent of the suggested retail selling price to go for wholesaler and retailer margins. He expected that UT's direct manufacturing costs would vary depending on the volume produced. Exhibit 1 presents these estimates. He expected direct labor costs to fall at higher production volumes due to the increased automation of the process and improved worker skills.

EXHIBIT 1   Estimated production costs of UT's video screen system

	Volume		
	0–5,000	5,000–10,000	10,001–20,000
Raw materials	$ 480	$460	$410
Direct labor	540	320	115
Total direct costs	$1,020	$780	$525

Material costs were expected to fall due to less waste due to automation. The equipment costs necessary to automate the product process were $70,000 to produce in the 0–5,000 unit range, an additional $50,000 to produce in the 5,001–10,000 unit range, and an additional $40,000 to produce in the 10,001–20,000 unit range. The useful life of this equipment was put at five years. Mr. Cowing was sure that production costs were substantially below those of current competitors including Sony. Such was the magnitude of UT's technological breakthrough. Mr. Cowing was unwilling to produce over 20,000 units a year in the first few years due to the limited cash resources of the company to support inventories, and so on.

MARKET STUDIES

Mr. Cowing wanted to establish a position in the consumer market for his product. He felt that the long-run potential was greater there than in the commercial market. With this end in mind he hired a small economic research consulting firm to undertake a consumer study to determine the likely reaction to alternative retail prices for the system. These consultants undertook extensive interviews with potential television pur-

chasers and examined the sales and pricing histories of competitive products. They concluded that: "UT's video screen system would be highly price elastic across a range of prices from $500 to $5,000, both in a primary and secondary demand sense." They went on to estimate the price elasticity of demand in this range to be between 4.0 and 6.5.

THE PRICING DECISION

Mr. Cowing was considering a number of alternative suggested retail prices. "I can see arguments for pricing anywhere from above Advent's to substantially below Muntz's lowest price," he said.

QUESTIONS

1. What factors should be considered in setting a price for UT's video system?

2. What price should Mr. Cowing set for UT's video screen system? Why?

██████████████

INTEGRATED MARKETING PROGRAMS

A firm's overall marketing program is a composite of many bits and pieces. Parts three through six of this text treated, in depth, specific decision areas in the development of an overall marketing program. The success of this program, however, is not only a function of the wisdom of these specific decisions but also depends upon: (1) how these decisions are integrated into a total program and (2) how effectively both specific decisions and the overall program are implemented. If these two things are accomplished well, the resultant marketing program will be, in a very real sense, more than the sum of its parts.

The following cases are broad in scope and permit consideration of a firm's total marketing strategy. They provide an opportunity to synthesize what has been covered previously in this text and to perceive how decisions in one area of marketing strategy affect decisions in other areas of marketing strategy. The marketing planning process outlined in Chapter 1 provides a useful framework for their analysis.

Cases for part seven

GUNTHER CANDY COMPANY (B)*

Quality Cookie Division

Development of a marketing strategy

INTRODUCTION

In April 1982 Jerome (Jerry) Schwartz, a recent graduate of a leading MBA program, was hired by the management of the Quality Cookie Division of the Gunther Candy Company. His task was to turn around the performance of the division after a two-year period of declining sales and profitability (see Exhibit 1). Quality Cookie Division's performance, although still marginally profitable, was slipping; and unless changes were made, the division would be operating in the red by the end of the summer.

The company was purchased by the Gunther Candy Company of Rochester, New York, in March 1978. Gunther, a well-established candy and tobacco wholesaler, was owned by Steve and Ken Goodman. These men believed that margins in the cookie business were better than in the candy business, and when Quality Cookies became available at what they considered a very low price, they bought the company.

After buying Quality, however, the Goodman brothers devoted very

---

*Written by Jeffrey Nagel, under the supervision of Professor Martin R. Warshaw, Graduate School of Business Administration, The University of Michigan. All names and numerical data are disguised.

EXHIBIT 1   Four-year performance of Quality Cookie Division

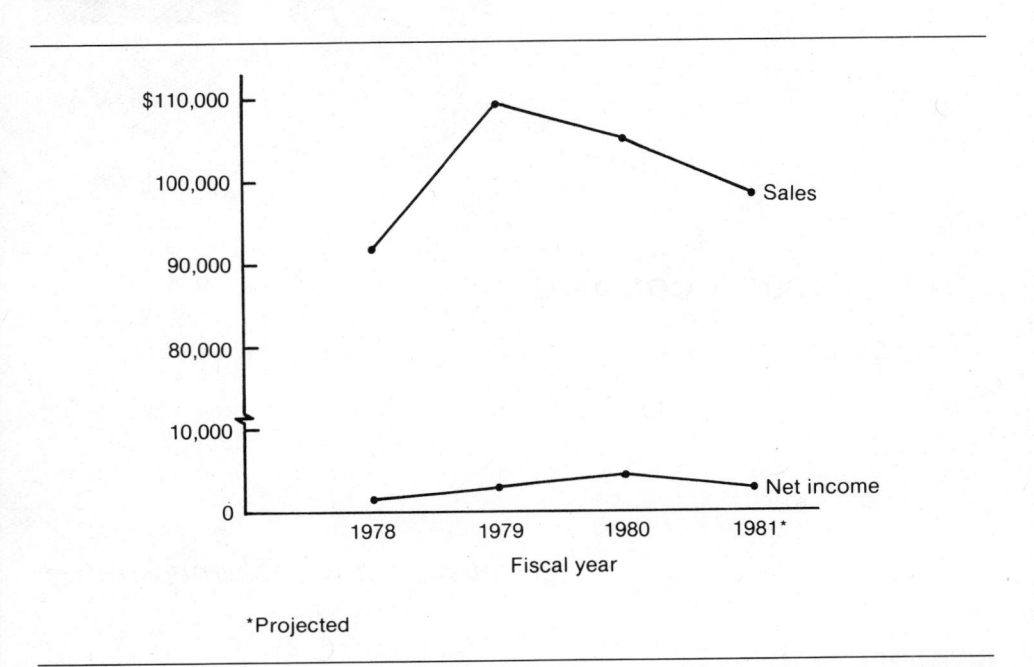

*Projected

little of their time to its operation. The candy and tobacco business continued to receive most of their attention. Cookie products were rarely promoted, sales declined, and a third of the customers were lost over a four-year period. Rather than face the total demise of the company, they hired Jerry and gave him a year to put Quality back on the track to profitability.

THE WHOLESALE CANDY AND COOKIE MARKET

The wholesale candy and cookie business is predominantly a commodity business in which every distributor has the same products and the major selling point is price. The industry is based on variable pricing, in which various customers are charged different prices.

The nature of the industry is that the retailer normally works on higher margins than the wholesaler. For the wholesaler to survive and be profitable, he must do a large volume.

Cookies are sold either by advance sales or "off the truck." The former method involves sending out a salesman to take orders and having the merchandise delivered within a few days. Cookies are usually serviced by the wholesaler. This involves pricing the product, putting it on the shelves, and setting up point-of-purchase material. Servicing is very important because the cookie business is considered a "thieves' market." Shelf space is very scarce. The wholesaler is always trying to get additional facings of his products, which means that competitors must lose facings.

The second method of selling is "off the truck." This involves sending a salesman into an account to take an order and then having him bring the merchandise into the store at that time. There are three major disadvantages to this: (1) the potential out-of-stocks resulting from the limited storage capacity of a truck, (2) errors resulting from invoices being handwritten, and (3) the difficulty of controlling inventory.

It is standard cookie and candy industry practice to guarantee both sales and merchandise free from damage. The largest problem is in handling seasonal merchandise. Customers expect the wholesaler to have seasonal merchandise and also to guarantee it. There are always unsold products remaining after the holidays, and the wholesaler must take the merchandise back from his customers and give them credit. Since the manufacturers do not give credit to the wholesalers, the products must be held until the following year—when they are resold if they are still in good condition. Cookies cannot be resold, since they do not have a long enough shelf life. Wholesale margins on seasonal merchandise are the same as on regular merchandise, which makes guaranteed sales unprofitable if there is even a small percentage of returns.

Manufacturers normally give 30-days credit, while wholesalers give two to four weeks, depending on the size of the account.

A number of stores in the Rochester area, both large and small, have gone out of business in the past year. This has led some wholesalers to sell on a "cash-and-carry" basis. Customers pick up their merchandise at low prices from the distributor and pay cash.

PRODUCT LINE

Quality Cookies carried the complete line of Mama's cookies, which was similar to Nabisco, Keebler, and Sunshine lines (Exhibit 2). The suggested retail price of Mama's cookies was 10 cents to 60 cents less than comparable Nabisco products, with Keebler and Sunshine priced between the two. (See Exhibit 3 for the volume price list of all cookie items.) Part of the Mama's line consisted of 12 varieties of five- to seven-ounce packages, prepriced at two for $1.00. This line constituted over

EXHIBIT 2   The Mama's Cookies product line

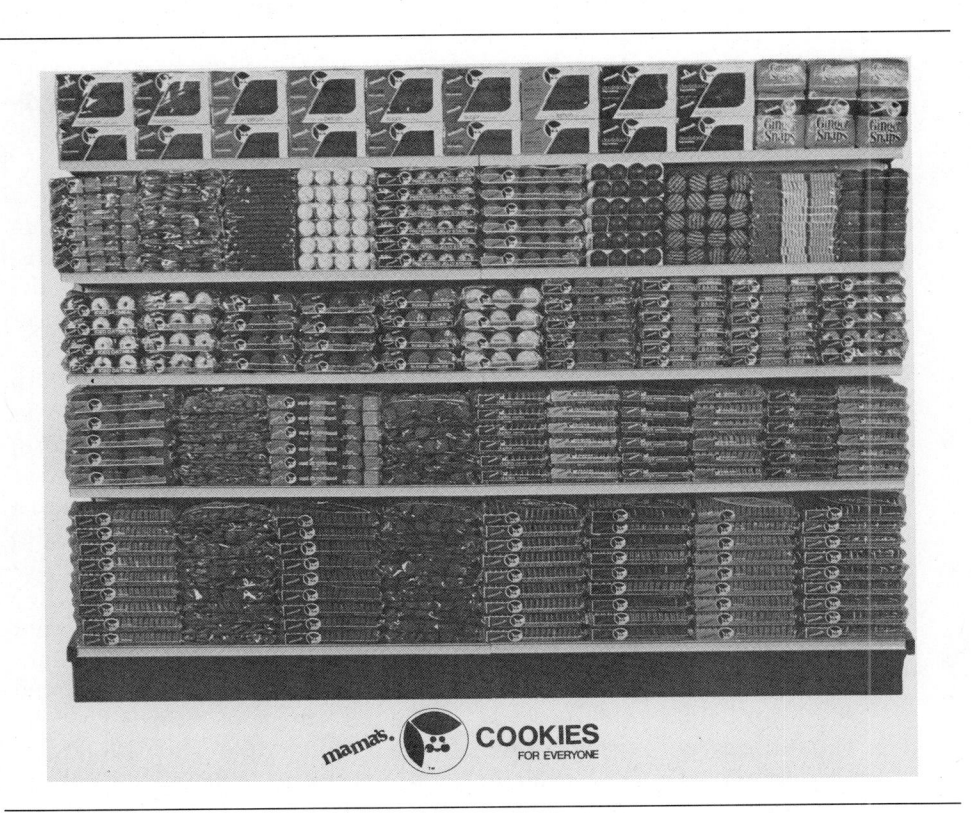

mama's. COOKIES FOR EVERYONE

50 percent of Quality's cookie sales. Total cookie sales comprised approximately 60 percent to 70 percent of sales, with gross margins from 22 percent to 28 percent.

The Mama's line had been carried only for the past two years. Before that time Quality Cookies carried Penn Dutch and Murray cookies. The Penn Dutch line was a bag line of cookies and crackers similar to those of Pepperidge Farm (Exhibit 4). There were three cookie varieties and four cracker varieties. One advantage to this line was the low minimum order quantity ($500) compared to Mama's 800-case minimum.

The Murray line of cookies consisted of five varieties of thins. The retail price of the thins was 99 cents for 11 dozen.

The manufacturers of both lines sold to any distributor who wanted them. When Murray raised the price of its products two years ago, Steve

EXHIBIT 3   Quality Cookies' wholesale price list for cookie items

Item	Weight (ounces)	Unit pack	Suggested retail
Two for $1.00			
Strawberry Creme	7	24	2/$1
Vanilla Creme	7	24	2/$1
Banana Creme	7	24	2/$1
Onyx Creme	7	24	2/$1
Fudge Creme	7	24	2/$1
Choozy Chips	5.75	24	2/$1
Shortbread and Butter	6.00	24	2/$1
Ginger Crisp	6.00	24	2/$1
Sugar Cookie	6.50	24	2/$1
Striped Dainty	4.50	24	2/$1
Iced Snow Bars	7.00	24	2/$1
Duplex Sugar Wafer	4.75	24	2/$1
Ring cookies			
Macaroon Rings	7.50	12	$ .79
Sugar Rings	7.50	12	.79
Pecan Rings	7.50	12	.79
Lemon Rings	7.50	12	.79
Devilsfood Rings	7.50	12	.79
Pounder line			
Coconut Bars	16	12	$1.29
Dutch Windmill	16	12	1.29
Iced Oatmeal	16	12	1.29
Cremes			
Onyx Cremes	20	12	$1.29
Vanilla Cremes	20	12	1.29
2-in-1 Cremes	20	12	1.29
Duplex Cremes	20	12	1.29
Fudge Cremes	20	12	1.29
Lemon Cremes	20	12	1.29
2-pounder			
Angel Cremes	32	12	$1.99
Duplex Cremes	32	12	1.99
Lemon Cremes	32	12	1.99
Fudge Cremes	32	12	1.99
Miscellaneous			
Jelly Stars	10	12	$ .99
Butter Cookies	10	12	.89
Dutch Windmill	10	12	.89
Choozy Chips	10	12	.89
Coconut Bars	10	12	.89
Brown Edge Lemon	10	12	.99
Sooper Chips	17	12	1.49
Ginger Snaps	16	12	.99
Fancy Puffs	9.5	12	1.09
Mallow Whirls	9.5	12	1.09
Fig Bars	14.5	12	1.19
Graham Squares	12	12	1.19

EXHIBIT 3 *(concluded)*

Item	Weight (ounces)	Unit pack	Suggested retail
Striped Delights	11.5	12	1.19
Fudge n' Mint	11.5	12	1.19
Coconut Macaroon	8	12	1.19
Preferred Assortment	13	12	1.19
Assorted Sugar Wafers	10	12	1.19
Royal 6 Assortment	17	12	1.49
Crackers			
Somerset Saltines	16	12	$ .99
Somerset Grahams	16	12	1.09
Somerset Snax Crax	11	12	.99

Goodman decided to switch to the Mama's line. Besides a price advantage, Mama's cookies offered a full line, which the other two companies did not. All of these cookies were hard cookies, as opposed to soft cookies like Archway. The former type have a shelf life of six months, while the latter have a two-month shelf life.

The second largest product line for Quality Cookies, in terms of sales, was the 89 cent Brach bag line of candy. There were 30 varieties of the bag line and 10 varieties of boxed chocolates, which retailed for $1.39 each (Exhibit 5). The box line was sold at one price, while the bags were sold at two prices, depending on the amount of competition in an account. The Brach line comprised approximately 20 percent to 25 percent of sales.

The rest of Quality 's product line consisted of a variety of large-bag candy, beer nuts, almonds, caramel corn, and Sunburst fruit drinks. These items were usually an afterthought in a sale and therefore constituted only 5 percent to 10 percent of sales. The wholesale price list for Quality Cookies products other than cookies is presented in Exhibit 6.

COMPETITION

There were three nationally advertised cookie brands being sold in the same geographical area as Quality Cookies: Nabisco, Keebler, and Sunshine. The small stores normally carried Nabisco and sometimes either Keebler or Sunshine. Rarely did a store carry both; only very large supermarkets and chain stores carried all three major brands.

EXHIBIT 4   The Penn Dutch product line

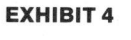

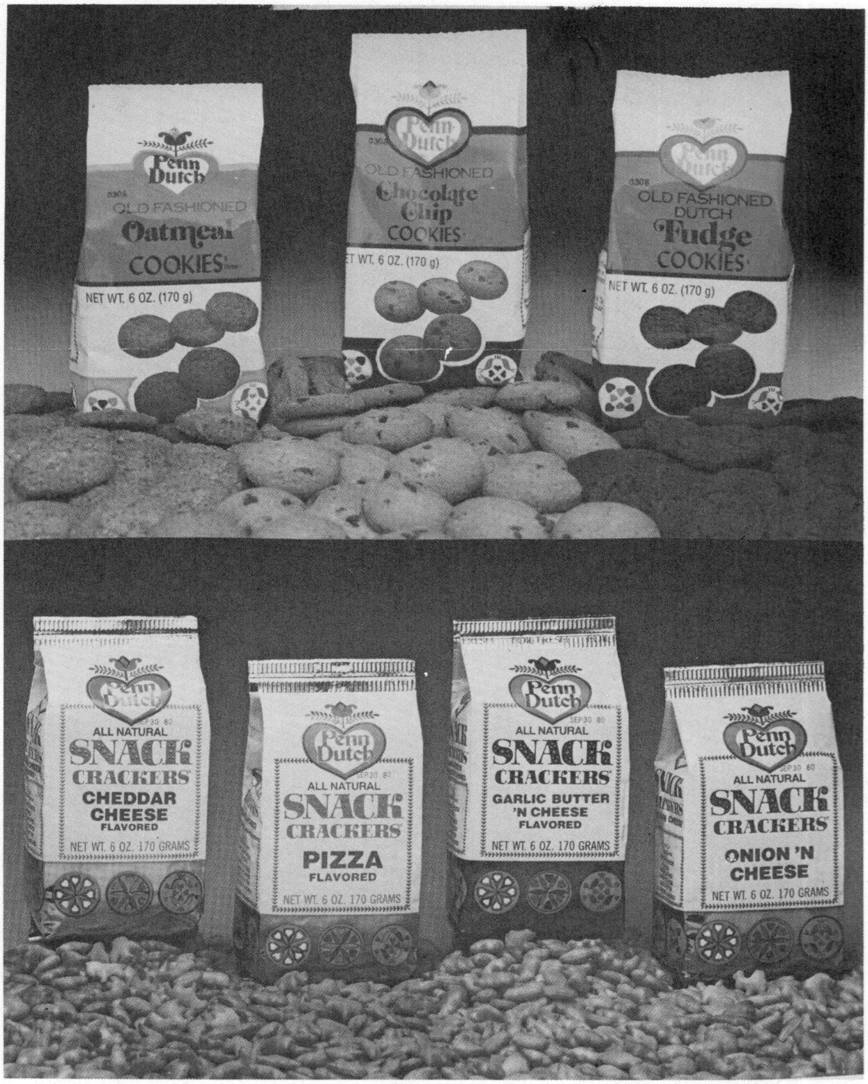

EXHIBIT 5 The Brach product line

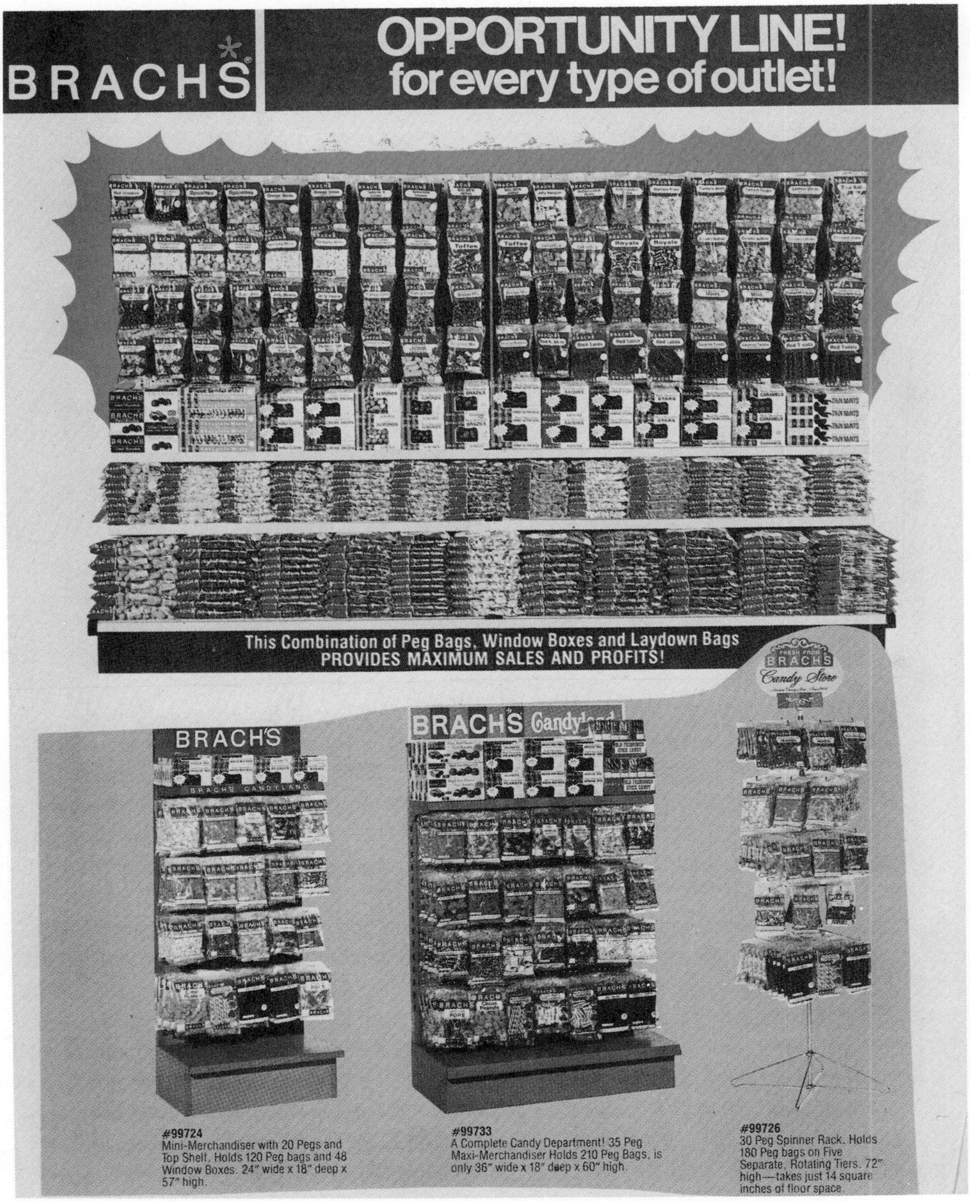
BRACH'S
OPPORTUNITY LINE!
for every type of outlet!
This Combination of Peg Bags, Window Boxes and Laydown Bags
PROVIDES MAXIMUM SALES AND PROFITS!
FRESH FROM BRACH'S
Candy Store
BRACH'S
BRACH'S Candyland
#99724
Mini-Merchandiser with 20 Pegs and Top Shelf. Holds 120 Peg bags and 48 Window Boxes. 24" wide x 18" deep x 57" high.
#99733
A Complete Candy Department! 35 Peg Maxi-Merchandiser Holds 210 Peg Bags, is only 36" wide x 18" deep x 60" high.
#99726
30 Peg Spinner Rack. Holds 180 Peg bags on Five Separate, Rotating Tiers. 72" high—takes just 14 square inches of floor space.

EXHIBIT 6   Quality Cookies wholesale price list for items other than cookies

Item	Case pack	Retail
Beer Nuts 12-oz. cans	12	$2.89
Beer Nuts 5½-oz. bags	4/12	.89
Beer Nuts 1¼-oz. bags	16/18	.30
Blue Diamond 16-oz. almond	4/12	.79
Blue Diamond ¾-oz. almond	6/24	.30
Caramel Corn	24	1.49
Foxy Pops—boxes	12/24	1.39
Foxy Pops—individual	48	.15
BRACH—boxes	4/12	$1.39
BRACH—bags	6	.89
Chelsea Chips	24	1.59
Goetze's Caramels 8 oz.	24	.89
Tootsie Midgees 7½ oz.	24	.99
Tootsie Pops 6¼ oz.	36	.99
Circus Peanuts	24	.89
Kimballs Candy	24	.99
Super Bubble	24	.89
Fizzers	24	.89
Bag-0-Kits 6 oz.	24	.79
Bag-0-Bats 7 oz.	24	.89
Kiddi Pops 10 oz.	24	.99
Mary Janes 6 oz.	24	.69
Licorice Nibs	24	.79
Slurpy	24	.89
Pearson Caramel Nip	12	.99
Pearson Coffee Nip	12	.99
Pearson Mint Parfait	12	.99
Pearson Pnutbutter Parfait	12	.99
Pearson Chocolate Parfait	12	.99
Pearson Licorice Nip	12	.99
Pearson Coffioca	12	.99
SUNBURST—Grape	48	.25
SUNBURST—Orange	48	.25
SUNBURST—Punch	48	.25

Retail gross margins (percent)

Mama's cookies	24–26
Brach	
Bags	23–34
Boxes	26
Bag candy	23–26
Sunburst	42
Nuts	21–33

Nabisco products were sold by salesmen through advance sales. The products were well known, carried high prices, and sold well. Using the manufacturer's suggested retail price, the margins to the retailer were kept at about 22 percent. Many smaller stores raised the retail prices to increase their margins.

At the end of May Nabisco announced that it would no longer service accounts with average purchases under $50. If a store wanted the product, it would have to call in an order to Nabisco. The product would then be delivered, and the store was responsible for putting it on the shelves. This annoyed many small retailers, but it was difficult for them not to carry the major-selling brand.

Sunshine was sold through a wholesale grocer who gave the retailers a gross margin of about 25 percent. Retailers thought that they were getting a higher margin on the product—the cost of the product to the retailer was listed on the invoice at 72 percent of retail—but a 3 percent delivery charge was added at the bottom of the invoice.

Keebler was sold through company salesmen and had better distribution than Sunshine. The gross margin to the retailer for Keebler products was also about 25 percent.

The only competitor for Quality Cookies' 2/$1.00 cookie line was a wholesaler located 70 miles away. The product it sold, called Sugar Kake, gave the retailer a 35 percent gross margin. The wholesaler came into the Rochester area only once each month and did not carry any other cookie lines.

Various other wholesalers in the area sold a variety of cookie products including the Barbara Dee, Murray, and Grandma's brands. None of these were full-line products. Barbara Dee had a 20-ounce creme line which retailed for 99 cents and a bag line of cookies. Murray offered a variety of thins priced at 99 cents for 11 dozen thins. Grandma's also offered a variety of cremes, but they were not as widely available in the marketplace. See Exhibit 7 for a comparison of the product lines of Quality Cookies and its wholesale competitors.

The only firm competing for Mama's cookies was M&R Distributors, a full-line wholesaler. The manufacturer generally had a policy of giving its products to only one distributor in an area, but in this case M&R was also given the Mama's line and eventually did three times the sales volume of Quality Cookies. M&R carried a variety of specialty items. Their large and diverse product line made each sales call very cost-effective. Cookie sales were usually an afterthought, since they were a hassle to handle. Only a few of Mama's cookies were used in the company's plan-o-gram, and it did not carry the 2/$1.00 line. Most of the distributor's sales of cookies were through the Grand Union supermarket chain.

Because M&R did not use all of Mama's cookies in its plan-o-gram, the manufacturer saw more potential growth with Quality Cookies,

EXHIBIT 7　　Comparison of Quality Cookies product line and theory of wholesale competitors

	Retail gross margin	Depth of product line	Service
Mama's	24–26%	Full-line, with 2/$1.00	Full-service Quality cookies
Nabisco	22	Full-line, no 2/$1.00	None to small accounts Company salespeople
Keebler	25	Full-line, no 2/$1.00	Full-service Company salespeople
Sunshine	25	Full-line, no 2/$1.00	None Wholesale grocers
Sugar Kake	35	Only 2/$1.00	Monthly deliveries Distributor
Barbara Dee	27–30	Bag line and 20-oz. cremes	Varied service Wholesalers
Murray	27	11 dozen thins	Varied service Wholesalers
Grandma's	27	Cremes	Varied service Wholesalers

which sold only Mama's cookies (see Exhibit 8 for Quality's plan-o-gram). The manufacturer made it clear, however, that Quality Cookies and M&R could not sell to the same accounts. This limited Quality Cookies' growth potential substantially since it had only small accounts, while its competitor had the large accounts. The manufacturer had threatened to stop supplying Quality Cookies with product if it tried to take business away from M&R. Jerry considered this a major factor limiting the growth of his company.

CUSTOMERS

By the end of fiscal 1981 the company had approximately 90 customers. These consisted predominantly of mom-and-pop grocery stores, with a few independent supermarkets and convenience stores. About 60 customers paid COD while the other 30 paid on account. The larger supermarkets paid monthly, while the smaller stores paid from invoice to invoice. The latter policy meant that the customer paid every other

EXHIBIT 8   Quality Cookies 5-shelf plan-o-gram I

1 row Vanilla Cremes 7 oz.	1 row Onyx Cremes 7 oz.	1 row Strawberry Cremes 7 oz.	1 row Fudge Cremes 7 oz.	1 row Banana Cremes 7 oz.	2 rows Ginger Snaps 16 oz.
1 row Assorted Sugar Wafers 10 oz.	1 row Dutch Windmill 10 oz.	1 row Graham Squares 12 oz.	1 row Pounder Iced Oatmeal 16 oz.	1 row Choozy Chips 10 oz.	
1 row Coconut Bars 10 oz.	1 row Brown Edge Lemon 9 oz.	1 row Striped Delight 11½ oz.	1 row Coconut Macaroon 8 oz.	1 row Fig Bars 14½ oz.	
1 row Jelly Star 10 oz.	1 row Sooper Chips 17 oz.	1 row Mallow Whirl 9½ oz.	1 row Royal 6 Assortment 17 oz.		
1 row Duplex Cremes 20 oz.	1 row Vanilla Cremes 20 oz.	1 row Fudge Cremes 20 oz.	1 row 2-in-1 Cremes 20 oz.		

week only if he made a purchase. Therefore, the receivables on those accounts sometimes stretched to four weeks.

The small Mom-and-Pop stores usually purchased only the Mama's 2/$1.00 line of cookies and, occasionally, Brach products. Purchases for a small account ranged from $8 to $30. The company had no four-foot sections of cookies in any account. (A four-foot section is four linear feet of shelf space, four or five shelves high.)

The larger accounts usually carried more than just cookies. The Brach line sold well off their racks, and Sunburst sold very well because of its low price.

Over the years Ken Goodman, one of the owners of Quality Cookies, had considered trying to get into some of the major supermarket chains in the area: Topps, Friendly Markets, Star, Wegman's, Bells, Super Duper, and Grand Union. To sell to these potential customers one had to see the chain buyer. It was rare that a sale was made on the first visit, and appointments usually took from four to six weeks to obtain. Sales depended on developing a relationship with the buyers.

A second consideration was whether delivery should be made directly

to the chains' warehouses or to the stores (store door delivery). The former method would require development of a new price structure and a way to service the accounts. Jerry considered this as a major opportunity for the firm.

The only Quality Cookie items that could be sold to these chains were cookies. The manufacturer of all the company's other products sold directly to the chains, while Mama's was sold only through distributors. If a Mama's sales representative sold a particular chain account, he would credit the account to the distributor in that area.

One potential customer in the area was the Convenient Food Mart chain. About 60 percent of the stores were franchises, while the other 40 percent were company-owned. The company-owned stores did almost all of their purchasing through central billing. The company had an unfortunate record of assigning charges and credits to wrong accounts, which caused a number of problems.

Quality Cookies sold to four Convenience Food Mart accounts. One of these, a company-owned store, owed Quality Cookies over $1,500 by March 1982. The company was making no effort to repay the money, so the store manager agreed to pay $100 per week out of the cash register until the debt was paid off. All sales to this store were made COD.

Two independent Convenience Food Mart stores were owned by Jay Lasky. No one really remembered how, but Laskey claimed that sometime in the past he had been given authorization to deduct 7 percent from his invoices. He paid through Convenient's central billing, even though his store was not company-owned. The payments did not usually match the charges, and over the years it became difficult to track the amounts that he owed Quality. This was a problem with a number of accounts which paid only a portion of an invoice at a time. Another problem was that Lasky had a habit of telling lots of people about his "deal." This put pressure on Quality Cookies to give the 7 percent discount to other stores in the chain.

Jerry felt that there was potential in the Convenient Food chain but not through central billing. It was possible for the stores to pay COD, since that is how most of them paid the bread men.

Another potential chain account was Stop N' Shop. There were about 80 to 100 Stop N' Shops in the Rochester area, and all were company-owned. The company had tried buying Nabisco products through its warehouse and found that it did not work. Nabisco products were the only cookies in the Stop N' Shop stores, and they were serviced store door.

Because the Stop N' Shops were very small, they could not carry many cookie items. In order to introduce a new cookie product in the chain, a distributor had to arrange to test the product in a few stores. There was one store manager in charge of arranging the tests. As with other buy-

ers, it was very important to develop rapport with him so that he would agree to test a new product. Jerry felt that there was some potential for the 2/$1.00 line. He estimated that, because of the size of the stores, he could get at most five different cookie items in each store and questioned whether sales from five items were enough to justify servicing the accounts.

SALES FORCE

The sales force consisted of one man, Langdon. Langdon was 60 years old and had been a bread route-man. This involved going into a store and filling up the shelves with bread from his truck. This was strictly a service job requiring no selling ability, which was good because Langdon had none.

Langdon was paid 10 percent of collections. Originally, Ken Goodman thought that he should be paid 7 percent, but Ken's accountant recommended 10 percent so that Langdon could figure out his commission more easily. (The services of that accountant were soon after terminated.)

Langdon complained about his low salary (about $10,000) but never tried to do anything about it. When he saw that sales were low for a particular week, he would overload his customers with merchandise, which greatly annoyed them. Langdon knew the names of only 70 percent of his customers, which added to his already poor rapport with them.

Langdon was generally lazy, although he swore that he wasn't. He rarely used the point-of-purchase (POP) material supplied to him, rarely kept his sections neat, and never checked codes on merchandise (in fact, he did not know how to read the codes). Consequently, there was a lot of out-of-date merchandise in the stores. Langdon only worked about 30 hours per week. His sales routes did not take him a full day, and Fridays were usually only half-days. Occasionally he worked part of Saturdays.

Over the years Langdon had lost dozens of accounts. He always had an excuse for everything he did wrong.

Langdon was given a sales book which contained pictures of all the cookie items, but he rarely used this book. The salesmen for Gunther Candy Company used sales books extensively since their product line was much broader and the salesmen could not possibly remember all of the items. Jerry thought that putting pictures of all of the items in Langdon's sales book might help sales; but, even more basic, Jerry felt a plan was needed to get Langdon to use his book.

GENERAL OPERATIONS

Quality Cookies operated out of the same warehouse as Gunther Candy Company. Each morning Langdon would come in and "cash out" with the bookkeeper. This involved checking to make sure that the money he received from the previous day matched his collection card, which he filled out. Every Wednesday the bookkeeper posted the invoices which were paid "on account" and the receipts to the accounts receivable. She then totaled Langdon's collections for the week to determine his commission.

After cashing out Langdon took the elevator up to the third floor, loaded it with merchandise, and then brought it down to the basement. There he loaded his truck with the inventory that he felt he needed for the day. Usually, he was just replacing products that he sold the day before.

Langdon then listed by group all of the items that he took from inventory and gave the list to Steve Goodman before he left. Since the items were grouped (e.g., six dozen Brach) and not itemized, actual inventory could not be tracked by this procedure. The purpose of the list was to make the salesman think that inventory controls did exist.

Langdon also listed on a Gunther invoice the products which he took from Gunther's inventory. Sunburst, for example, was considered part of Gunther's inventory, even though Quality Cookies also sold it. When the list became long, Steve paid Gunther for the products on the invoice.

As sales dropped over the years, Langdon began to take snack items from Gunther's inventory to sell. He did such a small volume with these items that it did not even seem worth the expense of keeping records. However, Ken Goodman felt that any extra sales could not hurt, so the practice continued.

After Langdon loaded his truck he drove to his first account. He had eight specific sales routes which he followed Monday through Thursday in a two-week cycle. A few accounts were visited each week. Fridays were used to visit accounts that he had missed during the week. Each route had from 6 to 15 accounts.

The method of selling was "off the truck." Most of the work that Langdon did was servicing as opposed to selling. He would normally go into an account, determine what cookie or candy items needed to be replaced, and replace them. The cashier or stockboy in the store would check to see that the merchandise Langdon brought in matched the invoice. Langdon then put the products on the shelves. If no products were needed, he would straighten up the section. He was then paid either in cash, by check, or on account. Often it was not even necessary to see the store manager.

Some customers decided what they wanted, and then Langdon might

try to talk the buyer into an extra case or two of cookies. Items such as nuts, caramel corn, and Sunburst required some selling, and since Langdon did not usually talk to the manager, very few of these products were sold.

FINANCIAL RESOURCES

The financial statements for the past four years of operations are shown in Exhibits 9 and 10. When Jerry began working at the end of April 1982, the financial statements for last quarter 1981 had not yet been finished. Jerry collected some of the information necessary to complete the income statement and found problems with the division's accounting system.

Gunther did not allocate any costs to the cookie division. Had such expenses as electricity, depreciation, supplies, office expenses, and payroll been allocated to Quality, the company would have been operating

---

EXHIBIT 9   GUNTHER CANDY COMPANY: QUALITY COOKIES DIVISION
Comparative statement of operations

| | December 1981 (9 months) | Year ended March 31, | | |
		1981	1980	1979
Sales	$74,969	$105,086	$109,741	$92,187
Less: Cost of goods sold	51,723	74,791	84,995	73,010
Gross profit	23,246	30,295	24,746	19,177
Expenses				
Payroll	7,380	10,871	10,887	8,367
Delivery	6,119	6,837	5,677	3,831
Insurance	1,870	2,719	1,674	1,501
Depreciation	1,336	2,457	1,558	1,301
Payroll taxes	1,536	1,023	853	804
Office	296	1,011	295	699
Travel	1,066	420	284	297
Audit	410	273	387	900
Total expenses	20,013	25,611	21,615	17,700
Net operating income	3,233	4,684	3,131	1,477
Franchise tax	323	472	320	250
Corporate tax	550	342	243	
	873	814	563	250
Net profit	$ 2,360	$ 3,870	$ 2,568	$ 1,227

EXHIBIT 10   GUNTHER CANDY COMPANY: QUALITY COOKIES DIVISION
Balance sheet
March 31, 1981

Assets

Cash		9,957
Accounts receivable		4,039
Inventory		10,260
Truck	10,069	
Less accumulated depreciation	(5,316)	4,753
Total assets		29,009

Liabilities and stockholder's equity

Accounts payable	5,430
Notes payable	6,727
Other current liabilities	1,284
Common stock	10,000
Retained earnings	5,568
Total liabilities and stockholder's equity	29,009

in the red for four years. After discussing this with Ken and Steve, Jerry decided to leave the accounting methods alone. It was felt that the paperwork involved was not worth the effort.

By the end of May Jerry had plotted the sales for the 1981 fiscal year (Exhibit 11). Before Jerry's arrival monthly sales figures had not been calculated. Monthly sales for 1981 were erratic, with very low sales for the two months preceding Christmas. Normally this was a large selling season for candy. Jerry asked Langdon for the cause of this problem and was told that he had no Christmas merchandise to sell. Ken later said that Langdon had been given free rein to take seasonal merchandise from Gunther's inventory and therefore that was not the problem.

One of the major expenses was gasoline. Langdon was not concerned with the expense and tended to drive the truck more than necessary to cover his routes. In addition, he drove the truck to and from home, which was about 20 miles from work. Jerry considered having Langdon leave the truck at the warehouse each night, but the neighborhood was not very safe and Langdon did not have a car in which to get to work. Jerry felt that there must be some incentive that could encourage Langdon to reduce the gas expense, but he did not know what it might be.

EXHIBIT 11   Quality Cookies' monthly sales for 1981

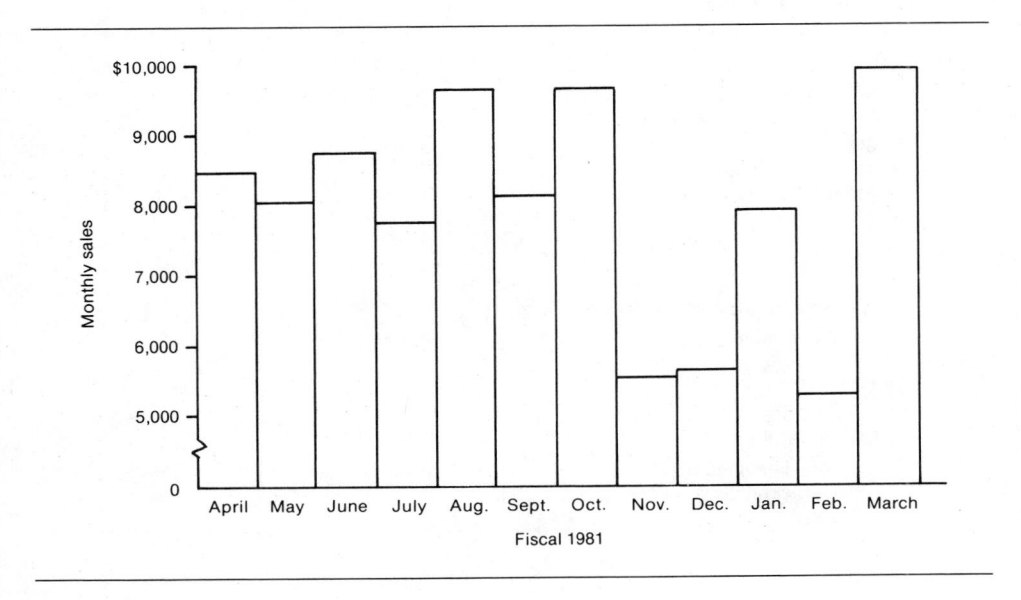

PURCHASING

Ken Goodman had been responsible for purchasing before Jerry Schwartz was hired. Because Ken did not devote much time to Quality Cookies, he did not check the inventory levels often enough, and consequently there were many out-of-stocks.

To compound the purchasing problem, sales were unpredictable. Cookie purchases were made approximately every four to six weeks. Langdon had a habit of only selling certain items. When the items were out of stock, he would start selling the other items. Therefore, if there were 20 cases of fudge cookies left in inventory when it was time to reorder, for example, the purchaser would assume that no more fudge cookies were needed at that time. However, if the company was out of stock on some items, Langdon would start to sell the fudge cookies. By the time the new cookie order arrived, the company would no longer have any of the fudge variety.

When Jerry started working, he found that very few records were kept. There were no price lists, customer lists, monthly sales figures, accounts receivable reports, product lists, credit terms, nor any business

plans. If the salesman had quit that day, the company would not know to whom its products were being sold or at what prices.

Jerry realized that he had to get the company to a profitable state by the end of summer. After that point he would have to figure a way to make the company grow. The manufacturer for Mama's cookies developed a 15 percent promotional campaign for Quality Cookies to use to gain new accounts (Exhibit 12). The manufacturer agreed to rebate half of the 15 percent upon proof of compliance.

Jerry questioned the worth of the promotional campaign since Quality Cookies was in too poor a position financially to cut its margins by an extra 7.5 percent. He also questioned whether this deal would be attractive enough to the chain accounts who were always asking for free setups (i.e., a free four-foot section of cookies).

Langdon was another problem which Jerry did not know how to resolve. The salesman was 60 years old and probably could not find another job at this age. Even if he were fired, it was questionable that Jerry could replace him at the same low salary.

Jerry also had to start ordering products for the Halloween season. He did not want to order a large amount because he did not want to get stuck with returns; if he ordered too little, however, his customers would get very annoyed.

Left with the problem of declining sales and an unorganized company, Jerry was not quite sure where to start. Yet he realized that something had to be done quickly.

EXHIBIT 12   Suggested promotional campaign for Mama's Cookies

---

SPECIAL INTRODUCTORY OFFER

Quality Cookies, Inc. agrees to rebate by one check at the end of a four-week period, the sum of 15 percent of net total per all invoices for all Mama's Cookies displayed on and off shelves.

Space allocation	Four-foot section (four or five shelves) minimum per all stores.
Delivery	Store door with servicing of shelves and displays (FREE).
Billing	1. Net—volume prices 2. Terms—1 percent 10 days, net 30 days.
Promotions	Minimum of one per month.

The above offer effective until further notice.

15% REBATE

QUESTIONS

1. What are the major problems and opportunities facing Jerry?
2. Is the situation favorable or unfavorable? Explain?
3. Develop a marketing plan for Quality. Consider pricing structure, credit terms, promotions, personal selling plans, service, depth of product line, and general method of operations in your analysis and recommendations.

GUNTHER CANDY COMPANY (C)*

Quality Cookie Division

Developing a product line strategy

By the end of August 1982, Jerry had reorganized the Quality Cookie Division. Sales were increasing, and the company was in the black. The problem of growth still existed, and Jerry was pondering what his next step should be to increase further Quality sales and profits. He had only seven months left to get the company firmly on the growth track.

It was at this point that Alan Toller, the sales rep from Mama's, informed Jerry that he could no longer supply Quality with the Mama's cookie line.

COMPANY CHANGES

During his four months with Quality, Jerry had instituted several major changes which he believed had been responsible for the improved performance of the company. These changes were as follows:

Pricing policies. Customary wholesale prices for Mama's cookies gave the retailers a gross margin of 24 to 26 percent. Jerry believed that

---

*Written by Jeffrey Nagel, under the supervision of Professor Martin R. Warshaw, Graduate School of Business Administration, The University of Michigan. All names and numerical data have been disguised.

price was an important part of the marketing strategy in selling products such as cookies, so he lowered his prices to dealers, enabling them to make a 27 percent margin across the board. This price was available to all customers.

Credit policies. Because the poor economic conditions had made the offering of credit a very risky undertaking, Jerry decided to extend credit only to large, financially strong customers. All other customers would have to pay cash on delivery. To gain retailer acceptance of this new policy, a 5 percent rebate was offered on all outstanding bills. The message was clear: pay cash and get lower prices.

Although some retailer resistance was felt by Quality, on the whole the policy was successful. Jay Lasky's two Convenient Food Mart Store accounts were lost, but Jerry believed that in the long run he would be better off without them.

Promotion policy. At the beginning of June, Jerry started using promotion sheets for the cookie line. These sheets had been used successfully by Gunther Candy Company for years. The sheets were placed in customer orders, and copies were put in the salesmen's selling books.

The promotion sheets had only a small positive effect on Quality's sales. Jerry analyzed the situation and saw that, inasmuch as orders were delivered to point of sale, there was very little to be gained by placing the sheet in the order. Second, Langdon, the salesman, rarely used his selling book. He kept the sheets folded up in his pocket. Jerry dropped the promotion sheets after three months and tried to get Langdon to inform his customers verbally of new items and new deals.

In addition to promotion sheets, Jerry instituted the policy of using PMs (promotional monies) to stimulate sales. He had noted that Gunther Candy had used PMs extensively and in one case had given its salesmen 50 cents per item sold.

Jerry sensed that if the "pull" approach to marketing cookies did not work, perhaps some "push" would be effective in gaining new accounts and additional shelf space in established accounts. Langdon was given a variety of PMs on a wide range of products. The PMs just did not work. Now Jerry had been disappointed by both "pull" and "push" efforts. Perhaps the PMs were too small to motivate Langdon, although they seemed to work with the Gunther sales force.

Personal selling. After two months Jerry decided to try some personal selling himself. He spent 80 percent of his time on the road trying to open new accounts. His selling point was the 15 percent promotion in which customers received a 15 percent rebate if they bought and displayed a specified amount of merchandise (see Case B). Jerry tried to use negative reinforcement on Langdon by shaving his commissions on accounts that Jerry opened from 10 to 7 percent. Although Jerry increased the number of customers by 20 percent, Langdon remained unimpressed and unmotivated.

Jerry concentrated his selling efforts on the Convenient Food Mart

chain because they had relatively large stores. All new accounts were sold COD. With the 15 percent promotion the new stores now had four-foot cookie sections with over 20 cookie varieties.

Chain buyer meetings.   In an attempt to gain entry to the major grocery and drug store chains in the market area, Jerry made appointments to see the various cookie buyers. He attempted to sell these people the 2/$1.00 line of Mama's cookies as an in—out promotion. This was a way of allowing the chains to test the rate of sales in the stores without putting the goods in the warehouses. Jerry's attempts were not too successful. First, it took time to develop rapport with the buyers before they would try the line. Second, 2/$1.00 cookies did not do well as in—out items as there was little opportunity for consumers to engage in comparison shopping. Last, cookie sales were down, in general, in most supermarket and drug stores.

Jerry was successful in convincing the Stop N' Shop chain to take on five items in the 2/$1.00 line on a trial basis. Jerry personally delivered the cookies to four stores. When he checked the stores one month later, hardly any cookies had moved off the shelves.

Stop N' Shop had over 100 stores in the area, and, if the cookies had moved, it would have meant a lot of business. Jerry racked his brain trying to find a way to get the product to move.

Salesman retraining.   Jerry decided that Langdon had to be replaced. He interviewed 12 persons but could find no suitable replacement. The people were capable, but because of low sales the commissions generated were insufficient to meet their salary needs.

Jerry believed that his only alternative was to retrain Langdon and to build up the sales volume to a level which would support a first-class salesperson. Each morning Jerry spent a half hour trying to train Langdon. These sessions lasted for four weeks. In the first of these sessions, Langdon was educated about the product line. The major selling points and techniques were described to him, and he was required to memorize them. After going over the attributes of the products, Jerry explained some objections that retailers might raise and how to respond to them. Finally, Langdon practiced his sales pitch with Jerry, who critiqued it.

To get Langdon enthused about selling, Jerry gave him new selling and order books. In an attempt to boost sales, Jerry gave Langdon large incentive bonuses. For every new account that Langdon opened he would receive a 20 percent commission on his first sale. On any account, present or new, in which he sold the Brach line he would receive a 25 percent commission on his first sale. These bonuses were effective for the month of August only.

The results of these efforts were minimal. Sales did increase during the month of August (see Exhibit 1) but mostly because of Jerry's personal selling efforts. Langdon's sales increased but not dramatically. He opened a few new accounts but with very small initial sales. This situation benefited the firm in that new accounts were opened without costing

EXHIBIT 1   Quality Cookies' monthly sales

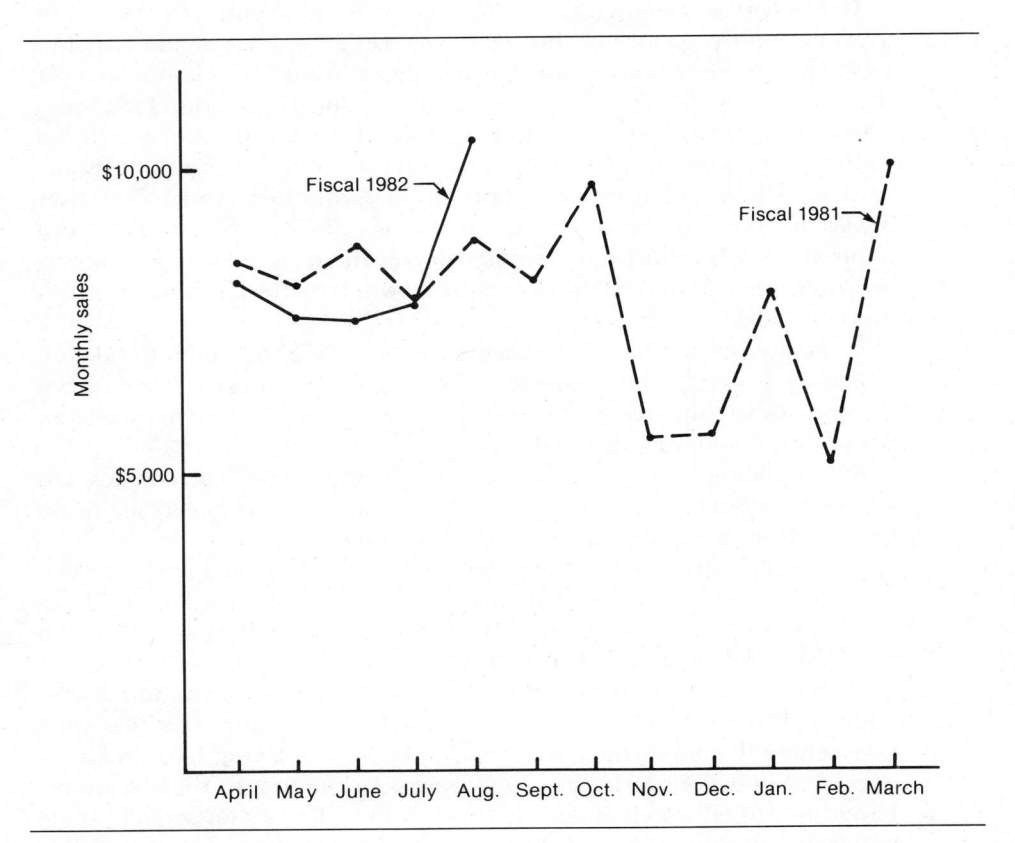

a great deal in bonuses. The effort showed, however, that Langdon could not be motivated by even large amounts of money.

Jerry felt that he personally could increase sales by opening new accounts, but that was not his job. Even after the accounts were opened, it was doubtful that Langdon would do anything to expand them. Sales had to be increased before the company could afford to hire a new salesman, but to increase sales a new salesman was needed. Jerry considered this to be a major stumbling block to growth.

PRODUCT LINE PROBLEMS

In the beginning of September, Jerry received word from Alan Toller, Mama's sales representative, that Quality would no longer be able to carry Mama's line. Jerry was very upset and went to see Alan at Mama's

regional sales office in Buffalo, New York, to question the decision. After considerable discussion and argumentation, Alan agreed to supply Quality with Mama's cookies only if the company would not compete with M&R Distributors.

This solution did not satisfy Jerry since it limited the company's growth potential. Alan then recommended that Quality sell Mama's Salerno line of cookies to new accounts. This would enable Quality to sell the M&R's accounts. Alan advised Jerry to combine Mama's 2/$1.00 line with the Salerno line.

The Salerno line was a better-quality and higher-priced line than Mama's. Because of the higher price, the manufacturer was able to promote the product more; however, no advertising was used.

Jerry saw two problems with switching to the Salerno line. First, one major selling point of Mama's was that it was a full line which included the 2/$1.00 cookies that people could trade up to larger sizes. Customers would now have to trade up to a different brand.

Second, the price of Salerno was 5 percent higher to the wholesaler and 10 cents to 30 cents higher at retail. The Mama's line had not been selling well, and Jerry questioned whether the new line would sell. If a customer wanted a low-priced cookie, he would buy a private label brand. If he wanted quality, he would only buy a nationally advertised brand such as Nabisco. Salerno seemed to fall between the two.

PRODUCT LINE ALTERNATIVES

Jerry considered the problem of choosing a new cookie line and came up with a number of alternatives:

First, Quality Cookies could stay with the Mama's line. This would not allow the company any substantial growth. On the other hand, the company had finally obtained good placement of its products in the stores, and Jerry questioned whether it was worth trying to switch retailers to a new brand.

Second, the company could take the Salerno line with the Mama's 2/$1.00 line, as Alan Toller had suggested. Jerry felt that he could not take the full line of Mama's since it would require double inventory and could cause stock-outs on the truck. Moreover, the price of the new product line would require a small investment on the part of the owners and would hurt the company's cash flow.

Third, the company could take the Salerno line and find a lower-priced 2/$1.00 line. Since over 50 percent of Quality's cookies sales were 2/$1.00 cookies, the company could make more money by selling a product with a higher margin. Jerry did not think that retailers or consumers would care about the brand switch in 2/$1.00 cookies. The major problem with this was that it would be difficult for Quality to meet the 800-case minimum shipment from Mama's.

Fourth, the company could take on a totally new line of cookies. This sounded like the best option, but after a month of searching for a full-line cookie, Jerry came up empty-handed.

Fifth, the company could take on a full line of soft cookies. There were a number of different lines available to him, but Jerry was not sure that the company could handle that type of cookie. Soft cookies have a very short shelf life and require a great deal of service. Also, the market for soft cookies is not as great as that for hard cookies.

Sixth, the company could take on a novelty type of cookie. When Jerry was in California on vacation, he had seen a box of chocolate chip cookies called People-Bones that looked just like a box of dog biscuits. He felt that this was a great item that would sell in college book stores and department stores. Jerry contacted the manufacturer and found out that it was willing to take on Quality Cookies as a distributor in New York State. The product would retail for $5.00 and cost Quality $2.75 per box FOB Los Angeles with a 5 percent freight alowance. The minimum order quantity was one case (36 boxes @ $99).

The price of the product seemed a little high, and Jerry wondered whether Quality's distribution operation was geared for selling the product. Yet, it seemed like a great item.

Although Jerry's major problem was to increase the company's growth, he first needed to have a product to sell that would achieve that growth. He analyzed the six alternatives and various combinations of them and felt that there must be some other alternatives that he had not considered. With only seven months left, Jerry had to decide what mix of products would help the company achieve its growth objectives.

QUESTIONS

1. Critically appraise the changes made by Jerry in the operation of Quality Cookies.

2. What kind of marketing strategy would you recommend to Quality in order to sell more products? (Do not restrict your ideas to the cookie line.)

3. Which product line alternative should Jerry choose? Explain. Has he overlooked any other alternatives?

4. Who should serve the Stop N' Shop stores and how? How should the 2/$1.00 items be promoted here?

5. What can be done about the Langdon situation?

6. Evaluate Jerry's new pricing policy.

THE MICHIGAN LEAGUE*

Developing a promotional strategy

Pat Lawson has been manager of the Michigan League for six years. She is in charge of the operation and maintenance of the League building. She acts as purchasing agent and is in charge of the accounting and financial management of the League's activities. As business manager, Pat Lawson is responsible to a Board of Governors and to the vice president for finance. She is expected to report regularly to both.

Recently the staff has noticed a continuing decrease in the number of customers in the cafeteria and coffee shop. However, at the same time the other League functions (conferences, banquets, special events) are operating near capacity. Pat is interested in finding the underlying causes of the decrease in the customer count. She would like to develop courses of action to reverse this trend.

BACKGROUND

The Michigan League is one of three University Activity Centers. The other two centers are the North Campus Commons and the Michigan

---

*Written by Leo Burnett Fellow Maureen Fanshawe under the direction of Professor Martin R. Warshaw, Graduate School of Business Administration, The University of Michigan. Names and numerical data may be disguised.

Union. The Michigan League was built in 1929 with funds raised by University of Michigan women. At the time of the League's construction, women were not permitted to use the Michigan Union. In response to the women's need, the University alumnae built the Michigan League "for the purpose of promoting the social and recreational welfare of the women students in the university." Through the years the emphasis has shifted, and presently for both men and women the primary student building (receiving the major university funding) is the Michigan Union. Currently the Michigan League serves not only the campus community but also the general public.

The League is centrally located one block from the main street of the campus area. It is situated on a highly trafficked street and is very visible. A large sign near the sidewalk advertises the cafeteria and other services. In addition to the cafeteria and coffee shop, the League building has a gift shop, study rooms, conference rooms, a ballroom, several large banquet rooms, student organization offices, and, on the fourth floor, hotel service consisting of 21 rooms. Over the past four years there has been a significant increase in the use of the building by students for study and meeting space.

CAFETERIA

The cafeteria is open Monday–Saturday, 11:30 A.M.–1:15 P.M. and 5:00 P.M.–7:15 P.M. Dinner is served on Sunday from 11:30 A.M. to 2:15 P.M. A full menu is provided for both lunch and dinner. Meal prices range from approximately $3.00 for lunch to $4.25 for dinner. The cafeteria does not serve alcohol. The League has a limited conference liquor license for scheduled events. A daily special is offered in addition to the other items. The luncheon and dinner entrees are on a three-week cycle and offer a different variety daily. Although there is no table service, the cafeteria maintains a full staff. The cafeteria has a pleasant atmosphere and emphasis is placed on cleanliness.

NATURE OF THE MARKET

The Michigan League is available to the general public as well as the campus community. Throughout the school year the cafeteria serves approximately 388 lunches and 350 dinners daily. The coffee shop serves 800–1,200 people daily. During the summer months the daily totals are considerably lower. Peak seasons are directly associated with the academic year. From May through August there is a steady decline in business (Exhibit 1 and Exhibit 1a). Special functions scheduled at the League are also affected by the "seasonality" factor. During the months of May–August the League facilities for weddings operate at capacity.

EXHIBIT 1

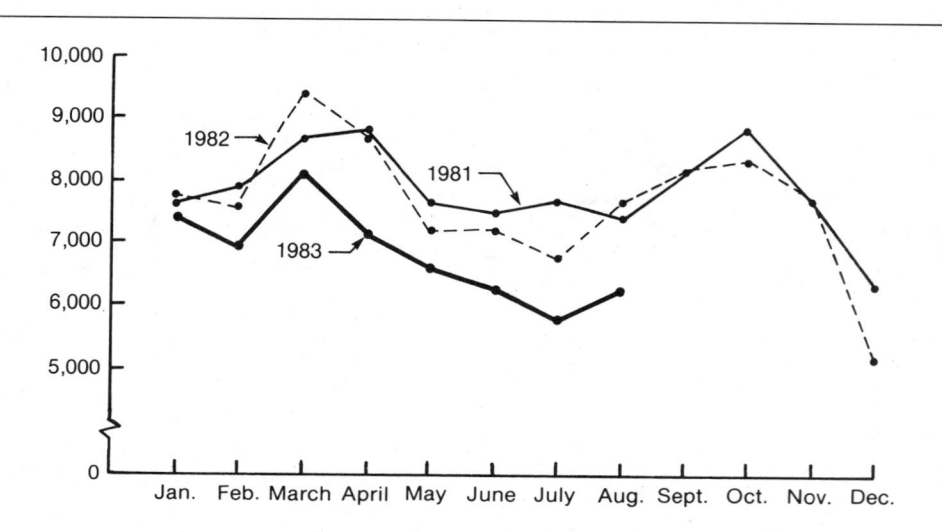

	Customer count: Lunch		
	1981	1982	1983
January	7,641	7,648	7,487
February	7,883	7,586	6,989
March	8,725	9,403	8,067
April	8,816	8,780	7,125
May	7,675	7,267	6,610
June	7,440	7,221	6,290
July	7,659	6,795	5,722
August	7,435	7,724	6,236
September	8,144	8,049	*
October	8,900	8,418	*
November	7,667	7,682	*
December	6,422	5,227	*

*Customer count not yet taken for September–December 1983.

Hill Auditorium and Powers Center are university cultural performance centers, each within one block of the League. Plays, concerts, and
ballet are frequently run. On performance nights the League adjusts its
regular schedule and menu. There is an increase in the cafeteria customer count on these evenings. This increase is not as high as Pat believes it could be. She has attributed this fact to the large number of area

EXHIBIT 1a

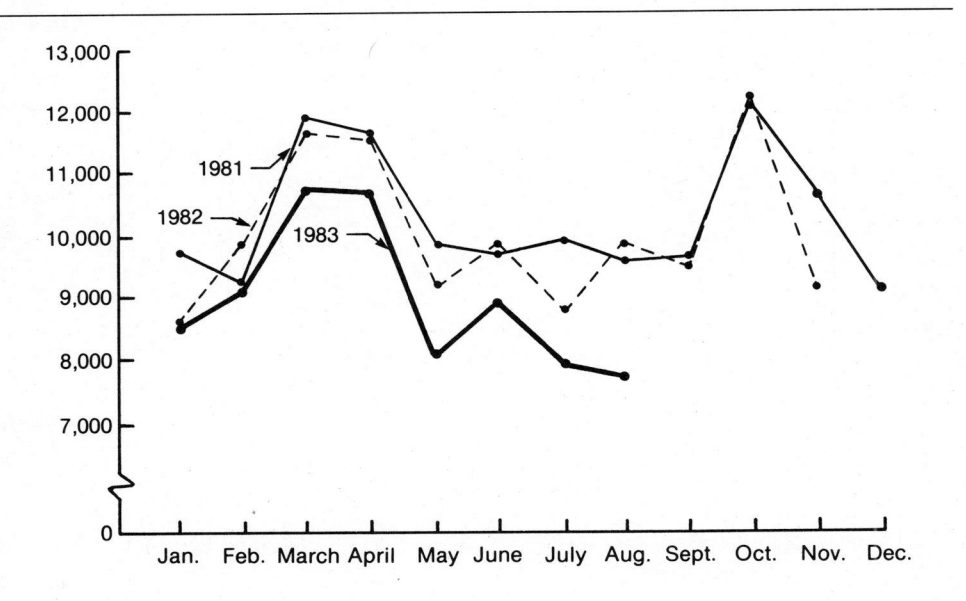

	Customer count: Dinner		
	1981	**1982**	**1983**
January	9,757	8,666	8,635
February	9,265	9,849	9,074
March	11,946	11,636	10,779
April	11,664	11,552	10,718
May	9,894	9,170	8,098
June	9,688	9,838	8,941
July	9,943	8,766	7,925
August	9,628	9,844	7,812
September	9,673	9,572	*
October	12,152	12,164	*
November	10,778	9,168	*
December	9,253	7,555	*

*Customer count not yet taken for September–December 1983.

restaurants serving alcohol which are available to the Hill Auditorium and Powers Center patrons.

The results of a 1978 survey performed by the League Cafeteria revealed that present customers use the cafeteria on a regular basis and for the following reasons: they enjoy the food, location, no tipping feature, cafeteria-style service, and atmosphere. Also provided by this survey were positive and negative comments about the cafeteria (Exhibits 2 and 2a).

A third and final part of the survey requested customer suggestions. Many of the suggestions were for bigger salads, a salad bar, to expand the variety of vegetarian dishes and specials, and to include a vegetable or salad with the student special. Presently the League has comment and

---

EXHIBIT 2   Survey results for Michigan League (1978)

	Tuesday noon (170 surveys)	Tuesday night (128)	Thursday night (130)	Sunday (140)
How Often				
First time	2	2	2	4
Infrequent	40	19	25	33
Often	125	107	88	102
Enjoy				
Food	128	117	101	132
Location	154	105	85	98
Cafeteria	126	98	86	122
No tipping	117	100	87	116
Atmosphere	91	91	88	117
Music				
Prefer music	41	54	43	37
Prefer no music	41	27	5	46

Cumulative results (568 surveys)

How Often	
First time	10
Infrequent	117
Often	422
Enjoy	
Food	478
Location	432
No tipping	426
Cafeteria	432
Atmosphere	387
Music	
Prefer music	175
Prefer no music	119

EXHIBIT 2a

Frequent comments: Positive
Enjoy the food   74
Variety   25
Reasonable price   32
International night   17
Service   51
Atmosphere   18

Frequent comments: Negative
Dull variety   23
Too much gravy   13
Student special   19
Prices too high   28
Cold food   25
Service
   Long, slow lines   38
   Discourteous staff   21
   Small portions   38
Parking   20

suggestion cards available in the cafeteria, coffee shop, and hotel rooms. After each special function, a short rating and suggestion card is sent to the person who made the arrangements.

SPECIAL FEATURES AT THE CAFETERIA

The League cafeteria offers daily specials. These specials are available to the students at a reduced price. A luncheon special costs $2.50, and a dinner student special costs $2.75. The cafeteria sells approximately 125 luncheon and 60 dinner specials daily. The student specials are less than the cost of dormitory dinners. Students find it the "best food for the price in town." Over the years, the board has felt "that providing good food to students at the lowest possible cost in an attractive university setting was an important responsibility of the League." The League has a student tax discount but does not have senior citizen discounts.

From October through July, every Thursday evening at the cafeteria is "International and American Heritage Night." Each Thursday night the menu consists of foods from the featured country or state. International night has been successful. On this night the cafeteria serves an average of 475 customers.

The Michigan League cafeteria "Command Performance dinner" of-

fered the customer a unique dining experience. The customers are encouraged through advertisements to make requests for their favorite foods, to be served at the Command Performance dinner. From these nominations the most requested items are selected to make up the menu for the evening. This special feature has been offered twice and was successful.

Sunday dinner at the cafeteria is served from 11:30 A.M. to 2:15 P.M. White linen cloths and fresh flowers are placed on the tables. The Sunday customer profile at the cafeteria is primarily senior citizens.

COMPETITION

The Michigan League is centrally located on the Michigan campus one block from the campus shopping street and three blocks from downtown Ann Arbor. There are approximately 143 restaurants in the downtown area. Eighty of these restaurants provide full service. The League cafeteria's 1982 share of the Ann Arbor restaurant market was 1.9 percent. In a recent report the Board of Governors recommended that, "The university administration officially recommend that all university departments use the university centers (League, Union, and North Campus Commons) food services, both within these buildings and for catering wherever needed on the university campus."

In direct competition with the League cafeteria is the Michigan Union. The recent revitalization of the union is expected to impact the League. Food revenue may decline as union revenue increases. The Union University Club offers a menu similar to the League's, with prices approximately one dollar higher per meal at lunch and two dollars higher at dinner. The union has table service and serves alcohol. Every Sunday night at the union from 5:30 P.M.–8:00 P.M. is an "all-you-can-eat" Italian Festival for $3.99. The Italian Festival night is successful. A recent addition to the union's lower level, the Michigan Union Grill (MUG), has a variety of food counters and primarily caters to student clientele. The prices are relatively low, to meet the students' budgets, and a student tax discount is offered. Dormitory food service does not operate on Sundays. The other area restaurants have a wide variety of menus but are priced slightly higher than the League. The recent restructuring of dorm food service to include breakfast and flexible hours affected the League's student count adversely.

The recent construction of the Ingalls Street pedestrian mall has drastically decreased parking availability for League patrons. Ingalls Street (which runs adjacent to the League), previously had 45 open-meter parking spaces. More than half of the spaces were destroyed. This loss of parking has been a problem for League patrons. There are two public parking structures, each within one block of the League. It costs two

dollars to park in the garage. Across the street from the League is a staff parking lot. Parking is permitted in this lot only after 5:00 P.M. Street parking on North University after 5:00 P.M. has recently been permitted, adding about 12 spaces.

PROMOTION

The League's 1982 advertising budget was $5,500. Of this budget, 91 percent was allocated to the cafeteria. The objective of the cafeteria advertising is to increase awareness in the community. The emphasis of weekly advertisements is usually placed on special-feature nights at the cafeteria. The Command Performance dinner was advertised twice in the *Ann Arbor News* (Exhibit 3). The League purchased a 2″ × 5″ ad (space is sold by column inch, $7.50 per inch) and ran the ad the week preceding the event. When the League is not advertising for a feature night, a 1½″ × 2″ ad is purchased for $22.50 and run once a week (Exhibit 4).

For several years the League ran a weekly advertisement for the cafeteria using a limerick theme. Readers would compose an advertising limerick for the cafeteria and mail their suggestions to Julie, Pat Lawson's administrative assistant. She would then select the best limerick entry weekly, to be used in the advertisement. The winning entry received two free dinners at the cafeteria. The League employed this promotional strategy for five years prior to its discontinuance in July 1983. The League staff felt that although they had received a tremendous response, the theme had become overused and repetitive and, as a result, had lost effectiveness.

Presently the League has no measurement of ad effectiveness. In addition, their promotional strategy uses a mass appeal, with minimal attention given to individual market segments. The staff wonders whether the advertising dollars could be more effectively spent by placing emphasis on slow nights rather than on already successful feature nights. To increase the customer count on slow nights, Pat is considering the extension of the feature-night concept to these nights. She also senses a need for an advertising strategy to define her key potential customers and then to target the advertising efforts to this market.

The League also advertises in the *Observer,* a monthly newspaper publication. The cafeteria is listed in the Restaurant Guide section. The price is $25.00/6 months for a four-line listing. The ad is clearly visible but is listed with many other Ann Arbor restaurants. A one-fourth page display advertisement in the *Observer* costs $246.00 (for a one-month edition). However, the *Observer* offers a frequency rate discount. The League has never purchased display ad space in the *Observer.* Presently they purchase only the service ad in the restaurant guide. (See Exhibit 4 for *Observer* advertising rates.)

EXHIBIT 3

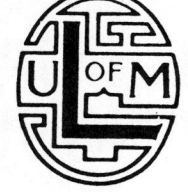 # COMMAND PERFORMANCE

The Michigan League invites your help in presenting two very special dinners in our cafeteria.

Thursday, September 22 and Thursday, September 29 will be Command Performance Nights. You can help us create the menus by filling out the form below suggesting your favorite Michigan League specialites.

When you turn in your suggestion card you will receive a special invitation.

See you at the League, 911 N. University, 764-0446

My League favorites are (you may list as many as you wish):

Salads _____

Breads _____

Entrees _____

Vegetables _____

Desserts _____

Be as specific as you can. If you aren't sure of the name describe the item and/or list as many of the ingredients as possible.

Name: _____ Phone: _____

Address: _____

The *Michigan Daily* is a student-run newspaper on the Ann Arbor campus of The University of Michigan. The *Daily* has approximately 5,000 subscribers. Advertising space costs $4.75/inch. Presently the League does not advertise in the *Michigan Daily.*

The remaining balance of the advertising budget is used to purchase flyers for the League cafeteria and coffee shop. These flyers are distributed to all new students and staff. Included on this flyer is a coupon for

EXHIBIT 4

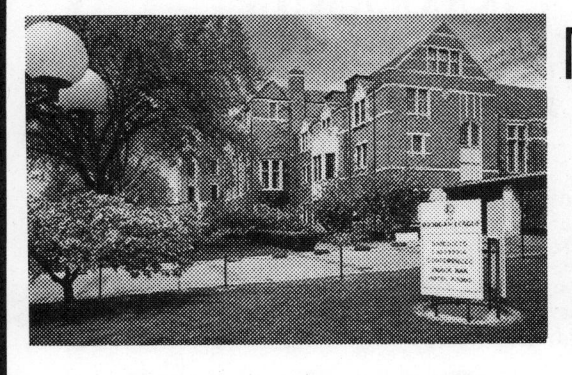

WELCOME TO THE

MICHIGAN LEAGUE

In the Heart of Campus

Serving fine food in a gracious atmosphere to alumni, staff, students and the public.

CAFETERIA • COFFEE SHOP
BANQUET & PARTY SERVICES

Michigan League
"A Tradition Since 1929"

911 N. University
764-0446

Observer Advertising Rates*

Observer Display Ads						Service Ads		
	Open	*3x*	*6x*	*9x*	*12x*		*1x*	*6x*
Full page	$700	$676	$641	$606	$571	1" by 2 5/16"	$34	$24
3/4 page	658	608	577	546	514	1 1/2" by 2 5/16"	50	35
1/2 page	464	422	400	378	347	2" by 2 5/16"	70	47
1/4 page	246	224	217	202	185			
1/8 page	139	125	119	112	102	*Display and Service Ad rates do not include production services.*		
1/16 page	86	78	74	69	57			

Premium Placement and Color Charges

A fixed rate* will be charged for the following guaranteed-placement ads:
Inside front page: $750 (Includes production & color)   **Table of contents:** $86 (Limited to 1/16 page ads)
Page three: $725   **Inside back page:** $700   **Black and one color per page:** $75
Back page: $775 (Includes production & color)   *10% discount for camera-ready ads.

Production Charges

The Ann Arbor Observer provides professional design and production services. The rates are as follows:
Design and production fee: $20 minimum   **Camera-ready modification fee:** $5 minimum
Copy change fee: $5 minimum   **Camera work:** halftones and reversals $6.50
Service ad design and production fee: $10   PMT/photostats $5

a free beverage, which is heavily used by students. The International and American Heritage Nights schedule is printed on a 2″ × 3″ card and is available throughout the university (Exhibit 5).

FINANCIAL RESOURCES

The University Activities Centers—North Campus Commons, Michigan Union, and the Michigan League—are owned by the university. The League uses earned revenue to meet its operating expenses. Financial support from the university is made available through allocations. All improvements have been financed from reserves and university loans. Loans are repaid on schedule, and there is only a small balance outstand-

---

EXHIBIT 5

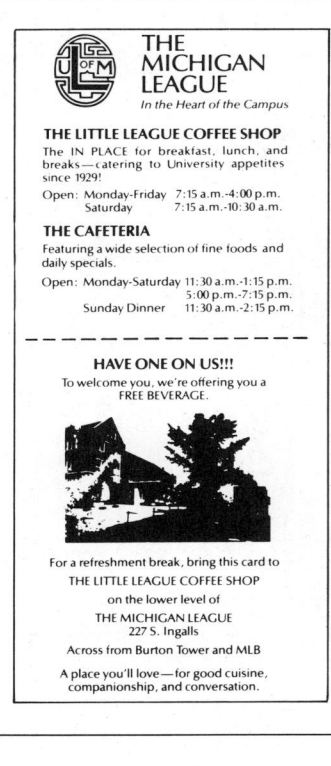

THE MICHIGAN LEAGUE
In the Heart of the Campus

THE LITTLE LEAGUE COFFEE SHOP
The IN PLACE for breakfast, lunch, and breaks—catering to University appetites since 1929!
Open: Monday-Friday   7:15 a.m.-4:00 p.m.
         Saturday   7:15 a.m.-10:30 a.m.

THE CAFETERIA
Featuring a wide selection of fine foods and daily specials.
Open: Monday-Saturday 11:30 a.m.-1:15 p.m.
                              5:00 p.m.-7:15 p.m.
         Sunday Dinner   11:30 a.m.-2:15 p.m.

- - - - - - - - - - - - - - - -

HAVE ONE ON US!!!
To welcome you, we're offering you a
FREE BEVERAGE.

For a refreshment break, bring this card to
THE LITTLE LEAGUE COFFEE SHOP
on the lower level of
THE MICHIGAN LEAGUE
227 S. Ingalls
Across from Burton Tower and MLB

A place you'll love—for good cuisine, companionship, and conversation.

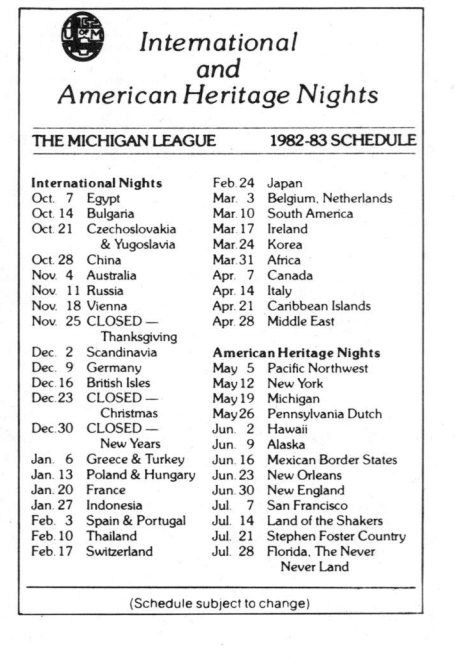

International and American Heritage Nights

THE MICHIGAN LEAGUE	1982-83 SCHEDULE

International Nights

Oct. 7	Egypt	Feb. 24	Japan
Oct. 14	Bulgaria	Mar. 3	Belgium, Netherlands
Oct. 21	Czechoslovakia & Yugoslavia	Mar. 10	South America
		Mar. 17	Ireland
Oct. 28	China	Mar. 24	Korea
Nov. 4	Australia	Mar. 31	Africa
Nov. 11	Russia	Apr. 7	Canada
Nov. 18	Vienna	Apr. 14	Italy
Nov. 25	CLOSED — Thanksgiving	Apr. 21	Caribbean Islands
		Apr. 28	Middle East
Dec. 2	Scandinavia		
Dec. 9	Germany	**American Heritage Nights**	
Dec. 16	British Isles	May 5	Pacific Northwest
Dec. 23	CLOSED — Christmas	May 12	New York
		May 19	Michigan
Dec. 30	CLOSED — New Years	May 26	Pennsylvania Dutch
		Jun. 2	Hawaii
Jan. 6	Greece & Turkey	Jun. 9	Alaska
Jan. 13	Poland & Hungary	Jun. 16	Mexican Border States
Jan. 20	France	Jun. 23	New Orleans
Jan. 27	Indonesia	Jun. 30	New England
Feb. 3	Spain & Portugal	Jul. 7	San Francisco
Feb. 10	Thailand	Jul. 14	Land of the Shakers
Feb. 17	Switzerland	Jul. 21	Stephen Foster Country
		Jul. 28	Florida, The Never Never Land

(Schedule subject to change)

ing. Presently the student fee allocation to the League is $3.50 per student.

The number of customers served at the cafeteria and coffee shop is declining. A statement of the League's revenues and expenses for the year 1982–83 is shown in Exhibit 6. Revenue for the Michigan League for fiscal year 1982–83 was 6 percent greater than for fiscal year 1981–82. This includes: guest room rentals (up 2 percent), meeting room rentals (up 25 percent), banquets and parties (up 16 percent), catering (up 79 percent), and beverages (up 12 percent). However, despite these growth areas cafeteria revenue is down $25,437 (3 percent) and coffee shop revenue is down $6,145 (2 percent). Food costs are in line, but labor costs are 50 percent of total earned income. In a report to the Board of Governors, Pat Lawson states, "A major staff training program is currently underway to increase productivity, but with an already lean, hard-working staff, it is unrealistic to expect much of a reduction in labor costs because of the AFSCME (union) wage rates."

EXHIBIT 6

MICHIGAN LEAGUE

Statement of Revenue and Expense
June 1983 and Fiscal 1982–83

	June 1983	June 1982	7/1/82– 6/30/83	7/1/81– 6/30/82
Revenue				
House				
Guest room rentals	$ 14,368	$ 14,335	$ 194,569	$ 189,848
Meeting room rentals	8,273	9,809	120,757	96,540
Front desk merchandise	7,976	8,877	113,718	113,372
Sundry	193	2,920	7,316	10,707
Food				
Cafeteria	59,191	67,692	725,102	750,539
Coffee shop	18,355	22,178	272,373	278,518
Banquets and parties	38,867	47,081	414,803	357,603
Catering	23,315	4,897	105,701	59,095
Beverage	6,401	15,487	83,757	74,582
NCC administrative services	450	450	5,400	5,400
Total operating revenue	$177,389	$193,726	$2,043,496	$1,936,204
Expense				
House				
Salaries and wages	$ 22,004	$ 21,360	$ 184,593	$ 174,272
Front desk merchandise	9,435	6,272	85,585	79,147
Supplies and general	991	1,214	9,893	10,300
Equipment repairs	1,306	92	4,010	4,327
Laundry	602	634	11,476	10,268

EXHIBIT 6 (*concluded*)

	June 1983	June 1982	7/1/82– 6/30/83	7/1/81– 6/30/82
Food				
Coffee shop salaries and wages	11,194	11,438	116,170	100,338
Food, salaries and wages	70,128	68,385	652,021	617,413
Food cost	37,276	41,201	533,873	540,594
Transportation	-0-	-0-	2,531	2,452
Supplies and general	4,260	2,187	37,275	35,429
Equipment repairs	383	704	9,940	9,353
Laundry	2,182	2,644	35,476	29,638
Beverage	(293)	5,163	25,692	27,192
General				
Administrative salaries	11,781	18,599	137,432	131,137
Maintenance wages	2,198	2,182	20,587	23,316
Office	930	613	7,936	6,002
Telephone	(82)	(150)	7,722	8,386
Building maintenance	4,475	4,877	37,901	41,978
Board of Governors	56	415	712	1,443
Publicity	419	281	4,245	5,970
Sales tax	3,485	4,270	51,312	45,618
Insurance	74	148	9,094	10,626
Unemployment insurance	-0-	-0-	2,107	503
Bad debts	-0-	-0-	17	60
Miscellaneous	2,408	850	17,479	15,243
Total operaing expense	185,842	193,379	2,005,079	1,931,005
Net operating income (loss)	$ (8,453)	$ 347	$ 38,417	$ 5,199
Other income and expense				
U-M allocation	$ 17,781	$ 48,877	$ 319,761	$ 295,919
Interest on investments	33,898	26,430	33,898	26,430
Development fund	6,376	100	62,707	200
Utilities	(12,486)	(15,255)	(214,863)	(204,080)
Student awards	(629)	-0-	(629)	(549)
Debt retirement	-0-	(4,837)	(58,272)	(58,040)
Equipment reserves	(950)	(397)	(11,393)	(4,761)
Building reserves	(1,570)	(466)	(18,854)	(5,589)
Total other income and expense	42,420	54,452	112,355	49,530
Net income (loss)	$ 33,967	$ 54,799	$ 150,772	$ 54,729
Total salaries and wages	$117,305	$121,964	$1,110,803	$1,046,476

The staff is presently considering several cafeteria improvement projects. The League is unwilling to borrow additional funds until the current loan is repaid. Alternative sources considered are: "A search for major donors (fund-raising committee and fund drive)" and additional financial assistance from the university. The League's fund raising for 1982 collected $69,000. The League is developing a cookbook for sale. The book will be ready for sale in June 1984 and is expected to earn

$50,000–$100,000. Pat Lawson believes that although revenue generated by the cafeteria is the most important source of operating funds, it is not a source of funds for projects that might be undertaken in the future.

FURTHER CONSIDERATIONS

In her report to the Board of Governors, Pat Lawson stated a need for financial assistance to meet necessary kitchen modernization costs (new appliances). The projected need totals $500,000. However, Pat is considering a complete remodeling of the cafeteria within the next three years. Total costs for complete remodeling are approximately $750,000. The project would include the necessary kitchen equipment, line restructuring, and a complete redecoration of the cafeteria. The plans for the cafeteria line restructuring are to change it from a straight line to an "open"-style square line (scramble system). This would improve efficiency and provide additional customer convenience by eliminating unnecessary waiting. Customers would be able to proceed directly to the section of items they desired. The development of an "open" line would decrease seating capacity. The cafeteria presently seats 250 persons.

As Pat considers the remodeling plans, she is also hoping to include plans to build a small extension to the cafeteria, which would help to recover the seating lost to the line restructuring. The extension as a "greenhouse"-style design is being considered. She believes that the extension should be built at the same time as the other remodeling is undertaken so that shutdown time is minimized. The greenhouse room is to extend from the front of the League building, which faces the main street.

Pat believes that the new room would provide several benefits: (1) make the League cafeteria more visible, (2) provide a direct entrance from the street to the cafeteria, (3) increase seating, and (4) improve cafeteria attractiveness. If remodeling plans include construction of the greenhouse room, estimated total costs could be approximately $1 million. Pat is interested in determining the feasibility of the League financing the remodeling project. She believes that the League's opportunities are limited to income provided by loans, fund raising, cookbook sales, and increased business at the cafeteria.

QUESTIONS

1. What are the problems and opportunities faced by Pat Lawson as the customer count continues to decrease?

2. What are your recommendations or alternative courses of action to improve the situation?

THE BATTLE OF THE BURGERS*

Developing a promotional strategy

A BBA student from The University of Michigan was hired in May as a summer intern in the National Sales Promotion Department of McDonald's Corporation, located in Oakbrook, Illinois. The intern was assigned to the director of the department to act as an assistant and also to undertake the management of independent promotional projects. That summer McDonald's was in the midst of what has become known as the "Battle of the Burgers." This battle was instigated by Burger King, the Number 2 fast-service restaurant chain in the industry. As seen in Exhibit 1, their extremely successful comparative advertising campaign closed the gap considerably between their Number 2 position and McDonald's Number 1 position. Thus, the marketing team at McDonald's could no longer feel as secure in their leadership position. This was a battle, and McDonald's needed a strategy to counter the aggressive moves of their competitors—especially those of Burger King. But, in order for the optimal strategy to be developed by the company executives, a thorough knowledge of the situation at hand and the events leading up to it was needed.

---

*Written by Kris Ralston, BBA student, under the supervision of Professor Martin R. Warshaw, Graduate School of Business Administration, The University of Michigan.

EXHIBIT 1   Burger franchise sales (in $000 per U.S. unit for fiscal year)

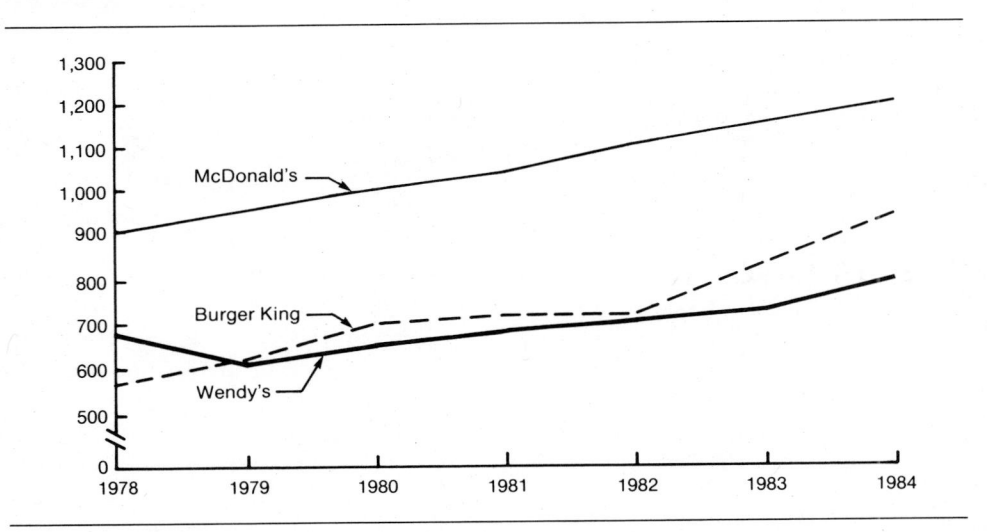

Source: *Chicago Tribune.*

BURGER KING STRATEGY

Prior to 1982, when Burger King set out to beat McDonald's at its own game of selling hamburgers, the restaurant chain had been plagued with problems which included a lack of clearly defined position in the market, a less concentrated menu selection due to the introduction and withdrawal of products, over-expansion of the physical plant, and inconsistency in the quality of store operations.

The fast-service restaurant industry is based on simplicity. Burger King's wide-ranging diversification produced confusion in the consumer's mind. And its marketing efforts at that time seemed to do little to position Burger King against its two major competitors, Wendy's and McDonald's.

When Burger King's performance sagged to marginal levels in 1981, the executives of the Pillsbury Company, which bought the chain in 1967 and received 25 percent of its earnings from this subsidiary, were alarmed. After its acquisition, Burger King turned in a string of double-digit profit increases. In 1981, by contrast, pre-tax earnings were up only 8 percent.

Burger King's reformulated strategy called for "getting back to basics"—namely, refocusing attention on its best-known product, the

"Whopper," and making it the symbol of the chain's high standards of quality and value.

With 3,500 stores systemwide and annual sales in the neighborhood of $2.5 billion, Burger King is second only to McDonald's—which has more than 7,000 units that, collectively, account for $7 billion in sales. Domestic Burger King stores average more than $750,000 per year in annual sales, and there are more than 300 units in the system that gross annually over $1 million apiece. (By comparison, more than half of all McDonald's stores exceed the $1 million mark.)

In 1979 Burger King made its first major move into menu expansion by introducing a line of nonbeef specialty sandwiches. At the same time, the firm's advertising strategy went into soft focus to provide a marketing umbrella for what had become a diverse product mix. With "Make It Special, Make It Burger King" (1980), the promotional emphasis shifted from product quality to "experiential" appeal. Burger King was clearly following the same advertising strategy as McDonald's but with only about one third of the media budget.

Specialty sandwiches started off well but soon ran into heavy competition as other chains introduced their own versions of these products. Burger King needed a long-range plan. Within three months, Burger King decision makers had developed the framework of a tactical action plan addressing marketing, productivity, restaurant development, quality/service/cleanliness/value, and return on invested capital. Burger King had returned to a marketing position it had had for the first 25 years of its existence: that of a purveyor of quality hamburger products.

Burger King had spent a tremendous amount of advertising dollars on the "warm fuzzies" (slice-of-life commercials), and they were not getting credit for their product being as good as it was. They were competing with McDonald's by using emotional appeals, and they were being outspent 3½ to 1.

By not advertising the Whopper, Burger King had abdicated their position in the consumer's mind. Wendy's had taken it away from them because they were targeting the prime audience and reaching its members with their "Hot and Juicy" campaign.

In 1982, Burger King also launched Operation Shape-Up to upgrade the consistency of store operations and, in turn, to reinforce the chain's marketing message. The program, for example, taught store operators how to serve Whoppers consistently at the right temperature (about 100 degrees F) after research indicated that the burgers were being served anywhere from 80 to 130 degrees.

With the onset of "Aren't You Hungry?" came a major shift in Burger King's audience targeting. Once a formidable advertiser to children, the chain now concentrated its media bucks on adults aged 18–49. Burger King had been competing in an area where they were not able to offer a distinctive benefit to kids. McDonald's and Burger King had the same

small burgers, drinks, and fries. Both competitors had kiddie-oriented characters—although the Magical Burger King was a more broadly appealing character than Ronald McDonald.

Burger King started to see consumer perceptions of products as becoming more positive on attributes such as broiling, fresh ingredients, and good quality. After a brief advertising lull in the second quarter, Burger King increased its summer efforts in conjunction with the introduction of the chain's bacon double cheeseburger. The new product propelled the company to a third quarter sales increase of 8 percent.

Launched in late September as an extension of the "Aren't You Hungry?" theme, Project BOB ("Battle of the Burgers") pitted the Whopper against McDonald's Big Mac and Wendy's "Single" in order to gain consumer preference.

To position itself as what it called the "Home of the Winner," Burger King initially plunked down $20 million for an eight-week schedule (primarily prime-time TV) to tell American fast-service food eaters that:

1. Independent research ranked the Whopper as best tasting when compared to both the Big Mac and Single.
2. Two thirds of survey respondents expressed a preference for having their fast-food hamburgers broiled.
3. Customization of burgers ("Have It Your Way") was preferred 3 to 1.
4. Burger King's regular hamburger patty had 20 percent more meat before cooking than McDonald's (2 ounces versus 1.6).

This comparative approach was seen as a way of getting more impact out of a sorely outdistanced media budget as well as getting consumers to ask themselves why they were eating at McDonald's when they preferred Burger King-type fast food.

On September 23, four days before the inaugural air date, McDonald's filed a lawsuit contesting Burger King's competitive claims. Wendy's subsequently did the same thing. By suing Burger King early, McDonald's did the one thing that no amount of money in the world could do—make people watch TV more intensely.

The ensuing legal squabble also turned the Battle of the Burgers into a national media event, with Burger King receiving some $20 million worth of free publicity. (An out-of-court settlement later reached wth McDonald's and Wendy's allowed Burger King to extend Project BOB advertising for an additional six weeks through the end of 1982.)

A unique twist in Project BOB's advertising/media strategy was the introduction of a "video coupon" during the week of October 20th. TV viewers were offered a "Buy one, get one free" deal on Whoppers that weekend if they said, "The Whopper beat the Big Mac" when ordering. It was a promotion that reinforced product quality, not a game that detracted from it. Burger King hyped the coupon with spot TV in more

than 150 markets, each weighted at about 250 gross rating points. Weekend radio schedules also ran in most of these markets. Burger King reported 60–70 percent sales increases during this period.

WENDY'S STRATEGY

Wendy's International entered the burger wars in summer 1983 with a campaign as hard-hitting as it was distinctive. The subtle comparative message was packaged in five eye-catching spots that were sure to draw the same level of attention from consumers and competitors as the earlier Burger King campaign did. Tongue-in-cheek aggressiveness was the advertising tone of the $20 million Wendy's campaign which broke in mid-June. The five spots showed the consumer, victimized by the restaurant chain's unnamed competitors, finding sanctuary at Wendy's.

Wendy's believed those spots would end the burger wars. The comic and slick style contrasted sharply with the All-American theme and head-on comparisons favored by Burger King and McDonald's. That approach allowed Wendy's to make sly comparisons, not only to the products but to the competitors' preparatory and service systems as well.

It was not a change in strategy for Wendy's. The tag line of the new spots continued the theme "Wendy's Kind of People." Wendy's had always positioned itself as the best fast-food restaurant. It was simply a new presentation of the same strategy.

Wendy's major points of comparison, dramatized in the new campaign, were fresh meat versus frozen, made-to-order meals, and special stations for drive-through take-out orders. They continued to position the product as one of of top quality.

One commercial, titled "Through the Mill," spoofed the Burger King assembly line, conveyor–broiler cooking system in order to emphasize Wendy's prepared-fresh message. Others, like "Step Aside," "Park It," and "Frozen Stiff," were exaggerated takeoffs on situations Wendy's felt happen daily in Burger King and McDonald's restaurants. All showed the consumer as a victim of the institutional disinterest Wendy's felt characterized its competitors.

The goal of Wendy's campaign was not only to dramatize the apparent differences, but to create an image of the restaurant chain that was itself a dramatic departure from traditional representations.

Timing was an important consideration in the decision to change campaigns and introduce the new spots. Wendy's was outspent by Burger King and McDonald's combined by seven to one. So they went for advertising that was not necessarily in the fast-food mold. Burger King's campaign opened the door for Wendy's to be more competitive. It gave them permission to be more explicit. And it changed the tone of their execution—Wendy's was able to tell a more persuasive story. The

primary goals of the new campaign were to achieve top-of-the-mind awareness, both in terms of the restaurant itself and the distinctive advertising.

The introduction of the new campaign represented more than 25 percent of Wendy's total budget of $75 million for 1983, up 19 percent from the previous year. Of the $20 million, $5 million went to network TV, and the rest went to local support-spot TV and radio and newspapers. In 1982, according to *Leading National Advertisers*, Wendy's spent $13,817,300 in network TV; $17,916,300 in spot TV; $1,119,861 in spot radio; and $676,000 in outdoor. Total traceable expenditures were $33,529,461.

McDONALD'S RESPONSE

The results of the aggressive actions taken by McDonald's competitors began to show in 1982. Many options available in developing an advertising–promotional strategy would allow McDonald's to fight in the Battle of the Burgers effectively. But McDonald's too had to step back and look at the position that they held in the consumer market, what events had led them to that position, and where the competition was making headway.

The major area in which the competition outperformed McDonald's, especially in 1982, was in message dominance. It occurred because the competition focused on singular themes, while McDonald's aired a number of different messages at any given time both locally and nationally. The focused weight and consistent message concentration of the competition helped them to achieve higher awareness levels than their media share would normally dictate.

McDonald's maintained a slight edge in network share of GRPs, or share-of-voice, over the competition during the first, second, and fourth quarters of 1982. However, a comparison of weekly weight levels by company shows that Burger King doubled McDonald's spending in July and led spending in October with 143 GRPs per week versus McDonald's 125 GRPs per week. Wendy's spending increased substantially in October, more than doubling their yearly averages.

As anticipated, McDonald's share of spending on the kid segment rose rapidly during 1982—to reach 100 percent by the fourth quarter—as Burger King abandoned the market. McDonald's dominated children's spending in 1982 with an average 161 GRPs per week compared with Burger King's average 76 GRPs per week.

McDonald's total adult network spending for 1982 averaged 27 percent of all fast-service restaurant advertising dollars, still ahead of Burger King with an average 21 percent share. McDonald's led total local TV spending (kids and adults) with an average 29 percent share,

with Burger King as the closest competitor at an average 9 percent share for the year. McDonald's outdistanced all other competitors in combined network and local TV spending during 1982.

In 1983, 1,250 people were questioned by telephone from May 1 through May 21. Under Ad Watch[1] methodology, an increase or decrease of 2.8 percentage points indicates a statistically significant change—one attributable to more than variations in the sample itself.

In the fast-food category, McDonald's suffered a 7.5-point decline in awareness to 42.3 percent of all responses (from 49.8 percent in April 1983). That was the second steepest drop, topped only by a 15.7-point decline the previous October, when Burger King launched its hard-hitting comparative campaign.

Unlike the pattern of previous months, when a rise or fall for McDonald's was accompanied by a Burger King move in the opposite direction, Burger King held steady with a score of 16.3 percent (versus 16.2 percent in April). Burger King phased out its broiling-versus-frying ads in mid-May 1983, at roughly the same time McDonald's began airing commercials that touted its Number 1 ranking in fast-food sales, the 11 million people served daily, and its array of products.

The content of McDonald's messages to the public had changed as well. However, from 1980–82 the messages shifted to a heavy emphasis on sales promotions in order to stop the declining transaction-count trends. The shift gave McDonald's the needed positive momentum but left the system vulnerable in the area of consumer product and attribute awareness and favorability.

Only in new-product introductions was McDonald's no longer leading the pack, partly because it rolled out market-broadening products, such as breakfast, years ago. With so much going right and so large a share of the market, McDonald's had the most to lose if it introduced a new product which consumers did not like.

QUESTION

1. Develop a promotional strategy for McDonald's. Be sure to include target markets, creative schemes, media plans, budget, and so forth in your plan.

---

[1]Ad Watch is a joint project of *Advertising Age* and SRI Research Center, Lincoln, Nebraska. Ad Awareness is measured by asking a national random sample of consumers to identify the advertising that first comes to mind of all seen or heard in the previous 30 days for each of 20 categories.

ROSEMOUNT, INC.

Industrial Products Division

In January 1975, John Williamson, vice president of marketing at Rosemount, Inc., listens intently as marketing department personnel identify opportunities that might fit into the long-range strategy for the company's Industrial Products Division. The meeting is a significant one for Rosemount as it must lead to a final version of a comprehensive marketing plan for 1975 that can shift attention from one product line (the Model 1151 series), which had provided dramatic growth for the company during the past five years, to new products and markets. The Model 1151 product line consists of expensive, high-precision electronic pressure transmitters.

Potential new products include (1) an original equipment manufacturer (OEM) offering of the Model 1151, (2) an inexpensive electronic gage pressure transmitter—the Model 1144, and (3) an electronic pressure transmitter designed for nuclear applications—the Model 1153.

This case was made possible through the cooperation of Rosemount, Inc. The case was prepared by William Rudelius, University of Minnesota, and Steven Hartley, University of Denver, as a basis for class discussion rather than for illustration of the appropriate or inappropriate handling of administrative situations. Copyright © 1982 by the Case Development Center, School of Management, University of Minnesota.

These products are all in late stages of development. A variety of new markets for current and new products are also under consideration. Rosemount has limited resources available to allocate to further research and development and to marketing efforts; therefore, an assessment of the products and markets with greatest potential is vital to the company.

THE COMPANY

Rosemount, Inc., was a spinoff of the University of Minnesota. During the Korean War, the university's Aeronautical Engineering Department operated the Rosemount Aeronautical Research Laboratories at Rosemount, Minnesota. In these labs students and engineers from the University of Minnesota worked on projects for the rapidly growing aerospace industry. One Rosemount project, sponsored by the U.S. Air Force, developed a temperature sensor for military aircraft. Unable to find a manufacturer for the new design, the Air Force offered the original project members a contract to produce the sensor they had designed. Shortly thereafter, in early 1956, Rosemount, Inc., was formed—with one product and one customer.

Early years.   That first contract provided the means for Rosemount to gain expertise in manufacturing sensors for precise temperature measurement. This, in turn, enabled Rosemount's participation in the U.S. space program starting in the late 1950s. As the space program grew, the need for advanced space technology provided the opportunity for Rosemount to gain research, development, and manufacturing expertise in sensing devices. Engineering excellence became the basis for success and provided the foundation for growth. In 1960 pressure-measurement technology developed by Rosemount allowed the company to introduce high-quality pressure sensors. Again, primary applications were in the space and aircraft markets.

By 1966 Rosemount's annual sales had reached $8.5 million. However, a severe problem was the overwhelming dependence on the U.S. space and defense programs. So in the late 1960s Rosemount tried to apply its unique temperature- and pressure-measurement technology to industrial markets. Several of these markets were growing and needed expensive, high-accuracy instruments.

Present situation.   Currently, Rosemount provides its products to four primary markets—commercial aviation, defense-and-space, energy, and process-and-manufacturing. Sales during fiscal year 1974 were well distributed among the four markets, exceeding a total of $32 million (see Exhibit 1). Rosemount considers this recent diversification into four markets to be a key strength for the company.

EXHIBIT 1   Rosemount financial data (in $1,000)

Summary of earnings	1970	1971	1972	1973	1974
Net sales	$13,388	$15,324	$19,012	$23,977	$32,875
Cost of sales	7,628	8,382	10,278	13,296	18,315
Research and development costs	1,137	942	847	780	1,125
Selling, general and admin. expenses*	3,744	4,450	5,526	7,051	9,135
Interest expense	151	134	133	237	623
Net income before taxes	849	1,576	2,268	2,792	3,462
Income taxes	393	757	1,194	1,393	1,895
Net income after taxes	456	819	1,074	1,399	1,567
Instrument sales by market:					
Commercial aviation	1,540	2,309	2,671	3,128	3,616
Defense and space	6,100	6,615	8,011	8,180	8,876
Energy	1,330	1,815	3,218	5,114	5,851
Process and manufacturing	3,880	3,880	3,648	4,990	10,916
Total instrument sales	12,850	14,619	17,548	21,412	29,259†
Pressure transmitter sales	100	600	1,350	3,740	8,533†

Source: Company financial statements.
*Marketing and sales personnel = 10 percent, advertising = 3 percent of selling, general and administrative expenses.
†Figures include noninstrument sales, and instrument sales include non-pressure transmitter sales.

PRODUCT LINES

John Williamson feels that now is the time for Rosemount to assess opportunities for its present and prospective product lines. He leans forward in his chair as George Mills, head of the Product Planning Group, and technical executives summarize opportunities for four key product lines.

Model 1151 series. As with temperature-related products, Rosemount elected to concentrate on high-quality technology when developing the pressure-related products. Using electrical capacitance to measure changes in pressure, the Rosemount Model 1151 series of pressure sensors established new standards of accuracy and reliability in a wide variety of applications. Very simply, the basic function of the Model 1151 is to monitor pressure, convert the pressure to an electrical signal, and transmit the signal to a control or monitoring station. The primary component of any pressure-measurement device, the sensor, is reponsible for the first steps. Because a change in pressure is proportional to such properties as temperature, velocity, weight, force, and strain, many types of sensors are available. The Rosemount product uses a unique

EXHIBIT 2   Estimated financial data on the alternative new products

| Product | R&D | Manufacturing | Incremental fixed costs ($) | | Miscellaneous marketing support |
			Personal selling	Advertising	
OEM					
1151	0	$10,000	0	0	$40,000
1144	$150,000	$50,000	$50,000	$60,000	$40,000
1153	$250,000	$100,000	$200,000	$40,000	$40,000

Source: Estimates made by casewriters.

technique in which the capacitance, varying directly with pressure, is converted to an electrical signal.

Rosemount manufactures an entire series of Model 1151 transmitters that are used to measure different types of pressure. They include: differential pressure (differences in pressures at two different points in a pipe or system), gage pressure (pressure in excess of atmospheric pressure), and absolute pressure (pressure above zero pounds per square inch). Of the many models, the differential pressure type accounts for more than 80 percent of Rosemount pressure transmitter sales.

Now in 1975 the Model 1151 has become the standard product offering for Rosemount and also a standard of the pressure-transmitter industry. In his presentation George Mills attributes the wide acceptance of the product and rapid growth in its sales to four key benefits: (1) high-quality performance, (2) ruggedness of design, (3) economical purchase and installation, and (4) reduced maintenance cost. Other benefits, such as specifications, materials of construction, and available options, also give the Model 1151 series a competitive advantage.

Model 1153 series.   In 1971 Rosemount initiated a program to develop a pressure transmitter qualified for nuclear applications—the Model 1153 series. One reason for this decision was the increased acceptance of the Model 1151 in the power-generating industry. Thus, extending the product line to include nuclear applications in the power-generating industry appeared to be an obvious move.

The design and manufacture of the sensor component of the Model 1151 and of the Model 1153 were very similar. But the transmitter component for the Model 1153 required major changes from the Model 1151 design. These transmitter changes were needed to enable the product to meet specifications established by the government for all instrumentation utilized in nuclear power facilities. Specifically, the stan-

dards require rigorous aging, radiation, and seismic tests. During the past three years a large portion of Rosemount's research and development (R&D) resources have been allocated to this effort. Although some success has been achieved, additional work is required to "qualify" the product fully for nuclear applications. The estimated unit variable cost for the Model 1153 was $560.00. Rosemount hoped to achieve a 14 percent pretax return on sales goal with this product.

Model 1144 series.   The proposed Model 1144 pressure transmitter represents an inexpensive version of the more reliable Model 1151 gage pressure transmitter. The Model 1144 would not have differential pressure-measurement capability. Preliminary design efforts indicated that the Model 1144, which would utilize pressure technology developed for the Model 1151, would meet most performance specifications of competitive products. The new design, which requires an additional $150,000 in research and development to reach the production stage, could also be priced below most other gage pressure transmitters. However, because the Model 1144 would be similar in function to the Model 1151—an extremely successful product to date—several managers have expressed concern about further development of the inexpensive model. The primary concern was the possibility that Model 1144 sales would reduce those of the Model 1151—that is, the products would compete with, rather than complement, each other. The estimated unit variable cost for the Model 1144 was $280. An 8 percent pretax return on sales objective was set for this product.

OEM Model 1151 series.   The OEM Model 1151 series pressure transmitter would simply be a Rosemount Model 1151 pressure transmitter with a different color paint. These transmitters would then be resold by another firm for use with its own products. Such an arrangement would (1) allow Rosemount to estimate production needs (through OEM production contracts) and (2) gain sales in new markets. A disadvantage, again, would be the possibility that the OEM products would compete directly with regular Rosemount products. The estimated unit variable cost for the OEM Model 1151 was $345.00. An 18 percent pretax return on sales objective was set for this product.

Support Costs

Each of the product line alternatives would require different levels of marketing, manufacturing, and R&D support. Mr. Mills had solicited rough estimates of these costs from various R&D, manufacturing, and marketing personnel and now presented them to John Williamson and the others in a summary table (see Exhibit 2). Although the information represented subjective judgments, George felt that it was important to get a "feel" for the costs involved. In addition, he noted that Rosemount achieved a 41 percent contribution margin and a 10.5 percent pretax return on sales in 1974 (see Exhibit 1).

COMPETITION

Number of Competitors

The number of competitors listed under the SIC heading of 3,823 "Industrial Instruments for Measurement, Display and Control of Process Variables and Related Products" was 119 in 1974. These companies manufacture a large number of products, including sensors, actuators, indicators, recorders, controllers, and transmitters.

Exhibit 3 depicts Rosemount's major competitors in the pressure-transmitter market. Foxboro, the largest competitor, offers a range of products from individual instruments to integrated process management and control systems. Foxboro also offers customized control panels and a host of customer support services, including repair, maintenance, and training programs. Despite the dominance of Foxboro in the pressure-transmitter market, Rosemount had been able to gain considerable market share over the past four years.

EXHIBIT 3   Pressure transmitter market (percent share of North American sales)

	1970	1971	1972	1973	1974
Fischer and Porter	10%	10%	10%	9%	8%
Foxboro	50	48	44	38	32
Statham	0	0	3	4	5
Honeywell	5	5	7	9	10
Leeds and Northrup	3	5	5	5	5
Rosemount	<1	3	6	12	20
Taylor	15	15	13	11	9
Other*	16	14	12	12	11
Total	100%	100%	100%	100%	100%
Market size ($1,000,000)	$15	$18	$20	$26	$32

Source: Estimates made by casewriters from company records.
*Includes Bourns, Barton, Bell and Howell, Westinghouse, Bailey, Robertshaw, and Teledyne-Tavis.

Competitive Products

Exhibit 4 provides information about competitive product offerings. For example, only Statham, Bourns, Bell and Howell, and Teledyne-Tavis offer a gage pressure transmitter similar in price and performance to the Model 1144. All other competitors offer products that compete directly with the Model 1151. None of the companies currently offer both products. Information regarding competitors' developmental efforts is difficult to obtain; however, two important points have been

EXHIBIT 4 Competitive product information and prices

| | Type of pressure transmitter | | | |
| | | | | Nuclear |
Manufacturer	*High-priced*	*OEM*	*Low-priced*	*qualified*
Bailey	yes	no	no	no
Barton	yes	no	no	no
Bell and Howell	no	no	yes ($435)	no
Bourns	no	no	yes ($450)	no
Fischer and Porter	yes ($585)	no	no	no
Foxboro	yes ($560)	no	no	yes
Honeywell	yes ($565)	no	no	no
Leeds and Northrup	yes	no	no	no
Robertshaw Controls	yes	no	no	no
Rosemount	yes ($555)	? ($465)	? ($430)	? ($900)
	Model 1151	OEM 1151	Model 1144	Model 1153
Statham	no	no	yes ($485)	no
Taylor	yes ($600)	no	no	no
Teledyne-Tavis	no	no	yes ($440)	no
Westinghouse	yes	no	no	no

Source: Estimates made by casewriters from company records and competitors' sales literature.

raised by Rosemount personnel. First, with the exception of the nuclear-qualified transmitter, the new products being considered by Rosemount could easily be added by competitors. Second, several competitors are probably spending research and development resources on the development of a new "generation" of pressure-measurement technology that, if successful, could greatly reduce the position of the Model 1151 series in the marketplace.

Annual Sales of Pressure Transmitters

Sales in the control instrument industry have been increasing at an annual rate of approximately 20 percent—reaching $1.5 billion in 1973. Instruments account for 60 percent of the industry sales, while 8 percent of the instrument sales are from electronic pressure transmitters. Currently, the North American market (United States and Canada) represents 38 percent of all pressure-transmitter sales. Pressure-transmitter sales in the United States and Canada grew at a rate of approximately 20 percent during the past four years. Market forecasts indicate that sales will continue to increase at a rate of at least 20 percent through 1980. Overseas markets are also expected to grow, although foreign manufacturers are challenging the once-dominant U.S. firms. In fact, non-U.S. firms are even expanding in the U.S. market. These changes

have been attributed to growth of the world market and increased technological and business skills in Western Europe and the Far East.

MARKETS

Although Rosemount has diversified into four major instrument markets, the majority of Rosemount and industry electronic pressure-transmitter sales are to the energy and process-and-manufacturing markets (see Exhibit 5).

EXHIBIT 5   Pressure transmitter sales in North America by market (in $000)

Industry	1970	1971	1972	1973	1974
Process-and-manufacturing	6,200	7,900	8,200	12,900	6,500
Pulp-and-paper	3,000	3,700	4,400	5,200	6,200
Chemical	3,200	4,200	3,800	7,700	10,300
Energy	8,600	9,900	11,300	12,900	15,000
Oil and gas production and distribution	5,300	6,100	6,700	7,700	9,000
Oil and gas refining	1,600	2,000	2,500	3,000	3,600
Electric utilities: fossil	1,600	1,700	1,900	2,000	2,100
Electric utilities: nuclear	100	100	200	200	300
Other	300	500	400	600	600
Total	15,100	18,300	19,900	26,400	32,100
Rosemount					
Process-and-manufacturing	100	500	580	1,550	4,140
Pulp-and-paper	0	200	260	620	1,240
Chemical	100	300	320	930	2,900
Energy	0	40	600	1,532	2,200
Oil and gas production and distribution	0	0	235	955	1,615
Oil and gas refining	0	0	65	162	195
Electric utilities: fossil	0	40	300	415	390
Electrical utilities: nuclear	0	0	0	0	0
Other	0	0	20	38	60
Total	100	540	1,200	3,120	6,400

Energy

Rosemount shipments to the energy market rose 63 percent in 1973 over 1972. Because of significant long-term growth potential, development efforts directed at the energy market have been encouraged. The market consists of three sub-markets—electrical power generation, oil

and gas production and distribution, and oil and gas refining—that have varied sales records.

Electrical power generation.   The electrical power generation sub-market consists of government- and investor-owned utilities. Rose-mount's Model 1151 competes primarily with Foxboro, Leeds and Northrup, Bailey, and Westinghouse products for the fossil-fueled utili-ties, while only Foxboro offers a competitive product for the nuclear power utilities. Leeds and Northrup and Bailey currently dominate the fossil-fueled segment of the market, but marketing managers feel that the lower-priced Model 1144 would be very attractive to these customers.

Although electric utilities will continue to account for a major portion of the U.S. market for electronic transmitters, they will represent a steadily declining share as market growth decreases (see Exhibit 6). This growth pattern reflects a fundamental change in the demand for electric power in the United States; historically, demand grew at an annual rate of 7 percent. Moreover, now in 1975 the U.S. is just coming out of the 1973–1974 international oil embargo, and energy experts expect a shift from fossil-fueled power generation to nuclear power generation. Each type of power plant requires approximately $150,000 worth of elec-tronic pressure transmitters. Twenty percent of Rosemount's sales to the energy market are to electric utilities.

Oil and gas production and distribution (pipeline).   The market for instrumentation utilized in the production and pipeline distribution of oil and gas is projected to have a favorable growth pattern of 15 percent annually through 1985. Underlying this growth pattern is an increasing level of capital expenditures to increase the production of oil and gas in the United States to make U.S. citizens less dependent on foreign oil. Although few new production fields are anticipated during the forecast period, modernization and upgrading projects for existing facilities as well as some replacement projects will continue to be a substantial factor in future market growth. Similarly, the number of new oil and gas pipe-line installations will be limited. Pipeline expenditures will consist of small-scale projects directed at expansion, modernization, upgrading, and replacement.

Despite increased capital expenditures, Rosemount has not been ex-tremely competitive in oil and gas production and distribution. Cur-rently, none of the pressure-transmitter manufacturers dominate the submarket. However, because a production field can require up to 600 transmitters for use on injection and recovery wells, low-priced trans-mitters such as those offered by Bourns, Statham, and Bell and Howell have a slight competitive advantage. Exhibit 7 provides electronic pres-sure-transmitter sales projections through 1985.

Oil and gas refining.   The least successful submarket for Rosemount has been oil and gas refining. What was previously believed to be a

EXHIBIT 6   Projected growth of electrical power generating capacity (domestic and foreign)

	1975	1976	1977	1978	1979	1980	1981	1982	1983	1984	1985
Total electric generating capacity at peak (millions of kilowatts)	476	502	528	555	584	613	641	675	707	745	773
Annual growth (%)	6.0	5.5	5.0	5.1	5.2	5.0	4.6	5.3	4.7	5.4	3.8
Plant construction:											
Fossil fuel											
Number	37	39	39	38	35	31	29	27	26	21	26
Size (megawatts × 1000)	15.0	16.0	16.1	15.3	15.6	15.7	12.7	14.6	12.8	11.6	14.8
Nuclear											
Number	5	7	8	6	11	11	12	15	16	20	12
Size (megawatts × 1000)	5.0	6.5	7.7	5.9	11.0	12.3	13.4	15.8	18.3	23.6	14.1

Source: Company estimates.

EXHIBIT 7   Projected sales of pressure transmitters to oil and gas markets (domestic and foreign, $ millions)

	1975	1976	1977	1978	1979	1980	1981	1982	1983	1984	1985
Oil and gas production and distribution	40.8	47.3	54.2	62.0	71.9	85.1	97.7	112.0	129.4	148.8	170.7
Oil and gas refining	16.5	17.6	18.5	19.5	20.7	21.8	23.1	24.8	26.1	27.8	29.4

Source: Company estimates.

shortage of refining capacity has actually become an excess. Uncertainties of supply, existence of government regulation, and reduced demand for gasoline all were contributing factors. This situation became apparent only recently as refineries trimmed, postponed, or cancelled their expansion plans. Foxboro and Honeywell have become the major suppliers of pressure transmitters to this submarket by also selling supervisory control computers. Rosemount is not yet able to supply a control system and therefore cannot assume responsibility for an entire refinery. Taylor and Fischer and Porter also serve as secondary suppliers to the oil and gas refining market. The Fischer and Porter company has expressed interest in purchasing Rosemount transmitters as an OEM product. Several Rosemount marketing managers feel that this may be the best alternative for gaining access to orders requiring complete systems.

Process-and-Manufacturing

The combined market for measurement and control instrumentation in the process-and-manufacturing industry now exceeeds $250 million in the United States alone. Although most sales are made to the chemical and pulp-and-paper industries, the market includes other industries such as mineral processing and food-and-beverage. The products manufactured by these industries have little in common, but their requirements for control systems and instruments are quite similar. Because accuracy and stability are of great importance in process-and-manufacturing plants, buyers look for very high performance specifications.

Rosemount is not yet a dominant supplier in this market. In fact, only recently has any progress been made against Taylor, Fischer and Porter, and Foxboro—the established competitors in the market. To encourage acceptance, Rosemount has adopted a "concentration" strategy that directs most marketing efforts at major, multinational companies (e.g., International Paper, Boise Cascade, DuPont, Union Carbide). Small firms are contacted through system suppliers and original equipment manufacturers.

Rosemount's annual sales to the process-and-manufacturing market increased over 110 percent from 1973 to 1974. Marketing managers feel that the market has additional growth potential for Rosemount as long as capital expenditures are at a high level. Both the paper and chemical industries have focused on pollution abatement in recent years, absorbing many of the capital equipment resources. Thus, growth potential for the next two or three years appears favorable.

Pulp-and-paper manufacturers.   U.S. pulp and paper consumption has grown at a rate of about 4.5 percent over the past several years. Industry experts now believe that the pulp-and-paper industry is approaching 95 percent of capacity utilization. Significant increases in capital spending also indicate that plans for expansions and new plants are in progress. Although recent increases in consumption have brought the

industry to record production levels, the rate of increase is declining. Growth rates are likely to continue to decline because domestic per-capita consumption is already quite high, many markets appear to be saturated, and the population is increasing at a slower rate. Future growth will come from foreign markets where per-capita consumption is still low.

Chemical. Although capital expenditures in process-and-manufacturing have fallen somewhat below expectations, oil companies seem to be diverting funds from refining to petrochemical production. Several factors may account for this shift in spending. First, refining capacity is adequate. Second, worldwide shortages of petrochemicals (particularly feedstocks and fertilizers) were caused by the 1973 Arab oil embargo. Capital spending for 1975 is expected to rise to 15.3 percent of sales, or about $4.3 million.

CURRENT MARKETING STRATEGY

Despite Rosemount's recent growth and the apparent success of the Model 1151 series, Mr. Williamson feels that a marketing plan is essential for future growth. Historically, the company has used over 50 percent of its research and development budget to develop new applications for current products, test competitive products, and investigate potential technical improvements in current temperature- and pressure-measurement technology. New product efforts typically receive "project" status to be reviewed on an annual basis. Marketing resources are allocated to areas of potential growth. As the number of new product and market alternatives increases, the need for an explicit allocation procedure increases. Focused marketing and research and development efforts seem increasingly important.

Appeals and Product Features Stressed

Company salesmen identify several factors that are critical in competing with other instrument manufacturers:

1. *Reputation.* Reputation is considered the strongest competitive factor. Users looked for reliable and fast service.
2. *Knowledge.* Thorough knowledge of the user's industry is considered critical. Users expect suppliers to know where instruments are required to maintain production efficiency or product quality and where instruments are unnecessary, thus reducing costs.
3. *Technology.* Product reliability and quality are extremely important to users, particularly in applications where product failure would shut down the factory or system or where production quality would be greatly reduced.

4. *Price.* Competitive bidding always plays a role in contract negotiations but is less important than other factors. In fact, many users do not even consider bids from unestablished suppliers.

Sales Efforts

Sales of new products or to new users are very difficult. Users of pressure transmitters are extremely loyal. If the equipment they have been using is reliable and functional, they are reluctant to change suppliers. Users are loyal because they feel the suppliers know their processes and needs. Reeducating a new supplier is too costly in terms of time and does not insure that the new supplier will be reliable. Even a reputation for high-quality performance in one industry is rarely enough to make a sale to a user in another industry.

Because users expect salesmen to be knowledgeable about Rosemount products, competitive products, and industry applications, significant sales training is required. The marketing department (1) provides regular product-line education sessions for new salesmen and (2) distributes evaluations of competitive products whenever possible. Salesmen often develop expertise in particular industries or applications. Introducing new products or markets has significant implications in terms of marketing costs as new technical information will be required or new customers will have to be called on.

PLANNING MEETING

A corporate planning meeting is scheduled for the last week of January, and Mr. Williamson must recommend and support specific resource allocations. First, he must set goals for Rosemount's industrial products and markets for 1975. Second, he must identify the market segments on which marketing effort must be focused and the product lines to which R&D effort will be allocated.

QUESTIONS

1. What product-line alternatives are available to Williamson?
2. What are the favorable and unfavorable effects of adding each of the new products to Rosemount's product line?
3. How can Rosemount segment the market for its line of pressure transmitters?
4. How can Rosemount use a product-market matrix to aid in the assessment of "where it is now," "where it wants to go with its new product," and "how it will get there"?

INDEX OF CASES

This book has been set Linotron 202, in 10 and 9 point Baskerville, leaded 2 points. Part numbers are 14 point Baskerville Italic and part titles are 12 point Helvetica Extra Bold. Chapter numbers are 11 point Helvetica Light and 72 point Baskerville Bold and chapter titles are 12 point Helvetica Extra Bold. The size of the type page is 30 by 47 picas.